TruCluster™ Server Handbook

TruCluster™ Server Handbook

Scott Fafrak, Jim Lola, Dennis O'Brien, Greg Yates, Brad Nichols

Digital Press
An imprint of Butterworth-Heinemann
Amsterdam Boston London New York Oxford Paris San Diego San Francisco Sydney Tokyo

Digital Press™ is an imprint of Elsevier Science.

 Recognizing the importance of preserving what has been written, Elsevier Science prints its books on acid-free paper whenever possible.

Library of Congress Cataloging-in-Publication Data
A catalog record for this book is available from the Library of Congress.

TruCluster server handbook / by Scott Fafrak ... [et al.].
p. cm.
Includes bibliographical references and index.
ISBN 1-55558-259-1 (paper)
1. Parallel processing (Electronic computers) 2. Electronic data processing--Distributed processing. 3. Client/server computing. I. Fafrak, Scott.
QA76.58 .T737 2002
004'.36--dc21
2002041294

British Library Cataloging-in-Publication Data
A catalog record for this book is available from the British Library.

The publisher offers special discounts on bulk orders of this book.
For information, please contact:

Manager of Special Sales
Elsevier Science
200 Wheeler Road
Burlington, MA 01803
Tel: 781-313-4700
Fax: 781-313-4882

For information on all Digital Press publications available, contact our World Wide Web home page at:
http://www.digitalpress.com or http://www.bh.com/digitalpress

10 9 8 7 6 5 4 3 2 1

Printed in the United States of America

Dedication

To our wonderful wives – Kris Fafrak, Kim Lola, Cheryl Dyment, Beth Yates, and Susan Nichols:

You supported us as we huddled around our computers writing and researching, often into the wee hours of the night. Without your support this project would never have been brought to fruition. Your love, encouragement, patience, and understanding gave us the strength to get started every day, stay focused during those unbelievably long hours, and complete this seemingly endless project.

Words cannot express the gratitude that is in our hearts.

Thank you.

Table of Contents

Part II: Design and Configuration of a Tru64 UNIX Cluster

Part III: Installing and Configuring Tru64 UNIX

Part IV: Cluster Hooks

Part V: Creating a Cluster

10 Creating a Single-Node Cluster 245

Part VI: Adding and Removing Cluster Members

11 Adding a Cluster Member/Deleting a Cluster Member 281

15
The Device Request Dispatcher (DRD) 403

16
The Cluster Alias Subsystem (CLUA) 433

Part IX: Application Deployment in a Cluster

23 Cluster Application Availability (CAA) 669

B
Resources 813

C
Index 821

Preface

A long, long time ago, Jim Lola approached me to write a book on the *TruCluster* Server product – I think that I was still young at the time. Now, many grey hairs later, I sit here on my recliner, my feet up, and my trusty (albeit quirky) laptop on my lap trying to put into words what an adventure it has been to create the book you now hold in your hands. Once upon a time we envisioned a nice, small, compact handbook – as you can see, we have no apparent concept of what small and compact are. So while it may not be compact, it is as complete as we could make it.

Jim, Dennis, Greg, Brad, and I attempted to cover as many aspects of the *TruCluster* Server product as possible while keeping the book under one million pages and not delving too deeply into the nether-workings of the product's implementation.

This book primarily focuses on version 5.1A of the *TruCluster* Server product, although we have tried to point out differences between V5.1A and the two previous version 5 releases. As a bonus (and due to our tendency to provide more rather than less information), some chapters include version 5.1B information as well.

As the cover indicates, this book reflects the collaborative effort of five authors, so although we aimed for a consistent look and feel, you will no doubt pick up on each author's individual voice and writing style. Jim was the primary author of chapters 1, 4, 5, 10, 11, 25, and appendix B; Dennis took the lead on chapters 2, 16, 18, 19, and 20; Greg was in charge of chapters 21, 22, 26, and appendix A; Brad had primary responsibility for chapter 3; and I wrote chapters 6 – 9, 12 – 15, 17, 23, and 24 as well as batting cleanup and pitching in out of the bullpen.

It is our sincere hope that you read this book, find it indispensable, dog-ear many, many pages, and end up buying copies for every member of your family, friends, co-workers, and the neighbor next door.

Enjoy!

Scott Fafrak
Chief Cook and Bottle Washer
November 2002

Acknowledgments

Welcome to the part of the book where we get a chance to thank and acknowledge those individuals who gave of their time and energy, willingly and quite often enthusiastically, to make this book so much better than it would have been without them. The behind-the-scenes efforts of the following people will not soon be forgotten.

Thank you so very much for your technical expertise, encouragement, and in some cases, bad jokes:

Dick Buttlar,
Ernie Heinrich,
Christian Klein,
Alan Brunelle

Greg Brown,
Wayne Cardoza,
Tim Donar,
Bruce Ellis,
Tom Ferrin,
Steve Gonzalez,
Bob Grosso,
Travis Gummels,
Jan Mark Holzer,
Chris Jankowski,
Fred Knight,
Diane Lebel,
Lorrin Lee,
Bruce Lutz,
Maria Maggio,
Dan McGraw,
Scooter Morris,
John Mundt,
Janice Parker,
Lauralee Reinke,
Alan Rose,
Susan Rundbaken,
Mike Schloss,
Thomas Sjolshagen,
Tom Smith,
Roy Takai,
Jem Treadwell,
Susan Verhulst,
Pelle Wahlstrom,
John Williams,
Laurel Zolfonoon,
and the Systems Operations and the Computing Technologies Groups at Genentech.

Also, to the many who contributed through your encouragement, support, comic relief, poetry, and tolerance during this project:

Pam Chester,
Cary Cose,
Marcie Dark,
Nancy King,
Evan Lola,
Karl Lola,
Lauren Lola,
Chris Manley,
Scott Manley,
Tracy McTernan,
Cecelia Nichols,
Daniel Nichols,
Timothy Nichols,
Theron Shreve,
Robert Trouard Jr.,
Abigail Yates,
Cherith Yates,
Gail Yates,
Horace Yates,
and the #unix-chat gang

Thank you.

And finally, to our amazingly supportive and downright wonderful wives, Kris Fafrak, Kim Lola, Cheryl Dyment, Beth Yates, and Susan Nichols, your patience and encouragement mean more than words can convey.

Scott
Jim
Den
Greg
Brad

Foreword

In March, 2000, those of us on the *TruCluster* project team were gratified to see our *TruCluster* Server product receive first place in 3 of 6 categories in D.H. Brown Associates, Inc.'s Competitive Analysis of Cluster Functionality. For Digital Equipment Corporation's engineers in Nashua, New Hampshire; Manalapan, New Jersey; Bellevue, Washington; and Galway, Ireland, taking top score in the categories of Cluster Concurrent Database Access, Cluster High-Availability Administration, and Cluster Single-System Image spelled a satisfying conclusion to more than three years of development. Unique technologies, such as a cluster file system (CFS) that enables a fully shared root file system and single file system namespace, the distributed lock manager (DLM), clusterwide graphic and command-line management interfaces, and the cluster application availability (CAA) failover framework, are integral to the success of the *TruCluster* technology. The *TruCluster* Server product has become the preferred high availability solution for industries that need continuous operation or require large numbers of compute cycles, such as biotech, mobile telephony, and information services. (When the human genome was decoded, *TruCluster* was there!)

Now, a few years and a couple of corporate acquisitions later, the *TruCluster* engineers are smarter, dressed more sensibly, and devastatingly attractive. Significant portions of the *TruCluster* technology have made their way into the Oracle 9i Real Application Cluster (RAC) product. We are now busy sustaining and improving *TruCluster* technology on HP's *Tru64* UNIX/Alpha platform and porting it to the HP-UX/Itanium platform. (Coincidentally, in the same D.H. Brown analysis, HP's cluster product, MC/ServiceGuard, took top spot in two of the remaining three categories. Coupled with the technology's VAXcluster heritage, the new HP-UX cluster product will have strong bloodlines.)

Scott, Jim, Greg, Brad, and Dennis have collectively logged over three hundred thousand hours of cluster time and, although not devastatingly attractive, they are decidedly not unattractive. Each of them has woken up in the middle of the night in recent weeks, reciting the cluster boot messages in exact order in their entirety. Seriously, these individuals have been on the front lines representing *TruCluster* products to customers for years, relaying ideas, as well as complaints, to engineering. They've assembled the tools and solutions they describe in this book while on active duty helping real customers configure and maintain large cluster configurations. They personify the care, commitment, and expertise that the *TruCluster* project team has put into the product and are trustworthy guides to the technology.

Dick Buttlar,
Senior Member of Technical Staff
Hewlett-Packard Company, Enterprise Systems Group, Business Critical Systems

1

Introduction

Imagine that you are the Data Center Manager or the Systems Manager for your company. Okay, quit imagining, you probably are, or may soon be, if you've already purchased this book. Every day, you are faced with challenges. One of the biggest challenges is keeping all your company's corporate critical applications available to your users, twenty-four hours per day, seven days per week, and 365 days per year. Another challenge is ensuring that all your systems are performing optimally, all the time, and will scale as your company grows. Finally, all of your systems have to be easy to manage by your existing staff – you know, do more with less.

This scenario probably sounds like someone higher up in the corporate "food chain" is saying, "I want my cake and I want to eat it too, and by the way, it must taste marvelous!" But that is the reality we face in a world where timely information is the key to corporate success.

While there are no guarantees that you will be the next CIO, the information to be gained by reading this book should go a long way in furthering your understanding of how to use the *TruCluster* Server product-and Clustering technology in general-to help you meet your primary challenges. Who knows, implementing *TruCluster* Server may even get you that well-deserved promotion.

1.1 What is a Cluster?

If this were a science fiction novel, then when we refer to clusters, we would be referring to stars. If this were a book on wine, then we would be referring to grapes. The term clusters has been bandied about and used to mean many things in Information Technology. With this in mind, let's define what clusters are. According to one definition in the Merriam Webster Dictionary (the online version of course) a cluster is "a number of similar individuals that occur together." Well, that's not quite right in terms of what a computer cluster is, but it's a good start.

For a more precise definition of what a cluster is, try this: "A cluster is a type of parallel or distributed computer system that forms, to varying degrees, a single, unified resource composed of several interconnected computers. Each interconnected computer has one or more processors, I/O capabilities, an operating-system kernel, and memory."[1]

What differentiates clustering from distributed computing is that with a cluster, a number of similar computers work together and form a cadre. This unifying relationship becomes the basis for providing the primary themes in clustering: increased application availability (or high availability), load balancing for scalability and performance, and ease of manageability.

This book provides a detailed description of how to create real, single-system image clusters from individual UNIX servers using Compaq's *Tru64* UNIX operating system and *TruCluster* Server software.

1.2 Overview of UNIX Cluster Types

There are three basic types of UNIX clusters: the Failover Cluster, the Single System Image (SSI) Application Cluster, and the Single Systems Image (SSI) Systems Cluster. There would be four different types of UNIX clusters if you count Linux or Beowulf Clustering, but the discussion in this book is limited to the first three types listed above.

1.2.1 Failover Cluster

The Failover Cluster is currently the most common form of UNIX clustering. In its many incarnations and flavors, it is available from most major computer hardware and system software vendors. While the main purpose of the failover cluster is high availability of applications, it is generally considered the most difficult to configure and manage due to the customizations required of application failover scripts.

In looking at a failover cluster from a hardware perspective, it usually has some kind of interconnect between cluster nodes, access to a common disk or storage subsystem from each node, and a network failover capability. Failover of applications is accomplished through scripts that start and stop the applications during cluster node failure and recovery.

Even though each node of a failover cluster is closely coupled through hardware, for the most part it is considered "shared-nothing" from a systems standpoint. Each cluster node must have its own copy of the operating system, and there can be no simultaneous access of disks or of memory between cluster nodes.

The difficulty in developing good, robust application failover scripts usually has to do with the timing and the synchronization for startup or failover of applications versus the common disk subsystem accessibility.

---

1 "Clusters: Moving Beyond Failover," by Bruce Walker, August 1998, UNIX Review.com

1.2.2 Single System Image (SSI) Application Cluster

The principal difference between a SSI application cluster and a failover cluster is the application software. The application software must not only be "cluster-aware" but also "parallelized" to operate on each node of the cluster at the same time. These multiple components of the application are presented as one application to the users and the application administrator. The most well-known application, providing a single view of the application and its data, is Oracle Parallel Server (OPS) from the Oracle Corporation.

For the most part, a SSI application cluster usually consists of the application, like OPS, and a fully configured failover cluster. All nodes of the failover cluster would run the application software, and failover scripts would control the actual failover of the application software.

1.2.3 Single System Image (SSI) Systems Cluster

It is generally accepted that adding more Single System Image features increases availability, performance and scalability, and manageability to a cluster. However, there has been a great deal of disagreement, among computer hardware and systems manufacturers, regarding which SSI features constitute a full SSI systems cluster. Not surprisingly, each manufacturer believes they are correct in how they define what constitutes a SSI systems cluster, regardless of what the customers think.

From a hardware perspective, again, there is little or no difference between a SSI systems cluster and a failover cluster. The real differences come in the software.

Features that are essential to any SSI systems cluster include the following:

- SSI device access - a common view and access to all storage devices.
- A cluster file system - a common view and access to the entire file system hierarchy.
- A cluster alias or cluster Internet Protocol (IP) addressing - clients view the cluster as one system.
- SSI systems management - the cluster is managed like a single system.

As these features provide the core functionality of any SSI cluster, they must be available prior to the addition of any other SSI related feature(s).

Additional SSI systems cluster features are:

- Batch-load leveling - allows for the running of certain processes on the least loaded cluster node.
- SSI interprocess communications (IPC) - allows for a single name space and the sharing of standard IPC capabilities like pipes, semaphores, and shared memory.
- SSI process management - allows for a single namespace for processes.
- Dynamic load balancing - along with SSI process management, allows for process relocation between cluster nodes thereby dynamically balancing the load on the cluster as a whole.

Inclusion of one or all of these additional SSI systems cluster features may or may not determine whether it is a full or partial SSI systems cluster. Rather than have a computer manufacturer's marketing department dictate what is a full or partial SSI systems cluster, we believe that the definition depends on whether the cluster's functionality meets the requirements that you, the user, have for a full or partial SSI cluster.

The three themes to consider for any type of cluster solution are high availability, performance and scalability, and manageability.

1.3 Evolution of *TruCluster* Server

While we will not delve into the complete history of the clustering of computer systems – we'll leave that for another book – we will provide a brief history of clustering as it pertains to the evolution of the *TruCluster* Server product.

In 1982, Digital Equipment Corporation (Digital) – or as many users still fondly remember as DEC – introduced the first commercially viable cluster: the VAXCluster. What made the VAXCluster such a success was that it was technologically the most complete general-purpose cluster on the market. It was a full feature implementation of a SSI systems cluster and, as many would say, "very cool stuff."

Later, as Digital started producing Alpha AXP based VMS systems, they extended the capabilities of VAXCluster to allow for a heterogeneous mix of Alpha AXP and VAX based systems. The product name was also changed from VAXCluster to OpenVMS Cluster to reflect the heterogeneity of the product and the inclusion of the new POSIX open systems standards into VMS.

In 1994, Digital announced the first commercially available UNIX based cluster – the DECsafe Available Server Environment (ASE) version 1.0. DECsafe ASE was a failover cluster but instead of using a cluster interconnect for intra-cluster communications, it used the existing TCP/IP based network. Access to common storage was the initial paradigm with DECsafe ASE. See Figure 1-1.

Over the next couple of years, DECsafe ASE was improved to support additional Alpha-based systems and to add greater functionality in line with customers' demands and expectations for the product. This also provided an opportunity to create a solid foundation for the next step in the evolution of clustering on Digital UNIX. See Table 1-1, Cluster Chronology.

When Digital shipped the *TruCluster* Software version 1.0 product in 1996, it saw the introduction of MEMORY CHANNEL as the cluster interconnect. This was the next step towards achieving what OpenVMS Clusters already had: the SSI systems cluster paradigm.

What made the *TruCluster* Software version 1.0 product truly unique compared to DECsafe ASE was that it was the first UNIX-based cluster product to include support for cluster-aware applications. This support for cluster-aware applications basically allowed for the creation of SSI application clusters.

Late 1996 saw the creation of a new *TruCluster* (TCR) Product umbrella consisting of three functionally overlapping yet distinct products: *TruCluster* Available Server (ASE) version 1.4, *TruCluster* Production Server (PS) version 1.4, and *TruCluster* Memory Channel Software (MC) version 1.4.

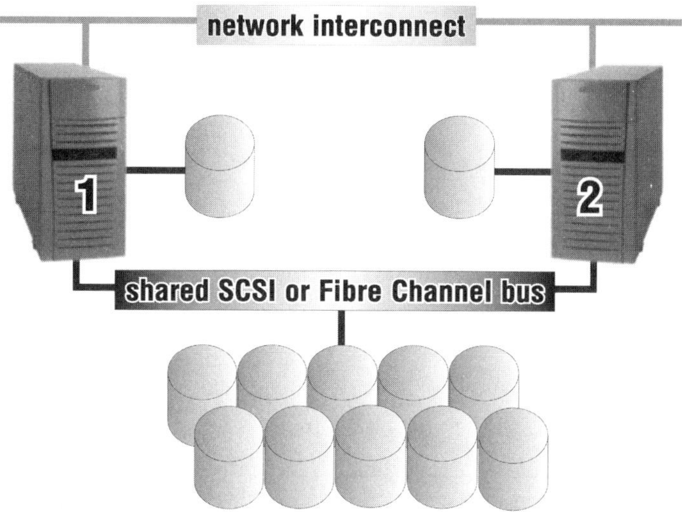

Figure 1-1: ASE-style Cluster

ASE was the failover cluster product. PS was the natural extension to ASE and the SSI application cluster product. MC allowed users to write applications to take advantage of the new cluster interconnect – very attractive from the standpoint of high performance technical computing (HPTC). Of these three *TruCluster* products, PS and MC required the use of the MEMORY CHANNEL interconnect.

The next couple of years brought further evolutionary advances in the ASE, TCR, and MC software to provide support for new Alpha-based server hardware and new customer-centric features like shared Tape access, online service[2] modification, and Year 2000 Readiness.

1998 to 1999 was a watershed year in which we saw many things change, yet stay the same. Digital Equipment Corporation was acquired by Compaq Computer Corporation (Compaq), and the product name changed from Digital UNIX to Compaq's *Tru64* UNIX.

In 1999, Compaq released TCR version 1.6, which offered many enhancements but nothing really new in terms of clustering technology. The enhancements included support for Enhanced Security (C2)[3], NetRAIN[4], NFS over TCP/IP, Switched Fibre Channel, and MEMORY CHANNEL 2.

---

[2] A "service" in the old ASE/TCR days is similar to a Cluster Application Availability (CAA) resource in *TruCluster* Server with the exception that you had to consider both the failover scripts and the associated storage for the service. CAA is covered in Chapters 23 and 24.

[3] C2 is a security level for computer systems and is defined by the U.S. Computer Security Center's "Orange Book."

[4] NetRAIN (Redundant Array of Independent Network interface controllers) is discussed in greater detail in Chapter 9.

Cluster Chronology

Date	Cluster Software	Operating System	Notes
1983	VAXcluster	VAX/VMS	The VAXcluster and VAX/VMS were renamed to the OpenVMS Cluster and OpenVMS respectively when ported to the Alpha AXP processor in the early 1990's. OpenVMS and the cluster software continue to be actively developed and supported.
1994	DECsafe ASE version 1.0	DEC OSF/1 version 2.0A	
	DECsafe ASE version 1.1	DEC OSF/1 version 3.0A	
1995	DECsafe ASE version 1.2	DEC OSF/1 version 3.2A	
1996	DECsafe ASE version 1.3	Digital UNIX version 3.2D and 3.2F	DEC OSF/1 is renamed to Digital UNIX.
	TruCluster Software version 1.0	Digital UNIX version 3.2E and 3.2G	
	TruCluster Available Server Software version 1.4 TruCluster Memory Channel Software version 1.4 TruCluster Production Server Software version 1.4	Digital UNIX version 4.0A and 4.0B	
1997	TruCluster Available Server Software version 1.4A TruCluster Memory Channel Software version 1.4A TruCluster Production Server Software version 1.4A		
1998	TruCluster Available Server Software version 1.5 TruCluster Memory Channel Software version 1.5 TruCluster Production Server Software version 1.5	Digital UNIX version 4.0D and 4.0E	Compaq Computer Corporation purchases Digital Equipment Corporation.
1999	TruCluster Available Server Software version 1.6 TruCluster Memory Channel Software version 1.6 TruCluster Production Server Software version 1.6	Tru64 UNIX version 4.0F and 4.0G	Digital UNIX is renamed to Tru64 UNIX.
	TruCluster Server version 5.0	Tru64 UNIX version 5.0	TruCluster Server version 5.0, was a VERY limited advanced release.
2000	TruCluster Server version 5.0A	Tru64 UNIX version 5.0A	
	TruCluster Server version 5.1	Tru64 UNIX version 5.1	
2001	TruCluster Server version 5.1A	Tru64 UNIX version 5.1A	
2002	TruCluster Server version 5.1B	Tru64 UNIX version 5.1B	Hewlett-Packard Company purchases Compaq Computer Corporation.

Table 1-1: Cluster Chronology

Later that same year, Compaq quietly released *TruCluster* Server version 5.0 as a limited release to a select group of customers. *TruCluster* Server version 5.0 was the very first version of *TruCluster* Server to have SSI systems cluster features. From a UNIX perspective, this version of *TruCluster* Server was no longer evolutionary but revolutionary! It was revolutionary to be able to write a file from one server to a common cluster file system and then be able to read this same file almost instantaneously from another server.

2000 signaled the release of *TruCluster* Server version 5.0A and later *TruCluster* Server version 5.1 to customers. This was the first general release of *TruCluster* Server software that had SSI systems cluster features. As of the release of *TruCluster* Server version 5.0A, any new version of *TruCluster* Server software will release with any new version of *Tru64* UNIX.

Tru64 UNIX version 5.1A and *TruCluster* Server version 5.1A was released in the fall of 2001.

That about brings us to the present (Summer, 2002). As of this writing, we expect the release of *Tru64* UNIX version 5.1B and *TruCluster* Server version 5.1B in the fall of 2002.

1.4 What is *TruCluster* Server?

Now that we know what a cluster is, what is *TruCluster* Server? *TruCluster* Server is an amalgam of *Tru64* UNIX software, storage devices, cluster interconnects, and two or more AlphaServer systems that operate together as a single virtual system. Each cluster member can share resources, storage, and cluster-wide file systems under a single systems management domain.

TruCluster Server versions 5.0A, 5.1, and 5.1A provide the following features:

- Cluster-wide namespace.
- Cluster-wide access to disk and tape storage.
- Cluster-wide Logical Storage Manager (LSM).
- Connection Manager[6].
- Cluster application availability (CAA).
- Cluster alias.
- Highly available NFS server using cluster alias.
- Cluster Communications Interconnect.
- Distributed Lock Manager (DLM)[5].
- Single-systems management.
- Single Security Domain.
- Rolling Upgrade/Patch.
- Expanded Process IDs (PIDs).

Again, with *TruCluster* Server, you are creating *real* single-systems image systems clusters from individual *Tru64* UNIX servers. We will provide a more in-depth overview of *Tru64* UNIX and *TruCluster* Server in Chapter 2.

---

[5] Distributed Lock Manager is discussed in detail in Chapter 18.

[6] Connection Manager is discussed in detail in Chapter 17.

1.5 What This Book Covers

We will cover a great deal of material in this book, but there are some topics that will not be covered. For instance, while we are aware of various techniques in which to deploy Stretch Clusters and Disaster Tolerant (DT) Clusters, at this time, it is neither recommended nor generally supported by Compaq. We will also not cover Compaq's AlphaServer SC Supercomputer implementation in this book because the subject would encompass an entire book on its own.

When we decided to write this book, it was and continues to be our goal to provide a comprehensive technical guide that can be used to design, implement, deploy, and administer a *TruCluster* Server environment. We also wanted to remove the mystery and "magic" from what a UNIX Cluster is and why IT managers may want to use this technology to help them decrease their overall systems management costs while increasing manageability and availability of their UNIX server infrastructure. To that end, we have organized the book into ten sections and an appendix for easy reference.

Section 1 – This is the Introduction and provides a certain amount of background on UNIX clustering and a good overview on *Tru64* UNIX and *TruCluster* Server. For folks not familiar with UNIX clustering and/or Compaq's *Tru64* UNIX, we strongly recommend that you start with this section as it lays the foundation for more to come.

Section 2 – This section is on Design and Configuration of a *Tru64* UNIX Cluster is a very important section as it discusses the design, planning, and configuration of a *TruCluster* Server environment. We recommend that before you even think about the mechanics of deploying *Tru64* UNIX for a *TruCluster* Server environment, you first design and carefully plan out your environment. As with most endeavors, a little up front design and planning will save you a lot of work in the long run.

Section 3 – This section provides information on how to build and configure *Tru64* UNIX in preparation for installing and configuring *TruCluster* Server.

Section 4 – Cluster Hooks covers those features in the *Tru64* UNIX operating system that are the enablers for clustering. This section provides the background to understanding the basis for what is needed in the operating system to allow for clustering on UNIX.

Sections 5 & 6 – The actual planning, installation, and deployment of a *TruCluster* Server environment. This section should be especially useful to systems architects and systems administrators.

Section 7 – Cluster Subsystems demystifies how a cluster operates. This section clarifies all the subsystems that make up *TruCluster* Server and is vital to understanding how a cluster really works.

Sections 8 & 10 – Cluster Systems Administration and Upgrading or Patching a Cluster should interest systems administrators who manage a *TruCluster* Server environment on a day-to-day basis.

Section 9 – Systems administrators and application programmers should find section 9 on Application Deployment in a Cluster particularly relevant as they start to design and deploy their applications in a clustered environment.

1.6 References

- Walker, Bruce. "Clusters: Moving Beyond Failover," In *UNIX Review.com*, August 1998.
- *Merriam Webster Dictionary* – Online version
- Pfister, Gregory F. *In Search of Clusters*. Upper Saddle River, NY: Prentice Hall PTR, 1995.
- *TruCluster* Server Technical Overview for *TruCluster* Server versions 5.0A/5.1.

2

Tru64 UNIX & *TruCluster* Server Overview

Before diving into the world of designing and configuring a *Tru64* UNIX cluster, a brief overview of the *Tru64* UNIX operating system will help set the table. Consider this chapter the appetizer, and the following chapters as the main meal. To enable you to digest the main topics in this book, we will prepare you by discussing several concepts and features of *Tru64* UNIX and the *TruCluster* Server software that is now part of the operating system.

2.1 *Tru64* UNIX Overview

The name of this operating system speaks volumes. First, it is a UNIX-based operating system. It falls towards the middle of the UNIX family tree because it draws some of its characteristics from both the BSD[1] and System V[2] sides of the family. It also has a healthy dose of core code created by Compaq engineers.

Figure 2-1 depicts several of the common UNIX variants. Note *Tru64* UNIX at the bottom of the diagram.

Second, *Tru64* Unix is truly a 64-bit operating system. The virtual addresses used in the system are indeed 64 bits, providing a huge virtual address space and supporting large file offsets and sizes. So, is that it? Are those the distinguishing features of the system? There are actually many more features of the operating system which we will visit in the first part of this chapter. If you are familiar with another UNIX system, you may want to take a quick look at the first section of this chapter but plan on slowing down and carefully reading the *TruCluster* Server Overview (section 2.7).

---

[1] Berkeley Standard Distribution (BSD), developed at the University of California at Berkeley.

[2] UNIX System V, developed by the UNIX System Development Lab at AT&T.

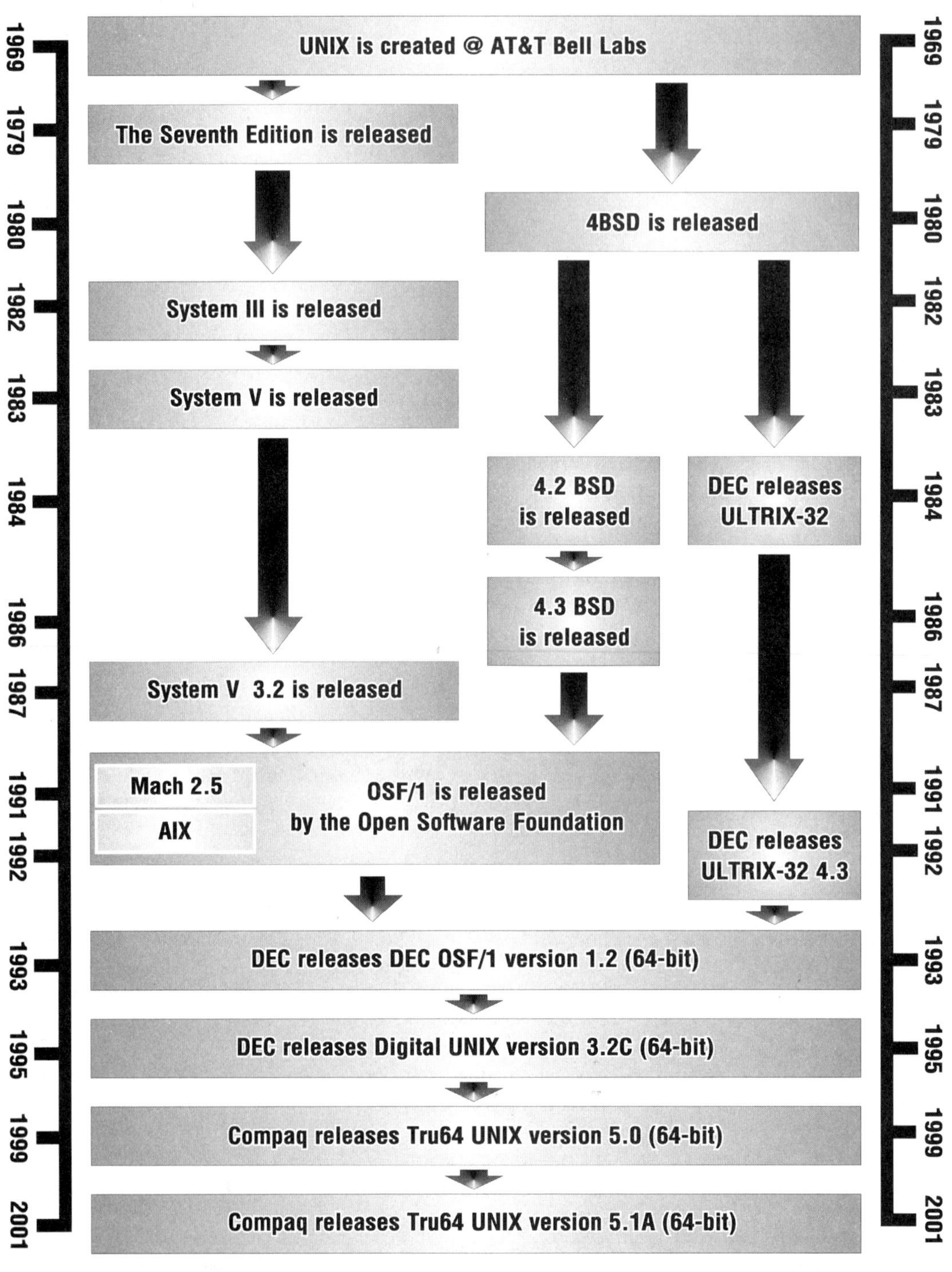

Figure 2-1: ***Tru64*** **UNIX History**

2.1.1 Operating System Features

Tru64 UNIX has rapidly expanded its capabilities to the point where it provides the ability to support a Single System Image (SSI) Cluster option (as discussed in the previous chapter). *Tru64* UNIX has been an integral part of the computer mix at many sites for many years – even before full-bodied clustering (SSI) was available.

Which features attracted customers to *Tru64* UNIX before the advent of clustering? As you will see, there are many. We'll point out some features in the next few sections and relate those features to *TruCluster* Server (the focus of this book).

2.1.2 Mach Kernel

Lurking at the very heart of *Tru64* UNIX are elements of the Mach kernel. Mach is a system created at Carnegie-Mellon University. It includes the notions of tasks and threads that figure prominently within the workings of *Tru64* UNIX. A "task" represents a running program, while a 'thread' is a schedulable entity within that program. Historically, programs were written with a single thread. Most of the advanced UNIX variants provide the ability to create multi-threaded programs such that better advantage can be taken of multiple CPU systems.

The Mach kernel is also touted as a "Microkernel" (a small, compartmentalized kernel supported by many kernel mode threads and user mode processes), despite the fact that earlier releases, such as the V2.5 upon which *Tru64* UNIX was built, were actually monolithic in nature. While not central to the function of *TruCluster* Server, this notion is important to the ongoing development of *TruCluster* Server and *Tru64* UNIX in general. Essentially, key alterations in the system kernel can be implemented much more rapidly with a microkernel (or even a pseudo-microkernel) since the subsystems are very well defined and somewhat isolated from one another. Note that *Tru64* UNIX is not strictly using the microkernel strategy but borrows heavily from it (we'd love to say the subsystems are completely distinct from one another, but that's just not true). This provides us with a flexible software product (*Tru64* UNIX and *TruCluster* Server) to which new features can be added relatively quickly. Indeed, *TruCluster* Server itself is an example of rapid adaptation of the operating system to include new features and subsystems.

Some cluster components are implemented as kernel threads. Others are implemented as process-based code consisting of one or more threads. Still others are subsystems within the kernel. These components ultimately rely on system functions partially derived from Mach. Many other cluster components are implemented as driver-level kernel code. The following sections will briefly develop and introduce many of the key system components and cluster components. All cluster components will be discussed in subsequent chapters of the book.

2.1.3 Virtual Memory

The system uses virtual addresses, which are translated into physical addresses to provide access to data and code in memory (or I/O space). The previous sentence could be used to describe just about any modern operating system. *Tru64* UNIX has solved the problem of representing a virtual address space consisting of 2^{64} bytes of potential addressability (most other UNIX variants are years behind

Compaq, now HP, in developing 64-bit systems). It does this using a clever three-level page table scheme that we don't need to detail here. The point is that it is a key feature of the system and is used heavily by all components including the *TruCluster* Server components.

2.1.4 Unified Buffer Cache

The Unified Buffer Cache (UBC) is an innovation through which *Tru64* UNIX can tune itself, at least partially. The memory caching needs of the file systems tend to be in direct conflict with the memory needs of processes. If the system is experiencing a burst of I/O activity, the file system caching memory count (generally referred to as the UBC page count) will increase. If the virtual memory requests from processes become heavy, the pages are taken back from the UBC and used for process memory. And so the pendulum can swing back and forth throughout the life of your system without your lifting a finger. Pretty impressive, huh?

To be fair, *Tru64* UNIX is not the only UNIX that uses this strategy.

As you will see, the UBC is used by several of the I/O components that make clustering possible.

2.1.5 Shared Libraries

Shared libraries provide for the sharing of code at the function level. UNIX has always been good at sharing code at the process level, meaning that two users who both happen to be running the `vi(1)` editor at the same time, for example, will be sharing the single copy of the `vi` code that is brought into memory. But UNIX has traditionally been weak at sharing at the function level. So if one process were running the `vi` editor and the other were running `emacs(1)` (we'll assume that these two editors use many of the same functions), traditional UNIX would have brought two copies of the potentially shared functions into memory.

Shared libraries provide a mechanism where any program that uses shared library functions (think `printf(3)`), will reference the single copy of the function code that has been brought into memory. Note that the system is an 'on demand' system, so none of the shared functions are in memory until the first request causes one to be brought in. Likewise, as soon as there are no users of the function, the memory that it occupies will be freed.

The process-level *TruCluster* Server code is linked against shared libraries. The following example shows that the Cluster Application Availability Daemon (`caad(8)`) is linked against shared libraries. We then document which shared libraries are referenced within the `caad` process.

```
# file /usr/sbin/caad
/usr/sbin/caad: COFF format alpha dynamically linked, demand paged executable or
 object module stripped - version 3.13-14
```

```
# odump -Dl /usr/sbin/caad

                        ***LIBRARY LIST SECTION***
        Name              Time-Stamp           CheckSum    Flags Version
/usr/sbin/caad:
        libpolicy.so Jan 16 04:39:17 2002 0x7958cdb5      0 osf.1
        libevm.so    Jan 15 17:37:17 2002 0xde4a5d09      0 osf.1
        libclu.so    Jan 15 17:36:05 2002 0xd148a817      0 osf.1
        libm.so      Jan 15 17:20:50 2002 0x07757304      0 osf.1
        libpthread.so Jan 15 17:26:48 2002 0x42a00c94     0 osf.1
        libcxx.so    Jan 15 17:29:14 2002 0x9060972e      0 cxx6.3
        libexc.so    Jan 15 17:20:58 2002 0xb0f9a902      0 osf.1
        libc.so      Jan 15 17:19:09 2002 0x1e4e245f      0 osf.1
```

The following command output lists the location and some of the shared library files available in *Tru64* UNIX.

```
# ls /usr/shlib
.mrg..so_locations     libarmui.so          libmsfs.so
.new..so_locations     libaud.so            libmxr.so
.proto..so_locations   libawt.so            libndb.so
TCR_libclu.so          libawt_g.so          libnet.so
X11                    libbkr.so            libnet_g.so
_null                  libc.so              libnuma.so
diagui__unix.uid       libc_r.so            libots.so
ev6                    libcdrom.so          libots3.so
generic                libcfg.so            libpacl.so
libDSNLinkAPI.so       libchf.so            libpolicy.so
libDXm.so              libclu.so            libproplist.so
libDXterm.so           libclua.so           libpset.so
libDeCOR.so            libcmalib.so         libpthread.so
libDtHelp.so           libcsa.so            libpthreaddebug.so
libDtMail.so           libcurses.so         libpthreads.so
...
```

2.1.6 Memory Wiring

Most of the physical memory on *Tru64* UNIX is pageable. This means that the contents of the memory pages may be paged out to swap space (on disk), or swapped out to swap space if the system's free page list becomes critically low. Certain applications may require that portions of its memory be treated as if it were non-pageable. This activity (referred to as "wiring down" a page) is limited to processes that are owned by root. The kernel may also wire down pageable pages to meet its dynamic memory requirements.

The following example concludes with a section displaying statistics on the wired pages within the system.

```
# vmstat -P
Total Physical Memory =    128.00 M
                      =     16384 pages

Physical Memory Clusters:

start_pfn     end_pfn        type  size_pages / size_bytes
        0         256         pal         256 /      2.00M
      256       16287          os       16031 /    125.24M
    16287       16384         pal          97 /    776.00k

Physical Memory Use:

 start_pfn     end_pfn        type  size_pages / size_bytes
       256         288    scavenge          32 /    256.00k
       288        1036        text         748 /      5.84M
      1036        1180        data         144 /      1.12M
      1180        1400         bss         220 /      1.72M
      1400        1594      kdebug         194 /      1.52M
      1594        1600     cfgmgmt           6 /     48.00k
      1600        1601       locks           1 /      8.00k
      1601        1615        pmap          14 /    112.00k
      1615        1811   unixtable         196 /      1.53M
      1811        1814        logs           3 /     24.00k
      1814        2046    vmtables         232 /      1.81M
      2046       16287     managed       14241 /    111.26M
                                   ============================
         Total Physical Memory Use:      16031 /    125.24M

Managed Pages Break Down:

       free pages = 582
     active pages = 1901
   inactive pages = 4839
      wired pages = 3869
        ubc pages = 3082
        ==================
            Total = 14273

WIRED Pages Break Down:

   vm wired pages = 705
  ubc wired pages = 0
  meta data pages = 1467
     malloc pages = 995
     contig pages = 88
   user ptepages = 585
  kernel ptepages = 21
    free ptepages = 8
        ==================
            Total = 3869
```

2.1.7 Non-Uniform Memory Access (NUMA)

Another example of the rapidly changing nature of *Tru64* UNIX is the inclusion of support for Non-Uniform Memory Access (NUMA) systems. Traditional Symmetric Multiprocessing (SMP) systems do not scale well as more processors are added. The Compaq (now HP) GS-series of computers (GS80, GS160, and GS320) can handle 8, 16, and 32 CPUs respectively (more in the future) in a manner yielding excellent scalability. This requires specialized hardware, but the operating system software is, once again, nothing more than good, old *Tru64* UNIX. While some folks refer to the GS-series as a "cluster in a box," that is definitely not the intent of these machines (and certainly nothing that we recommend), although the hardware will support it.

The next sequence will take you through the conceptual developments in the world of computers that led to the notion of clusters. Along the way, several of the *Tru64* UNIX features will be mentioned.

2.2 Single CPU Computer

Pull apart any computer and you will find some common hardware components. There is a Central Processing Unit (CPU), which is responsible for executing instructions. It is typically considered to be the brains of the computer.

There is some physical memory. The memory holds the code that is being executed and the data that is being accessed by the CPU currently. The CPU is designed to execute code that exists in memory. If the code is still out on the disk, the system will complain (cause an exception) and a page fault will take place. Upon completion of the page fault, the on-disk page containing the faulting instruction will have been brought into memory and placed into a page frame (in physical memory). The same instruction that caused the fault will then be re-executed.

There will also be some I/O capability. This can vary wildly from machine to machine but usually consists of disks, tapes, printers, network interface, and other hardware items.

Figure 2-2 depicts a single CPU computer with some physical memory and I/O capability.

Most of the software features discussed in this chapter do not appear in the above list of hardware components. *Tru64* UNIX and *TruCluster* Server are primarily software mechanisms. The software that is charged with managing the hardware is the operating system (*Tru64* UNIX in our case). If you are wondering why we're taking you through a review of basic computer concepts, be patient. Our goal is to raise the issues and problems involved in implementing a cluster and to determine how the *TruCluster* Server software and components solve these problems.

The first step is to consider a standalone system. It allows no access to its resources other than by software running on the system itself. The resources in this case may be memory, disks, other I/O components, or even the CPU itself. The coordination and synchronization necessary to keep the various components of the system from stepping on each other (or causing corruption of some sort) is achieved through the use of processing modes and System Priority Levels (SPLs).

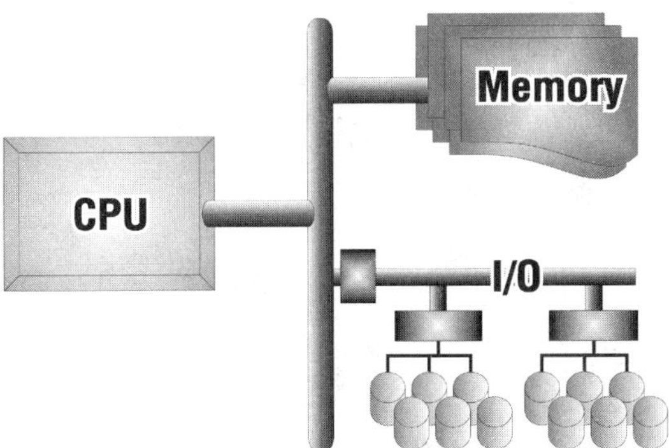

Figure 2-2: Computer Hardware Components

NOTE:

SPLs are sometimes referred to as Interrupt Priority Levels (IPLs).

In essence, the CPU is always running in one of 8 SPLs (0-7) with the higher SPLs being more important than the lower SPLs.

The system will also be in one of two possible processing modes: user mode or kernel mode. Most of the standard processing in the machine will take place at SPL 0 and in user mode. If a more important event needs to take precedence over the current processing, an interrupt is issued, and an Interrupt Service Routine (ISR) executes in kernel mode.

You may be thinking that this is related to process priorities (or thread priorities). Nope. All of the process/thread activities (with certain kernel mode exceptions) take place at SPL 0 and in user mode. Even the payroll program that generates your paycheck executes at SPL 0. So what exactly is more important than the program generating your paycheck? Bear in mind that the system sees the payroll program as just another user-mode program. The more important processing is the software that has to execute in response to an interrupt and other kernel mode processing that may need access to system support structures such as device drivers and kernel routines.

The ISR must run in such a way that it will not be interrupted by subsequent interrupts at the same level or below. This is achieved by setting bits in a CPU register (the Processor Status or PS register) to indicate at which SPL the processor is currently running. There is another bit in the PS register that indicates kernel or user mode. Note carefully that the SPL is a per-CPU phenomenon since every CPU has a PS register.

For the purposes of our discussion, interrupts are generated by hardware devices to indicate that an event has taken place (I/O completion, for example). So the various devices can be assigned an SPL at which to run their ISR. A device that interrupts at a higher SPL takes precedence over the ISR of a device that interrupts at a lower SPL. When all of the ISRs have finished processing, the system lowers the SPL to the level it occupied before the interrupt occurred.

If you're wondering how this pertains to a clustered environment, keep in mind that a clustered environment includes multiple systems with many I/O devices, and each system has one or more CPUs, and each CPU has its own PS register. Therefore, each CPU in a computer in a cluster may be at a different SPL from the other cluster members' CPU(s) at any one instant. The point is that

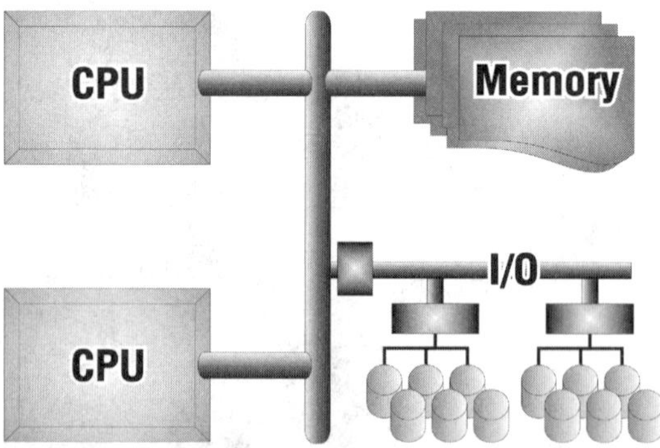

Figure 2-3: Dual-CPU Hardware Components

there have to be other synchronization mechanisms available both to processes and to the systems themselves in order to maintain a level of sanity and synchronization in a cluster. The next few sections will introduce a number of system mechanisms to handle synchronization and communication as the complexity of the system approaches full-blown clusterhood.

2.3 Multiple CPU Systems

Adding a second CPU to the computer increases the complexity of synchronizing the system's activities. Each CPU has its own set of registers including the PS register containing the SPL and mode information. Therefore, any attempt by software to set the SPL to a non-zero value with the goal of synchronizing with an ISR will be faulty. It will provide synchronization but only with ISRs that happen to run on that particular CPU. The ISRs and other kernel mode code running on another CPU will not be aware of the SPL setting on this CPU.

Figure 2-3 depicts a two CPU system. Note that either CPU can access any of the physical memory or I/O devices on the system.

2.3.1 Asynchronous Multiprocessing (ASMP)

One solution to the synchronization issue would be to force all code that runs in kernel mode (including ISRs) to run on a particular CPU. This is a form of 'funneling' that forces activities to run on a particular CPU (usually the primary CPU). Forcing all of the kernel mode activities to run on a single CPU in a multiprocessor system (more than one CPU in the box) is a solution referred to as Asymmetric Multiprocessing (ASMP). ASMP is relatively simple to implement and allows the SPL synchronization for kernel mode activities to continue working even though there are multiple CPUs involved. However, it causes high scheduling overhead as each process that needs to get into kernel mode (for a system call, for example) must be rescheduled to run on the primary CPU.

ASMP worked, but didn't work well enough, and it scaled poorly. As more CPUs were added, fewer of their CPU cycles could actually be utilized. There had to be another way to synchronize between multiple CPUs. Remember, we are still talking about a single computer. We have not yet reached a point where we are adding more computers or clustering computers, but we will.

Figure 2-4 shows a two-CPU system in an asymmetric arrangement. The top CPU has been designated as the primary CPU and will handle all interrupts and run all kernel mode code.

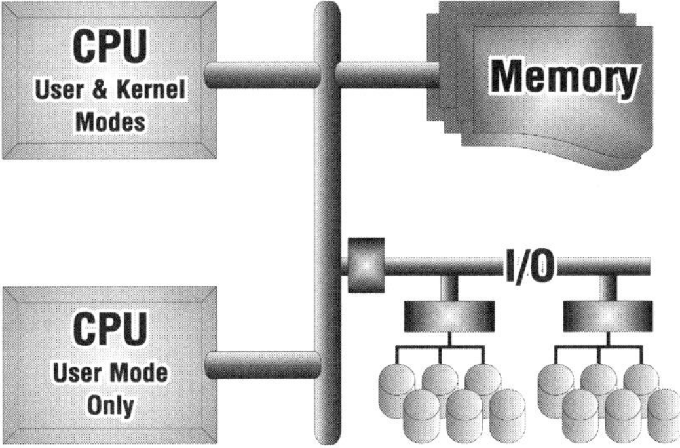

Figure 2-4: Asynchronous Multiprocessing

2.3.2 Symmetric Multiprocessing (SMP) – Tightly Coupled

In order for a system to be deemed Symmetric, all of the CPUs in the system must be able to execute all modes of processing. In UNIX, the two modes are user mode and kernel mode. Software running on any CPU in a multiprocessor system needs to be coordinated with respect to access to kernel data structures that may be referenced (perhaps simultaneously) by other kernel mode software (including ISRs) running on other CPUs. The CPU-centric SPL synchronization method is not sophisticated enough to handle multiple CPUs.

Tru64 UNIX uses a memory interlocking mechanism and special 'load-locked', 'store-conditional' instructions to achieve the necessary extra level of synchronization. Memory is accessible to all CPUs in the system. The idea is to protect kernel structures or arrays with a spinlock bit. The spinlock is nothing but a bit in memory that is designated to coordinate access to a particular structure, field, array, device, etc. The term 'spinlock' is generic. *Tru64* UNIX refers to these locks as 'simple locks'. Let's face it, on the surface, they are about as simple as they can get. If you can set the bit, you have access to the resource represented by the bit; if you cannot (because it is already set), you do not have access to the resource represented by the bit. When access is denied, the requestor usually will 'spin' and repetitively check to see if the bit is clear. Once it is clear, the requestor can set it and access the protected resource. Do not get this confused with application level file locks and related activities. File locks are available to an application program, while spinlocks ('simple locks') are available to the operating system kernel. User mode application code will never directly request a simple lock.

Now we have a mechanism that provides synchronization between multiple CPUs within a system. The next step is to figure out how to coordinate access to resources when the accessing code is running on multiple systems. For the record, we have just discussed synchronization between 'tightly coupled' CPUs that use the same memory copy of the operating system software running on more than one CPU.

Figure 2-5 depicts a 'tightly coupled' system with two CPUs in an SMP arrangement. Note that both CPUs can run user mode and kernel mode code.

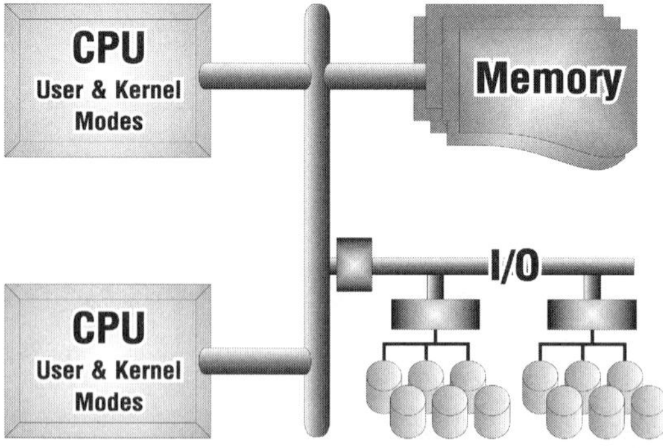

Figure 2-5: Symmetric Multiprocessing

2.4 Network – Loosely Coupled

Each computer in a network has its own operating system, its own memory, and its own I/O subsystem. If there needs to be some communication between software running on one node in a network and software running on another node in the network, there has to be an agreement to accept the coordination and complete the communication. By the way, this notion of 'accepting the coordination' is not totally foreign. In the previous section, the kernel mode code had to have been built with requests for simple locks and the raising of an SPL inherent within the code. In effect, this was the kernel code's agreement to accept the coordination. Network coordination and synchronization can be particularly dicey because the operating systems and hardware platforms can vary forming a heterogeneous environment.

Fortunately, most modern operating systems contain TCP/IP software (or other related network software such as Remote Procedure Calls (RPCs)). TCP/IP provides the necessary synchronization (when requested) between processes running on multiple nodes. The cluster software will be intimately involved with the network software and hardware in order to present a single target on the network, or to prepare for network interface failure, or to communicate using Remote Procedure Calls (RPCs).

Figure 2-6 shows a close-up of one system in a network connected with several other systems (each of which consist of similar components).

2.5 Cluster – Closely Coupled

The *TruCluster* Server product provides for the close interaction of multiple systems. A cluster is generally considered to be "closely coupled" in that the systems have an awareness of each other but do not access the system code in common memory (as tightly coupled systems would) and do not

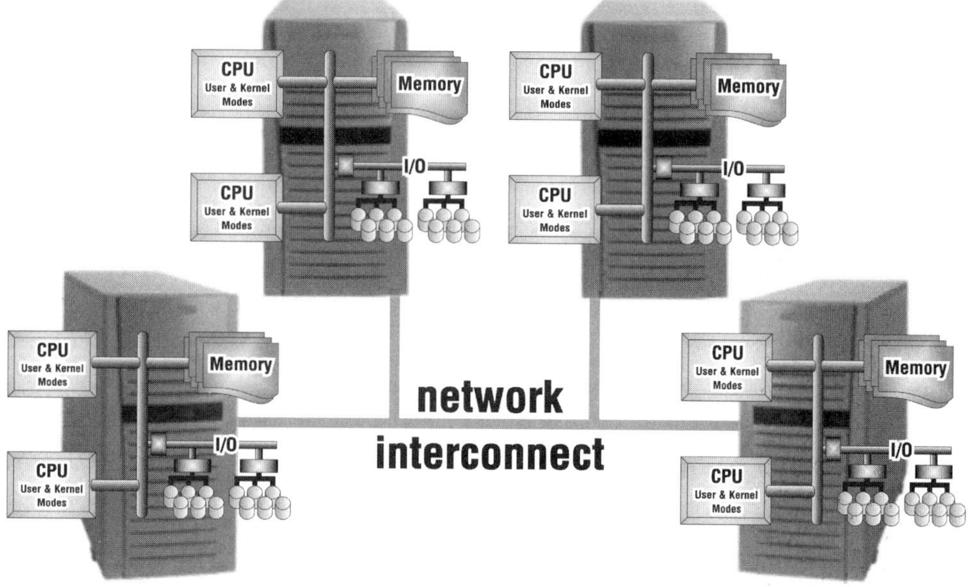

Figure 2-6: Loosely-Coupled Computers

rely on a traditional network for communications (as a loosely coupled arrangement would be). It may help to think of a cluster as having the characteristics of both loosely coupled and tightly coupled systems. It is like a loosely coupled system because it is easy to add more horsepower by adding a new member to the cluster (similar to adding another CPU in a tightly coupled arrangement), and if one member goes down, you're not necessarily sunk. It also resembles a tightly coupled system in that the machines directly share storage, file system, and hostname (sort of – each member will have a unique name, but there will also be a name for the entire cluster) and act as one virtual entity (despite the fact that each system has its own physical memory).

Figure 2-7 shows two members in a cluster with three connections between the members: cluster interconnect, shared bus, and network interconnect. At least one cluster-specific interconnect mechanism (Memory Channel or LAN[3]) must be in place to form a cluster. Note that the network interconnect shown below is used for network traffic such as NFS, while the cluster interconnect is used for intra-cluster communication. The shared bus is common and highly recommended but optional.

A cluster is coupled in one of two ways. It may either use specialized hardware such as Memory Channel or use a LAN-based interconnect for a slower but less expensive communications alternative. Cluster members must be aware of the state of the cluster. Communication and synchronization must be achieved in order to determine the viability of the cluster.

You may have several questions by now, including: "Should a cluster continue operations if one member of a three member cluster goes down?," "What happens to the applications that were running on the failed member?," "How do the other members decide whether to continue?," "How does the cluster appear to other nodes in the network?," and "How is I/O coordinated between cluster members sharing a common bus and I/O access?" These questions will be addressed in the following sections. The issues of kernel mode versus user mode, interrupts, synchronization, and cooperation among applications will all be revisited, only this time within the context of a cluster.

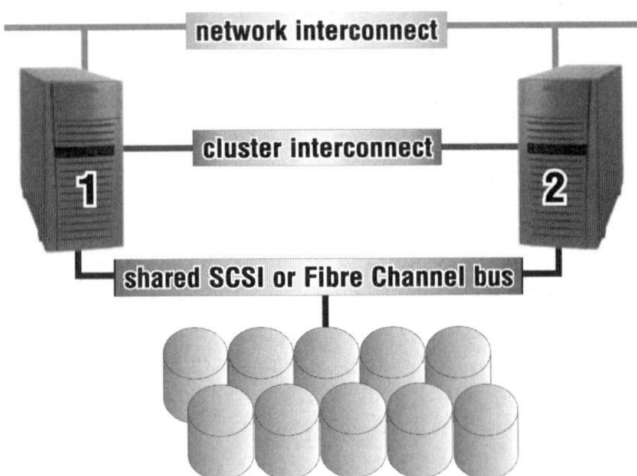

Figure 2-7: Two-Member Cluster

[3] Local Area Network

2.6 Cluster Definition

According to HP specifications, the *TruCluster* Server V5.1A for *Tru64* UNIX "provides highly available and scalable solutions for mission-critical computing environments." The specification (Quick Specs for *TruCluster* Server) goes on to describe a combination of features from SMP, distributed computing, and fault resilience that provide very high availability and scalability.

So a cluster is a mechanism whereby a closely coupled group of computers can combine their resources and present itself to an application, administrator, or even to the network as a single, highly available machine. The *TruCluster* Server product attempts to eliminate as many points of failure as possible in order to provide consistent access to a company's critical resources. It also provides administration mechanisms through which cluster administration becomes only slightly more complex than single node administration. In a cluster, product installations, system monitoring, and most other management tasks can be done a single time, rather than once for each member of the cluster. A cluster can appear as a single node in a network if desired.

In the remainder of this chapter, we will introduce you to the cluster components that provide the mechanisms for making the above-mentioned features happen.

2.7 *TruCluster* Server Overview

This might be a good place for a quick comparison of the V1.X *TruCluster* product and the V5.X *TruCluster* Server product. As we mentioned in Chapter 1, there has been a steady evolution of the clustering software. In the early days (1994), the cluster was referred to as the Available Server Environment (ASE). Most of the cluster support daemons ran in user mode and used TCP/IP to interface with the Memory Channel once it became available in 1996. Also, each member of the cluster had its own copy of the operating system, thereby eliminating any possibility for ease of management. In 1996, the product (V1.4) involved three major components (ASE, Production Server, and Memory Channel). A cluster site could graduate from using ASE for application failover support to the Production Server (PS), which would include support for a Connection Manager, Distributed Lock Manager, and Distributed Raw Disks. (Note that Oracle Parallel Server was an example of a PS V1.*X* application.)

The PS environment encompassed ASE and Memory Channel. As such, it prepared the foundation for a significant leap forward to today's *TruCluster* Server software product (V5.x). Prior to *TruCluster* V5.0A, administering a cluster was actually more difficult than managing a single system or group of systems. Each system would require separate installation efforts. Today most administrators find the cluster relatively easy to manage.

With its inclusion of the Cluster File System (CFS), the Cluster Application Availability Subsystem (CAA) replacing ASE, and the Cluster Alias Subsystem (CLUA), the *TruCluster* software provides excellent availability through CAA and component failure detection techniques. Using CFS, applications are able to access file data transparently from any cluster member. The following subsections introduce many of the cluster software components. Subsequent chapters will provide more detail on each component.

2.7.1 Communication between Cluster Members

Remember how difficult it was to synchronize code running on multiple CPUs in an SMP environment? The solution was to design the kernel mode and ISR code such that it acquired the simple lock protecting the requested resource before going forward and accessing it. What happens in the world of clusters when code running on two nodes needs to access a common database of information? The answer includes several levels. First we need to discuss the mechanism for communication between cluster members. Then we'll look at the software that uses the medium. In order to use *TruCluster* Server version 5.0A or 5.1, the systems have to have Memory Channel adapters installed and be connected directly (for a two member cluster) or be connected through a hub for more than two members. In *TruCluster* Server version 5.1A, the LAN hardware can be used as the cluster interconnect alternatively.

2.7.2 Memory Channel (MC)

Cluster-based code will be executing on one (or more) CPUs within each member of the cluster (remember that a cluster member can be an SMP-based multiprocessor). We saw earlier that multiple CPUs within one member can remain synchronized through simple locks, but simple locks require access to memory that is equally accessible to the two CPUs. Through the Memory Channel, portions of the memory of one cluster member can be mapped into the address space of another member. Don't jump to conclusions here. Standard, *Tru64* UNIX simple locks are not used in this instance due to their reliance on inter-processor interrupts and CPU specific registers (note that the Memory Channel will set aside a page for MC spinlocks). Interestingly, the fact that there is some ability to access data over a common medium (Memory Channel) opens up many possibilities for speedy communications between members. Normal memory access across the Memory Channel should complete within 3 – 5 microseconds.

Figure 2-8 shows two cluster members connected by a cluster interconnect. Currently, the cluster interconnect can be implemented through Memory Channel hardware or Ethernet hardware[4] (new for V5.1A).

Figure 2-8: Cluster Interconnect

4 V5.1A supports 100Mb/Full Duplex connections with a switch; 100Mb/half duplex with a hub (this is supported but not recommended). Gigabit Ethernet is also supported.

2.7.3 Internode Communication Subsystem

No hardware, even something as sophisticated as Memory Channel, can communicate without the help of software. The software responsible for communications across the Memory Channel is referred to as the Internode Communication Subsystem (ICS). Just as a disk has a disk driver, and a terminal has a terminal driver, you can consider the ICS as the software that interacts with the device driver for the MC.

In a very basic sense, the MC is present to provide a speedy communication path between the members of a cluster. Remove the MC from the picture for a minute. Don't we still have a mechanism to communicate between the members? A network interconnect should also suffice as the communication medium.

In version 5.1A of *TruCluster* Server, the Ethernet is also supported as the Cluster Interconnect. This changes the equation slightly since the ICS will also drive the data across the Ethernet. The Ethernet is supported by the Ethernet driver. Don't think about TCP/IP here. That's further up the food chain. Consider the fact that the same Ethernet driver (and device) can send TCP/IP, LAT[5], DECnet[6], and other network protocols across the medium. If that's true, why shouldn't we be able to create a portion of the ICS code such that it handles cluster communication over the Ethernet rather than relying on having a memory channel adapter installed?

From this point forward, we will refer to the Cluster Interconnect (CI), rather than specifically mention the Memory Channel. Essentially, the rest of the concepts will be the same whether the MC or the LAN hardware is used for the CI. As you will see, there are many major cluster components that use the ICS (and indirectly the CI). Note that ICS actually has communication channels for every cluster subsystem.

Figure 2-9 shows the ICS above the CI. Note that the cluster interconnect will exist on each member in the cluster and have some kind of medium connecting the members.

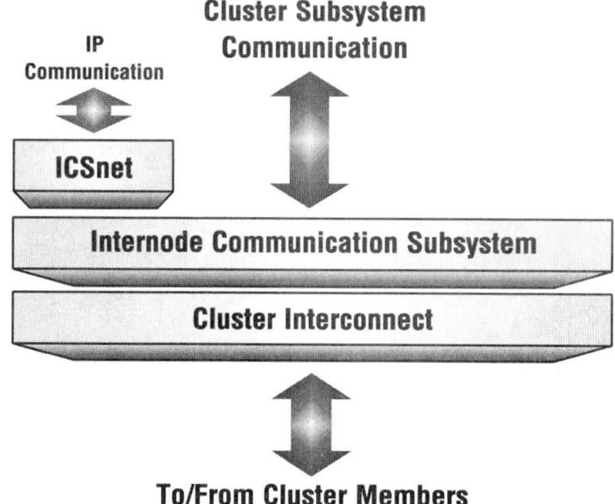

Figure 2-9: ICS to CI Subsystem Relationship

---

5 Local Area Transport – An aging, non-routable network protocol used in terminal servers.

6 DECnet – HP's OSI based network software.

See Chapter 18 for more information on the Internode Communication Subsystem.

2.7.4 Connection Manager

In order for the cluster to function as a unit, there must be a component responsible for checking and maintaining the status of the members. The Connection Manager (CNX) is built into the kernel of *Tru64* UNIX. It runs on each member in a cluster and provides the software glue to keep the cluster stuck together (or to unstick it as the case may be). The CNX on each member in a cluster establishes communication with each other and periodically checks to be sure that the communication path is intact. In the event of a communication path error, the ICS notifies the CNX so that it can take appropriate action, such as removing a member from the cluster and notifying other cluster components of the cluster's change in state.

During cluster formation, the heavy lifting is done by the CNXs as they check for a predetermined number of votes from the members in order to establish the cluster. This agreement is referred to as the cluster quorum. The cluster will not form if enough votes to establish quorum are not present. The CNXs and the quorum mechanism also prevent cluster partitioning, where some members come up as a cluster separate from and unaware of the rest of the cluster.

The CNX uses the ICS and the CI to communicate with the other members (or potential members) of the cluster. The CNX will also communicate with the *Tru64* UNIX Event Manager (EVM) in order to log/report cluster events and communicate with the Cluster Application Availability daemon. The CNX is also responsible for notifying other cluster subsystems when certain events occur. Finally, the CNX must rebuild the Distributed Lock Manager (DLM)[7] and Kernel Group Services (KGS)[8] when members leave the cluster.

Figure 2-10 depicts the CNX as a kernel component interacting with the ICS and the Event Manager.

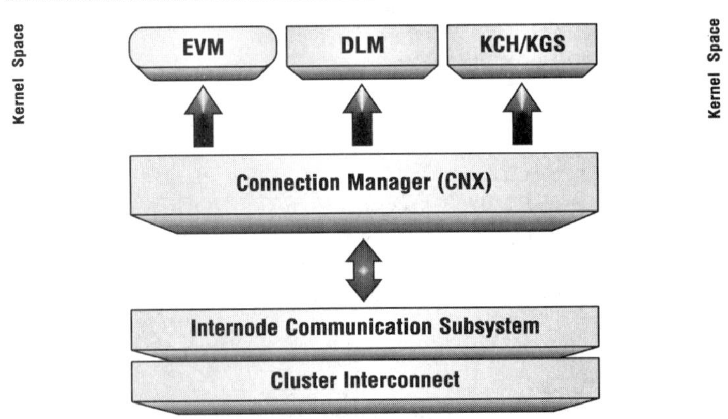

Figure 2-10: Connection Manager Subsystem Relationships

7 See section 2.7.7.

8 See Chapter 18 for more information on KGS.

2.7.5 Cluster Application Availability

Applications can be created to run on the cluster in one of two ways. They can either be cluster-aware or cluster-unaware. Most cluster-unaware applications will need some software intervention if the member on which the application is running goes down. Assuming that it is possible to get the application running on another member in the cluster, the Cluster Application Availability (CAA) component will be responsible for reacting to EVM messages (which may have emanated from CNX or another cluster component such as NIFF – Network Interface Failure Finder) and starting the application on another member. Once the application has restarted, CAA will resume its indirect watch over the cluster-unaware applications. Note that CAA can directly check the status of an application if the application script contains a "check" entry point. See Chapters 23 and 24 for more information on CAA. Take note that cluster-unaware applications come in two flavors: single instance – the software can run on one cluster member at a time; and multi instance – the application can run on multiple members at a time. A multi-instance cluster-unaware application could be using system calls (such as `fcntl(2)`) to synchronize file access, in which case CAA would not be necessary for failover situations since the application code might already be running a synchronized instance on each cluster member. However, a multi-instance cluster-unaware application that uses an interprocess communication (IPC) method such as shared memory and semaphores is a candidate for CAA.

Figure 2-11 shows the CAA software responsible for marshalling cluster-unaware applications. Note that CAA is implemented as a user mode software mechanism.

2.7.6 Cluster-Aware Applications

A cluster-aware application is one that has been written with full use of the cluster based APIs such as the Distributed Lock Manager (DLM) or the MC API. The cluster-aware application can be arranged in several ways. It can be organized such that some processing takes place on multiple

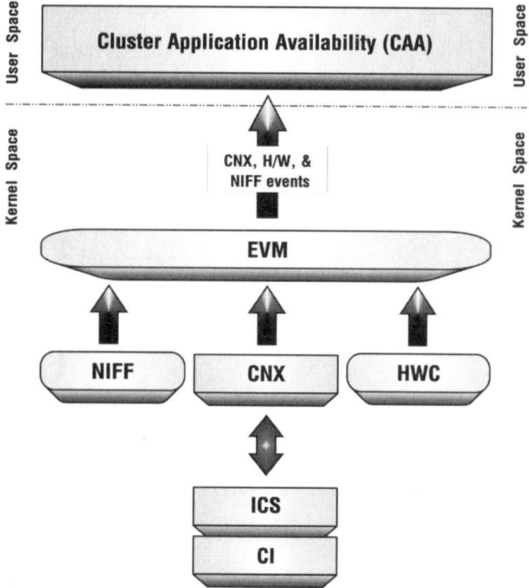

Figure 2-11: CAA Component Relationship

cluster members, or it can be arranged such that parallel processing occurs, or there can be duplication of service. But in each of these cases, there will inevitably be the need to coordinate process-based activities. DLM is available for exactly that kind of synchronization.

2.7.7 Distributed Lock Manager

The Distributed Lock Manager (DLM) is used by cluster-aware applications and by some of the cluster components themselves for cluster-wide synchronization. DLM goes far beyond standard file locking capabilities (although it can be used for file locking as well). In essence, DLM represents a resource (which can be just about anything) with a Resource Name. The Resource Name will have queues of locks (i.e., granted, waiting, waiting for conversion) that represent the applications contending for the resource. Each requested lock will contain the Process Identifier (PID) of the requesting process. Note that in V5.X, PIDs are unique cluster-wide (see Chapter 6 for more information). Therefore each lock can be traced back to a process and a cluster member.

Note that the component is called the DISTRIBUTED Lock Manager. This is because the lock database is distributed across all of the members of the cluster. The DLM database is not fully replicated on all cluster members. Portions of the lock database will live on each member in the cluster. Upon a cluster state transition, one of the items to be resolved is the redistribution of the lock database.

The beauty of the DLM is that it is a cluster-wide mechanism for synchronization. It is one of the few ways that processes can quickly communicate when they exist on separate cluster members. Another way to communicate is to put data into shared files. But file sharing is one of those good news, bad news situations. The good news is that the file can be accessed by several processes at once. The bad news is the same: the file can be accessed by several processes at once. File locking can be used by the applications to coordinate their access to shared files. Furthermore, disk access tends to be much slower than memory access, even when the access is through MC or other ICS options. The lock manager is used by cluster components as well as user processes through the DLM API. Figure 2-12 includes the kernel mode DLM component.

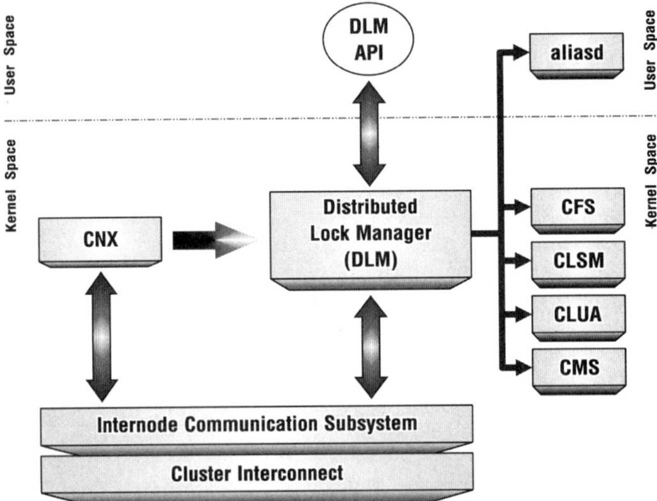

Figure 2-12: DLM Subsystem Relationships

2.7.8 Cluster File System

File system level access to disk storage is supported by the Cluster File System (CFS). CFS makes all file systems mounted on any member in the cluster visible to any other member in the cluster. CFS is implemented using a client-server strategy, where the first member to mount a file system will be the serving member for the rest of the cluster. All file systems created on disks that are found on a non-shared bus will be served by the local member. The Virtual File System (VFS) software (part of the *Tru64* UNIX kernel) will interact with the CFS, which will then issue the request to the physical file system. The physical file system will most likely be the Advanced File System (AdvFS) but could be the Unix File System (UFS), which is currently supported in read-only mode when mounted cluster wide. Note that in V5.1A, a UFS (and MFS – Memory File System) can be available in read-write mode if mounted using the "`-o server_only`" option on the `mount(8)` command. The physical file system will need to interact with another software level that will be responsible for accessing the correct disk.

Figure 2-13 shows the *Tru64* UNIX VFS kernel mode code, which feeds the CFS code and ultimately the local disk driver to get access to file system data. Note that a portion of the CFS client activities is still under wraps but will be examined in the next section. Specifically, there must be a component that is responsible for identifying the target disk if it exists on another member in the cluster.

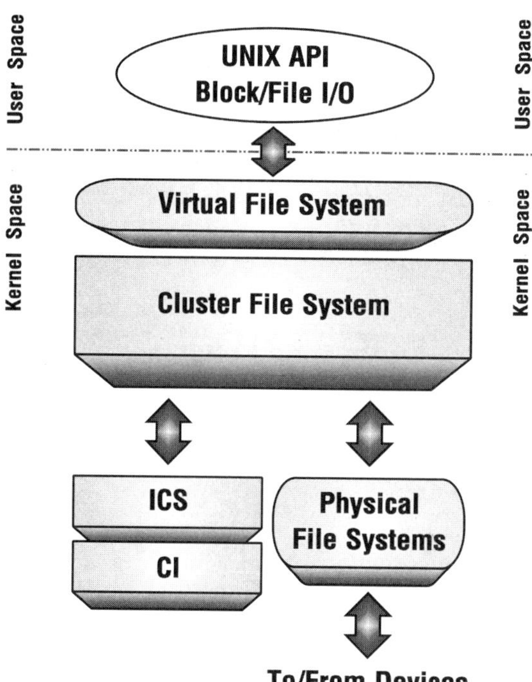

Figure 2-13: CFS Subsystem Relationships

2.7.9 Device Request Dispatcher

The Device Request Dispatcher (DRD) accepts requests for data from the physical file systems and sends the request to the appropriate serving member. Note that the CFS is organized as client-server as is the DRD in some cases. The DRD is at a lower level than the CFS and does not concern itself with file system specifics. It dispatches the requests for data to be retrieved from the devices (thus the name).

The DRD provides cluster-wide access to disk storage regardless of whether the disk storage is accessible locally. The DRD will use the ICS and ultimately the CI to send its requests for data to the appropriate serving member. Note that DRD is not limited to providing access to disks. It also provides access to tape drives, floppy drives, CD-ROM, and DVD-ROM devices.

Be aware that prior to V5.0, DRD stood for Distributed Raw Disk. After V5.0, the Device Request Dispatcher provides access to raw disks and other block devices. Thus the change in the acronym was made.

Figure 2-14 includes the DRD handling requests for device access.

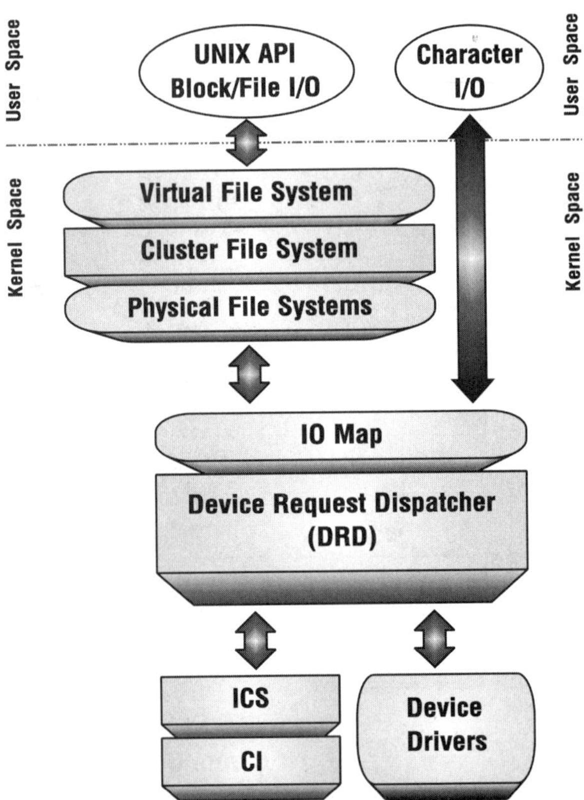

Figure 2-14: DRD Subsystem Relationships

2.7.10 Cluster LSM

The Logical Storage Manager (LSM) provides the ability to create logical storage devices referred to as volumes. The volumes can be arranged in a mirrored fashion, or striped, or concatenated. In any of these cases, LSM presents to the system a pseudo-device that potentially represents multiple physical devices. For this reason, many *Tru64* UNIX users consider LSM to be a software RAID option.

LSM is supported in a cluster except for use on some specialized storage such as the quorum disk and the member's boot disk (discussed later in this book). Note that LSM will ultimately need to specify the I/O to be performed to the lower levels of the software. It would be easy to say that LSM (which is primarily implemented as a pseudo-device driver) will ultimately pass its request to the local driver for processing. The statement would be true on a standalone system. However, on a cluster, LSM must ask the DRD to deliver its data requests to the device drivers. Consider the fact that the device may only be physically accessible to another member of the cluster. DRD will deliver the request to the correct target member.

Figure 2-15 positions the Cluster LSM component just above the DRD.

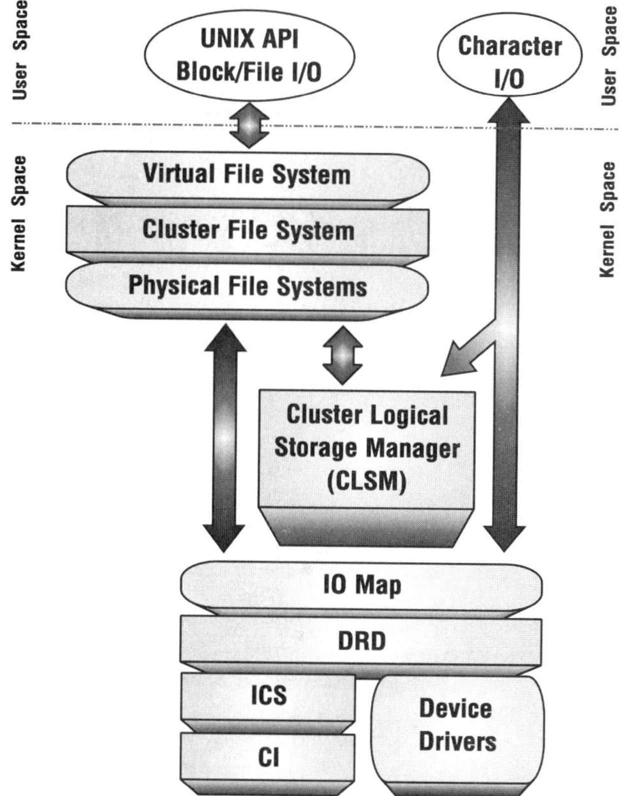

Figure 2-15: CLSM Subsystem Relationships

2.7.11 Cluster Alias

As a closely coupled computing system, a cluster may need to present itself to network applications (such as `telnet(1)` or `ftp(1)`) as a single entity. A cluster may in fact consist of up to eight members, and all eight members may have network interfaces. A client system will be able to reference a single IP address that can represent all of the cluster members. The single cluster alias will transparently provide access to the cluster. Note that multiple aliases can be defined representing subsets of the cluster members if desired.

Let's go back to the problem of the cluster presenting itself to the network as a single entity. This is achieved through the use of the Cluster Alias (CLUA) software. The CLUA software allows client systems (`telnet`, `ftp`, NFS, etc.) to request a connection to the cluster as a server for NFS, FTP, telnet, or other network options. The CLUA software would direct the request to a target member within the cluster and attempt to load balance and distribute the client requests. Later on (in Chapter 16), we will discuss the mechanisms behind CLUA (in addition to the other components for that matter).

Each cluster member may have multiple network interfaces for redundancy, but even with a single network interface, the cluster member will want to be a 'member' of one or more cluster aliases. Notice that the network interfaces are supported by the Network Interface Failure Finder (NIFF) software, which is responsible for reporting an event involving the network interface, to the EVM, which forwards the event to the CAA software, CLUA software, or other software relying on the network. The routing tables would be altered to reflect the current usable interfaces. NIFF would

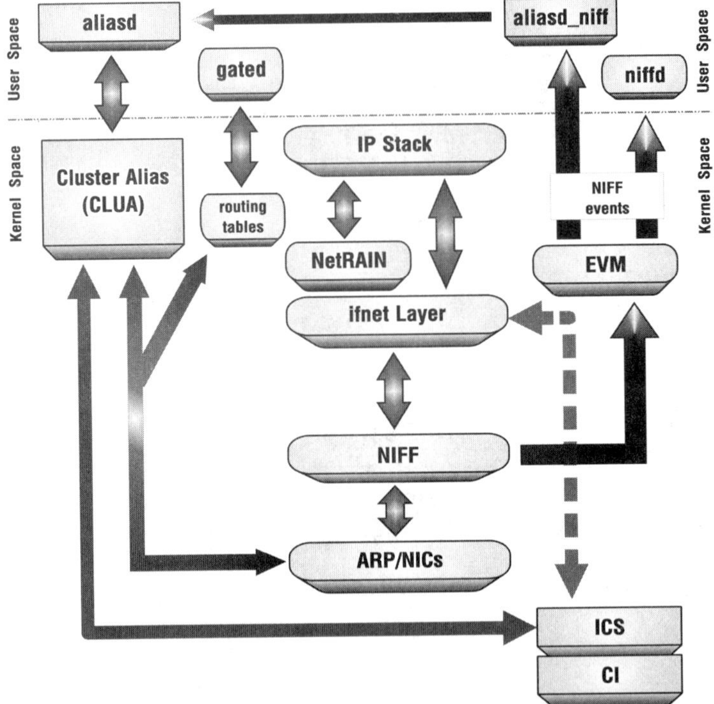

Figure 2-16: CLUA Subsystem Relationships

ultimately interact with Redundant Array of Independent Network interfaces (NetRAIN), which would attempt to fail over the network activities such that another interface is used.

Figure 2-16 includes the user mode NIFF components, as well as the kernel mode NIFF and NetRAIN components. Note that this picture positions the CLUA software in both user mode space (`aliasd`) and kernel mode space.

2.7.12 Cluster Big Picture

Figure 2-17 should give you an appreciation of the complexity of the *TruCluster* software. Each component is there to solve a particular implementation problem. Subsequent chapters will build a full meal out of the appetizers presented in this chapter. You may want to dog-ear this page for reference as you move through the book as it helps to drop back occasionally and look at the big cluster picture.

2.8 References

- *Tru64* UNIX Technical Overview
- *TruCluster* Server Technical Overview
- *Tru64* UNIX QuickSpecs
- *TruCluster* Server QuickSpecs

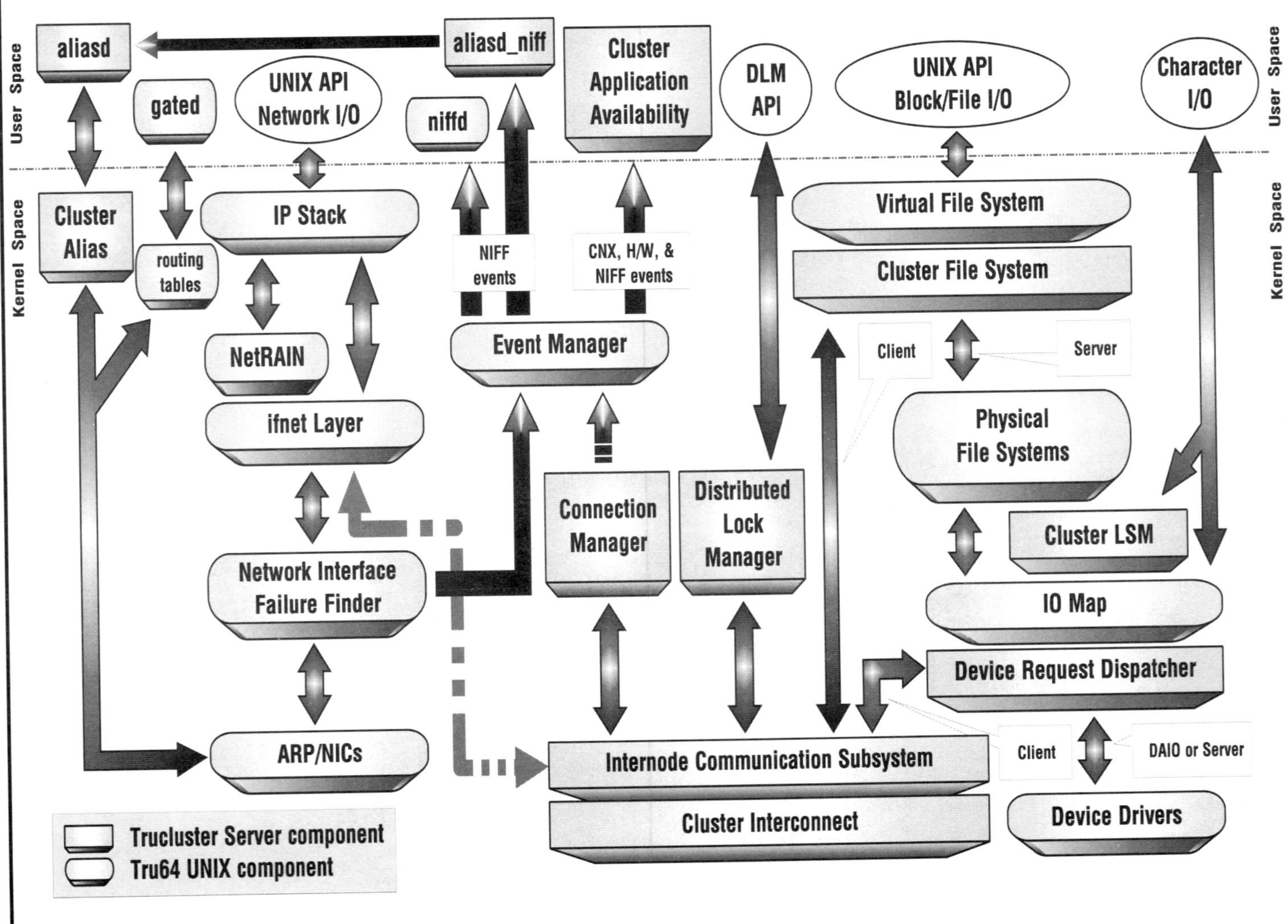

Figure 2-17: Cluster Subsystem Components

3

Designing and Planning a Cluster

3.1 Introduction

A cluster can have many benefits over an otherwise non-clustered solution, but there are many configuration options in designing a *TruCluster* Server cluster solution which have a direct impact on how beneficial it will be over a standalone system. How do you make these configuration choices in order to meet the goals for your solution? This chapter will walk you through these configuration choices beginning with basic high-level options and working towards more detailed levels including:

- Model, configuration, and number of member systems
- Whether or not to include a Quorum Disk
- Type of cluster interconnect
- Number and type of external network connections
- Use of Hardware and/or Software RAID solutions for storage
- Number of storage Host Bus Adaptors and Fabrics

In each of these areas, we will cover the following trade-offs concerning the solution's end goals:

- Availability
- Performance
- Ease of Management and Workload Consolidation

3.1.1 Default Options for Most Solutions

Before addressing each area in detail, it is useful to summarize a best practice or "all other things being equal" configuration that should be your default starting point when evaluating options. Note, these are suggestions and in each case the alternative is a configuration supported by HP for *TruCluster* Server as of this writing (reference the QuickSpecs for the latest supported information). That being said, "safe" default configuration choices are as follows:

- Keep to a moderate size (i.e., something below the currently supported maximum size).

  This is recommended for a number of reasons:

  - Despite *TruCluster* Server being the easiest cluster to manage due to its Single System Image, the larger the cluster, the more complex it is to manage, especially when problems occur.
  - Choosing the largest possible configuration means choosing a less typical and field proven solution. To pick the largest possible cluster is to pick something that is "not the norm" in the *TruCluster* Server user community and hence puts you more towards the bleeding edge.
  - It is wise to leave room for additional cluster members to be added in the future to accommodate growth in the solution.

- Stick with homogeneity of members.

  Keep your cluster with members of the same model and computing resources. In heterogeneous clusters, it is harder to manage workloads because some members cannot take as much work or maybe cannot take the same classes of work that are being run in the cluster. This complicates your administration and failover planning. Heterogeneous members can also complicate patching and support as different hardware models may need different patches, drivers, and kernel builds.

- Use redundant Memory Channel as the cluster interconnect.

  As of this writing, Memory Channel is the older, more established, and better performing interconnect. Unless distance or cost factors are significant, choose Memory Channel.

- Use Fibre Channel based storage backed by hardware RAID[1] with dual-redundant fabrics connected by two Host Bus Adapters (HBAs) on each host.

  Your solution is only as available as its data. Give each host at least two HBAs with paths to storage endpoints to ensure multiple paths for failover. Also, implement at least two fabrics that connect all HBAs from the servers to all the storage end points. This is done so that a failure or need to perform maintenance on a fabric (firmware, addition of more switches, etc.) doesn't leave you high and dry. Finally, most enterprise sites will require a storage solution that will include RAID controllers simply to get the necessary Gigabytes or Terabytes of storage in a convenient manageable package.

- Use redundant network interface cards (NICs) configured for NetRAIN[2] to interface with public networks.

  On the networks that connect your cluster to client systems, utilize the NetRAIN facility to make sure that your network connections stay up even with the loss of an individual NIC card.

3.1.2 Example: A TruCluster Server for a Biotech Research Department

To illustrate the trade-offs and decision process covered in this chapter, a common example will be used and revisited as each major concept is presented. The example is a hypothetical Biotech Company

---

1 Redundant Array of Independent (or Inexpensive) Disks.

2 Redundant Array of Independent NICs

planning a new *TruCluster* Server cluster. The cluster is intended for a research department that has a mixture of custom written and off-the-shelf applications. They currently have a collection of individual standalone systems that host various applications and share data using network protocols such as NFS and FTP.

3.2 The Big Picture – Applications, Member Systems, and the Goal of the Cluster

The first task is to determine the member systems and their configuration as computing resources. This is based on the performance needs of the application(s), the need to ensure capacity for future application growth and to ensure the overcapacity required for availability. This section will discuss meeting these needs by posing a series of questions:

- What are the applications?
- Are multiple applications going to be run in the cluster?
- Are any of the applications parallel (multi-instance)?
- What are the computing resource requirements of each application?
- Will multiple applications run on a single member?
- Is there room to scale out the cluster's size in terms of number of members?
- Is there room to scale up an individual member's computing capacity?
- Will there be homogeneity of member systems (will the systems be similar)?
- Is there required overcapacity in terms of computing resources available in the cluster for failover?

Be forewarned, the process of sizing the basic member systems is often an iterative one as different goals and options are considered.

3.2.1 What Are The Applications?

Sometimes we get caught up in the component technology of a cluster. To state the obvious, therefore, a solution is configured to run applications. So the starting point of designing a *TruCluster* Server cluster-based solution is to specify the applications and then determine the basic platform or platforms and their resources required to run the applications at the desired performance levels.

So what are the applications intended for your cluster? The variety of possible applications is as diverse as that for a standalone server – a Database server, WebServer, Application Server, Compute Server, NFS Server, Mail server, Network Services Server such as DHCP, DNS, BIND etc., and many more possibilities.

3.2.2 Are Multiple Applications Going to be Run in the Cluster?

One important issue is whether more than one application will exist in the cluster. Just like a standalone platform, a cluster can host multiple applications. This can have both up and downsides. On the benefit side, running multiple applications within the cluster can be viewed as a server consolidation strategy. On the negative side, multiple applications within the cluster can make it more complex and error prone to manage.

Running multiple applications on a single large system is commonly referred to as "Server Consolidation." Most system vendors including HP with its Alpha-based GS series and PA-RISC-based Superdomes have implemented special facilities in system partitioning and resource management to compartmentalize the running of multiple applications on a single system to increase robustness, control, and predictability. In a sense, a cluster has its own feature to meet these goals. Each member system can run a specific application or applications of the total workload and be its own unit of resource application, control, and robustness.

Multiple applications do not come without a downside. They will require a larger and more complex environment – and size and complexity are enemies of stability. For instance, applications may have very different system resource needs. If they run on the same cluster member, then it can be difficult to tune and size that member for the combination of the workloads, which may have diametrically opposed optimal tuning requirements. Running workloads with drastically different characteristics on different members solves the immediate problem, but what about when failover is required? If the member systems are then tuned or sized for a specific application, then when failover occurs, behavior will be sub-optimal.

Even if you think you are running one application, be sure to outline all the minor pieces of the application solution that could be thought of separately. For instance, an application where users first log in to the host and then use tools to access a database could be thought of as two pieces, the user login and the database server. Another example would be backup of the data being used by the application. If the data in the cluster is small or unchanging, then backup could be a secondary consideration. On the other hand, if backup requires large resources and time, it may be wise to list it as a separate application.

3.2.2.1 Example

For the Biotech research cluster project, the following applications are identified for the new cluster:

- Home written compute application
- Small standard database application
- Web server application
- User logins for development environment and job dispatching

3.2.3 Are Any of the Applications Parallel (Multi-Instance)?

Parallel applications run as separate instances on multiple cluster members. Together, the instances cooperate to do the work of the application utilizing the resources on each of the cluster member systems on which they run. Multi-instances versions of applications are typically offered as a performance enhancement feature over the single-instance version of the same product. To achieve more throughput or processing by the application, simply start additional instances on additional members in the cluster. In addition to performance benefits, multi-instance applications can also offer faster failover. Rather then having to cold-start the application on a surviving member (when a traditional single-instance application or the member it runs on fails), for multi-instance applications, an instance is already running on additional members at the time any given instance or its member host fails.

The common example for *TruCluster* Server would be Oracle Server and Oracle RAC[3]. Oracle Server is the standard single-instance version of the database product. Oracle RAC is the parallel multi-instance implementation. Although Oracle RAC is the most common case, there are other parallel applications including:

- NFS Serving

  In a *TruCluster* Server, all members can be used to export files over NFS to NFS clients mounting exported file systems from the cluster.

- Web Serving

  Popular Web Servers can be configured to run on multiple members exporting the same HTML[4] files from a common file system to browsers running on clients.

- Advanced Server for UNIX (ASU)

  The HP product for Serving PC file systems and NT Domains from *Tru64* UNIX can be configured as single-instance or multi-instance in a cluster.

- NIS Server

  Once built, all NIS servers on all members will export NIS data to clients.

- Multiple user logins

  In a *TruCluster* Server cluster, the common shared file system means that users can be logged in to multiple cluster members and see the same home directories and shell configuration.

There are some potential downsides for multi-instance applications. The ability of a multi-instance application to scale is dependent on the workload that it is given. The workload you are presenting to the application may not run any faster with multiple instances. The second is that the application vendor may charge a premium in terms of license fee for a multi-instance version of the applications. Finally, the additional complexity of running multiple instances can increase administrative overhead over that of traditional single-instance applications. In the case of *TruCluster* Server, this has been minimized with

---

3 Real Application Clusters

4 HyperText Markup Language

the single common file system. In the case of Oracle, the database itself can be placed in the common file system rather than on raw devices. Please refer to Chapter 13 for more on the cluster file system.

At this step in the cluster solution design process, we would like to simply mark which applications are potentially multi-instance. Note that depending on the workload, etc., it may not be worth the additional complexity.

3.2.3.1 Example

Which of the applications planned for the Biotech cluster could potentially run as multi-instance and which, if any, have been chosen by the site to run multi-instance?

- Home written compute application

  This application is launched in a batch manner and accesses a large collection of input files in read-only mode. It then writes to an output file that can be specified as an argument to the process. The application is inherently multi-instance as long as separate output files are specified for each instance. Multiple instances of the application can be started on a single system, or in the case of the cluster, on multiple members sharing access to common input data and each having its own private output file. These private output files, such as log files, can be implemented by way of Context Dependent Symbolic Links (CDSLs), which are discussed in Chapters 6 and 12. The decision to run the application as a single-instance on a single large member system or multi-instance on multiple smaller systems will come down to the cost of the systems and the scaling across multiple members to obtain the best price-to-performance ratio.

- Small industry standard database application

  The database vendor supplies a multi-instance as well as single-instance version of their product. For this particular usage, the database is small and has very low performance requirements. It is unlikely that going with a multi-instance configuration is worth the additional cost and complexity.

- Web Server application

  The Web Server in question exports a series of read-only HTML files and also has active content to query or update the database mentioned previously. The Web Server could be run multi-instance because the HTML files are read-only, and the database in the backend can guarantee transactional properties if multiple queries or updates come in simultaneously from multiple Web Server instances. On the other hand, the amount of traffic and performance needs are such that it is unlikely that multiple Web Servers will be needed.

- User logins

  User logins could be made to be multi-instance. As long as a user can log in to any system and see the same home directories, shells, and tools, then it doesn't matter whether a group of active logged in users are all on one member system or spread over multiple member systems. The major activity of the logged in users is to submit computational jobs. In addition, some users also access the database or work on developing the applications. For this cluster, the user application could be deployed on a single host or multiple hosts. The final decision can be based on cost-effectiveness by comparing the price of one larger platform with multiple smaller platforms.

3.2.4 How Much Computing Resources Do The Applications Require?

This must be done for each application individually. If the single application were running on a standalone platform (or multiple, if multi-instance), what class, model, and configuration of system(s) would be required to meet its performance needs? The details include CPU, Memory, Network I/O Bandwidth, Storage I/O Bandwidth, and total Storage.

Application sizing performance for a platform is not always easy. This task is independent of the cluster technology except for the scaling factor as the member count is increased for multi-instance applications. For some standard popular software applications, such as Oracle, some references exist. In other cases, sizing a new platform for an application can be based on the site's experience running the application on an existing smaller or older platform.

3.2.4.1 Example

Like many sites, the Biotech Company has previous experience running either the same or the current incarnation of the applications on standalone servers in the environment. To size the new platforms for the new cluster, they will start out by studying the performance resource consumption rates on the current environments. Next, they will evaluate the latest server models and choose memory and cpu counts for the servers in the new cluster.

- Home written compute application

  If run on a single system, it would require a GS160 class system. The GS160 would require twelve CPUs, 32GBs of Memory, six HBAs, and approximately one TB of storage. Alternatively, the application could be split over multiple systems in a cluster, the best option being three ES45 class systems. Each of these servers would have four CPUs, 8GB of Memory, and two HBAs. The network interface requirements are low. A single, logical interface implemented with two Fast Ethernet physical NICs would be adequate.

- Small standard database application

  Assuming it is run on a single node as a single instance, a DS20 system with two CPUs, 4GB of memory, and two HBAs would be adequate. The total storage required is 400 GB. Network interface requirements would be low. A single logical interface implemented with two Fast Ethernet physical NICs would be adequate.

- Web Server application

  Assuming it is run on a single node as a single instance, a DS10 system with one CPU, 2GB of memory, and two HBAs would be adequate. The total storage required is 200 GB. Network interface requirements would be low. A single logical interface implemented with two Fast Ethernet physical NICs would be adequate.

- User logins and development environment application

  If run on a single system, a single ES45 with four CPUs, 8GB of memory, and two HBAs would be more then adequate. The total storage required would be 400 GB. Network interface requirements would be moderate. A single logical interface implemented with two Fast Ethernet physical NICs would be adequate.

3.2.5 Will Multiple Applications Run on a Single Member?

When we plan how the applications will be mapped to cluster members, we have the choice of dedicating specific members to a specific application or running multiple applications on a single cluster member. One to one mapping of applications to servers in a cluster (or standalone servers) can simplify tuning, support, and computing resource management for the members. On the other hand, maximizing the investment in platforms is an incentive to run multiple applications on the same box.

This decision can have a lot to do with the nature of the applications and the services available in the operating system to simplify and control the running of multiple applications using resource management.

- Do the applications have extreme resource consumption patterns that make sharing a host difficult to optimize?
- Would utilizing the *Tru64* UNIX Operating system's resource management facilities (including processor sets, class scheduling, and the ARMTech fair share scheduler) simplify resource management on a server?
- Would multiple applications conflict because they run at different times of the day?
- Even if a set of applications can share a host, how does the combination of applications affect the system if they were to failover to another cluster member, which is already running a different set of jobs?
- Would the doubling up of applications allow the overall cluster to be smaller, thus simplifying the cluster at large configuration and management?

3.2.5.1 Example

In the case of the Biotech cluster, some of the applications could be run on the same member without major risk:

- The web server and database can run on a common platform because neither is expected to be an excessive resource consumer. Also, the web server interfaces with the database so running them on the same platform will improve the performance seen by the web server's clients.

After this, the resulting workloads could be reduced to:

- Home written compute application

  No change from earlier description.

- Small standard database application and Web Server Application

  A single ES40 system with four CPUs, 8 GB of memory, two HBAs, and 600GB of storage would be adequate.

- User logins and development environment application

  If run on a single system, one ES45 with four CPUs, 8GB of memory, and two HBAs would be more than adequate. The total storage required would be 400GB. Network interface requirements would be moderate. A single logical interface implemented with two Fast Ethernet physical NICs would be adequate.

3.2.6 Will There Be Homogeneity of Member Systems?

The *TruCluster* Server software supports homogeneous or heterogeneous cluster configurations. Homogeneous clusters have members that consist of the same model and computing resources and have the advantage of simplifying management of the cluster in a number of ways. First, the site does not need to worry about keeping track of which systems have which computing resources when assigning applications within the cluster either statically or when failover occurs. Moreover, tuning and hardware and software maintenance through patches can be more standardized. Heterogeneous environments can be more cost-effective as the site either pulls together existing hardware of different model types to make the cluster, or exactly matches systems to the applications when they are drastically different needs.

3.2.6.1 Example

In the Biotech cluster, no legacy servers will be included in the cluster, and the ease of management of a homogeneous cluster is deemed a priority so the design will center on a homogeneous configuration.

- 3 ES45s – Compute application
- 1 ES45 – Database and Web Server
- 1 ES45 – User Logins

Note that in the case of the Database and Web Server system, the server will have more power than is absolutely required by the application in the interest of keeping the cluster homogeneous.

3.2.7 Is Availability Insured By Providing Additional Computing Capacity?

Almost all cluster solutions have high availability as a design criterion. In this case, the cluster must have enough spare computing power so that if a member fails, the applications running on it can be moved to another cluster member and continue to run. The major question is what level of service is required for the application when moved to a new member. If it is the same as before the original member failed, then free computing capacity of the same amount as the failed member must be available to failover to. For example, if the cluster has one application running on one member, another member of the same size is required to meet this requirement. The key is that this additional member is idle until such time as the first member fails, causing the application to failover. Having 100% idle computing power is the worst case and can be reduced if you do the following:

- As cluster size increases, the overhead of the spare capacity can be amortized over a number of members. For instance, if the cluster has two applications on two members, it requires a third idle member to take either of the two applications if the current member fails.

- The site may be willing to live with degraded level of service or the termination of less essential applications when a failure condition exists. For instance, a two-node cluster with two applications could either allow both applications to run on a single member when one fails with degraded performance, or terminate the less important application when failover occurs.

Complicating all of this failover planning is the computing resources required by the applications of the cluster and whether or not the cluster will be homogeneous in member systems. For instance, if one workload requires an extremely large server, and other applications in the cluster do not, an additional large server would be required for failover of the large application – independent of the smaller needs of the remaining applications.

3.2.7.1 Example

The Biotech cluster design has already been narrowed down to a homogeneous cluster. This makes failover planning easier. The minimum number of members to support the applications without considering failover is already 5. The cost of adding a 6th member as a failover host is not excessive to the site's plans so that solution will be taken. This results in a cluster as follows:

- 3 ES45s – Compute application
- 1 ES45 – Database and Web Server
- 1 ES45 – User Logins
- 1 ES45 – Failover host for the other jobs

3.2.8 Is There Room to Scale Out Cluster Size In Terms of Number of Members?

Many sites like to be able to design into a solution the ability to grow in computing capacity over time. Sometimes it is known up front that the application load will increase over time; other times it's simply the desire to be ready in case it does, due to an unforeseen event. With a cluster, the computing power can be grown in two dimensions – the size of the members and the number of members.

The changes that can trigger a need to grow the cluster by adding new members are:

- The addition of new applications
- The number of members running instances of a multi-instance application
- Moving applications that were sharing member systems onto their own member systems

In the case of the number of cluster members, the currently supported maximum is eight nodes. This means that if a site would like to be able to grow, it needs to start with a cluster size of less than this value.

3.2.8.1 Example

In the Biotech cluster solution, as it stands there are six members. This leaves room to add two more members either for new applications or because in the case of the multi-instance compute jobs, more computing power is to be supplied by adding instances.

3.2.9 Is There Room to Scale Up Individual Member Computing Capacity/Size?

As we discussed previously, the capability to grow in computing resources is often a requirement for computing solutions. Growing the cluster in number of members can be useful for certain types of requirements but not others. A key growth that can only be met by increasing the size of an individual member is:

- A single-instance application that needs additional computing resources on the member where it is running.

In this case, we are looking at the traditional growth mechanisms for a standalone platform: increasing the number of CPUs, memory, HBAs, etc., or replacing the system with a larger server model.

The largest single platform in the AlphaServer stable has been the GS320. Recently coming onto the scene is the even larger GS1280 "Marvel" class systems. In the case of both models, they are moduler and scalable. A site can start with a small configuration, which can later be expanded/upgraded to many times its initial installed size.

3.2.9.1 Example

The Biotech cluster solution is currently centered on ES45 servers. The next size platform would be a GS-series platform, which would have plenty of scalability beyond the ES45 in terms of CPU count, memory, etc.

3.3 The Remaining Details – Cluster Interconnect, Network Connections, and Storage

Once the number of hosts and their size have been chosen, there is a second level of decisions concerning the configuration of the cluster. This includes whether to have a quorum disk, the configuration of the cluster interconnect, external network interfaces, and storage.

3.3.1 Should a Quorum Disk be Configured?

The *TruCluster* Server Connection Manager (CNX) component is responsible for maintaining a list of which cluster members are actively participating members at any moment in time. This "list" is made available to the cluster software running on all members. This current membership list takes into account hardware failures that cause some systems to crash or if the cluster interconnect communication were to fail between members. As part of the CNX design, a quorum disk is a configuration option. Its necessity or usefulness is dependent on the number of members of the cluster configuration. We will discuss it briefly here, but you can read more about the quorum disk in Chapter 17.

3.3.1.1 When is a Quorum Disk "Required"?

The short answer is for two-node clusters. The longer explanation starts with a note about the word "required". The *TruCluster* Server software never insists that a quorum disk be defined for any node count cluster for that cluster to boot and become operational. Yet, if we want to be ready in the event of an individual node failure for the remaining member to stay operational, then a quorum disk is a "requirement" for two-node clusters. If a quorum disk is not configured for a two-node cluster, and either member or all redundant cluster interconnect rails were to fail, the cluster would suspend operations.

3.3.1.2 When is a Quorum Disk Beneficial (As Opposed to "Required")?

A quorum disk is beneficial for four, six and eight node clusters. For a cluster with an even number of members, the quorum disk allows one additional member system to be unavailable and the cluster will continue to operate (that would be the case for a same size cluster not configured with a quorum disk). For instance, in a four-node cluster without a quorum disk, if two nodes are down, fail, or become unreachable on the cluster interconnect, the cluster will suspend operation. If a quorum disk is added to the four-node cluster's configuration, then it takes three nodes to be unavailable for the cluster to suspend operation. Note that this benefit does not exist with odd-node count clusters.

See Chapter 17 for more details.

3.3.1.3 Example

The Biotech cluster is at six nodes. So, they will add a quorum disk to increase the threshold at which the cluster suspends operations from three to four nodes.

3.3.2 What Type of Cluster Interconnect Should Be Used?

TruCluster Server now supports two types of cluster interconnects: Memory Channel and LAN-based. In addition, either interconnect type can be configured as either a single rail or in a dual-redundant configuration. The short and conservative answer is to use Memory Channel because it has been supported the longest and has the best performance characteristics. Of course there are some overriding reasons to use a LAN based cluster interconnect instead – cost, distance, and slot restrictions on the host member. These will be discussed in more detail in the following sections.

3.3.2.1 The Role of the Cluster Interconnect

The performance and integrity of the cluster interconnect is critical to the operation of the cluster. The cluster interconnect is used for communication and synchronization between the cluster software running on all the members. For instance, in the case of the Connection Manager (CNX) component of *TruCluster* Server, partial or total failure of the cluster interconnect can result in individual cluster members suspending or the entire cluster suspending operation. With this in mind, it is critical to a successful cluster to use a redundant interconnect configuration and to select a cluster interconnect which has the best performance possible.

The cluster interconnect is presented to the system and users as an IP network whether it is Memory Channel or LAN-based. A conservative approach to ensure that the full performance of the cluster interconnect is available to the cluster software is to not utilize this IP network between cluster members for any application or administrative high bandwidth consuming tasks. If high performance communication between members were required between applications on different members, a conservative solution would be to implement an additional network common to all members for this traffic.

3.3.2.2 Memory Channel Interconnect

The Memory Channel is the original and longest supported cluster interconnect for the *TruCluster* Server software. It is based on PCI-based Memory Channel cards that reside in the members that in the standard configuration are connected in a star fashion to a Memory Channel Hub. If only two hosts are being connected, the hub can be omitted with setting jumpers on the memory channel boards (this is covered in detail in Chapter 4). In this configuration, the maximum point-to-point distance between two members is twenty meters. Memory channel has high bandwidth and very low latency compared to traditional network technology making it attractive for use between tightly connected cluster members. As an alternative configuration option that trades off performance for distance, instead of one hub, two hubs with a Fibre Channel bridge between them can be used to span larger distances of up to 6000 meters point to point. For high availability, two memory channel rails should be configured between member systems. The cluster automatically detects the two interconnects and uses one as active and the other as a passive standby LAN-Based Cluster Interconnect

Starting with V5.1A, *TruCluster* Server supports LAN-based cluster interconnects built from industry standard fast Ethernet or gigabit Ethernet hardware. Both technologies offer an industry standard hardware solution for cluster interconnects with a trade-off in varying degrees of performance when compared with memory channel. Gigabit Ethernet can be nearly comparable to memory channel in both bandwidth and latency, but FastEthernet is significantly slower in both cases. Also be aware that LAN interconnect support is not a wildcard that allows you to use any "network" you might otherwise be able to configure between two systems. You should know that restrictions exist concerning distance and public or private nature of the network. First the total point-to-point distance for NSPOF LAN interconnect configurations is finite at 1100 meters, and although this is much greater than a standard Memory Channel configuration, the memory channel configuration with a fibre bridge can actually span longer distances at 6000 meters. Various restrictions exist for the physical LAN interconnect configuration related to the number of switches allowed between members (currently three), which are described in the Cluster LAN Interconnect guide that is part of the *TruCluster* Server documentation set from HP.

Additionally, the LAN interconnect is expected to be a private network solely to the cluster and no other systems or applications. With a memory channel configuration, it is difficult if not impossible to get non-cluster systems connected to the interconnect. With a "network," it would be easy to do but disastrous if the additional traffic made the interconnect unusable by the cluster members.

For availability, the LAN interconnect should be configured as dual redundant at the hardware level. It is then required that the two rails be configured using the base system's NetRAIN facility so that they are treated as one logical rail. The NetRAIN facility is a standard component of the *Tru64* UNIX operating system.

3.3.2.3 Comparing and Contrasting Memory Channel and LAN-Based Interconnects

Table 3-1 lists the attributes of Memory Channel and LAN-based cluster interconnects.

Note the following:

- In performance, Memory Channel has a bandwidth comparable to Gigabit but a much better latency performance characteristic.
- In the area of maximum distances, LAN-Based solutions are better unless you use the fibre-bridge configuration for Memory Channel.
- In relative cost metric, the highest option is memory channel. In absolute terms, however, Memory Channel cards and hub are not excessive vis-à-vis Gigabit hardware.
- In NSPOF configurations, Memory Channel and LAN-based cluster interconnects are comparable in supporting multiple rails in an active/passive mode until the active rail fails. Memory channel configurations support a maximum of two physical rails. The LAN interconnect supports as many as the NetRAIN subsystem allows (two is typically adequate).
- In the area of release history, although both types of interconnects are fully supported by HP for *TruCluster* Server, Memory Channel hardware and the *TruCluster* Server software to drive it have been around longer and have significantly more test and deployed hours behind it at the current time.
- Memory Channel will detect communication failures much more quickly since it doesn't have to wait for IP timeouts to occur.

The conservative approach and recommended rule of thumb is to use Memory Channel unless you have a compelling reason to do otherwise – i.e., distance, cost, or member system slot restrictions.

3.3.2.4 Example

For the Biotech research department, they started with the assumption they'd use Memory Channel. Looking at cost, they do not find the cost of the Memory Channel components disproportionate to the cost of LAN-Based components or the total cost of the cluster. In addition, the six ES45 nodes of the cluster will be located in a pair or racks in a common equipment room with no greater than five meters between the furthest systems point-to-point.

3.3.3 Should the Cluster Interconnect Be Dual-Redundant?

Given the previous discussion of the critical role of the cluster interconnect in the operation of the cluster, the answer is "Yes." Note that although the cluster software does not insist on redundant interconnect hardware as an active software-enforced hardware configuration rule, it is the reasonable thing to do to protect the stability and availability of the cluster as a whole.

Interconnect Type	Relative Performance		Point to Point Max Distance Supported in a NSPOF Config	Relative Cost	Slots Consumption	Redundancy Model	1st Supported Release
	Bandwidth	Latency					
Memory Channel	High	Low	20 meters	High	1 PCI slot/rail	Active/Passive	5.0
Memory Channel with Fibre Bridge	Medium	Medium	6000 meters	High	1 PCI slot/rail	Active/Passive	5.0
Fast Ethernet	Medium	Med/High	1100 meters	Low	¼ slot/rail (4-port card)	Active/Passive (NetRAIN)	5.1A
Gigabit Ethernet	High	Med/High	1100 meters	Med/High	1 PCI slot/rail	Active/Passive (NetRAIN)	5.1A

Table 3-1: Memory Channel Vs LAN Comparison

3.3.3.1 Example

For the Biotech cluster, a dual-redundant Memory Channel cluster interconnect configuration will be used.

3.3.4 Should Network Interfaces be Highly Available?

If clients and users cannot access the cluster over network interfaces, it is as good as down. So yes, configure network interfaces for high availability.

How is it done? *TruCluster* Server solutions have mechanisms at two levels to insure that network connectivity stays up in the face of failure. At the first level, the *TruCluster* Server software's Cluster Alias capability can be used. The cluster alias can be configured so that if a member's network interface fails, another member with a working interface can act as a proxy, accepting and forwarding network traffic from the original member over the cluster interconnect. At the *Tru64* UNIX level, the NetRAIN and LAG[5] interfaces provide a means to create a single logical IP interface from multiple physical network cards and remain highly available when one of the physical interface cards fail. You can read about NetRAIN and LAG in more detail in Chapters 9 and 12.

---

5 Link Aggregation (or trunking)

3.3.5 Default Basic Remedy to a Failed Network Interface on a Member - Using a CLUA Common-Subnet Alias

The Cluster Alias (CLUA) subsystem is a component of *TruCluster* Server software that allows virtual network addresses to be created and used to allow clients to connect to services in the cluster, independent of the member's native IP addresses and any failures to those interfaces or members. The Cluster Alias subsystem is described in detail in Chapter 16. Here we will briefly describe configuration options and alternatives when designing a cluster solution.

Using the Cluster Alias with the default, common subnet alias type, requires no special hardware beyond each member systems having a network interface to the public network, which would be the norm anyway. Under this configuration scheme, if the one network interface of a member currently receiving traffic from the outside world fails, then the Cluster Alias subsystem will automatically choose another member to receive incoming traffic on its interface on the same subnet and forward any traffic destined to the original host over the cluster interconnect to reach it. This scheme will meet most requirements by offering the following:

- Configuring member systems with only a single NIC to a public network, network traffic will be delivered to a member even when its single physical NIC to that network fails.

In rare cases, the routing incoming traffic over the cluster interconnect could cause the following issues:

- For some applications, the additional step of being rerouted over the cluster interconnect might result in an unacceptable performance impact.
- The additional traffic on the cluster interconnect could, in extreme cases, impact the ability of the cluster to use the cluster interconnect for other purposes, such as the Connection Manager subsystem and forwarding I/O for devices and file systems.

If you encounter a situation where you believe using the Alias is causing excessive traffic on the cluster interconnect, you can use software configuration options and additional hardware to minimize the effect. These methods are described next.

3.3.6 Additional Options That Eliminate Any Potential Network Traffic Being Re-Routed Over the Network Interconnect

As described in the previous section, using the default cluster alias with single network interfaces can result in undesirable network traffic on the cluster interconnect. If this is an issue for the cluster you are designing, you have four options.

3.3.6.1 Use CAA to Relocate an Application When a Network Interface Fails

Utilize the Cluster Application Availability (CAA) framework to create a dependency between an application and a network interface to trigger failover of the application to a member with a working external network interface when the network interface on the member it is running has a failure. This option has the following pros and cons:

- Does not require additional hardware in terms of physical NICs
- Does result in downtime for the application as it is relocated to another member.

3.3.6.2 Use a CLUA Virtual Subnet Alias

Create your alias as a CLUA "virtual subnet alias" and have two external network interfaces on each member, connected to two different subnets, which are connected by a common router. In this scheme, if one network interface fails, the router will recognize the other network interface of the member as a valid path and forward network traffic to the same host using this alternative path. This option has the following pros and cons:

- Eliminates the need to re-route network traffic over the cluster interconnect when a single physical network interface fails
- Is transparent to the application and does not require it to restart
- Not only survives the failure of an individual NICbut also survives the failure of an entire subnet between the members and a router
- Requires multiple physical network interfaces
- Requires an additional network interface
- Requires all members to be configured on two subnets connected by a common router

3.3.6.3 Utilize Tru64 UNIX NetRAIN Feature

Utilize *Tru64* UNIX's NetRAIN configuration option for network interfaces. NetRAIN is independent of the cluster and allows a logical network interface to be created from multiple physical network interfaces on the same host. If one interface fails, the kernel transparently fails over to another physical network interface in the set without disruption to the application. This option has the following pros and cons:

- Eliminates the need to re-route network traffic over the cluster interconnect when a single physical network interface fails
- Is transparent to the application and does not require it to restart
- Requires multiple physical network interfaces

3.3.6.4 Utilize Tru64 UNIX LAG Feature

Tru64 UNIX's LAG feature, like NetRAIN, allows multiple physical network interfaces to be used to create a single logical network interface with high availability characteristics. The advantage of LAG is that all physical network interfaces are used in parallel in an active/active scheme to increase aggregate bandwidth of the logical interface. Though LAG can survive the failure of a physical network interface in the set, this performance gain comes at the availability downside that all of the physical network interfaces must be connected to a common network switch. This option has the following pros and cons:

- Eliminates the need to re-route network traffic over the cluster interconnect when a single physical network interface fails
- Is transparent to the application and does not require it to restart
- Offers performance scaling
- Requires multiple physical network interfaces
- The switch that all NICs have to be connected to becomes a single point of failure

As stated earlier, utilizing single network interfaces and the default-style common subnet alias will be sufficient for most clusters and applications. Only if excessive network traffic on the cluster interconnect is known to be unacceptable should further measures be considered.

3.3.6.5 Example

For the Biotech cluster, two networks are required. One network will be used only by cluster members. It will be for communications between the user "login" system and compute farm. An additional network will connect all members to the outside world. The primary traffic will come in to the login system and the web server.

For both networks, the site will start out with single NICs and utilize the Cluster Alias subsystem to reroute traffic in the event of a failure. In the case that the private network cannot provide the required performance, the site is prepared to invest in additional NICs and convert the interface to LAG.

3.3.7 How Should Storage Be Configured?

The cluster and applications that run in it need dependable, reliable, and redundant access to storage devices. The minimum disk configuration for a cluster is the following:

- A disk with three partitions for cluster root (`/`), `/usr`, and `/var` file systems
- A disk for each member of the cluster to contain the member's `boot_partition`, `swap`, and a `cnx` data areas
- An additional disk to be used as a quorum disk for clusters configurations with an even number of members

Beyond these minimum configuration requirements, a cluster can have its cluster root (`/`), `/usr`, and `/var` over multiple disks and will certainly have additional disks for use in file systems for applications and users.

The availability features at your disposal to make these storage containers highly available in *TruCluster* Server are at different levels in the I/O hierarchy:

- Using LSM and/or Hardware RAID to create highly available volumes
- Using multiple paths from different members relying on the *TruCluster* Server software's Device Request Dispatcher (DRD) to ensure that if all paths to storage from one member fail, another member can access the device on behalf of the member and transfer any required I/O across the cluster interconnect
- Using the Multi-Pathing between HBAs on the same host (intrinsic in *Tru64* UNIX)
- Implementing redundant fabrics connecting HBAs to storage endpoints

As a general rule, try and make the storage architecture for the cluster as symmetrical as possible for ease of implementation, management, and troubleshooting.

General default rule of thumb:

- Have at least two HBAs in each host.
- Have at least two fabrics between the hosts and their storage.
- Assume the use of hardware RAID Arrays unless it is a small storage cluster and cost is an issue. Evaluate the use of LSM for ease of management or additional features on a case by case basis.

3.3.8 Use Hardware RAID and/or LSM?

In today's computing environments for standalone systems as well as clusters, two methods are available to implement highly available RAID configurations for disk devices – software based RAID and hardware based RAID. In *Tru64* UNIX and the *TruCluster* Server software, these are available as Logical Storage Manager (LSM) and the StorageWorks family of RAID Arrays respectively. The standard question is, "Which of these two solutions should be used?"

3.3.8.1 Enterprise Servers with 100GB+ of storage

The original question of software versus hardware RAID is lightly off target for almost all Enterprise solutions utilizing *Tru64* UNIX. The reason is that in these cases, the site will already be investing in StorageWorks devices, which come with RAID capability simply to physically attach and reasonably manage the amount of total physical storage connecting to the cluster. In other words, hardware RAID is almost always a given as available to use, so the real question becomes: "I've already paid for hardware RAID capability in the storage hardware. Do I also utilize software RAID in LSM?"

The answer is usually "No," for cost and simplicity, unless the following factors cause the site to choose LSM:

- The site wants to gain additional performance benefits by creating stripe sets that include hardware RAID sets being hosted by different RAID Arrays. Making use of this capability is rarely used as it only makes sense for sites with very large amounts of storage and very high bandwidth requirements.
- The site is ultra paranoid and wants to mirror storage with LSM across hardware cabinets.
- The site wants to make use of additional features in LSM other than RAID for their own merits. These include flexible volume management and the ability to create a volume of any arbitrary size independent of physical disk or hardware RAID properties.

3.3.8.2 Small Scale Cost-Conscious Configurations

You may ask, "What if the solution I'm putting together does not have 100+ GB of storage and could be put together with simple storage devices, which do not have RAID capability built in?" In this case, we get into the classic question of hardware RAID versus software RAID and the general answer will come down to cost.

- Can a simpler hardware solution with LSM be less expensive than a more complex hardware solution without LSM and still provide the total bytes of storage to the cluster?

Another lesser consideration is that LSM cannot be used with specific file systems (and partitions) used in the cluster. The quorum disk, if configured, and any member boot disks cannot be used as LSM volumes (swap can be an LSM volume, but the entire boot disk – `boot_partition`, CNX partition, and `swap` – cannot be under LSM control which is our point here). How much of a disadvantage is this?

- If a member boot disk fails, that member will crash. If quorum is configured properly and all other hosts are available, the cluster will continue to operate. Any applications running on the failed node will need to be restarted on a surviving node.
- If the quorum disk fails on a cluster that has not lost any members, the cluster will continue to operate. So there is no immediate impact. It can only impact the cluster if its failure goes undetected and is not repaired, and one of the member hosts fails or shuts down causing the cluster to lose quorum.

  Online replacement procedures for both member boot disks and the quorum disk are covered in Chapter 22.

Taking these two factors into account, the major non-cost availability difference in behavior between a cluster configured with software RAID versus hardware RAID is that in the event of a member boot disk failure, a software RAID configured cluster will result in an application restart.

3.3.9 Independent Paths from Each Member to All Storage Devices

The next level of storage availability in a *TruCluster* Server is that if a cluster member does not have a working path to a storage device but another member does, the member with a working path will "serve" the I/O to the member without the path. This feature is implemented in the Device Request Dispatcher (DRD) subsystem of the *TruCluster* Server software and is described in more detail in Chapter 15. This means that as long as one member has a working path to a storage device, all members can continue to access it.

This encourages us to configure paths from more than one member to all storage containers the cluster uses. Before we think too deeply on this and ponder which two members will be have connections to which storage, etc., the issue becomes moot with the typical use of Fibre Channel today. The overwhelming configuration of *Tru64* UNIX and the *TruCluster* Server software is to connect all members to a Fibre Channel fabric that is connected to all storage devices. This symmetry is the simplest, most cost-effective means and utilizes the ability of Fibre Channel to address a large number of devices and host bus adaptors through a single Fabric.

So, assuming that all members are connected by a common fabric to all storage devices, is utilizing DRD the final answer? Not quite.

- The DRD alone cannot protect us if we have a single fabric between all members, and the storage or the fabric fails.
  - The solution here is to implement multiple redundant fabrics between the hosts and the storage. This implies at least two HBAs in each host connected to two different fabrics, and the storage arrays connected through different ports to the two different fabrics.
- The DRD's rerouting of I/O over the cluster interconnect in an extreme case might impact the performance of the application or the stability of the cluster as a whole. To alleviate this concern:
  - Utilize CAA to detect failure of storage paths on the host an application is running on and re-start the application on a host that does have working connectivity, or
  - Utilize *Tru64* UNIX's multi-pathing capability and have multiple redundant host bus adaptors from the same member to the storage. Not that performance reasons alone promotes the use of this, but a single member will also utilize all HBAs in an active/active scheme that scales performance with the number of paths.

3.3.9.1 Example

The Biotech Company's six-node ES45 cluster will contain two HBAs on each system for availability and to meet performance requirements. Two fabrics using two switches will be implemented to connect each member to each HSG raid array through two different independent paths. LSM will also be used as convenience for database volumes.

4

Cluster Configuration Planning

"Planning without action is futile, action without planning is fatal."

– Japanese Proverb

"Long-range planning does not deal with future decisions, but with the future of present decisions."

– Peter Drucker

The key to any successful endeavor is careful planning and preparation. Successful implementation of a cluster takes planning – planning for the short term and planning for the long term – but planning nonetheless. This chapter provides ideas for carefully and logically planning and preparing a successful *TruCluster* Server implementation – both for the short term and for the long term.

4.1 Memory Requirements for *TruCluster* Server

As of this writing, the memory requirement for a *TruCluster* Server cluster member is the amount of memory to install *Tru64* UNIX plus at least an additional 64 MB for the cluster software. So, if it takes 128 MB of memory to install and operate *Tru64* UNIX, each cluster member is required to have at least 192 MB of memory to operate in a *TruCluster* Server environment.

4.2 Planning the Disk Devices

Frequently, the planning for the system disk(s) for both the initial *Tru64* UNIX installation and the *TruCluster* Server implementation is overlooked. In fact, even experienced Systems Administrators fail to consider how big or little a partition on a system disk should be or what file system goes where until it is too late and they are already installing the system.

This lack of planning creates serious problems both in the short and long term. At best, you will end up rebuilding your system before you have any users and wasting valuable time in the process. At worst, you may have to have an extended amount of down time on a production system that is supposedly highly available. Bottom line: failure to plan is a poor practice.

We recognize that you are eager to start the implementation of *TruCluster* Server right away. But wait. Take a minute and think about what you are about to do.

Take your eagerness to start and channel it into planning the devices that you will use for the initial *Tru64* UNIX system disk and the eventual *TruCluster* Server system disks.

4.2.1 Planning the Tru64 UNIX System Disk

Very often, we hear from Systems Administrators – both experienced and inexperience – that "Planning the initial *Tru64* UNIX systems disk is not a big deal, especially if we will be installing and configuring *TruCluster* Server. After all, once the installation and configuration of *TruCluster* Server is complete, we'll never use that original *Tru64* UNIX system disk again. In fact, we can just "nuke" that old system disk and use that space for something constructive like another scratch area."

While it is true that the initial *Tru64* UNIX system disk is used to build the *TruCluster* Server environment and then little used later, it should be retained and used as an "Emergency Repair" disk. Additionally, you can utilize the swap partition and/or configure a separate, local `/tmp` file system on this disk for use within the cluster to remove additional I/O from the shared buses, since both swap and `/tmp` are used on a per member basis as of this writing[1].

The Emergency Repair disk is essential to the repair and recovery of your cluster configuration should you encounter any problems in the future. For more information on the Emergency Repair disk, please refer to Chapter 22 on Cluster Maintenance and Recovery.

In any event, the importance in planning the *Tru64* UNIX system disk should not be minimized. This system disk can still play an active role in the day-to-day operation of your cluster and can play an essential roll in the recovery of a cluster should problems occur.

As an aside, while this discussion and the discussions in the *Tru64* UNIX Installation guides suggest using a local disk for the initial *Tru64* UNIX installation, this is not a hard and fast rule. Disk devices on the shared bus may also be used for the initial *Tru64* UNIX installation system disk.

4.2.1.1 How Much Space Is Enough?

Determining the disk partition sizes for each of the operating system's file systems is based on the software subsets that are to be installed and the usage of the file systems. The amount of space occupied by the software subsets can be easily determined ahead of time. This information is contained in the Release Notes for the version of the *Tru64* UNIX that is to be installed. The amount of space to be used for each file system, based on actual daily usage, is usually discovered through experience so this information is usually harder to come by.

According to the *Tru64* UNIX Installation guide, if you were to use a disk that is greater than 3 GB, the partition sizes used for: `root (/)` should be 384 MB, `swap` should be 384 MB, and `/usr` (including the `/var`) should be 2.235 GB. Based on the software subset sizes from the *Tru64*

---

1 See Chapter 21 on configuring a separate `/tmp` file system.

UNIX Release Notes for version 5.1A, if all the software subsets from the *Tru64* UNIX Operating System CD, the Associated Products Vol. 1 CD, and Associated Products Vol. 2 CD were to be installed, the amount of space used for the `root` (`/`) file system would be 122.35 MB, `/usr` would be 3004.86 MB, and `/var` would be 135.01 MB. We certainly do not recommend blindly installing everything from all of these CDs, but this information provides us with a baseline from which we have derived our own recommendations for partition sizes.

In the *TruCluster* Server Cluster Installation guide, HP strongly recommends, "that, unless prohibited by site policy, you load all subsets when installing the *Tru64* UNIX system." Alternatively, you might consider installing only those software subsets that are needed to support your hardware configuration and/or that you expect your users will need based on the requirements for the implementation of your system. This approach to installing *Tru64* UNIX can enhance basic system security and availability, and will be discussed in more depth in Chapter 5.

Our recommendations for the partitions used for the initial *Tru64* UNIX disk are presented in Table 4-1.

We know, you are looking at this table and thinking to yourself that the sizes of these partitions are quite large. Well, given that 18 GB hard drives are now under $1,000, think of this as you would a rather inexpensive insurance policy – you may not think you need it but when you do, you will be quite happy to have it. Actually, the sizes of these system disk partitions are closely representative of implementations on clustered systems that we have seen.

4.2.1.2 Partitioning and Disk Layout

Obviously, the disk that you will use for the initial *Tru64* UNIX installation will most likely differ from the disk we will use in our examples. This is to be expected, as you will probably use the latest and greatest disks available for your configuration. With this in mind, please use the partition sizes in our examples and recommendations as a starting point. Additionally, when considering your own *Tru64* UNIX system disk layout, be sure to include space for other software components that you

Disk Partition	Size	File System Type	File System	Usage by Tru64 UNIX or TruCluster Server
`a`	512 MB	AdvFS	/	Tru64 UNIX
`b`	2 to 3 times size of memory	**swap**	**swap**	Optionally Both
`f`	2 GB	AdvFS	**/tmp***	Optionally Both
`g`	3 to 4 GB	AdvFS	**/usr**	Tru64 UNIX
`h`	1 to 2 GB	AdvFS	**/var**	Tru64 UNIX

* - See Chapter 21 on configuring a separate **/tmp** file system.

Table 4-1: Standalone Operating System Disk Partition Layout

expect to install from HP, third party vendors, or Open Source.

Partitioning the initial *Tru64* UNIX system disk can be performed either before you start the *Tru64* UNIX installation or during the *Tru64* UNIX installation. We will show you two ways in which this can be done, and will leave it to you to determine which way is easier and more efficient.

4.2.1.2.1 Partitioning Using the `disklabel(8)` Command

Partitioning the *Tru64* UNIX system disk using the `disklabel(8)` command is performed before you actually start the installation of *Tru64* UNIX. We know, you are asking yourself "How can you use a UNIX command like `disklabel` and not have *Tru64* UNIX installed yet?" Let's look and see how we do this:

- At the first prompt for the Installation of *Tru64* UNIX, you would exit the Installation program to edit and write a new disk label on the disk that you will use for *Tru64* UNIX.

```
          Welcome to the Tru64 UNIX Installation Procedure
This procedure installs Tru64 UNIX onto your system.  You will be asked a
series of system configuration questions.  Until you answer all questions,
your system is not changed in any way.
...
o   The "Exit Installation" option stops the installation and puts your
    system in single-user mode with superuser privileges.  This option
    is intended for experienced UNIX system administrators who want to
    perform file system or disk maintenance tasks before the installation.
    This option may also be used for disaster recovery on a previously
    installed system.

Remember, you can always get extra information by typing help.

1) U.S. English Installation
2) Installation with Worldwide Language Support
3) Exit Installation
Enter your choice: 3
```

- At the shell prompt, set the appropriate terminal type and editor that you will be using to edit the disk label. In our example, we have found that the `vt100` terminal type with the `vi(1)` editor work well.

```
# TERM=vt100; export TERM
# EDITOR=/bin/vi; export EDITOR
```

- The next step is to determine which disk to use. You should already have a good idea which disk to use. The issue is finding the right one. In this case, we will use `dsk0` as it is the hard disk that is local to the server.

```
# /sbin/hwmgr -view device
...
   67: /dev/disk/cdrom0c        COMPAQ    CD-224E           bus-1-targ-0-lun-0
   68: /dev/disk/dsk0c          COMPAQ    BD018635C4        bus-5-targ-0-lun-0
...
```

- Now that we know which disk to use, it's just a matter of editing and writing out the disk's label, right? Well, kind of. We know what the partition sizes in MB are for the system disk, but we still have to know what to change each partition size to in the disk label. Since the sizes for each partition are in 512-byte blocks, use the following algorithm to obtain the appropriate size for each partition:

  Partition Size in MB * 2048 = Partition Size in 512-byte blocks

  Here are a couple of examples:

  If we need a partition that is 512 MB, let's say for root (/), we calculate the partition size as follows:

  ```
  512 * 2048 = 1048576
  ```

  If we need a partition that is 4.5 GB for swap[2], the partition size is calculated to be:

  ```
  (4.5 * 1024) * 2048 = 9437184
  ```

  We use the same algorithm for calculating the other three disk partitions that we will use on this soon-to-be system disk. See Table 4-2 for an example of the partitions that we plan to use for our local *Tru64* UNIX system disk.

- Now that we have identified the disk that we will use and the sizes of each partition, it comes down to writing a default label on the disk before we can edit this label.

  ```
  # disklabel -r -w dsk0
  ```

- Finally, we edit the disk label for this disk and write it out to the disk itself.

  ```
  # disklabel -e -r dsk0
  ```

- To restart the Installation of *Tru64* UNIX, it is just a matter of executing the command `restart`.

  ```
  # cd /
  # restart
  ```

4.2.1.2.2 Partitioning Using the Disk Configuration Application

If you are performing a Full Installation of *Tru64* UNIX with the graphical user interface (GUI), custom modification of the partitions of the system disk can be accomplished without exiting the installation. How? From the installation's GUI, view the selected disk partition information by

---

2 See section 4.2.2 regarding the swap.

Disk Partition	Size (MB/GB)	Size (512-byte blocks)	File System Type	File System
a	512 MB	1048576	AdvFS	/
b	4.5 GB	9437184	swap	swap
e	3.9 GB	8302104	unused	unused
f	2 GB	4194304	AdvFS	/tmp*
g	4 GB	8388608	AdvFS	/usr

* - See Chapter 21 on configuring a separate /tmp file system.

Table 4-2: Example Disk Partition Sizes

clicking on the "Edit Partitions..." button on the Custom File System Layout box to open the Disk Configuration application. See Figure 4-1 for an example.

The Disk Configuration application can also be run outside of the *Tru64* UNIX Installation program by executing the command `/usr/sbin/diskconfig`. For more information on the `diskconfig(8)` command, please see its reference page.

4.2.1.2.3 The Disk Label After the Tru64 *UNIX Installation*

Using our example, after the Full Installation of *Tru64* UNIX, the disk label for our new system disk should look something like this:

```
# disklabel dsk0 | grep -p "8 part"

8 partitions:
#          size       offset    fstype  fsize  bsize   cpg  # ~Cyl values
  a:    1048576            0     AdvFS                      #      0 - 206*
  b:    9437184      1048576      swap                      #    206*- 1857*
  c:   35565080            0    unused      0      0        #      0 - 7000
  d:          0            0    unused      0      0        #      0 - 0
  e:    8302104     10485760    unused      0      0        #   1857*- 3491*
  f:    4194304     18787864    unused      0      0        #   3491*- 4316*
  g:    8388608     22982168     AdvFS                      #   4316*- 5967*
  h:    4194304     31370776     AdvFS                      #   5967*- 7000
```

Notice that disk partitions "e" and "f" still have an `fstype` of `unused`. At this time, we have only "prepared" the disk to have a separate `/tmp` file system. See Chapter 21 on creating a cluster member's `/tmp` as a separate file system.

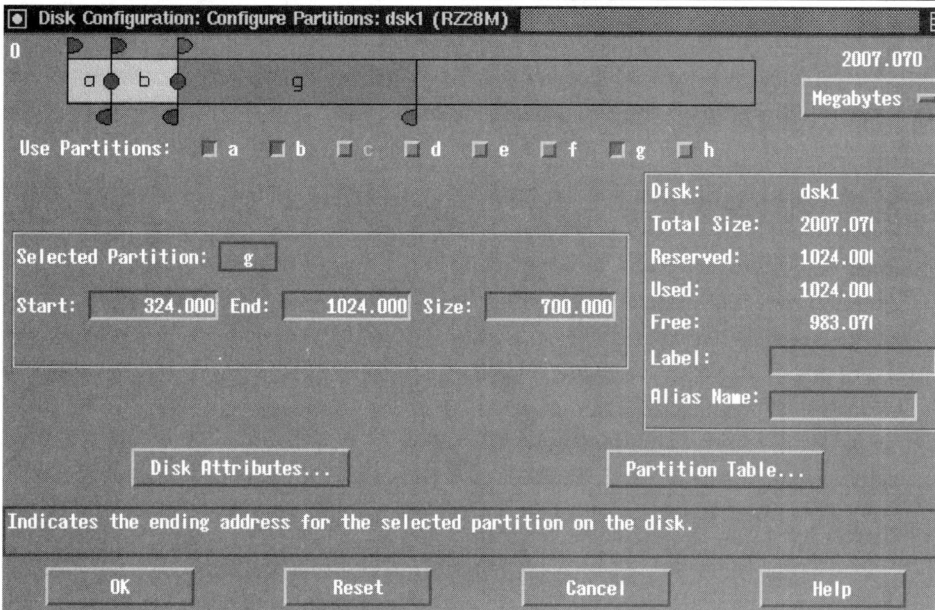

Figure 4-1: The Disk Configuration (`diskconfig(8)`) Program

4.2.2 Planning the Swap Areas for the Cluster

When a cluster member is initially configured, by default, its primary swap is located on the "`b`" partition of the same hard disk as the cluster member's `boot_partition`. Normally this is also on the cluster's shared bus, which has its advantages especially when it comes to high availability of the swap device and the ability to save the crash dump of a cluster member that is down.

Configuring swap on a shared bus, however, can have performance consequences. For example, if an individual cluster member starts to aggressively use its swap space, all the I/O would go across the shared bus and potentially impact the other cluster member(s). While this is not an ideal condition, we should emphasize that with a properly configured system, aggressive usage of the swap space should occur very rarely.

If a member's swap space is configured on the shared bus, the Device Request Dispatcher (DRD) server for the disk where the swap partition resides does not necessarily have to be located on the cluster member that is actually using the swap space. This situation could occur if the host bus adapter (HBA) or cable from the member to the storage fails and is an excellent automatic recovery scenario from a pure high availability standpoint. If a cluster member starts to use the swap space aggressively while the DRD server is not local to the member, however, all the swap-related I/O would be routed through the cluster interconnect. This scenario, while **extremely** rare, could saturate the cluster interconnect and impact the entire cluster.

In planning your cluster, and in planning the swap for your cluster, you must consider issues of high availability as well as performance. You also must examine what is an acceptable failure scenario for the applications and the users on the cluster. By default, the installation of a *TruCluster* Server environment attempts to provide high availability for as much as possible, including swap. In our two examples, this high availability of swap has consequences for a system that's not properly configured. The consequences relate to the performance and availability of the cluster itself. This underscores the importance of designing your cluster carefully and thoughtfully considering the applications and the user community that the cluster will be supporting.

Imagine that instead of having each cluster member's swap partition on the shared bus, it resides on a disk locally accessible to each member. Let's analyze the pros and cons of this arrangement.

- The pros of having swap on a locally accessible disk:
  - The swap-related I/O is not on the shared bus.
  - The swap-related I/O will not be routed through the cluster interconnect.
  - The swap activity of one cluster member has little or no impact on any of the other cluster members because the resources involved are no longer shared.
  - The swap-related I/O is now local to the server that is doing the swapping. From a performance standpoint, this should give better performance.

- The cons of having swap on a locally accessible disk:
  - The swap for the cluster member is no longer highly available. If swap is not available for whatever reason (i.e., the HBA fails), the cluster member may crash.
  - Should a cluster member crash and is down, you will not be able to access the crash dump for that member from any other cluster member. This information would be available only after the cluster member reboots.

Another option to consider is to keep a small primary swap partition on the member boot disk that is large enough to hold a partial dump and add a larger secondary swap partition on a bus that is accessible only to the cluster member.

The decision on where you have each cluster member's swap partition should ultimately be based on your cluster's availability criteria. If you decide to have each cluster member's swap on a local disk, please refer to Chapter 21 on how to implement this.

One last note about the swap partition: regardless of where the primary swap partition physically resides, we recommend that if you are using the eager swap mode algorithm (the default), you should allocate a swap space of at least two to three times the size of the cluster member's physical memory, which can be distributed on one or more swap partitions. Also, should you later increase the memory of a server, don't forget to increase the size of the swap space.

If your cluster members are Very Large Memory (VLM)[3] systems and used for a specific application like a database, please refer to the application vendor's documentation on how much swap space is required and which swap algorithm to use. Based on this information, please plan accordingly. If the swap algorithm that you are to use is lazy mode or deferred mode, your swap space requirements can vary widely, from as little as configuring swap to contain only a partial dump to three times the size of memory.

---

3 VLM systems are by definition systems, which utilize 64-bit architecture, multiprocessing, and at least 2 GB of memory for memory intensive applications.

4.2.3 Hardware Storage Configuration

When you think about a *TruCluster* Server environment, a couple of the things that come to mind are the Cluster File System, a shared bus, and how everything magically works together. *TruCluster* Server may not be magic, but it is very cool technology. It is a technology that can easily be aligned with your company's business goals if those goals include high availability and scalability.

We believe that if you have chosen to deploy a *TruCluster* Server implementation, you have done so with both high availability and scalability in mind. In order to implement *TruCluster* Server, in addition to the software "bits and bytes," the servers, adapter cards, hubs, switches, cluster interconnects, and cables, we need storage - storage for the cluster's system disks and for the users applications and data. We also recommend that if you are going to deploy any type of highly available cluster, please use RAID-based storage for the protection and availability it provides.

The storage subsystem is an integral part of any *TruCluster* Server implementation. In this section, we will be discussing the hardware RAID array storage that is necessary to support *TruCluster* Server in a highly available configuration.

NOTE:

While hardware-based RAID is generally accepted as the better performing RAID solution, there is a software-based RAID option known as the Logical Storage Manager (LSM) that can be used as a lower-cost alternative. See Chapter 14 for more information.

4.2.3.1 Supported Hardware RAID Array Controllers

Table 4-3 provides a list of HP StorageWorks hardware RAID array controllers, along with the each controller's minimum firmware requirements, that support the implementation of *TruCluster* Server V5.1A.

Storage Controller	Minimum Firmware Version
HSZ40	Version 3.7 or higher
HSZ50	Version 5.7 or higher
HSZ70	Version 7.7 or higher
HSZ80	Version 8.3-1 or higher
HSG60	Version 8.5 or higher
HSG80	Version 8.5 or higher

Table 4-3: RAID Controller Minimum Supported Firmware Version

For more detailed information and restrictions on the usage of these hardware storage controllers, we highly recommend reviewing the *TruCluster* Server Cluster Release Notes, *TruCluster* Server Cluster Hardware Configuration guide, and the *TruCluster* Server Cluster Installation guide for the version that you will be implementing. For more information on configuring the storage controller that you expect to use, please refer to the StorageWorks Installation and Configuration Guide for Compaq *Tru64* UNIX that comes with your controller.

4.2.3.2 Transparent Failover Mode vs. Multi-bus Failover Mode

Before we start our discussion on what a failover mode is, let's assume that we have a pair of RAID array storage controllers from those listed in Table 4-3 and configured in a dual-redundant configuration. A dual-redundant configuration means that if one controller should fail, the other controller picks up the slack, and the cluster continues to operate without interruption.

For the purposes of this discussion, we will be using the HSG80 controller to represent all the StorageWorks RAID array controllers that are supported for a *TruCluster* Server configuration. While all of the RAID array storage controllers that we have listed in Table 4-3 are capable of Transparent Failover Mode, only the HSZ70, HSZ80, HSG60, and HSG80 storage controllers are capable of Multi-bus Failover Mode.

What is failover mode? Failover mode is a way to keep the shared storage array available to the attached servers or hosts if one of the storage controllers goes down or becomes unresponsive. Failover mode provides for the remaining storage controller to take control and allows the storage array to remain available.

There are two different failover modes: Transparent and Multi-bus. Transparent failover is handled by the remaining controller and as such is "transparent" to the hosts connected to the storage. The hosts handle multi-bus failover.

The primary characteristics of transparent failover mode include:

- The hosts attached to the storage are unaware that a failover has occurred.
- The logical storage units presented to the hosts, and managed by the controllers, are divided between controller host ports 1 and 2. Storage units 0-99 are accessible through port 1 with storage units 100-199 accessible through port 2.
- In a dual-redundant controller configuration, only host port 1 on one of the controllers will be active with the host port 1 on the other controller in standby. The same is true of host port 2. Only one host port 2 on one of the controllers will be active with the host port 2 on the other controller in standby. Please see Figure 4-2 for an illustration of this configuration.

How does transparent failover work? If one of the two controllers fails, then both ports on the remaining controller become active and serve out all the storage units.

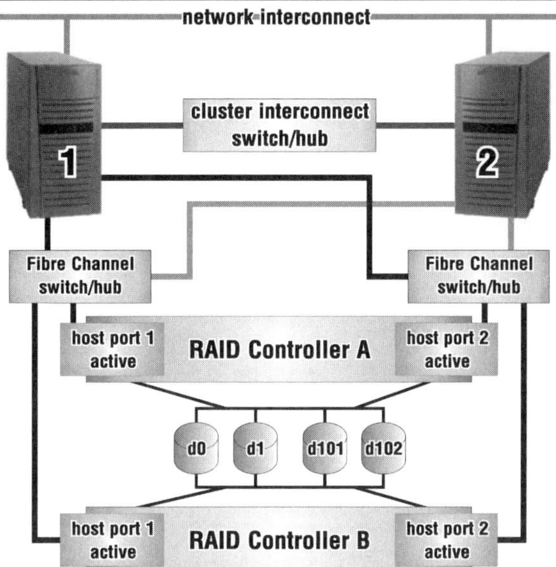

Figure 4-2: RAID Controller Multi-Bus Failover

While transparent failover compensates for the failure of a controller, it does not address the failure of a host bus adapter in the server or the storage link.[4] This is where multi-bus failover really shines. Multi-bus failover compensates for the failure of a controller, host bus adapter, or storage link.

Some of the characteristics of multi-bus failover mode include:

- All storage units are accessible through all host ports of the controllers (unlike transparent failover).
- Each host has at least two paths to the storage units. This is accomplished by using multiple host bus adapters in each host.
- All hosts attached to the storage must have the appropriate operating system software that supports multi-bus failover.
- The hosts control the process of moving the storage units from one controller to another during a failover scenario. When access to storage units from one path fails, the host(s) issues the command to access the storage units through another path. Please see Figure 4-3 for an illustration of this configuration.
- Although all storage units are accessible through all host ports on the controllers, you can specify which storage units are normally serviced by a specific controller.
- The I/O load from a host can be redistributed between controllers.

---

4 The storage link can be either a storage hub or Fibre Channel switch but also includes the cables and components attached to these.

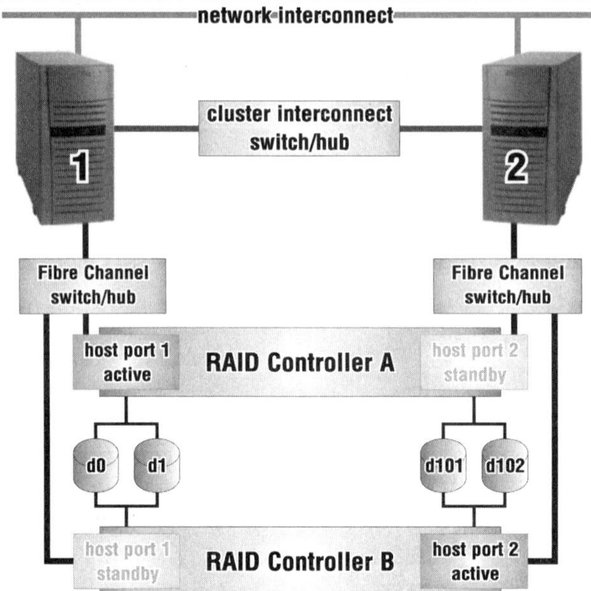

Figure 4-3: RAID Controller Transparent Failover

4.2.3.3 Clustering in a Heterogeneous SAN Environment

The HSG60 and the HSG80 RAID array controllers are by their nature Storage Area Network (SAN) ready controllers. This means that you can attach multiple, heterogeneous servers to this storage array by connecting them to a SAN Fibre Channel Switch that is a part of this type of storage configuration. While this can potentially provide a huge benefit to the data center by consolidating storage for many servers, it can also be quite dangerous for a *TruCluster* Server configuration if it is not well thought out and planned.

Although we will not describe in detail how to deploy a cluster in a heterogeneous SAN environment – we will leave this for another book – we can say that this is entirely possible and very easy to implement. We will also provide warnings on deploying such a configuration.

When deploying multiple *TruCluster* Server environments on one SAN, use selective storage presentation[5] and, although not necessary, try to create separate zones (for each cluster) at the Fibre Channel Switch.[6] As *TruCluster* Server uses persistent reservations on all the storage devices that it sees, we want to protect storage used for one cluster from being accessed by another cluster.

When deploying other servers (i.e., HP-UX, Solaris, Windows 2000, etc.) in addition to a *TruCluster* Server into a SAN environment, there are several considerations:

---

5 See section 4.2.3.4 for more information on selective storage presentation.

6 For more information on creating zones on a Fibre Channel Switch, see the StorageWorks Fibre Channel SAN Management Guide.

- The storage controllers must be configured for multi-bus failover mode and all servers should have multiple host bus adapters.
- All servers must also have installed software that supports multi-bus failover. Tru64 UNIX and TruCluster Server automatically have this software. For other servers, HP StorageWorks has a product called SecurePath that provides these "bits and bytes."
- Zoning at the Fibre Channel Switch should be done for each class of servers. There should be separate zones for HP-UX, Solaris, Windows 2000, and *TruCluster* Server. This helps prevent servers of different classes from interfering with each other's storage.
- Selective storage presentation should always be used. Again, this prevents servers from accessing each other's storage within the same zone.

4.2.3.4 Selective Storage Presentation

What is selective storage presentation? Selective storage presentation is a feature of the HSG60 and the HSG80 controllers that allows specific hosts to access specific storage units and is a means by which we can restrict host access to storage units.

If you have more than one cluster connected to a storage subsystem, or if you have other servers that are not part of a cluster connected to this same storage subsystem, then the access path to the individual storage units must be specified. This is accomplished through selective storage presentation.

Selective storage presentation is supported in Transparent Failover Mode or Multi-bus Failover Mode.

How do you use selective storage presentation for a cluster? The process is very straightforward.

- From each server's console, determine the World Wide Name or World Wide ID (wwid) for the host bus adapter(s) that are connected to the storage subsystem.

```
P00>>> wwidmgr -show adapter
item     adapter                     WWN                      Cur. Topo  Next Topo
pga0.0.0.7.1 - Nvram read failed
[ 0] pga0.0.0.7.1          2000-0000-c924-7c58            FABRIC     UNAVAIL
[9999] All of the above.
```

The "`Nvram read failed`" message indicates that the host bus adapter's (a KGPSA) NVRAM has not been initialized or formatted. The "`Next Topo`" field shows up as `UNAVAIL` because the host bus adapter has an unformatted NVRAM. In a cluster configuration, as the server and the storage subsystem will be operating in fabric mode, both messages can be safely ignored.

Even though these messages are benign, they can be corrected using the "`wwidmgr`" command with the "`-set adapter`" option at the SRM console prompt:

```
P00>>> wwidmgr -set adapter -item 9999 -topo fabric
```

```
P00>>> wwidmgr -show adapter

item     adapter                    WWN                    Cur. Topo  Next Topo
[ 0] pga0.0.0.7.1         2000-0000-c924-7c58              FABRIC     FABRIC
[9999] All of the above.
```

In this example, we obtained the wwid for the host bus adapter for only one of the cluster's servers. Use this same process for each server in the cluster to determine the wwid for each host bus adapter connected to the storage subsystem

- Next, connect to the HSG60/HSG80 controller's command console and determine the host connections for the adapters attached to the storage subsystem.

```
HSG> show connections

Connection
   Name       Operating system    Controller    Port    Address    Status

!NEWCON1          WINNT              THIS          1      011600    OL this        0
           HOST_ID=2000-0000-C924-7C58          ADAPTER_ID=1000-0000-C924-7C58

!NEWCON2          WINNT              OTHER         2      011600    OL other     100
           HOST_ID=2000-0000-C924-7C58          ADAPTER_ID=1000-0000-C924-7C58

!NEWCON3          WINNT              THIS          1      011700    OL this        0
           HOST_ID=2000-0000-C924-3514          ADAPTER_ID=1000-0000-C924-3514

!NEWCON4          WINNT              OTHER         2      011700    OL other     100
           HOST_ID=2000-0000-C924-3514           ADAPTER_ID=1000-0000-C924-3514
```

Notice that by default, the "`Operating system`" is noted to be `WINNT` even though we are using *Tru64* UNIX. We will change that to something more meaningful later in our discussion, but we are currently interested in the address of the `HOST_ID`. It should be the same as the wwid of the host bus adapter(s) as seen from the server's console.

Let's change the operating system type to *Tru64* UNIX and make the connection names more meaningful.

```
HSG> set !NEWCON1 TRU64_UNIX
HSG> set !NEWCON2 TRU64_UNIX
HSG> set !NEWCON3 TRU64_UNIX
HSG> set !NEWCON4 TRU64_UNIX
HSG> rename !NEWCON1 MOLR1A1
HSG> rename !NEWCON2 MOLR1B2
HSG> rename !NEWCON3 SHER1A1
HSG> rename !NEWCON4 SHER1B2
```

That's better, now let's see what we have in terms of host connections.

```
HSG> show connections

Connection
   Name       Operating system    Controller     Port    Address    Status

MOLR1A1          TRU64_UNIX           THIS        1       011600    OL this         0
           HOST_ID=2000-0000-C924-7C58          ADAPTER_ID=1000-0000-C924-7C58

MOLR1B2          TRU64_UNIX           OTHER       2       011600    OL other      100
           HOST_ID=2000-0000-C924-7C58          ADAPTER_ID=1000-0000-C924-7C58

SHER1A1          TRU64_UNIX           THIS        1       011700    OL this         0
           HOST_ID=2000-0000-C924-3514          ADAPTER_ID=1000-0000-C924-3514

SHER1B2          TRU64_UNIX           OTHER       2       011700    OL other      100
           HOST_ID=2000-0000-C924-3514          ADAPTER_ID=1000-0000-C924-3514
```

- Now that we know the connections from the cluster nodes to the storage, for every storage unit that we create for the cluster, we would set the accessibility so that only the nodes of the cluster have access to this storage. First, we would disable access to all connections; then selectively enable access to only those connections connected to the cluster nodes.

```
HSG> add unit d101 m2 partition=1 disable_access_path=all
```

```
HSG> show d101
    LUN                                      Uses                Used by
------------------------------------------------------------------------------

  D101                                       M2            (partition)
        LUN ID:      6000-1FE1-0001-6950-0009-1420-0755-0047
        IDENTIFIER = NONE
        Switches:
          RUN                      NOWRITE_PROTECT         READ_CACHE
          READAHEAD_CACHE          WRITEBACK_CACHE
          MAX_READ_CACHED_TRANSFER_SIZE = 32
          MAX_WRITE_CACHED_TRANSFER_SIZE = 32
        Access:
          None
        State:
          ONLINE to the other controller
        Size:              2133378 blocks
        Geometry (C/H/S): ( 420 / 20 / 254 )
```

```
HSG> set d101 enable_access_path=(MOLR1A1,MOLR1B2,SHER1A1,SHER1B2)
```

```
HSG> show d101
    LUN                                                     Uses              Used by
-------------------------------------------------------------------------------

  D101                                                      M2               (partition)
        LUN ID:       6000-1FE1-0001-6950-0009-1420-0755-0047
        IDENTIFIER = NONE
        Switches:
          RUN                     NOWRITE_PROTECT          READ_CACHE
          READAHEAD_CACHE         WRITEBACK_CACHE
          MAX_READ_CACHED_TRANSFER_SIZE = 32
          MAX_WRITE_CACHED_TRANSFER_SIZE = 32
        Access:
          MOLR1A1, MOLR1B2, SHER1A1, SHER1B2
        State:
          ONLINE to the other controller
        Size:             2133378 blocks
        Geometry (C/H/S): ( 420 / 20 / 254 )
```

From this example, only the individual cluster nodes, `sheridan` and `molari`, have selective access to storage unit `D101`.

Another way to do selective storage presentation is to set the offsets for each host connection. Setting offsets establishes the beginning of the range of storage units that a host connection can access. For the purposes of simplicity of design and implementation, we do not recommend that you use offsets in a *TruCluster* Server configuration – especially if you are dealing with multiple clusters attached to one storage subsystem. For more information on using offsets, please refer to Chapter 1 of the HSG80 ACS Solution Software – Installation and Configuration Guide.

4.2.4 Hardware RAID Configuration

By selecting *TruCluster* Server, one assumes that high availability is of concern. For this reason, we recommend using a RAID solution for root ((`/`) or `cluster_root`), `/usr` (or `cluster_usr`), and `/var` (or `cluster_var`) as well as any other file systems that your requirements deem critical. In this section, we will discuss configuring RAID 1, RAID 0+1, and RAID 5 using HP StorageWorks HSZ or HSG controllers to support the cluster systems disks in a *TruCluster* Server configuration.

Before we get into the details of why you may want to use one level of RAID over another and the implementation process, let's go over a generalized procedure that will be used to create and make available multiple storage units from a RAID set.

- Creating and initializing the RAID set
- Partitioning the RAID set
- Creating the storage units
- Configuring the storage units

As we provide examples on how to build the cluster's system disks using the different levels of RAID, this generalized procedure will become more specific.

RAID sets can be very large, but since modern individual disk drives are very large, the devices that are required for the cluster's system disks tend to be small by comparison, so storage set partitioning at the controller can be useful. Storage set partitioning is a means of dividing a storage set into smaller pieces. It is these smaller pieces that are presented to the hosts as separate storage units of the appropriate size.

The following are limitations on partitioning of storage sets or RAID sets:

- Each partition is created as a percentage of the RAID set or storage set.
- The maximum number of partitions per storage set for the HSZ70, HSZ80, HSG60, and HSG80 controllers is eight.
- The maximum number of partitions per storage set for the HSZ40 and the HSZ50 controllers is four.
- In transparent failover mode, partitions from the same storage set must be on the same host port.
- On HSZ controllers, storage partitioning is only supported in transparent failover mode. On HSG controllers, storage partitioning is supported in both transparent failover mode and multi-bus failover mode.
- In multi-bus failover mode, partitions from the same storage set must be on the same controller.
- Unless within a single *TruCluster* Server environment, separate storage partitions from the same storage set or RAID set should not be used between different individual systems.

At their simplest, the disks and UNIX partitions required to build a two-node cluster are illustrated in Table 4-4.

Please note that the quorum disk requires its own disk without anything else on it. Is this necessary? Absolutely! For more information on the quorum disk and when to use a quorum disk, see Chapter 17.

Disk	Partition or File System		Disk	Partition or File System	
dsk1	a	member1 boot_partition	dsk2	a	member2 boot_partition
	b	member1 swap partition		b	member2 swap partition
	h	member1 cnx partition		h	member2 cnx partition
dsk3 (quorum disk)	h	cnx partition	dsk4	b	cluster_root
				g	cluster_usr
				h	cluster_var

Table 4-4: *TruCluster* Server Disk Layout

Now, let's look at specifically what we will need in terms of disks, partitions, and partition sizes for a two-node cluster. Table 4-5 not only illustrates what is needed for a two-node cluster, but it also provides the information necessary to grow and expand this cluster.

Disk	UNIX Partition	Size	File System Type	File System	AdvFS Domain
dsk1	a	256 MB	AdvFS	member1 boot_partition	root1_domain
	b	1.5 GB or 4.5 GB	swap	swap	swap
	h	1 MB	cnx	n/a	n/a
dsk2	a	256 MB	AdvFS	member2 boot_partition	root2_domain
	b	1.5 GB or 4.5 GB	swap	swap	swap
	h	1 MB	cnx	n/a	n/a
dsk3 dsk4	a	256 MB	unused	n/a	n/a
	b	1.5 GB or 4.5 GB	unused	n/a	n/a
	h	1 MB	unused	n/a	n/a
dsk5	h	1 MB	cnx	quorum disk	quorum disk
dsk6	a	512 MB	AdvFS	/	cluster_root
	g	4.0 GB	AdvFS	/usr	cluster_usr
	H	4.0 GB	AdvFS	/var	cluster_var

The "**b**" partition(s) used for swap are 1.5 GB (the size of memory) if the primary swap is on the local disk. In our example, as we are using eager swap, and if there is no local disk for primary swap, the "**b**" partition is three times the size of memory.

dsk3 and **dsk4** are created for future cluster members 3 and 4. This is to support the expected expandability of the cluster.

Table 4-5: *TruCluster* Server Disks, Partitions, and File Systems

It is important to note that before you start to install *Tru64* UNIX on the local disk, all RAID storage sets should be properly configured and initialized. The following sections will detail ways to configure and initialize different types of RAID storage sets to support a cluster's system disks.

4.2.4.1 RAID 1 vs. RAID 0+1 vs. RAID 5 for the Cluster's System Disks

In this section, we will briefly discuss what RAID 1, RAID 0+1, and RAID 5 are and why you might want to use one RAID level over another in a cluster configuration.

- RAID 1

  RAID level 1 is also known as mirroring. The redundancy of mirroring is exactly what happens with the data. All data is simultaneously written to two of more drives at the same time. From a performance standpoint, access to data is faster on reads than on writes; however, should a drive ever fail in a RAID 1 set there should be no loss of data. The minimum number of drives to implement a RAID 1 set is two. The effective storage utilization space is approximately the size of one drive in a two drive RAID 1 set.

- RAID 0+1[7]

  This is a combination of mirroring (RAID level 1) and striping (RAID level 0). This provides for the complete redundancy of mirroring with the write performance that comes with striping the data across all drives. A RAID 0+1 set offers the highest level of redundancy with the greatest level of performance but at a higher cost in terms of hard drive spindles. The minimum number of drives to implement a RAID 0+1 set is four. The effective storage utilization space is approximately the size of two drives of the four drive RAID 0+1 set.

- RAID 5

  RAID level 5 stripes data across all disks, but it also distributes parity among all the disks in the RAID 5 set. The parity information provides for recovery of the RAID set should any single drive fail. Performance on writes is decent while performance on reads is just okay. The minimum number of drives to implement a RAID 5 set is three. Optimally, we recommend that three to six drives be used for a RAID 5 set. The effective storage utilization space is approximately the size of all the drives in the RAID 5 set less one drive, which is necessary for parity. In sum, while RAID 5 may not be the best in terms of performance, it is the most cost effective.

Now that we know about the RAID levels that provide for high availability of the storage, why might one be preferable to another in a *TruCluster* Server configuration?

This decision should be made based on requirements versus cost. All three RAID levels discussed provide for high availability but at varying costs and performance levels. If cost is not an issue, we recommend using RAID 0+1 for everything. Again, this provides for the highest availability at the

---

7 RAID 0+1 is a bit of a misnomer. 1+0 might be more accurate as we are creating striped mirror sets and not mirrored stripe sets.

greatest performance. If cost is an issue and you want a sound foundation upon which to build your cluster, we recommend using RAID 1 for the system disks and RAID 5 for all the users' file systems.

Bottom line: deciding which RAID level to use is situational. What we can do here is offer ideas for the various implementations of the cluster system disks on the different levels of RAID.

4.2.4.2 Planning for Future Cluster Expansion

In planning for your cluster, plan not only for the impending implementation of your cluster but also for its future expansion. If you plan for the future expansion of your cluster, then increasing the number of cluster members is easy, straightforward, and should not take any longer than 45 minutes per additional cluster node.

Okay, so does this have anything to do with building RAID sets or are the authors a little "whacked?" There is, as they say, a method to our madness. The upcoming sections on building RAID sets for the cluster's system disks will include building an extra amount of storage for cluster nodes that may be added six months or a year down the line. It is prudent to build all your storage units sooner rather than later.

4.2.4.3 Building a RAID 5 Set for the Cluster's System Disks

In this section, we will build all the storage units necessary to support a cluster's system disks using a RAID 5 set. RAID 5 provides the best availability at the best cost per byte of storage.

As disk drives tend to be very large, any RAID set will generally be very large. This is especially true with the smallest RAID 5 set. In general, with the exception of the space requirement for swap, the amount of space to support a cluster's system disks is relatively small. While some Systems Administrators would say that this is a good problem to have, others would cringe at the thought of wasting valuable disk space.

In our example of building a RAID 5 set for the cluster's system disk, we will be using 18 GB drives – three 18 GB drives.

- Create and initialize the RAID 5 set.

  As you can see, building a three disk RAID 5 set is a relatively easy operation.

```
HSG> add raidset r0 disk10000 disk20000 disk30000
```

```
HSG> initialize r0 save_configuration
```

  After the RAID set is created and as it is initialized, the RAID configuration is actually saved to the RAID set using the `save_configuration` flag. It is important to save the RAID configuration information to a RAID set on the controller so that if a catastrophic failure is encountered and both storage controllers are lost at the same time, we can easily recover all the RAID sets without any loss of data. How is this done? After replacing the failed storage controllers, the recovery of the saved RAID configuration information is read off the RAID set to which it was originally saved.

- Partition the RAID 5 set.

  This next step of partitioning the RAID 5 set takes planning. It is here that we use the information from Table 4-5 to determine what percentage of the effective storage utilization space of the RAID 5 set each partition will be. As the effective storage utilization space for a three drive (each with a 18 GB drive) RAID 5 set is approximately 36 GB, each partition `size` is a percentage of this number.

```
HSG> create_partition r0 size=14
HSG> create_partition r0 size=14
HSG> create_partition r0 size=14
HSG> create_partition r0 size=14
HSG> create_partition r0 size=1
HSG> create_partition r0 size=largest
```

  In this example, the first partition is created with a partition size of 14% of 36 GB. The `size=largest` allows us to utilize all the remaining space on the drive without having to set a percentage.

- Create the partitioned storage units.

  Now that the RAID 5 set has been partitioned, each new storage unit is created from each storage partition. These storage units are presented to the hosts – the cluster members.

```
HSG> add unit d1 r0 partition=1 disable_access_path=all
HSG> add unit d2 r0 partition=2 disable_access_path=all
HSG> add unit d3 r0 partition=3 disable_access_path=all
HSG> add unit d4 r0 partition=4 disable_access_path=all
HSG> add unit d5 r0 partition=5 disable_access_path=all
HSG> add unit d6 r0 partition=6 disable_access_path=all
```

IMPORTANT:

As each new storage unit is created, we disable the access path to all hosts. This prevents accidental access by a host connected to the storage subsystem.

- Configure the partitioned storage units.

  In this final step, we set the `identifier` for each new storage unit and selectively enable the access path to allow only the host connections for each of the cluster nodes.

```
HSG> set d1 identifier=1 enable_access_path=(MOLR1A1,MOLR1B2,SHER1A1,SHER1B2)
HSG> set d2 identifier=2 enable_access_path=(MOLR1A1,MOLR1B2,SHER1A1,SHER1B2)
HSG> set d3 identifier=3 enable_access_path=(MOLR1A1,MOLR1B2,SHER1A1,SHER1B2)
HSG> set d4 identifier=4 enable_access_path=(MOLR1A1,MOLR1B2,SHER1A1,SHER1B2)
HSG> set d5 identifier=5 enable_access_path=(MOLR1A1,MOLR1B2,SHER1A1,SHER1B2)
HSG> set d6 identifier=6 enable_access_path=(MOLR1A1,MOLR1B2,SHER1A1,SHER1B2)
```

If only one cluster is connected to the storage subsystem, it is unnecessary to disable and then re-enable the access path to the storage. Disabling the access path and then selectively enabling the access path for certain host connections is an example of selective storage presentation. The default flag setting when you create any storage unit is to `enable_access_path=all` – or enable access for all host connections.

4.2.4.4 Building a RAID 1 Set for the Cluster's System Disk

In the previous section, we built all the storage units necessary to support a cluster's system disks; in this section, we will build only the majority of these storage units. As we are using eager swap allocation, we recommend that you allocate three times the size of memory for a swap partition. We assume that the primary swap partitions for each cluster member will be on other drives.[8] The swap space set aside when we configure these storage units will be the same size as memory for each cluster member and may eventually be used as the secondary swap partition for each cluster member.

Using RAID 1 for the cluster's system disks provides a sound foundation for availability in a cluster. While it is not the best performing for writes in the event a disk drive in a RAID 1 fails, you can be reasonably assured that your data will be safe.

Similar to our example of building a RAID 5 set, we will be use 18 GB drives – two 18 GB drives-- in this example of building a RAID 1 set for the cluster's system disks.

- Create and initialize the RAID 1 or Mirror set.

```
HSG> add mirrorset m0 disk10100 disk20100
```

```
HSG> initialize m0 save_configuration
```

  Be sure to use the `save_configuration` flag to preserve RAID configuration information on the Mirror set.

- Partition the RAID 1 or Mirror set.

  Partitioning is performed in precisely the same way as in the previous example using the RAID 5 set. The only difference is that the partition sizes are different. Instead of having an effective storage utilization space of 36 GB as with the RAID 5 set, we have an effective storage utilization space of only 18 GB. As the `size` is a percentage of the space available, it makes sense that the percentages would differ given the different space availability and especially given that we do not account for all the swap space.

---

8 See Chapter 21 on configuring swap on a local disk.

```
HSG> create_partition m0 size=12
HSG> create_partition m0 size=12
HSG> create_partition m0 size=12
HSG> create_partition m0 size=12
HSG> create_partition m0 size=1
HSG> create_partition m0 size=largest
```

- Create the partitioned storage units.

```
HSG> add unit d11 m0 partition=1 disable_access_path=all
HSG> add unit d12 m0 partition=2 disable_access_path=all
HSG> add unit d13 m0 partition=3 disable_access_path=all
HSG> add unit d14 m0 partition=4 disable_access_path=all
HSG> add unit d15 m0 partition=5 disable_access_path=all
HSG> add unit d16 m0 partition=6 disable_access_path=all
```

- Configure the partitioned storage units.

```
HSG> set d11 identifier=11 enable_access_path=(MOLR1A1,MOLR1B2,SHER1A1,SHER1B2)
HSG> set d12 identifier=12 enable_access_path=(MOLR1A1,MOLR1B2,SHER1A1,SHER1B2)
HSG> set d13 identifier=13 enable_access_path=(MOLR1A1,MOLR1B2,SHER1A1,SHER1B2)
HSG> set d14 identifier=14 enable_access_path=(MOLR1A1,MOLR1B2,SHER1A1,SHER1B2)
HSG> set d15 identifier=15 enable_access_path=(MOLR1A1,MOLR1B2,SHER1A1,SHER1B2)
HSG> set d16 identifier=16 enable_access_path=(MOLR1A1,MOLR1B2,SHER1A1,SHER1B2)
```

The two previous bullet points are exactly the same as in the RAID 5 example.

4.2.4.5 Building a RAID 0+1 Set for the Cluster's Systems Disk

In this section, we will build all the storage units necessary to support a cluster's system disks using a Striped Mirror set (aka a RAID 0+1 set). RAID level 0+1 provides the highest availability with the greatest performance but at a cost.

As with our RAID 5 example, the smallest RAID 0+1 set is actually very large. It is large enough to support all our space requirements for the cluster's system disk – including our large swap space recommendation.

Again, as with our example of building a RAID 5 set, we will use four 18 GB drives to build our RAID 0+1 set to support the storage requirements for our cluster's system disks.

- Create and initialize the RAID 0+1 (Striped Mirror) set.
  - First, we create all the Mirror sets that we will need.

```
HSG> add mirror m1 disk10200 disk20200
HSG> add mirror m2 disk10300 disk20300
```

- Now we create a Striped set from the two Mirror sets that we had just created.

```
HSG> add stripeset clu_sys m1 m2
```

- Finally, we initialize and save the RAID configuration to the newly created Striped Mirror set.

```
HSG> initialize clu_sys save_configuration
```

- Partition the RAID 0+1 set.

  You may notice that partitioning the RAID 0+1 set and creating and configuring the partitioned storage units pretty much duplicates the RAID 5 example. There is nothing new to this.

```
HSG> create_partition clu_sys size=14
HSG> create_partition clu_sys size=14
HSG> create_partition clu_sys size=14
HSG> create_partition clu_sys size=14
HSG> create_partition clu_sys size=1
HSG> create_partition clu_sys size=largest
```

- Create the partitioned storage units.

```
HSG> add unit d21 clu_sys partition=1 disable_access_path=all
HSG> add unit d22 clu_sys partition=2 disable_access_path=all
HSG> add unit d23 clu_sys partition=3 disable_access_path=all
HSG> add unit d24 clu_sys partition=4 disable_access_path=all
HSG> add unit d25 clu_sys partition=5 disable_access_path=all
HSG> add unit d26 clu_sys partition=6 disable_access_path=all
```

- Configure the partitioned storage units.

```
HSG> set d21 identifier=21 enable_access_path=(MOLR1A1,MOLR1B2,SHER1A1,SHER1B2)
HSG> set d22 identifier=22 enable_access_path=(MOLR1A1,MOLR1B2,SHER1A1,SHER1B2)
HSG> set d23 identifier=23 enable_access_path=(MOLR1A1,MOLR1B2,SHER1A1,SHER1B2)
HSG> set d24 identifier=24 enable_access_path=(MOLR1A1,MOLR1B2,SHER1A1,SHER1B2)
HSG> set d25 identifier=25 enable_access_path=(MOLR1A1,MOLR1B2,SHER1A1,SHER1B2)
HSG> set d26 identifier=26 enable_access_path=(MOLR1A1,MOLR1B2,SHER1A1,SHER1B2)
```

4.2.4.6 Building RAID Sets for Other "Important" File Systems

As we indicated earlier, all RAID storage sets and storage units should be configured ahead of time and before you install *Tru64* UNIX. We further recommend that other important file systems would certainly benefit from using RAID sets, including the users' home directory area, the file systems used for your users' applications and application data, and the file systems required for a data base (if you have a data base installed).

In any event, creation and allocation of RAID sets takes careful planning prior to implementation. If you invest the time to plan appropriately, you can be guaranteed that the planning will reap large rewards in terms of availability and scalability.

4.2.4.7 Spare Set for Your RAID Sets

Before we end this section on Hardware RAID configuration, let's discuss one last and sorely overlooked topic – the use of Spare Sets to support the RAID configuration. We have seen countless situations where the RAID configuration and implementation were absolutely beautiful except when it came to having an online Spare Set. Please remember that any hardware RAID set built on a RAID controller should always have a Spare Set with at least one disk drive in it. What is the purpose of the drive(s) in the Spare Set? If a drive that is a member of a RAID set fails, a good drive in the Spare Set will automatically take the place of the failed drive. This is one of those high availability issues that are too often overlooked.

Here is an example of adding two disk drives to a Spare Set.

```
HSG> add spareset disk10400
HSG> add spareset disk20400
```

4.2.5 Getting Storage Devices Seen at the Console – `wwidmgr`[9]

Now that we have all our storage sets configured for the cluster's system disks, there will be a point where we will need to see and access each cluster member's `boot_partition` or boot disk from the system console. Unfortunately, this is not something that happens automatically. When will this need to be done? After the complete installation and configuration of *Tru64* UNIX but before the installation of *TruCluster* Server. During the installation and operation of *TruCluster* Server, it is necessary to see and to access each cluster member's boot disk from each cluster member's system console.

We will use `wwidmgr` commands from the system console to view and to make viewable each cluster member's boot disk. How is this done and what are we really looking for? We are looking for the identifier or the wwid of the cluster member's `boot_partition` disk that we created on the RAID storage array.

Before we start using `wwidmgr` commands, please note that if the cluster member is an AS1200, AS4x00, AS8x00, GS60, GS60E, or GS140, the console must be set to diagnostic mode.

---

9 This only applies to the use of Fibre Channel based storage (HSG60 or HSG80 controllers). This step can be skipped if using SCSI-based storage.

```
P00>>> set mode diag
  Console is in diagnostic mode
```

After using the wwidmgr commands, the system must be reinitialized to return to the SRM console. This is done using the init command at the console.

The following example shows how we discover and make viewable a cluster member's boot disk. This example assumes that a cluster has not been previously installed.

Moreover, for the purposes of this example, the cluster member's boot disk that we are interested in has an identifier of 1 and this maps to storage unit D1.

- Display existing devices at the system console.

```
P00>>> show dev
dkc0.0.0.7.0          DKC0                          RZ2DD-LS  0306
dqa0.0.0.105.0        DQA0                           CD-224E  9.5B
dva0.0.0.0.0          DVA0
eia0.0.0.9.1          EIA0               00-50-8B-AE-F3-23
pga0.0.0.7.1          PGA0          WWN 2000-0000-c924-7c58
pka0.7.0.6.0          PKA0                     SCSI Bus ID 7
pkb0.7.0.106.0        PKB0                     SCSI Bus ID 7
pkc0.7.0.7.0          PKC0                     SCSI Bus ID 7
…
```

- Use wwidmgr to clear any wwid entries and check for the reachability of devices.

```
P00>>> wwidmgr -clear all
```

```
P00>>> init
```

```
P00>>> show ww*
wwid0
wwid1
wwid2
wwid3
```

```
P00>>> show n*
N1
N2
N3
N4
```

The "wwidmgr -clear all" command cleared the stored Fibre Channel wwid1, wwid2, wwid3, wwid4, N1, N2, N3, and N4 console variables.

```
P00>>> wwidmgr -show reachability
Disk assignment and reachability after next initialization:
```

```
P00>>> init
```

- Display the devices found by `wwidmgr`.

```
P00>>> wwidmgr -show wwid
[0] UDID:1 WWID:01000010:6000-1fe1-0001-6950-0009-1420-0755-0048(ev:none)
[1] UDID:2 WWID:01000010:6000-1fe1-0001-6950-0009-1420-0755-000b(ev:none)
[2] UDID:3 WWID:01000010:6000-1fe1-0001-6950-0009-1420-0755-0046(ev:none)
[3] UDID:4 WWID:01000010:6000-1fe1-0001-6950-0009-1420-0755-004b(ev:none)
[4] UDID:5 WWID:01000010:6000-1fe1-0001-6950-0009-1420-0755-0049(ev:none)
[5] UDID:6 WWID:01000010:6000-1fe1-0001-6950-0009-1420-0755-0047(ev:none)
[6] UDID:10 WWID:01000010:6000-1fe1-0001-6950-0009-9210-0896-0029(ev:none)
[7] UDID:11 WWID:01000010:6000-1fe1-0001-6950-0009-9210-0926-005f(ev:none)
[8] UDID:12 WWID:01000010:6000-1fe1-0001-6950-0009-9210-0896-0028(ev:none)
[9] UDID:13 WWID:01000010:6000-1fe1-0001-6950-0009-9210-0896-0027(ev:none)
...
```

The device that we are interested in has the identifier of `1`, which is the same as the entry with `UDID` of `1`.

- Use the `wwidmgr` command to make the device we are interested in accessible so we can eventually boot from it.

```
P00>>> wwidmgr -quickset -item 0 -unit 1
```

```
P00>>> init
```

The "`wwidmgr -quickset`" command actually sets the "`wwid*`" and "`N*`" console variables.

- Verify that we can see the new device at the console.

```
P00>>> wwidmgr -show wwid
[0] UDID:1 WWID:01000010:6000-1fe1-0001-6950-0009-1420-0755-0048(ev:wwid0)
[1] UDID:2 WWID:01000010:6000-1fe1-0001-6950-0009-1420-0755-000b(ev:none)
[2] UDID:3 WWID:01000010:6000-1fe1-0001-6950-0009-1420-0755-0046(ev:none)
[3] UDID:4 WWID:01000010:6000-1fe1-0001-6950-0009-1420-0755-004b(ev:none)
[4] UDID:5 WWID:01000010:6000-1fe1-0001-6950-0009-1420-0755-0049(ev:none)
[5] UDID:6 WWID:01000010:6000-1fe1-0001-6950-0009-1420-0755-0047(ev:none)
[6] UDID:10 WWID:01000010:6000-1fe1-0001-6950-0009-9210-0896-0029(ev:none)
[7] UDID:11 WWID:01000010:6000-1fe1-0001-6950-0009-9210-0926-005f(ev:none)
[8] UDID:12 WWID:01000010:6000-1fe1-0001-6950-0009-9210-0896-0028(ev:none)
[9] UDID:13 WWID:01000010:6000-1fe1-0001-6950-0009-9210-0896-0027(ev:none)
...
```

```
P00>>> init
```

```
P00>>> show ww*
wwid0   1 1  WWID:01000010:6000-1fe1-0001-6950-0009-1420-0755-0048
wwid1
wwid2
wwid3
```

In this example, we see by the "show wwid*" command that the wwid0 console variable is set to the cluster member's boot disk.

```
P00>>> show n*
N1  50001fe100016952
N2
N3
N4
```

Let's also take a quick look at the HSG80 controller:

```
HSG> show this
Controller:
        HSG80 ZG14100634 Software V86F-8, Hardware  E16
        NODE_ID            = 5000-1FE1-0001-6950
        ALLOCATION_CLASS = 0
        SCSI_VERSION       = SCSI-3
        Configured for dual-redundancy with ZG14200755
            In dual-redundant configuration
        Device Port SCSI address 7
        Time: 29-JUL-2002 08:54:46
        Command Console LUN is lun 0 (NOIDENTIFIER)
Host PORT_1:
        Reported PORT_ID = 5000-1FE1-0001-6951
        PORT_1_TOPOLOGY   = FABRIC (fabric up)
        Address           = 011000
Host PORT_2:
        Reported PORT_ID = 5000-1FE1-0001-6952
        PORT_2_TOPOLOGY   = FABRIC (standby)
        Address           = 011100
        NOREMOTE_COPY
Cache:
        256 megabyte write cache, version 0012
        Cache is GOOD
        Unflushed data in cache
        CACHE_FLUSH_TIMER = 300 (seconds)
Mirrored Cache:
        Not enabled
Battery:
        NOUPS
        FULLY CHARGED
        Expires:             15-FEB-2004
```

As we can see from the "show n*" command at the SRM console vs. the "show this" command at the HSG80's console, the "N1" SRM console variable contains the PORT_ID of the controller that is serving out the cluster member's boot disk. This indicates accessibility through the HSG80 ports.

```
P00>>> show dev

dga1.1001.0.7.1      $1$DGA1                       HSG80    V86F
dkc0.0.0.7.0          DKC0                     RZ2DD-LS    0306
dqa0.0.0.105.0        DQA0                      CD-224E    9.5B
dva0.0.0.0.0          DVA0
eia0.0.0.9.1          EIA0            00-50-8B-AE-F3-23
pga0.0.0.7.1          PGA0        WWN 2000-0000-c924-7c58
pka0.7.0.6.0          PKA0                SCSI Bus ID 7
pkb0.7.0.106.0        PKB0                SCSI Bus ID 7
pkc0.7.0.7.0          PKC0                SCSI Bus ID 7
...
```

A new device also shows up when we enter the "`show dev`" command. This will be the device that we use to boot the cluster node after the *TruCluster* Server software is properly installed and configured.

This process of identifying the cluster member's boot device should be performed on each cluster member's system console before the installation and configuration of the *TruCluster* Server software.

4.3 Firmware for a Cluster

Firmware on the AlphaServer and the StorageWorks storage subsystem components is the first software that is executed when the hardware powers up and usually the last software to execute as the hardware is powered down. It is also the software that directly controls the hardware and as such is platform dependent.

Although firmware is platform dependent, it is operating system independent. There have been many modifications to the operating system that are designed to interoperate with newer firmware features. For this reason, you should always install the latest firmware available from HP for the AlphaServers and for the StorageWorks storage subsystem of your cluster. All too frequently, operating system problems encountered by users can be traced to not having the appropriate firmware and operating system combination. As one colleague once said, "the PAL code makes the difference."[10]

4.3.1 Alpha Firmware

Alpha Firmware updates usually come on new Alpha Firmware Release CDs that accompany the release of a new version of *Tru64* UNIX. Alpha Firmware updates can also be found on the Web at:

`ftp://ftp.digital.com/pub/Digital/Alpha/firmware/`

---

10 PAL code or Privileged Architecture Library (PAL-code) is made up of non-interruptible functions required to support the lowest level of activities on an AlphaServer system such as context switching, system call initiation, and interrupt/exception dispatching.

Before updating the Alpha Firmware for any AlphaServer, always review the Firmware's Release Notes for new features, caveats, and known anomalies. Be certain to review the Firmware Release Notes that correspond to the AlphaServer to be updated for the exact procedure for updating the firmware on your AlphaServer.

IMPORTANT:

While performing any upgrade of the Alpha Firmware, do not abort the update. Furthermore, you should avoid any situation that can lead to the loss of power to the AlphaServer during the upgrade (i.e., don't upgrade your firmware during a thunderstorm unless the AlphaServer is connected to a UPS). Should either event happen, please contact your local HP Field Engineer to check the system.

The following example provides a brief procedure on how to update the firmware for a specific AlphaServer[11].

- Insert the firmware CD into the CDROM and determine which device is the CDROM.

```
P00>>> show dev

dga1.1001.0.7.1         $1$DGA1          HSG80    V86F
dkc0.0.0.7.0            DKC0             RZ2DD-LS 0306
dqa0.0.0.105.0          DQA0             CD-224E  9.5B
dva0.0.0.0.0            DVA0
...
```

- Re-initialize the server.

```
P00>>> init
```

- Boot from the Alpha Firmware CD.

```
P00>>> boot DQA0
...
[Release notes are displayed.]
```

- When prompted, enter the boot file or press enter to accept the default boot file that you will use on the Firmware CD.

```
...
The default bootfile for this platform is

        [DS20]DS20_V6_1.EXE

Hit <RETURN> at the prompt to use the default bootfile.
```

---

11 According to the AlphaServer DS20 V6.2 Console Firmware Release Notes.

```
Bootfile:
...
***** Loadable Firmware Update Utility *****
-------------------------------------------------------------------
Function Description
-------------------------------------------------------------------
Display Displays the system's configuration table.
Exit    Done exit LFU (reset).
List    Lists the device, revision, firmware name,update rev
Update  Replaces current firmware with loadable data image.
Verify  Compares loadable and hardware images.
?       or Help Scrolls this function table.
-------------------------------------------------------------------
UPD>
```

- Update the firmware.

```
UPD> update

Confirm update on:
fsb
nt
pga0
srm

[Y/(N)] y
```

```
WARNING: updates may take several minutes to complete for each device.

                         DO NOT ABORT!

fsb          Updating to 3.2...   Verifying 3.2...   PASSED.

nt           Updating to 5.71...   Verifying 5.71...   PASSED.

pga0         Updating to DS3.81A4...   Verifying DS3.81A4...   PASSED.

srm          Updating to 6.1-2...   Verifying 6.1-2...   PASSED.

UPD> exit
```

That's really all there is to it.

4.3.2 ECU Firmware

For some older AlphaServers that have the Extended System Integrated Architecture (EISA) bus, the EISA Configuration Utility (ECU) should be run if you have added devices or if the system is a dual-boot system (with OpenVMS). This utility updates the EISA NVRAM.

The following outlines how to update the ECU firmware:

- Insert the ECU diskette into the floppy disk drive.
- Boot the system from the floppy disk drive.
- Follow the instructions on the screen to display the Main Menu.

- Select the following menu items from the Main Menu:
  - CMOS setup
  - Advanced CMOS setup
  - Console Selection: Digital UNIX Console (SRM)
- Press the F10 key to save your selections.
- Power off and then power on the system.

4.3.3 Host Bus Adapter Firmware

As of Alpha Firmware update version 6.1, the host bus adapter firmware and the Alpha Firmware are updated at the same time. Included on the list of devices to update is the KGPSA host bus adapter – this is the `pga0` device. Just make sure that the firmware is updated for this device.

4.3.4 HSZ/HSG RAID Array Controller Firmware

Updating the HSZ/HSG RAID Array Controller firmware should be left to the HP Field Service Engineers. Only those customers who really know what they are doing should attempt this update and only after performing a full backup of any data that may be on the storage subsystem.

The minimum HSZ/HSG firmware revisions to support *TruCluster* Server are represented in Table 4-3.

To determine the firmware level of your HSZ/HSG controller, use the following command:

```
HSG> show this
Controller:
        HSG80 ZG14100634 Software V86F-8, Hardware  E16
...
```

In this example, the HSG80 controller is at the ACS firmware revision `V86F-8`. The "`-8`" usually signifies the patch level of the firmware. The same conventions and caveats that apply to the HSG ACS firmware can also be applied to the HSOF firmware of the HSZ family of controllers.

4.3.5 Fibre Channel Switch Firmware

Again, as with the HSZ/HSG Raid Array Controller firmware, only HP Field Service Engineers should perform updates to the Fibre Channel Switch Firmware.

4.4 Configuring and Verifying the Cluster Interconnect Hardware

Implementing a cluster requires a dedicated Cluster Interconnect in which all cluster members are connected. The cluster interconnect provides the foundation for a virtual private network that allows communications among all cluster members. This cluster interconnect provides for Internode Communications (via the ICS[12]) between cluster nodes or members. The *TruCluster* Server software creates this virtual private network within the cluster, and this virtual private network exists side-by-side with the physical communications channel provided by the cluster interconnect.

How does this work? For each member, the cluster software creates a virtual network device for the cluster interconnect. In V5.1A, this device is named `ics0`. In V5.0A and V5.1, this device was named `mc0` as only Memory Channel adapter cards were supported as cluster interconnects. In any event, this device has its own IP name and IP address, which are used when establishing the system's membership in the cluster.

The hardware that may be used for the cluster interconnect can be either the Memory Channel (MC) adapter or an Ethernet local area network (LAN) card but not a mix of both.

The Cluster Interconnect is used to provide the following functions within a cluster:

- Health and status messaging between cluster members. The Connection Manager uses this information to monitor the cluster members and to coordinate membership. For more information on the Connection Manager subsystem, see Chapter 17.
- Distributed lock manager (DLM) locking between cluster members. This is used to coordinate access to shared resources. For more detailed information on the DLM, please see Chapter 18.
- Accessing file systems between cluster members. For storage located on a cluster member's private bus but visible to all members of the cluster, all reads and writes from other cluster members are performed across the cluster interconnect. As Cluster File System uses a client-server model, this is also true for file systems on the shared bus.
- The cluster interconnect, through the ICSnet, includes a full IP stack. While this usage is not recommended for general-purpose network traffic, nothing can prevent an application from taking advantage of this with the exception of the bandwidth of the interconnect hardware. All non-cluster-related traffic should be kept off the cluster interconnect, and if a private network is needed, one should be added.
- Cluster alias routing. For more information, please see Chapter 16 on Cluster Alias.

To repeat, as of this writing, there are two approved types of Cluster Interconnect hardware for use with *TruCluster* Server – the Memory Channel (MC) adapter card and the Ethernet Local Area Network (LAN) card[13]. *TruCluster* Server supports up to eight members in a cluster regardless of which type of cluster interconnect is used.

In this section we will discuss how to configure and verify these different cluster interconnects, and why you may want to use one interconnect over another.

---

12 The Internode Communication Subsystem is covered in Chapter 18.

13 Ethernet Local Area Network card support as a cluster interconnect began in *TruCluster* Server version 5.1A.

Memory Channel 1 Jumper Settings	
Hub Mode	Jumper Pin Outs
Standard Hub	J4: Pins 1 to 2
Virtual Hub 0: VH0	J4: Pins 2 to 3
Virtual Hub 1: VH1	J4: All open

Table 4-6: Memory Channel 1 – Jumper Settings

4.4.1 Memory Channel as a Cluster Interconnect

There are three variants of Memory Channel adapter cards supported: Memory Channel 1, Memory Channel 1.5, and Memory Channel 2. The older Memory Channel 1 adapter card and Memory Channel 1.5 adapter card are collectively referred to as Memory Channel 1 (or MC1). Only the newer Memory Channel 2 (MC2) adapter card is supported on the DS, ES, and GS[14] classes of AlphaServers.

Memory Channel (MC) as a cluster interconnect can be used in either a virtual hub mode configuration or a standard hub mode configuration. A virtual hub mode configuration is only supported on two-node clusters. A standard hub mode configuration may be used for two-node clusters but is required for clusters that have three or more cluster members. A Memory Channel Hub is also a requirement for a cluster in a standard hub mode configuration.

4.4.1.1 Virtual Hub Mode

As stated earlier, using the MC as a cluster interconnect in a virtual hub mode is only supported in two-node cluster configurations. It consists of both cluster members directly connected together via the Memory Channel adapter cards using a MC cable. Each of the Memory Channel adapter cards is physically jumpered for virtual hub mode. The Memory Channel adapter card variant determines the proper jumper settings.

On MC1, there is an adapter jumper J4 that determines whether the configuration is in virtual hub mode or standard hub mode. For virtual hub mode, the Memory Channel adapter jumper J4 on one cluster node is configured to be virtual hub 0 (VH0) and the Memory Channel adapter jumper J4 on the other cluster node is configured to be virtual hub 1 (VH1). Table 4-6 represents the Hub Mode and the Memory Channel adapter jumper J4 pin outs for the MC1 adapter card.

Unlike the older MC1 adapter card, the MC2 adapter card has six jumpers – J1, J3, J4, J5, J10, and J11 – see Figure 4-4. Setting the MC2 adapter card for virtual hub mode is similar to setting the MC1 adapter card; all you need to do is set the adapter jumper J1.

---

14 The GS60 and GS140 AlphaServer systems support MC1.

Memory Channel 2 Jumper Settings	
Jumper	Description
J1: Hub Mode	Standard Hub: Pins 1 to 2
	Virtual Hub 0 (VH0): Pins 2 to 3
	Virtual Hub 1 (VH1): All open
J3: Window Size	512 MB: Pins 2 to 3
	128 MB: Pins 1 to 2
J4: Page Size	8 KB Page Size: Pins 1 to 2 (Default for UNIX)
J5: AlphaServer 8x00 mode	8x00 mode selected: Pins 1 to 2
	8x00 mode not selected: Pins 2 to 3
J10 and J11: Fiber Optic Mode Enabled	Fiber Off: Pins 1 to 2
	Fiber On: Pins 2 to 3

Table 4-7: Memory Channel 2 – Jumper Settings

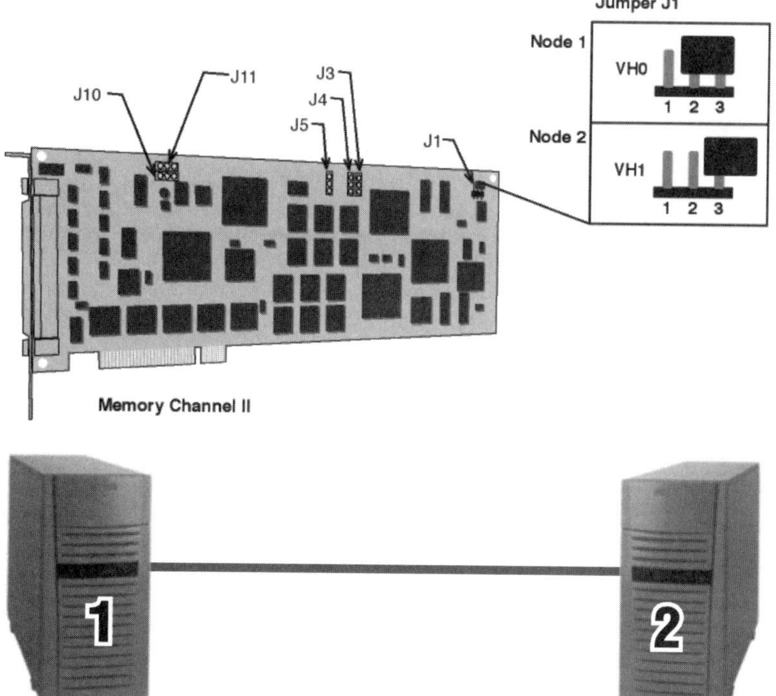

Figure 4-4: Memory Channel 2 – Virtual Hub Configuration

Table 4-7, provides a description of the MC2 adapter jumpers - what each is for and the possible jumper settings.

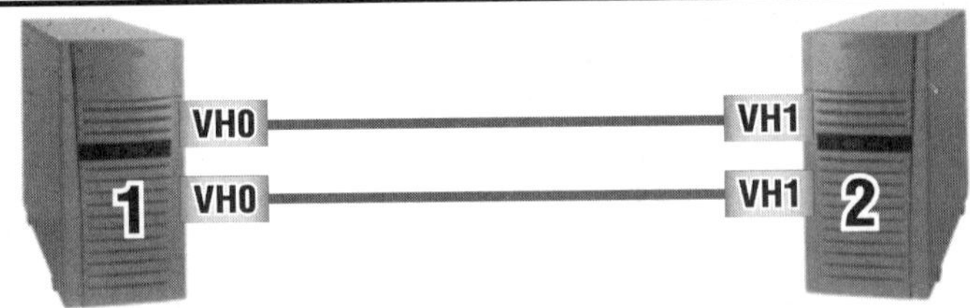

Figure 4-5: Redundant MC Virtual Hub Configuration

For more information on the other individual Memory Channel 2 jumper settings, please refer to Chapter 5 in the *TruCluster* Server Cluster Hardware Configuration Guide.

For the purposes of redundancy of the cluster interconnect, dual-rail MC is supported in a virtual hub mode. Dual-rail MC occurs when you have two Memory Channel adapter cards in one cluster node directly connected to another two Memory Channel adapter cards in another cluster node. How would this be configured from a Memory Channel adapter card perspective? You would identically jumper both Memory Channel adapters in cluster `member1` as `VH0`. In the other cluster member, `member2`, both Memory Channel adapters cards would be jumpered as `VH1`. Each of the adapters cards with the `VH0` setting in `member1` would then be cabled to an adapter with the `VH1` setting in `member2`. See Figure 4-5.

4.4.1.2 Standard Hub Mode

In standard hub mode, Memory Channel adapter cards are again in each cluster member, but instead of being directly connected to a Memory Channel adapter card in another cluster member, each is connected to a Memory Channel Line card in a central Memory Channel hub. All internode communications flows between the Memory Channel adapter cards through the Memory Channel Hub. Please see Figure 4-7 for an illustration.

Like the Memory Channel adapter cards in a virtual hub mode configuration, the Memory Channel adapter cards in standard hub mode configuration must be properly jumpered. For an MC1 adapter card jumper J4 is set accordingly for standard hub mode - see Table 4-6. For an MC2 adapter card jumper J1 is set for standard hub mode - see Table 4-7.

Dual-rail Memory Channel is also supported in a standard hub mode. How would this work? To implement a dual-rail Memory Channel configuration in a standard hub mode, it would require two Memory Channel adapter cards per cluster member and the use of two separate Memory Channel Hubs. As each primary Memory Channel adapter card is connected to a Memory Channel Line card in the primary Memory Channel Hub, take note of the physical slot of the Memory Channel Line card that is being used. When the secondary Memory Channel adapter card is connected to a Memory Channel Line card in the secondary Memory Channel Hub, it must use the same numbered slot in the secondary Memory Channel Hub as the primary Memory Channel Hub.

Let's illustrate how to implement a dual-rail configuration on a three-node cluster as an example. In the primary Memory Channel Hub, the primary Memory Channel card in cluster `member1` is physically connected to the Memory Channel Line card in slot 0. The primary Memory Channel card in cluster `member2` is connected to the Memory Channel Line card in slot 1. The primary Memory Channel card in cluster `member3` is connected to the Memory Channel Line card in slot 2. This same Memory Channel Hub configuration is replicated for the secondary Memory Channel Hub using the secondary Memory Channel adapter cards in each cluster node. See Figure 4-6.

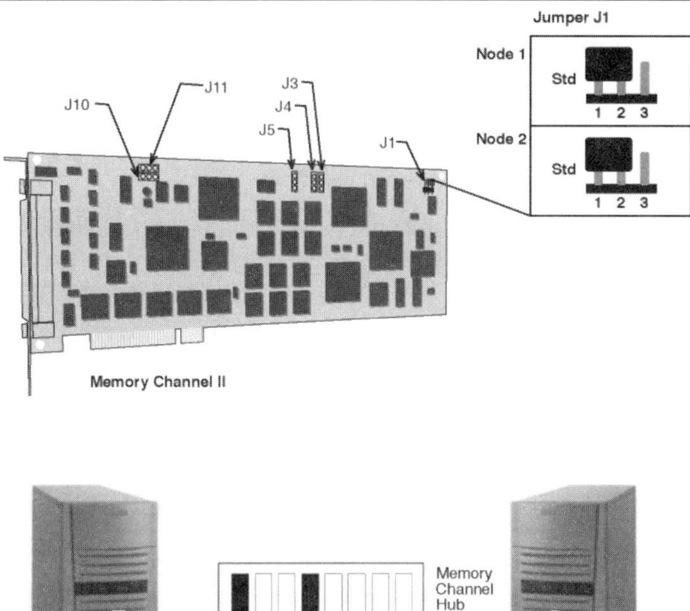

Figure 4-7: Memory Channel 2 – Standard Hub Configuration

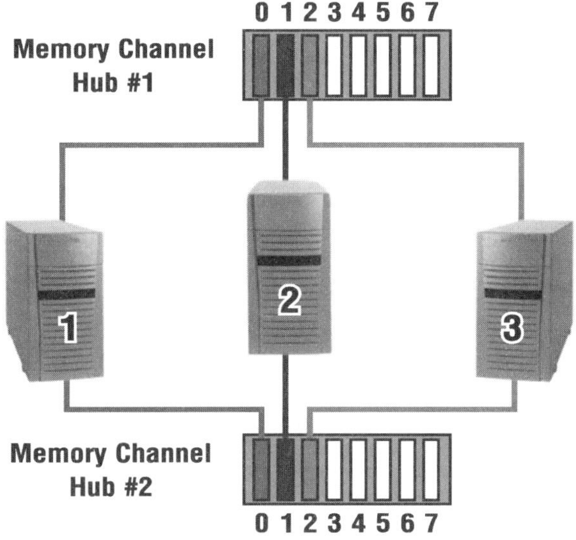

Figure 4-6: Redundant MC Standard Hub Configuration

4.4.1.3 Caveats on Using Memory Channel Adapter Cards

In planning the deployment of a cluster, there are a couple of caveats to keep in mind when using Memory Channel adapter cards. These apply to the use of Memory Channel adapter cards in both virtual and standard hub modes. They are as follows:

- The MC cable connectors have 100-pins, and extreme care should be taken in connecting or disconnecting the MC cable. Bending or breaking even one pin can be disastrous to the operation of a cluster.
- MC1 and MC2 can exist in the same cluster but cannot be intermixed on the same Memory Channel rail.
- Only one MC2 may be jumpered to a 512 MB memory window per PCI bus (reference Table 4-7).
- Although not specific to either Memory Channel cards or Ethernet LAN cards, ICS names and ICS IP addresses should never be registered with DNS.

4.4.1.4 Testing and Verifying the Memory Channel Adapter Cards

After the Memory Channel hardware is installed and configured, it should be tested to verify that it's working properly before starting the installation of the *TruCluster* Server software. To do this, there are two different Memory Channel diagnostic commands that are available at the system console: `mc_diag` and `mc_cable`.

4.4.1.4.1 `mc_diag` diagnostic

The main purpose of the `mc_diag` diagnostic command is to test out the Memory Channel adapter card. In detail, the `mc_diag` diagnostic command provides the following:

- Tests all the Memory Channel adapters on the system.
- This is executed as part of the initialization sequence when the system is powered up.
- This can be run on a stand-alone cluster member while other clusters are up and available.

Below is an example of the execution of the `mc_diag` diagnostic command:

```
P00>>> mc_diag
Testing MC-Adapter(s)
Adapter mca0, Passed
Adapter mcb0, Passed
```

As this server is configured for dual-rail Memory Channel, both Memory Channel adapter cards passed this hardware diagnostic test.

The `mc_diag` command can output detailed "diagnostic" information by using the "`-d`" option. See Appendix A for more information.

4.4.1.4.2 `mc_cable` diagnostic

The `mc_cable` diagnostic command's main purpose is to provide an end-to-end interconnect data flow check. This verifies that data can flow from one cluster member to all the other cluster members and vice versa. In detail, the following must be considered when using the `mc_cable` diagnostic command:

- This command should be run on all systems simultaneously so all cluster members must be down at the system console.
- This diagnostic is designed to isolate problems among the cables and hardware components that make up the complete Memory Channel interconnect – from the Memory Channel adapter cards, through the Memory Channel cables, to the Memory Channel Line cards, and, to a certain extent, the Memory Channel Hub.
- Indications of data flow through the Memory Channel interconnect are by response messages.
- While this diagnostic does not produce error messages, the change in connection state is an indication of the data flow between different points in the Memory Channel interconnect.
- This diagnostic can be run in either a virtual hub mode or a standard hub mode.
- Once the `mc_cable` command is executed on a system, it runs continuously until it is terminated using <CTRL/C>.

WARNING:

Never execute the `mc_cable` command on any node of a cluster if a portion of that cluster is still up. This command will crash all members in a running cluster.

The following are examples of the execution of the `mc_cable` diagnostic command.

- `mc_cable` in a virtual hub mode with dual-rail Memory Channel.

  The `mc_cable` command is executed on System 2. The two Memory Channel cards are online for this system, but there is no response from the MC card in the other system.

```
>>> mc_cable
To exit MC_CABLE, type <Ctrl/C>
mca0 node id 1 is online
No response from node 0 on mca0
mcb0 node id 1 is online
No response from node 0 on mcb0
```

  The `mc_cable` command is then executed on System 1. The Memory Channel cards on this system are online, and a response is received from the other system that is running the `mc_cable` command.

```
>>> mc_cable
To exit MC_CABLE, type <Ctrl/C>
mca0 node id 0 is online
Response from node 1 on mca0
mcb0 node id 0 is online
Response from node 0 on mcb0
```

System 2 receives a response from the `mc_cable` command running on System 1.

```
Response from node 0 on mca0
Response from node 0 on mcb0
```

On System 1, we then issue `<CTRL/C>` to abort the `mc_cable` command.

```
<CTRL/C>
>>>
```

On System 2, we receive a response that there is no further communication with System 1. On System 2, we also issue `<CTRL/C>` to abort the `mc_cable` command running there.

```
mcb0 is offline
mca0 is offline
<Ctrl/C>
```

- `mc_cable` in a standard hub mode with two cluster members.

  The `mc_cable` command is executed on System 1. Notice that the Memory Channel card is online for this system, but there is no response from any others.

```
>>> mc_cable
To exit MC_CABLE, type <CTRL/C>
 mca0 node id 0 is online
 No Response from node 1 on mca0
 No Response from node 2 on mca0
 No Response from node 3 on mca0
 No Response from node 4 on mca0
 No Response from node 5 on mca0
 No Response from node 6 on mca0
 No Response from node 7 on mca0
```

  The `mc_cable` command is then executed on System 2. The Memory Channel card on this system is online, and a response is received from the other system that is running the `mc_cable` command.

```
P00>>> mc_cable
To exit MC_CABLE, type <CTRL/C>
mca0 node id 2 is online
Response from node 0 on mca0
No Response from node 1 on mca0
No Response from node 3 on mca0
No Response from node 4 on mca0
No Response from node 5 on mca0
No Response from node 6 on mca0
No Response from node 7 on mca0
```

  System 1 receives a response from the `mc_cable` command running on System 2. On System 1, we then issue `<CTRL/C>` to abort the `mc_cable` command.

```
Response from node 2 on mca0
<CTRL/C>
>>>
```

On System 2, we receive a response that there is no further communication with System 1. On System 2, we also issue <CTRL/C> to abort the mc_cable command running there.

```
No Response from node 0 on mca0
<CTRL/C>
>>>
```

In this example, notice that although we only have two nodes in this cluster, the mc_cable diagnostic command is referring to these nodes as node 0 and node 2. Why? Because of the connections to the slots for the Memory Channel Line cards in the Memory Channel Hub. In this case, slots 0 and 2 are used to connect to the two cluster members. If we had used slots 0 and 1, the nodes would be identified as node 0 and node 1.

4.4.1.5 Memory Channel Information for the Creation of a Cluster

During the creation of a cluster or the addition of a new member to an existing cluster, certain information is required to identify the cluster interconnect. For a cluster using Memory Channel, the IP name and IP address for the virtual cluster interconnect device on each cluster member is needed. This is also known as the ICS name and ICS IP address.

By default, the cluster installation programs, clu_create(8) and clu_add_member(8), offer the IP address on the 10.0.0 subnet for the virtual cluster interconnect with the host portion of the IP address the same as the memberid of the cluster member. The IP name is set to the short host name of the cluster member followed by "-ics0" [15]. Both the IP address and the IP name of virtual cluster interconnect should not be in DNS.

The following shows an example of the cluster interconnect IP names and IP addresses for two members of the babylon5 cluster, molari and sheridan. This information is from the /etc/hosts file of the cluster. This cluster is running on a Memory Channel cluster interconnect:

```
10.0.0.1 molari-ics0       # member1's virtual interconnect IP name and address
10.0.0.2 sheridan-ics0     # member2's virtual interconnect IP name and address
```

In planning for the implementation of a cluster, determine ahead of time not only what the cluster's Name and IP address will be but also the IP name and address for each of the virtual cluster interconnects. See the *Tru64* UNIX/*TruCluster* Server Planning Worksheet in section 4.8.

---

15 In V5.1A, the name of a member's cluster interconnect virtual device has changed from mc0 to ics0.

4.4.2 Ethernet Local Area Network (LAN) Card as a Cluster Interconnect

With the release of *TruCluster* Server version 5.1A came support for an additional type of cluster interconnect from the usual Memory Channel adapter card – the Ethernet LAN card. The Ethernet LAN card automatically provides for a lower cost alternative to Memory Channel, but does that mean you should go out and replace your cluster interconnect hardware with Ethernet LAN? It depends. In section 4.4.3, we will review the advantages and disadvantages of both cluster interconnects. For the time being, let's see what it takes to deploy Ethernet LAN as a cluster interconnect.

4.4.2.1 Hardware Requirements for the LAN Interconnect

Any supported Ethernet adapter, switch, or hub that operates in a standard LAN environment at 100 Mb/sec or 1000 Mb/sec should, in theory, work within a LAN cluster interconnect. Fiber Distributed Data Interface (FDDI), ATM LAN Emulation (LANE), and 10 Mb/s Ethernet are not supported in a LAN interconnect. For more detail information, please see Chapter 22.

The following is required of the Ethernet hardware to operate in a LAN cluster interconnect:

- The LAN interconnect must be a private LAN accessible only to cluster members.
- Cluster members in the LAN interconnect must all be operating at the same network speed and can be half-duplex or full-duplex for the transmission mode. Half-duplex transmission mode is not recommended for use in a LAN interconnect because it may limit cluster performance.
- A LAN interconnect can be a single direct half-duplex or full-duplex connection between two cluster members on either switches or hubs but not both.
- One or more switches or hubs are required for a cluster of three or more members.
- No more than two switches are allowed between two cluster members.
- All cluster members must have at least one point-to-point connection to all other cluster members.
- The Spanning Tree Protocol (STP) must be disabled on all Ethernet switch ports specifically connected to cluster members. STP should be enabled on ports connecting Ethernet switches together for supporting a highly available LAN interconnect configuration.
- For the LAN interconnect, link aggregation of Ethernet adapters is not supported as of this writing.

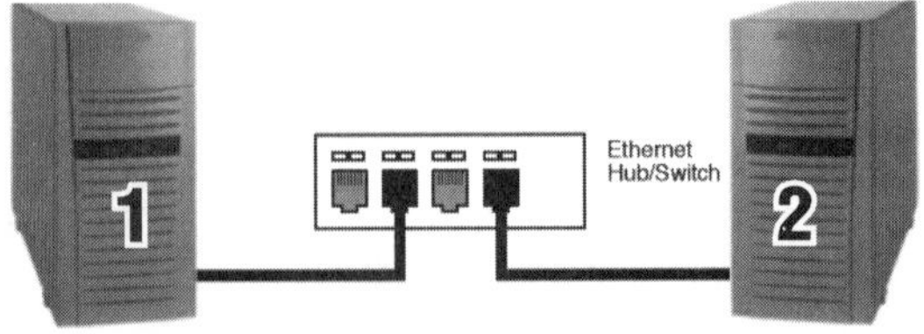

Figure 4-8: LAN Cluster Interconnect

4.4.2.2 Basic Hardware Configurations for LAN Interconnect

There are three basic hardware configurations that support a LAN cluster interconnect. In this section, we will go over these three configurations.

- For a two-node cluster only, a single crossover network cable directly connects one member's Ethernet card to the Ethernet card of the second cluster member. The crossover network cable provides a direct point-to-point Ethernet connection between the two cluster nodes without the necessity of a switch or a hub. Dual-redundant crossover cables between two cluster members is not supported because the method used to enable a redundant configuration is NetRAIN, so each NIC must be connected to the same physical subnet.

- A single Ethernet hub or switch could be used for a cluster that has two to eight members. In this type of configuration, a single Ethernet hub or switch would be used to connect to the Ethernet LAN cards in each of the two to eight cluster members. See Figure 4-8 for an example.

  An Ethernet hub operating at half-duplex transmission mode should not be used in this configuration as it would limit the performance of the cluster.

- An Ethernet LAN cluster interconnect configuration that has the greatest amount of redundancy is one in which you have two switches (with two crossover cables connecting the switches), with two or more Ethernet LAN cards in each member, configured as a NetRAIN virtual interface, but with each LAN card connected to a different switch. This configuration can survive not only the loss of a cluster member or a break in a LAN interconnect connection but also the loss of a switch or a crossover cable.

4.4.2.3 LAN Interconnect Information for the Creation of a Cluster

Before starting the creation and configuration of a cluster using a LAN cluster interconnect, you should have certain basic information about the LAN interconnect. In this section, we will discuss how to have this information ready and available for when it is needed during the creation of the cluster.

To obtain the device name, speed, and transmission mode of the LAN cards on your system, use the following command.

```
# hwmgr get attr -cat network -a name -a media_speed -a full_duplex

137:
  name = alt0
  media_speed = 1000
  full_duplex = 1
138:
  name = alt1
  media_speed = 1000
  full_duplex = 1
```

From our example, we see that our two LAN cards (devices alt0 and alt1) are operating at 1000 Mb/sec and at full-duplex.

A cluster that is using a LAN interconnect needs the following information:

- An IP name and IP address for the virtual cluster interconnect device for each cluster member.
- The clu_create and clu_add_member programs provide, by default, IP addresses on the 10.0.0 subnet for the virtual cluster interconnect. The host portion of the IP address is set to the memberid of the cluster member being configured, and the IP name is the short form of the member's host name followed by "-ics0". Again, as with the Memory Channel configuration, the IP addresses and the IP names for the virtual cluster interconnect should not be in DNS.
- For the physical LAN interface for each cluster member, an IP name and address is needed on a different subnet from the virtual cluster interconnect.
- The cluster creation programs also provide defaults for the physical LAN interface. By default, IP addresses on the 10.1.0 subnet are provided with the host portion of the IP address set to the memberid of the cluster member being configured, and the word "member" applended with the member ID and "-icstcp0". The IP addresses and the IP names for the physical LAN interface should not be in DNS.

The following example provides the cluster interconnect IP names and addresses for two members of the clue cluster, mustard and plum, operating on a LAN interconnect. This information is also contained in the /etc/hosts file of the cluster.

```
#
# member1's cluster interconnect
#

10.0.0.1 mustard-ics0          # virtual interface IP name and address
10.1.0.1 member1-icstcp0       # physical interface IP name and address

#
# member2's cluster interconnect
#

10.0.0.2 plum-ics0             # virtual interface IP name and address
10.1.0.2 member2-icstcp0       # physical interface IP name and address
```

As we stated in the section on the Memory Channel interconnect, you should determine ahead of time not only the cluster's Name and the cluster's IP address but also the IP name and IP address for each of the cluster interconnects – both virtual and physical. See the *Tru64* UNIX/*TruCluster* Server Planning Worksheet in section 4.8.

4.4.3 Why Use One Interconnect over Another?

We have had the opportunity to examine both the Memory Channel interconnect and the Ethernet LAN interconnect. We have discussed the hardware requirements for each interconnect, the configuration, and how to obtain interconnect information that is required to create a cluster.

Why use one interconnect over another? Unfortunately, this is not a question we can answer satisfactorily because, well, it depends. It depends on which applications will be run on the cluster, how many users will be on the cluster, how storage will be utilized, and what the cluster's purpose in life is. It depends on many variables, but it does come down to this – the user requirements that are used to do the planning for the deployment of the cluster.

To assist you in selecting which interconnect to use, we provide the following table - Table 4-8. This table compares Memory Channel to LAN Interconnect.

Memory Channel	LAN Interconnect
Higher cost • High bandwidth (100MB/s). • Low latency (~3μs).	Generally lower cost • Medium bandwidth, medium to high latency for 100 Mb/s. • High bandwidth, medium to high latency for 1000 Mb/s.
Up to eight members are supported as this is limited by the capacity of the Memory Channel hub.	Up to eight members are supported with the initial release; however, more members may be supported in the future.
The distances supported between members using copper cable is up to 20 meters (65.6 feet) and up to 2000 meters (1.2 miles) with fiber-optic cable in virtual hub mode, and up to 6000 meters (3.7 miles) with fiber-optic cable using a physical hub.	The distances supported between members using LAN interconnect hardware is determined by the length of a network segment and by the capabilities of and options allowed for the • Maximum Fast Ethernet distance is ~.4Km. • Maximum Gigabit Ethernet distance is ~1.6Km (SPOF) or ~1Km (NetRAIN).
Supports the use of the Memory Channel application programming interface (API) library.	Does not support the Memory Channel API library.
Dual-rail redundant Memory Channel configuration provides for internode communications redundancy.	Internode communications redundancy is achieved by configuring multiple network adapters as a redundant array of independent network adapters (NetRAIN). The virtual interface on each member is accomplished by distributing their connections across multiple switches.*

* - For more specific information, please review the Chapter on NetRAIN and the TruCluster Server Cluster LAN Interconnect guide.

Table 4-8: Memory Channel vs. LAN Interconnect

4.5 Console Level Preparation

As part of the planning process for installing either *Tru64* UNIX or *TruCluster* Server, we need to verify that the hardware, firmware, and console variables are set appropriately.

4.5.1 Verify the Hardware

4.5.1.1 Verify the Memory Requirements

In section 4.1 we discussed how we needed at least 192 MB of memory to install and operate *Tru64* UNIX and *TruCluster* Server on one server. Now let's verify that we meet those requirements.

```
P00>>> show memory

Array #         Size       Base Addr
-------      ----------    ---------
   0            512 MB     040000000
   1           1024 MB     000000000

Total Bad Pages = 0
Total Good Memory = 1536 Mbytes
```

Or

```
P00>>> show config
...
MEMORY

Array #         Size       Base Addr
-------      ----------    ---------
   0            512 MB     040000000
   1           1024 MB     000000000

Total Bad Pages = 0
Total Good Memory = 1536 MBytes
...
```

4.5.1.2 Verify the Network Hardware

We also need to verify the network hardware and settings.

```
P00>>> show config
...
PCI Hose 01
...
    Bus 00  Slot 09: DE600-AA
                                        eia0.0.0.9.1    00-50-8B-AE-F3-23
...
```

Given that we know how our network is configured, we make the appropriate network mode changes from Twisted-Pair (the default setting) to 100 MB Full Duplex.

```
P00>>>show eia0_mode
eia0_mode              Twisted-Pair
```

```
P00>>>set eia0_mode fastfd
Changing to selected mode.
```

```
P00>>>show eia0_mode
eia0_mode               FastFD (Full Duplex)
```

For more information on what settings to use for your own network configuration, please refer to your switch or hub manufacturer's reference documentation, the hardware documentation for your AlphaServer system(s), and the hardware documentation for the NIC card that you will be using.

4.5.1.3 Verify the Memory Channel Interconnect Hardware

Finally, if we are using Memory Channel as the cluster interconnect hardware, we need to verify it and its firmware revision.

```
P00>>>show config
...
     Bus 00  Slot 08: DEC PCI MC
                                        mca0.0.0.8.0          Rev: 22, mca0
...
```

This shows that we are using MC2 with firmware revision 0x22 (module revision 34). This satisfies the cluster interconnect hardware requirement and the firmware requirement for MC2.

	Module Revision
• MC1 –	11
• MC1.5 –	14
• MC2 –	32 or greater

```
>>> show config

11       DEC PCI MC                                 Rev: b,mc0a

Slot     Option Name                   Type      Rev     Name
2        DEC PCI MC                    181011    000E    mc0
3        DEC PCI MC                    181011    000E    mc1

Bus 00  Slot 08: DEC PCI MC
                           mca0.0.0.8.0           Rev: 20, mca0
```

4.5.2 Verify the Firmware

Although we updated the Alpha Firmware in section 4.3.1, let's verify the updated firmware.

```
P00>>> show version
version                  V6.1-2 Oct 15 2001 13:36:04
```

Or

```
P00>>> show config
                     COMPAQ AlphaServer DS20E 666 MHz

SRM Console:    V6.1-2
PALcode:        OpenVMS PALcode V1.93-75, Tru64 UNIX PALcode V1.88-70
...
```

4.5.3 Console Variables

Given that the hardware and firmware are appropriately verified, we need to modify specific console variables to support an installation of *Tru64* UNIX and *TruCluster* Server.

4.5.3.1 Processor-Specific Console Variables

The following is the processor-specific console variables for systems that can be members of a cluster.

System	Console Variable Settings
AlphaServer 800 AlphaServer 1200 AlphaServer 2100/2100A AlphaServer 4000/4100 AlphaServer 4100A	`P00>>> set bus_probe_algorithm new`
AlphaServer 1000/1000A	`P00>>> set bus_probe_algorithm new` `P00>>> set boot_file ""`
AlphaServer 8200 AlphaServer 8400	`P00>>> set os_type unix` `P00>>> set console serial`

These console settings should be implemented prior to the installation of *Tru64* UNIX.

4.5.3.2 General Console Variables

4.5.3.2.1 The `boot_osflags` Environment Variable

During the installation and configuration of *Tru64* UNIX and *TruCluster* Server, set the `boot_osflags` variable so that if the system should crash, it does not reboot.

```
P00>>> set boot_osflags "h"
```

After the cluster is built, reset the `boot_osflags` variable so that the system will automatically boot to multi-user mode after a crash. Remember, one of the themes of *TruCluster* Server is high availability; therefore, should a cluster member go down for any reason, we would want the cluster member up and a part of the cluster ASAP.

```
P00>>> set boot_osflags "a"
```

4.5.3.2.2 The boot_reset Environment Variable

Set the boot_reset variable so that when the system boots, it does a system reset first.

```
P00>>> set boot_reset on
```

4.5.3.2.3 The bootdef_dev Environment Variable

Before installing *TruCluster* Server, we would want to clear the bootdef_dev variable. This variable is used to specify the device from which to boot the system.

```
P00>>> set bootdef_dev " "
```

The clu_create and the clu_add_member programs automatically set this variable with the appropriate boot device when the cluster is created or a new cluster member is added.

4.5.3.2.4 The auto_action Environment Variable

During the installation and configuration of *Tru64* UNIX and *TruCluster* Server, set the auto_action variable so that if the system is ever initialized or powered on, it would not automatically start booting.

```
P00>>> set auto_action halt
```

After the installation is complete, reset the auto_action variable so that when the system is initialized it automatically boots.

```
P00>>> set auto_action restart
```

4.5.3.2.5 Miscellaneous Console Variables

We include a couple of miscellaneous console variables that we have found useful. We set the os_type variable to indicate the system is a UNIX system.

```
P00>>> set os_type UNIX
```

If we connect a console to the serial port and plan on a command line interface (CLI) installation of *Tru64* UNIX and *TruCluster* Server, we must also set the console variable to serial.

```
P00>>> set console serial
P00>>> init
```

4.6 Licensing Requirements

The licensing requirements or License Product Authorization Keys (License PAKs) information for implementing *Tru64* UNIX and *TruCluster* Server are rather simple.

- For *Tru64* UNIX, the following license PAKs are required:
  - OSF-BASE
  - OSF-USR
  - OSF-SVR (depending on the hardware)
- *TruCluster* Server only requires the `TCS-UA` license PAK.
- Additional licenses that may be required, depending on implementation, are:
  - AdvFS Advanced Utilities (`ADVFS-UTILITIES`)
  - Logical Storage Manager License (`LSM-OA`)

Software licensing on a cluster is done on a per node basis so be prepared to have separate license PAKs for each cluster node. We recommend that you make a copy of your original license PAKs and store the originals in a very safe and secure place. Make sure that each cluster node's license PAKs are available prior to the installation of *Tru64* UNIX and *TruCluster* Server so that they can be used when needed.

4.7 Network Planning for the Cluster

Network planning for a cluster should be very similar to network planning for an individual server except that you have a lot more names – hosts and cluster – and IP addresses to deal with. In this section, we will discuss some issues around network planning for a cluster that may help in the overall implementation of the cluster.

4.7.1 Network Information for the Cluster

Before starting the installation of *Tru64* UNIX, plan ahead and have all your network information ready and available. Network information should include the following:

- Host names for each cluster member
- Host IP addresses for each cluster member
- Cluster name
- Cluster IP address
- Network Mask

- DNS network domain
- Primary and Secondary DNS server name
- Primary and Secondary DNS server IP address
- Primary and Secondary NTP server name
- NIS domain
- Primary NIS server name
- Enable remote directory mounting or directory exporting using NFS

4.7.2 To `gated` or not to `gated`?

While `gated` is not required for a stand-alone *Tru64* UNIX server, prior to version 5.1A Patch Kit 1, it is required to implement *TruCluster* Server. If you are implementing a version of *TruCluster* Server prior to version 5.1A Patch Kit 1, we recommend that when routing configuration is performed on the *Tru64* UNIX server, as part of the configuration setup, that you choose to use `gated` in preparation for the implementation of *TruCluster* Server. For more information, please review Chapter 20 on Network Administration Tasks.

4.8 Cluster Preparation Checklist

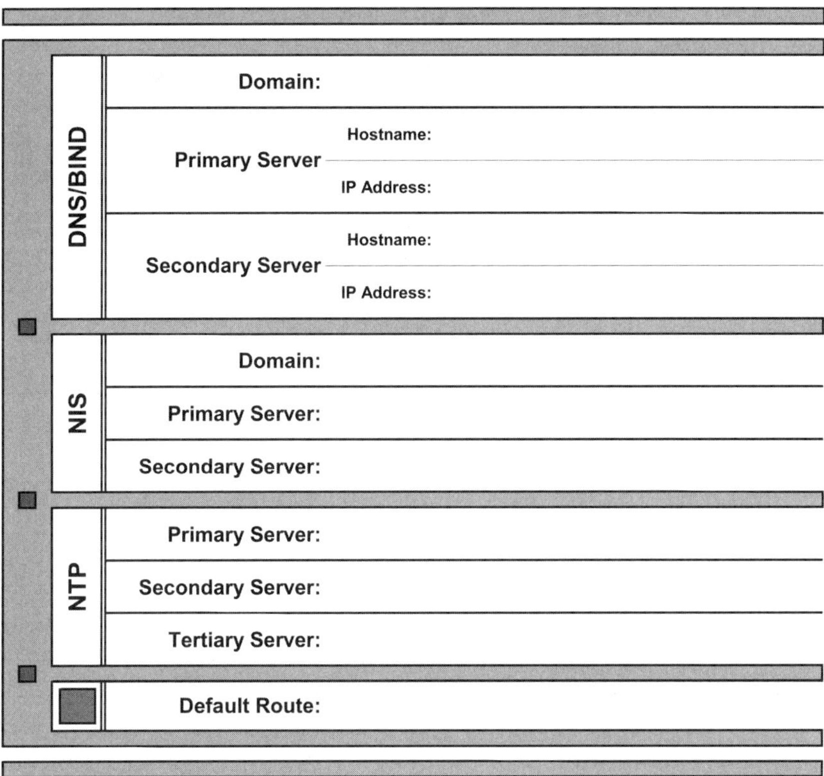

Table 4-9: Network Setup Information

		DSF Disk Name	DSF Partition	SRM Disk Name	Controller Unit ID	Size	Block Size	Firmware Disk/Controller
O/S (ER)	root							
	swap							
	usr							
	var							
	tmp							
cluster-common	cluster_root							
	cluster_usr							
	cluster_var							
	quorum disk		h			1MB	2048	
member boot disks 1	boot_partition		a					
	swap		b					
	cnx		h			1MB	2048	
2	boot_partition		a					
	swap		b					
	cnx		h			1MB	2048	
3	boot_partition		a					
	swap		b					
	cnx		h			1MB	2048	
4	boot_partition		a					
	swap		b					
	cnx		h			1MB	2048	
5	boot_partition		a					
	swap		b					
	cnx		h			1MB	2048	
6	boot_partition		a					
	swap		b					
	cnx		h			1MB	2048	
7	boot_partition		a					
	swap		b					
	cnx		h			1MB	2048	
8	boot_partition		a					
	swap		b					
	cnx		h			1MB	2048	

Table 4-10: Disk/Partition Layout

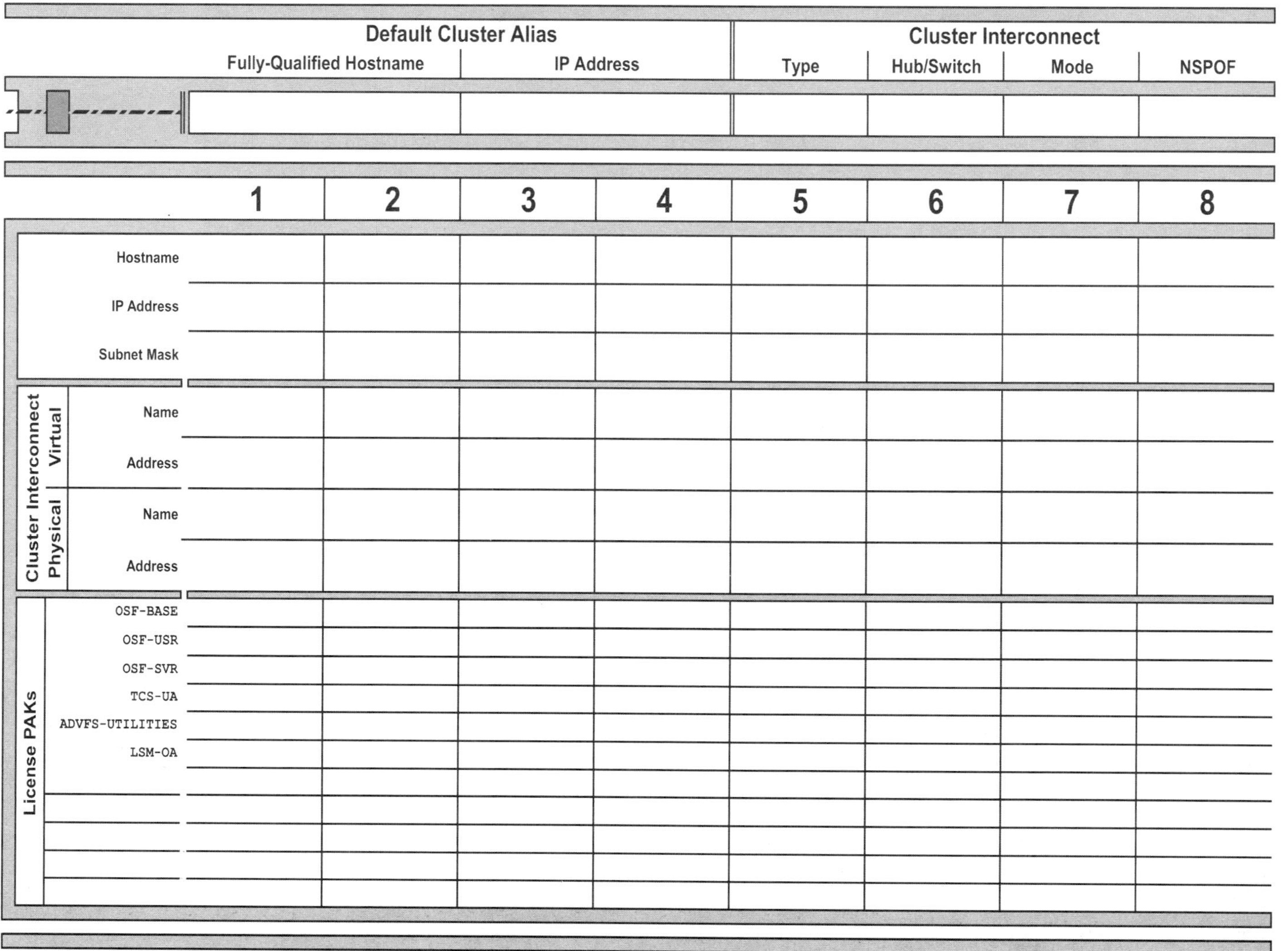

Default Cluster Alias	
Fully-Qualified Hostname	IP Address

Cluster Interconnect			
Type	Hub/Switch	Mode	NSPOF

Member Information

			1	2	3	4	5	6	7	8
		Hostname								
		IP Address								
		Subnet Mask								
Cluster Interconnect	Virtual	Name								
		Address								
	Physical	Name								
		Address								
License PAKs		OSF-BASE								
		OSF-USR								
		OSF-SVR								
		TCS-UA								
		ADVFS-UTILITIES								
		LSM-OA								

Table 4-11: Member Information and Default Cluster Alias

4.9 References

- *Tru64* UNIX Release Notes (V5.1, August 2000).
- *Tru64* UNIX Release Notes (V5.1A, June 2001).
- *TruCluster* Server Release Notes (V5.1, August 2000).
- *TruCluster* Server Cluster Release Notes (V5.1A, June 2001).
- *Tru64* UNIX Installation Guide (V5.1, August 2000).
- *Tru64* UNIX Installation Guide – Advanced Topics (V5.1, August 2000).
- *Tru64* UNIX Installation Guide (V5.1A, June 2001).
- *Tru64* UNIX Installation Guide – Advanced Topics (V5.1A, June 2001).
- *Tru64* UNIX Software Installation guide (V5.1, August 2000).
- *TruCluster* Server Cluster Installation guide (V5.1A, June 2001).
- *TruCluster* Server Cluster Hardware Configuration guide
- Compaq StorageWorks HSG80 ACS Solution Software V8.6 for Compaq *Tru64* UNIX – Installation and Configuration Guide
- Compaq StorageWorks Fibre Channel SAN Management Guide, 2nd Edition, (Nov. 2001), Compaq Part No. AA-RMMJB-TE
- Hardware Configuration Technical Update for Fibre Channel for *TruCluster* Server 5.0A
- AlphaServer DS20 V6.2 Console Firmware Release Notes
- *TruCluster* Server Cluster LAN Interconnect guide
- *TruCluster* Server Software Product Description (SPD)

5

Installation and Configuration of *Tru64* UNIX

"Whatever is worth doing at all is worth doing well."

– Earl of Chesterfield, Letters

In the last four chapters, we've shown you what a cluster is, provided quick overviews of *Tru64* UNIX, *TruCluster* Server, some technology considerations, designing a cluster, and finally, planning for a cluster configuration. If you're like many System Administrators and System Architects we know, you've probably felt ready to build your own cluster since picking up this book.

In this chapter, we will discuss how to install and configure *Tru64* UNIX to support the successful deployment of *TruCluster* Server. In addition to providing guidance on how to perform an installation, we will "walk you through" an actual installation that we performed.

We will cover a great deal of material in this chapter. As a point of comparison, HP has devoted two entire reference manuals to *Tru64* UNIX Installation (and that is for each version of *Tru64* UNIX that is released). Given this body of work, we defer to these reference manuals as the ultimate authority on this subject. Our purpose is to demonstrate what it takes to install *Tru64* UNIX to properly support a basic *TruCluster* Server deployment.

As with any successful implementation of a system, planning is always mandatory. In this case, the planning leads to a strong foundation on which to deploy *TruCluster* Server. *Tru64* UNIX is that foundation on which *TruCluster* Server is built. If you have not reviewed Chapters 3 and 4 of this handbook, we highly recommend that you go back and review them before proceeding any further. If you have already tackled Chapters 3 and 4, you are ready to get on with the show.

5.1 Philosophy on Installing *Tru64* UNIX

We can imagine your groans upon reading the title of this subsection. Having worked with many, many Systems Administrators over the years and having heard their lengthy criticisms of other books intended for Systems Administrators, we felt it was important to discuss the whys and hows of our methodology for installing and configuring *Tru64* UNIX.

In a *TruCluster* Server environment, *Tru64* UNIX is installed once, and only once, no matter if you have two or eight cluster nodes. As *Tru64* UNIX is the basis for *TruCluster* Server, it is crucial that the installation of *Tru64* UNIX be done properly the first time.

We have encountered two approaches when it comes to installing a UNIX server. The first is to install **all** software components of the operating system. HP advocates this approach in Chapter 3 of the *TruCluster* Server Cluster Installation guide. This is by far the simplest approach and if a user or System Administrator needs a software component, it will automatically be there.

The second approach is to install the minimum number of software components of the UNIX operating system required by the users of the system. The rational here is that maintenance should be easier (including the installation of future patches and additional software components), management should be easier because in theory, the system administration staff would have a better idea of what applications the users require, and system security should be easier to control.

In the example of the installation and the configuration of our *Tru64* UNIX, we will use the second approach. When it comes to deploying your own *Tru64* UNIX server to support the eventual creation of a *TruCluster* Server environment, we recommend that you first review your own requirements and then use the examples presented here as prototypes upon which to build.

5.2 Important Documents for *Tru64* UNIX and *TruCluster* Server

Before starting the installation of *Tru64* UNIX to support a deployment of *TruCluster* Server, we recommend that you always review the following documents for the version of *Tru64* UNIX and *TruCluster* Server you plan to install:

- *Tru64* UNIX Release Notes.
- *TruCluster* Server Release Notes.
- *Tru64* UNIX Installation guide.
- *TruCluster* Server Cluster Installation guide.
- *TruCluster* Server Cluster Administration guide.
- *Tru64* UNIX QuickSpecs (or Software Product Description prior to version 5.1A)
- *TruCluster* Server QuickSpecs (or Software Product Description prior to version 5.1A)

Please pay particular attention to the installation and hardware sections of these documents. The Release Notes are designed to provide important information about changes to the software, firmware, and hardware in addition to late breaking software bugs, "workarounds", and typos to the documentation that are not covered in the standard *Tru64* UNIX documentation set.

5.3 Preparing to Install *Tru64* UNIX

If you have not reviewed Chapter 4, stop right now! Please return to Chapter 4, as it is imperative to review Cluster Configuration Planning because it also covers what is necessary to prepare for the installation of *Tru64* UNIX. Remember, you are installing *Tru64* UNIX only once in a *TruCluster* Server environment so aim on doing it right the first time. Moreover, Chapter 4 has a handy Cluster Preparation Checklist[1] that includes *Tru64* UNIX options.

5.4 Installation of *Tru64* UNIX

In this section, we will cover an actual installation of *Tru64* UNIX. For our example of this installation, we will use *Tru64* UNIX version 5.1A on one node of what will be a two-node cluster.

As we stated earlier in this chapter, as we will be installing *Tru64* UNIX in preparation for building a *TruCluster* Server environment, we will need to install the operating system only once – no matter how many cluster nodes we may eventually have[2].

The following is a list of individual tasks that we will go over to perform the installation of *Tru64* UNIX:

	Section
• Boot from the Operating System CD.	5.4.1
• Start the installation.	5.4.2
• Setup information for a full installation.	5.4.3
• Select the software to install.	5.4.4
▪ Select mandatory software subsets.	5.4.4.1
▪ Select only some of the optional software subsets.	5.4.4.2
• Select the kernel options to build into the kernel.	5.4.5
• Choose a file system type to use for the operating system's file systems.	5.4.6
▪ Determine the File System Layout – what goes where.	5.4.6.1
• Confirm the selections before starting the installation.	5.4.7
• Create the file systems and install the software subsets.	5.4.8
• Configure the software subsets.	5.4.9
• Configure and build the UNIX kernel.	5.4.10

Well, now that we know what we are going to do, let's get on with it!

---

[1] See section 4.8 of Chapter 4.

[2] As of this writing, up to eight nodes are supported in a *TruCluster* Server environment.

5.4.1 Boot from the Installation CD

Before we actually boot from the *Tru64* UNIX Installation CD (that's the CD entitled Compaq *Tru64* UNIX Version 5.1A Operating System Volume 1), let's first initialize the system. At the console prompt, use the `init` command.

```
P00>>> init
```

Let's identify the CDROM from which we will be booting by using the "`show device`" command at the console prompt.

```
P00>>> show device

dga62.1001.0.7.1      $1$DGA62                       HSG80  V86F
dkc0.0.0.7.0          DKC0          COMPAQ BD009635CB  BDC4
dqa0.0.0.105.0        DQA0                    CD-224E  9.5B    ← CDROM
dva0.0.0.0.0          DVA0
eia0.0.0.9.1          EIA0              00-50-8B-AE-FE-DC
pga0.0.0.7.1          PGA0         WWN 2000-0000-c924-3514
pka0.7.0.6.0          PKA0                   SCSI Bus ID 7
pkb0.7.0.106.0        PKB0                   SCSI Bus ID 7
pkc0.7.0.7.0          PKC0                   SCSI Bus ID 7
```

Now that we have identified the CDROM, let's boot the *Tru64* UNIX Operating CD and start our installation.

CAUTION:

Before proceeding, make sure that you have performed the necessary preparatory steps in Chapter 4 such as setting environment variables and installing the latest firmware.

```
P00>>> boot dqa0
...
*** Performing CDROM Installation
```

5.4.2 Start the Installation

The first decision you must make after booting the *Tru64* UNIX operating system installation CD is as follows:

```
Remember, you can always get extra information by typing help.

1) U.S. English Installation
2) Installation with Worldwide Language Support
3) Exit Installation

Enter your choice: 1
```

By selecting "1", we choose to perform a "U.S. English Installation" of *Tru64* UNIX.

NOTE:

If you are using the non-GUI installation procedure and need a customized disk label on your installation disk, you would select option "3" and proceed to label the disk as described in section 4.2.1.

5.4.3 Setup Information for a Full Installation

The Installation program prompts for information needed to build our system as you'll see in the output that follows.

```
Enter a password to use as the root (superuser) password.
Be sure to remember this password, because it is needed to
log in as the user "root" following installation.  The
password must be at least six characters long, and at least
one of the first eight characters must be a number, special
character or uppercase letter (A-Z).

Enter root password:  xxxxxxxx
Retype root password: xxxxxxxx
```

One of the first things the Installation software does, aside from asking what type of installation you want, is to prompt for the root password. While we encourage the use of "good and strong passwords"[3] for any user on any computer system, it is especially imperative for the root user. And please, please do not put your password on a sticky note and attach it to your monitor!

```
Choose a hostname for this system.  The hostname identifies the
system on the network.  The hostname must start with a letter,
and may include letters, numbers, periods and hyphens.

Enter the hostname for this system: molari
```

Next, we are prompted for the hostname of the system that we are installing.

The next few prompts are for selecting the location and area (or time zone) the system is in.

```
Select the location that best describes your site.  This is to
determine what time zone your site is in.  If your location includes
multiple time zones (for example, Asia), the next question will
ask you which of those you want.

 1) Africa          7) Australia     13) Etc          19) MST
 2) America         8) CET           14) Europe       20) MST7MDT
 3) Antarctica      9) CST6CDT       15) Factory      21) PST8PDT
 4) Arctic         10) EET           16) HST          22) Pacific
 5) Asia           11) EST           17) Indian       23) SystemV
 6) Atlantic       12) EST5EDT       18) MET          24) WET
```

```
Enter your choice: 12
```

Next, you will be prompted to enter the date and time.

```
Enter the current date (as mm/dd/[cc]yy): 08/17/2002
```

```
Enter the current time in 24-hour format (as hh:mm): 23:22
```

```
The date and time has been set to: Sat Aug 17 23:22:00 EDT 2002
Is this correct (y/n) ? y
```

[3] A "good and strong password" is a password with mixed case letters and numbers. At this point in the installation, only the base security is supported so just the first eight characters of the password have meaning.

5.4.4 Select the Software to Install

In this section of the Installation, we are prompted for the software subsets that we will be installing.

```
                    *** Software Selection ***

** Reviewing available software for:
     Tru64 UNIX V5.1A Operating System ( Rev 1885 )
   Please wait ...

The following options are available:
o  Select "All Software" to install all mandatory and all optional
   software for the operating system.  You will be given the opportunity to
   view all software after selecting this option and to confirm your choice.

o  Select "Mandatory Only" to install the minimum required software.  No
   optional software will be installed.  You will be given the opportunity
   to view the mandatory software after selecting this option and to
   confirm your choice.

o  Select "Customize" to interactively select software from a numbered list
   of software subsets.  You will then be given the opportunity to confirm
   your choices.

1) All Software
2) Mandatory Only
3) Customize
```

```
Enter your choice: 3
```

We chose "3" or "`Customize`" because we want to select the software subset that will be installed.

5.4.4.1 Select Mandatory Software Subsets

The following output shows the mandatory software components that are installed as the result of a customized installation:

```
The following base operating system subsets are mandatory and will be
installed automatically unless you choose to exit without installing
any subsets:

  * AdvFS Kernel Modules
  * Base System
  * Base System - Hardware Support
  * Base System Management Applications and Utilities
  * Basic Networking Configuration Applications
  * Basic Networking Services
  * Basic X Environment
  * CDE Desktop Environment
```

```
 * CDE Mail Interface
 * CDE Minimum Runtime Environment
 * Compaq Management Agents Version 2.1b
 * Compiler Back End
 * DECwindows 100dpi Fonts
 * DECwindows 75dpi Fonts
 * Doc. Preparation Tools
 * Graphical Base System Management Utilities
 * Graphical Print Configuration Application
 * Graphical System Administration Utilities
 * Hardware Kernel Header and Common Files
 * Hardware Kernel Modules
 * Java 1.1.8-10 Environment
 * Kernel Header and Common Files
 * Local Printer Support
 * Logical Storage Manager Kernel Modules
 * NFS(tm) Configuration Application
 * NFS(tm) Utilities
 * Netscape Communicator V4.76
 * PCXAL Keyboard Support
 * Service Tools
 * Standard Kernel Modules
 * Tcl Commands
 * Tk Toolkit Commands
 * Tru64 UNIX Base System
 * X Fonts
 * X Servers Base
 * X Servers for PCbus

Space used after mandatory subsets (root/usr/var): 81.3 MB/307 MB/4.9 MB
```

5.4.4.2 Select Only Some of the Optional Software Subsets

In this section of the Installation, we are prompted for the software subsets that are considered optional to the operation of *Tru64* UNIX.

As we want our cluster to be able to grow and scale to meet our computer needs now and into the future, we recommend that all hardware-related subsets be installed so that if you add a system with a different hardware configuration, it will automatically be recognized without the need for installing additional software subsets. We also recommend that you use your best judgment to determine which software subsets to install by reading the description of the subsets in Appendix C of the *Tru64* UNIX Installation Guide. In other words, take the time and plan what you are going to install before you do the installation. You should really know and understand what software will be installed on your system and why it is there.

NOTE:

The output shown is from a V5.1A installation. The number of subsets will differ from version to version.

Optional *Tru64* UNIX software subsets are grouped into the following categories:

- General Applications
- Kernel Build Environment
- Kernel Software Development[4]
- Mail Applications
- Network-Server/Communications
- Obsolete Components
- Printing Environment
- Reference Pages
- Software Development
- Supplemental Documentation
- System Administration
- Text Processing
- Windowing Environment
- Windows Applications

The following output is trimmed to save a tree or two. Each category will contain one or more subsets to choose.

```
Optional software subsets are listed below.  There may be more optional
subsets than can be presented on a single screen.  If this is the case, you
can choose subsets one screen at a time.  At any prompt, you can enter "a"
to install all of the subsets, "m" to install only the mandatory subsets,
or "c" to cancel your selections and redisplay this menu.  All of the
choices you make will be collected for your confirmation before continuing
the installation.  Refer to the "Installation Guide" for descriptions of
individual subsets.


 - General Applications:
 1) Additional Terminfo databases
 2) Computer Aided System Tutor
 3) DOS tools
 4) Java 1.2.2-8 Environment
 5) Local Area Transport (LAT)
 6) UNIX(tm) SVID2 Compatibility
 7) UNIX(tm) to UNIX(tm) Copy Facility
 8) perl 5.6.0 Runtime
 9) xemacs Runtime

 - Kernel Build Environment:
 - Mail Applications:
 - Network-Server/Communications:
 - Obsolete Components:
 - Printing Environment:
 - Reference Pages:
 - Software Development:
 - Supplemental Documentation:
 - System Administration:
 - Text Processing:
 - Windowing Environment:
 - Windows Applications:
…
64) Virtual X Frame Buffer
```

---

[4] Subsets cannot be chosen in the initial installation.

```
Space used (root/usr/var): 93.6 MB/589 MB/10.1 MB
Add to your choices, or press RETURN to confirm choices.
Enter "c" to cancel your choices and redisplay this menu.
Choices (for example, 1 2 4-6): 1 3-4 6 8-9 12 14 18-39 41-49 51-55 57-59 62 63
```

5.4.4.3 Verification of Optional Software Subsets

The installation software asks that we verify that we want to install all the selected software subsets and that these software subsets will be loaded for the installation.

```
The following subsets will be loaded:
```

At this point, the selected (and mandatory) subsets will be displayed followed by the disk space required and a prompt to verify that the selection is correct. (The output has been trimmed.)

```
Space required in (root/usr/var): 93.6 MB/600 MB/10.3 MB

Are these the software subsets that should be loaded (y/n) ? y
```

Now that we have selected everything that we want to have installed, we should be all set. Right? Well, not quite yet.

5.4.5 Select the Kernel Options to Build into the UNIX Kernel

Now that we have told the installation software what software subsets we want to install, we next have to tell it how to build the UNIX kernel once it completes the installation and configuration of all the software subsets. There are three choices as shown in the following output.

```
                  *** Kernel Options Selection ***

The following options are available:
o  Select "All Options" to automatically build all mandatory
   and all optional kernel components into the tailored kernel.

o  Select "Mandatory Only" to automatically build only the mandatory
   kernel components into the tailored kernel.

o  Select "Customize" to manually select the optional kernel components.
   You will be prompted for your selection later in the installation
   process after all software subsets have been loaded and the system has
   been rebooted from the new system disk.  The mandatory kernel components
   will be automatically included in the custom-built kernel.
```

```
1) All Options
2) Mandatory Only
3) Customize
```

```
Enter your choice: 3
```

We will choose option "3" to select the kernel options that we know we will use. Selecting only the kernel options that we need will produce a smaller UNIX kernel that can potentially perform better and more efficiently than if the kernel is built with all kernel options.

NOTE:

By choosing option "1" or "2," the installation program will build the kernel without any further input from you. In other words, once the installation process begins, it will continue unattended. By choosing option "3," the installation process will stop prior to building the kernel to request the options to add to the kernel.

5.4.6 Choose a File System Type to Use for the Operating System's File Systems

These next few prompts have to do with whether or not we will be using the Logical Storage Manager (LSM), what type of file system we will be using, and the file system layout for the local system disk. The prompt for LSM is for encapsulating the operating system disk. As this is not propagated to the cluster disks during the creation of the cluster, we recommend you answer "no" when prompted.

```
                        *** File System Selection ***
The Logical Storage Manager (LSM) is a disk storage management tool that can
help protect against data loss through the use of disk mirroring, can
improve disk I/O performance through the use of disk striping, and can
dynamically extend available disk storage through the use of disk
concatenation.  Mirroring and striping through LSM require a separate
license PAK.

By choosing LSM, all file systems and swap areas created by the installation
process will be under LSM control.

Enter "help" for more information about LSM.
```

```
Would you like to use LSM (y/n) ? n
```

5.4.6.1 Determine the File System Layout

In Chapter 4, we partitioned the local disk in preparation for the *Tru64* UNIX installation. You can do this by either:

- Escaping to the shell and using the `disklabel(8)` command, or
- Using the `diskconfig(8)` command (part of the GUI installation).

The disk partition layout used for the system disk was based on the space needed for our chosen subsets, expected configuration, and future growth. Note the specific layout later in this section.

In this section of the installation, we will be prompted to choose both the device onto which we will install the operating system and the partition layout for each of file systems. By choosing the custom file system layout instead of the default file system layout, we can leverage the disk partitions that were created earlier.

For the standalone operating system disk, you must use the Advanced File System (AdvFS) for all file systems – this is a requirement for creating a cluster.

```
Choose your file system layout:
o  The default file system layout installs the operating system onto a
   single disk, and provides the most typical file system configuration:

        * root file system on the "a" partition
        * swapping area on the "b" partition
        * /usr file system on the "g" partition
        * /var in the /usr file system

   This option also provides a recommended disk partition table that is
   calculated based on existing software selections and future growth
   considerations.  Additionally, you may select either the UFS or
   AdvFS file system type.

o  The custom file system layout lets you choose the partition and
   file system type individually for each of the file systems created by
   the installation process.  You should choose this option if:

        * You want to place the file systems across multiple disks.
        * You want to place the file systems on a single disk, but there is
            existing data on that disk that must be protected.
        * You do not want the same file system type for each file system.
        * You want to create more than one swap area.

1) Default file system layout
2) Custom file system layout
```

```
Enter your choice: 2
```

In this section, we select the hard drive onto which we will install root (/). By default, this is installed on the "a" partition of the drive. We also elect to use AdvFS as the file system that will be used for root (/).

```
Select a disk for the root file system.  The root file system will be
placed on the "a" partition of the disk you choose.

To visually locate a disk, enter "ping <disk>", where <disk> is the device
name (for example, dsk0) of the disk you want to locate.  If that disk has
a visible indicator light, it will blink until you are ready to continue.
      Device       Size  Controller  Disk
      Name        in GB  Type        Model            Location
1)    dsk0         18.2  SCSI        BD018635C4       bus-5-targ-0-lun-0
...
```

```
Enter your choice: 1
```

```
Select the file system type for the root file system.
1) UFS -- UNIX File System
2) AdvFS -- Advanced File System
```

```
Enter your choice: 2
```

For the /usr file system, we select the "g" partition of the same device on which root (/) is installed. We use AdvFS for the file system type for /usr.

```
Select the disk where the /usr file system will reside, or
enter "ping <disk>" where <disk> is the device name (for example, dsk0)
to physically identify a particular disk.

      Device       Size  Controller  Disk
      Name        in GB  Type        Model            Location
1)    dsk0         18.2  SCSI        BD018635C4      bus-5-targ-0-lun-0
...
```

```
Enter your choice: 1
```

```
Select the dsk0 partition where the /usr file system will reside.
This partition must be at least 482MB in order to fit the software that
you have selected.  However, a size of 700 MB or greater is recommended to
allow for additional layered software and future upgrade considerations.

                            Start       End
   Partition     Size       Block       Block      Overlaps
1)      b        4.5GB    1048576    10485760       c
2)      e        3.9GB   10485760    18787864       c
3)      f        2.0GB   18787864    22982168       c
4)      g        4.0GB   22982168    31370776       c
5)      h        2.0GB   31370776    35565080       c
```

```
Enter your choice: 4
```

```
Select the file system type for the /usr file system.
1) UFS -- UNIX File System
2) AdvFS -- Advanced File System
```

```
Enter your choice: 2
```

The swap partition will also go on the same device as root (/). This time we will use the "b" partition for swap as this is approximately three times the size of memory.

```
Select the disk where the first swapping area (swap1) will reside, or
enter "ping <disk>" where <disk> is the device name (for example, dsk0)
to physically identify a particular disk.

      Device        Size   Controller  Disk
      Name         in GB   Type        Model            Location
1)    dsk0          18.2   SCSI        BD018635C4      bus-5-targ-0-lun-0
...
```

```
Enter your choice: 1
```

```
Select the dsk0 partition where the first swapping area (swap1) will reside.

                            Start       End
   Partition     Size       Block       Block      Overlaps
1)      b        4.5GB    1048576    10485760       c
2)      e        3.9GB   10485760    18787864       c
3)      f        2.0GB   18787864    22982168       c
4)      h        2.0GB   31370776    35565080       c
```

```
Enter your choice: 1
```

As we have chosen not to have a secondary swap partition, we answer "no" when prompted.

```
You may choose to have a second swapping area (swap2).
Do you want a second swapping area (y/n) ? n
```

In this section, we are prompted if we want to have a separate `/var` from `/usr`. In our case, we normally do keep `/usr` and `/var` as separate file systems. In keeping with tradition, we keep `/var` on the "h" partition. The `/var` file system is also on an AdvFS file system.

```
You can make /var a separate file system, or you can have it
share space on the /usr file system.
```

```
Should /var be a separate file system (y/n) ? y
```

```
Select the disk where the /var file system will reside, or
enter "ping <disk>" where <disk> is the device name (for example, dsk0)
to physically identify a particular disk.

      Device       Size  Controller  Disk
      Name        in GB  Type        Model            Location
1)    dsk0         18.2  SCSI        BD018635C4     bus-5-targ-0-lun-0
...
```

```
Enter your choice: 1
```

```
Select the dsk0 partition where the /var file system will reside.
                        Start       End
   Partition    Size    Block      Block    Overlaps
1)     e        3.9GB  10485760  18787864    c
2)     f        2.0GB  18787864  22982168    c
3)     h        2.0GB  31370776  35565080    c
```

```
Enter your choice: 3
```

```
Select the file system type for the /var file system.
1) UFS -- UNIX File System
2) AdvFS -- Advanced File System
```

```
Enter your choice: 2
```

Finally, we verify our disk partition selections for our *Tru64* UNIX system disk's file systems.

```
You have requested this file system layout:
  * root file system on dsk0a, type AdvFS
  * /usr file system on dsk0h, type AdvFS
  * /var file system on dsk0h, type AdvFS
  * first swapping area (swap1) will be on dsk0b
  * no second swapping area (swap2)
```

```
Is this the correct file system layout (y/n) ? y
```

Table 5-1 contains the partition layout for the system disk that we just configured.

It should be noted that while we were using an 18.2 GB hard disk drive for the system disk, we were not using the guidelines from HP for the layout of the system disk. HP recommends that for a system disk over 3 GB, the system's root (/) should be 384 MB and the swap should be 384 MB (if not larger)[5]. It has been our experience that for the original system disk of a system that will be used as the basis for building a cluster, the system's root (/) should be at least 512 MB and the swap should be two to three times the size of memory. As this system has 1.5 GB of memory, swap is

Tru64 UNIX Operating System Disk Layout			
Mount Point	File System	Partition Size	Partition
`root (/)`	`root_domain#root`	512 MB	`dsk0a`
`/usr`	`usr_domain#usr`	4.0 GB	`dsk0g`
`/var`	`var_domain#var`	2.0 GB	`dsk0h`
`swap`	`swap`	4.5 GB	`dsk0b`

Table 5-1: Standalone O/S Disk Partition Layout

[5] Table 6-7: Recommended Partition Table by Disk Capacity, Tru64 UNIX Installation Guide.

created to be 4.5 GB in size. For this system disk, though, we won't get too concerned about the swap size. It's likely to be used only long enough to build the cluster, or if we need a standalone operating system disk to troubleshoot a cluster problem.

So should you follow our example or use what HP recommends? What HP has published in their documentation are guidelines based on input from the designers, developers, and customers of *Tru64* UNIX and *TruCluster* Server. What we present is based mostly on experience. We believe that you should start with HP's recommendations, deviating when necessary based on what you know about your system's expected workload.

5.4.7 Confirm the Selections Before Starting the Installation

This next section will allow you to verify or modify any earlier selections made for the installation.

```
You have now answered all questions needed to install
the operating system.  Press CTRL/C to cancel the
installation; or type "history" to modify your earlier
answers; or press RETURN to proceed with installation:
```

In our case, we were satisfied with all our selections so we continue with the installation.

5.4.8 Create the File Systems and Install the Software Subsets

There really isn't much for us to do except monitor the creation of all the file systems and the loading of the software subsets that we had selected. So grab lunch or enjoy a long coffee break...

```
Continuing installation...

Restoring the existing disk label on device dsk0
Creating the root file system on device dsk0a
Creating the usr file system on device dsk0h
Creating the var file system on device dsk0g
Creating the swap1 file system on device dsk0b

The installation procedure will now load a total of 85 software subsets
on your disk partitions.  This total includes the following products:

        * 85 Base Operating System subsets


This process will take from 45 to 120 minutes to complete depending on
your distribution media and processor type.

LOADING THE BASE OPERATING SYSTEM SOFTWARE SUBSETS
```

```
Checking file system space required to install specified subsets:

File system space checked OK.

85 subsets will be installed.

Loading subset 1 of 85
Base System
   Copying from /ALPHA/BASE (disk)
        Working....Tue Jan 22 20:16:15 PST 2002
   Verifying
...
85 of 85 subsets installed successfully.
```

To spare you the repetition of seeing 84 additional software subset loads, we have provided one software subset load as representative of the other 84.

5.4.9 Configure the Software Subsets

Now that all the operating system software subsets are loaded, we start the configuration phase of these same software subsets. This phase is typically started by a reboot of the system in which instead of booting off the CDROM, it boots off the newly created system disk.

After the reboot is complete, the system starts configuring the previously loaded software subsets.

```
Checking for Installation Tasks...
...
Executing Installation Tasks...

*** SYSTEM CONFIGURATION ***

Configuring "Base System" (OSFBASE520)
...
Configuring "AdvFS Daemon" (OSFADVFSDAEMON520)

The Advanced File System Daemon includes support for the License
Management Facility (LMF).  A Product Authorization Key (PAK) is
required to use the file-system utilities.  See the AdvFS Installation
Guide for information on registering and activating the PAK.
...
The system name assigned to your machine is 'molari'.
```

Again, to save you from the repetition of seeing all the additional software subset configurations, we have provided two software subset configurations. The first is representative of the others. The second software subset configuration, for the "AdvFS" Daemon, is included because it indicates that we must install a License Management Facility (LMF) Product Authorization Key (PAK) in order to use the AdvFS file system utilities.

5.4.10 Configure and Build the UNIX Kernel

Earlier, when we were prompted for kernel configuration options, we selected to do a customized kernel. In this section of the Installation, we are given the opportunity to identify exactly which options are needed for our system's kernel.

If we had selected "All Options" or "Mandatory Only" for the Kernel configuration options, we would not be receiving this dialogue at all. We believe that by selecting only those options that we use, we should have a smaller and better performing kernel.

```
*** KERNEL CONFIGURATION AND BUILD PROCEDURE ***
*** KERNEL OPTION SELECTION ***
    Selection   Kernel Option
--------------------------------------------------------------
        1       System V Devices
        2       NTP V3 Kernel Phase Lock Loop (NTP_TIME)
        3       Kernel Breakpoint Debugger (KDEBUG)
        4       Packetfilter driver (PACKETFILTER)
        5       IP-in-IP Tunneling (IPTUNNEL)
        6       IP Version 6 (IPV6)
        7       Point-to-Point Protocol (PPP)
        8       STREAMS pckt module (PCKT)
        9       Data Link Bridge (DLPI V2.0 Service Class 1)
        10      X/Open Transport Interface (XTISO, TIMOD, TIRDWR)
        11      Digital Versatile Disk File System (DVDFS)
        12      ISO 9660 Compact Disc File System (CDFS)
        13      Audit Subsystem
        14      All of the above
        15      None of the above
        16      Help
        17      Display all options again
--------------------------------------------------------------
Enter your choices, choose an overriding action or
press <Return> to confirm previous selections.
```

```
Choices (for example, 1 2 4-6): 2 4 8 11 13
```

```
You selected the following kernel options:
        NTP V3 Kernel Phase Lock Loop (NTP_TIME)
        Packetfilter driver (PACKETFILTER)
        STREAMS pckt module (PCKT)
        Digital Versatile Disk File System (DVDFS)
        Audit Subsystem
```

```
Is that correct? (y/n) [y]: y
```

```
Do you want to edit the configuration file? (y/n) [n]: n
```

The *Tru64* UNIX kernel is then built based on the kernel configuration options selected.

As of this writing, IP Version 6 is not supported on *TruCluster* Server so please do not select IP Version 6 when you do your own *Tru64* UNIX kernel configuration. At a minimum, please review the *TruCluster* Server Release notes on what is and is not supported when it comes to kernel configuration options.

```
       The system will now automatically build a kernel
       with the selected options and then reboot.  This can take
       up to 15 minutes, depending on the processor type.

       When  the login prompt appears after the system
       has rebooted, use 'root' as the  login name and
       the SUPERUSER  password that was entered during
       this procedure, to log into the system.

*** PERFORMING KERNEL BUILD ***
        Working....Tue Jan 22 20:35:41 PST 2002

The new version ID has been successfully set on this system.
The entire set of new functionality has been enabled.

This message is contained in the file /var/adm/smlogs/it.log for
future reference.
```

At this point, the system will reboot. As soon as the system restarts, it will run on the newly built *Tru64* UNIX kernel.

5.5 Configuration of *Tru64* UNIX

In the previous section, we discussed what it takes to do an actual installation of *Tru64* UNIX. In this section, we will continue with our example and do a quick configuration of *Tru64* UNIX. Remember that our ultimate goal in presenting this example is to perform a successful deployment of *TruCluster* Server.

As you can see, the installation of *Tru64* UNIX in the previous section went quite smoothly. Now that the Installation is complete, the actual configuration of *Tru64* UNIX takes place.

The following is a list of tasks to be performed to get a standalone *Tru64* UNIX configured and on the network:

	Section
• Provide `OSF-BASE` Licensing Information.	5.5.1.2
• Configure the Network Interface Card (NIC).	5.5.1.3
• Setup Network Routing.	5.5.1.4
• Specify the Domain Name Service (DNS)/Bind Server.	5.5.1.5
• Specify the Network Time Protocol (NTP) Server.	5.5.1.6
• Specify the Network Information Service (NIS) Server.	5.5.1.7
• Specify NFS Services.	5.5.1.8
• Specify E-mail Server.	5.5.1.9
• Set a Default Printer and Print Server.	5.5.1.10

Once these task tasks have been completed, we are ready for the next step – the installation and configuration of *TruCluster* Server.

```
The system is ready.
```

```
Compaq Tru64 UNIX V5.1A (Rev. 1885) (molari) console

login: root
Password: xxxxxxxx
```

```
Can't find an OSF-BASE, UNIX-WORKSTATION, or UNIX-SERVER license PAK
```

```
Compaq Tru64 UNIX V5.1A (Rev. 1885); Sun Aug 18 00:56:22 EDT 2002

The installation software has successfully installed your system.

There are logfiles that contain a record of your installation.  These are:

        /var/adm/smlogs/install.cdf     - configuration description file
        /var/adm/smlogs/install.log     - general log file
        /var/adm/smlogs/install.FS.log  - file system creation logs
        /var/adm/smlogs/setld.log       - log for the setld(8) utility
        /var/adm/smlogs/fverify.log     - verification log file
```

```
        Tru64 UNIX Version V5.1A (Rev. 1885) System Setup

To prepare this system for general use, the Product Authorization Keys (PAKs)
that were purchased with it must be installed to allow users to log in and
access licensed software packages. In addition, several Tru64 UNIX subsystems,
such as networking, mail, printing, and others, must be configured.

This setup utility, in addition to allowing for the configuration of
Tru64 UNIX subsystems, provides information on other tasks that
you may want to do during or after the setup utility runs. You can access
this information from the following menu. If you want to view this information,
do so before choosing option 5. This information is also available in the
Installation Guide, a printed document shipped with your system.

1) Read this first!
2) Information about loading license PAKs
3) Information about accessing online documentation
4) Information about adding users
5) Begin system configuration
6) Exit
```

```
Please enter a number (1 to 6): 5
```

As you see from the warning message above, the system could not find a base (Operating System) License PAK. Please have the following License Product Authorization Keys (PAKs) available in preparation for the configuration of *Tru64* UNIX:

- `OSF-USR` – Multi-user License
- `OSF-BASE` and/or `OSF-SVR` – Base Operating System License
- `TCS-UA` – *TruCluster* Server License

And optionally:

- `ADVFS-UTILITIES` – Advanced File System Advanced Utilities License
- `LSM-OA` – Logical Storage Manager License

These are the License PAKs that you will need at a minimum to configure your system. If you are installing other software that requires a License PAK, please have those License PAK(s) available as well.

5.5.1 Selecting Quick Setup

In this section, we will perform a quick setup to configure *Tru64* UNIX in preparation for the installation of *TruCluster* Server. Our configuration is relatively simple because our environment is rather uncomplicated. Your environment may be more complex. We encourage you to take the time and configure *Tru64* UNIX to meet your needs first before you continue with the installation and configuration of *TruCluster* Server. Remember that you need a solid and strong foundation before you can build on it.

In our example (see Figure 5-1), we select a "1" for "Quick Setup". The "Quick Setup" program starts up various SysMan application menus and assists the system administrator in configuring basic services. The basic services allow the server to be on the network, do printing, and potentially send and receive e-mail.

NOTE:

SysMan is a common interface used to configure and manage *Tru64* UNIX systems and is available in GUI, menu, and command line formats.

If your system is graphics capable, then instead of seeing the `setup(8)` program, the `checklist` clipboard will appear as shown in Figure 5-2.

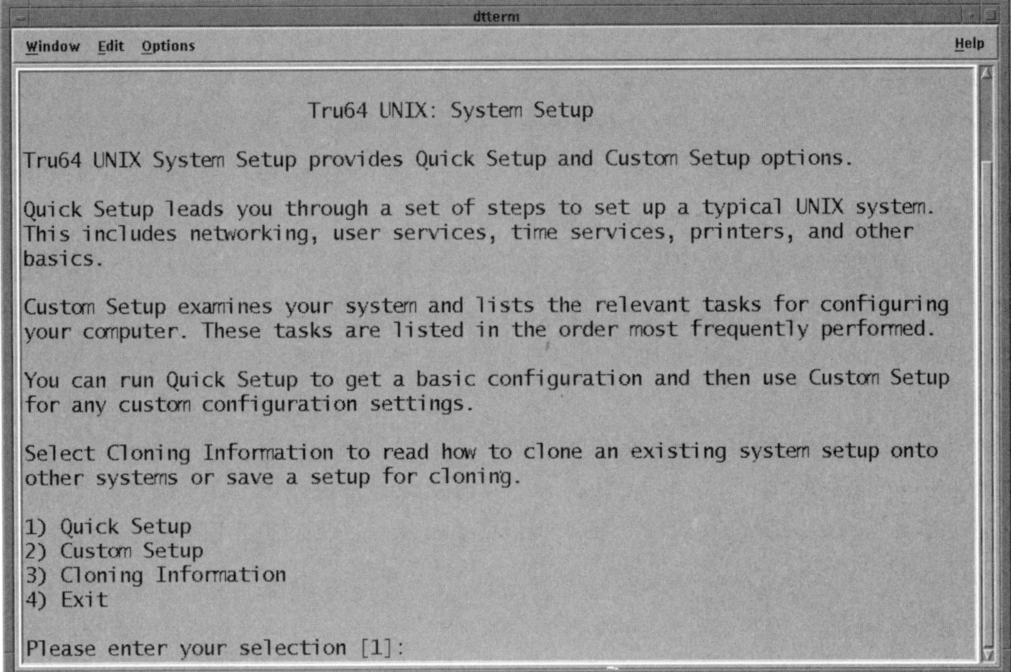

Figure 5-1: The Tru64 UNIX `setup` Program

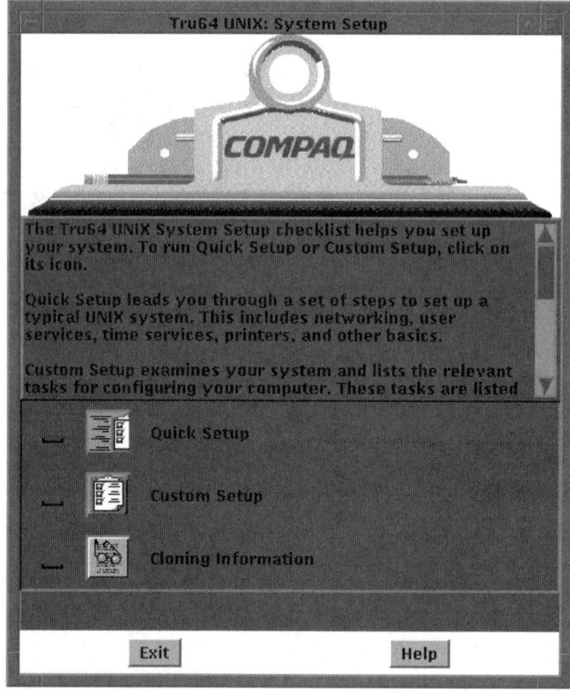

Figure 5-2: The `checklist` Clipboard

5.5.1.1 Quick Setup Main

Once you select the "Quick Setup" option, instructions will be displayed on how to navigate through to tool (see Figure 5-3).

As you can see in Figure 5-4, this screen outlines everything that the "Quick Setup" program does.

5.5.1.2 Provide `OSF-BASE` Information

Remember the LMF License PAKs that we discussed in section 5.5? Here is where you enter the license information for the `OSF-BASE` License PAK. Please have these License PAKs available before the system is configured (see Figure 5-5).

Enter the License PAK information for the `OSF-BASE` License. For more information on licenses, see the *Tru64* UNIX Software License Management Guide.

5.5.1.3 Configure the Network Interface Card (NIC)

The "`Host name*`" field will most likely be filled in already. We will need to enter the IP address and the network mask for our network (see Figure 5-6).

5.5.1.4 Setup Network Routing

On this SysMan screen, we are given the ability to setup network routing. In order to do this, we need to know how routing is performed on our network.

In Figure 5-7, we use gated for network routing. While it is not essential to use gated during the configuration of a standalone, non-clustered *Tru64* UNIX system, gated is a requirement for Cluster Alias to operate properly within *TruCluster* Server.

For your *Tru64* UNIX server, you will need to determine how routing is done on your network before you can make an appropriate selection. We strongly recommend that you check with your networking group to determine this information or check the configuration of another server on your network and use that information as a prototype for your own server. For more information on networking administration, refer to Chapter 20.

5.5.1.5 Specify the Domain Name Service (DNS/BIND) Server

This next "Quick Setup" screen (Figure 5-8) allows us to specify the DNS Server(s) information.

Here we enter the DNS network domain and the DNS server name(s) and IP address(es).

5.5.1.6 Specify the Network Time Protocol (NTP) Server

This "Quick Setup" screen (Figure 5-9) allows us to enter our NTP Server information.

The NTP server information is the hostname or the hostname's alias of the NTP server.

We recommend that you configure NTP prior to configuring the *TruCluster* Server software. *TruCluster* Server requires that the member system clocks be kept synchronized. Please refer to Chapter 20 for details on configuring NTP, including tips on using the local reference clock address (127.127.0.1) if needed.

If you choose not to use NTP Services, then we recommend that you use a time protocol that adheres to the RFC 1035 and that you not use `timed(8)`.

5.5.1.7 Specify the Network Information Service (NIS) Server

Figure 5-10 is the next "Quick Setup" screen. It allows you to configure NIS Services. If you use NIS in your environment, we recommend that the system be fully configured for NIS prior to the installation and configuration of *TruCluster* Server. Why is this our recommendation? Because if you configure NIS on the standalone server first, then when you create the cluster, it will be propagated to each cluster member. Please note that the NIS domain is not the same as a DNS Network Domain.

For more information on setting up NIS, see the *Tru64* UNIX Network Administration Guide for versions 5.0A and 5.1, or the *Tru64* UNIX Network Administration: Services Guide for version 5.1A and newer.

5.5.1.8 Specify NFS Services

Figure 5-11 allows us to specify the NFS Services that we will be using.

Here we are enabling remote directory mounting and directory exporting. For your system, please do what is in the best interests of your users.

5.5.1.9 Specify E-mail Server

As most UNIX servers either send e-mail, receive e-mail, or both, we need to specify an E-mail Server to use in our configuration. This configuration is primarily for forwarding SMTP mail. For more on configuring e-mail in a cluster, please review Chapter 21.

We enter the system name for our E-mail Server as shown in Figure 5-12.

5.5.1.10 Specify a Default Printer and Print Server

This "Quick Setup" screen (Figure 5-13) allows us to specify a default printer and print server.

5.5.1.11 Quick Setup Summary and Completion

That about does it for performing a simple *Tru64* UNIX configuration. These next two "Quick Setup" screens (see Figure 5-14) allow us to verify and potentially correct any mistakes we may have made during the selections for configuration of the system.

As we are satisfied with all entries, we select "Finish" and the Quick Setup program configures the system.

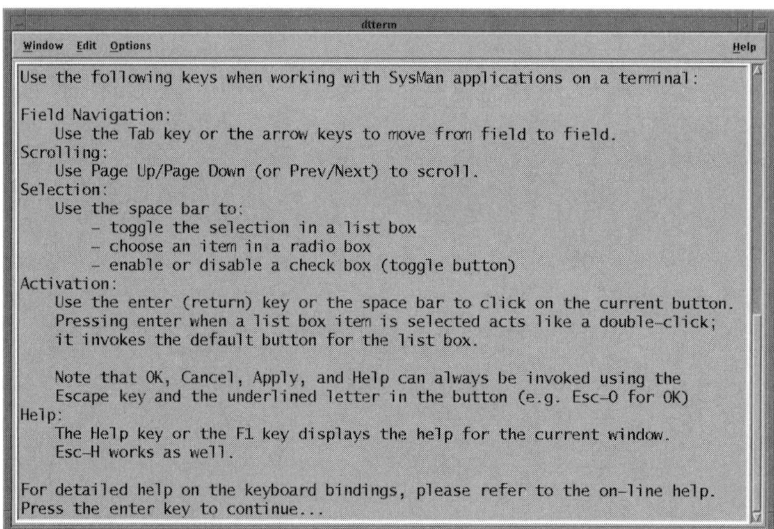

Figure 5-3: SysMan Navigational Information

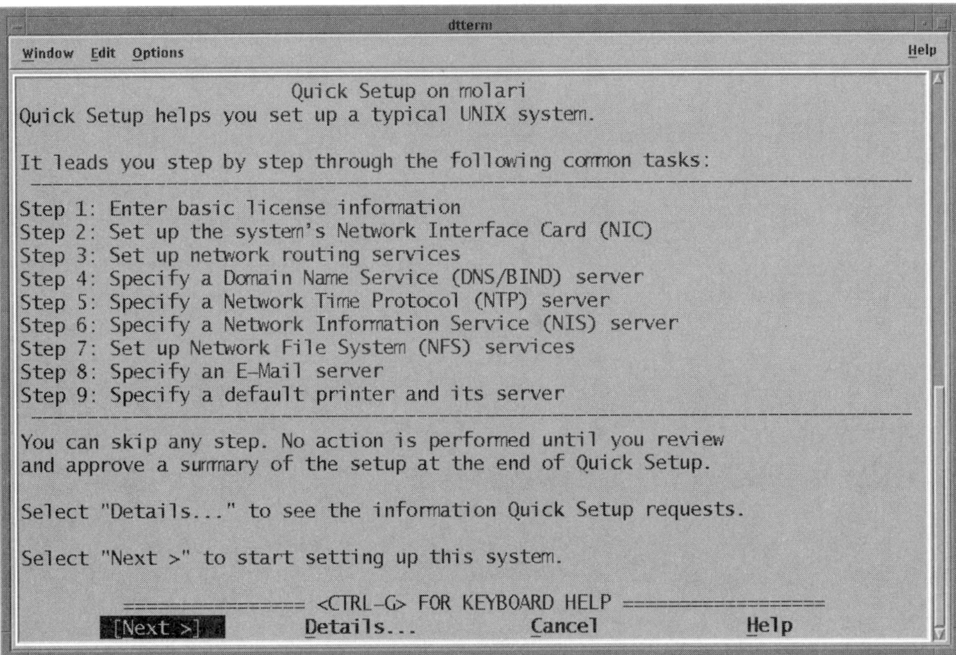

Figure 5-4: Quick Setup – Main Screen

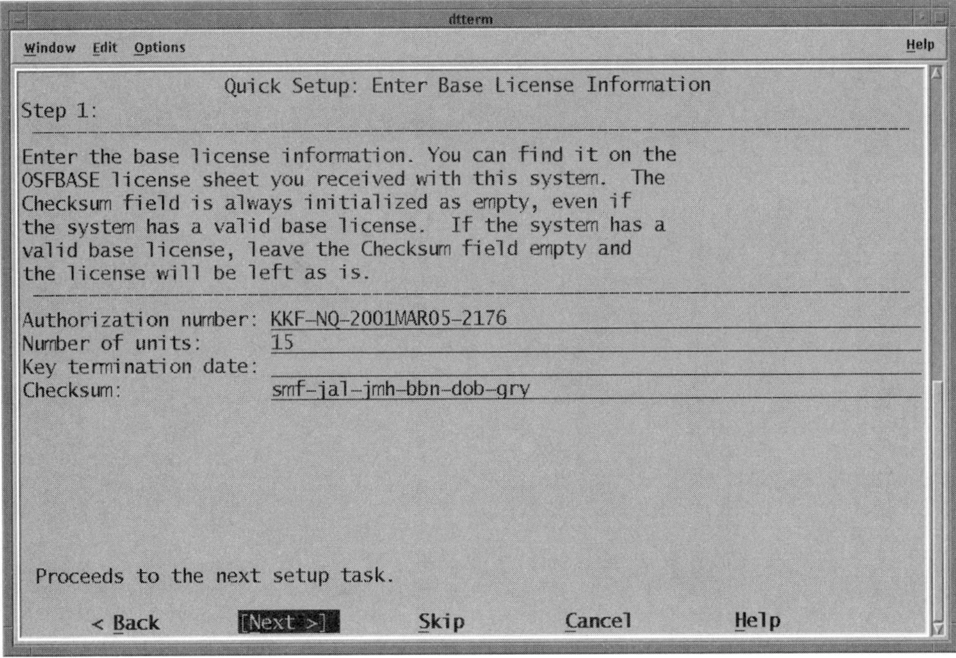

Figure 5-5: Quick Setup – `OSF-BASE` License PAK

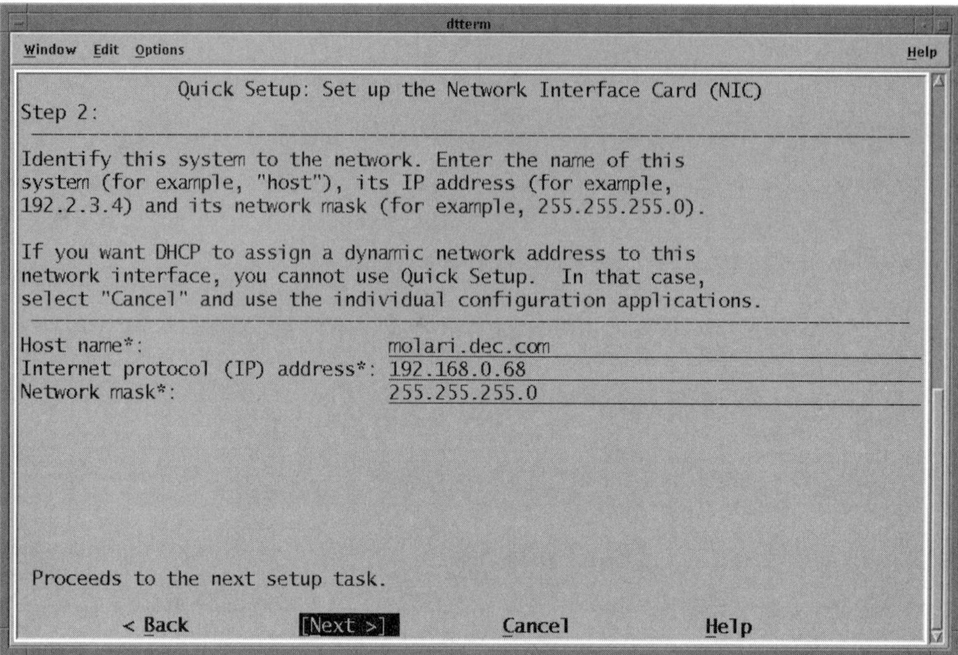

Figure 5-6: Quick Setup – NIC Setup

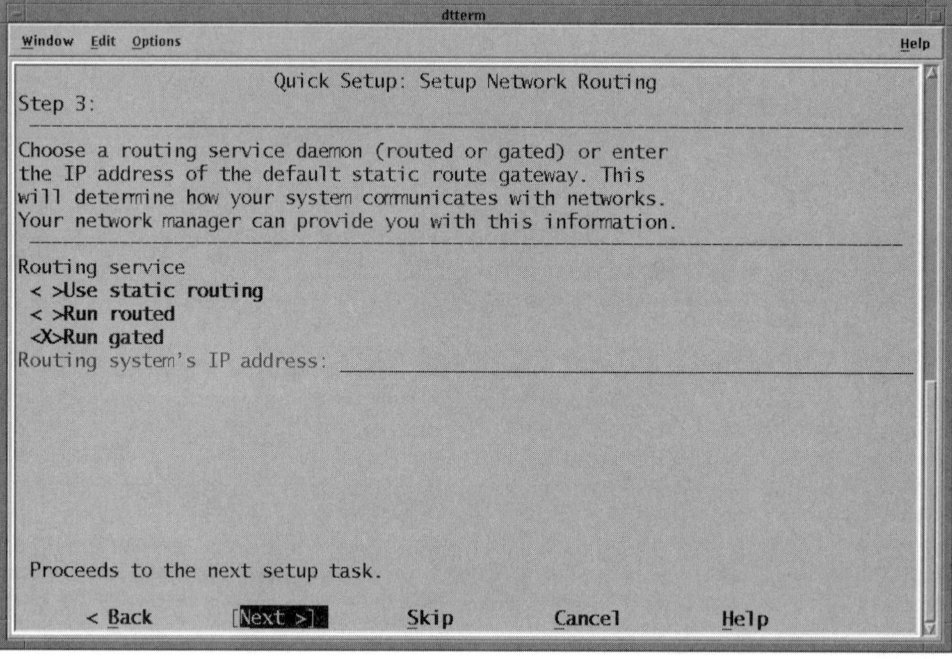

Figure 5-7: Quick Setup – Network Routing

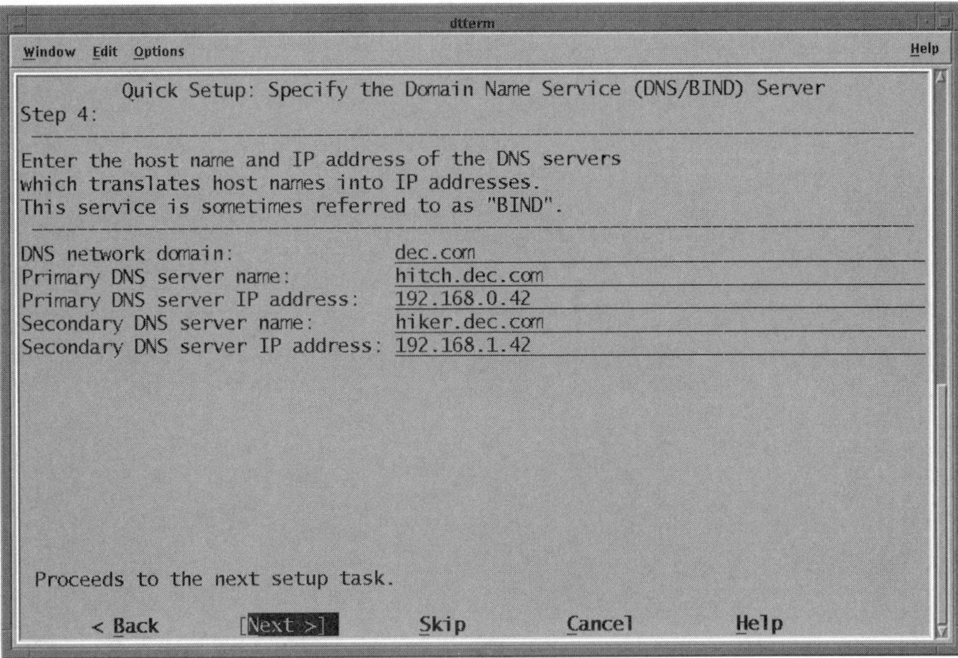

Figure 5-8: Quick Setup – DNS/BIND

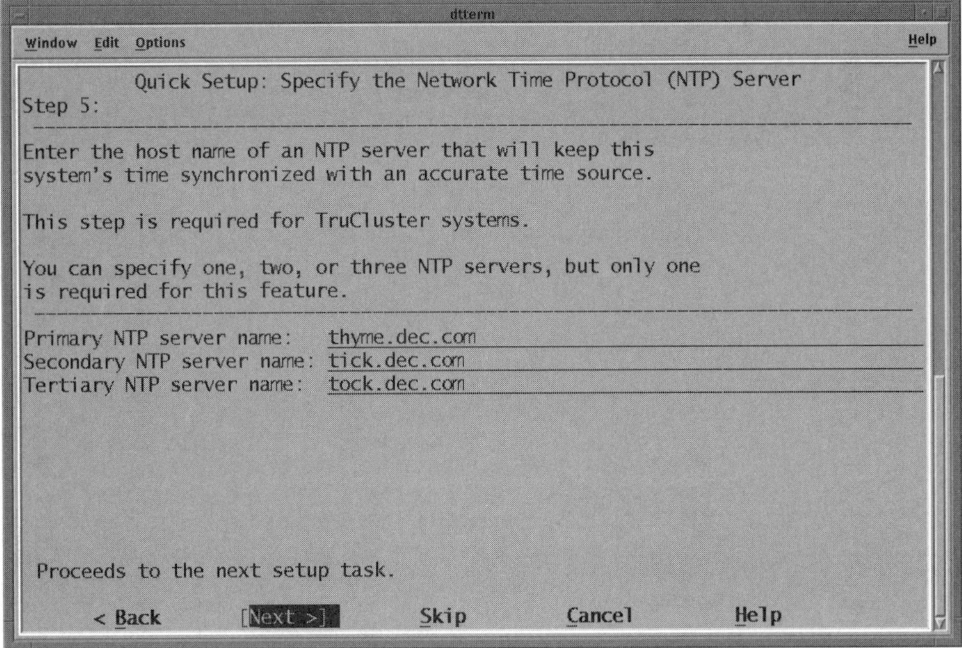

Figure 5-9: Quick Setup – NTP Server

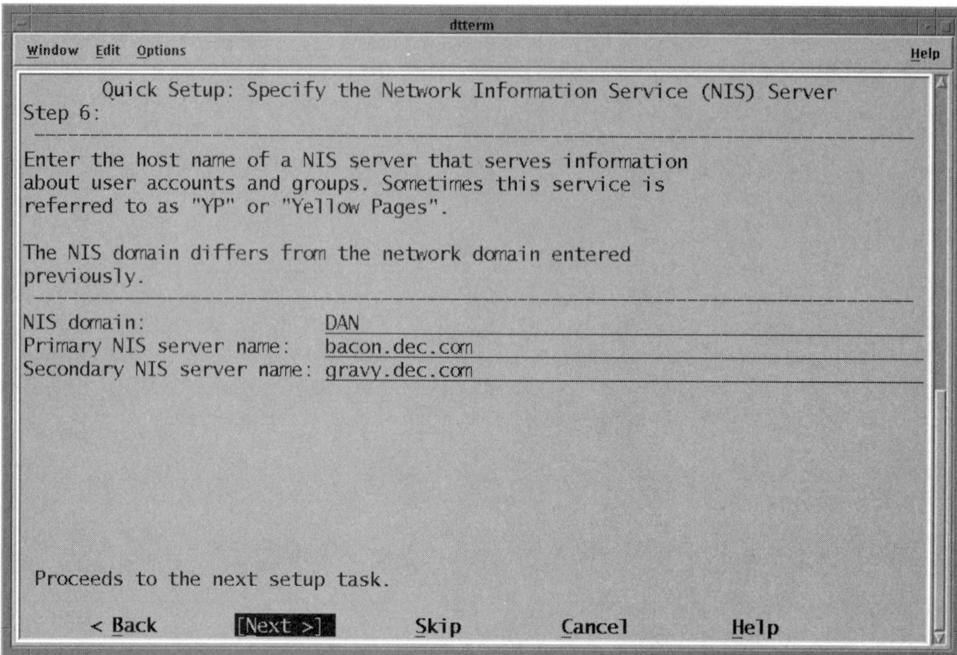

Figure 5-10: Quick Setup – NIS

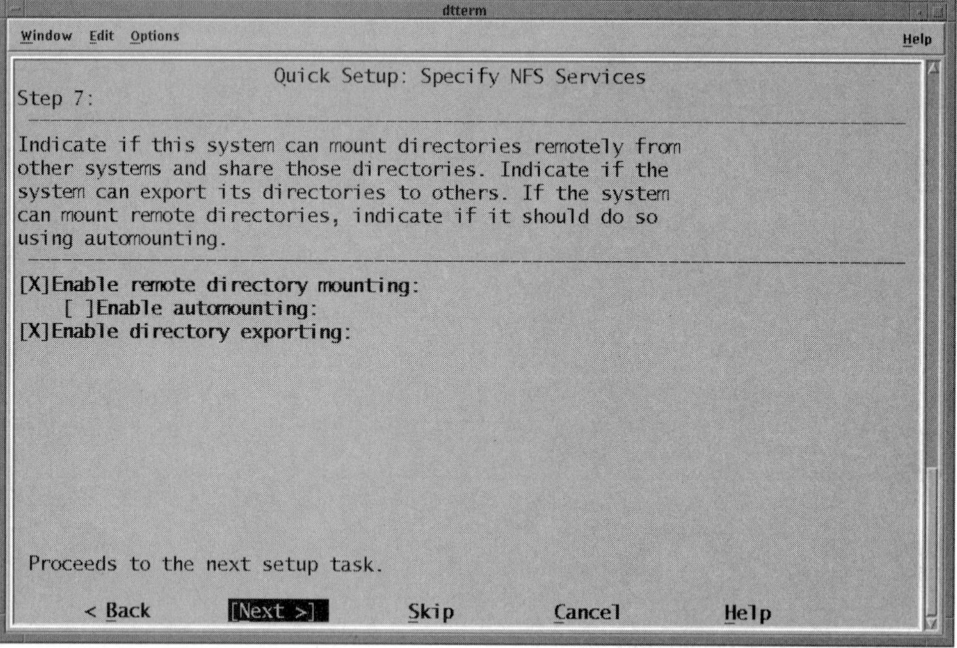

Figure 5-11: Quick Setup – NFS

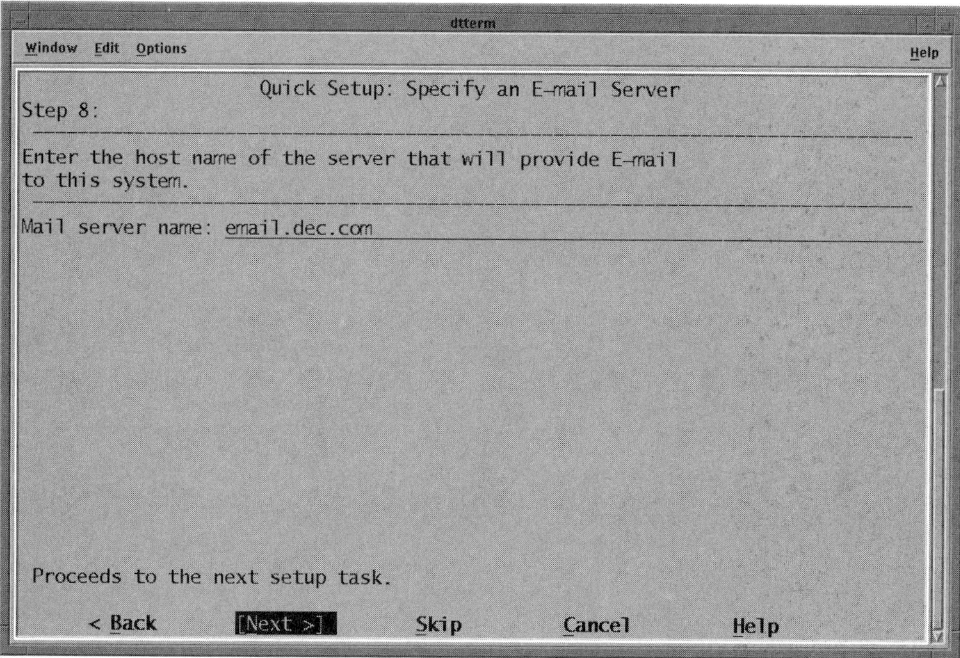

Figure 5-12: Quick Setup – E-mail Server

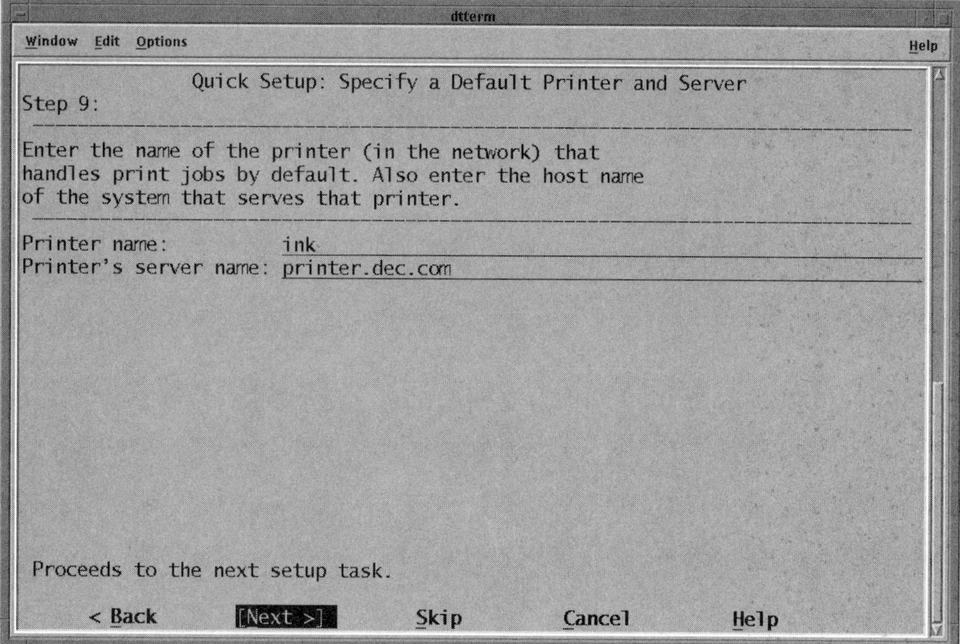

Figure 5-13: Quick Setup -- Default Printer & Print Server

```
dtterm
Window  Edit  Options                                          Help
                    Quick Setup: Summary: 1st Page
This is the first page of the setup information you entered.
Please review it, make any changes needed here (or in
previous dialog boxes by using the "< Back" button), then
select "Next >" to see the last page of setup information.
------------------------------------------------------------------
Base authorization number:          ALS-NQ-2001MAR05-2176
Number of units:                    15
Key termination date:
Checksum:                           smf-jal-jmh-bbn-dob-gry
Host name*:                         molari.dec.com
IP address*:                        192.168.0.68
Network mask*:                      255.255.255.0
Routing service:                    Run gated=
Routing system's IP address:
DNS network domain:                 dec.com
Primary DNS server name:            hitch.dec.com
Primary DNS server IP address:      192.168.0.42
Secondary DNS server name:          hiker.dec.com
Secondary DNS server IP address:    192.168.1.42

 Proceeds to the last page of setup information.

        < Back          [Next >]          Cancel          Help
```

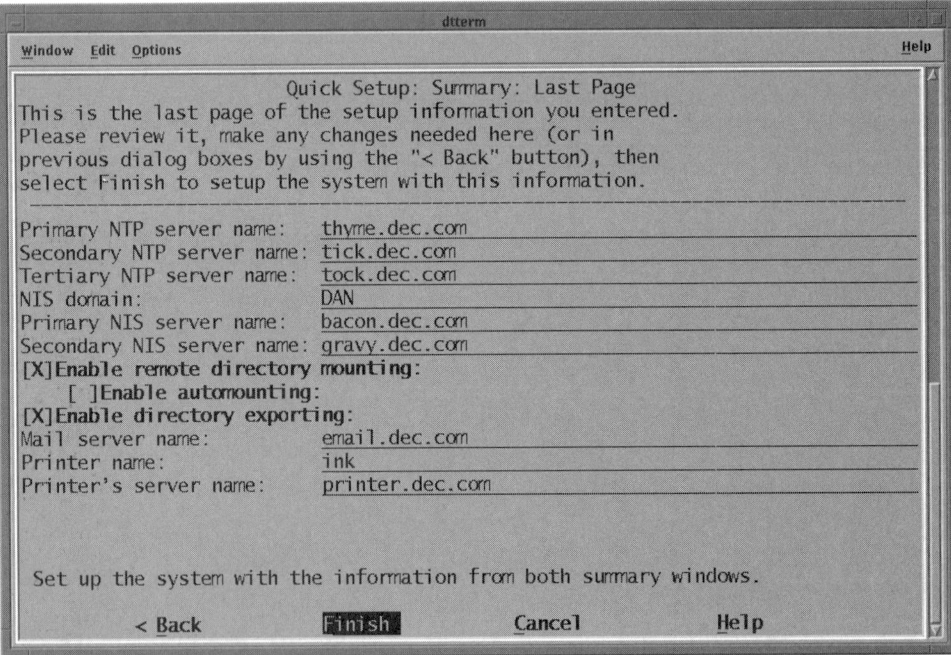

Figure 5-14: Quick Setup – Summary Pages (1 & 2)

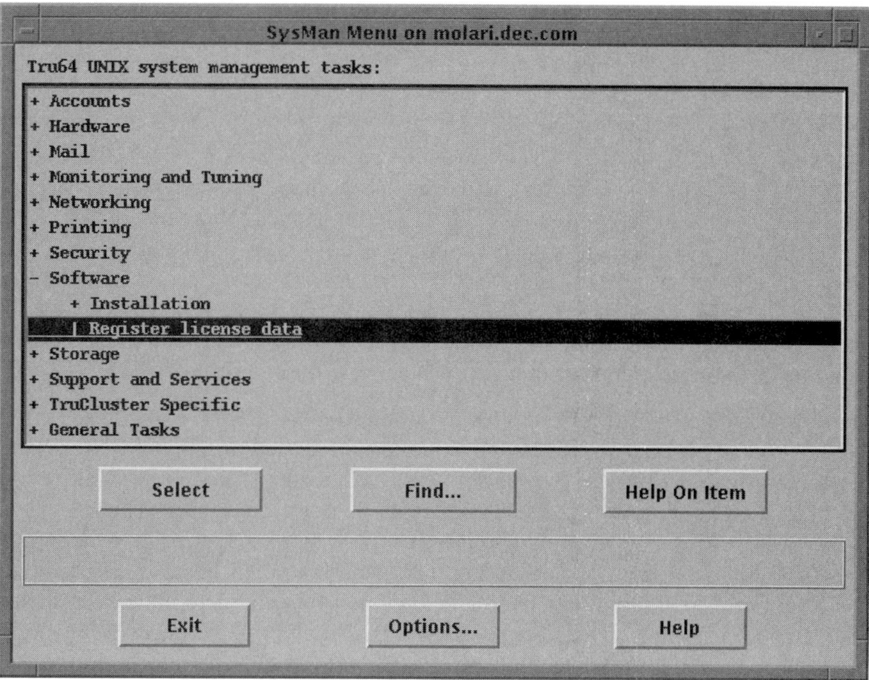

Figure 5-15: SysMan Menu

5.5.2 More on Licensing

Are we done with the configuration of our example of *Tru64* UNIX? Just about. We have one last thing to do – install our other licenses.

There are three ways to install License PAKs:

- `lmfsetup`.
- "`lmf register`".
- `sysman`, go to the "`Register license data`" under the "`Software`" management task. Alternately, you can use the "`sysman lmfsetup`" accelerator.

The LMF program will prompt for the proper license fields. Please see Figure 5-15 for an example using SysMan to register a License PAK.

5.6 A Final Note on Configuring a *Tru64* UNIX System

In our example presented in this chapter, we installed and configured a *Tru64* UNIX server for the purpose of deploying *TruCluster* Server. Our system was relatively uncomplicated in terms of what it does and how it needed to be configured. We highly recommend that you completely install and configure everything you need, from a systems perspective, on your standalone *Tru64* UNIX system first before you start your installation and configuration of *TruCluster* Server. Why? Consider this scenario: if you configure C2 security on the standalone system, at the time you create the cluster, it will be propagated to each member. However, if you configure C2 security after the cluster is created, you must reboot each member in order to enable the new security level.

If there are third party software applications that you need to install for your users, we recommend that you install, configure, and test these applications on the standalone *Tru64* UNIX system. If the application requires the *TruCluster* Server software be installed before it will allow itself to be installed cluster-aware, then wait until the cluster is built. As you are testing these applications, do as much characterization of the application as possible – characterize how they startup and shutdown, where they write data (including log files), and how their licensing is performed. After the cluster is built and configured, test these applications again and determine if these applications can be multi-instance or single-instance. In other words, can multiple instances of an application run on each node of a cluster at the same time or can only one instance of the application run on the cluster? This will determine whether or not you must use Cluster Application Availability (CAA) to control these applications. For more information on CAA, please see Chapters 23 and 24.

5.7 References

- *Tru64* UNIX Release Notes (V5.1 and V5.1A).
- *TruCluster* Server Release Notes (V5.1 and V5.1A).
- *Tru64* UNIX Installation Guide (V5.1 and V5.1A).
- *Tru64* UNIX Installation Guide: Advanced Topics (V5.1 and V5.1A).
- *Tru64* UNIX Network Administration (V5.0A and V5.1).
- *Tru64* UNIX Network Administration: Connections (V5.1A).
- *Tru64* UNIX Network Administration: Services (V5.1A).
- *TruCluster* Server Software Installation Guide (V5.1).
- *TruCluster* Server Cluster Installation Guide (V5.1A).

6

Tru64 UNIX Cluster Hooks: File System Hierarchy, CDSL, & PID

In this chapter we will begin the discussion of the various components included in the base Tru64 UNIX operating system that enable a more seamless transition from a standalone system to a cluster.

We will cover the following components:

	Section
• The Context Dependent Symbolic Link (CDSL)	6.1.1, 6.4
• Changes to the Runtime Configuration	6.1.2
• The File System Hierarchy	6.2
• Expanded Process IDs	6.5

The first and most significant change that was made to Tru64 UNIX was to have a transparent method for the operating system to locate its configuration information, executables, layered applications, etc., as well as to structure the basic file system hierarchy in such a way that it would not matter whether the system is standalone or in a cluster.

The method adopted is to split information into member-specific and cluster-common files for all Tru64 UNIX systems, whether they are in a cluster or standalone configuration. The cluster-common files are located in the files' normal location, while the member-specific files are located somewhere new (but appear to be located in the files' normal location – more on this in the following sections). The member-specific files are actually located in one of three primary locations:

- `/cluster/members/member`*n*
- `/usr/cluster/members/member`*n*
- `/var/cluster/members/member`*n*

(Where "*n*" is a number between 0 and 63 inclusive.)

NOTE:

The member0 directories are primarily used as a standalone system's member-specific directories. While technically it is unnecessary for a standalone system to have member-specific directories (since it is not a member of anything except your computer room), it keeps the layout consistent between standalone and clustered environments. In a cluster, it is used as a repository for generic versions of member-specific files. Cluster member IDs range from 1 to 63.

6.1 Is it Member-Specific or Cluster-Common?

Once a system joins or forms a cluster, it becomes a member of the cluster. So if something needs to be uniquely configured, such as a network interface, then its configuration information must be contained in a member-specific file. On the other hand, if something needs to be configured identically for every member in the cluster, such as NIS, then its configuration information must be located in a cluster-common file.

As of Tru64 UNIX version 5.0, the /etc/rc.config file has been split into two files with an optional third file as follows:

- rc.config
- rc.config.common
- rc.config.site (optional)

The rc.config file is member-specific and the rc.config.common file is, you guessed it, cluster-common. The rc.config.site file is for any site-specific configuration information.

```
# ls /etc/rc.config*
/etc/rc.config          /etc/rc.config.common
```

So, what makes /etc/rc.config member-specific? Let's take a closer look at both files.

```
# file /etc/rc.config*
/etc/rc.config: symbolic link to ../cluster/members/{memb}/etc/rc.config
/etc/rc.config.common:  /bin/sh shell script -- commands text
```

Notice that the rc.config file appears to be in the /etc directory when in actuality it is located in the "../cluster/members/{memb}/etc" directory. The /etc/rc.config file is not a regular file at all, but rather a special type of symbolic link known as a context-dependent symbolic link (CDSL).

6.1.1 Enter the CDSL

So, what is this CDSL thing? A CDSL is a symbolic link with the "{memb}" variable as part of the path. The "{memb}" is the "context", or more appropriately, what is resolved to determine what the context is. Figure 6-1 shows how a CDSL is resolved.

Notice that "{memb}" is equal to the word "member" with the member's ID appended. The member's ID is stored in the attribute memberid in the generic subsystem. A standalone system will always have a memberid of zero. Therefore, a CDSL with value of "../cluster/members/{memb}/etc/rc.config" on a standalone system would resolve to the path "../cluster/members/member0/etc/rc.config".

```
[/etc]
# ls -i ../cluster/members/{memb}/etc/rc.config
 1817 ../cluster/members/{memb}/etc/rc.config
```

```
[/etc]
# ls -i ../cluster/members/member0/etc/rc.config
 1817 ../cluster/members/member0/etc/rc.config
```

If you examine both files listed in the "ls -i" output, you will see that the files are the exact same file. The "-i" option displays a file's serial number (e.g., an inode in a UFS file system or a tag in an AdvFS file system).

```
[/etc]
#  cd /.tags && /sbin/advfs/tag2name 1817
/cluster/members/member0/etc/rc.config
```

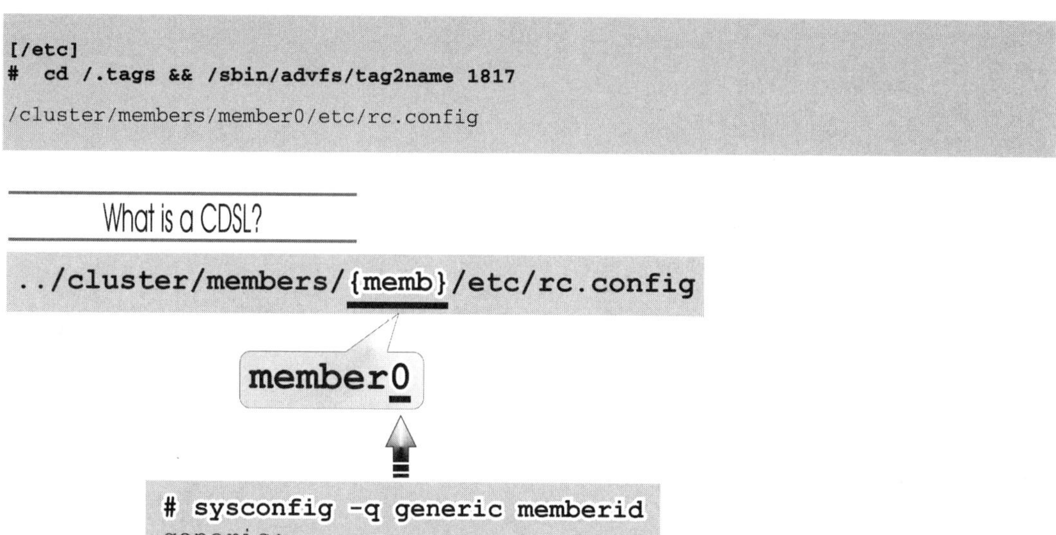

Figure 6-1: CDSL Resolved

Now that we have shown how you can differentiate a member-specific file from a cluster-common file, it bears mentioning that for every rule there is an exception. In other words, this is not the only way that member-specific files exist. Another method (although much less common) of creating a member-specific file is instead of placing the file in a member-specific directory and creating a CDSL to it, simply rename the file with a unique extension. An example of this second method is provided in Chapter 16 where the Cluster Alias subsystem is described. The Cluster Alias subsystem uses `gated.conf` files by creating a member-specific `gated.conf` file and appending "member*n*" to the file name (e.g. `/etc/gated.conf.member1`).

6.1.2 Is it in `rc.config` or `rc.config.common`?

We mentioned earlier that configuring a network interface was a member-specific task and that configuring NIS was a cluster-wide task, so how is this implemented in our `rc.config` files? Since NIS is configured cluster-wide, then all the NIS variables should be in `/etc/rc.config.common`, but not in `/etc/rc.config`.

```
# grep NIS /etc/rc.config
<nothing is returned>
```

```
# grep NIS /etc/rc.config.common
NIS_DOMAIN="DAN"
export NIS_DOMAIN
NIS_CONF="YES"
export NIS_CONF
NIS_TYPE="CLIENT"
export NIS_TYPE
NIS_ARGS="-s -S DAN,bacon.dec.com,gravy.dec.com"
export NIS_ARGS
```

The next question you might be asking is, "In what order are these files being called during startup?" In order to avoid unnecessary changes, since many of the `init` scripts already called `rc.config`, it was decided that `rc.config` would call `rc.config.common`.

```
# cat /etc/rc.config
#!/bin/sh
#
...
# Read in the cluster attributes before overriding them with the member
# specific options.
#
. /etc/rc.config.common
#
...
```

Note the comment right before `rc.config.common` is called: "Read in the cluster attributes before overriding them...". Since everything between "`#!/bin/sh`" and "`. /etc/rc.config.common`" are comments, the execution of `rc.config` does not set any variables until after `rc.config.common` has finished execution.

NOTE:

If you have any site-specific variables you want to set during system startup, create a file in `/etc` called `rc.config.site`, and call it from `rc.config.common` in the same relative position as `rc.config.common` is called from `rc.config`. It is important that site-specific variables are set before the cluster-common variables are set so that nothing in `rc.config.site` will inadvertently override anything in `rc.config.common` or `rc.config`. Note that the name `rc.config.site` is significant in that the `rcmgr` command can be used to manipulate your site-specific file (provided it has the correct name).

When the `init` daemon is started during system initialization, it uses the `/etc/inittab` file to tell it what initialization tasks need to be started or stopped at particular run levels.

```
# grep -E "^s[023]" /etc/inittab
s0:0:wait:/sbin/rc0 off < /dev/console > /dev/console 2>&1
s2:23:wait:/sbin/rc2 < /dev/console > /dev/console 2>&1
s3:3:wait:/sbin/rc3 < /dev/console > /dev/console 2>&1
```

Within `/etc/inittab` are lines that direct the `init` daemon to execute three particular scripts (`rc0`, `rc2`, and `rc3`). These scripts in turn execute a series of other scripts in subdirectories under `/sbin` (see Figure 6-2).

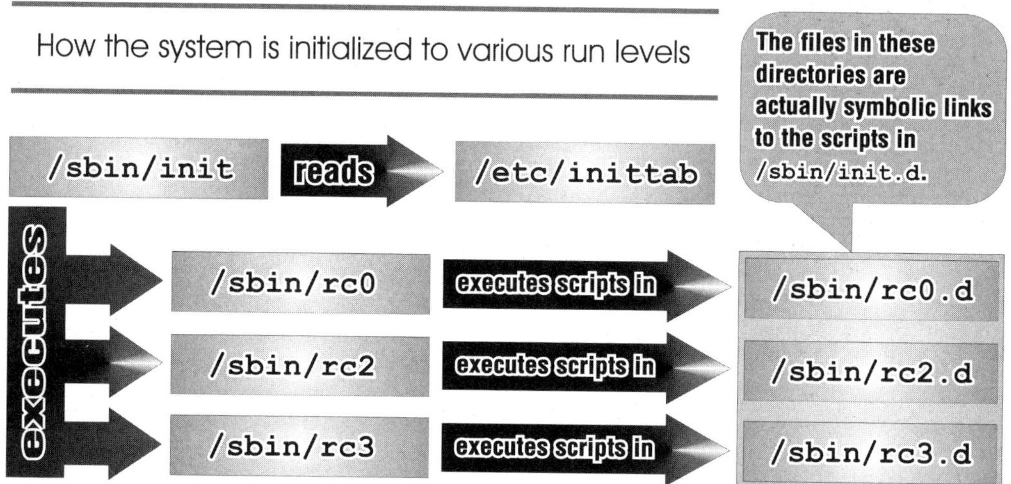

Figure 6-2: Runlevel Initialization

These subdirectories (`rc0.d`, `rc2.d`, and `rc3.d`) contain symbolic links to scripts located in `/sbin/init.d`. The links are named in such a way as to force the order in which they are executed.

```
# ls -l /sbin/rc2.d | awk '{ printf ("%15s  %3s  %s\n",$9,$10,$11) }'

         K00lpd   ->  ../init.d/lpd
         K03lat   ->  ../init.d/lat
        K04dhcp   ->  ../init.d/dhcp
...
     S25enlogin   ->  ../init.d/enlogin
     S35streams   ->  ../init.d/streams
         S45atm   ->  ../init.d/atm
```

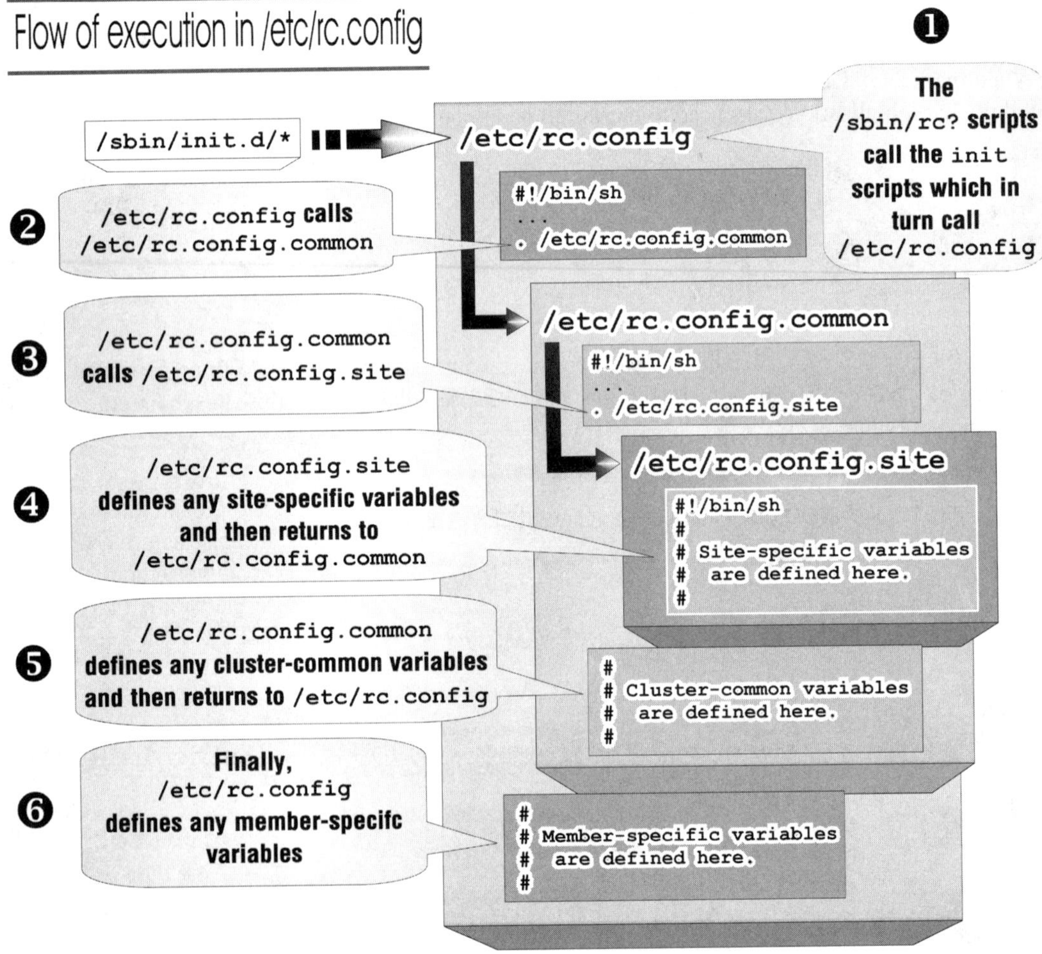

Figure 6-3: Runtime Configuration Execution Flow

Links that begin with a "K" indicate that the scripts associated with those links will be executed when the system is changing to the run level from a higher run level.

Links that begin with an "S" are executed when the system is changing to the run level from a lower run level. These scripts use variables that are set by the /etc/rc.config* scripts.

Figure 6-3 depicts the execution flow for the rc.config files. As you can see from the figure, the init scripts (that are executed from the /sbin/rc? scripts) execute rc.config, which in turn calls rc.config.common before it sets any variables. The rc.config.common file will immediately call rc.config.site (if one exists). Once rc.config.site returns to rc.config.common, then rc.config.common sets the variables in its file and returns to rc.config. Finally, rc.config sets its variables.

What happens if a variable is set in more than one file?

- If a variable is defined in rc.config and rc.config.common, then the value in rc.config is used.
- If a variable is defined in rc.config.common and rc.config.site, then the value in rc.config.common is used.

6.1.2.1 Using the rcmgr(8) command

The rcmgr command is the recommended method for modifying the rc.config files on Tru64 UNIX. Using rcmgr enables you to set variables as well as retrieve (get) variables. The rcmgr command has four command options that allow you to direct which rc.config file is used. See Table 6-1.

Let's see how rcmgr responds by setting and retrieving some variables.

First, let's set the same variable in both rc.config and rc.config.common.

```
# rcmgr set TCRHB from Member-specific file
# grep TCRHB /etc/rc.config*
/etc/rc.config:TCRHB="from Member-specific file"
/etc/rc.config:export TCRHB
```

```
# rcmgr -c set TCRHB from Cluster-common file
# grep TCRHB /etc/rc.config*
/etc/rc.config:TCRHB="from Member-specific file"
/etc/rc.config:export TCRHB
/etc/rc.config.common:TCRHB="from Cluster-common file"
/etc/rc.config.common:export TCRHB
```

rcmgr(8) command options

Option	Description	Example	Explanation
c	Use rc.config.common	# rcmgr -c set TCRHB 1	Set the "TCRHB" variable to the value "1" in rc.config.common.
h	Use rc.config on the member whose memberid equals the id input after the "-h". With get or mget also rc.config.common & rc.config.site.	# rcmgr -h 3 get GATED	Get the "GATED" variable from member3's rc.config file.
n	Use the rc.config on the member whose memberid equals the id input after the "-n".	# rcmgr -n 2 mget	Get all variables set in member2's rc.config file.
s	Use rc.config.site (if it exists)	# rcmgr -s get TCRHB	Get the variable "TCRHB" from rc.config.site (if it exists). If the site-specific file does not exist the following error is returned: "Error: Cannot open /etc/rc.config.site"

Table 6-1: The rcmgr Command Options

Now that we have set the variable in both files, let's see what value is returned when using the various command switches.

The "-c" switch:

```
# rcmgr -c get TCRHB
from Cluster-common file
```

The "-h" switch:

```
# rcmgr -h 0 get TCRHB
from Member-specific file
```

The "-n" switch:

```
# rcmgr -n 0 get TCRHB
from Member-specific file
```

No switch:

```
# rcmgr get TCRHB
from Member-specific file
```

Now let's remove the variable from `/etc/rc.config` and then repeat the test.

```
# rcmgr delete TCRHB
```

Verify that the variable is no longer in `/etc/rc.config`.

```
# grep TCRHB /etc/rc.config*
/etc/rc.config.common:TCRHB="from Cluster-common file"
/etc/rc.config.common:export TCRHB
```

We will skip the "`-c`" test since it will return the contents from `/etc/rc.config.common`, and as you can see from the previous output, the variable is still defined in the common file.

The "`-h`" switch:

```
# rcmgr -h 0 get TCRHB
from Cluster-common file
```

The "`-n`" switch:

```
# rcmgr -n 0 get TCRHB
< no output >
```

No switch:

```
# rcmgr get TCRHB
from Cluster-common file
```

Notice that the "`-n`" switch searches only the member-specific file. The "`-h`" switch, however, searches the `rc.config` first and then, if the variable is not there, it will search the `rc.config.common` file. When no switch is provided, both the "`-n`" and "`-h`" search sequences are executed. For additional information regarding the `rcmgr` command, see the associated reference page.

6.2 File System Hierarchy

The file system hierarchy in Tru64 UNIX version 5 has been modified slightly from the version 4 layout.

The version 5 file system layout is illustrated in Figure 6-4. The root (/), /usr, and /var directories have a new directory, named /cluster, added to each directory. Underneath each cluster directory is the members directory. The members directory is where the member-specific directories will be located. As you can see by the figure, each members directory currently contains two files:

- member
- member0

The member0 file is the standalone system's member-specific directory, while the member file is a member-neutral identity link, a CDSL, to allow you to get to that member's member-specific directory quickly.

```
# for i in / /usr /var
> do
>   cd ${i}/cluster/members
>   print "\n[${PWD}]"
>   ls -ld *
> done

[/cluster/members]
lrwxr-xr-x    1 root     system          6 Jan 26 08:46 member -> {memb}
drwxr-xr-x    9 root     system       8192 Feb  6 18:41 member0

[/usr/cluster/members]
lrwxr-xr-x    1 root     system          6 Jan 26 08:47 member -> {memb}
drwxr-xr-x    7 root     system       8192 Jan 26 08:47 member0

[/var/cluster/members]
lrwxr-xr-x    1 root     system          6 Jan 26 08:51 member -> {memb}
drwxr-xr-x   22 root     system       8192 Feb  6 17:02 member0
```

The other CDSL in the diagram is a hidden file in the root (/) directory called ".local..".

```
# ls -l /.local.. | awk '{ print $9,$10,$11 }'
/.local.. -> cluster/members/{memb}
```

This example illustrates a quick way to show a file name and its link. Since this command will come in handy throughout this chapter (and the rest of the book), let's create a function to use this command so you can save on typing. To make this change even more permanent, you can place it in your ".profile" file. Note: this particular function works in the Korn shell.

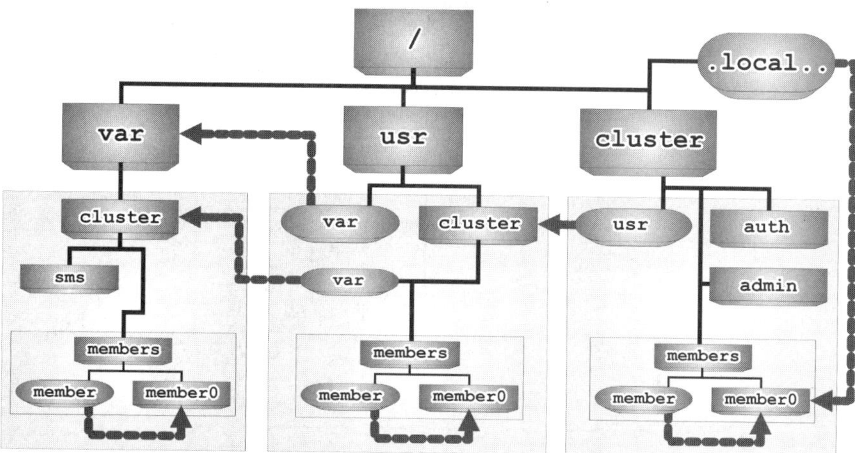

Figure 6-4: File System Hierarchy (V5+)

```
# function fln
> {
>    ls -l $@ | awk '{ print $9,$10,$11 }'
> }
```

```
# fln /.local..
/.local.. -> cluster/members/{memb}
```

To see the hierarchy information for the Tru64 UNIX version on your system, see the `hier(5)` reference page.

6.3 Is it Member-Specific or Cluster-Common? (redux)

Let's take a closer look at the root (`/`), `/usr`, and `/var` directories and see what has been moved to the "member-specific status". Figure 6-5 shows the `member0` directory hierarchy. Note that we use the term "`member`" in the figure since this directory could pertain to any member in a cluster.

The next three tables use the `find(1)` command to locate symbolic links in the root file system. The `awk(1)` command searches the output from the `find` command for a CDSL and prints out the link and the link's destination. Table 6-2 shows the CDSLs for the root (`/`) partition.

In Table 6-3, we explore the `/usr` file system. Note: we have edited the following output so that all of the "`.sts`" files in "`/usr/.smdb.`" are shown as one entry, "`/usr/.smdb./*.sts -> ../cluster/members/{memb}/.smdb./*.sts`".

In the final table, Table 6-4, the `/var` file system is displayed.

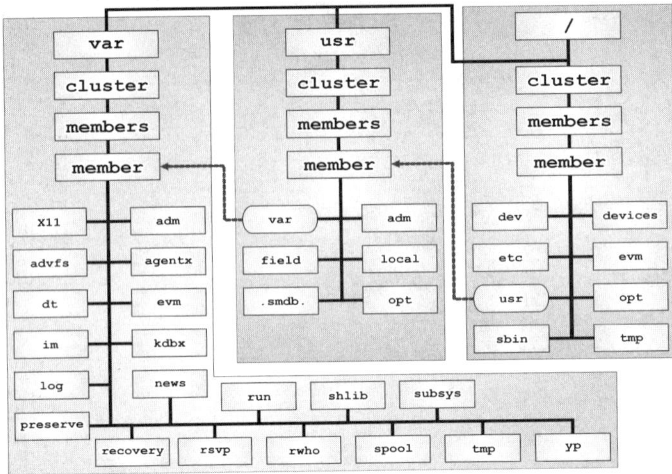

Figure 6-5: The `member0` directory hierarchy

```
# find / -xdev -type l -ls | awk '/\{memb\}/ { print $11,$12,$13 }'

/cluster/members/member ➔ {memb}
/etc/autopush.conf ➔ ../cluster/members/{memb}/etc/autopush.conf
/etc/binlog.conf ➔ ../cluster/members/{memb}/etc/binlog.conf
/etc/cfginfo ➔ ../cluster/members/{memb}/etc/cfginfo
/etc/rc.config ➔ ../cluster/members/{memb}/etc/rc.config
/etc/strsetup.conf ➔ ../cluster/members/{memb}/etc/strsetup.conf
/etc/syslog.conf ➔ ../cluster/members/{memb}/etc/syslog.conf
/etc/gated.conf ➔ ../cluster/members/{memb}/etc/gated.conf
/etc/ifaccess.conf ➔ ../cluster/members/{memb}/etc/ifaccess.conf
/etc/inet.local ➔ ../cluster/members/{memb}/etc/inet.local
/etc/inetd.conf.local ➔ ../cluster/members/{memb}/etc/inetd.conf.local
/etc/ntp.conf ➔ ../cluster/members/{memb}/etc/ntp.conf
/etc/ogated.conf ➔ ../cluster/members/{memb}/etc/ogated.conf
/etc/ppp ➔ ../cluster/members/{memb}/etc/ppp
/etc/remote ➔ ../cluster/members/{memb}/etc/remote
/etc/routes ➔ ../cluster/members/{memb}/etc/routes
/etc/slhosts ➔ ../cluster/members/{memb}/etc/slhosts
/etc/snmpd.conf ➔ ../cluster/members/{memb}/etc/snmpd.conf
/etc/dhcptab ➔ ../cluster/members/{memb}/etc/dhcptab
/etc/latautopush.conf ➔ ../cluster/members/{memb}/etc/latautopush.conf
/etc/dfsl.dat ➔ ../cluster/members/{memb}/etc/dfsl.dat
/etc/atm ➔ ../cluster/members/{memb}/etc/atm
/etc/atm.conf ➔ ../cluster/members/{memb}/etc/atm.conf
/etc/dfsl.bak ➔ ../cluster/members/{memb}/etc/dfsl.bak
/etc/gateways ➔ ../cluster/members/{memb}/etc/gateways
/etc/dfsl.h00 ➔ ../cluster/members/{memb}/etc/dfsl.h00
/sbin/it.d/data ➔ ../../cluster/members/{memb}/sbin/it.d/data
/sbin/it.d/23.d ➔ ../..//cluster/members/{memb}/sbin/it.d/23.d
/sbin/init.d/autosysconfig ➔ ../../cluster/members/{memb}/sbin/init.d/autosysconfig
/dev ➔ cluster/members/{memb}/dev
/tmp ➔ cluster/members/{memb}/tmp
/.local.. ➔ cluster/members/{memb}
```

Table 6-2: The `root` (`/`) Partition CDSLs – standalone system

```
# find /usr -xdev -type l -ls | awk '/\{memb\}/ { print $11,$12,$13 }'
```

```
              /usr/.smdb./*.sts ➔ ../cluster/members/{memb}/.smdb./*.sts
    /usr/cluster/members/member ➔ {memb}
      /usr/lib/X11/Xserver.conf ➔ ../../var/cluster/members/{memb}/X11/Xserver.conf
```

Table 6-3: The `/usr` Partition CDSLs – standalone system

```
# find /var -xdev -type l -ls | awk '/\{memb\}/ { print $11,$12,$13 }'
```

```
          /var/cluster/members/member ➔ {memb}
                      /var/adm/smlogs ➔ ../cluster/members/{memb}/adm/smlogs
                /var/adm/binary.errlog ➔ ../cluster/members/{memb}/adm/binary.errlog
                       /var/adm/crash ➔ ../cluster/members/{memb}/adm/crash
                        /var/adm/cron ➔ ../cluster/members/{memb}/adm/cron
                     /var/adm/lastlog ➔ ../cluster/members/{memb}/adm/lastlog
                         /var/adm/lmf ➔ ../cluster/members/{memb}/adm/lmf
                    /var/adm/messages ➔ ../cluster/members/{memb}/adm/messages
    /var/adm/sendmail/protocols.map ➔ ../../cluster/members/{memb}/adm/sendmail/protocols.map
      /var/adm/sendmail/sendmail.st ➔ ../../cluster/members/{memb}/adm/sendmail/sendmail.st
                      /var/adm/syslog ➔ ../cluster/members/{memb}/adm/syslog
                /var/adm/syslog.dated ➔ ../cluster/members/{memb}/adm/syslog.dated
           /var/adm/sysman/shutdown ➔ ../../cluster/members/{memb}/adm/sysman/shutdown
/var/adm/sysman/sysman_station/logs ➔ ../../../cluster/members/{memb}/adm/sysman/sysman_station/logs
      /var/adm/sysman/system_census ➔ ../../cluster/members/{memb}/adm/sysman/system_census
    /var/adm/sysman/checklist.dates ➔ ../../cluster/members/{memb}/adm/sysman/checklist.dates
                        /var/adm/utmp ➔ ../cluster/members/{memb}/adm/utmp
                        /var/adm/wtmp ➔ ../cluster/members/{memb}/adm/wtmp
                         /var/adm/lpd ➔ ../cluster/members/{memb}/adm/lpd
                /var/adm/collect.dated ➔ ../cluster/members/{memb}/adm/collect.dated
                         /var/adm/fee ➔ ../cluster/members/{memb}/adm/acct/fee
                        /var/adm/acct ➔ ../cluster/members/{memb}/adm/acct
                       /var/adm/pacct ➔ ../cluster/members/{memb}/adm/acct/pacct
                       /var/adm/qacct ➔ ../cluster/members/{memb}/adm/acct/qacct
                             /var/tmp ➔ ./cluster/members/{memb}/tmp
               /var/evm/adm/logfiles ➔ ../../cluster/members/{memb}/evm/adm/logfiles
                      /var/evm/evmlog ➔ ../cluster/members/{memb}/evm/evmlog
                     /var/evm/sockets ➔ ../cluster/members/{memb}/evm/sockets
                             /var/log ➔ ./cluster/members/{memb}/log
                        /var/preserve ➔ ./cluster/members/{memb}/preserve
                             /var/run ➔ ./cluster/members/{memb}/run
                      /var/spool/cron ➔ ../cluster/members/{memb}/spool/cron
                     /var/spool/locks ➔ ../cluster/members/{memb}/spool/locks
                       /var/spool/lpd ➔ ../cluster/members/{memb}/spool/lpd
                      /var/spool/uucp ➔ ../cluster/members/{memb}/spool/uucp
                /var/spool/uucppublic ➔ ../cluster/members/{memb}/spool/uucppublic
                /var/X11/Xserver.conf ➔ ../cluster/members/{memb}/X11/Xserver.conf
                          /var/agentx ➔ ./cluster/members/{memb}/agentx
                            /var/rwho ➔ ./cluster/members/{memb}/rwho
                              /var/dt ➔ cluster/members/{memb}/dt
              /var/advfs/daemon/logs ➔ ../../cluster/members/{memb}/advfs/daemon/logs
            /var/advfs/daemon/socket ➔ ../../cluster/members/{memb}/advfs/daemon/socket
                       /var/advfs/gui ➔ ../cluster/members/{memb}/advfs/gui
                            /var/rsvp ➔ ./cluster/members/{memb}/rsvp
            /var/kdbx/system.kdbxrc ➔ ../../var/cluster/members/{memb}/kdbx/system.kdbxrc
                              /var/im ➔ ./cluster/members/{memb}/im
                        /var/recovery ➔ /var/cluster/members/{memb}/recovery
```

Table 6-4: The `/var` Partition CDSLs – standalone system

6.4 More on the CDSL

The previous section showed that even on a standalone Tru64 UNIX system, CDSLs are everywhere. In this section, we will discuss how to manage those CDSLs.

IMPORTANT CDSL PUBLIC SERVICE ANNOUNCEMENT:

We of the "Citizens to Promote Transparency in Cluster Environments (CPTCE)" – "Kaput-see" – yeah, we know our name needs work – would like it known that CDSLs exist as a transparent method for accessing files, by the name you know and love, regardless of where they are. Pay no attention to the author behind the computer!

In all seriousness, CDSLs are a "behind-the-scenes" feature to make your life as an administrator easier. In a perfect world, nothing ever goes wrong, but you need to know what to do in the real world, so humor us as we discuss how to manage CDSLs.

As we have stated, a CDSL is a special type of symbolic link that contains a "`{memb}`" in the path. It is the kernel's path resolution software within the Virtual File System that resolves the "`{memb}`" to the member-specific directory as we demonstrated earlier in this chapter. A CDSL is a symbolic link and is treated as a symbolic link by the underlying physical file systems. Therefore, some issues may arise with exporting a file system via NFS or restoring a `tar(1)` backup that contains CDSLs to a non-Tru64 UNIX system. In the case of NFS, if `member1` were exporting the file system, all CDSLs would resolve to `member1`'s member-specific files. As for `tar`, the restored CDSLs will be unusable on systems not running at least version 5.0 of Tru64 UNIX.

6.4.1 Creating a CDSL using the `mkcdsl(8)` command

Since a CDSL is a symbolic link, you can use the `ln(1)` command with the "`-s`" option, although it is highly recommended that you use the `mkcdsl` command. The `mkcdsl` command does the following:

- Creates a CDSL.
- Optionally, copies the file to the destination of the CDSL.
- Updates the CDSL inventory file (`/var/adm/cdsl_admin.inv`). See the next section for more details on this.

In the first example, we create a CDSL (`myFirstCDSL`) in the root(`/`) directory using the `mkcdsl` command and print out the result.

```
# cd / && mkcdsl myFirstCDSL && fln myFirstCDSL
myFirstCDSL -> cluster/members/{memb}/myFirstCDSL
```

NOTE: although we have created a CDSL that points to somewhere, that somewhere points to nowhere.

```
# wc -l myFirstCDSL
wc: myFirstCDSL : No such file or directory
```

This is not an error, but rather the nature of a symbolic link. You can remedy this situation by simply copying a file to /myFirstCDSL.

```
# cp .profile myFirstCDSL && wc -l myFirstCDSL
      74 myFirstCDSL
```

Next, let's create a directory under root (/) to illustrate the mkcdsl command with the "-c" option. The "-c" option copies the file (or in this case, the directory) from its location to a member-specific location while leaving a CDSL in the file's location.

```
# C=cluDir && mkdir $C && mkcdsl -c $C && fln $C
cluDir -> cluster/members/{memb}/cluDir
```

6.4.2 Maintaining CDSLs

There are two commands that can be used to maintain CDSLs on a system:

- cdslinvchk(8)
- mkcdsl(8)

6.4.2.1 Using the cdslinvchk(8) command

The cdslinvchk command verifies that all the CDSLs installed on the system exist by searching the subset inventory files located in /usr/.smdb. (the *.inv files) and the /var/adm/cdsl_admin.inv file. If the command detects any errors, it writes them in the cdsl_check_list file located in /var/adm. The cdslinvchk command checks only for missing CDSLs; it does not recreate missing links. To recreate a missing CDSL, use the mkcdsl command.

```
# cdslinvchk
Successful CDSL inventory check
```

Let's remove a CDSL to demonstrate an error condition.

```
# mv /etc/rc.config /etc/rc.config.cdsl
```

Rerun the CDSL inventory check program.

```
# cdslinvchk
Failed CDSL inventory check. See details in /var/adm/cdsl_check_list
```

Check the contents of the error log.

```
# cat /var/adm/cdsl_check_list
Expected CDSL: ./etc/rc.config -> ../cluster/members/{memb}/etc/rc.config
An administrator or application has removed this CDSL.
```

How would you correct this? Use the `mkcdsl` command as we discussed earlier in this chapter.

```
#  mkcdsl /etc/rc.config
```

Rerun the `cdslinvchk` program to make sure we put everything back together correctly.

```
# cdslinvchk
Successful CDSL inventory check
```

Do not forget to remove the saved link.

```
# rm /etc/rc.config.cdsl
```

6.4.2.2 Using the mkcdsl(8) command

The `mkcdsl` command is designed not to create just a CDSL, but to create a CDSL that can be maintained. As we have stated before, a CDSL is a symbolic link. Sure, it is a special symbolic link with the "`{memb}`" variable sandwiched into the path, but it is a symbolic link nonetheless. In other words, you can create a CDSL using the `ln` command with the "`-s`" switch as mentioned in the previous section, but what we haven't yet told you is why it is a bad idea to use the `ln` command. Simply put, the `ln` command does not make any log that the CDSL was ever created. Consequently, if you created a CDSL for your application so that every member can write to its own log file, for instance, you might want to know if that link were deleted, wouldn't you? By using the mkcdsl command, when the CDSL is created, an entry is added to the /var/adm/cdsl_admin.inv inventory file. How is the inventory file maintained? By using the "-i" option to the mkcdsl command.

Using the mkcdsl command with the "-i" switch permits you to do the following:

- Add a new entry or update an existing entry in the /var/adm/cdsl_admin.inv file if the name you input to the command is a CDSL.
- Remove an entry from the /var/adm/cdsl_admin.inv file if the name you input to the command is a non-existent CDSL.

Remember those two CDSLs we created in the previous section? Let's verify that they were entered into the cdsl_admin.inv file.

```
# grep -E "myFirstCDSL|cluDir" /var/adm/cdsl_admin.inv
0          34          00000     0          0          120777    2/26/01  010          s
./myFirstCDSL    cluster/members/{memb}/myFirstCDSL        -
0         29          00000     0          0          120777    2/26/01  010       s          ./cluDir
cluster/members/{memb}/cluDir     -
```

Now remove the CDSL "myFirstCDSL" and run the mkcdsl command with the "-i" switch.

```
# C=myFirstCDSL ; rm $C && mkcdsl -i $C && grep $C /var/adm/cdsl_admin.inv
< no output >
```

Although we do not recommend this method for creating a CDSL, this time let's use the ln command. The ln command can also create a CDSL (since a CDSL is a symbolic link) but does not update /var/adm/cdsl_admin.inv.

```
# cd / && ln -s cluster/members/{memb}/$C && fln $C
myFirstCDSL -> cluster/members/{memb}/myFirstCDSL
```

Check /var/adm/cdsl_admin.inv.

```
# grep $C /var/adm/cdsl_admin.inv
< no output >
```

It is not there because ln does not update the CDSL inventory file. However, with the mkcdsl command, we can have /var/adm/cdsl_admin.inv automatically updated.

```
# mkcdsl -i $C && grep $C /var/adm/cdsl_admin.inv
0          34         00000     0          0          120777   2/26/01  010          s
./myFirstCDSL   cluster/members/{memb}/myFirstCDSL        -
```

6.4.3 CDSL and the mv(1) command

Special care needs to be taken in using the mv command when a CDSL is involved. The mv command will not follow the link and therefore will replace the link with the file. In a standalone configuration, this may or may not be a big deal (of course, cdslinvchk will return an error); however, in a cluster this will have unpredictable (and possibly not very pleasant) results.

To illustrate this problem, create a file (we'll call it "mover") and move it to the link we created in the previous section.

```
# cat > mover
la dee da
tweedledee
tweedledum
^D
```

```
# ls -lid mover myFirstCDSL | awk '{ print $1,$10,$11,$12 }'
2112 myFirstCDSL -> cluster/members/{memb}/myFirstCDSL
2894 mover
```

```
# mv mover myFirstCDSL ; ls -lid myFirstCDSL | awk '{ print $1,$10,$11,$12 }'
2894 myFirstCDSL
```

You can see by the serial number that the file is the same file, but more importantly, the CDSL is gone! It is recommended that you use the cp(1) command instead of the mv command when CDSLs are involved. If you accidentally remove a CDSL, don't worry, just recreate it with the mkcdsl command.

6.4.4 CDSL and Shells

The Korn shell '88 (ksh) and Korn shell '93 (dtksh) do not display symbolic links in the same way that the Bourne shell (sh) or C shell (csh) do. The Korn shells hide the symbolic links in output, when possible, whereas the other shells display the actual path you are in. Table 6-5 illustrates each shell's response when changing the current working directory using a CDSL as the directory. Three alternate shells from the Tru64 UNIX Open Source CD are also shown in the table. Notice that the bash and zsh shells are like ksh whereas tcsh is similar to csh.

6.5 Expanded Process IDs

You might be wondering, "What do expanded process IDs have to do with CDSLs and the file system hierarchy?" Nothing really, but we thought you might be interested in this bit of information and chose to offer it here.

Process IDs have been expanded to a 32-bit integer beginning in Tru64 UNIX version 5.0 (although it appears that the maximum value is 2147483647 which is actually 31-bits). In a standalone environment, you will not see any appreciable difference; for instance PID 0 is still [kernel_idle] and PID 1 is still the init daemon. The PID structure in a TruCluster environment, however, is defined to provide a unique range of process IDs (524288 PIDs/member) and is defined as follows:

1. Process ID (19-bits)
2. Member ID (8-bits)
3. Sequence Number (4-bits)

Shell response to CDSLs

/.local.. ➔ cluster/members/{memb}

sh (/sbin/sh, /usr/bin/sh)	csh (/usr/bin/csh)	ksh (posix) (/usr/bin/ksh, /usr/bin/posix/sh)	dtksh (ksh93) (/usr/dt/bin/dtksh)
# cd /.local..	# cd /.local..	# cd /.local..	# cd /.local..
# pwd	# pwd	# pwd	# pwd
/cluster/members/member0	/cluster/members/member0	/.local..	/.local..

tcsh (/usr/local/bin/tcsh)	bash (/usr/local/bin/bash)	zsh (/usr/local/bin/zsh)
# cd /.local..	# cd /.local..	# cd /.local..
# pwd	# pwd	# pwd
/cluster/members/member0	/.local..	/.local..

Table 6-5: Shell Responses to Symbolic Links

4. Sign-bit (1-bit) – this is reserved for future use.

The PID structure is defined in `/usr/include/sys/types.h`. The initial PID for each member is shown in Table 6-6.

Let's take a closer look at the PID of the `init` daemon on a cluster to explore how the PID structure in a cluster affects the PID. On `member1`, the PID for `init` would be `524589`.

```
# sysconfig -q generic memberid

generic:
memberid = 1
```

```
# ps -eo pid,command | grep "/sbin/init" | grep -v grep

524289 /sbin/init -a
```

PID Range by Member ID

memberid × 2^{19}

Member ID	PID	Member ID	PID	Member ID	PID
1	524288	22	11534336	43	22544384
2	1048576	23	12058624	44	23068672
3	1572864	24	12582912	45	23592960
4	2097152	25	13107200	46	24117248
5	2621440	26	13631488	47	24641536
6	3145728	27	14155776	48	25165824
7	3670016	28	14680064	49	25690112
8	4194304	29	15204352	50	26214400
9	4718592	30	15728640	51	26738688
10	5242880	31	16252928	52	27262976
11	5767168	32	16777216	53	27787264
12	6291456	33	17301504	54	28311552
13	6815744	34	17825792	55	28835840
14	7340032	35	18350080	56	29360128
15	7864320	36	18874368	57	29884416
16	8388608	37	19398656	58	30408704
17	8912896	38	19922944	59	30932992
18	9437184	39	20447232	60	31457280
19	9961472	40	20971520	61	31981568
20	10485760	41	21495808	62	32505856
21	11010048	42	22020096	63	33030144

Table 6-6: PID Range by Member

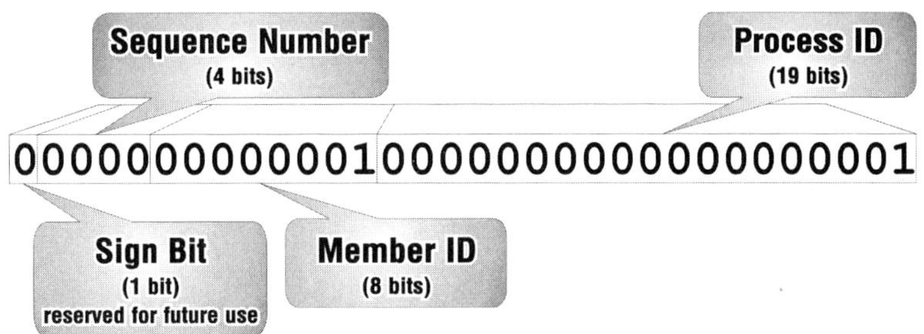

Figure 6-6: PID Structure Illustrated

If we convert the PID from decimal to binary, we can see the how the PID is composed.

```
# perl -e 'printf ("%b\n", 524289);'
10000000000000000001
```

Figure 6-6 shows the bit field breakout.

6.6 References

- Tru64 UNIX System Administration Guide – versions 5.1 and 5.1A.
- TruCluster Server Technical Overview – versions 5.1 and 5.1A.
- Reference pages (noted within the text).

7

Tru64 UNIX Cluster Hooks: Device Naming & Hardware Management

In the last chapter, we showed how the directory hierarchy had been altered in *Tru64* UNIX, starting with version 5.0, to ease the transition from a standalone environment to a clustered one. In this chapter, we will dig a little deeper into this modified hierarchy as we explore how device locations have been altered as well.

We will cover the following:

7.1 Device Special File Names and Locations

In *Tru64* UNIX prior to version 5.0, all devices were located in the `/dev` subdirectory. In version 5.0 and above, this has changed; to the casual observer, though, it will look the same. It bears mentioning up front that the device special file naming convention for storage devices has changed. Gone is the `bus-target-lun` (`b-t-l`) mnemonic for disks and cdrom devices; gone is the cryptic tape device naming convention. Table 7-1 shows the device special file naming changes.

Why did the `b-t-l` naming convention get replaced? First, to enable *Tru64* UNIX to support multiple paths to a device, and second, to enable every member in a cluster to see the same device by the same device special file name regardless of its physical location. How is this accomplished? We will answer that question in the next section.

Device Special File Naming									
	Version 4 and below				Version 5.0 and above				
	directory (/dev)	basename	instance	partition or density	directory (/devices)	basename	instance	partition or density	
CDROM	.	rz	n	[ac]	./disk	cdrom	n	[ac]	block
		rrz	n	[ac]	./rdisk		n	[ac]	character
Disk	.	rz	n	[a-h]	./disk	dsk	n	[a-h]	block
		rrz	n	[a-h]	./rdisk		n	[a-h]	character
Tape	.	rmt	n	[almh]	./tape	tape	n	_d[0-7]	rewind
		nrmt	n	[almh]	./ntape		n	_d[0-7]	no rewind
CCL	.	rz	n	c	./cport	scp	n		
Changer	.	mc	n	[a-h]	./changer	mc	n		
LSM	./vol/dg	user-defined volume name			./vol/dg	user-defined volume name			block
	./rvol/dg				./rvol/dg				character

n = device number

Table 7-1: Device Special File Naming

Another fundamental change that has occurred is the location of the device special files. Storage devices have been relocated to the `/devices` directory tree. The `/dev` file is now a CDSL pointing to a member-specific `/dev` directory and contains member-specific devices (e.g., the console, keyboard, mouse, pseudo terminals, etc.). Figure 7-1 shows the device directory hierarchy.

Let's explore the hierarchy. First, what are the device files in the root (`/`) directory?

```
# file /dev*

/dev:    symbolic link to cluster/members/{memb}/dev
/devices:        directory
```

Notice that `/dev` is now a CDSL, whereas `/devices` is actually a cluster-common directory. If we look more closely at what is in `/devices` we see that the storage device directories are located there. This is done because storage devices are shared in a cluster.

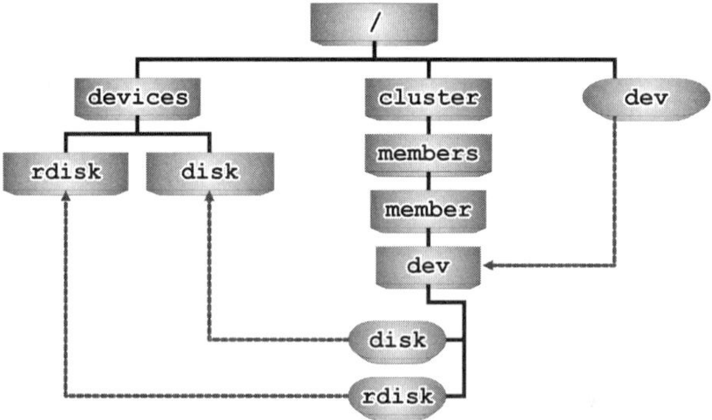

Figure 7-1: Device Directory Hierarchy

```
# file /devices/*

/devices/changer:       directory
/devices/cport: directory
/devices/disk:  directory
/devices/dmapi: directory
/devices/ntape: directory
/devices/rdisk: directory
/devices/rvol:  directory
/devices/tape:  directory
/devices/vol:   directory
```

Although the directory hierarchy has changed, it looks the same. That is to say we can still `cd(1)` to `/dev`, and all devices, including the storage device directories, are there. However, the storage device directories are actually symbolic links to the `/devices` directory.

```
# find /dev/ -type l -ls | awk '{ print $11,$12,$13 }'

/dev/none -> ../devices/none
/dev/cport -> ../../../../devices/cport
/dev/disk -> ../../../../devices/disk
/dev/rdisk -> ../../../../devices/rdisk
/dev/tape -> ../../../../devices/tape
/dev/ntape -> ../../../../devices/ntape
/dev/changer -> ../../../../devices/changer
/dev/dmapi -> ../../../../devices/dmapi
/dev/vol -> ../../../../devices/vol
/dev/rvol -> ../../../../devices/rvol
```

7.2 Worldwide Identifiers (WWID)

In the previous section, we discussed the device special file naming change and why it changed from the `b-t-l` naming convention of previous *Tru64* UNIX releases. We said that we would tell you how unique cluster-wide naming was accomplished in the next section, and here we are. Unique device special file names are accomplished by using a SCSI worldwide identifier (WWID) to identify storage devices on a standalone system or in a cluster.

Every device is assigned a name the first time it is detected by the operating system. The name starts with a base name (`dsk`, `cdrom`, `tape`, etc.) followed by a number. The numbering begins with zero. Once the device has been recognized, it can be relocated to another bus or another target, etc., and the name remains the same. A WWID is a unique identifier, not unlike a serial number, that most SCSI devices should have. There are exceptions, however, and these include how *Tru64* UNIX identifies units from HSZ RAID controllers and older SCSI devices.

7.2.1 WWID formats

Currently, ten WWID formats are defined in the camdb.h header file located in the /usr/sys/include/io/cam directory. The maximum defined size for a WWID is currently 276 bytes (the size of the wwid_dec_unique and wwid_serial_num structures).

NOTE:

The wwid_decoder program can be used to decode the WWID header. The WWID header is the hexadecimal value found after the "SCSI-WWID" in the "name" attribute of a device. This header contains the following information:

- The type of the WWID.
- The length of the WWID.
- Whether or not the WWID is ASCII.

The wwid_decoder program can be downloaded from the *TruCluster* Server Handbook Web site (see Appendix B for the URL). The following example illustrates the wwid_decoder program.

Get the WWID header from hwmgr(8). First, get the HWID of a storage device.

```
# hwmgr -view devices
 HWID: Device Name           Mfg       Model            Location
 ------------------------------------------------------------------------------
    4: /dev/kevm
   30: /dev/disk/floppy0c              3.5in floppy     fdi0-unit-0
   40: /dev/disk/dsk0c       COMPAQ    BB009235B6       bus-2-targ-0-lun-0
   41: /dev/disk/dsk1c       COMPAQ    BB009235B6       bus-2-targ-1-lun-0
   45: /dev/disk/cdrom0c     COMPAQ    CRD-8402B        bus-0-targ-0-lun-0
```

Second, get the WWID header.

```
# hwmgr -get attribute -a name -id 41
41:
  name = SCSI-WWID:0c000008:0000-0e11-0012-5205
```

Finally, run the wwid_decoder.

```
# wwid_decoder 0c000008

IEEE EUI (64-bit):
  Uses the wwid_p83_ieee64 structure in /usr/sys/include/io/cam/camdb.h.
  This is a Page 0x83, ID type 2 (IEEE) WWID -- length is 8 bytes.
```

Let's return to the WWID issue and the HSZ RAID controllers. What's the big deal? Well, since a unit can be a number of physical devices, it was determined that units from HSZ RAID controllers would be defined by the combination of the HSZ's serial number concatenated to the unit number. Here's an example.

The first thing we need to do is get a HWID from a device attached to an HSZ.

```
# hwmgr -view devices -dsf dsk13
 HWID: Device Name          Mfg       Model              Location
 ------------------------------------------------------------------------------
   81: /dev/disk/dsk13c     DEC       HSZ70              bus-4-targ-3-lun-3
```

Next, we get the attributes for the device that is identified by HWID 81. Note: we are using the cut(1) command to trim off everything but the actual WWID for the device.

```
# hwmgr -get attribute -a name -id 81 | cut -d = -f2
81:
SCSI-WWID:0910003c:"DEC     HSZ70           ZG81110558ZG81110725:d00t00003100003"
```

Figure 7-2 shows the composition of a WWID for a device that is connected to an HSZ controller.

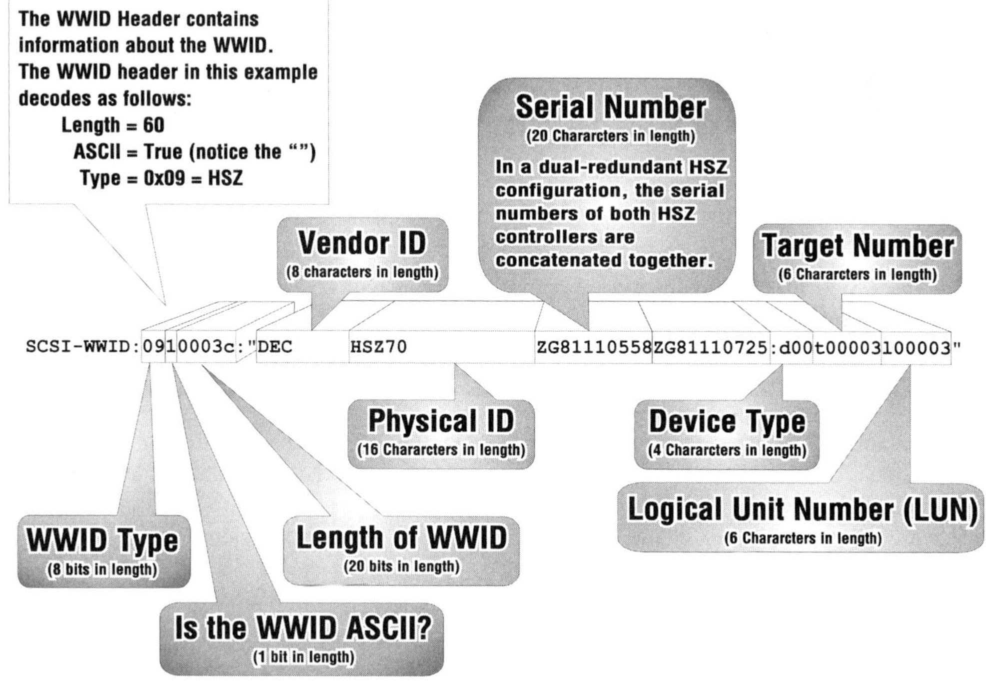

Figure 7-2: WWID for the HSZ explained

Let's see what the wwid_decoder program says about the WWID.

```
# wwid_decoder 0910003c

HSZ Algorithm:
  Uses wwid_hsz_this_other structure in /usr/sys/include/io/cam/camdb.h.
  This is an HSZ Algorithm WWID (ascii) -- length is 60 bytes.
```

As pointed out in the figure and confirmed by the output above, this is an HSZ WWID, which is an ASCII WWID of 60 bytes in length. Notice that the "ZG81110558ZG81110725" portion of the WWID is the serial numbers of the two HSZ controllers concatenated together. Let's see if we can verify this fact. From the console on the HSZ, type "show this". The output will show the serial number of each HSZ controller.

```
HSZ70> show this
Controller:
        HSZ70 ZG81110558 Firmware V77Z-0, Hardware  H01
        Configured for dual-redundancy with ZG81110725
            In dual-redundant configuration
...
```

The "this" controller's serial number is "ZG81110558", and the "other" controller's serial number is "ZG81110725".

7.3 Hardware Management Databases

IMPORTANT:

Many of the ASCII formatted files we are about to discuss will very likely be converted to binary files in a future release of *Tru64* UNIX, so we highly recommend not becoming dependent on the fact that these files are currently ASCII.

Given the hardware changes that have occurred with the V5.0 release of *Tru64* UNIX, several databases are used to keep track of the configuration information. Note that these files **must** **not** be edited manually. There are programs (see hwmgr and dsfmgr(8) below) that can be used to modify some of these databases while others are modified by kernel subsystems. Note that all of the following files are located in the /etc directory.

- dccd.dat

The dccd.dat file is the Category to Class-Directory, Prefix Database used by dsfmgr to create device special files. This is an ASCII file but should not be modified. The following information is contained in the file:

- The device category.
- The device name.
- The device type (block, character, rewind, norewind, sgeneric, storage, *).
- The subdirectory where the device special file is to be located.
- The device special file type (block or character).
- The file mode permission bits (in octal).
- The device prefix.
- The instance width (e.g., a cdrom device will always have at least one digit in the instance field: cdrom0).

Note that the kevm device instance width is zero and has a device name of only kevm, and a hardwired terminal with an instance width of two would be named tty00.

```
# more /etc/dccd.dat
  disk        cdrom       block    disk     b 600 cdrom    1
  disk        cdrom       char     rdisk    c 600 cdrom    1
...
  pseudo      kevm        *        .        c 600 kevm     0
...
  terminal    hardwired   *        .        c 666 tty      2
...
```

- dcdd.dat

The dcdd.dat file is the Device Class Directory Default Database. It is used by the dsfmgr command to create the device directories. This is an ASCII file and should not be modified. The file contains the directory location (local - /dev, or cluster - /devices), the directory mode permission bits (in octal), and the directory name.

```
# cat /etc/dcdd.dat
  l  0755  .
  l  0755  none
  c  0755  cport
  c  0755  disk
  c  0755  rdisk
  c  0755  tape
  c  0755  ntape
  c  0755  changer
  c  0755  dmapi
```

- ddr.db

The Dynamic Device Recognition (DDR) database is used to describe SCSI CAM (common access method) device parameters and characteristics so that devices can be dynamically created. This is a data file and is created by ddr_config(8) using the ddr.dbase(4) file as input. See the ddr.dbase(4) reference page for more information.

- dec_devsw_db

This refers to the primary device switch table database file. It contains the device driver major numbers and device switch entries. This is a binary data file and is maintained by the kernel but can be viewed using the devswmgr(8) program.

- dec_hw_db

This binary file holds the hardware topology for the system. Contained within this file is the hardware persistence information for buses and controllers. The file is maintained by the kernel driver framework and can be modified and queried by the hwmgr command using the "name" subsystem. For example:

```
# hwmgr -show name

 HWID:  NAME     HOSTNAME          PERSIST TYPE     PERSIST AT
-------------------------------------------------------------------------------
   33:  ata0     sheridan          BUS              pci0 slot 13
   49:  isp0     sheridan          BUS              pci0 slot 15
   44:  itpsa1   sheridan          BUS              pci0 slot 14
   36:  itpsa0   sheridan          BUS              pci0 slot 15
   51:  mchan0   sheridan          CONTROLLER       pci0 slot 16
    5:  pci0     sheridan          BUS              nexus
   50:  scsi3    sheridan          CONTROLLER       isp0 slot 0
   37:  scsi2    sheridan          CONTROLLER       itpsa0 slot 0
   35:  scsi1    sheridan          CONTROLLER       ata0 slot 1
   34:  scsi0    sheridan          CONTROLLER       ata0 slot 0
   32:  tu1      sheridan          CONTROLLER       pci0 slot 11
   31:  tu0      sheridan          CONTROLLER       pci0 slot 9
```

- dec_hwc_cdb and dec_hwc_ldb

These are the hardware component database files. The "ldb" file is the local (or member-specific) database file for this system, while the "cdb" file is the common (or cluster-wide) database file. These databases contain information for all the registered hardware components for the system.

The "cdb" file contains storage devices and some of their information, like the WWID. This can be verified by typing the following command: "strings /etc/dec_hwc_cdb".

The "ldb" file contains information for the other hardware components (adapters, cpu, keyboard, mouse, etc.) as well as some storage device information (user_name, phys_location, etc.). Component information can be seen in the following example:

```
# hwmgr -show component

 HWID:  HOSTNAME   FLAGS SERVICE COMPONENT NAME
-----------------------------------------------
    1:  sheridan   ----- none    COMPAQ AlphaStation XP900 466 MHz
    2:  sheridan   r---- none    CPU0
    3:  sheridan   r-d-- none    scp
    4:  sheridan   r-d-- none    kevm
    5:  sheridan   r---- none    pci0
...
   53:  sheridan   -cds- iomap   SCSI-WWID:0c000008:0000-0e11-0019-9fbe
   54:  sheridan   -cds- iomap   SCSI-WWID:0c000008:0000-0e11-0019-9492
   55:  sheridan   -cds- iomap   SCSI-WWID:0c000008:0000-0e11-0018-ba75
   56:  sheridan   -cds- iomap   SCSI-WWID:0c000008:0000-0e11-0018-9f1f
   57:  sheridan   -cd-- iomap   SCSI-WWID:0c000008:0000-0e11-0018-9f33
   58:  sheridan   -cd-- iomap   SCSI-WWID:0c000008:0000-0e11-0018-9f1a
```

- dec_scsi_db

This file is owned by the SCSI/CAM subsystem and is used to store the WWIDs and track the SCSI devices that are known to the system. This binary data file is also used by the hwmgr command. For example:

```
# hwmgr -show scsi


       SCSI                 DEVICE     DEVICE  DRIVER NUM  DEVICE FIRST
 HWID: DEVICEID HOSTNAME    TYPE       SUBTYPE OWNER  PATH FILE   VALID PATH
--------------------------------------------------------------------------
    0: 0        sheridan    cdrom      none    0      1    (null)
   40: 1        sheridan    disk       none    2      1    dsk0   [2/0/0]
   41: 2        sheridan    disk       none    2      1    dsk1   [2/1/0]
   45: 3        sheridan    cdrom      none    0      1    cdrom0 [0/0/0]
   53: 4        sheridan    disk       none    0      1    dsk2   [3/0/0]
   54: 5        sheridan    disk       none    0      1    dsk3   [3/1/0]
   55: 6        sheridan    disk       none    0      1    dsk4   [3/2/0]
   56: 7        sheridan    disk       none    0      1    dsk5   [3/3/0]
   57: 8        sheridan    disk       none    0      1    dsk6   [3/4/0]
   58: 9        sheridan    disk       none    0      1    dsk7   [3/5/0]
```

- dcc_unid_db

This database contains unique IDs. According to the *Tru64* UNIX System Administration guide, "This is a binary database that stores the preceding highest hardware identifier (HWID) assigned to a hardware component. This database is used to generate the next HWID to be assigned to a newly-installed hardware component." There is other information contained in the file, as shown by the output from using the `strings(1)` command, which indicates that the file is used for unique IDs other than just the HWID, although that may be its most common function.

```
# strings /etc/dec_unid_db

DEC_UNID
hardware
dsf_group_id
cluster_minor
control_port_id
```

- `dfsc.dat` and `dfsl.dat`

The device file status data files are ASCII files that are maintained by the `dsfmgr` command. The `dfsl.dat` file is for both local (or member-specific) device special files status and the old device special files names. The `dfsc.dat` file contains the common (or cluster-wide) device special files status. The files are split into three sections:

1. Instance

   The instance record contains three fields:

   - Type
   - Base Name
   - Instance

   For instance (excuse the pun):

   ```
   "I: dsk 8"
   ```

2. Version

   This record looks like a comment, but it contains the version of the file format as well as the hostname and O/S version.

   ```
   "#  1.0    sheridan  V5.1 (Rev. 732)  Tue Mar 20 01:23:34 2001"
   ```

3. Status

   The status record currently contains 12 fields:

   - Status (`A`, `C`, or `d`)
   - Cluster Dev Major/Minor #
   - Basename ID
   - Device Type
   - (`block` or `character`)
   - Device Path
   - Device Instance
   - Local Dev Major/Minor #
   - Hardware ID
   - Device Node ID
   - Old Node Name
   - Device Prefix
   - Device Suffix

Here are a few examples:

The first example is from /etc/dfsc.dat and shows the "A" (active) status for a cluster device.

```
A:         0  1300041        45        10        0   b  ""          /dev/disk/ cdrom 0 a
```

The second example is also from /etc/dfsc.dat and shows the "d" (deactivated) status for a cluster device.

```
d:         0  1300043        45        10        1   b  ""          /dev/disk/ cdrom 0 b
```

The last example shows two entries from /etc/dfsl.dat illustrating the "C" (cluster) status for a local device.

```
C:  5500000  1300001        30         6        0   b  fd0a        ~ "" "" ""
C:  5500000  1300002        30         6        0   c  rfd0a       ~ "" "" ""
```

- gen_databases

This file contains the list of hardware databases, the files used by them, and (optionally) the database handler. This is an ASCII text file but should not be modified.

7.4 The Hardware Manager (hwmgr)

The hwmgr command is a new tool that is akin to "one-stop shopping" when it comes to hardware management. It replaces the scsimgr(8) utility and can perform many functions that the scu(8) utility does – although scu is not obsolete. The hwmgr command is cluster-aware, and many of its options can be directed on a specified member or on the entire cluster. The hwmgr command manages three hardware subsystems:

- component

  The component subsystem maintains information about all hardware components on the system. This information is stored in two databases: dec_hwc_ldb (local) and dec_hwc_cdb (cluster).

- name

  The name subsystem maintains hardware persistence information for hardware components such as buses and controllers. This information is stored in dec_hw_db.

- scsi

  The scsi subsystem maintains information about SCSI devices. This information is stored in dec_scsi_db.

For additional information on the various hardware databases, see section 7.3 earlier in this chapter.

The absolute best information regarding the hwmgr command, as of this writing, is the hwmgr command itself.

```
# hwmgr -help | grep -E "^Usage|^ *or"

Usage: hwmgr -flash light
   or: hwmgr -get attribute [ saved | default | current ]
   or: hwmgr -get category
   or: hwmgr -help [ <command> ] [ <subsystem> ]
   or: hwmgr -set attribute [ saved | current ] -a <attribute>=<value>
   or: hwmgr -view cluster
   or: hwmgr -view devices
   or: hwmgr -view hierarchy
   or: hwmgr -view env
   or: hwmgr -view timestamps
   or: hwmgr -view transaction
   or: hwmgr <command> <subsystem> <args>
```

We only included the basic command usage using the grep(1) command, although the last hwmgr command usage, "or: hwmgr <command> <subsystem> <args>", actually has many permutations.

```
# hwmgr -help | grep -p -E "(^Where <command>)"

Where <command> is:
        -add
        -delete
        -edit
        -locate
        -online
        -offline
        -power
        -redirect
        -refresh
        -reload
        -remove
        -scan
        -show
        -status
        -unconfigure
        -unindict
        -unload
```

We will not attempt to show you every possible option to the hwmgr command but will focus instead on a few of the more useful options.

For further information see the hwmgr(8) reference page on V5.0A and V5.1. In V5.1A the hwmgr(8) reference page is augmented by four additional reference pages:

- hwmgr_get(8) – reference page for the get and set command options.
- hwmgr_show(8) – reference page for the show commands options.
- hwmgr_view(8) – reference page for the view commands options.
- hwmgr_ops(8) – reference page for the other commands options: add, delete, edit, locate, offline, online, power, redirect, refresh, reload, remove, scan, status, unconfigure, unindict, unload.

7.4.1 How Can I Show Devices on the System?

```
# hwmgr -view devices
 HWID: Device Name            Mfg      Model            Location
 ----------------------------------------------------------------------------
    4: /dev/kevm
   30: /dev/disk/floppy0c              3.5in floppy     fdi0-unit-0
   40: /dev/disk/dsk0c        COMPAQ   BB009235B6       bus-2-targ-0-lun-0
   41: /dev/disk/dsk1c        COMPAQ   BB009235B6       bus-2-targ-1-lun-0
   45: /dev/disk/cdrom0c      COMPAQ   CRD-8402B        bus-0-targ-0-lun-0
```

NOTE:

The hwmgr command options can be abbreviated to uniqueness. For example:

```
# hwmgr -view devices
```

This can be abbreviated to:

```
# hwmgr -v d
```

Also, note that the main keyword does not require a hyphen (-) although subsequent options do. For example, "view" is equivalent to "-view", the "-dsf" option must contain a "-".

```
# hwmgr view device -dsf dsk3
```

You can just show specific devices too. For example, let's search for only tape devices on a system:

```
# hwmgr -v d -category tape
 HWID: Device Name           Mfg       Model             Location
 ---------------------------------------------------------------------------
   75: /dev/ntape/tape0      COMPAQ    SDT-9000          bus-6-targ-0-lun-0
```

As stated earlier, many command options can be focused on a member or the entire cluster. How do you know which options can be focused on another member or the entire cluster? Ask `hwmgr`.

```
# hwmgr -help view dev
Usage: hwmgr -view devices
        [ -dsf <device-special-filename> ]
        [ -category <hardware-category>  ]
        [ -member <cluster-member-name>  ]
        [ -cluster ]
```

Another way to show devices using `hwmgr` is to look at the `scsi` subsystem.

```
# hwmgr -show scsi

        SCSI                    DEVICE    DEVICE  DRIVER NUM  DEVICE FIRST
 HWID:  DEVICEID HOSTNAME       TYPE      SUBTYPE OWNER  PATH FILE   VALID PATH
-------------------------------------------------------------------------
    0:  0        sheridan       cdrom     none    0      1    (null)
   40:  1        sheridan       disk      none    2      1    dsk0   [2/0/0]
   41:  2        sheridan       disk      none    2      1    dsk1   [2/1/0]
   45:  3        sheridan       cdrom     none    0      1    cdrom0 [0/0/0]
   53:  4        sheridan       disk      none    0      1    (null)
   54:  5        sheridan       disk      none    0      1    (null)
   55:  6        sheridan       disk      none    0      1    (null)
   56:  7        sheridan       disk      none    0      1    (null)
   57:  8        sheridan       disk      none    0      1    (null)
   59:  9        sheridan       disk      none    0      1    (null)
```

Notice the "`(null)`" in the output above. This indicates that there is no active path to some of the devices that were previously seen by the system. In this particular instance, the storage cabinet is not powered on. Let's give the storage some juice and rerun the command. First, let's scan the bus.

```
# hwmgr -scan scsi
hwmgr: Scan request successfully initiated
```

Now, let's see what has changed.

```
# hwmgr -show scsi

        SCSI                DEVICE    DEVICE  DRIVER NUM  DEVICE FIRST
 HWID:  DEVICEID HOSTNAME   TYPE      SUBTYPE OWNER  PATH FILE   VALID PATH
-------------------------------------------------------------------------
    0:  0        sheridan   cdrom     none    0      1    (null)
   40:  1        sheridan   disk      none    2      1    dsk0   [2/0/0]
   41:  2        sheridan   disk      none    2      1    dsk1   [2/1/0]
   45:  3        sheridan   cdrom     none    0      1    cdrom0 [0/0/0]
   53:  4        sheridan   disk      none    0      1    dsk2   [3/0/0]
   54:  5        sheridan   disk      none    0      1    (null) [3/1/0]
   55:  6        sheridan   disk      none    0      1    (null) [3/2/0]
   56:  7        sheridan   disk      none    0      1    (null) [3/3/0]
   57:  8        sheridan   disk      none    0      1    (null) [3/4/0]
   59:  9        sheridan   disk      none    0      1    (null) [3/5/0]
```

Notice that we now see an active path but still do not see a device name. This is where we can have the `dsfmgr` command give us a hand. The `dsfmgr` command with the "`-K`" option creates all newly detected devices. Note: this additional step should be unnecessary (and is unnecessary in V5.1A). In V5.1 (where this example was created), however, it was necessary.

```
# dsfmgr -K
```

Now rerun the original command.

```
# hwmgr -show scsi

        SCSI                DEVICE    DEVICE  DRIVER NUM  DEVICE FIRST
 HWID:  DEVICEID HOSTNAME   TYPE      SUBTYPE OWNER  PATH FILE   VALID PATH
-------------------------------------------------------------------------
    0:  0        sheridan   cdrom     none    0      1    (null)
   40:  1        sheridan   disk      none    2      1    dsk0   [2/0/0]
   41:  2        sheridan   disk      none    2      1    dsk1   [2/1/0]
   45:  3        sheridan   cdrom     none    0      1    cdrom0 [0/0/0]
   53:  4        sheridan   disk      none    0      1    dsk2   [3/0/0]
   54:  5        sheridan   disk      none    0      1    dsk3   [3/1/0]
   55:  6        sheridan   disk      none    0      1    dsk4   [3/2/0]
   56:  7        sheridan   disk      none    0      1    dsk5   [3/3/0]
   57:  8        sheridan   disk      none    0      1    dsk6   [3/4/0]
   59:  9        sheridan   disk      none    0      1    dsk7   [3/5/0]
```

Notice that the "`-view devices`" option to the `hwmgr` command (abbreviated to "`-v d`") now sees the devices as well.

```
# hwmgr -v d
HWID: Device Name              Mfg       Model              Location
-------------------------------------------------------------------------------
   4: /dev/kevm
  30: /dev/disk/floppy0c                 3.5in floppy       fdi0-unit-0
  40: /dev/disk/dsk0c          COMPAQ    BB009235B6         bus-2-targ-0-lun-0
  41: /dev/disk/dsk1c          COMPAQ    BB009235B6         bus-2-targ-1-lun-0
  45: /dev/disk/cdrom0c        COMPAQ    CRD-8402B          bus-0-targ-0-lun-0
  53: /dev/disk/dsk2c          COMPAQ    BD009635C3         bus-3-targ-0-lun-0
  54: /dev/disk/dsk3c          COMPAQ    BD009635C3         bus-3-targ-1-lun-0
  55: /dev/disk/dsk4c          COMPAQ    BD009635C3         bus-3-targ-2-lun-0
  56: /dev/disk/dsk5c          COMPAQ    BD009635C3         bus-3-targ-3-lun-0
  57: /dev/disk/dsk6c          COMPAQ    BD009635C3         bus-3-targ-4-lun-0
  59: /dev/disk/dsk7c          COMPAQ    BD009635C3         bus-3-targ-5-lun-0
```

Let's get back to the "`-show scsi`" option for a moment. If the system contains multiple paths to a device, adding an additional qualifier to the command "`-full`" will show the paths to you. Although it is not necessary, it is often cleaner if you only look at one device at a time. For example:

```
# hwmgr -show scsi -full -id 65

        SCSI                  DEVICE    DEVICE  DRIVER NUM  DEVICE FIRST
 HWID:  DEVICEID HOSTNAME     TYPE      SUBTYPE OWNER  PATH FILE   VALID PATH
-------------------------------------------------------------------------
   65:  6        jaffa        disk      none    0      4    dsk5   [5/0/9]

      WWID:01000010:6060-1aa1-000f-1a40-0009-0361-3888-0007

      BUS   TARGET  LUN   PATH STATE
      ------------------------------
      5     0       9     valid
      5     1       9     valid
      6     0       9     valid
      6     1       9     valid
```

Note the output from the last command was taken from a different system that contained a multi-path/multi-bus configuration. As you can see, there are actually four paths to the device. This system has two adapters connected to two Fibre Channel switches, each connected to two Fibre Channel RAID controllers (with dual ports) – in other words, "No Single Point of Failure" (NSPOF).

7.4.2 How Can I See All the Hardware on My System?

```
# hwmgr -view hierarchy

HWID:  hardware component hierarchy
-------------------------------------------------------
  46:  platform COMPAQ AlphaServer DS10 466 MHz
   2:    cpu CPU0
   5:    bus pci0
   6:      connection pci0slot7
  18:        bus isa0
  19:          connection isa0slot0
  20:            keyboard keyboard0
  21:            pointer mouse0
  22:          connection isa0slot2
  23:            serial_port tty00
  24:          connection isa0slot3
  25:            serial_port tty01
  26:          connection isa0slot4
  27:            parallel_port lp0
  28:          connection isa0slot5
  29:            fdi_controller fdi0
  30:              disk fdi0-unit-0 floppy0
   8:      connection pci0slot9
  31:        network tu0
  10:      connection pci0slot11
  32:        network tu1
  12:      connection pci0slot13
  33:        ide_adapter ata0
  34:          scsi_bus scsi0
  45:            disk bus-0-targ-0-lun-0 cdrom0
  35:          scsi_bus scsi1
  42:      connection pci0slot14
  44:        scsi_adapter itpsa1
  37:          scsi_bus scsi2
  40:            disk bus-2-targ-0-lun-0 dsk0
  41:            disk bus-2-targ-1-lun-0 dsk1
  14:      connection pci0slot15
  49:        scsi_adapter isp0
  50:          scsi_bus scsi3
  53:            disk BA356 Slot 1 (top) cluster-common
  54:            disk BA356 Slot 2 sheridan boot
  55:            disk BA356 Slot 3 molari boot
  56:            disk BA356 Slot 4 quorum
  57:            disk bus-3-targ-4-lun-0 dsk6
  59:            disk bus-3-targ-5-lun-0 dsk7
  47:      connection pci0slot16
  51:        cluster_interconnect mchan0
  52:        legacy_driver Legacy-driver-(mchan0)
  16:      connection pci0slot17
  38:        graphics_controller comet0
```

7.4.3 How Can I Remove a Broken Component?

Identify the bad component, such as a bad disk.

```
# hwmgr -show scsi

        SCSI                  DEVICE    DEVICE  DRIVER NUM  DEVICE FIRST
 HWID:  DEVICEID HOSTNAME   TYPE      SUBTYPE OWNER  PATH FILE   VALID PATH
---------------------------------------------------------------------------
...
   56:  7        sheridan   disk      none    0      1    (null)
...
```

Delete the component.

```
# hwmgr -delete component -id 56
hwmgr: Delete operation was successful
```

7.4.4 How Can I See Newly Added Devices?

If you have added a device while the system was up, you will need to `scan` the bus.

```
# hwmgr -scan scsi
hwmgr: Scan request successfully initiated
```

NOTE:

In a cluster environment, the "`hwmgr -scan scsi`" command will need to be performed cluster-wide. There is not a "`-cluster`" option to the command. There is, however, a "`-member`" option that can be used to direct the command to a specific member. We have written a script (`clu_scan_scsi`) to dispatch `hwmgr` commands to all cluster members.

```
# ./clu_scan_scsi

molari: "/sbin/hwmgr scan scsi"
  hwmgr: Scan request successfully initiated

sheridan: "/sbin/hwmgr scan scsi"
  hwmgr: Scan request successfully initiated
```

The `clu_scan_scsi` script is available on the web (see Appendix B for the URL).

7.4.5 How Can I See All the Information for a Specific Component?

```
# hwmgr -get attribute -id 46
46:
  name = COMPAQ AlphaServer DS10 466 MHz
  category = platform
  memory_size_MB = 256
  registration_time = Tue Mar 20 12:39:23 2001
  user_name = (null) (settable)
  location = (null) (settable)
  software_module = (null)
  state = available
  state_previous = unknown
  state_change_time = none
  event_count = 0
  last_event_time = none
```

7.4.6 How Can I See Only a Few Attributes for Some Components?

You can see as little as one attribute by specifying that particular attribute with the "`-a attribute`" option.

```
# hwmgr -get attribute -a dev_base_name -id 59
59:
  dev_base_name = dsk7
```

Here is an example showing several attributes, including searching for an attribute NOT containing a certain value.

```
# hwmgr get a -a name -a dev_base_name -a power_mgmt_capable!=1
2:
  name = CPU0
  power_mgmt_capable = 0
30:
  name = FDI-fdi0-unit-0
  dev_base_name = floppy0
  power_mgmt_capable = 0
45:
  name = SCSI-WWID:0710002c:"COMPAQ  CRD-8402B       :d05b000t00000100000"
  dev_base_name = cdrom0
  power_mgmt_capable = 0
```

Here is a similar example where we are searching for an attribute that contains a particular value. We are also limiting our search to the "`disk`" category.

```
# hwmgr -get a -a dev_base_name -a cluster_disables=1 -cat disk

45:
  dev_base_name = cdrom0
  cluster_disables = 1
```

Note that some of the conditional parsing does not work as expected. For example, the component at `HWID 40` has "`COMPAQ`" listed as the manufacturer.

```
# hwmgr -get a -a manufacturer -id 40

40:
  manufacturer = COMPAQ
```

Yet, when we specifically state "`manufacturer!=COMPAQ`", we get the opposite of what we would expect.

```
# hwmgr -get a -a manufacturer!=COMPAQ

40:
  manufacturer = COMPAQ
...
```

If we look for "`manufacturer=COMPAQ`", we do not see any output.

```
# hwmgr -get a -a manufacturer=COMPAQ

<no output>
```

We considered that it might be a string parsing problem, but:

```
# hwmgr -get a -a dev_base_name -a state=available -cat disk

30:
  dev_base_name = floppy0
  state = available
40:
  dev_base_name = dsk0
  state = available
...
```

This appears to be a bug, and we have notified COMPAQ's Customer Support Center.

7.4.7 How Can I Set the "settable" Attributes for a Component?

Some components have user settable attributes like a name (user_name) or physical location (phys_location). In large configuration, the ability to give a device a name that is meaningful to you, such as "my boot disk" or its location, can be very useful. First, let's find the "settable" attributes for a particular device.

```
# hwmgr -get attr -id 46 | grep "(settable)"
  user_name = (null) (settable)
  location = (null) (settable)
```

What device is this?

```
# hwmgr -get attr -id 46 -a name
46:
  name = COMPAQ AlphaServer DS10 466 MHz
```

It's the system. Well, let's set the "user_name" to the system's hostname. Note that the "user_name" attribute is currently limited to fifteen characters. For example:

```
# hostname | wc -c
17
```

Notice that the fully qualified hostname of this system is sixteen characters ("wc -c" returns an extra character, probably the newline character). So let's try to set the attribute with more than fifteen characters.

```
# hwmgr -set attr -a user_name=$(hostname) -id 46
hwmgr:  46: Attribute "user_name" value is too large.
```

Now let's set the "user_name" attribute by using only the base hostname.

```
# hwmgr -set attr -a user_name=$(hostname -s) -id 46
46:
  user_name = sheridan (settable)
```

Verify that the change has taken place.

```
# hwmgr -get attr -id 46 -a name -a user_name

46:
  name = COMPAQ AlphaServer DS10 466 MHz
  user_name = sheridan (settable)
```

7.4.8 How Can I Find a Device?

If you happen to have a large cabinet with a bunch of disks in it, wouldn't it be nice to be able to find the device you are looking for quickly? Well, it can be. Try this:

```
# hwmgr -flash light -dsf dsk3
```

Although this only works on SCSI disks, most disks are currently still SCSI, so for the immediate future, this is a useful command. By the way, if the flashing is too slow or fast due to other disk activity in the cabinet, try the "`-nopause`" option.

7.4.9 How Can I Find a Device with Inconsistent Data?

You can use the "`hwmgr show component`" command with the "`-inconsistencies`" command to locate software inconsistencies in the hardware component database files. An "inconsistency" is a possible internal error in the `dec_hwc_cdb` and `dec_hwc_ldb` files.

```
# hwmgr show comp -i

 HWID:  HOSTNAME   FLAGS SERVICE COMPONENT NAME
-----------------------------------------------
  106:  molari     rcd-i iomap   SCSI-WWID:0c000008:0000-0e11-0018-9f1f
```

You can obtain additional information by adding the "`-full`" option.

7.5 The Device Special File Manager (dsfmgr)

7.5.1 The `dsfmgr(8)` Command

The `dsfmgr` command is used to manage device special files using the new naming convention defined in *Tru64* UNIX version 5.0. The following database files are used by `dsfmgr`:

- dccd.dat
- dcdd.dat
- dfsl.dat
- dfsc.dat

We will not attempt to show every permutation of every command option but instead will concentrate on the most useful options.

7.5.1.1 How Can I See Device Special File Information for My System?

Show information on device special files for the system (output not shown).

```
# dsfmgr -s
```

7.5.1.2 How Can I Create a Device Special File for a Newly Added Device?

Create the device special file for a newly added device (output not shown).

```
# dsfmgr -k
```

7.5.1.3 How Can I Rename a Device Special File?

Rename a device special file to a non-existent instance.

```
# ls /dev/disk/dsk9
ls: /dev/disk/dsk9* not found
```

```
# dsfmgr -m dsk7 dsk9
  dsk7a=>dsk9a  dsk7b=>dsk9b  dsk7c=>dsk9c  dsk7d=>dsk9d  dsk7e=>dsk9e  dsk7f=>d
sk9f  dsk7g=>dsk9g  dsk7h=>dsk9h  dsk7a=>dsk9a  dsk7b=>dsk9b  dsk7c=>dsk9c  dsk7
d=>dsk9d  dsk7e=>dsk9e  dsk7f=>dsk9f  dsk7g=>dsk9g  dsk7h=>dsk9h
```

7.5.1.4 How Do I Fix a "second device status is active" Error?

Occasionally when you replace a device, the dfsl.dat and dfsc.dat files need to be updated; otherwise, when you attempt to rename the new device back to the old device special file, you will see the following:

```
# dsfmgr -m dsk7 dsk9
dsfmgr: ERROR: second device status is active: dsk9a
```

First, you will need to identify which HWID is associated with dsk9. You will probably already know which it is, because you probably deleted the component when you replaced the device. If you do not know the HWID, however, you can still find it by searching the dfsc.dat file.

```
# grep "dsk 9 a" /etc/dfsc.dat
A:       0  13000b1      59       17       0   b  ""          /dev/disk/ dsk 9 a
A:       0  13000b2      59       17       0   c  ""          /dev/rdisk/ dsk 9 a
```

Or try:

```
# awk '/dsk 9 / { print $4 }' < /etc/dfsc.dat | uniq
59
```

We printed for the 4th field because it is HWID (see section 7.3). Also, be very careful with the search string; make sure the pattern is: /dsk<space><instance number><space>/

The <space> characters are very important.

The HWID is 59, and this is the one we need to remove from the files. Now that we have the HWID, we can remove it from the dfsl.dat and dfsc.dat files. We will do this using an undocumented switch "-Z" to the dsfmgr command.

```
# dsfmgr -Z rm_hwid 59 0
 -dsk9a -dsk9b -dsk9c -dsk9d -dsk9e -dsk9f -dsk9g -dsk9h -dsk9a -dsk9b -dsk9c -dsk9d
-dsk9e -dsk9f -dsk9g -dsk9h
```

This will remove the HWID entries from the dfsc.dat and dfsl.dat database files. Alternatively, if you need to remove entries from only one file, you can use the "rm_local_hwid" flag to remove the HWID from the dfsl.dat file or the "rm_cluster_hwid" flag to remove the HWID from the dfsc.dat file.

At this point, the "dsfmgr -m" command should work.

NOTE:

In V5.1A, a new option "-R" has been added to the dsfmgr command that **is** documented and can be used to remove the HWID entries from the dfsc.dat and dfsl.dat database files. The "-R" option takes two parameters:

- Where to remove the HWID
  - cluster_hwid – remove the HWID from dfsc.dat
  - local_hwid – remove the HWID from dfsl.dat
  - hwid – remove the HWID from all locations
- The HWID

```
# dsfmgr -R hwid 59
 -dsk9a -dsk9b -dsk9c -dsk9d -dsk9e -dsk9f -dsk9g -dsk9h -dsk9a -dsk9b -dsk9c -
dsk9d -dsk9e -dsk9f -dsk9g -dsk9h
```

For additional information, see the dsfmgr(8) reference page for V5.1A.

7.5.1.5 How Can I Exchange a Device Special File with Another Device Special File?

Exchange two device special file instances.

```
# dsfmgr -e dsk6 dsk7
  dsk6a<==>dsk7a  dsk6b<==>dsk7b  dsk6c<==>dsk7c  dsk6d<==>dsk7d  dsk6e<==>dsk7e
  dsk6f<==>dsk7f  dsk6g<==>dsk7g  dsk6h<==>dsk7h  dsk6a<==>dsk7a  dsk6b<==>dsk7b
  dsk6c<==>dsk7c  dsk6d<==>dsk7d  dsk6e<==>dsk7e  dsk6f<==>dsk7f  dsk6g<==>dsk7g
  dsk6h<==>dsk7h
```

7.5.1.6 How Do I Fix a "Device record not found in status database" Error?

This problem is similar to the "second device status is active" error but occurs when using the "dsfmgr -e" command.

The error will look like this:

```
# dsfmgr -e dsk7 dsk9
dsfmgr: ERROR: find device node dsk9   : Device record not found in status database
dsfmgr: ERROR exchange failed: Device record not found in status database
```

Follow the "How Do I Fix a "second device status is active" Error?" procedure (section 7.5.1.4) to resolve the problem.

7.5.1.7 How Can I Verify that My Device Special File Databases are Error Free?

```
# dsfmgr -v
dsfmgr: verify all datum for system at /

Default File Tree:
    OK.

Device Class Directory Default Database:
    OK.

Device Category to Class Directory Database:
    OK.

Dev directory structure:
    OK.

Device Status Files:
    OK.

Dev Nodes:
    OK.
```

7.5.1.8 How Can I Repair Errors in My Device Special File Databases?

Fix database errors or inconsistencies (output not shown). Note this may need to be run a few times to correct errors.

```
# dfsmgr -vF
```

NOTE:

The "-o" and "-O" options are used to create the pre-V5 device names that are not supported in a *TruCluster* Server environment.

For more information, see the dsfmgr(8) reference page as well as the *Tru64* UNIX System Administration guide.

7.5.2 The dn_setup Command

The dn_setup command uses dsfmgr to create device special files for the system. This command is run every time the system is rebooted. The dn_setup command can also be used to recreate the devices in /dev and /devices.

To create a tape device when booting from the installation CD to restore the operating system, you can use dn_setup with the "-install_tape" switch. As a general rule, dn_setup should not be used except in those situations where the devices and device databases reach a state where no other command (dsfmgr or hwmgr) can clear things up.

Caution should be taken whenever using the dn_setup command with the "-init" or "-clean" options, especially if you are using LSM, because dn_setup will not recreate the LSM devices. See Chapter 14 ("Cluster Logical Storage Manager") for a detailed discussion.

7.5.2.1 How Can I Reinitialize My /dev and /devices Directories?

```
# dn_setup -init
```

After executing this command, it is important to run "dsfmgr -K" immediately afterward. Furthermore, if you are using LSM, you must also run the following commands:

If the system is in multi-user mode (or in single-user mode with /usr mounted):

```
# /usr/sbin/volinstall update
# /sbin/voldctl enable
```

If the system is in single-user mode and /usr cannot be mounted (likely because /usr is encapsulated within LSM):

```
# mknod /dev/volconfig c 41 0
# mknod /dev/voltrace c 41 1
# mknod /dev/voliod c 41 2
# mknod /dev/volinfo c 41 3
# bcheckrc
```

These additional steps are necessary when using LSM because "dn_setup -init" completely deletes the /devices directory as well as the contents of /dev, and dn_setup does not know about LSM. We'll cover LSM in greater detail in Chapter 14.

7.5.2.2 How Can I Check My Device Special Files and Directory Hierarchy for Inconsistencies?

```
# dn_setup -sanity_check
    Passed.
```

Note that this is effectively the same as running "dsfmgr -zx", although the "-z" switch is undocumented.

7.5.2.3 How Can I Create a Tape Device Special File from the Installation CD?

```
# dn_setup -install_tape
```

As of this writing, there is no reference page for the dn_setup command. However, it is documented in the *Tru64* UNIX System Administration manual prior to version 5.1B and the *Tru64* UNIX Hardware Management manual as of version 5.1B.

7.6 References

- *Tru64* UNIX System Administration – versions 5.1, 5.1A, and 5.1B.
- *Tru64* UNIX Hardware Management – version 5.1B.
- Reference pages (noted within the text).

8

Tru64 UNIX Cluster Hooks: Event Manager

The Event Manager (EVM) is a new component added to *Tru64* UNIX in the version 5.0 release of the operating system in response to customer requests to have common access to all system (and cluster) event information.

In previous releases, events that occurred on the system would likely be logged to one of two main loggers: the System Message Logger (`syslogd`) and the Binary Error Logger (`binlogd`) – although other logging methods could also be used. EVM works in cooperation with these other event loggers to consolidate information. Figure 8-1 illustrates the event path to EVM.

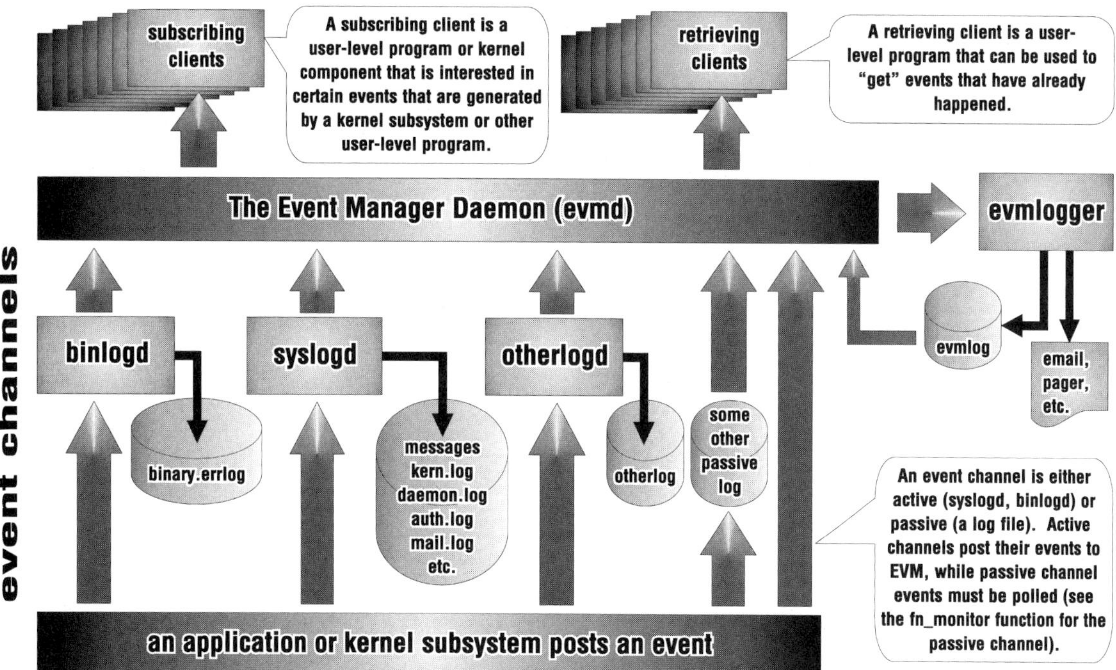

Figure 8-1: EVM Event Path

1. An application or kernel subsystem generates an event.
2. That event may be sent to one of the legacy *Tru64* UNIX loggers, another logger or a log file, or posted directly to EVM.
3. Once the EVM daemon (`evmd`) receives the event, it sends the event to any program or kernel component that takes out an EVM subscription to that event.

Think of EVM as a publishing company or a favorite bookstore, events as magazines, and applications as subscribers. You (or your application in this case) subscribe to only those magazines (or events) that are of interest. Every time there is a new issue (or event), it is delivered to you. The same thing happens here. EVM receives the event and sends it to the subscribers. On occasion, you may go to the bookstore to pick up some magazines. You can get events from EVM in much the same way, using the `evmget(1)` program.

You can even wait for events to occur using the `evmwatch(1)` program (kind of like waiting in line all night to get concert tickets – except without the lawn chair).

8.1 What is an Event Anyway?

An event is something of interest that occurs on the system or cluster. "Of interest to whom?" you might ask. Anyone, from the engineers who wrote the *Tru64* UNIX and *TruCluster* Server products to everyday users, might have an interest in at least some of the events that EVM handles and dispatches. But EVM is not used for human interest alone. In fact, many applications use EVM to wait for events to occur and then act upon the information received. An event might be:

- A system timestamp.
- A task completed successfully.
- A disk error occurred.
- An application started.
- A file system was mounted.
- A system panic.

Let's see where events are defined and how to define our own.

8.2 EVM Components

EVM components are located in the root (/), `/usr`, and `/var` directory trees. The root (/) tree (shown in Figure 8-2) contains the EVM configuration files (in `/etc`), the `init` startup script (in `/sbin/init.d`), the kernel EVM device special files (in `/dev`), and the EVM API shared library (not shown). The `/usr` directory tree (shown in Figure 8-3) contains the EVM CLI and GUI programs, the resident components, the EVM filters, templates, and channel service routines, as well as a slew of other files (reference pages, examples, the static EVM API libraries, etc.) that are not shown. The `/var` tree (Figure 8-4) contains the logs, sockets, and site-defined filters, template, and channel service routines directory hierarchy.

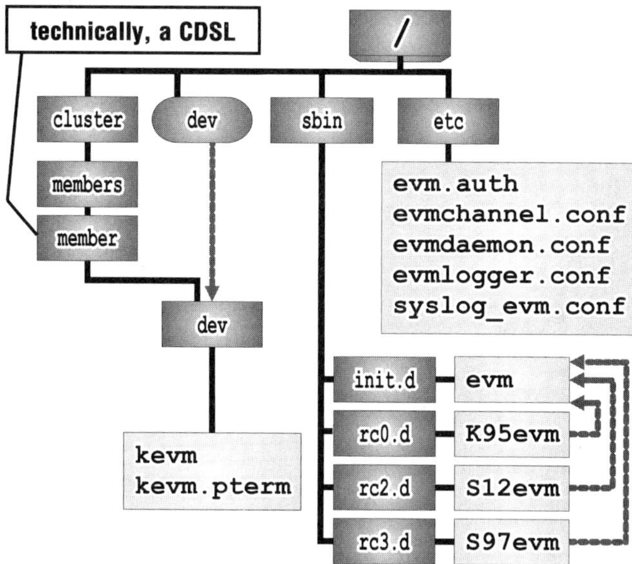

Figure 8-2: EVM root directory hierarchy

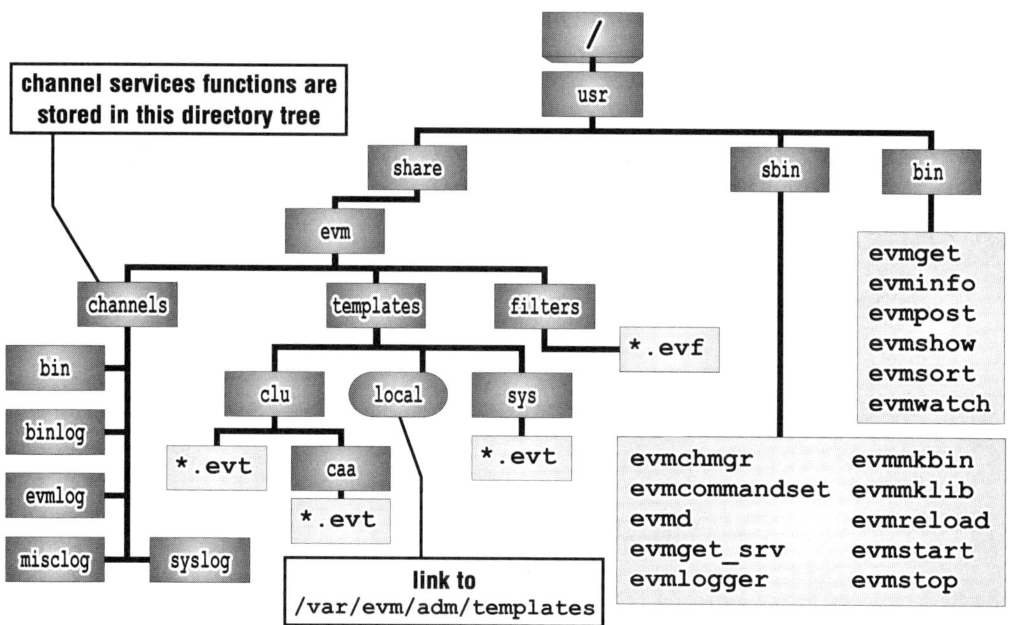

Figure 8-3: EVM /usr directory hierarchy

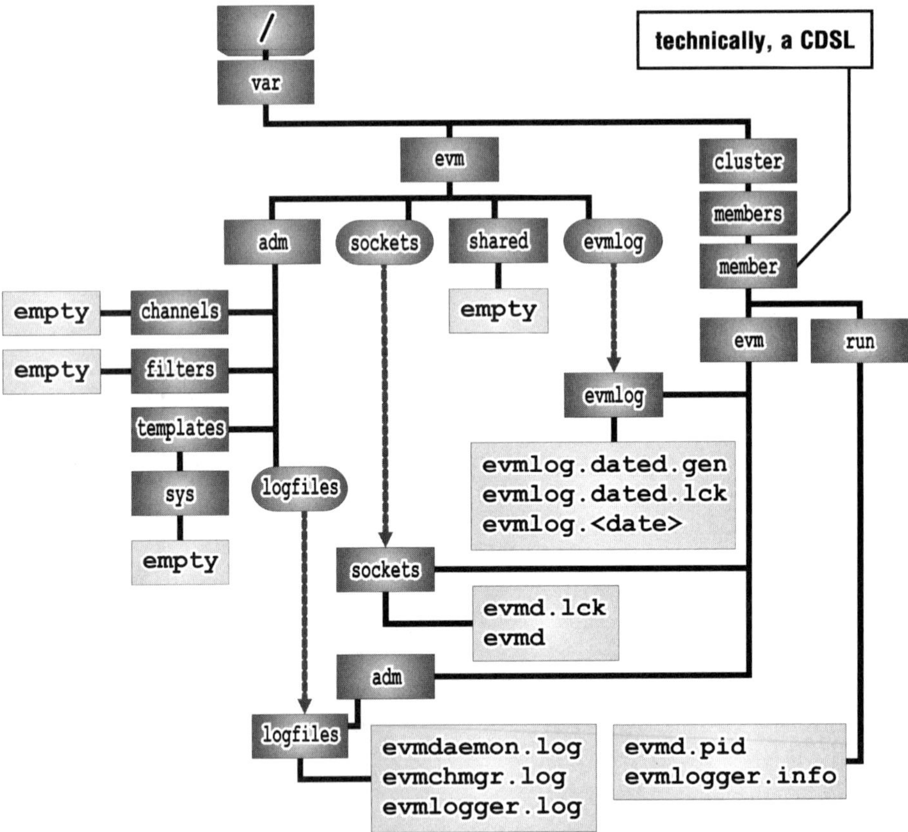

Figure 8-4: EVM /var directory hierarchy

8.2.1 EVM Resident Components

EVM has three primary components for event management:

- `evmd`
- `evmchmgr`
- `evmlogger`

8.2.1.1 The EVM Daemon (`evmd`)

The EVM daemon is the main distribution hub for EVM. It is started during system initialization at runlevel 2, although it cannot access remote connections until runlevel 3. Communication to `evmd` is handled via socket connections. Posting and subscription requests are handled directly by `evmd`.

However, event retrieval is handled by forking an `event_get` service program (actually, `/usr/sbin/evmget_srv`. See `/etc/evmdaemon.conf`).

The EVM daemon starts both the Channel Manager and the Logger processes as defined in the `/etc/evmdaemon.conf` file. In fact, it can be configured to start any site-defined synchronizing client process as well.

For more information, see the `evmd(8)` and the `evmdaemon.conf(4)` reference pages.

8.2.1.2 The EVM Channel Manager (**evmchmgr**)

The channel manager is responsible for the monitoring and cleanup of channels defined in the `/etc/evmchannel.conf` file, provided they have a monitor (`fn_monitor`) or cleanup (`fn_cleanup`) service routine defined. The channel manager is started automatically by the `evmd` daemon and should not be run as a standalone program.

By default, `evmchmgr` will write any error output to `stderr`.

For additional information, see the `evmchmgr(8)` and the `evmchannel.conf(4)` reference pages.

8.2.1.3 The EVM Logger (evmlogger)

The logger program is a subscriber of EVM events as defined in the `/etc/evmlogger.conf` file. This daemon subscribes to events and then writes them to an `eventlog` (such as `/var/adm/evmlog/evmlog.dated`) or forwards them using a `forward` command (such as sending email to the `root` account). The logger is started automatically by the `evmd` daemon but can be run as a standalone program by creating a configuration file and starting an `evmlogger` process with the "`-c`" switch. For example:

```
# evmlogger -c $HOME/evm/myEVMlogger.conf
```

By default, the `evmlogger` will write any error output to `stderr`.

For additional information, see the `evmlogger(8)` and the `evmlogger.conf(4)` reference pages.

8.2.2 EVM Configuration Files

The EVM configuration files are located in the /etc directory. We have already mentioned a few configuration files in the previous section: here we show them again along with additional files not mentioned earlier:

- evm.auth

  The evm.auth file is the event authorization file. It defines who can post or access events and service routines. See section 8.6.1or the evm.auth(4) reference page for more information.

- evmchannel.conf

  The evmchannel.conf file is where EVM channels and their functions are configured. This file is read by evmchmgr (see section 8.2.1.2). Table 8-1 shows the services that can be defined for each channel.

  For more information, see the evmchannel.conf(4) reference page.

- evmdaemon.conf

  The evmdaemon.conf file is the configuration file for evmd. Among other things, this file tells the evmd daemon to start the evmchmgr and evmlogger processes, which event_get service program to use, and whether to accept remote connections.

  For more information, see the evmdaemon.conf(4) reference page.

- evmlogger.conf

  The evmlogger.conf file is used to configure the evmlogger (see section 8.2.1.3). For more information, see the evmlogger.conf(4) reference page.

- syslog_evm.conf

  The syslog_evm.conf configuration file is used by the syslogd daemon to define what syslog events should be forwarded to the EVM daemon. See the syslog_evm.conf(4) reference page for additional information.

After making any changes to a configuration file, you need to tell EVM about the change by telling the EVM resident components (see section 8.2.1 for more information) to reload the configuration files.

Event Channel Services		
Function	**Keyword**	**Description**
Cleanup	`fn_cleanup`	This function is called daily by the **evmchmgr** daemon to archive and/or remove log files used by this channel.
Event Detail	`fn_details`	This function is called by "**evmshow -d**" to get a detailed view of the contents of the event from the channel.
Event Explanation	`fn_explain`	This function is called by "**evmshow -x**" to get an explanation of the event from the channel, and if appropriate, any necessary action.
Retrieval	`fn_get`	This function is called by the **evmget_srv** program to retrieve events from the channel. Note, this happens when you run the **evmget** command.
Monitor	`fn_monitor`	This function is called periodically by the **evmchmgr** daemon to check the status of the channel, and to post EVM events as necessary. Monitor functions are usually defined for passive event channels.

Table 8-1: EVM Channel Services

To reconfigure all the EVM resident components:

```
# evmreload
```

To reconfigure only the EVM daemon:

```
# evmreload -d
```

To reconfigure only the EVM channel manager process:

```
# evmreload -c
```

To reconfigure only the EVM logger process:

```
# evmreload -l
```

If you make changes to an event template, check the template syntax before reconfiguring the EVM daemon with the following command.

```
# evmreload -n
```

For more information, see the `evmreload(8)` reference page.

8.2.3 EVM Channels

A channel is a source for events. There are two types of channels:

- Active

  An example of an active channel is the syslogd daemon. The syslogd daemon receives events from an application or kernel subsystem and traditionally logged the event to one or more log files as defined in /etc/syslog.conf. The syslogd daemon has been modified to also act as a channel to EVM. Now, syslogd daemon receives an event, logs the event, and sends the event to the evmd daemon.

- Passive

  An example of a passive channel is a log file. The log file is not active in that it does not "actively" send events to the evmd daemon. However, if a subscribing client is looking for an event of the type defined by the event channel, then the evmget_svr program will retrieve the event from the log and pass it to the subscriber.

Channels are defined in the /etc/evmchannel.conf file; channel services are defined in the /usr/share/evm/channels/<channel> directory tree; channel filters are defined in /usr/share/evm/filters/<channel>.evf; and channel event templates are defined in /usr/share/evm/templates/sys/<channel>.evt. For example:

What channels are defined?

```
# /usr/bin/evminfo -lc

syslog
binlog
misclog
evmlog
```

Choose one of the channels. In this example, let's pick "binlog".

```
# ls /usr/share/evm/channels/binlog

binlog2evm       binlog_details  binlog_get
binlog_cleanup   binlog_explain  binlogshow
```

The channels directory contains the service routines for the binlog channel. We can verify this by referring back to the /etc/evmchannel.conf file.

```
# cat /etc/evmchannel.conf
...
# ===================================
# Event channel:  binary error log
# ===================================
channel {
        name            binlog
        path            /usr/share/evm/channels/binlog
        events          @SYS_VP@.binlog
        fn_get          "binlog_get -r 8d"
        fn_details      "binlog_details -decevent -ca localhost"
        fn_explain      "binlog_explain"
        fn_cleanup      "binlog_cleanup"
}
...
```

Before you ask, "What are those `binlog2evm` and `binlogshow` files?"…

```
# grep binlog2evm *
binlog_get:CONVTOOL=$DIR/binlog2evm                  # Converts binlog events to EVM
events
```

```
# grep binlogshow *
binlog_details:CONVTOOL=`${DIRNAME} $0`/binlogshow
```

Finally, filters and templates are defined in the `/usr/share/evm/filters/binlog.evf` and `/usr/share/evm/templates/sys/binlog.evt` files (see sections 8.2.4 and 8.2.5).

One final note on channels: if you plan to define your own channel, place the definition in `/etc/evmchannel.conf`, but place the supporting files in the `/var/evm/adm` directory tree instead of `/usr/share/evm`.

8.2.4 EVM Filter Files

EVM filter files are located in the `/usr/share/evm/filters` directory (site-defined filter files should be placed in the `/var/evm/adm/filters` directory). Filter files should end with the suffix "`.evf`".

See section 8.5 for additional information.

8.2.5 EVM Commands

Examples of using the EVM commands are in section 8.7, except for the `evmreload(8)` command, which was shown in section 8.2.2. EVM commands are shown in Table 8-2.

EVM Commands

Run?*	Command	Location	Man	Type	Description
✓	evmget	/usr/bin	1	binary	This program retrieves events from log files, and writes them to `stdout` in the form of binary EVM events.
✓	evminfo	/usr/bin	1	binary	This program provides information regarding the EVM subsystem. It also provides configuration file syntax verification.
✓	evmpost	/usr/bin	1	binary	This program allows posting of an event from the command line or script. It provides the ability for administrators and users to post quick (or simple) messages to EVM.
✓	evmshow	/usr/bin	1	binary	This program displays EVM events.
✓	evmsort	/usr/bin	1	binary	This program sorts EVM events.
✓	evmwatch	/usr/bin	1	binary	This program monitors the system or cluster for events to occur. It can also list the registered events that are known to the EVM subsystem.
✗	evmchmgr	/usr/sbin	8	binary	The evmchmgr program is the EVM channel manager. **DO NOT RUN THIS PROGRAM ON THE COMMAND LINE.**
✗	evmcommandset	/usr/sbin	-	sh	This shell script defines commands and their locations primarily for EVM's multi-platform implementation.
✗	evmd	/usr/sbin	8	binary	This program is the EVM daemon. **DO NOT RUN THIS PROGRAM ON THE COMMAND LINE.**
✗	evmget_srv	/usr/sbin	-	binary	The **`evmget_srv`** program is called by the **`evmd`** daemon when the **`evmget`** command requests retrieval of EVM events.
✓	evmlogger	/usr/sbin	8	binary	This program is the EVM logger.
✗	evmmkbin	/usr/sbin	-	binary	This program is used by the **`evmmklib`** command to compile the event templates into a binary format for the **`evmd`** daemon.
✗	evmmklib	/usr/sbin	-	sh	This script is used by **`evmd`** and the **`evmreload`** command to setup the environment for the **`evmmkbin`** program.
✓	evmreload	/usr/sbin	8	sh	This shell script posts an event to have the EVM daemons reread their configuration files. It also verifies the syntax of event template files and configuration files.
✓	evmstart	/usr/sbin	8	sh	This shell script starts the EVM daemon.
✗	evmstop	/usr/sbin	8	sh	This shell script stops the EVM daemon, although it should not be run under normal circumstances.

*The ✓ indicates that the program can be run. The ✗ indicates that the program **should not** be run.

Table 8-2: EVM Commands

8.2.6 EVM Template Files

EVM template files for *Tru64* UNIX are located in `/usr/share/evm/templates/sys` directory; *TruCluster* Server templates are located in `/usr/share/evm/templates/clu`; and site-defined template files should be placed in `/usr/share/evm/templates/local` (which is actually a link to `/var/evm/adm/templates`).

Template file names must end with the suffix "`.evt`", and the files must be owned by `root` or `bin` and must have permissions of `0400`, `0600`, `0440` or `0640` to be recognized. If the owner or permissions are incorrect, you may see a warning:

```
# evmreload
2001-03-26 05:04:04 evmmklib: Warning: /usr/share/evm/templates/local/tcrhb/tcrhb.evt ignored - incorrect owner or permissions
```

See section 8.4 for additional information.

8.2.7 EVM Graphical User Interface

The Event Viewer is the GUI for EVM. It is invoked via the `sysman` program.

```
# sysman event_viewer
```

Image 8-1 shows a screen shot of the Event Viewer from the curses interface, while Image 8-2 shows the CDE GUI. For additional information, see the `evmviewer(8)` reference page.

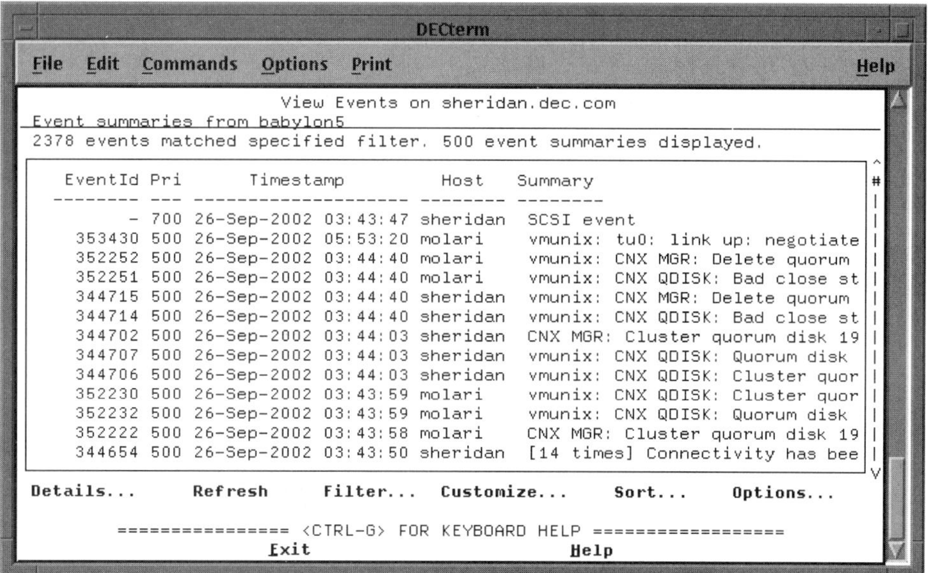

Image 8-1: EVM curses-style interface

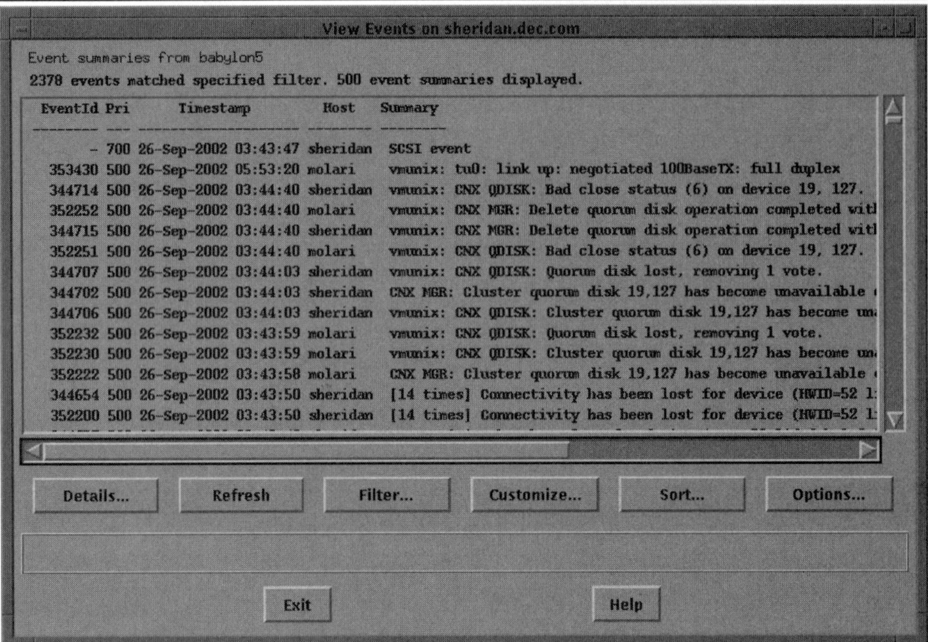

Image 8-2: EVM CDE GUI

8.3 EVM Priorities versus syslog and binlog Priorities

Event priorities are shown in Table 8-3. EVM priorities range from 0-700, with 700 intended to be the highest priority, whereas `syslog` priorities range from 7-0, with 0 (zero) being the highest. The `binlog` priority range, with only three effective priorities, is not nearly as granular.

Event Priorities			
Name	**EVM**	**syslog**	**binlog**
process-to-process	0	-	
debug	1 - 99	7	low (5)
information	100 - 199	6	
notice	200 - 299	5	
warning	300 - 399	4	high (3)
error	400 - 499	3	
critical	500 - 599	2	
alert	600 - 699	1	severe (1)
emergency	700	0	

Table 8-3: Event Priorities

The EVM priority of zero is reserved for events that are not to be viewed by anyone. These low priority events are useful for applications to communicate amongst themselves, such as a heartbeat event from another process to keep itself alive (as you will see in the NetRAIN Events section [chapter 9, section 9.2.3], all the registered events have a priority of zero). By default, events lower than a priority of 200 are not logged by the EVM logger.

The `EvmEvent(5)` reference page lists the EVM priorities and their intended use.

8.4 Event Templates

We have talked about what an event is and how events are handled but not how an event is defined. In order to post the event, the event has to be defined.

The events template files that are provided with *Tru64* UNIX and *TruCluster* Server have events grouped in a template file by the type of the event; for example, hardware network events are located in the `hw.net.evt` file, and AdvFS file system events are located in the `fs.advfs.evt` file.

A template file has the following format:

```
event {
       name           event_name
       format         format_specifier
       priority       priority
       cluster_event  true | false
       i18n_catalog   i18n_cat
       i18n_set_id    i18n_set
       i18n_msg_id    i18n_msg
       reference      reference_string
       var {
            name      variable_name
            type      variable_type
            value     variable_value
           }
       }
```

- `name`

  Every event must have a `name` attribute that consists of at least three components. Components are separated by a period (`.`). For example:

  `tcrhb.timeEvent.overdue`

- `format`

  The `format` attribute is the text of the event. For example:

  “`TCR Handbook: this book is overdue`”

- `priority`

  The `priority` is any value between 0 (zero) and 700. See the `EvmEvent(5)` reference page for the priority definitions.

- `cluster_event`

  The `cluster_event` attribute is used to define the scope of the event. If `cluster_event` is "`true`", then if this event occurs on any member in the cluster, every member in the cluster will see it. If `cluster_event` is "`false`", then only the member that generates the event will see the event. As you can see from the previous example, all events in the `hw.evt` template file default to a `cluster_event` value of "`true`".

- `i18n_catalog`, `i18n_set_id`, `i18n_msg_id`

  If you are using message catalogs, the "i18n" attributes can be used to index into the catalog message for the event text. See the `evmtemplate(5)` reference page for more information.

- `reference`

  This is a text string that is to be used by the event channel's explanation function. The string's format is defined by the event channel.

- `var`

  You can also pass variables to your event by defining a "`var`" block. The variable has three attributes: `name`, `type`, and `value`. The "name" attribute is the name of variable, and the "`type`" attribute can be any of several different types as defined in the `EvmEvent(5)` reference page. The type "`STRING`" is the default. The "`value`" attribute is the default value that you want the variable to have.

Here is a template for our fictional event that includes a variable:

```
event {
    name        tcrhb.timeEvent.overDue
    format      "TCR HB: this book is overdue.  $dueDate is the due date."
    priority    400
    var         {name dueDate  type STRING  value "Today"}
}
```

Type the event template into a file.

```
# cd /usr/share/evm/templates/local ; mkdir tcrhb ; cd tcrhb
```

```
# cat > tcrhb.evt
event {
    name        tcrhb.timeEvent.overDue
    format      "TCR HB: this book is overdue.  $dueDate is the due date."
    priority    400
    var         {name dueDate  type STRING  value "Today"}
}
^D
```

Set the owner and permissions.

```
# chown root tcrhb.evt

# chmod 640 tcrhb.evt
```

Check the template file for syntax errors.

```
# evmreload -n
```

Tell EVM about the new template.

```
# evmreload
```

Post the new event.

```
# echo "event { name tcrhb.timeEvent.overDue }" | evmpost
```

Check to see if the event was posted.

```
# evmget -A -f "[name tcrhb]"

TCR Handbook: this book is overdue.  Today is the due date.
```

Post the event again. This time, pass a value to the "`dueDate`" variable.

```
# print "event
> { name tcrhb.timeEvent.overDue
>   var {name dueDate value \"$(date)\"} }" | evmpost
```

Retrieve the events. This time you should see two events since this is the second time we have posted an event.

```
# evmget -A -f "[name tcrhb]"

TCR Handbook: this book is overdue.  Today is the due date.
TCR Handbook: this book is overdue.  Mon Mar 26 05:34:29 EST 2001 is the due date.
```

Finally, you can define a default attribute value for all events in a template file by placing the attribute entry outside of the `event` definition. An attribute within an `event` definition will override the "global" attribute value. Here is an excerpt from the `hw.evt` template file that illustrates the point:

```
#============ Hardware event defaults ============================

cluster_event    true
priority         200
ref              cat:evmexp.cat:800

#============ Hardware event templates ===========================
...
event {
    name         @SYS_VP@.hw.deregistered
    priority     400
    format       "A hardware component has been de-registered (HWID=$_hwid)"
    var          {name _hwid      type UINT64      value 0}
}
...
event {
    name         @SYS_VP@.hw.scan_completed
    format       "A hardware scan has just completed"
}
...
```

Notice that the `cluster_event`, `priority`, and `ref` attributes are not defined within an `event` template. This means that any event templates below these entries will have these attribute defaults unless specifically overridden within the event template. So, the `@SYS_VP@.hw.scan_completed` event template would have the "default" `priority` of `200`, but the `@SYS_VP@.hw.deregistered` event template would override the default `priority` and assign a `priority` of `400`.

For additional information regarding event templates, see the `evmtemplate(5)` and `EvmEvent(5)` reference pages.

8.5 Event Filters and Filtering Events

An event filter is what you use to get certain events from the EVM subsystem. Think of it as putting qualifiers on the items on your shopping list.

If you were to say, "I want to buy a musical recording," that would bring you to a store with hundreds or even thousands of recordings.

By saying "I want to buy a musical recording on CD," you've narrowed down your search a little. But let's get a little more specific.

"I want to buy a musical recording on CD that was recorded in the last two years by a popular Blues guitarist."

8.5.1 Event Keywords

Event filters help us to narrow down the number of events that we're looking for. *Tru64* UNIX defines several keywords (see Table 8-4) to assist with narrowing the scope of events.

Event keywords can also be combined to form complex filters. A complex filter is two or more keywords combined with one of the defined logical operators:

- `AND` (you can use the `AND` keyword or the "`&`").
- `OR` (you can use the `OR` keyword or the "`|`").
- `NOT` (you can use the `NOT` keyword or the "`!`").

Event Filter Keywords*

Keyword	Values	Example	Description

Name	event-name-specifier	`[name *.clu]`
		`![name *.clu.*]`
		`[name sys.unix.?]`
		`[name ?.?.?]`
			The name of the event as defined in an event template or wildcard string. Valid wildcards are: * (0 or more components) or ? (exactly one component).

Priority	equality-operator[1] integer	`[prio >= 200]`	The priority range is from 0 - 700.
Timestamp	time-range-specifier[2]	`[time *:6:1-3:*:*:*:*]`	The time-range-specifier is shown below. Any field can have a "*" wildcard that matches all possible values. You can also a range of values as show in the example.
Age	equality-operator[1] age-specifier	`[age < 1d]` `[age > 1d]`	The age-specifier is an integer followed by a letter. Valid letters are: w (weeks), d (days), h (hours), m (minutes), s (seconds)
Before	absolute-time-specifier[3]	`[before 2000:6:1:03:00:00]`	Absolute time value. No Wildcards.
Since	absolute-time-specifier[3]	`[since 2000:6:1:03:00:00]`	Absolute time value. No Wildcards.
Host_name	hostname	`[host sheridan]`	Any valid hostname.
Cluster_name	cluster_name	`[cluster babylon5]`	Any cluster name.
Event_id	equality-operator[1] integer	`[id <= 10]`	An integer representing the event ID. See EvmEvent(5).

1- equality-operator	=	`eq`	equal to
	<	`lt`	less than
	>	`gt`	greater than
	<=	`le`	less than or equal to
	>=	`ge`	greater than or equal to
	!=	`ne`	not equal to
2 - time-range-specifier	year:month-of-year:day-of-month:day-of-week:hours:minutes:seconds		can use range (-) specifier and wildcard (*)
3 - absolute-time-specifier	year:month-of-year:day-of-month:day-of-week:hours:minutes:seconds		cannot use range or wildcard

*See the EvmFilter(5) reference page for additional information.

Table 8-4: Event Filter Keywords

For example:

```
[name *.evm] AND [prio <= 500] AND NOT [before 2001:03:24:00:00:00]
```

Return all "evm" events with a priority less than or equal to 500 before March 24, 2001.

To ensure proper sequence of a complex filter, you can include filters in parentheses "(" and ")" as well.

```
([name *.evm] | [name ?.?.?]) & [age <= 2d]
```

Return all "evm" events or any event that contains three components and is less than or equal to two days old.

To utilize a filter, you use the "-f" switch on the evmget, evmwatch, evmshow(1), or evmsort(1) commands. For example:

```
# evmget -f "([name *.evm] | [name ?.?.?]) & [age <= 2d]"
```

For more information, see the EvmFilter(5) reference page.

8.5.2 Event Filter Files

In addition to event keywords, there is a way to create complex filters and store them for reuse (kind of like an environment variable). These reusable filters can be stored in filter files.

Tru64 UNIX and *TruCluster* Server include several filter files. These filter files are located in /usr/share/evm/filters. Event filter files have an extension of ".evf". Table 8-5 shows the filter file directories and the order in which they are searched.

To override the file search order, you can define the EVM_FILTERDIR environment variable.

Event Filter File Directories

Directory	Search Order *	Description
current working directory	1	
$HOME/.sysman/evmfilters	2	User-defined filter files should be placed in this directory.
/var/evm/adm/filters	3	Site-specific filter files should be placed in this directory.
/usr/share/evm/filters	4	Filter files provided by Tru64 UNIX and TruCluster Server are located in this directory.

* - can be overridden by the **EVM_FILTERDIR** environment variable

Table 8-5: EVM Filter File Directories

Event filter files have the following syntax:

```
filter {
       name     filter_name
       value    filter_value
       include  filter_element
       exclude  filter_element
       title    filter_title
       }
```

The `filter_name` is the name of your filter. The `filter_value` is a keyword filter string. The `filter_element` for the "`include`" (logical `OR`) and "`exclude`" (logical `AND NOT`) attributes are keyword filter strings you can use to further refine your filter. Finally, the `filter_title` attribute is a description of the filter. For example:

```
filter {
    name "scsi"
    value "[name @SYS_VP@.binlog.hw.scsi]"
    title "Binlog SCSI events"
}
```

This filter is from the `binlog.evf` file located in the `/usr/share/evm/filters` directory. To use this filter, you would use the following syntax: "`@filter_file:filter_name`". To use the `scsi` filter from the `binlog` filter file, use: "`@binlog:scsi`". Notice that this filter does not contain an "`include`" or "`exclude`" attribute. There can be any number of "`include`" or "`exclude`" attributes per filter definition.

```
filter
{
  name          net
  value         "[name @SYS_VP@.hw.net]"
  include       "[name @SYS_VP@.clu.clua]"
  exclude       "[prio < 200]"
  exclude       "[age > 1w]"
}
```

This is an example that defines a filter by the name of "`net`" that will retrieve events that match the name of `sys.unix.hw.net` or `sys.unix.clu.clua`, as long as the events have a priority greater than 200 and the events have not occurred longer than one week ago.

In other words, you could create a filter file and use this command:

```
# evmget -A -f @myFilterfile:net
```

Or type this command:

```
# evmget -A -f "[name *.hw.net] | [name *.clu.clua] & ![prio < 200] & ![age > 1w]"
```

NOTE:

The @SYS_VP@ value is a macro that defines "vendor" and "product name". What does the macro resolve to?

```
# evminfo -vp
sys.unix
```

You should use this value instead of using the actual value. This will accomplish two tasks:

1. It makes your filter files portable.
2. It gives the vendor the freedom to change their product name without giving you more work to do.

For additional information on event filter files, see the evmfilterfile(5) reference page.

8.6 Miscellaneous EVM Topics

8.6.1 EVM Security

The /etc/evm.auth file defines which users and/or groups are authorized to post, subscribe (monitor), or retrieve particular events. The evm.auth file contains two types of entries:

- event_rights

  This entry type defines the rights for a particular event class. Each event_rights entry contains three fields:

  ```
  event_rights {
               class  event_class
               post   rights_list
               access rights_list
              }
  ```

  The class field contains the event class (e.g. @SYS_VP@.evm.msg.admin). The event must have a base template. See section 8.4 for more information.

The post field contains the list of who has permission to post this event class.

The access field contains the list of who has permission to retrieve or subscribe to this class of event.

The rights_list is defined in Table 8-6.

The rights_list must be enclosed in double-quotes ("") if it contains spaces. Multiple users and/or groups in the rights_list must be separated by a comma (,). The root user has implicit rights to all events and services unless explicitly denied.

For example:

```
event_rights {
              class   @SYS_VP@.binlog      # binary error log events
              post    root
              access "root, group=adm"
             }
```

The root user can post events of type "sys.unix.binlog", and the root user and users in the adm group can retrieve the events. If you are concerned about future portability, you should use the @SYS_VP@ macro to refer to system (sys.unix) events.

- service_rights

This entry type defines the rights for a particular service to be performed by the daemon for a requesting client. Each service_rights entry contains two fields:

```
service_rights {
                service   service_name
                execute   rights_list
               }
```

The service field contains the particular service. Services must be defined in /etc/evmdaemon.conf. User-defined services are not supported as of this writing.

Event Authorization Rights	
[+|-][user | group=groupname]	
Attribute	**Value**
user	any login username
groupname	any group
+	grant access
-	deny access

Table 8-6: Event Authorization Rights

The execute field contains the users and/or groups that are authorized to execute this service.

For example:

```
service_rights {
                service    event_get         # event_get  service  -  handles  evmget
requests
                execute   +
               }
```

All users can execute the event_get service. The event_get service is used by the evmget program.

For additional information, see the *Tru64* UNIX System Administration Guide, chapter 13, and the evm.auth(4) reference page.

8.6.2 EVM Remote Access

Remote access is disabled by default. To enable remote access, modify the remote_connection attribute to "true" in /etc/evmdaemon.conf.

As of this writing, there is no authentication for remote users. Remote users are granted the lowest level of access or posting privileges. For additional information, see the *Tru64* UNIX System Administration Guide, chapter 13.

8.6.3 EVM API

Writing applications that use EVM falls beyond the scope of this book. However, we would be remiss if we did not mention that there is a full API for EVM that enables you to write programs that can post events or subscribe to events. For additional information, see the *Tru64* UNIX Programmer's Guide, chapter 14, as well as the reference pages in section 3 for the EVM API. To find all the "Evm*" calls, try the following command:

```
# man -k evm | grep -E '^(Evm)(.*)\(3\)'
```

Alternatively, you can use our sman script (see Appendix B for the URL) which is a section-based "man -k" script with formatted output.

```
# sman 3 Evm
```

There are also program examples in the /usr/examples/evm directory.

8.7 Using EVM

This section will not attempt to cover every possible function within the EVM subsystem; instead, it will discuss some of the interesting uses we have discovered and how they relate to the *TruCluster* Server product. For more in depth analyses of EVM, we suggest the *Tru64* UNIX System Administration Guide, or the following reference pages:

- evmget(1)
- evminfo(1)
- evmpost(1)
- evmshow(1)
- evmsort(1)
- evmwatch(1)
- evm(5)
- EvmEvent(5)
- EvmFilter(5)
- evmreload(8)
- evmstart(8)
- evmstop(8)
- evmviewer(8)

A complete list of reference pages can be obtained by using the "man -k" command, or our section-based sman script (see Appendix B for where to get it).

8.7.1 How Can I Find Out Which Events are Registered with EVM?

You can retrieve the registered events by using the evmwatch command with the "-i" switch.

NOTE:

Prior to *Tru64* UNIX version 5.1, the "-A" command option did not exist for the evmwatch and evmget commands. The "-A" switch added to the evmwatch command automatically invokes evmshow, whereas the evmget command automatically invokes the evmsort command.
If you are using *Tru64* UNIX version 5.0A, use the following command in place of the "-A" command option to evmwatch:

```
# evmwatch -i | evmshow
```

```
# evmwatch -A -i
```

Since that command gives us a lot of events, we may want to limit our search to just network-related events.

With V5.0A, use "evmwatch -i -f "[name *.net]" | evmshow".

With V5.1 (and newer), use "evmwatch -A -i -f "[name *.net]"".

```
# evmwatch -A -i -f "[name *.net]"
NIFF: node sheridan detected a failed network connection on network  via interface
NIFF: node sheridan has detected an available network connection on network  via
interface
NIFF: node sheridan has declared a connectivity alert with network  via interface
NetRAIN: node sheridan detected a failed network connection on network  via
interface
NetRAIN: node sheridan has detected an available network connection on network  via
interface
NetRAIN: node sheridan has declared a connectivity alert with network  via interface
```

Okay, so we narrowed it down, but what if we want to see the name of the event instead of the format text? The EvmEvent(5) reference page defines the "Standard Data Items" that can be used to create a "show-template". A "show-template" can be created with the "-t" switch to the evmget, evmshow, evmsort, and evmwatch commands (or if you use the same show-template, you can set the EVM_SHOW_TEMPLATE environment variable with your favorite format).

With V5.0A, use: "evmwatch -i -f "[name *.net] " | evmshow -t "@name""

With V5.1 (or newer), use: "evmwatch -A -i -f "[name *.net]" -t "@name""

```
# evmwatch -A -i -f "[name *.net]" -t "@name"
sys.unix.hw.net.niff.down
sys.unix.hw.net.niff.up
sys.unix.hw.net.niff.alert
sys.unix.hw.net.netrain.down
sys.unix.hw.net.netrain.up
sys.unix.hw.net.netrain.alert
```

8.7.2 How Can I Wait for an Event to Happen?

Waiting for events to occur on the system or cluster is easily accomplished using the evmwatch command without the "-i" switch.

With V5.0A (or newer):

```
# evmwatch | evmshow
```

With V5.1 (or newer):

```
# evmwatch -A
```

Note that until an event occurs, no output will appear. Using the `evmwatch` command works similarly to using the "`tail -f`" command to display the output from the `/var/adm/messages` file. The difference, however, is that with the `evmwatch` command you have the power of filtering and formatting the events and seeing the events as they occur from a variety of sources on not just one system but on every member in a cluster!

8.7.3 How Can I Retrieve Events that Have Occurred?

If the event was logged, it can be retrieved with the `evmget` command.

With V5.0A (or newer):

```
# evmget | evmshow
```

With V5.1 (or newer):

```
# evmget -A
```

Remember that you can filter the events as well.

```
# evmget -A -f "[name *.hw] AND [prio > 400]"
Correctable error reporting state changed
Correctable error reporting state changed
```

By default, only the event text is reported. To see additional information, you can use a "show-template".

```
# evmget -A -f "[name *.hw] AND [prio > 400]" -t "@timestamp [@priority] @name @@"
22-Mar-2001 09:22:56 [700] sys.unix.binlog.hw.correctable_rpt_switch Correctable
error reporting state changed
22-Mar-2001 09:30:16 [700] sys.unix.binlog.hw.correctable_rpt_switch Correctable
error reporting state changed
```

8.7.4 How Can I See which Channels are Configured?

```
# evminfo -lc

syslog
binlog
misclog
evmlog
```

8.7.5 How Can I Get Events from One Particular Channel?

You can limit the scope of your search to a particular channel using the "`-C`" flag to `evmget`. This was added to EVM in *Tru64* UNIX version 5.1.

```
# evmget -A -C binlog -f "[age < 1d]" -t "@timestamp @name @@"

28-Mar-2001 07:36:13 sys.unix.binlog.op.timestamp System timestamp
28-Mar-2001 07:37:41 sys.unix.binlog.hw.scsi SCSI event
28-Mar-2001 07:37:41 sys.unix.binlog.hw.scsi SCSI event
28-Mar-2001 07:37:41 sys.unix.binlog.hw.scsi SCSI event
28-Mar-2001 16:17:42 sys.unix.binlog.op.timestamp System timestamp
```

To retrieve information from more than one channel, use multiple "`-C`" switches.

```
# evmget -A -C binlog -C syslog -f "[age < 1d]" -t "@timestamp @name @@"
```

8.7.6 How Can I Format the "timestamp" Received from the Event?

As you have seen, you can retrieve the time and date using the "`@timestamp`" filter, but this gives you both the time and date. If you only want a specific portion to the timestamp, you can use `evmshow` and specify the time format with the "`-T`" switch. The format you use is the same format used for the `date(1)` command.

```
# evmget -f "[prio >= 700]" | evmshow -T "%A (%D) %H:%M"

Thursday (03/22/01) 09:22  Correctable error reporting state changed
Thursday (03/22/01) 09:30  Correctable error reporting state changed
```

8.7.7 How Can I Send an Event?

You can send (or post) an event using the evmpost command. The evmpost command receives its input from an input stream (or file), converts the input to EVM's binary format, and then sends the event to the EVM daemon for distribution to subscribers.

```
# echo "event { name tcrhb.timeEvent.overDue }" | evmpost
```

This simply posts the "tcrhb.timeEvent.overdue" event to EVM using the default values defined in the event template file (see section 8.4 for more information).

You can also pass variables to the event as defined in the template for the event. For example, in the "tcrhb.timeEvent.overdue" event, we defined the variable "dueDate" which was defined as a string with a default value of "Today".

```
event {
    name        tcrhb.timeEvent.overDue
    format      "TCR Handbook: this book is overdue.  $dueDate is the due date."
    priority    400
    var         {name dueDate  type STRING  value "Today"}
}
```

In order to post the event with an alternate value to the "dueDate" variable, we could do the following:

```
# echo "event { name tcrhb.timeEvent.overDue var {name dueDate value \"`date`\"}}" \
| evmpost
```

If you do not want to type the event on the command line to post it, you can place it in a file and have evmpost read the file instead.

```
# evmpost myEvent
```

You can also post simple messages to EVM with the "-a" (administrator) and "-u" (user) switches.

```
# evmpost -a "Starting the upgrade for the C++ compiler" -p 201

# evmpost -u "I am here!"
```

NOTE:

If you are using the csh shell, you will need to escape the "!" character like "\!". This is necessary to be able to print the "!" character. Omitting the "\" will result in an "" : Event not found." error. Note further that the "Event" in the error message does not refer to an EVM event but is the C shell's way of saying that the command you were trying to recall was not found. The "!" is how you recall a command from your history list.

8.7.8 How Can I Send an Event from a Script?

You can post an event from a script by using the evmpost command from within your script. There is also a small excerpt of a script in the evmpost(1) reference page.

8.7.9 How Can I Format the Event Information I Receive?

Formatting event information can be done using the "-t" switch to the evmwatch, evmget, or evmshow commands. The "-t" enables you to create a "show-template" for the command. The format can use any valid EVM data item as defined in the EvmEvent(5) reference page. When using a data item in the "show-template", prefix it with "@". The data items are listed in uppercase in the EvmEvent(5) reference page, but you can use lowercase. Note that the "@@" is the actual event text with any variable values, referred to in the text, substituted in place of their references.

```
# evmget -A -t "@pid [@priority] @name: @@" -f "[prio > 600]"
- [700] sys.unix.binlog.hw.correctable_rpt_switch: Correctable error reporting state
changed
- [700] sys.unix.binlog.hw.correctable_rpt_switch: Correctable error reporting state
changed
302 [700] sys.unix.hw.net.niff.down: NIFF: node sheridan detected a failed network
connection on network 192.168.0.69 via interface tu0
```

If you find that you are constantly using the same format, you may wish to define the format in the EVM_SHOW_TEMPLATE environment variable.

```
# export EVM_SHOW_TEMPLATE="@pid [@priority] @name: @@"
# evmget -A -f "[name *.hw]"
21667 [300] sys.unix.hw.dev_base_name_changed.tape._hwid.123: Device base name
changed from unknown to tape0 (HWID=123)
21667 [300] sys.unix.hw.dev_base_name_changed.tape._hwid.124: Device base name
changed from unknown to tape1 (HWID=124)
```

As of V5.1A, newline (`\n`) and tab (`\t`) characters can be used to increase the readability of your event output. For example, you can insert a newline into the event output by using a "`\n`".

```
# evmget -A -f "[age < 1d]" \
> -t "\n@timestamp - @event_id [@priority]\n@name\n@@" | more

26-Sep-2002 03:43:59 - 344680 [200]
sys.unix.clu.drd.server_leave._hwid.52
DRD: Removed (unmapped) DRD server molari
```

Using the "`%`" character next to a filter keyword allows you set a minimum field width. For example, to set the minimum field width of a `cluster_event` field to five you can use the following command.

```
# evmget -A -f "[age < 1d]" \
> -t "@cluster_event%5 - @name" | more

True  - sys.unix.hw.net.niff.alert
False - sys.unix.evm.logger.log_closed
False - sys.unix.evm.logger.log_started
False - sys.unix.evm.mark
False - sys.unix.binlog_chan.binlog_size
False - sys.unix.binlog.hw.scsi
True  - sys.unix.clu.drd.server_leave._hwid.52
False - sys.unix.binlog.hw.scsi
True  - sys.unix.clu.drd.server_add._hwid.52
True  - sys.unix.clu.drd.new_accessnode._hwid.52
True  - sys.unix.clu.drd.new_accessnode._hwid.52
...
```

8.7.10 How Can I Find Out Which Filters are Available?

Filter keywords are defined in the `EvmFilters(5)` reference page. You can find filters defined in the filter files located in the `/usr/share/evm/filters` (system) and `/var/evm/adm/filters` (site defined) directories.

```
# ls /var/evm/adm/filters /usr/share/evm/filters

/usr/share/evm/filters:
binlog.evf    evm.evf       sys.evf       syslog.evf

/var/evm/adm/filters:
<no output>
```

Also, the *TruCluster* Server Handbook web site (see Appendix B for the URL) contains a Korn Shell script called `evf(1)` that can be used to find out which filters are available in a filter file.

evf [-v] [-d FilterFileDir] [file1 file2...filen]

The evf script will use the current working directory, /var/evm/adm/filters, and /usr/share/evm/filters as the default search path if either the "-d" switch or the EVF_DIR_PATH environment variable is not used.

```
# evf binlog

/
  [no event filter files found]


/var/evm/adm/filters
  [no event filter files found]
/usr/share/evm/filters

  binlog.evf

    @binlog:binlog
    @binlog:scsi
    @binlog:lsm
    @binlog:info
    @binlog:msg
    @binlog:startup
    @binlog:shutdown
    @binlog:panic
    @binlog:timestamp
    @binlog:unknown
```

In this example, the "-d" switch is used to search only the /usr/share/evm/filters directory; the "-v" switch displays the details of the filter by performing an "evmshow -f filter_exp -F".

```
# evf -v -d /usr/share/evm/filters binlog

/usr/share/evm/filters

  binlog.evf

    @binlog:binlog       ->  [name sys.unix.binlog]
    @binlog:scsi         ->  [name sys.unix.binlog.hw.scsi]
    @binlog:lsm          ->  [name sys.unix.binlog.sw.lsm]
    @binlog:info         ->  [name sys.unix.binlog.op.info]
    @binlog:msg          ->  [name sys.unix.binlog.op.info.ascii_msg]
    @binlog:startup      ->  [name sys.unix.binlog.op.startup]
    @binlog:shutdown     ->  [name sys.unix.binlog.op.shutdown]
    @binlog:panic        ->  [name sys.unix.binlog.op.panic]
    @binlog:timestamp    ->  [name sys.unix.binlog.op.timestamp]
    @binlog:unknown      ->  [name sys.unix.binlog.unknown_class]
```

You can see all the filters in every file in the specified directory with the following command:

```
# evf -d /usr/share/evm/filters
```

If you just want to see a couple of files, separate them by white space.

```
# evf syslog binlog
```

The `evf` command also accepts standard shell wildcards for file specs, provided that file spec is enclosed in double quotes (`""`). The following example will search the `EVF_DIR_PATH` for all filter files that end in "`log`", all filter files that start with a "`c`" followed by either an "`l`" or an "`a`" followed by either a "`u`" or an "`a`", and any four-letter filter files.

```
# export EVF_DIR_PATH="/var/evm/adm/filters /var/share/evm/filters"
# evf -v "*log" "c[la][ua]" "????"
```

For more information on the `evf` command, see the `evf(1)` reference page included in the `evf.tar.gz` kit.

8.7.11 How Can I See the Format of a Filter in a Filter File?

If you are using a filter from a filter file and would like to see what it is actually filtering, you can look at the filter file (if you know where it is), or you can ask `evmshow` to show you.

```
# evmshow -f @binlog:scsi -F
 ( [name sys.unix.binlog.hw.scsi] )
```

8.7.12 How Can I Check the Syntax of the Template I Created?

If you are an administrator, you can use the "`evmreload -n`" command.

```
# evmreload -n
```

If you are a user, you can use `evmpost`.

```
# cat New_Events.evt | evmpost -r -M | evmshow -D
```

8.7.13 How Can I Sort the Events?

Since events can come from a variety of channels, the order in which they are displayed is not always the order in which you may expect to see them. Furthermore, you may wish to see the events sorted by different data items. The `evmsort` command was designed to accomplish this task.

NOTE:

As of *Tru64* UNIX version 5.1, the `evmget` command automatically invokes the "`evmsort -A`" command when the "`-A`" switch is used.

To sort events, you use the "`-s`" switch followed by a "Sort-Spec". The "Sort-Spec" is defined as a colon (`:`) delimited string of EVM data types. The sort order is determined by placing either a "+" or "`-`" after an EVM data type in the "Sort Spec" (the "+" indicates an ascending sort order while a "`-`" indicates a descending sort order). If you do not specify the sort order it will default to ascending order.

For example:

`@timestamp+:@name:@priority-`

This sorts each event by the `timestamp` (in ascending order), then by the `name` (in ascending order), and then by `priority` (in descending order).

The following examples will deliver the same results.

```
# evmget | evmsort -s "@timestamp+:@name:@priority-" | \
> evmshow -t "@timestamp [@priority] @name"
```

Or:

```
# evmget | \
> evmsort -A -s "@timestamp+:@name:@priority-" -t "@timestamp [@priority]  @name"
```

Or:

```
# evmget -A -s "@timestamp+:@name:@priority-" -t "@timestamp [@priority] @name"
```

Returns:

```
...
27-Mar-2001 02:00:01 [200] sys.unix.evm.chmgr.cleanup_done
27-Mar-2001 02:00:39 [500] sys.unix.syslog.mail
28-Mar-2001 07:37:41 [200] sys.unix.sysman.station.update_object.HOST.elroy
28-Mar-2001 07:37:43 [300] sys.unix.hw.dev_base_name_changed.tape._hwid.123
28-Mar-2001 07:37:43 [300] sys.unix.hw.dev_base_name_changed.tape._hwid.124
29-Mar-2001 18:02:41 [200] sys.unix.evm.mark
29-Mar-2001 18:15:41 [500] sys.unix.syslog.mail
29-Mar-2001 18:17:44 [200] sys.unix.binlog.op.timestamp
```

If you find that you are constantly using the same format, you may wish to define the sort order in the `EVM_SORT_SPEC` environment variable. If, for instance, `EVM_SHOW_TEMPLATE` and `EVM_SORT_SPEC` were both defined, then your `evmget` command could be shortened to:

```
# export EVM_SHOW_TEMPLATE="@timestamp [@priority] @name"
# export EVM_SORT_SPEC="@timestamp+:@name:@priority-"
# evmget -A
```

8.7.14 How Can I Find Out More Information about the Event(s) I Retrieved?

There are three options to the `evmshow` command that will return additional information (if available) about the event:

- "`-d`" returns the details of the event from the "`fn_details`" routine of the channel.
- "`-x`" returns an explanation of the event from the "`fn_explain`" routine of the channel.
- "`-D`" returns a formatted dump of the event's full contents.

Say you retrieve a series of events from the system. One of them looks interesting, and you decide you want more information. Here is an example using each switch:

```
# evmget -f "[id = 4817]" | evmshow
29-Mar-2001 12:44:36 [200] sys.unix.syslog.auth
```

```
# evmget -f "[id = 4817]" | evmshow -x
    Syslog authorization events are posted by Security Integration
    Architecture (SIA) components to report actions such as granting of
    superuser privileges to a user through the "su" command, or refusal
    to grant access.

    Authorization events should be monitored by the System
    Administrator.
```

```
# evmget -f "[id = 4817]" | evmshow -D

Formatted Message:
    login: ROOT login on /dev/pts/1

Event Data Items:
    Event Name          : sys.unix.syslog.auth
    Priority            : 200
    PID                 : 302
    PPID                : 1
    Event Id            : 4817
    Timestamp           : 29-Mar-2001 12:44:36
    Host IP address     : 192.168.0.69
    Host Name           : sheridan
    User Name           : root
    Format              : login: ROOT login on /dev/pts/1
    Reference           : cat:evmexp.cat:200

Variable Items:
    None
```

```
# evmget -f "[id = 4817]" | evmshow -d
============================ Syslog event ============================
EVM event name: sys.unix.syslog.auth

    Syslog authorization events are posted by Security Integration
    Architecture (SIA) components to report actions such as granting of
    superuser privileges to a user through the "su" command, or refusal
    to grant access.

    Authorization events should be monitored by the System
    Administrator.

======================================================================

Formatted Message:
    login: ROOT login on /dev/pts/1

Event Data Items:
    Event Name          : sys.unix.syslog.auth
    Priority            : 200
    PID                 : 302
    PPID                : 1
    Event Id            : 4817
    Timestamp           : 29-Mar-2001 12:44:36
    Host IP address     : 192.168.0.69
    Host Name           : sheridan
    User Name           : root
    Format              : login: ROOT login on /dev/pts/1
    Reference           : cat:evmexp.cat:200

Variable Items:
    None
======================================================================
```

As you probably noticed, the "-d" switch is a combination of both the "-x" and "-D" switches. The fn_details scripts actually call the evmshow command with the "-x" and "-D" switches.

Here is the details script from the evmlog channel (as defined in /etc/evmchannel.conf):

```
# grep evmshow evmlog/evmlog_details

/usr/bin/evmshow -n 1 -t "EVM event name: @name" < $TEMPFILE 2>&1
/usr/bin/evmshow -n 1 -x < $TEMPFILE 2>&1
/usr/bin/evmshow -D < $TEMPFILE 2>&1
```

8.8 References

- Tru64 UNIX System Administration Guide – versions 5.1 and 5.1A.
- Reference pages (noted within the text).

9

Tru64 UNIX Cluster Hooks: NIFF, NetRAIN, & LAG

In this chapter we will discuss the various network components included in the base Tru64 UNIX operating system that can be used to increase availability and throughput.

We will cover the following components:

	Section
• The Network Interface Failure Finder (NIFF)	9.1
• The Redundant Array of Independent Network Interfaces (NetRAIN)	9.2
• Link Aggregation	9.3

9.1 Network Interface Failure Finder (NIFF)

The Network Interface Failure Finder is a new component to Tru64 UNIX that enables network interfaces to be monitored for connectivity issues. In order for a network interface to be monitored on a Tru64 UNIX standalone environment, you need to inform NIFF using the `niffconfig(8)` command.

NOTE:

In a TruCluster Server environment, configured network interfaces are automatically monitored by NIFF.

Once an interface is added via `niffconfig`, the kernel-level portion of NIFF, called the Traffic Monitor Thread (`nifftmt(7)`), monitors the interface. If the interface fails to respond, `nifftmt` posts an event to EVM.

The user-level NIFF daemon (niffd(8)) subscribes to the EVM events generated by nifftmt. When a connectivity issue arises, it is niffd's job to generate traffic on the interface that has been marked inactive by nifftmt to verify whether the interface is truly down.

NIFF is used in conjunction with NetRAIN (see below) to provide a high-availability network solution for a standalone system. In a cluster, NIFF is also used by the Cluster Alias (CLUA) subsystem as well as the Cluster Application Availability (CAA) subsystem. We will cover CLUA and CAA in more detail in chapter 16 and chapter 23 respectively.

To add an interface to be monitored by NIFF, type the following command (replace tu0 with the interface you wish to monitor).

```
# niffconfig -a tu0
```

To examine the state of the interface according to NIFF, you can use either the "-u" or "-v" switches as shown in the following examples:

```
# niffconfig -u
Interface:   tu0, status: UP
```

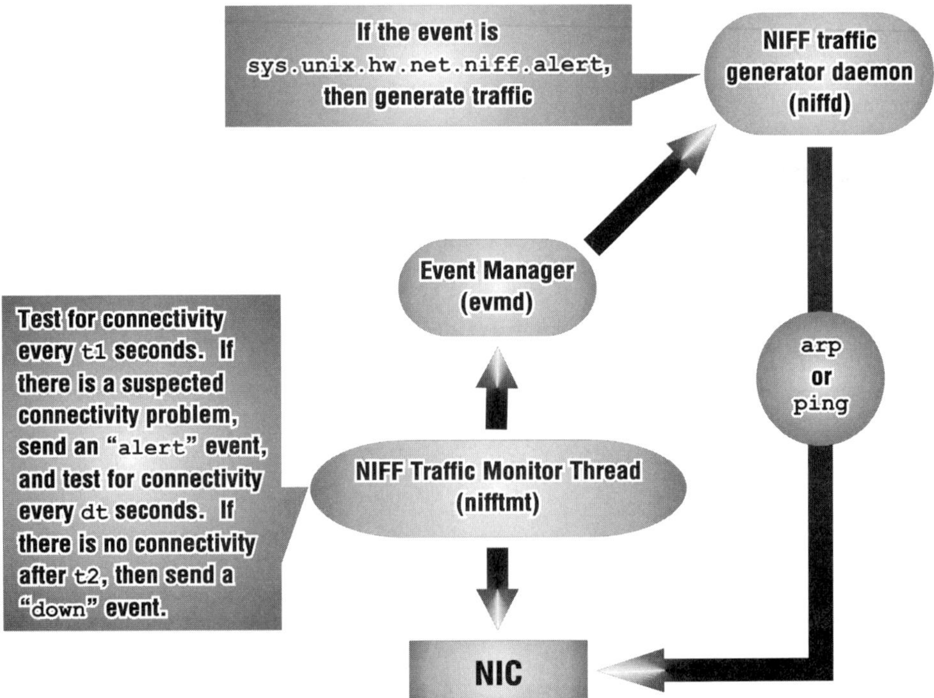

Figure 9-1: NIFF Flow

```
# niffconfig -v
Interface:   tu0, description:     , status: UP, event: ALERT, state: GREEN
t1: 20, dt: 5, t2: 60, time to dead: 30, current_interval: 20, next time: 20
```

Figure 9-1 shows the nifftmt to niffd communication path.

The nifftmt thread checks the monitored interface every t1 seconds. If nifftmt detects a connectivity problem, then it posts a sys.unix.hw.net.niff.alert event to EVM and then starts checking the monitored interface every dt seconds. The niffd daemon receives the sys.unix.hw.net.niff.alert event from EVM and begins generating traffic on the interface until it receives a sys.unix.hw.net.niff.down or sys.unix.hw.net.niff.up event. If t2 seconds elapse without the monitored interface's counters increasing, then the interface is marked as DEAD, and a sys.unix.hw.net.niff.down event is sent by nifftmt.

9.1.1 NIFF Events

NIFF events are defined in /usr/share/evm/templates/sys/hw.net.evt. Below are the registered NIFF events:

```
# evmwatch -A -i -f "[name *.niff]" -t "[@priority] @name"
[600] sys.unix.hw.net.niff.down
[200] sys.unix.hw.net.niff.up
[200] sys.unix.hw.net.niff.alert
```

For additional information regarding NIFF, see the Tru64 UNIX Network Administration Guide for version 5.0A and version 5.1, or the Tru64 UNIX Network Administration: Connections Guide for version V5.1A. You might also check out the niff(7), nifftmt(7), niffd(8), and niffconfig(8) reference pages.

9.2 Redundant Array of Independent Network Interfaces (NetRAIN)

Tru64 UNIX provides a method of taking multiple network interface cards (NICs) and grouping them together to function as one highly available network, more commonly known as a redundant array of independent network adapters or NetRAIN.

NetRAIN is a virtual interface that works by grouping two or more NICs into an array seen by the operating system as one interface. Each NetRAIN interface uses only one IP address, and there is only one active NIC at any time (for multiple active NICs with one IP address, see "Link Aggregation" in the following section). If the active NIC fails, an idle NIC comes online. The coolness factor in this is that if you happen to be connected to the system via the NetRAIN interface when a NIC fails, you may experience a brief pause while the new NIC comes online, but you will not be disconnected!

The number of arrays currently supported is `nr_maxdev - 1`. The `nr_maxdev` attribute is defined in the `netrain` subsystem and has a default value of `128`.

```
# sysconfig -q netrain nr_maxdev
netrain:
nr_maxdev = 128
```

For the most up-to-date information on the `netrain` subsystem for the version of Tru64 UNIX that you are using, see the `sys_attrs_netrain(5)` reference page.

9.2.1 Network Configuration without NetRAIN

A network configuration without NetRAIN is shown in Figure 9-2. There is no redundancy, so if the network interface fails, the system can no longer communicate on that subnet.

When configuring a network interface without NetRAIN, you (or your favorite network configuration program) modifies the following parameters in `/etc/rc.config`:

- `MAX_NETDEVS`

  The `MAX_NETDEVS` attribute is the maximum network devices that can be configured. This should be greater than or equal to `NUM_NETCONFIG`.

  ```
  # rcmgr get MAX_NETDEVS
  2
  ```

- `NUM_NETCONFIG`

  The NUM_NETCONFIG attribute is the number of network devices to configure. This must be equal to the number of `NETDEV_#/IFCONFIG_#` pairs configured.

  ```
  # rcmgr get NUM_NETCONFIG
  2
  ```

- `NETDEV_#` (where "#" is the instance of the network configured)

  Get the interface to configure.

  ```
  # rcmgr get NETDEV_0
  tu0
  ```

- IFCONFIG_# (where "#" is the instance of the network)

  The configuration information to pass to the ifconfig(8) program for the NETDEV_# interface.

```
# rcmgr get IFCONFIG_0
192.168.0.69 netmask 255.255.255.0
```

There are several programs that can be used to configure a network interface in Tru64 UNIX: "netconfig", "sysman net_wizard", "sysman interface", "setup", and "checklist". Configuring NetRAIN, however, does not yet have a program to walk you through the task.

9.2.2 Configuring NetRAIN

CAUTION:

Configuring NetRAIN for a LAN Cluster Interconnect is quite a bit different than the method we will be discussing in this section. We will cover configuring a LAN Cluster Interconnect in Chapter 10.

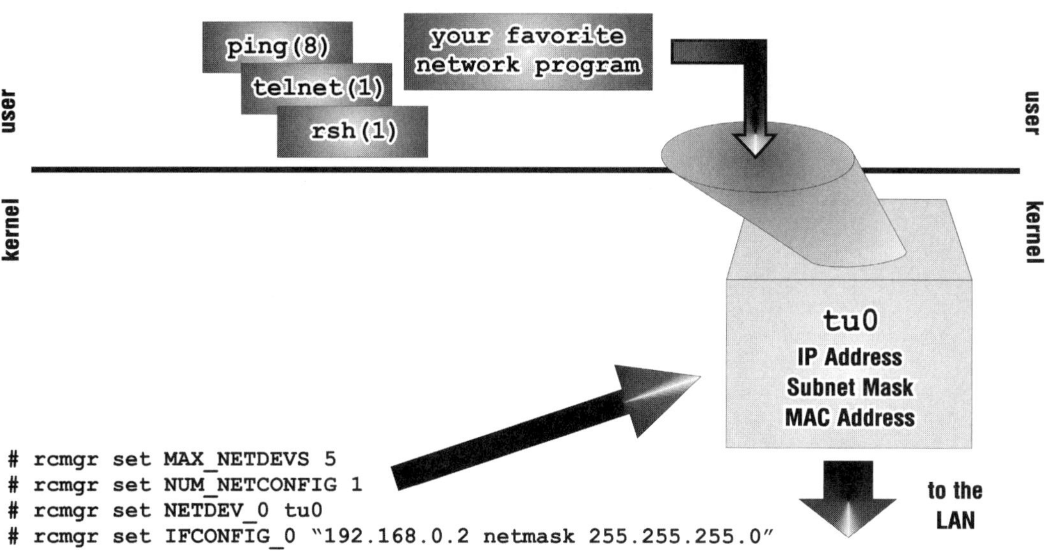

Figure 9-2: Traditional Network Interface Configuration

NetRAIN is fairly easy to configure, but there are some rules that need to be followed to ensure success.

- All NICs in the array must be physically connected to the same subnet but should have separate paths to the subnet for redundancy. In other words, you probably do not want two NICs connected to the same hub because if the hub breaks, your connection to the subnet would be lost from both NICs.
- All NICs in the array must be of the same type (Ethernet, FDDI, ATM, etc.).
- All NICs in the array must be the same speed and operational mode (full duplex, half duplex).
- All NICs to be configured in the NetRAIN set must be idle (e.g., not currently configured).
- You cannot run LAT on a NetRAIN virtual interface (`nr`) or any of the NICs that are configured within a NetRAIN set.

A network configuration with NetRAIN is shown in Figure 9-3.

9.2.2.1 Delete the In-Use Interfaces (if any)

If one or more of the NICs are currently in use, delete them. The easiest method for doing so is to use the "`sysman`" command with the "`interface`" accelerator.

```
# sysman interface
```

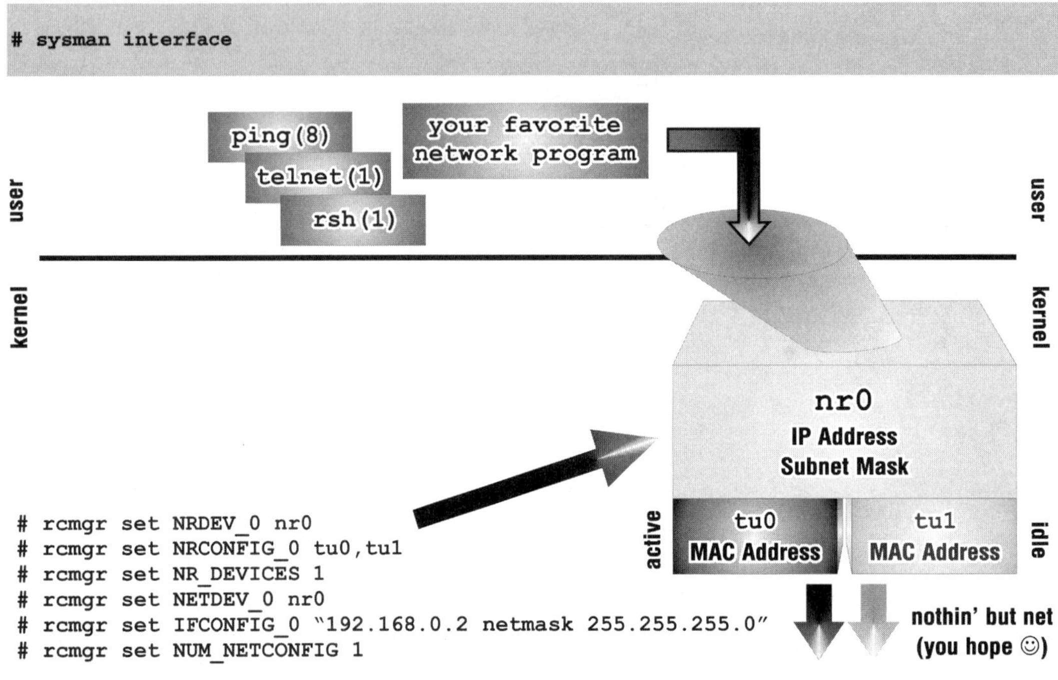

Figure 9-3: NetRAIN Interface Configuration

However, you can remove the interface using the manual approach as well.

1. Delete the running interface.

```
# ifconfig delete tu0
tu0: delete inet address 192.168.0.69
```

```
# ifconfig delete tu1
tu1: delete inet address 192.206.126.69
```

2. Decrease the NUM_NETCONFIG attribute by the number of interfaces that you are going to delete.

```
# rcmgr get NUM_NETCONFIG
2
```

```
# rcmgr set NUM_NETCONFIG 0
```

3. Find the NETDEV_# attributes for the interfaces you are removing.

```
# grep -E "tu0|tu1" /etc/rc.config
NETDEV_0="tu0"
NETDEV_1="tu1"
```

4. Delete the NETDEV_# and IFCONFIG_# attributes.

```
# for i in `grep -E "tu0|tu1" /etc/rc.config`
> do
>    DELNUM="${i##*_%%=*}"
>    print "deleting NETDEV_${DELNUM}"
>    rcmgr delete NETDEV_${DELNUM}
>    print "deleting IFCONFIG_${DELNUM}"
>    rcmgr delete IFCONFIG_${DELNUM}
> done
deleting NETDEV_0
deleting IFCONFIG_0
deleting NETDEV_1
deleting IFCONFIG_1
```

9.2.2.2 Configure the NetRAIN Interface

If you are configuring the NetRAIN interface on a NETDEV_# other than instance number zero, then increment NRDEV_# and NRCONFIG_# to be the same instance number as NETDEV_# and IFCONFIG_#. This only applies to the attribute itself and not the value. In other words, if the instance number was "1", then the attributes would be NETDEV_1, IFCONFIG_1, NRDEV_1, NRCONFIG_1. The NetRAIN interface would remain nr0.

1. Define the NetRAIN interface.

```
# rcmgr set NRDEV_0 nr0
```

2. Specify the array of adapters.

   Make sure you do not use any space between "tu0", the "," and "tu1".

```
# rcmgr set NRCONFIG_0 "tu0,tu1"
```

3. Define or update the number of NetRAIN devices configured.

   This number is analogous to NUM_NETCONFIG for NetRAIN interfaces.

```
# rcmgr get NR_DEVICES
<no output>
```

```
# rcmgr set NR_DEVICES 1
```

4. Set the NETDEV_# to the NetRAIN interface.

```
# rcmgr set NETDEV_0 nr0
```

5. Set the IFCONFIG_# attribute.

```
# rcmgr set IFCONFIG_0 "192.168.0.69 netmask 255.255.255.0"
```

6. Increment NUM_NETCONFIG.

```
# rcmgr get NUM_NETCONFIG
0
```

```
# rcmgr set NUM_NETCONFIG 1
```

7. Reboot the system.

```
# shutdown -sr now
```

8. Login to the system and check the interface.

```
# niffconfig -v

Interface:   tu1, description: NetRAIN internal, status:      UP, event:   ALERT
, state: GREEN
         t1: 4, dt: 2, t2: 10, time to dead: 2, current_interval: 4, next time: 4
Interface:   nr0, description: NetRAIN internal, status:      UP, event:   ALERT
, state: GREEN
         t1: 4, dt: 2, t2: 10, time to dead: 2, current_interval: 4, next time: 2
Interface:   tu0, description: NetRAIN internal, status:      UP, event:   ALERT
, state: GREEN
         t1: 4, dt: 2, t2: 10, time to dead: 2, current_interval: 4, next time: 4
```

So which interface is active? Check the network counters using the `netstat(1)` command.

```
# netstat -i | grep -E "tu0|tu1|nr0"

nr0    1500   <Link>       2:10:64:30:16:12       1861      0      1734     0     0
nr0    1500   DLI          none                   1861      0      1734     0     0
nr0    1500   192.168      sheridan               1861      0      1734     0     0
tu0    1500   <Link>       0:10:64:30:12:31        254      0       317     0     0
tu0    1500   DLI          none                    254      0       317     0     0
tu1    1500   <Link>       2:10:64:30:16:12       1607      0      1417     0     0
tu1    1500   DLI          none                   1607      0      1417     0     0
```

Generate some traffic. You can just `ping(8)` the interface.

```
# ping -f -c 100000 -I nr0 sheridan

PING sheridan (192.168.0.69): 56 data bytes
.

----sheridan PING Statistics----
100000 packets transmitted, 100000 packets received, 0% packet loss
round-trip (ms)  min/avg/max = 0/0/3 ms
```

Check the network counters again.

```
# netstat -i | grep -E "^(tu0|tu1|nr0|Name)"

Name   Mtu    Network      Address               Ipkts Ierrs    Opkts Oerrs  Coll
nr0    1500   <Link>       2:10:64:30:16:12       2014      0      2016     0     0
nr0    1500   DLI          none                   2014      0      2016     0     0
nr0    1500   192.168      sheridan               2014      0      2016     0     0
tu0    1500   <Link>       0:10:64:30:12:31        257      0       320     0     0
tu0    1500   DLI          none                    257      0       320     0     0
tu1    1500   <Link>       2:10:64:30:16:12       1757      0      1696     0     0
tu1    1500   DLI          none                   1757      0      1696     0     0
```

The `tu1` interface is active.

9.2.3 NetRAIN Events

NetRAIN events are defined in `/usr/share/evm/templates/sys/hw.net.evt`. Below are the registered NetRAIN events:

```
# evmwatch -A -i -f "[name *.netrain]" -t "[@priority] @name"
[0] sys.unix.hw.net.netrain.down
[0] sys.unix.hw.net.netrain.up
[0] sys.unix.hw.net.netrain.alert
```

For additional information regarding NetRAIN, see the Tru64 UNIX Network Administration Guide for version 5.0A and version 5.1, or the Tru64 UNIX Network Administration: Connections Guide for version 5.1A. Also check out the `nr(7)` and `sys_attrs_netrain(5)` reference pages.

9.3 Link Aggregation (LAG)

NOTE:

As of this writing, Link Aggregation is not supported for the LAN Cluster Interconnect.

Link Aggregation (or trunking) is a new feature that was added to Tru64 UNIX starting with version 5.1A. It is similar to NetRAIN in that it provides increased redundancy for your network. Unlike NetRAIN, though, all NICs in the set can be simultaneously active, allowing for load sharing and increased network bandwidth.

Both inbound and outbound traffic is distributed to all interfaces in the link aggregation group. According to the `lag(7)` reference page, "When transmitting packets, the system uses a load distribution algorithm to determine on which attached port to transmit the packets. The following load distribution algorithm is supported:

- For IP packets, the port is selected based on a hash of the destination IP address. For non-IP packets, the port is selected based on a hash of the destination MAC address. All traffic addressed to a specific destination system uses the same port in the link aggregation group. This ensures that the packets arrive in order."[1]

---

[1] The `lag(7)` reference page from Tru64 UNIX version 5.1A.

9.3.1 Configuring a Link Aggregation Group (LAG)

Configuring a LAG is straightforward provided that the following conditions are met:

- All NICs in the array must be on the same subnet and dedicated to the same server or switch.
- All NICs in the array must be of the same type (currently only Ethernet).
- All NICs in the array must be the same speed and running in full duplex mode.
- All NICs to be configured in the LAG set must be idle (e.g., not currently configured).
- You cannot run LAT on a LAG virtual interface (`lag`) or any of the NICs that configured within a LAG set.

Currently, to configure a LAG you must edit the `/etc/inet.local` file. Do not be surprised if this configuration method changes in a future release because NetRAIN was configured in a similar manner in V4.0F but was moved to `/etc/rc.config` in V5.0.

1. Verify that the link aggregation subsystem is configured in the kernel.

```
# sysconfig -q lag
framework error: subsystem 'lag' not found
```

   If it is not configured, add "`options LAG`" to your kernel configuration file (`/usr/sys/conf/HOSTNAME`), rebuild the kernel, copy the kernel to the root (`/`) directory, and reboot.

2. Verify that the NICs are not in use. If they are configured, see section 9.2.2.1 for information on how to unconfigure the interfaces.

3. Edit the `/etc/inet.local` file.

```
# cat >> /etc/inet.local
lagconfig -c
lagconfig -p tu0 key=1
lagconfig -p tu1 key=1
ifconfig lag0 192.168.0.69 netmask 255.255.255.0 up
^D
```

4. Reboot the system.

```
# shutdown -sr now
```

5. Login and verify that the LAG interface is configured and functioning.

```
# lagconfig -s lag=lag0

  lag0: Attached Interfaces: ( tu1 tu0 )
        key = 1
        Max ports = 8
```

```
# ifconfig lag0

lag0: flags=c63<UP,BROADCAST,NOTRAILERS,RUNNING,MULTICAST,SIMPLEX>
     inet 192.168.0.69 netmask ffffff00 broadcast 192.168.0.255 ipmtu 1500
```

Are both interfaces active? Check the network counters using the `netstat` command.

```
# netstat -i | grep -E "^(tu0|tu1|lag0|Name)"

Name  Mtu   Network      Address               Ipkts Ierrs    Opkts Oerrs  Coll
lag0  1500  <Link>       0:10:64:30:3a:29         50     0       36     0     0
lag0  1500  192.168      sheridan                 50     0       36     0     0
tu0   1500  <Link>       0:10:64:30:3a:29         45     0       41     0     0
tu1   1500  <Link>       0:10:64:30:3a:29          9     0        0     0     0
```

There is some traffic on both interfaces. Notice, though, that the `lag0` interface shows no traffic itself. Generate some traffic.

```
# ping -f -c 100000 192.168.0.255

PING 192.168.0.255 (192.168.0.255): 56 data bytes
.

----192.168.0.255 PING Statistics----
100534 packets transmitted, 100000 packets received, +534 duplicates, 0% packet loss
round-trip (ms)  min/avg/max = 0/80/85 ms
```

Check the counters again.

```
# netstat -i | grep -E "^(tu0|tu1|lag0|Name)"

Name  Mtu   Network      Address               Ipkts Ierrs    Opkts Oerrs  Coll
lag0  1500  <Link>       0:10:64:30:3a:29     201057     0   100109     0     0
lag0  1500  192.168      sheridan             201057     0   100109     0     0
tu0   1500  <Link>       0:10:64:30:3a:29     100643     0      326     0     0
tu1   1500  <Link>       0:10:64:30:3a:29     100692     0   100534     0     0
```

It appears that the `tu1` interface sent the pings, and both interfaces received them due to the address we chose to `ping`.

For additional information regarding LAG, see the Tru64 UNIX Network Administration: Connections Guide for version 5.1A. Also check out the `lag(7)`, `lagconfig(8)`, and `sys_attrs_lag(5)` reference pages.

9.4 References

- Tru64 UNIX Network Administration Guide – version 5.1.
- Tru64 UNIX Network Administration: Connections Guide – version 5.1A.
- Reference pages (noted within the text).

10

Creating a Single-Node Cluster

"A mind stretched to a new idea never goes back to its original dimensions."

– Oliver Wendell Holmes

In Chapter 4, we discussed Cluster Configuration Planning. This included the configuration planning for *Tru64* UNIX to support *TruCluster* Server and the configuration planning for *TruCluster* Server. In Chapter 5, we discussed the actual installation of *Tru64* UNIX, again in support of the installation of *TruCluster* Server. In Chapters 6 through 9, we discussed what makes it easier to implement a cluster in *Tru64* UNIX – the "Cluster Hooks." Now, finally, in this chapter we will discuss the installation and configuration of *TruCluster* Server and the creation of a single-node cluster.

In this chapter, careful planning and preparation come together to help us create something quite tangible and quite remarkable – a highly available, highly scalable UNIX cluster. We will therefore assume that you have done all your planning and preparation for installing and configuring *TruCluster* Server and for the creation of your UNIX cluster.

10.1 Before the Cluster Installation

If you've already skipped ahead to this chapter without reading Chapters 3, 4, and 5, we recommend that you stop and carefully review these three chapters at a minimum before continuing. Generally speaking, planning is essential to success.

For the best understanding of what it takes to design and plan a cluster, we suggest that you review Chapters 2 through 9, in addition to using the Cluster Preparation Worksheet and Checklist from section 4.8, to help design and plan your cluster implementation. Planning without a solid foundation of knowledge and understanding usually produces wasted time and energy.

Before we actually start the installation of the *TruCluster* Server software, we should explore some things on the standalone *Tru64* UNIX installation. As we have stated in earlier chapters, *Tru64* UNIX is the core foundation for any *TruCluster* Server cluster.

10.1.1 A Quick View of the *Tru64* UNIX File Systems

Let's take a quick look at a *Tru64* UNIX system before it is clustered and examine what file systems are mounted using the `mount(8)` command:

```
# mount
root_domain#root on / type advfs (rw)
/proc on /proc type procfs (rw)
usr_domain#usr on /usr type advfs (rw)
var_domain#var on /var type advfs (rw)
```

If we examine only the system level file systems, we see pretty much what is expected for a *Tru64* UNIX system – root (/), /usr, /var, and /proc. In this case, all file systems, except /proc, are AdvFS file systems. Nothing unusual, right?

Now let's expand on what we have seen by looking at where the file system domains for these system level AdvFS file systems reside.

```
# ls /etc/fdmns
.advfslock_fdmns          .advfslock_var_domain    var_domain/
.advfslock_root_domain    root_domain/
.advfslock_usr_domain     usr_domain/
```

Again, this is what is expected, but let's use this as a baseline for comparison later -- after the creation of the cluster.

10.1.2 Disks for the Cluster

Before we start the creation of the cluster, let's briefly review what disks and partitions are required to build the cluster-common file systems, the member-specific file systems, and the quorum disk.[1] We'll also discuss some specifics about partition sizes to support these file systems and disk(s).

The following details what disks are required to build a single-node cluster:

- One or more disks on the shared bus to hold the clusterwide AdvFS file systems: cluster_root (/), cluster_usr (/usr), and cluster_var (/var).
- One boot disk per cluster member on the shared bus.
- Depending on the number of members in the cluster, one entire disk on the shared bus to act as the quorum disk.

---

[1] This was also specified earlier in Table 4.4.

This list does not include the original system disk for *Tru64* UNIX.

What needs a disk and what needs a partition? During the initial creation of the cluster, it is expected that physical disk partitions will be needed for the following cluster-common file systems:

- `cluster_root`
- `cluster_usr`
- `cluster_var`

While the member boot disk will also use partitions for the creation of its two file systems and cluster status partition, the `clu_create(8)` program will only ask for the entire disk and then use the "`a`", "`b`", and "`h`" partitions. As for the quorum disk, while an entire disk is asked for and used, only the "`h`" partition has a `cnx` label on it.

As an aside, if you want to use LSM to mirror file systems on the cluster, you can set up LSM on the original *Tru64* UNIX system but hold off on the mirroring of any file systems until after the first member of the cluster is booted. During the initial creation of the cluster using the `clu_create` command, LSM volumes may not be used.

After you have created a single-member cluster, you can use the `volmigrate(8)` command to move the `cluster_root` domain to an LSM volume and then mirror that volume. Please be aware that using the `volmigrate` command to move `cluster_root` actually moves the data from the disk partition you specified in the initial cluster creation command, `clu_create`, to new target storage that you must specify when you run `volmigrate`. For more information on using LSM within a *TruCluster* Server configuration, please refer to Chapter 14.

Information from Table 10-1, taken along with information from Table 4-5, provides a basis for determining the disks and the disk partitions that should be used in our *Tru64* UNIX/*TruCluster* Server Planning Worksheet and Checklist from section 4.8. We will use this completed Worksheet as the blueprint to build our cluster.

The "*TruCluster* Server Handbook Recommendations on Partition Sizes" column, from Table 10-1, contains average sizes taken from clusters in production at several sites so this is a more realistic recommendation. The term "`currently_used`" refers to the currently used partition sizes for the *Tru64* UNIX system disk.

When a member is initially created or added to a cluster, the default disk partition sizes are used for the partitions – not the existing disk partitions. While the sizes of the partitions for `boot_partition` and for the "`cnx`" partition are appropriate (see Table 10-1), we expect that the partition used for swap will most likely be larger than the default partition. How can we create and use a partition of the appropriate size for swap when we do not have control over what the `clu_create` program does to the disk partitions for the member disk? Basically, we work "around" the `clu_create` program.

According to the *TruCluster* Server Installation Manual, "For disks that contain file systems, the installation procedure calculates whether the sizes are acceptable. If the required partitions are usable, the installation procedure prompts whether you want to use the existing partition sizes." Using this information, we can write a disklabel with the appropriate partition size information and a `fstype` of "`AdvFS`" for partition "`a`", a `fstype` of "`swap`" for partition "`b`", and a `fstype` of

File System (Type)	Partition	HP Recommended Minimum Partition Sizes	Comments from HP on Partition Sizes	*TruCluster* Server Handbook Recommendations on Partition Sizes
Cluster Root (/) AdvFS	a	200 MB	The minimum partition size requirement is the larger of 125 MB or (1.125 x currently_used root size).	512 MB
Cluster /usr (AdvFS)	g	1000 MB	The minimum partition size requirement is the larger of 675 MB or (1.125 x currently_used /usr size). The absolute minimum partition size is 675 MB.	4.0 GB
Cluster /var (AdvFS)	h	1000 MB	The minimum partition size requirement is the larger of 360 MB or (1.125 x currently_used /var size). The absolute minimum partition size is 360 MB.	4.0 GB
Member boot disk: root (AdvFS)	a	256 MB	The only required file systems on member boot disks are root, swap, and a 1 MB partition used for cluster status.	256 MB
Member boot disk: swap (swap)	b	Depends on system.	The remainder of the member boot disk after the "a" and "h" partitions are allocated. The minimum size requirement is 256 MB.	Depends on the system. See section 4.2.2 for the discussion on swap in a cluster.
Member boot disk: CNX cluster status	h	Exactly 1 MB	The "h" partition (fstype cnx) stores cluster state information. The installation procedure creates this partition on each member's boot disk.	Exactly 1 MB
Quorum disk	h	Exactly 1 MB	Use a small disk as the quorum disk. As all cluster members must be able to retrieve the information from the quorum disk, no I/O barriers are placed on this disk. Therefore, no file systems should be on this disk.	Exactly 1 MB

Table 10-1: Cluster Partition Sizes

"`cnx`" for partition "`h`" to the disk that will be used as the member's boot disk. When we use this disk as the member's boot disk, the `clu_create` command will re-use the existing partition sizes because it sees the partitions are in-use.

How can we partition the member's boot disk setting the appropriate partitions in-use? The following provides an example on how this can be done. Before going any further, we partition the disk that will be used for the first member's boot disk.

- Write a default label to the disk.

```
# disklabel -rw dsk1
```

- Edit and write out the disklabel of the disk providing the appropriate partition sizes.

```
# disklabel -re dsk1
```

Note, if you're GUI inclined, you can also use the `diskconfig(8)` command.

- Change the `fstype` for the partitions that we are interested in from "`unused`" to the appropriate in-use type.

```
# disklabel -sF dsk1a AdvFS
# disklabel -sF dsk1b swap
# disklabel -sF dsk1h cnx
```

Note, as of this writing, the `diskconfig` command does not support setting a "`cnx`" `fstype`.

Since you will likely have more than a one-member cluster and the members' boot disks will probably be identical, you can quickly partition the additional member boot disks by saving the first member's disklabel to a file and then writing it to the other member boot disks. For example, we plan to use `dsk2` as our second member's boot disk.

Save the disklabel.

```
# disklabel -r dsk1 > /tmp/bd.lbl
```

Write the disklabel.

```
# disklabel -Rr -t advfs dsk2 /tmp/bd.lbl
```

10.1.3 About the Quorum Disk

One of the Connection Manager's (CNX) responsibilities is to ensure data integrity within the cluster in the event of a communications failure. It does this through a voting mechanism in which processing and I/O are allowed to occur but only when there is a majority of votes present or a quorum. The quorum disk can add to that voting mechanism; therefore, it can potentially add to the high availability of a cluster.

Although the quorum disk is not very large, a minimum of 1 MB, we want to emphasize that the entire disk is used. It should also be noted that the quorum disk does not require a disklabel and that there will be no file systems occupying any of its partitions. The `clu_create` program will write a 1 MB label of `fstype:` "`cnx`" to the "`h`" partition of the quorum disk.

When should you use a quorum disk? If you have a two-node cluster, a quorum disk is highly recommended. If your cluster is larger than two nodes, then it depends on how many nodes are in your cluster, although you should not configure a quorum disk in a cluster with an odd number of members. For more information on the Connection Manager and quorum within a cluster, please see Chapter 17.

During the initial creation of the cluster using the `clu_create(8)` command, you will be asked to provide a quorum disk. If your cluster will contain an even number of members and you plan to use a quorum disk, you can certainly provide the quorum disk when prompted. If you plan to operate the cluster as a single-member cluster for a while to "get the feel of the cluster," then we recommend that you refrain from creating the quorum disk during the initial creation of the cluster. After the second member is added to the cluster, the quorum disk can easily be added using the following command:

```
clu_quorum -d add <disk> <# of votes>.
```

If you find that you do not require a quorum disk and yet you plan to increase the number of members in your cluster at a much later date, then it would make sense to set aside a small disk on the shared bus that could be used as quorum disk.

10.1.4 Using the Cluster Preparation Worksheet and Checklist

In section 4.8, we created a *Tru64* UNIX/*TruCluster* Server Planning Worksheet and Checklist. Using this Worksheet, you should be able to plan the implementation of your cluster in a very straightforward manner. Please use this as a guide upon which to build.

10.2 Installation of the *TruCluster* Server Software

Now that we have completed the planning and understand what it takes to build a cluster, let's start by loading the *TruCluster* Server License PAK and installing the *TruCluster* Server software subsets. If you have already loaded the *TruCluster* Server License PAK onto your system, please jump ahead to section 10.2.2 on Installing the *TruCluster* Server Software.

10.2.1 Load the *TruCluster* Server License PAK

A quick and easy way to load a license PAK is to use `lmfsetup(8)`. We load the license PAK for *TruCluster* Server on the system that we will be installing and configuring the *TruCluster* Server software subsets.

```
# /usr/sbin/lmfsetup

Register PAK (type q or quit to exit)  [template]
                 Issuer : dec
   Authorization Number : ala-nq-xxxxxxx-xxxx
           Product Name : tcs-ua
               Producer : dec
        Number of units : 1050
                Version :
   Product Release Date :
   Key Termination Date :
Availability Table Code : h
    Activity Table Code :
            Key Options : mod_units,alpha
          Product Token :
            Hardware-Id :
               Checksum : 2-wwww-xxxx-yyyy-zzzz
PAK registered for template successfully
Register PAK (type q or quit to exit)  [template] q

You have registered at least one new PAK. Until it is loaded by use of
the lmf reset, lmf load for each newly registered PAK, or rebooting your
system, software dependent on them will be treated as if the registrations
had not been performed.

Would you like a lmf reset to be performed at this time?  [Yes] Yes
```

Let's now verify that the license PAK for *TruCluster* Server is loaded and active. To do this we use the `lmf(8)` command.

```
# /usr/sbin/lmf list for tcs-ua

TCS-UA                    active                                  unlimited
```

10.2.2 Install the *TruCluster* Server Software

Please note that while it is a good practice to load the *TruCluster* Server License PAK prior to installing the *TruCluster* Server software subsets, it is not required. The *TruCluster* Server software subsets may be installed without the *TruCluster* Server License PAK, but you will not be able to use any of these software subsets without the License PAK being active.

Now let's go ahead and install the *TruCluster* Server software subsets.

- First let's mount the *Tru64* UNIX Associated Products Volume 2 CD-ROM. This contains the *TruCluster* Server software subsets.

```
# mount -r /dev/disk/cdrom0c /mnt
```

- Now let's "cd" to the *TruCluster* Server kit and see what we will be installing.

```
# cd /mnt/TruCluster/kit && ls
TCRBASE520      TCRMAN520       TCRMIGRATE520   instctrl/
```

The *TruCluster* Server installation contains three software subsets:

Software Subset	Description	Contents
TCRBASE520	*TruCluster* Server Base Components	All the mandatory components to implement *TruCluster* Server.
TCRMAN520	*TruCluster* Server Reference Pages	Reference Pages.
TCRMIGRATE520	*TruCluster* Server Migration Tools	Migration tools for migrating from *TruCluster* Production Server and *TruCluster* Available Server. This also contains tools that are useful in troubleshooting general cluster related issues.

- Using the setld(8) command, we perform the installation of the *TruCluster* Server software subsets. We choose to install all the *TruCluster* Server subsets, although if you do not plan to perform a migration from *TruCluster* version 1.[56] (see Chapter 26), the TCRMIGRATE subset is not necessary.

```
# /usr/sbin/setld -l .

*** Enter subset selections ***

The following subsets are mandatory and will be installed automatically
unless you choose to exit without installing any subsets:

     * TruCluster Base Components

The subsets listed below are optional:

    There may be more optional subsets than can be presented on a single
    screen. If this is the case, you can choose subsets screen by screen
    or all at once on the last screen. All of the choices you make will
    be collected for your confirmation before any subsets are installed.

 - TruCluster(TM) Software :
    1) TruCluster Migration Components
    2) TruCluster Reference Pages
```

```
Or you may choose one of the following options:

     3) ALL mandatory and all optional subsets
     4) MANDATORY subsets only
     5) CANCEL selections and redisplay menus
     6) EXIT without installing any subsets

Estimated free diskspace(MB) in root:293.1 usr:1428.5 var:1200.6

Enter your choices or press RETURN to redisplay menus.

Choices (for example, 1 2 4-6): 3
```

- After selecting to install all the *TruCluster* Server software subsets, we are asked to verify our selection.

```
You are installing the following mandatory subsets:

        TruCluster Base Components

You are installing the following optional subsets:

 - TruCluster(TM) Software :
        TruCluster Migration Components
        TruCluster Reference Pages

Estimated free diskspace(MB) in root:293.1 usr:1428.5 var:1200.6

Is this correct? (y/n): y
```

- After we verify our selection of software subsets that we want to install, the installation starts.

```
Checking file system space required to install selected subsets:

File system space checked OK.

3 subsets will be installed.

Loading subset 1 of 3 ...

TruCluster Migration Components
   Copying from . (disk)
   Verifying

Loading subset 2 of 3 ...

TruCluster Reference Pages
   Copying from . (disk)
   Verifying

Loading subset 3 of 3 ...
TruCluster Base Components
   Copying from . (disk)
   Verifying

3 of 3 subsets installed successfully.
```

- As soon as the software subset installation is complete, the individual subsets are configured as part of the system.

```
Configuring "TruCluster Migration Components" (TCRMIGRATE520)

Configuring "TruCluster Reference Pages" (TCRMAN520)
Running : /usr/lbin/mkwhatis : in the background...

Configuring "TruCluster Base Components" (TCRBASE520)

Use /usr/sbin/clu_create to create a cluster.
```

- We can then verify that all the *TruCluster* Server software subsets are properly installed before we start to create the cluster.

```
# /usr/sbin/setld -i | grep -i TCR
TCRBASE520          installed           TruCluster Base Components (TruClust
er(TM) Software)
TCRMAN520           installed           TruCluster Reference Pages (TruClust
er(TM) Software)
TCRMIGRATE520       installed           TruCluster Migration Components (Tru
Cluster(TM) Software)
```

10.3 Install the *Tru64* UNIX and *TruCluster* Server Patches

Before we start the creation of the cluster, there are quite often patches or late fixes to the *Tru64* UNIX and/or *TruCluster* Server software. As the installation of patches using HP's `dupatch(8)` facility installs patches for all "installed" software subsets instead of all "configured" or "active" software subsets, it would be most efficient to install the patches at this point in the process.

As of this writing, the latest patches for *Tru64* UNIX and *TruCluster* Server can be obtained from the following website: http://www.support.compaq.com/patches

If you're asking, "Why are they installing patches now instead of after the creation of the cluster?," there are two answers. First, it takes less time to install patches at this point in the process than after the cluster is created as we do not have to go through the time-consuming process of performing a rolling upgrade of the cluster[2]. The second and more important reason is that when we actually create the cluster, we want to have the best and most up-to-date software available to do so.

---

[2] Note a "No Roll" patch procedure is available in V5.1A patch kit 2 and later which will allow for a faster patching process in a cluster. See Chapter 25 for more information.

While you can certainly install patches in multi-user mode, we recommend that you install patches in single-user mode to prevent potential problems like having two systems administrators working on the same system at the same time.

The following illustrates the start of the installation of patches to *Tru64* UNIX and to *TruCluster* Server. This is performed after the installation of the *TruCluster* Server software had been completed but before the actual configuration of the cluster.

```
# ./dupatch

Enter path to the top of the patch distribution,
or enter "q" to quit : .

        * A new version of patch tools required for patch management
          is now being installed on your system.

        * Tools updated, invoking the updated Patch Utility...

Tru64 UNIX Patch Utility (Rev. 32-02)
==========================
        - This dupatch session is logged in /var/adm/patch/log/session.log

    Main Menu:
    ---------

    1)  Patch Installation
    2)  Patch Deletion
    3)  Patch Documentation
    4)  Patch Tracking
    5)  Patch Baseline Analysis/Adjustment
    h)  Help on Command Line Interface
    q)  Quit

Enter your choice: 1
```

```
 Tru64 UNIX Patch Utility (Rev. 32-02)
 ==========================
        - This dupatch session is logged in /var/adm/patch/log/session.log

     Patch Installation Menu:
     -----------------------

    1)  Pre-Installation Check ONLY
    2)  Check & Install patches in Single-User Mode
    b)  Back to Main Menu
    q)  Quit

Enter your choice: 2
```

```
     There may be more optional products than can be presented on a single
     screen. If this is the case, you can choose products screen by screen
     or all at once on the last screen. All of the choices you make will
     be collected for your confirmation before any products are installed.

     1) Patches for Tru64 UNIX V5.1A
     2) Patches for TruCluster Server V5.1A

Or you may choose one of the following options:

     3) ALL of the above
     4) CANCEL selections and redisplay menus
     5) EXIT without installing any products

Enter your choices or press RETURN to redisplay menus.

Choices (for example, 1 2 4-6): 3
```

```
You are installing patches (to be selected) from the following products:

        Patches for Tru64 UNIX V5.1A
        Patches for TruCluster Server V5.1A

Is this correct? (y/n): y
...
```

For more information on installing patches on *Tru64* UNIX, please review the *Tru64* UNIX and *TruCluster* Software Products Patch Kit Installation Instructions guide for the patch kit that you will be installing.

10.4 Create the Cluster

Now comes the "fun" part – creating a single-node cluster. To create a cluster, we use the `clu_create(8)` command. The `clu_create` command performs the following:

- It prompts the System Administrator for configuration information necessary for the creation of a single-node cluster.
- It labels disks, creates `root` (/), `/usr`, and `/var` file systems, and the first member's boot disk, copies data to the newly created file systems, creates CDSLs, and updates system configuration information.
- A quorum disk is optionally configured.
- The next step is the kernel build of the first cluster member. At this point, the System Administrator will be given the opportunity to modify the kernel configuration file.
- The final step is the configuration of boot-related SRM console variables: `bootdef_dev`, `boot_reset`, and `boot_dev`. This allows for the boot of the cluster from the cluster member's `boot_partition`.

Now without further ado, let's build a cluster!

10.4.1 The `clu_create(8)` Command

Let's start the process by issuing the `clu_create` command. A nice feature of the `clu_create` command is that it tells you exactly what it will do and then prompts you to verify if that is indeed what you really want to do.

```
# /usr/sbin/clu_create

This is the TruCluster Creation Program

You will need the following information in order to create a cluster:

    - Cluster name (a hostname which is also used as the
      default cluster alias)
    - Cluster alias IP address
    - Clusterwide root disk and partition (for example, dsk4b)
    - Clusterwide usr  disk and partition (for example, dsk4g)
    - Clusterwide var  disk and partition (for example, dsk4h)
    - Quorum disk device (for example, dsk4)
    - Number of votes assigned to the quorum disk
    - Member ID
    - Number of votes assigned to this member
    - First member's boot disk (for example, dsk5)
    - First member's virtual cluster interconnect IP name
    - First member's virtual cluster interconnect IP address
    - First member's physical cluster interconnect devices
    - First member's NetRAIN device name
    - First member's physical cluster interconnect IP address

The program will prompt for this information, offering a default
value when one is available.  To accept the default value, press Return.
If you need help responding to a prompt, either type the word 'help'
or type a question mark (?) at the prompt.

The program does not begin to create a cluster until you answer
all the prompts, and confirm that the answers are correct.

Cluster creation involves the following steps:

    Labeling disks (when required)
    Creating AdvFS domains
    Copying the files on the current root, usr, and var
      partitions to the clusterwide partitions
    Creating additional CDSLs
    Updating configuration files
    Building a kernel and copying it to the first member's boot disk

After the kernel is built and copied, you will halt the system and boot
it using the first member's boot disk.

Do you want to continue creating the cluster? [yes]: [Enter]
```

10.4.1.1 Enter the Cluster Alias Name

The first thing that we are prompted for is the cluster alias name. Here we check the Cluster Preparation Checklist and Worksheet for the cluster alias name and IP address that we had planned to use.

```
Each cluster has a unique cluster name, which is a hostname
used to identify the entire cluster.

Enter a fully-qualified cluster name []:babylon5.dec.com
Checking cluster name: babylon5.dec.com

You entered 'babylon5.dec.com' as your cluster name.
Is this correct? [yes]: ↵Enter
```

This will become the value of the clubase:cluster_name attribute, also known as the Default Cluster Alias (see Chapter 16 for more information).

10.4.1.2 Enter the Cluster Alias IP Address

```
The cluster alias IP address is the IP address associated with the
default cluster alias.  (192.168.168.1 is an example of an IP address.)

Enter the cluster alias IP address [ ]:
Checking cluster alias IP address: 192.168.0.70

You entered '192.168.0.70' as the IP address for the default cluster alias.
Is this correct? [yes]: ↵Enter
```

The cluster alias IP address is placed in the host file in the /etc directory.

10.4.1.3 Enter the cluster_root, cluster_usr, and cluster_var Partitions

Using the disk and partition planning information from the Cluster Preparation Checklist and Worksheet, we enter the partitions set aside for cluster_root, cluster_usr, and cluster_var.

```
The cluster root partition is the disk partition (for example, dsk4b)
that will hold the clusterwide root (/) file system.

    Note: The default 'a' partition on most disks is not large
    enough to hold the clusterwide root AdvFS domain.
```

```
Enter the device name of the cluster root partition []:dsk6a
Checking the cluster root partition: dsk6a

You entered 'dsk6a' as the device name of the cluster root partition.
Is this correct? [yes]: Enter
```

```
The cluster usr partition is the disk partition (for example, dsk4g)
that will contain the clusterwide usr (/usr) file system.

    Note: The default 'g' partition on most disks is usually
    large enough to hold the clusterwide usr AdvFS domain.

Enter the device name of the cluster usr partition []:dsk6g
Checking the cluster usr partition: dsk6g

You entered 'dsk6g' as the device name of the cluster usr partition.
Is this correct? [yes]: Enter
```

```
The cluster var device is the disk partition (for example, dsk4h)
that will hold the clusterwide var (/var) file system.

    Note: The default 'h' partition on most disks is usually
    large enough to hold the clusterwide var AdvFS domain.

Enter the device name of the cluster var partition []:dsk6h
Checking the cluster var partition: dsk6h

You entered 'dsk6h' as the device name of the cluster var partition.
Is this correct? [yes]: Enter
```

10.4.1.4 Enter the Quorum Disk

In planning this cluster, we set aside a quorum disk as we plan to have an even number of members in the cluster. In this section, we are prompted for the name of the quorum disk that was set aside.

```
Do you want to define a quorum disk device at this time? [yes]: Enter
The quorum disk device is the name of the disk (for example, 'dsk5')
that will be used as this cluster quorum disk.

Enter the device name of the quorum disk []:dsk5
Checking the quorum disk device: dsk5
The device you have selected for the quorum disk must be re-labeled
with new cnx partition data. Performing this operation may cause data
contained on this device to be destroyed.
Do you want to use this device anyway? [yes]: Enter
```

```
You entered 'dsk5' as the device name of the quorum disk device.

Is this correct? [yes]: ↵Enter
```

Next, we are prompted for the number of votes the quorum disk will have. We choose to have the quorum disk be assigned 1 vote; however, if we were to operate the cluster as a single-member cluster for awhile, then this should be set to zero votes.

```
By default the quorum disk is assigned '1' vote(s).
To use this default value, press Return at the prompt.

The number of votes for the quorum disk is an integer usually 0 or 1.
If you select 0 votes then the quorum disk will not contribute votes to the
cluster. If you select 1 vote then the quorum disk must be accessible to
boot and run a single member cluster.

Enter the number of votes for the quorum disk [1]: ↵Enter
Checking number of votes for the quorum disk: 1

You entered '1' as the number votes for the quorum disk.

Is this correct? [yes]: ↵Enter
```

10.4.1.5 Enter the Member ID

Here we are prompted for the cluster member ID. As this is the first member of the cluster, we select the default of "1"; however, it can be any integer from 1 to 63.

By default, no matter what the member ID of the first cluster member, it is required that the first cluster member is assigned 1 vote.

```
The default member ID for the first cluster member is '1'.
To use this default value, press Return at the prompt.

A member ID is used to identify each member in a cluster.
Each member must have a unique member ID, which is an integer in
the range 1-63, inclusive.

Enter a cluster member ID [1]: ↵Enter
Checking cluster member ID: 1

You entered '1' as the member ID.

Is this correct? [yes]: ↵Enter

By default the 1st member of a cluster is assigned '1' vote(s).
Checking number of votes for this member: 1
```

This will become the value of the `generic:memberid` attribute.

10.4.1.6 Enter the Member Boot Disk

From the planning we have done, enter the disk that we will use for this member's boot disk. Given that we had pre-configured our disk's partitions differently than the default partition sizes (and set the partitions "in-use"), notice the dialogue around the partition sizes. This is how we were able to use the appropriate partition sizes for swap.

```
Each member has its own boot disk, which has an associated
device name; for example, 'dsk5'.

Enter the device name of the member boot disk []:dsk1
Checking the member boot disk: dsk1

The specified disk contains the required 'a', 'b', and 'h'
partitions.  The current partition sizes are acceptable for a member's
boot disk.  You can either keep the current disk partition layout or have
the installation program relabel the disk.  If the program relabels the disk,
the new label will contain the following partitions and sizes (in blocks):

    Current                  New
    -------                  ---
    a: 524288                a: 524288
    b: 1572864               b: 16777216
    h: 2048                  h: 2048

Do you want to use the current disk partitions? [yes]: [Enter]
You entered 'dsk1' as the device name of this member's boot disk.
Is this correct? [yes]: [Enter]
```

10.4.1.7 Enter the Cluster Interconnect IP Name

Prior to *TruCluster* Server version 5.1A, there was only one type of cluster interconnect supported – the Memory Channel card. As such, at this point in the creation of the cluster, instead of "`ics0`" as the virtual cluster interconnect device, "`mc0`" would be presented as the cluster interconnect interface device. If you are building either a version 5.0A or a version 5.1 cluster, please substitute "`mc0`" for "`ics0`".

By default, the cluster interconnect IP name is the individual system's name with "`-ics0`" appended to it.[3] Prior to *TruCluster* Server version 5.1A, the default interconnect IP name is the individual system's name appended with "`-mc0`". For more information on this subject, please see section 4.4.1.5.

As this cluster interconnect IP name will be used for the internode communications among the cluster members, we recommend using this default value.

---

[3] This is for TruCluster Server version 5.1A or higher.

```
Device 'ics0' is the default virtual cluster interconnect device
Checking virtual cluster interconnect device: ics0

The virtual cluster interconnect IP name 'molari-ics0' was formed by
appending '-ics0' to the system's hostname.
To use this default value, press Return at the prompt.

Each virtual cluster interconnect interface has a unique IP name (a
hostname) associated with it.

Enter the IP name for the virtual cluster interconnect [molari-ics0]: ↵Enter
Checking virtual cluster interconnect IP name: molari-ics0

You entered 'molari-ics0' as the IP name for the virtual cluster interconnect.
Is this name correct? [yes]: ↵Enter
```

10.4.1.8 Enter the Cluster Interconnect IP Address

By default, the subnet `10.0.0` is used as the private network for internode communications between the cluster members. Any subnet that is or will be a private network and that is not in your DNS configuration should also work. For more information, please see sections 4.4.1.5 and 4.4.2.3.

Also by default, the `10.0.0` subnet appended with the member ID is provided as a default cluster interconnect IP address. For simplicity purposes and since it is a reserved address per RFC 1918 (private and non-routable), using this default as the cluster interconnect IP address makes good sense.

```
The virtual cluster interconnect IP address '10.0.0.1' was created by
replacing the last byte of the default virtual cluster interconnect network
address '10.0.0.0' with the previously chosen member ID '1'.
To use this default value, press Return at the prompt.

The virtual cluster interconnect IP address is the IP address
associated with the virtual cluster interconnect IP name.  (192.168.168.1
is an example of an IP address.)

Enter the IP address for the virtual cluster interconnect [10.0.0.1]: ↵Enter
Checking virtual cluster interconnect IP address: 10.0.0.1

You entered '10.0.0.1' as the IP address for the virtual cluster interconnect.
Is this address correct? [yes]: ↵Enter
```

10.4.1.9 Enter the Cluster Interconnect Type

This section of the inputs for the `clu_create` command is new and not found in *TruCluster* Server version 5.0A or 5.1. With the addition of the Ethernet Local Area Network (LAN) as a cluster interconnect in *TruCluster* Server version 5.1A, there had to be some way to specify between using Memory Channel and LAN as a cluster interconnect. In this section, we will be allowed to select which cluster interconnect type to use for our cluster. For more detailed information on configuring the different types of cluster interconnect hardware, please review section 4.4.

Here we will provide two separate examples using the different cluster interconnect types. The first example uses the Memory Channel, and the second uses the Ethernet LAN.

- Using Memory Channel as a cluster interconnect is very straightforward. We simply select Memory Channel as the type of interconnect, verify that this is what we want, and we are done.

```
What type of cluster interconnect will you be using?

    Selection   Type of Interconnect
----------------------------------------------------------------------
         1      Memory Channel
         2      Local Area Network
         3      None of the above
         4      Help
         5      Display all options again
----------------------------------------------------------------------
Enter your choice [1]: 1
```

```
You selected option '1' for the cluster interconnect
Is that correct? (y/n) [y]: y
```

```
Device 'mc0' is the default physical cluster interconnect interface device
Checking physical cluster interconnect interface device name(s): mc0
```

- Using an Ethernet LAN as a cluster interconnect is a bit more complex than using a Memory Channel card. Instead of selecting Memory Channel, we select Local Area Network as the type of interconnect and then verify that this is indeed the interconnect that we want. However, we are not finished with our selections.

```
What type of cluster interconnect will you be using?

    Selection   Type of Interconnect
----------------------------------------------------------------------
         1      Memory Channel
         2      Local Area Network
         3      None of the above
         4      Help
         5      Display all options again
----------------------------------------------------------------------
Enter your choice [1]: 2
```

```
You selected option '2' for the cluster interconnect
Is that correct? (y/n) [y]: [Enter]
```

In this example, we use a gigabit Ethernet LAN card as a cluster interconnect, and we must now tell the software the type of device that it is. In this case, the device is "alt0". For the purposes of our example and as we are only using one Ethernet device as a cluster interconnect, we choose not to put this Ethernet device into a NetRAIN set. For more information on NetRAIN and the benefits of using NetRAIN, please refer to Chapters 9 and 12.

```
The physical cluster interconnect interface device is the name of the
physical device(s) which will be used for low level cluster node
communications. Examples of the physical cluster interconnect interface
device name are: tu0, ee0, and nr0.

Enter the physical cluster interconnect device name(s) []:alt0
Would you like to place this Ethernet device into a NetRAIN set? [yes]:no
Checking physical cluster interconnect interface device name(s): alt0

You entered 'alt0' as your physical cluster interconnect interface

device name(s). Is this correct? [yes]: ↵Enter
```

Now that the software knows what the physical cluster interconnect device is, we need the physical cluster interconnect IP name and IP address. The physical cluster interconnect IP name is created from the word "member" appended with the member ID and "-icstcp0". In our example, this would be member1-icstcp0. This is done automatically for us.

- The default physical cluster interconnect IP address is created by appending the member ID "1" to the default private subnet 10.1.0. Again, we decide to accept this default for the sake of simplicity as it is a reserved address per RFC 1918 (private and non-routable) and it is a good choice to meet our needs in creating a cluster.

```
The physical cluster interconnect IP name ' member1-icstcp0' was formed by
appending '-icstcp0' to the word 'member' and the member ID.
Checking physical cluster interconnect IP name: member1-icstcp0

The physical cluster interconnect IP address '10.1.0.1' was created by
replacing the last byte of the default cluster interconnect network address
'10.1.0.0' with the previously chosen member ID '1'.
To use this default value, press Return at the prompt.

The cluster physical interconnect IP address is the IP address
associated with the physical cluster interconnect IP name. (192.168.168.1
is an example of an IP address.)

Enter the IP address for the physical cluster interconnect [10.1.0.1]:↵Enter
Checking physical cluster interconnect IP address: 10.1.0.1

You entered '10.1.0.1' as the IP address for the physical cluster interconnect.

Is this address correct? [yes]: ↵Enter
```

For more information on configuring an Ethernet LAN card as a cluster interconnect, please see section 4.4.2.

10.4.1.10 Input Summary

Now that we have completed all the inputs required to create a single node cluster, we are given a chance to review all that we have entered. Given that we have two separate examples using the different cluster interconnect types, we also have two different configuration summaries.

- This first configuration summary is when we used Memory Channel as a cluster interconnect. If all the entries look good, we just answer "`yes`" when prompted if we want to create the cluster.

```
You entered the following information:

    Cluster name:                                           babylon5.dec.com
    Cluster alias IP Address:                               192.168.0.70
    Clusterwide root partition:                             dsk6a
    Clusterwide usr  partition:                             dsk6g
    Clusterwide var  partition:                             dsk6h
    Clusterwide i18n partition:                             Not-Applicable
    Quorum disk device:                                     dsk5
    Number of votes assigned to the quorum disk:            1
    First member's member ID:                               1
    Number of votes assigned to this member:                1
    First member's boot disk:                               dsk1
    First member's virtual cluster interconnect device name: ics0
    First member's virtual cluster interconnect IP name:     molari-ics0
    First member's virtual cluster interconnect IP address:  10.0.0.1
    First member's physical cluster interconnect devices     mc0
    First member's NetRAIN device name                       Not-Applicable
    First member's physical cluster interconnect IP address  Not-Applicable

If you want to change any of the above information, answer 'n' to the
following prompt. You will then be given an opportunity to change your
selections.

Do you want to continue to create the cluster? [yes]: ↵Enter
```

- This last configuration summary is for when we used the Ethernet LAN as a cluster interconnect. Again, if we agree that all the entries look good, we just answer "`yes`" when prompted if we want to create the cluster.

  Notice that there is a subtle difference between using the Memory Channel and the Ethernet LAN as a cluster interconnect. Aside from the physical cluster interconnect device being different, can you tell if anything else is different? What about the physical cluster interconnect IP address? When we use the Ethernet LAN as a cluster interconnect, we are actually asked for this as an input.

```
You entered the following information:

    Cluster name:                                                babylon5.dec.com
    Cluster alias IP Address:                                    192.168.0.70
    Clusterwide root partition:                                  dsk6a
    Clusterwide usr  partition:                                  dsk6g
    Clusterwide var  partition:                                  dsk6h
    Clusterwide i18n partition:                                  Not-Applicable
    Quorum disk device:                                          dsk5
    Number of votes assigned to the quorum disk:                 1
    First member's member ID:                                    1
    Number of votes assigned to this member:                     1
    First member's boot disk:                                    dsk1
    First member's virtual cluster interconnect device name:     ics0
    First member's virtual cluster interconnect IP name:         molari-ics0
    First member's virtual cluster interconnect IP address:      10.0.0.1
    First member's physical cluster interconnect devices         alt0
    First member's NetRAIN device name                           Not-Applicable
    First member's physical cluster interconnect IP address      10.1.0.1

If you want to change any of the above information, answer 'n' to the
following prompt. You will then be given an opportunity to change your
selections.

Do you want to continue to create the cluster? [yes]: ↵Enter
```

Now that we are satisfied with all our entries and it matches our plan for the creation of our cluster, from the Cluster Preparation Worksheet and Checklist, we are ready to configure the cluster.

10.4.1.11 Configuring the Cluster

As we have already provided the `clu_create` software and all the inputs required to create a single-node cluster, let's see what happens during the actual configuration and creation of the cluster.

First, the member disk and the quorum disk are labeled, and the `cnx` partition on each is initialized.

```
Creating required disk labels.
  Creating disk label on member disk : dsk1
  Initializing cnx partition on member disk : dsk1h
  Creating disk label on quorum disk : dsk5
  Initializing cnx partition on quorum disk : dsk5h
```

Next, the AdvFS domains for all our system level file systems are created for the cluster and for the first cluster member. These AdvFS domains are `cluster_root`, `cluster_usr`, `cluster_var`, and finally, the first cluster member's `boot_partition` (`root1_domain`).

```
Creating AdvFS domains:
  Creating AdvFS domain 'root1_domain#root' on partition '/dev/disk/dsk1a'.
  Creating AdvFS domain 'cluster_root#root' on partition '/dev/disk/dsk6a'.
  Creating AdvFS domain 'cluster_usr#usr' on partition '/dev/disk/dsk6g'.
  Creating AdvFS domain 'cluster_var#var' on partition '/dev/disk/dsk6h'.
```

Now that the cluster-common file systems are created, we start to populate these file systems with data from the original *Tru64* UNIX system disk. As we have stated previously, *Tru64* UNIX provides the foundation for *TruCluster* Server. And you thought we were just kidding…

```
Populating clusterwide root, usr, and var file systems:
  Copying root file system to 'cluster_root#root'.
  Copying usr file system to 'cluster_usr#usr'.
  Copying var file system to 'cluster_var#var'.
```

Once all the data is copied from the original *Tru64* UNIX system disk, Context Dependent Symbolic Links (CDSLs) are created in all the new system level file systems. Now we start to see a bit of the magic that we call the "Cluster Hooks." We will expand on our discussion of the "Cluster Hooks" in Chapter 12.

```
Creating Content Dependent Symbolic Links (CDSLs) for file systems:
  Creating CDSLs in root file system.
  Creating CDSLs in usr  file system.
  Creating CDSLs in var  file system.
  Creating links between clusterwide file systems
```

In the next stage, the first cluster member's root file system is populated.

```
Populating member's root file system.
```

Finally, in this next section, system level files are either created or updated based upon the configuration entries that we previously provided. As we provided separate configurations for the two examples using the different types of cluster interconnects, we will continue to use separate examples for the two different cluster interconnect configurations.

- This is the output from the configuration using Memory Channel as a cluster interconnect.

```
Modifying configuration files required for cluster operation:
  Creating /etc/fstab file.
  Configuring cluster alias.
  Updating /etc/hosts - adding IP address '192.168.0.70' and hostname
'babylon5.dec.com'
  Updating member-specific /etc/inittab file with 'cms' entry.
  Updating /etc/hosts - adding IP address '10.0.0.1' and hostname 'molari-ics0'
  Updating /etc/rc.config file.
  Updating /etc/sysconfigtab file.
  Retrieving cluster_root major and minor device numbers.
  Creating cluster device file CDSLs.
  Updating /.rhosts - adding hostname 'babylon5.dec.com'.
  Updating /etc/hosts.equiv - adding hostname 'babylon5.dec.com'
  Updating /.rhosts - adding hostname 'molari-ics0'.
  Updating /etc/hosts.equiv - adding hostname 'molari-ics0'
  Updating /etc/ifaccess.conf - adding deny entry for 'ee0'
  Updating /etc/ifaccess.conf - adding deny entry for 'sl0'
  Finished updating member1-specific area.
```

- This is the output from a configuration using Ethernet LAN as the cluster interconnect.

```
Modifying configuration files required for cluster operation:
  Creating /etc/fstab file.
  Configuring cluster alias.
  Updating /etc/hosts - adding IP address '192.168.0.70' and hostname
'babylon5.dec.com'
  Updating member-specific /etc/inittab file with 'cms' entry.
  Updating /etc/hosts - adding IP address '10.0.0.1' and hostname 'molari-ics0'
  Updating /etc/hosts - adding IP address '10.1.0.1' and hostname 'member1-
icstcp0'
  Updating /etc/rc.config file.
  Updating /etc/sysconfigtab file.
  Retrieving cluster_root major and minor device numbers.
  Creating cluster device file CDSLs.
  Updating /.rhosts - adding hostname 'babylon5.dec.com'.
  Updating /etc/hosts.equiv - adding hostname 'babylon5.dec.com'
  Updating /.rhosts - adding hostname 'molari-ics0'.
  Updating /etc/hosts.equiv - adding hostname 'molari-ics0'
  Updating /.rhosts - adding hostname 'member1-icstcp0'.
  Updating /etc/hosts.equiv - adding hostname 'member1-icstcp0'
  Updating /etc/ifaccess.conf - adding deny entry for 'ee0'
  Updating /etc/ifaccess.conf - adding deny entry for 'sl0'
  Finished updating member1-specific area.
```

- Next, the new kernel for the first cluster member is built and copied into place.

```
Building a kernel for this member.
  Saving kernel build configuration.
  The kernel will now be configured using the doconfig program.

*** KERNEL CONFIGURATION AND BUILD PROCEDURE ***

Saving /sys/conf/MOLARI as /sys/conf/MOLARI.bck

*** PERFORMING KERNEL BUILD ***
        Working....Mon Mar 25 12:03:40 PST 2002

The new kernel is /sys/MOLARI/vmunix
  Finished running the doconfig program.

  The kernel build was successful and the new kernel
   has been copied to this member's boot disk.
  Restoring kernel build configuration.
```

10.4.1.12 Updating the SRM Console Variables

In this next section, the boot-dependent SRM console variables are either created or updated to allow for the boot from the newly created cluster member's boot disk. It is important to note that these boot-dependent SRM console variables are **not** being set to root (/) but to the cluster member's boot disk.

```
Updating console variables
  Setting console variable 'bootdef_dev' to dsk1
  Setting console variable 'boot_dev' to dsk1
  Setting console variable 'boot_reset' to ON
  Saving console variables to non-volatile storage
```

10.4.1.13 Completing the Creation of the New Single-Node Cluster

Finally, the `clu_create` command completes and asks if we want to reboot the system to bring up the newly created single-node cluster.

```
clu_create: Cluster created successfully.

To run this system as a single member cluster it must be rebooted.
If you answer yes to the following question clu_create will reboot the
system for you now. If you answer no, you must manually reboot the
system after clu_create exits.

Would you like clu_create to reboot this system now? [yes] ↵Enter
```

10.4.2 Check the Cluster Configuration

After the system is rebooted, it comes back up as a new single-node cluster. Let's check and see what has changed.

10.4.2.1 Checking the File Systems

With regard to the file systems, things look a little different. Using the `mount` command, we see three new cluster file systems that are used for `root` (/), `/usr`, and `/var`. We also see the new cluster member's `boot_partition` is separate.

```
# /sbin/mount
cluster_root#root on / type advfs (rw)
cluster_var#var on /var type advfs (rw)
root1_domain#root on /cluster/members/member1/boot_partition type advfs (rw)
cluster_usr#usr on /usr type advfs (rw)
/proc on /proc type procfs (rw)
```

Taking a closer look, we see that four new AdvFS domains have been created for these file systems. We also see that the AdvFS domains for the original *Tru64* UNIX system level file systems are still available but not mounted.

```
# ls /etc/fdmns
.advfslock_cluster_root      cluster_root/
.advfslock_cluster_usr       cluster_usr/
.advfslock_cluster_var       cluster_var/
.advfslock_root1_domain      root1_domain/
.advfslock_root_domain       root_domain/
.advfslock_usr_domain        usr_domain/
.advfslock_var_domain        var_domain/
```

By looking at the directories for the domains, you can verify that the devices we chose were set. Here is one possible approach:

```
# for i in $(ls -l /etc/fdmns | awk '/^d/ { print $9 }')
> do
>   cd /etc/fdmns/$i
>   print "\n[$PWD]"
>   ls -l | awk '{ print "\t",$9,$10,$11 }'
> done
```

```
[/etc/fdmns/cluster_root]

         dsk6a -> /dev/disk/dsk6a

[/etc/fdmns/cluster_usr]

         dsk6g -> /dev/disk/dsk6g

[/etc/fdmns/cluster_var]

         dsk6h -> /dev/disk/dsk6h

[/etc/fdmns/root1_domain]

         dsk1a -> /dev/disk/dsk1a

[/etc/fdmns/root_domain]

         dsk0a -> /dev/disk/dsk0a

[/etc/fdmns/usr_domain]

         dsk0g -> /dev/disk/dsk0g

[/etc/fdmns/var_domain]

         dsk0h -> /dev/disk/dsk0h
```

10.4.2.2 Checking the SRM Console Variables

We also see that the boot-related SRM console variables are still set from the creation of the cluster.

```
# /sbin/consvar -v -l | grep boot

boot_dev = dsk1
bootdef_dev = dsk1
booted_dev = dsk1
boot_file =
booted_file =
boot_osflags = A
booted_osflags = A
boot_reset = ON
```

10.4.2.3 Checking the `clu_create` Command Logs

To review what occurred during the creation of the single-node cluster, we encourage you to review the logs created by the `clu_create` command. This log file is `/cluster/admin/clu_create.log` and is created or updated every time the `clu_create` command is executed.

10.4.2.4 Checking the Cluster Using `hwmgr(8)` Command

Using the `hwmgr` command, you can also obtain information about the new cluster.

```
# /sbin/hwmgr -view cluster

Member ID         State    Member HostName
---------         -----    ---------------
    1             UP       molari.dec.com (localhost)
```

10.5 Cluster Verification

There is an old saying, "Trust but verify." In this next section, we will verify that the single-node cluster was created properly and is operational. It is important to verify that the configuration of the cluster actually works before proceeding any further and adding additional cluster nodes. We do this by checking and verifying each of the cluster's software subsystems.

10.5.1 Check the Overall Cluster Configuration

The `clu_check_config(8)` command allows us to check the overall configuration of the new cluster and its subsystems. This command executes other commands that check the individual subsystems.

```
# /usr/sbin/clu_check_config

Starting Cluster Configuration Check...
***************** Log Start *****************
Sun Apr 21 00:59:06 PDT 2002

*****
*****   Output from running clu_get_info -full
*****
Cluster information for cluster babylon5

Number of members configured in this cluster = 1
memberid for this member = 1
Cluster incarnation = 0x15512
Cluster expected votes = 2
Current votes = 2
Votes required for quorum = 1
Quorum disk = dsk5h
Quorum disk votes = 1
```

```
Information on each cluster member

Cluster memberid = 1
Hostname = molari.dec.com
Cluster interconnect IP name = molari-ics0
clu_check_config : no configuration errors or warnings were detected
Cluster interconnect IP address = 10.0.0.1
Member state = UP
Member base O/S version = Compaq Tru64 UNIX V5.1A (Rev. 1885)
Member cluster version = TruCluster Server V5.1A  (Rev. 1312)
Member running version = INSTALLED
Member name = molari
Member votes = 1
csid = 0x20001

*****
*****   Output from running cfsmgr -v
*****

 Domain or filesystem name = cluster_root#root
 Mounted On = /
 Server Name = molari
 Server Status : OK

 Domain or filesystem name = root1_domain#root
 Mounted On = /cluster/members/member1/boot_partition
 Server Name = molari
 Server Status : OK

 Domain or filesystem name = cluster_var#var
 Mounted On = /var
 Server Name = molari
 Server Status : OK

 Domain or filesystem name = cluster_usr#usr
 Mounted On = /usr
 Server Name = molari
 Server Status : OK
*****
*****   Output from running cluamgr -s all
*****
*****   Running cluamgr on member molari-ics0

Status of Cluster Alias: babylon5.dec.com

netmask: 0
aliasid: 1
flags: 7<ENABLED,DEFAULT,IP_V4>
connections rcvd from net: 29
connections forwarded: 22
connections rcvd within cluster: 14
data packets received from network: 8364
data packets forwarded within cluster: 943
datagrams received from network: 2190
datagrams forwarded within cluster: 37
datagrams received within cluster: 3063
fragments received from network: 0
fragments forwarded within cluster: 0
fragments received within cluster: 0
Member Attributes:
memberid: 1, selw=3, selp=1, rpri=1 flags=11<JOINED,ENABLED>
```

```
*****
*****   Checking daemons on members *****
*****
*****   Checking member molari-ics0 daemons
        aliasd is RUNNING
        aliasd_niff is RUNNING
        /sbin/kloadsrv is RUNNING
        /usr/sbin/evmd is RUNNING
        /usr/sbin/niffd is RUNNING
        /usr/sbin/portmap is RUNNING
        /usr/sbin/caad is RUNNING
        /usr/sbin/clu_wall is RUNNING
        /usr/sbin/xntpd is RUNNING
        /usr/sbin/gated is RUNNING
        /usr/sbin/clu_mibs is RUNNING
        /usr/sbin/rdginit is RUNNING
        /usr/sbin/snmpd is RUNNING
        /usr/sbin/syslogd is RUNNING
        /usr/sbin/binlogd is RUNNING
        /usr/sbin/mountd is RUNNING
        /usr/sbin/nfsd is RUNNING
        /usr/sbin/smsd is RUNNING
        /usr/sbin/clu_wall is RUNNING
        /usr/sbin/xntpd is RUNNING
        /usr/sbin/gated is RUNNING
        /usr/sbin/clu_mibs is RUNNING
        /usr/sbin/rdginit is RUNNING
        /usr/sbin/snmpd is RUNNING
        /usr/sbin/syslogd is RUNNING
        /usr/sbin/binlogd is RUNNING
        /usr/sbin/mountd is RUNNING
        /usr/sbin/nfsd is RUNNING
        /usr/sbin/smsd is RUNNING
*****
*****   Checking time synchronization between members *****
*****
molari-ics0: delay:0.000976 offset:0.000488  Sun Apr 21 00:59:10 2002

check_cdsl_config : Checking installed CDSLs
check_cdsl_config : Successfully verified CDSLs configuration
```

10.5.2 Check the Connection Manager Subsystem

Let's now check the Connection Manager subsystem. The `clu_get_info(8)` command provides detailed information about the cluster and all the cluster members. This command is also executed from the `clu_check_config` command.

```
# /usr/sbin/clu_get_info -full

Cluster information for cluster babylon5

Number of members configured in this cluster = 1
memberid for this member = 1
Cluster incarnation = 0xb63fd
Cluster expected votes = 2
Current votes = 2
Votes required for quorum = 1
Quorum disk = dsk5h
Quorum disk votes = 1

Information on each cluster member

Cluster memberid = 1
Hostname = molari.dec.com
Cluster interconnect IP name = molari-ics0
Cluster interconnect IP address = 10.0.0.1
Member state = UP
Member base O/S version = Compaq Tru64 UNIX V5.1A (Rev. 1885)
Member cluster version = TruCluster Server V5.1A  (Rev. 1312)
Member running version = INSTALLED
Member name = molari
Member votes = 1
csid = 0x10001
```

The clu_quorum(8) command is used for configuring or deleting a quorum disk and adjusting the quorum disk votes, individual member node votes, and overall expected votes. This command can also be used to display information about what quorum is in a cluster. For more detailed information concerning the clu_quorum command, please read Chapter 17 on the Connection Manager or the clu_quorum(8) reference page.

In any event, let's look at quorum in our new single-node cluster using the clu_quorum command.

```
# /usr/sbin/clu_quorum

Cluster Quorum Data for: babylon5 as of Sun Apr 21 01:27:16 PDT 2002

Cluster Common Quorum Data
Quorum disk:    dsk5h
File:           /etc/sysconfigtab.cluster

Attribute                                  File Value
expected votes                                      2

Member 1 Quorum Data
Host name:      molari.dec.com           Status:                 UP
File:           /cluster/members/member1/boot_partition/etc/sysconfigtab

Attribute              Running Value         File Value
current votes                      2                N/A
quorum votes                       1                N/A
expected votes                     2                  2
node votes                         1                  1
qdisk votes                        1                  1
qdisk major                       19                 19
qdisk minor                      384                384
```

10.5.3 Check the Cluster Alias Subsystem

The cluamgr(8) command is used to manage and report information and statistics about cluster aliases. As this cluster was just created, there should only be information about one cluster alias – the default cluster alias. Let's see what information is provided.

```
# /usr/sbin/cluamgr -s all

Status of Cluster Alias: babylon5.dec.com

netmask: 0
aliasid: 1
flags: 7<ENABLED,DEFAULT,IP_V4>
connections rcvd from net: 30
connections forwarded: 22
connections rcvd within cluster: 17
data packets received from network: 8796
data packets forwarded within cluster: 1361
datagrams received from network: 2190
datagrams forwarded within cluster: 37
datagrams received within cluster: 3068
fragments received from network: 0
fragments forwarded within cluster: 0
fragments received within cluster: 0
Member Attributes:
memberid: 1, selw=3, selp=1, rpri=1 flags=11<JOINED,ENABLED>
```

As we can see, the cluster alias is "babylon5.dec.com" and it only has one cluster member in the cluster. This is evident by the memberid field.

More information on cluster aliases can found in Chapter 16 on the Cluster Alias Subsystem.

10.5.4 Check the Device Request Dispatcher (DRD) Subsystem

The command used to configure and report on the DRD subsystem is the drdmgr(8) command. Let's use the drdmgr command to look at the properties of the disk containing the cluster_root file system.

First, let's find out what disk is used for the cluster_root domain.

```
# /sbin/showfdmn cluster_root

               Id              Date Created  LogPgs  Version  Domain Name
3d013c89.0000fc70  Thu Apr 21 16:06:49 2002     512        4  cluster_root

  Vol   512-Blks        Free  % Used  Cmode  Rblks  Wblks  Vol Name
   1L    1048576      769360     27%     on    256    256  /dev/disk/dsk6a
```

Now let's use the drdmgr command to examine dsk6.

```
# /sbin/drdmgr dsk6

  View of Data from member molari as of 2002-04-21:01:24:17

                Device Name: dsk6
                Device Type: Direct Access IO Disk
              Device Status: OK
          Number of Servers: 1
                Server Name: molari
               Server State: Server
         Access Member Name: molari
        Open Partition Mask: 0xc1 < a g h >
 Statistics for Client Member: molari
   Number of Read Operations: 8189
  Number of Write Operations: 910513
        Number of Bytes Read: 145510400
     Number of Bytes Written: 8068251648
```

Notice that molari is both the server and the client (Access Member Name) for this disk. Also notice that three partitions are open on this disk (from the Open Partition Mask) – partitions a, g, and h. These partitions correspond to the AdvFS domains for cluster_root, cluster_usr, and cluster_var.

Now let's look at the quorum disk.

```
# /sbin/drdmgr dsk5

  View of Data from member molari as of 2002-04-21:01:29:39

                Device Name: dsk5
                Device Type: Direct Access IO Disk
              Device Status: OK
          Number of Servers: 1
                Server Name: molari
               Server State: Server
         Access Member Name: molari
        Open Partition Mask: 0
 Statistics for Client Member: molari
   Number of Read Operations: 200979
  Number of Write Operations: 200977
        Number of Bytes Read: 205805568
     Number of Bytes Written: 102903808
```

As you can see, there appears to be quite a bit of I/O activity to this disk but there does not appear to be any open partitions. As this is the quorum disk, the Connection Manager does not have any partitions open.

For more detailed information on the DRD subsystem, please review Chapter 15 on the Device Request Dispatcher.

10.5.5 Check the Cluster File System (CFS) Subsystem

The cfsmgr(8) command is used to manage and gather information on the mounted file systems in a cluster.

With the creation of a single-node cluster, let's see what information the cfsmgr command provides.

```
# /sbin/cfsmgr

 Domain or filesystem name = cluster_root#root
 Mounted On = /
 Server Name = molari
 Server Status : OK

 Domain or filesystem name = root1_domain#root
 Mounted On = /cluster/members/member1/boot_partition
 Server Name = molari
 Server Status : OK

 Domain or filesystem name = cluster_var#var
 Mounted On = /var
 Server Name = molari
 Server Status : OK

 Domain or filesystem name = cluster_usr#usr
 Mounted On = /usr
 Server Name = molari
 Server Status : OK
```

Since this is a single-node cluster, it is reasonable to expect that the server for all the file systems is the only member in the cluster. For more detailed information on the Cluster File System subsystem, please refer to Chapter 13.

10.5.6 Check the Cluster Application Availability (CAA) Subsystem

The caa_stat(8) command is used to obtain status of applications under CAA subsystem control. Applications under CAA subsystem control can usually run on only one cluster node at a time. CAA is the high availability mechanism to failover an application if the cluster node where it was running becomes unavailable.

By default, usually cluster_lockd is configured as a CAA on a new cluster. Using the caa_stat command provides for statistics on its state.

```
# /usr/bin/caa_stat -t
Name           Type         Target    State     Host
------------------------------------------------------------
cluster_lockd  application  ONLINE    ONLINE    molari
dhcp           application  OFFLINE   OFFLINE
named          application  OFFLINE   OFFLINE
```

For more information on CAA, please review Chapters 23 and 24 on Cluster Application Availability.

10.5.7 Check the Network Aliases

From the following output, we can see that we have a network up and available on the Memory Channel interconnect.

```
# netstat -I ics0
Name  Mtu   Network   Address              Ipkts Ierrs   Opkts Oerrs  Coll
ics0  7000  <Link>    ics0:42.0.0.0.0.1    82417     0   82791     0     0
ics0  7000  10.0.0    molari-ics0          82417     0   82791     0     0
```

Notice that the alias for our cluster, `babylon5`, does not appear on the interface associated with the subnet that we are using.

```
# netstat -I ee0
Name  Mtu   Network       Address              Ipkts Ierrs    Opkts Oerrs  Coll
ee0   1500  <Link>        0:50:8b:ae:fe:dc   1172451     0   115869     0     0
ee0   1500  DLI           none               1172451     0   115869     0     0
ee0   1500  138.127.89    molari             1172451     0   115869     0     0
```

10.6 References

- The *TruCluster* Server Cluster Installation Guide.
- The *TruCluster* Server Cluster Administration Guide.
- The *Tru64* UNIX and *TruCluster* Software Patch Summary and Release Notes.
- The *Tru64* UNIX and *TruCluster* Software Patch Kit Installation Instruction Guide.
- Reference pages (noted within the text).

11

Adding a Cluster Member/Deleting a Cluster Member

"Out of clutter, find Simplicity. From discord, find Harmony. In the middle of difficulty lies opportunity."

- Albert Einstein

In Chapter 10, we discussed how to create a single-node cluster based on careful cluster configuration planning and preparation. In this chapter, we will expand on that discussion. We will discuss the next step in creating a cluster, that is, expanding a cluster by adding a new member. To round off our review of creating and expanding a cluster, we will discuss how to delete a cluster member.

With the proper care, planning, and preparation, adding a new member and deleting a member from a cluster are straightforward and simple activities that can be done very quickly. It's therefore very important to continue to use the Cluster Preparation Checklist and Worksheet from section 4.8 as a guide. The Checklist and Worksheet are like the blueprint to a house – you would never want to start building a house without first having the plans in place showing what its architecture will look like.

As a rather non-scientific test, we timed ourselves to see how long it would take to add and configure a new AlphaServer into an existing *TruCluster* Server environment. Our fastest time from initial power on of the system to the new system being booted and operational as a cluster member was 32 minutes. While we certainly wouldn't qualify as members of a pit crew at the Indy 500, consider the normal time it takes to install and configure a single server. If it takes an hour and a half to two hours to build one server, and building two servers takes three to four hours. Building a two-member cluster on the other hand would take approximately two to two and a half hours. Not bad!

Does that give us bragging rights on how quickly we can add a new member to an existing cluster? No, but it does show that with the proper planning and preparation, and the *TruCluster* Server software, adding a new member to a cluster is a straightforward and simple task. The same applies to deleting a member from a cluster.

11.1 Preparation

It is said that a failure to prepare is preparing to fail. With that in mind, take your time to plan and prepare for the deployment of your cluster. Start with the Cluster Preparation Checklist and Worksheet from section 4.8 to develop your plan of deployment, and then execute your plan.

11.1.1 Planning on Adding Another Cluster Member

All elements to adding members to a cluster are carefully discussed in Chapter 4. Please review Chapter 4 for more information and again, please use the Cluster Preparation Checklist and Worksheet as a guide to planning your cluster.

11.1.2 Getting Ready

You should start with at least one single-node cluster that has been successfully configured. Assuming you have planned and prepared to add a member to the cluster, you are ready to add a new member to a cluster. The following subsections cover some last minute items.

11.1.2.1 Add or Delete One Member at a Time

As it is so very easy to add a new member or delete a member, it is important to note that you should completely add or delete a cluster member before initiating another add or delete of another cluster member. Why? To avoid any cluster quorum problems. In the context of the cluster, it is vital that quorum be maintained and adjusted as necessary as we add or delete cluster members.

11.1.2.2 The New Member Boot Disk

The boot disk or `boot_partition` for the cluster member to be added should be identified by now. If not, please review Chapter 4 and your plan for the deployment of the cluster.

At this point, use the information from section 10.1.2 to properly partition the member boot disk and write an appropriate disklabel to it. After the disklabel has been written, it should have the appropriate in-use `fstype` for the partitions used for the member `boot_partition`, swap, and the cluster status partition. If this is not the case, please refer to section 10.1.2, review your plan for the deployment of your cluster, and again create the appropriate disklabel.

11.1.2.3 Initialize SRM Console Variables

If the boot-related SRM console variables for the new cluster member have not already been initialized to prevent the new cluster member from booting during the installation, then this should be done before starting the process to add that member to the cluster. For more information, please see section 4.5.3.

11.2 Adding a New Cluster Member

To add a new system or new member to a cluster, we execute the clu_add_member(8) command on an existing cluster member. The clu_add_member command does the following:

- Creates directories and files for the new member in the cluster_root, cluster_usr, and cluster_var file systems.
- Labels and populates a boot disk for the new member.
- Configures layered product software subsets.
- Builds a new kernel and copies it into place in the new member's boot_partition.
- Writes a record of the session to a log file, clu_add_member.log, which is located in the /cluster/admin directory. It also writes the new member's configuration information to the .member*n*.cfg file (where *n* is the memberid of the new member) located in the same directory.
- There are no software installations on the new cluster member. As this is a cluster, we only need to install software once, and this was performed when the cluster was first created.

Execute the clu_add_member command on an existing cluster member. Notice that like the clu_create command in Chapter 10, the clu_add_member command tells us what information is required and exactly what it will do to create the new cluster member.

```
# /usr/sbin/clu_add_member

This is the TruCluster Add Member Program

You will need the following information in order to add a member to
the cluster:

     - Hostname
     - Member ID (1-63)
     - Members Votes
     - Member's boot disk (for example, dsk7)
     - Member's virtual cluster interconnect IP name
     - Member's virtual cluster interconnect IP address
     - Member's physical cluster interconnect devices
     - Member's NetRAIN device name
     - Member's physical cluster interconnect IP address
     - Member's cluster license

The program will prompt for this information, offering a default
value when one is available.  To accept the default value, press Return
If you need help responding to a prompt, either type the word 'help'
or type a question mark (?) at the prompt.

The program does not begin to add the member until you answer
all the prompts, and you confirm that the answers are correct.
```

```
Adding a member involves the following steps:

    Labeling the boot disk (when required)
    Creating AdvFS domains
    Creating additional CDSLs
    Updating configuration files

You then boot genvmunix from the new member's boot disk. At the first
boot the new member:

    Configures layered product subsets
    Builds a kernel and copies it to the member's boot disk
    Boots the new kernel
```

The first thing we must do to add a new cluster member is to acknowledge that this is what we intend to do.

```
Do you want to continue adding this member? [yes]: yes
```

11.2.1 Enter the Hostname

In the next dialogue that we have with the `clu_add_member` program, we are prompted to enter the fully qualified hostname that we reserved for the new cluster member. We refer to our planning document – the Cluster Preparation Checklist and Worksheet – for what we have decided to call this system.

```
Each cluster member has a hostname, which is assigned to the HOSTNAME
variable in /etc/rc.config.

Enter the new member's fully qualified hostname []:sheridan.dec.com
Checking member's hostname: sheridan.dec.com

You entered 'sheridan.dec.com' as this member's hostname.
Is this name correct? [yes]: yes
```

11.2.2 Enter the Member ID and the Expected Vote

Next, we are prompted to enter the `memberid` for this new cluster member. By default, the next available `memberid` in sequential order is presented. In this case, it is 2; however, we can use any number up to 63. Of course, this is only if the `memberid` is not currently in use by another cluster member.

```
The next available member ID for a cluster member is '2'.
To use this default value, press Return at the prompt.

A member ID is used to identify each member in a cluster.
Each member must have a unique member ID, which is an integer in
the range 1-63, inclusive.

Enter a cluster member ID [2]: 2
Checking cluster member ID: 2

You entered '2' as the member ID.
Is this correct? [yes]: yes
```

By default, this new cluster member is given 1 vote. In this case, it makes perfect sense to accept this default value. For more detailed information on quorum and the Connection Manager, please review Chapter 17.

```
By default, when the current cluster's expected votes are greater then 1,
each added member is assigned 1 vote(s). Otherwise, each added member is
assigned 0 (zero) votes.
To use this default value, press Return at the prompt.

The number of votes for a member is an integer usually 0 or 1
Enter the number of votes for this member [1]: 1
Checking number of votes for this member: 1

You entered '1' as the number votes for this member.
Is this correct? [yes]: yes
```

11.2.3 Enter the Member Boot Disk

As each individual cluster member must have its own boot device or `boot_partition`, we are prompted to enter the name of the disk that will be used for this new cluster member. Given that we had planned for this, we refer to our completed Cluster Preparation Checklist and Worksheet for the information on the disk that has been reserved and already properly partitioned for the `boot_partition` of this new cluster member.[1]

```
Each member has its own boot disk, which has an associated
device name; for example, 'dsk5'.

Enter the device name of the member boot disk []:dsk2
Checking the member boot disk: dsk2
```

---

[1] Please refer to section 11.1.2.2 on The New Member Boot Disk and section 10.1.2 on Disks for the Cluster.

```
The specified disk contains the required 'a', 'b', and 'h'
partitions.  The current partition sizes are acceptable for a member's
boot disk.  You can either keep the current disk partition layout or have
the installation program relabel the disk.  If the program relabels the disk,
the new label will contain the following partitions and sizes (in blocks):

    Current                  New
    -------                  ---
    a: 524288                a: 524288
    b: 1572864               b: 16777216
    h: 2048                  h: 2048

Do you want to use the current disk partitions? [yes]: yes
You entered 'dsk2' as the device name of this member's boot disk.
Is this correct? [yes]: yes
```

As you can see, we have successfully used the custom partitioned member boot disk. For more information on the special technique that we used to do this, please refer to section 10.2.1.

11.2.4 Enter the Cluster IP Name

As we had stated in Chapters 4 and 10, with the release of *TruCluster* Server version 5.1A and the addition of Ethernet LAN as an alternate cluster interconnect to Memory Channel, the cluster interconnect device name was changed from "`mc0`" to "`ics0`". This was done so that the cluster interconnect device could now be virtual. This change was accompanied by the change in some default naming conventions so by default, the new cluster member's virtual cluster interconnect IP name is the hostname appended with "`-ics0`". Prior to *TruCluster* Server version 5.1A, this default cluster interconnect IP name would be the hostname appended with "`-mc0`". While any IP name, which is not in your DNS configuration, should work, we recommend using the default for simplicity and consistency and because it is already highly descriptive.

```
Device 'ics0' is the default virtual cluster interconnect device
Checking virtual cluster interconnect device: ics0

The virtual cluster interconnect IP name 'sheridan-ics0' was formed by
appending '-ics0' to the system's hostname.
To use this default value, press Return at the prompt.

Each virtual cluster interconnect interface has a unique IP name (a
hostname) associated with it.

Enter the IP name for the virtual cluster interconnect [sheridan-ics0]:sheridan-ics0
Checking virtual cluster interconnect IP name: sheridan-ics0

You entered 'sheridan-ics0' as the IP name for the virtual cluster interconnect.
Is this name correct? [yes]: yes
```

11.2.5 Enter the Cluster IP Address

In Chapter 10, the subnet `10.0.0` is used as the private network for internode communications between the cluster members. By default, the 10.0.0 subnet plus the member ID is provided as a default cluster interconnect IP address for this new member. In the interest of consistency, and since it is a reserved address per RFC 1918 (private and non-routable), using this default as the virtual cluster interconnect IP address is a good choice.

```
The virtual cluster interconnect IP address '10.0.0.2' was created by
replacing the last byte of the virtual cluster interconnect network address
'10.0.0.0' with the previously chosen member ID '2'.
To use this default value, press Return at the prompt.

The virtual cluster interconnect IP address is the IP address
associated with the virtual cluster interconnect IP name.  (192.168.168.1
is an example of an IP address.)

Enter the IP address for the virtual cluster interconnect [10.0.0.2]: 10.0.0.2
Checking virtual cluster interconnect IP address: 10.0.0.2

You entered '10.0.0.2' as the IP address for the virtual cluster interconnect.
Is this address correct? [yes]: yes
```

11.2.6 Enter the Cluster Interconnect Type[2]

Starting with *TruCluster* Server version 5.1A, the `clu_add_member` command, like the `clu_create` command, gives us the option to use either Ethernet LAN or Memory Channel as the cluster interconnect.[3] At this point in adding a new member, we are prompted to select a cluster interconnect type.

For the purposes of illustration, we are providing two examples of what the selection of a cluster interconnect type should look like. The first example is using the Memory Channel and the second is using the Ethernet LAN.

- Using Memory Channel is very straightforward. We just select "`mc0`" as the physical cluster interconnect device, confirm the selection, and we are done.

```
Device 'mc0' is the default physical cluster interconnect interface device
To use this default value, press Return at the prompt.
```

---

[2] This section of the `clu_add_member` is not present in *TruCluster* Server version 5.0A and *TruCluster* Server version 5.1.

[3] *TruCluster* Server version 5.0A and *TruCluster* Server version 5.1 only support Memory Channel as a cluster interconnect.

```
The physical cluster interconnect interface device is the name of the
physical device(s) which will be used for low level cluster node
communications. Examples of the physical cluster interconnect interface
device name are: tu0, ee0, and nr0.

Enter the physical cluster interconnect device name(s) [mc0]: mc0
Checking physical cluster interconnect interface device name(s): mc0

You entered 'mc0' as your physical cluster interconnect interface
device name(s). Is this correct? [yes]: yes
```

- When adding a new cluster member, using Ethernet LAN as a physical cluster interconnect is a more complex than using Memory Channel. First, we are prompted for the physical cluster interconnect device. In our example, we use a gigabit Ethernet LAN card – "`alt0`".

```
The physical cluster interconnect interface device is the name of the
physical device(s) which will be used for low level cluster node
communications. Examples of the physical cluster interconnect interface
device name are: tu0, ee0, and nr0.

Enter the physical cluster interconnect device name(s) []:alt0
Would you like to enter another Ethernet device? [yes]:no
Checking physical cluster interconnect interface device name(s): alt0

You entered 'alt0' as your physical cluster interconnect interface
device name(s). Is this correct? [yes]:yes
```

We are then prompted to specify whether the interfaces should be configured in a NetRAIN virtual interface. For more information on NetRAIN, please review Chapter 9. In our example, we choose not to select anything for a NetRAIN interface device name as we have only one Ethernet device for a cluster interconnect.

```
Enter a NetRAIN interface device name []:
```

Given that the software now knows what the physical cluster interconnect device is, we need the physical cluster IP name and address. As discussed in Chapters 4 and 10, this name is created from the word "`member`" appended with the `memberid` and "`-icstcp0`". This is automatically created for us.

Appending the `memberid` to the default private subnet `10.1.0` creates the default physical cluster IP address. In our example, this IP address would be `10.1.0.2`. Again, we accept this default.

```
The physical cluster interconnect IP name 'member2-icstcp0' was formed by
appending '-icstcp0' to the word 'member' and the member ID.
Checking physical cluster interconnect IP name: member2-icstcp0

The physical cluster interconnect IP address '10.1.0.2' was created by
replacing the last byte of the physical cluster interconnect network address
'10.1.0.0' with the previously chosen member ID '2'.
To use this default value, press Return at the prompt.

The cluster physical interconnect IP address is the IP address
associated with the physical cluster interconnect IP name. (192.168.168.1
is an example of an IP address.)

Enter the IP address for the physical cluster interconnect [10.1.0.2]:10.1.0.2
Checking physical cluster interconnect IP address: 10.1.0.2

You entered '10.1.0.2' as the IP address for the physical cluster interconnect.
Is this address correct? [yes]:yes
```

For more information on configuring and using an Ethernet LAN card as a cluster interconnect, please review section 4.4.2.

11.2.7 *TruCluster* Server License PAK

Finally, the `clu_add_member` command prompts us for the last input – the *TruCluster* Server License PAK. With this prompt, we can choose to either add the license PAK for the new cluster member now or use the `lmfsetup` command later after we boot the new cluster member. In our example, we choose to enter the *TruCluster* Server License PAK.

```
Each cluster member must have its own registered TruCluster Server
license. The data required to register a new member is typically located on
the License PAK certificate or it may have been previously placed on your
system as a partial or complete license data file. If you are prepared to
enter this license data at this time, clu_add_member can configure the new
member to use this license data. If you do not have the license data at this
time you can enter this data on the new member when it is up and running.
Do you wish to register the TruCluster Server license for this new member at
this time? [yes]: yes
```

```
By default the TruCluster Server license data is entered by invoking
the editor that is defined by your EDITOR environment variable. If the
environment variable is undefined, the vi editor will be invoked.
clu_add_member will display a template that includes all the fields on a PAK
and an additional field for your comment. You must transfer the values from
your License Pak certificate to the template, then save and exit the editor.
Do you wish to enter the data using the 'vi' editor? [yes]: yes
```

```
Licensed Software Product Authorization Key

Enter data on lines terminated with :
                 Issuer : dec
   Authorization Number : alq-nq-2000dec30-zzzz
           Product Name : tcs-ua
               Producer : dec
        Number of units : 1050
                Version :
   Product Release Date :
   Key Termination Date :
Availability Table Code : h
    Activity Table Code :
            Key Options : mod_units,alpha
          Product Token :
            Hardware-Id :
               Checksum : 2-wwww-xxxx-yyyy-zzzz

Creating new license database
Warning creating new history file
Checking TruCluster Server license data
```

11.2.8 Summary of Inputs

Given that we have completed all the required inputs to add a member to a cluster, we are given a chance to review and accept all that we have entered. As we had two examples using the different types of cluster interconnect devices, we have two different summaries.

- This first input summary is based on using Memory Channel as a cluster interconnect.

```
You entered the following information:

    Member's hostname:                                   sheridan.dec.com
    Member's ID:                                         2
    Number of votes assigned to this member:             1
    Member's boot disk:                                  dsk2
    Member's virtual cluster interconnect devices:       ics0
    Member's virtual cluster interconnect IP name:       sheridan-ics0
    Member's virtual cluster interconnect IP address:    10.0.0.2
    Member's physical cluster interconnect devices:      mc0
    Member's NetRAIN device name:                        Not-Applicable
    Member's physical cluster interconnect IP address:   Not-Applicable
    Member's cluster license:                            Entered

If you want to change any of the above information answers 'n' to the
following prompt. You will then be given an opportunity to change your
selections.
Do you want to continue to add this member? [yes]: yes
```

- This next input summary is based on using Ethernet LAN as a cluster interconnect.

```
You entered the following information:

    Member's hostname:                                    sheridan.dec.com
    Member's ID:                                          2
    Number of votes assigned to this member:              1
    Member's boot disk:                                   dsk2
    Member's virtual cluster interconnect devices:        ics0
    Member's virtual cluster interconnect IP name:        sheridan-ics0
    Member's virtual cluster interconnect IP address:     10.0.0.2
    Member's physical cluster interconnect devices:       alt0
    Member's NetRAIN device name:                         Not-Applicable
    Member's physical cluster interconnect IP address:    10.1.0.2
    Member's cluster license:                             Entered

If you want to change any of the above information answers 'n' to the
following prompt. You will then be given an opportunity to change your
selections.
Do you want to continue to add this member? [yes]: yes
```

In either example, we confirm the summary and answer "yes" when prompted to continue adding the cluster member.

11.2.9 Configuring the Cluster

This next section does not require any input as all selections and entries have already been made. Let's examine what is being done.

First, a disk label is written to the new cluster member's boot disk. The cnx partition on this disk is then initialized.

```
Creating required disk labels.
  Creating disk label on member disk : dsk2
  Initializing cnx partition on member disk : dsk2h
```

The AdvFS domain for the new cluster member's boot disk is created along with member-specific files for the new cluster member.

```
Creating AdvFS domains:
  Creating AdvFS domain 'root2_domain#root' on partition '/dev/disk/dsk2a'.

Creating cluster member-specific files:
  Creating new member's root member-specific files
  Creating new member's usr  member-specific files
  Creating new member's var  member-specific files
  Creating new member's boot member-specific files
```

Next, as part of the addition of the new cluster member, configuration modifications and updates to system files are performed. Again, as we have two different examples of configurations using the different cluster interconnect types, we also have two different examples of modifications to system files.

- If a Memory Channel is used as a cluster interconnect, the updates to system files looks like this:

```
Modifying configuration files required for new member operation:
  Updating /etc/hosts - associating IP address '10.0.0.2' with hostname
'sheridan-ics0'
  Updating /etc/rc.config
  Updating /etc/rc.config
  Updating /etc/sysconfigtab
  Updating member-specific /etc/inittab file with 'cms' entry.
  Updating /.rhosts - adding hostname 'sheridan-ics0'
  Updating /etc/hosts.equiv - adding hostname 'sheridan-ics0'
  Updating /etc/cfgmgr.auth - adding hostname 'sheridan.dec.com'
  Configuring cluster alias.
  Configuring Network Time Protocol for new member
  Adding interface 'molari-ics0' as an NTP peer to member 'sheridan.dec.com'
  Adding interface 'sheridan-ics0' as an NTP peer to member 'molari.dec.com'
  Registering TruCluster Server License
```

- If an Ethernet LAN is used as a cluster interconnect, the updates to system files look like this:

```
Modifying configuration files required for new member operation:
  Updating /etc/hosts - associating IP address '10.0.0.2' with hostname
'sheridan-ics0'
  Updating /etc/hosts - adding IP address '10.1.0.2' and hostname 'member2-
icstcp0'
  Updating /etc/rc.config
  Updating /etc/sysconfigtab
  Updating member-specific /etc/inittab file with 'cms' entry.
  Updating /etc/securettys - adding ptys entry
  Updating /.rhosts - adding hostname 'sheridan-ics0'
  Updating /etc/hosts.equiv - adding hostname 'sheridan-ics0'
  Updating /.rhosts - adding hostname 'member2-icstcp0'
  Updating /etc/hosts.equiv - adding hostname 'member2-icstcp0'
  Updating /etc/cfgmgr.auth - adding hostname 'sheridan.dec.com'
  Configuring cluster alias.
  Configuring Network Time Protocol for new member
  Adding interface 'molari-ics0' as an NTP peer to member 'sheridan.dec.com'
  Adding interface 'sheridan-ics0' as an NTP peer to member 'molari.dec.com'
  Registering TruCluster Server License
```

Once the entire configuration for the addition of the new cluster member is complete, a list of instructions on what to do next on the new cluster member is displayed.

```
Configuring automatic subset configuration and kernel build.
CNX MGR: Adjust expected votes operation completed with quorum.

clu_add_member: Initial member 2 configuration completed successfully.
From the newly added member's console, perform the following steps to
complete the newly added member's configuration:

   1. Set the console variable 'boot_osflags' to 'A'.
   2. Identify the console name of the newly added member's boots device.

      >>>show device

      The newly added member's boot device has the following properties:

      Manufacturer: DEC
      Model: HSG80
      Target: IDENTIFIER=2
      Lun: UNKNOWN
      Serial Number: SCSI-WWID:01000010:6000-1fe1-0001-6950-0009-1420-0755-0038

      Note: The SCSI bus number may differ when viewed from different members.

   3. Boot the newly added member using genvmunix:

       >>>boot -file genvmunix <new-member-boot-device>

      During this initial boot the newly added member will:

      o  Configure each installed subset.

      o  Attempt to build and install a new kernel. If the system cannot
         build a kernel, it starts a shell where you can attempt to build
         a kernel manually. If the build succeeds, copy the new kernel to
         /vmunix. When you are finished exit the shell using ^D or 'exit'.

      o  The newly added member will attempt to set boot related console
         variables and continue to boot to multi-user mode.

      o  After the newly added member boots you should setup your system
         default network interface using the appropriate system management
         command.
```

11.3 Booting the New Cluster Member

Let's follow the instructions that were displayed at the completion of the `clu_add_member` command.

First, let's set the `boot_osflags` console variable.

```
P00>>> set boot_osflags 'a'
```

Next, let's identify the boot device of the new cluster member.[4]

```
P00>>> show device
Dga2.1001.0.7.1              $1$DGA2                        HSG80   V86F
...
```

IMPORTANT:

If you are using a SCSI device for your member boot disk, the location of the device on the new cluster member may differ from the location of the device as seen by the cluster member that ran the clu_add_member command. Since device naming at the operating system level is independent of the physical device location (i.e., not dependent on bus-target-lun symantics), this may potentially lead to misidentifying the device from the new member's perspective.

For example, if dsk2 (the new member's boot disk) were a SCSI disk, its location would be determined by its bus-target-lun (b-t-l) not a Fibre Channel identifier. However, the b-t-l would not determine the device name (see Chapter 7).

From the current cluster member:

```
# hwmgr -v d -dsf dsk2
 HWID: Device Name           Mfg       Model              Location
 ------------------------------------------------------------------------
   49: /dev/disk/dsk2c       COMPAQ    BD009635C3         bus-2-targ-0-lun-0
```

This equates to DKB0 at the current cluster member's console.

```
>>> show dev
dka0.0.0.14.0                DKA0                 COMPAQ BB009235B6   B017
dka100.1.0.14.0              DKA100               COMPAQ BB009235B6   B017
dkb0.0.0.15.0                DKB0                 COMPAQ BD009635C3   B017
dkb100.1.0.15.0              DKB100               COMPAQ BD009635C3   B017
dkb200.2.0.15.0              DKB200               COMPAQ BD009635C3   B017
dkb300.3.0.15.0              DKB300               COMPAQ BD009635C3   B017
dkb400.4.0.15.0              DKB400               COMPAQ BD009635C3   B017
dkb500.5.0.15.0              DKB500               COMPAQ BD009635C3   B017
```

There is no requirement, however, that the new system have the same bus numbering as the current cluster member. Therefore, bus 2 on member1 may be bus 3 on member2 resulting in dsk2 being seen at location DKC0 from member2's console (see Figure 11-1).

---

[4] For more information on determining the boot device in a Fibre Channel switched environment and having this device seen at the SRM console, please see section 4.2.5.

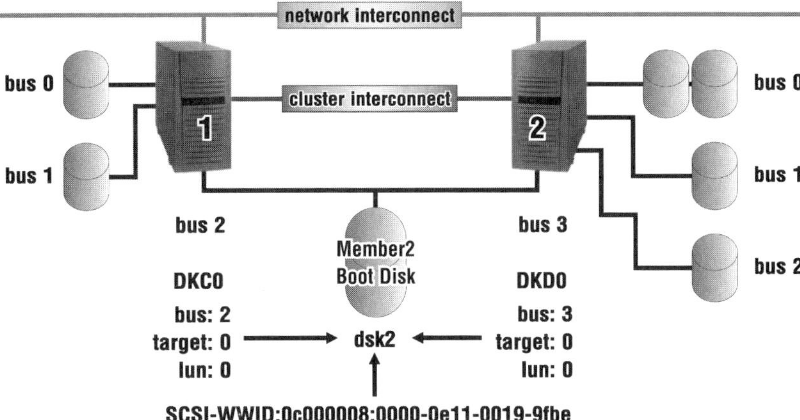

Figure 11-1: SCSI Device Location vs. Naming

If you are unsure of the location of the device, you can locate the device from the current cluster member using the `hwmgr` command with "`flash`" option.

```
# hwmgr flash light -dsf dsk2 -seconds 60 -nopause
```

This command will illuminate the activity light on the disk for 60 seconds (the default is 30 seconds). Note the "`-nopause`" option will cause the light to not flash but stay on for the duration of the command. Once you locate the device, you can physically trace the cable to the host bus adapter if needed.

It is extremely important that you know your hardware configuration.

Now let's boot the generic kernel from the new cluster member's boot device.

```
P00>>> boot -file genvmunix dga2
```

As the new cluster member continues to boot, it will configure all installed software subsets.

```
Executing Installation Tasks...

*** SYSTEM CONFIGURATION ***
...

[Configure installed software subsets.]

[Configure installed patch kit.]
...
```

After all the installed software subsets are configured, a new UNIX kernel is built for the new cluster member. This new kernel is then copied into place.

```
*** KERNEL CONFIGURATION AND BUILD PROCEDURE ***

*** PERFORMING KERNEL BUILD ***

A log file listing special device files is located in /dev/MAKEDEV.log
        Working....Wed Mar 27 16:35:42 PST 2002

The new kernel is /sys/SHERIDAN/vmunix
Copying new kernel to /vmunix ...
```

As soon as this is done, the new cluster member continues to boot to multi-user mode.

11.4 Configuring the New Cluster Member

Once in multi-user mode, the configuration of the new cluster member continues with the setup of the system default network interface. The first prompt asks if we are prepared to add the network interface configuration for the new cluster member. We can opt to do this later using the "sysman net_wizard" command or the clu_netsetup(8) command or we can choose to configure the network interface now. For our cluster, we choose to configure the interface now.

```
clu_add_member was unable to determine the network configuration for the
interface associated with this system's hostname. You may configure this
interface using the clu_netsetup by answering 'yes' to the following
question. If you decide not to run clu_netsetup, then the time it takes the
system to boot will be considerably longer.
Would you like to run clu_netsetup at this time? [yes]: yes

   **** TruClusters Add Member Network Interface Configuration ****

                 1  Configure Interface

                 2  Exit

Enter the number for your choice: 1
***** CONFIGURE/DELETE NETWORK INTERFACES *****

You can configure or delete network interfaces.  Configuration information
is updated in /etc/rc.config and /etc/hosts.  Choose "configure" or "delete"
at the prompt.

Enter whether you want to "(c)onfigure" or "(d)elete" network interfaces.
If you are finished, press the RETURN key: c
```

Next, we are asked to select the network interface we want to configure. In our case, we select the "ee0" device. Your configuration will most likely be different, so plan which devices you want to use for your network interface.

```
You will now be asked a series of questions about the system.
Default answers are shown in square brackets ([]).  To use a
default answer, press the RETURN key.

This machine contains the following network interfaces:
         ee0
         sl0

Which interface do you want to configure [ee0]: ee0
You want to configure "ee0".  Is this correct [yes]? yes
```

We are then prompted for the hostname and network IP address we will use for this network interface.

```
Enter the hostname for interface "ee0" []: sheridan.dec.com
The hostname for interface "ee0" is "sheridan.dec.com".
Is this correct [yes]? yes

Enter the Internet Protocol (IP) address for interface "ee0"
in dot notation []: 192.168.0.69
The IP address for interface "ee0" is "192.168.0.69".
Is this correct [yes]? yes
```

We are then prompted for the subnet mask for our local network and asked if we use any additional `ifconfig(8)` flags for the network interface.

```
Subnetworks allow the systems on a local area network to be on different
physical networks.  For the following question, use the default answer
unless the existing local area network is using subnet routing.
If the local area network is using subnet routing, you need to know
the subnet mask.

Enter the subnet mask in dot notation [255.255.255.0]: 255.255.255.0
The subnet mask for "ee0" is "255.255.255.0".
Is this correct [yes]? yes

For the following question USE THE DEFAULT ANSWER unless you would like
to add additional flags (found in the ifconfig reference page) to the
ifconfig command.  Normally, you will USE THE DEFAULT ANSWER.

Do you want to use additional ifconfig flags for this interface [no]? no
```

Finally, we are asked to confirm the network interface information that we entered before configuration begins.

```
The configuration looks like:

        interface "ee0" hostname: "sheridan.dec.com"
        ifconfig ee0 192.168.0.69 netmask 255.255.255.0

Is this correct [yes]? yes
```

```
***** UPDATING /etc/rc.config *****

"ee0" is configured in /etc/rc.config

Do you want to configure another network interface [yes]? no

Enter whether you want to "(c)onfigure" or "(d)elete" network interfaces.
If you are finished, press the RETURN key:

   **** TruClusters Add Member Network Interface Configuration ****

                1  Configure Interface

                2  Exit

Enter the number for your choice: 2

***** Interface Configuration Completed *****
```

As soon as the network interface is complete, the boot-related SRM console variables are set for the new cluster member.

```
Setting console variables
set bootdef_dev = dsk2
set boot_dev = dsk2
set boot_reset = on
```

If email is configured, it is then clusterized so that all members of the cluster – both existing members and the newly added member – can send and/or receive email.

```
Clusterizing mail...
```

11.5 Install All License PAKs

One of the last things to be done on the new cluster member is to install all the remaining License PAKs specific for that cluster member. Note: as part of the addition of a new member to the cluster, we already entered the *TruCluster* Server License PAK so this does not need to be reinstalled.

We recommend the use of the `lmfsetup(8)` command especially for the installation of multiple License PAKs. This is by far the easiest and most straightforward mechanism for the installation of License PAKs.

```
# /usr/sbin/lmfsetup
```

As soon as all the License PAKs are installed and the License Management Facility's database reset, we verify that all the License PAKS are active by using the `lmf(8)` command.

```
# /usr/sbin/lmf list
Product                 Status                    Users: Total      Active

OSF-SVR                 active                           unlimited
OSF-USR                 active                           unlimited
OSF-BASE                active                           unlimited
OSF-BASE                active, multiple                 unlimited
TCS-UA                  active                           unlimited
```

11.6 Verify the New Cluster Member

Finally, let's explore the newly added cluster member and verify that everything is configured and operational.

First, let's take a look at the cluster using the `hwmgr(8)` command.

```
# /sbin/hwmgr -view cluster
Member ID       State   Member HostName
---------       -----   ---------------
    1           UP      molari.dec.com
    2           UP      sheridan.dec.com (localhost)
```

Now let's see what file systems are mounted. As we can see, the new cluster member's `boot_partition` is mounted.

```
# mount
cluster_root#root on / type advfs (rw)
root2_domain#root on /cluster/members/member2/boot_partition type advfs (rw)
cluster_var#var on /var type advfs (rw)
root1_domain#root on /cluster/members/member1/boot_partition type advfs (rw)
cluster_usr#usr on /usr type advfs (rw)
/proc on /proc type procfs (rw)
```

Finally, let's check the cluster configuration and see what it looks like. To examine the cluster configuration, we use the `clu_check_config(8)` command, which checks the majority of the *TruCluster* Server's individual subsystems. We have trimmed the output to show only `member2`'s information.

```
# /usr/sbin/clu_check_config

Starting Cluster Configuration Check...
**************** Log Start ****************
Sun Apr 21 00:59:06 PDT 2002

*****
*****   Output from running clu_get_info -full
*****
Cluster information for cluster babylon5

Number of members configured in this cluster = 2
memberid for this member = 1
Cluster incarnation = 0x15512
Cluster expected votes = 3
Current votes = 3
Votes required for quorum = 2
Quorum disk = dsk5h
Quorum disk votes = 1

Information on each cluster member
…
Cluster memberid = 2
Hostname = sheridan.dec.com
Cluster interconnect IP name = sheridan-ics0
Cluster interconnect IP address = 10.0.0.2
Member state = UP
Member base O/S version = Compaq Tru64 UNIX V5.1A (Rev. 1885)
Member cluster version = TruCluster Server V5.1A  (Rev. 1312)
Member running version = INSTALLED
Member name = sheridan
Member votes = 1
csid = 0x20002

*****
*****   Output from running cfsmgr -v
*****
…
 Domain or filesystem name = root2_domain#root
 Mounted On = /cluster/members/member2/boot_partition
 Server Name = sheridan
 Server Status : OK

*****
*****   Output from running cluamgr -s all
*****
…
*****   Running cluamgr on member sheridan-ics0

Status of Cluster Alias: babylon5.dec.com

netmask: 0
aliasid: 1
flags: 7<ENABLED,DEFAULT,IP_V4>
connections rcvd from net: 16
connections forwarded: 4
connections rcvd within cluster: 34
data packets received from network: 1050
```

```
data packets forwarded within cluster: 325
datagrams received from network: 884
datagrams forwarded within cluster: 878
datagrams received within cluster: 30
fragments received from network: 0
fragments forwarded within cluster: 0
fragments received within cluster: 0
Member Attributes:
memberid: 1, selw=3, selp=1, rpri=1 flags=11<JOINED,ENABLED>
memberid: 2, selw=3, selp=1, rpri=1 flags=11<JOINED,ENABLED>
*****
*****   Checking daemons on members *****
*****
…
*****   Checking member sheridan-ics0 daemons
        aliasd is RUNNING
        aliasd_niff is RUNNING
        /sbin/kloadsrv is RUNNING
        /usr/sbin/evmd is RUNNING
        /usr/sbin/niffd is RUNNING
        /usr/sbin/portmap is RUNNING
        /usr/sbin/caad is RUNNING
        /usr/sbin/clu_wall is RUNNING
        /usr/sbin/xntpd is RUNNING
        /usr/sbin/gated is RUNNING
        /usr/sbin/clu_mibs is RUNNING
        /usr/sbin/rdginit is RUNNING
        /usr/sbin/snmpd is RUNNING
        /usr/sbin/syslogd is RUNNING
        /usr/sbin/binlogd is RUNNING
        /usr/sbin/mountd is RUNNING
        /usr/sbin/nfsd is RUNNING
        /usr/sbin/smsd is RUNNING
        /usr/sbin/clu_wall is RUNNING
        /usr/sbin/xntpd is RUNNING
        /usr/sbin/gated is RUNNING
        /usr/sbin/clu_mibs is RUNNING
        /usr/sbin/rdginit is RUNNING
        /usr/sbin/snmpd is RUNNING
        /usr/sbin/syslogd is RUNNING
        /usr/sbin/binlogd is RUNNING
        /usr/sbin/mountd is RUNNING
        /usr/sbin/nfsd is RUNNING
        /usr/sbin/smsd is RUNNING
*****
*****   Checking time synchronization between members *****
*****
     molari-ics0: delay:0.000976 offset:0.000488  Sun Apr 21 00:59:10 2002
     sheridan-ics0: delay:0.000976 offset:-0.000093  Sun Apr 21 00:59:10 2002

check_cdsl_config : Checking installed CDSLs
check_cdsl_config : Successfully verified CDSLs configuration
```

As we can see from the `clu_check_config` output, this cluster looks like it is indeed configured and operational.

11.7 Removing a Member from the Cluster

To end the chapter, we will discuss removing a member from the cluster. In order to avoid any quorum problems, you should remove only one cluster member at a time and adjust the votes on the quorum disk as appropriate to maintain quorum for the cluster. To remove a member from a cluster, we use the `clu_delete_member(8)` command. Let's see what the `clu_delete_member` command actually does before we see an example of its execution.

11.7.1 The `clu_delete_member` Command

The `clu_delete_member` command does the following:

- It mounts the soon-to-be deleted member's `boot_partition` and deletes all files in the file system. From this point on, this cluster member can no longer boot from this disk.

WARNING:

If the "`clu_delete_member -f`" command is used, it will delete a member even when that member's boot disk is inaccessible. This lets you delete a member whose boot disk has failed or is inaccessible for any reason.

- If the member-to-be-deleted has votes, and if its boot disk is accessible, it adjusts the value of `cluster_expected_votes` throughout the cluster.

WARNING:

If the `clu_delete_member` command cannot mount the boot partition, it is unable to determine the number of votes held by the member-to-be-deleted. The value of `cluster_expected_votes` will therefore not be reset throughout the cluster. If you encounter this scenario, after the `clu_delete_member` command completes, use the `clu_quorum(8)` command to check the value of `cluster_expected_votes`.[5] Most likely an adjustment of the value will be necessary.

- It removes all member-specific directories and files from the cluster-common file systems (`cluster_root`, `cluster_usr`, and `cluster_var`) for the member-to-be-deleted.

[5] For more detailed information on quorum, please see Chapter 17 on the Connection Manager.

IMPORTANT:

As the System Administrator can create member-specific files in other directories, such files must be manually removed after the completion of clu_delete_member command.

- It removes the soon-to-be deleted member's host name for its cluster interconnect interface from the /.rhosts and /etc/hosts.equiv files.
- It writes a log file, clu_delete_member.log, in the /cluster/admin directory.

The clu_delete_member command can be run either interactively or with a simple command line argument. For example, to delete member3 from a cluster, use the following command:

```
# /usr/sbin/clu_delete_member -m 3
```

11.7.2 Steps to Deleting a Cluster Member

Now that we know what the clu_delete_member command actually does, let's go over the actual steps needed to delete a cluster member.

1. First, we need to determine whether the member-to-be-deleted is a critical voting member of the cluster. This is an essential step since we do not want to impact the cluster's operation by losing quorum.

   Before halting the member-to-be-deleted, we use the clu_quorum(8) command to determine whether it is safe to do so.[6]

2. Shut down the cluster member-to-be-deleted.
3. Make sure that all remaining cluster members are up and operational. Use the "clu_get_info -full" command for verification.
4. Now comes the actual deletion of a cluster member-. On another cluster member, run the clu_delete_member command to remove the halted member from the cluster. The clu_delete_member command can be run either interactively or with command line arguments
5. Prior to the deletion of the member, if the cluster had an even number of members and a configured quorum disk, then it is important to delete the quorum disk or change the quorum disk's votes from 1 to 0.

[6] For more information on adjusting votes for quorum, please see Chapter 17 on Connection Manager.

```
# /usr/sbin/clu_quorum -d remove
 Collecting quorum data for Member(s): 1 2

 qdisk_major: reconfigured
 qdisk_minor: reconfigured
 qdisk_votes: reconfigured
 qdisk_oper: reconfigured

 Quorum disk successfully removed.
```

Or

```
# /usr/sbin/clu_quorum -d adjust 0
Collecting quorum data for Member(s): 1 2

CNX MGR: Adjust quorum disk votes operation completed with quorum.

Quorum disk votes successfully adjusted.
```

If, on the other hand, deleting the member reduces the number of members to an even number, then either the quorum disk should be added and/or the quorum disk's votes should be changed from 0 to 1.

```
# /usr/sbin/clu_quorum -d add dsk5 1
 Collecting quorum data for Member(s): 1 2

 Initializing cnx partition on quorum disk : dsk5h
 qdisk_major: reconfigured
 disk_minor: reconfigured
 qdisk_votes: reconfigured
 qdisk_oper: reconfigured

 Quorum disk votes successfully adjusted.
```

Or

```
# /usr/sbin/clu_quorum -d adjust 1
Collecting quorum data for Member(s): 1 2

CNX MGR: Adjust quorum disk votes operation completed with quorum.

Quorum disk votes successfully adjusted.
```

WARNING:

Never add, delete, or modify a quorum disk while either the `clu_delete_member` or the `clu_add_member` commands are in process.

11.7.3 Execution of the clu_delete_member Command

In our example, let's execute the clu_delete_member interactively. Like the other commands needed to create a cluster or to add a new cluster member, the clu_delete_member command reveals exactly what it will do and then asks the user if he wants to continue.

```
# /usr/sbin/clu_delete_member

This is the TruCluster Delete Member Program

You will need the following information in order to delete a member from
the cluster:

    - Member ID (1-63)

The program will prompt for this information, offering a default
value when one is available.  To accept the default value, press Return
If you need help responding to a prompt, either type the word 'help'
or type a question mark (?) at the prompt.

The program does not begin to delete the member until you answer
all the prompts, and confirm that the answers are correct.

Deleting a member involves the following steps:

    Removing the files from the member boot disk. (If accessible)
    Removing member specific areas from the /, /usr, and /var file systems.
    Removing the deleted members entries in shared configuration files.

Do you want to continue deleting a member from this cluster? [yes]: yes
```

Next, the clu_delete_member command prompts the cluster member to be deleted. If this cluster member is not halted and ready to be deleted, do not proceed and please review section 11.7.2.
In our example, we are deleting cluster member3.

```
A member ID is used to identify each member in a cluster.
Each member must have a unique member ID, which is an integer in
the range 1-63, inclusive.

Enter a cluster member ID []: 3
Checking cluster member ID: 3

You entered '3' as the member ID.
Is this correct? [yes]: yes

You entered the following information:

    Member's ID: 3

If any of this information is incorrect, answer 'n' to the following
prompt.  You can then enter the correct information.

Do you want to continue to delete a cluster member?:[no] yes
```

Finally, we are presented with messaging of what the `clu_delete_member` command is doing as it occurs.

```
Deleting member disk boot partition files
  Member disk boot partition files deleted

Initial cluster deletion successful, member '3' can no longer join the
cluster. Deletion continuing with cleanup
cluster_expected_votes: reconfigured

Removing deleted member entries from shared configuration files
  Removing cluster interconnect interface 'tester-ics0' from /.rhosts

…
Deleting Member Specific Directories
  Deleting: /cluster/members/member3/
  Deleting: /usr/cluster/members/member3/
  Deleting: /var/cluster/members/member3/

clu_delete_member: The deletion of cluster member '3' completed successfully.
```

After the `clu_delete_member` command has completed, we must adjust the number of votes for the quorum disk. Since we have a cluster with an even number of members, we change the number of votes on the quorum disk from 0 to 1.

```
# /usr/sbin/clu_quorum -d adjust 1
Collecting quorum data for Member(s): 1 2

CNX MGR: Adjust quorum disk votes operation completed with quorum.

Quorum disk votes successfully adjusted.
```

That's really about it when it comes to deleting a member from a cluster, which, as promised, is a straightforward and simple process.

11.8 References

- The *TruCluster* Server Cluster Installation Guide
- The *TruCluster* Server Cluster Administration Guide
- The *Tru64* UNIX and *TruCluster* Software Patch Summary and Release Notes
- The *Tru64* UNIX and *TruCluster* Software Patch Kit Installation Instruction document
- Reference pages (noted within the text)

12

Cluster Hooks Revisited

Now that we have a cluster up and running, it is time to expand upon those "hooks" within *Tru64* UNIX that are used to more easily enable clustering. Our initial discussion started in chapter 6 and continued through chapter 9. In this chapter we will revisit the following topics:

	Revisited Coverage in **Section**	Original Coverage in **Chapter**
• File System Hierarchy	12.1	6
• Member-Specific or Cluster-Common?	12.1.1	6
• Context Dependent Symbolic Link (CDSL)	12.2	6
• Hardware Management Databases	12.3.1	7
• Hardware Manager (`hwmgr(8)`)	12.3.2	7
• Device Special File Manager (`dsfmgr(8)`)	12.3.3	7
• Event Manager (EVM)	12.4	8
• Network Interface Failure Finder (NIFF)	12.5	9
• NetRAIN	12.6	9
• Link Aggregation (LAG)	12.7	9

12.1 File System Hierarchy Revisited

We begin our journey with the changes to the file system hierarchy now that the cluster has been created. The first change is the location of the file systems. In our standalone system, we had three file systems on two AdvFS domains:

- `root_domain#root` – the root (`/`) file system
- `usr_domain#usr` – the `/usr` file system
- `usr_domain#var` – the `/var` file system

Now that we have a two-member cluster, there are five file systems:

- `cluster_root#root` – the root (/) file system
- `cluster_usr#usr` – the `/usr` file system
- `cluster_var#var` – the `/var` file system
- `root1_domain#root` – `member1`'s boot disk
- `root2_domain#root` – `member2`'s boot disk

Figure 12-1 shows the *TruCluster* Server file system layout.

The second change you will see is that there are more member directories.

```
# for i in / /usr /var
> do
>   cd ${i}/cluster/members
>   print "\n[${PWD}]"
>   ls -ld *
> done

[/cluster/members]
lrwxr-xr-x    1 root     system         6 Dec 13 16:39 member -> {memb}
drwxr-xr-x    9 root     system      8192 Dec 13 16:43 member0
drwxr-xr-x    9 root     system      8192 Dec 13 16:54 member1
drwxr-xr-x    9 root     system      8192 Dec 14 13:12 member2

[/usr/cluster/members]
lrwxr-xr-x    1 root     system         6 Dec 13 16:40 member -> {memb}
drwxr-xr-x    7 root     system      8192 Dec 13 16:40 member0
drwxr-xr-x    7 root     system      8192 Dec 13 16:43 member1
drwxr-xr-x    7 root     system      8192 Dec 14 13:04 member2

[/var/cluster/members]
lrwxr-xr-x    1 root     system         6 Dec 13 16:42 member -> {memb}
drwxr-xr-x   21 root     system      8192 Dec 13 16:42 member0
drwxr-xr-x   21 root     system      8192 Dec 13 16:42 member1
drwxr-xr-x   21 root     system      8192 Dec 14 13:05 member2
```

This is to be expected because we now have a two-member cluster. A more interesting directory, however, lies within each cluster member's member directory – that directory is the member's boot partition (`boot_partition`).

12.1.1 The Boot Partition

The boot partition is the directory where files are located that are required by a member in order to boot. It is the boot partition, and not the root partition, that a member uses to boot. When we created the cluster, the root partition which was formerly `root_domain#root` was replaced by `cluster_root#root`. Since the root partition is mounted clusterwide it cannot be a bootable partition; therefore, it became necessary to have a member-specific boot partition with a boot block

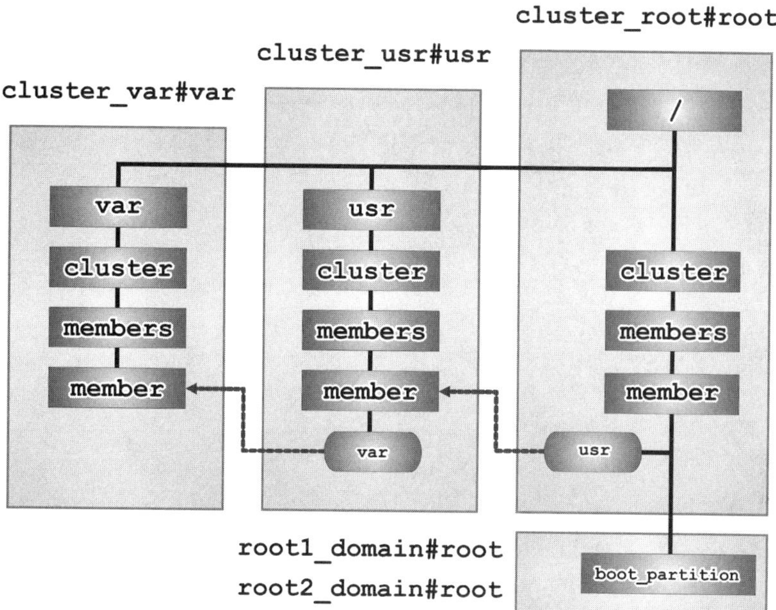

Figure 12-1: File System Hierarchy in a Cluster

that each member could use to boot itself into the cluster. Each member has its own boot partition that is mounted at `/cluster/members/member/boot_partition`.

Two questions immediately spring to mind when considering this new file system hierarchy:

- If root is cluster-common and that is where the kernel is located, how can I boot without root?
- If I now have a boot partition, what is in it?

To answer the first question, let's expand upon what we stated earlier in this section. Every member must have its own boot disk. Why? First of all, every member must have its own kernel due to potential hardware differences between members. Second, another member when attempting to boot from it cannot open the boot partition. So we need a separate disk that only one member will attempt to access, solving the second problem, and on that disk we will place the kernel and associated support files thus solving the first problem.

A member boot disk contains three partitions:

- The boot partition – the "`a`" partition at the head of the disk.
- The primary swap partition – the "`b`" partition.
- The `cnx` partition – the "`h`" partition, a 1MB partition at the end of the disk.

At block 0 of the member's boot disk is the boot block (`rzboot.advfs` for an AdvFS domain). This boot block points to the primary bootstrap code (`bootrz.advfs`) located at logical block number (LBN) 64. It is this bootstrap code that opens the `osf_boot` executable, which in turn loads the kernel. Both the `osf_boot` file and the kernel are located on the boot partition. Besides osf_boot and the kernel, what else should we expect? How about the sysconfigtab file? What about some of the hardware databases?

Returning to the second question, "If I now have a boot partition, what is in it?," let's take a look.

```
# ls -R /.local../boot_partition
.tags          genvmunix      osf_boot       quota.user
etc            mdec           quota.group    vmunix

/.local../boot_partition/.tags:

/.local../boot_partition/etc:
clu_bdmgr.conf      dec_devsw_db        dec_hwc_ldb         dvrdevtab
clu_recover.dat     dec_devsw_db.bak    dec_hwc_ldb.bak     fwevdb
ddr.db              dec_hw_db           dec_scsi_db         gen_databases
ddr.dbase           dec_hw_db.bak       dec_scsi_db.bak     sysconfigtab

/.local../boot_partition/mdec:
bootblks
```

As you can see, the entire partition contains a small number of files, many of which you have probably seen once or twice before. In fact, the boot partition currently uses about 35MB on our test cluster.

```
# du -sk /.local../boot_partition
35645   /.local../boot_partition
```

12.1.2 Member-Specific or Cluster-Common? (Revisited)

Now that we have a cluster, it should be easier to understand why we must have both member-specific and cluster-common files. Since the purpose of a cluster is to act like one large system instead of many smaller systems working independently, the cluster members share many files. In fact, the cluster members share most of the files. They also share a common configuration for many applications but not **all** applications.

As we pointed out in the previous section, every member requires its own files in order to boot. The kernel must be tailored to the member's specific hardware configuration, for example. Since the member is likely to have a unique hardware configuration, each member has its own /dev directory as well as member-specific hardware databases. Each member will need its own hostname and IP address; therefore, the rc.config file is member-specific. We discussed much of this in chapter 6 but felt it important enough to reiterate here.

12.2 CDSLs Revisited

We also want to point out that member-specific locations are not only located directly under the cluster/members/member directories of the root(/), /usr, and /var directories.

For example, /etc/rc.config is a link to /.local../etc/rc.config, but /etc/sysconfigtab points to /.local../boot_partition/etc/sysconfigtab. Both files are member-specific.

```
# fln /etc/rc.config /etc/sysconfigtab
/etc/rc.config -> ../cluster/members/{memb}/etc/rc.config
/etc/sysconfigtab -> ../cluster/members/{memb}/boot_partition/etc/sysconfigtab
```

Remember that /.local.. is a CDSL that points to /cluster/members/{memb}.

In section 6.3, we showed the CDSLs that exist on a standalone system. Table 12-1 shows the CDSLs

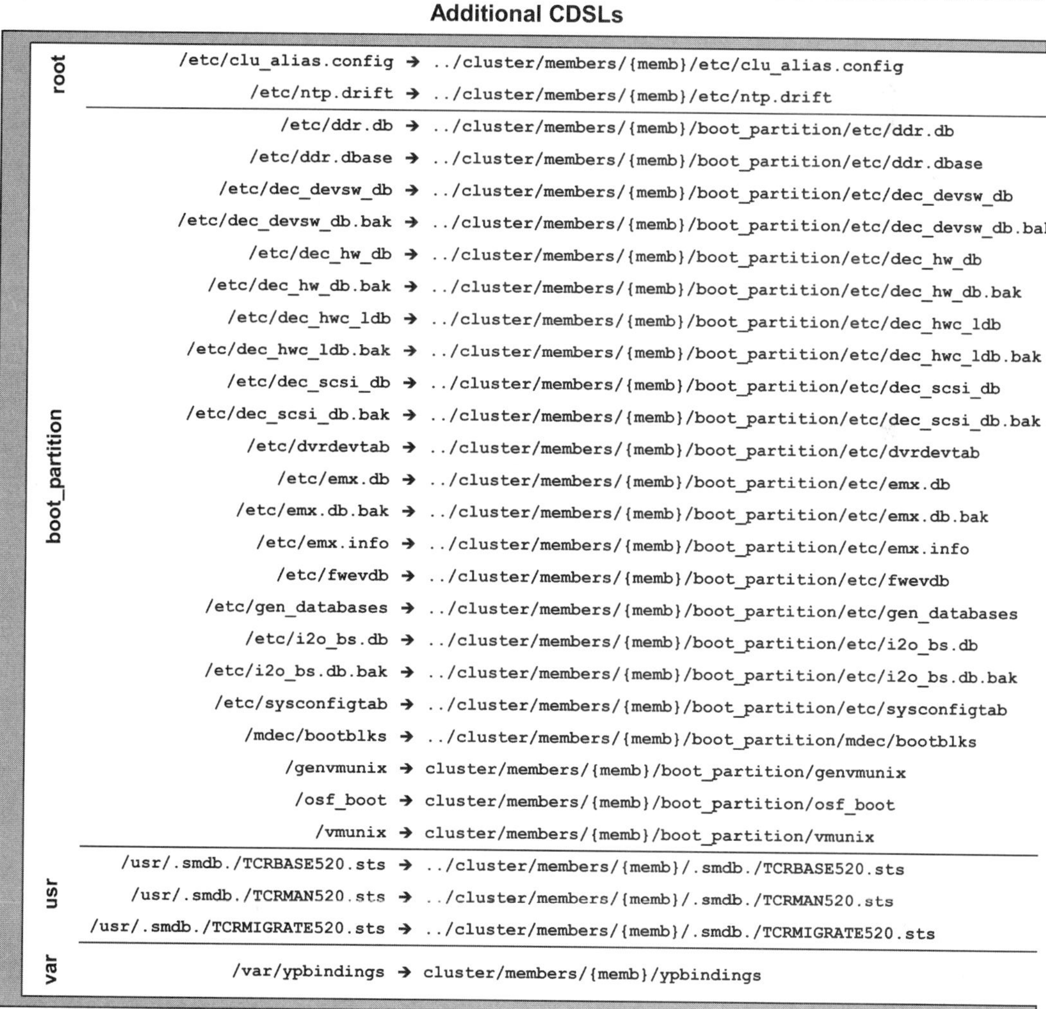

Additional CDSLs

	CDSL		Target
root	/etc/clu_alias.config	→	../cluster/members/{memb}/etc/clu_alias.config
	/etc/ntp.drift	→	../cluster/members/{memb}/etc/ntp.drift
boot_partition	/etc/ddr.db	→	../cluster/members/{memb}/boot_partition/etc/ddr.db
	/etc/ddr.dbase	→	../cluster/members/{memb}/boot_partition/etc/ddr.dbase
	/etc/dec_devsw_db	→	../cluster/members/{memb}/boot_partition/etc/dec_devsw_db
	/etc/dec_devsw_db.bak	→	../cluster/members/{memb}/boot_partition/etc/dec_devsw_db.bal
	/etc/dec_hw_db	→	../cluster/members/{memb}/boot_partition/etc/dec_hw_db
	/etc/dec_hw_db.bak	→	../cluster/members/{memb}/boot_partition/etc/dec_hw_db.bak
	/etc/dec_hwc_ldb	→	../cluster/members/{memb}/boot_partition/etc/dec_hwc_ldb
	/etc/dec_hwc_ldb.bak	→	../cluster/members/{memb}/boot_partition/etc/dec_hwc_ldb.bak
	/etc/dec_scsi_db	→	../cluster/members/{memb}/boot_partition/etc/dec_scsi_db
	/etc/dec_scsi_db.bak	→	../cluster/members/{memb}/boot_partition/etc/dec_scsi_db.bak
	/etc/dvrdevtab	→	../cluster/members/{memb}/boot_partition/etc/dvrdevtab
	/etc/emx.db	→	../cluster/members/{memb}/boot_partition/etc/emx.db
	/etc/emx.db.bak	→	../cluster/members/{memb}/boot_partition/etc/emx.db.bak
	/etc/emx.info	→	../cluster/members/{memb}/boot_partition/etc/emx.info
	/etc/fwevdb	→	../cluster/members/{memb}/boot_partition/etc/fwevdb
	/etc/gen_databases	→	../cluster/members/{memb}/boot_partition/etc/gen_databases
	/etc/i2o_bs.db	→	../cluster/members/{memb}/boot_partition/etc/i2o_bs.db
	/etc/i2o_bs.db.bak	→	../cluster/members/{memb}/boot_partition/etc/i2o_bs.db.bak
	/etc/sysconfigtab	→	../cluster/members/{memb}/boot_partition/etc/sysconfigtab
	/mdec/bootblks	→	../cluster/members/{memb}/boot_partition/mdec/bootblks
	/genvmunix	→	cluster/members/{memb}/boot_partition/genvmunix
	/osf_boot	→	cluster/members/{memb}/boot_partition/osf_boot
	/vmunix	→	cluster/members/{memb}/boot_partition/vmunix
usr	/usr/.smdb./TCRBASE520.sts	→	../cluster/members/{memb}/.smdb./TCRBASE520.sts
	/usr/.smdb./TCRMAN520.sts	→	../cluster/members/{memb}/.smdb./TCRMAN520.sts
	/usr/.smdb./TCRMIGRATE520.sts	→	../cluster/members/{memb}/.smdb./TCRMIGRATE520.sts
var	/var/ypbindings	→	cluster/members/{memb}/ypbindings

Table 12-1: Additional CDSLs Since Cluster Creation

that have been added to the system since installing the *TruCluster* Server software and creating the cluster.

Getting back to our boot partition discussion, if the kernel and `osf_boot` files are now in `/.local../boot_partition`, then we have changed where we would normally look for these files, right? Well, yes and no. While the files are technically in a different location, we can still reference them from their previous location in the root directory because there are CDSLs there.

```
# fln / | grep boot_partition
genvmunix -> cluster/members/{memb}/boot_partition/genvmunix
osf_boot -> cluster/members/{memb}/boot_partition/osf_boot
vmunix -> cluster/members/{memb}/boot_partition/vmunix
```

12.2.1 CDSLs and the `mv(1)` command

It is because of the output from the last example that we find ourselves compelled to discuss the importance of **not** using the `mv` command when replacing a file that is a CDSL. As you can see, the kernel (`/vmunix`) is now a CDSL. For many years we have all built a new kernel and moved it from its build location to the root directory. In fact, it was taught that way. We must now unlearn what we have learned and use the `cp(1)` command instead.

Build the kernel as you always have.

```
# doconfig -c MOLARI

*** KERNEL CONFIGURATION AND BUILD PROCEDURE ***

Saving /sys/conf/MOLARI as /sys/conf/MOLARI.bck

Do you want to edit the configuration file? (y/n) [n]:


*** PERFORMING KERNEL BUILD ***
        Working....Mon Dec 17 11:59:58 EST 2001

The new kernel is /sys/MOLARI/vmunix
```

Copy the kernel.

```
# cp /sys/MOLARI/vmunix /
```

Remove the kernel from the build directory, keeping in mind that that kernel is a hard link.

```
# cd /sys/MOLARI ; ls -i vmunix* | sort
26247 vmunix.swap
26711 vmunix
26711 vmunix.MOLARI
26711 vmunix.sys
```

```
# rm vmunix vmunix.MOLARI vmunix.sys
```

12.2.2 Repairing a Broken CDSL

If you accidentally (or otherwise) remove a CDSL, you can repair it with the mkcdsl(8) command.

For example, we accidentally move a new kernel to the root directory out of habit.

```
# mv /sys/MOLARI/vmunix /
```

The kernel is now in the root directory and vmunix is no longer a CDSL.

```
# file /vmunix
/vmunix:        COFF format alpha executable or object module not stripped - ver
sion 3.13-14
```

We know that /vmunix is a supposed to be a CDSL, but what if we didn't know that? Well, we can run the cdslinvchk(8) command, and it should tell us that there is a missing link and what it should be. It should also be noted that the clu_check_config(8) also executes cdslinvchk.

```
# cdslinvchk
Failed CDSL inventory check. See details in /var/adm/cdsl_check_list
```

```
# cat /var/adm/cdsl_check_list
Expected CDSL: ./vmunix -> cluster/members/{memb}/boot_partition/vmunix
An administrator or application has replaced this CDSL with:
-rwxr-xr-x   1 root     system   21009120 Dec 17 12:00 ./vmunix
```

Now that we know what the link should be, we can repair it with the mkcdsl command. We will use the "-b" option to create the CDSL, have it point to the boot_partition, and use the "-c" option to copy the file to the location pointed to by the CDSL.

```
# mkcdsl -bc /vmunix
```

Verify that the procedure was successful.

```
# cdslinvchk
Successful CDSL inventory check
```

For more information on CDSLs, as well as the cdslinvchk and mkcdsl commands, see chapter 6 and/or the cdslinvchk(8) and mkcdsl(8) reference pages.

12.3 Hardware Management Revisited

In a cluster, hardware management is by and large unchanged from a standalone system, but then again, the way that hardware is handled in *Tru64* UNIX (starting with version 5.0) was redesigned specifically to accommodate two things:

- Multiple paths to storage devices.
- *TruCluster* Server.

However, a few things have changed, and we thought that it would be a good idea to let you in on the differences.

12.3.1 Hardware Management Databases Revisited

The first minor change that occurs when the cluster is created is that some of the hardware databases that were previously located in the `/etc` directory have been relocated to each member's boot partition and replaced with CDSLs (see Figure 12-2).

Table 12-2 lists the databases and their locations respective to a cluster or standalone system.

12.3.2 The `hwmgr(8)` Command Revisited

The `hwmgr` command is cluster aware. It must, however, be focused on the cluster in order to see clusterwide results or you will see only member-specific information. For example, if you want to view the devices on you cluster you would use the "`hwmgr –view device`" command.

```
[sheridan]
# hwmgr view device | tee hwmgr_view_device.sheridan
 HWID: Device Name            Mfg       Model             Location
 --------------------------------------------------------------------------
    3: /dev/dmapi/dmapi
   50: /dev/disk/dsk1c        COMPAQ    BD009635C3        bus-3-targ-0-lun-0
   51: /dev/disk/dsk2c        COMPAQ    BD009635C3        bus-3-targ-1-lun-0
   52: /dev/disk/dsk3c        COMPAQ    BD009635C3        bus-3-targ-2-lun-0
   53: /dev/disk/dsk4c        COMPAQ    BD009635C3        bus-3-targ-3-lun-0
   54: /dev/disk/dsk5c        COMPAQ    BD009635C3        bus-3-targ-4-lun-0
   55: /dev/disk/dsk6c        COMPAQ    BD009635C3        bus-3-targ-5-lun-0
   58: scp                              (unknown)         (unknown)
   59: /dev/kevm
   89: /dev/disk/floppy1c               3.5in floppy      fdi0-unit-0
  102: /dev/disk/cdrom1c      COMPAQ    CRD-8402B         bus-0-targ-0-lun-0
  103: /dev/disk/dsk8c        COMPAQ    BB009235B6        bus-2-targ-0-lun-0
  104: /dev/disk/dsk9c        COMPAQ    BB009235B6        bus-2-targ-1-lun-0
```

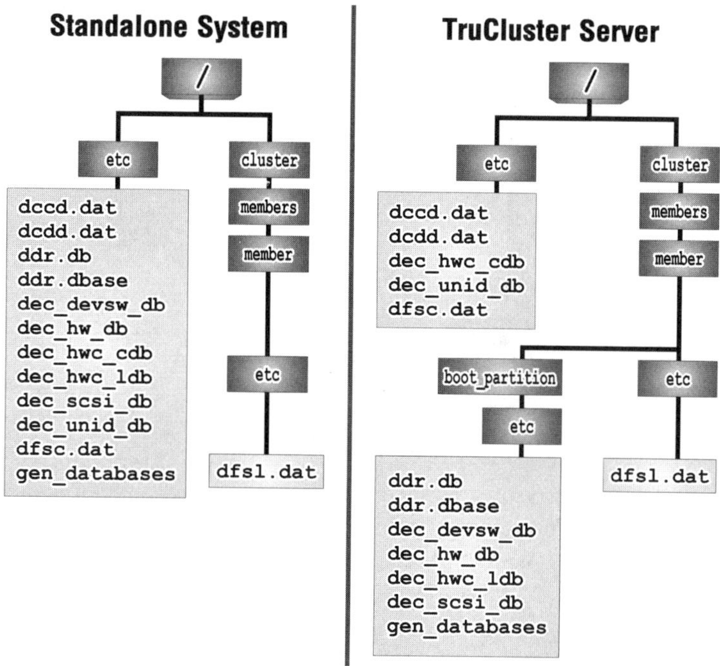

Figure 12-2: Hardware and Device Special Files Database Locations

Hardware and Device Special File Databases in `/etc`

Database	Cluster	Standalone
`dccd.dat`	file	file
`dcdd.dat`	file	file
`ddr.db`	cdsl*	file
`ddr.dbase`	cdsl*	file
`dec_devsw_db`	cdsl*	file
`dec_hw_db`	cdsl*	file
`dec_hwc_cdb`	file	file

Database	Cluster	Standalone
`dec_hwc_ldb`	cdsl*	file
`dec_scsi_db`	cdsl*	file
`dec_unid_db`	file	file
`dfsc.dat`	file	file
`dfsl.dat`	cdsl	cdsl
`gen_databases`	cdsl*	file

* - this CDSL resolves to the member's **boot_partition/etc** directory

Table 12-2: Hardware and Device Special File Databases in `/etc`

```
[molari]
# hwmgr view device | tee hwmgr_view_device.molari
HWID: Device Name              Mfg        Model            Location
-------------------------------------------------------------------------------
    3: /dev/dmapi/dmapi
    4: scp                                (unknown)        (unknown)
    5: /dev/kevm
   35: /dev/disk/floppy0c                 3.5in floppy     fdi0-unit-0
   46: /dev/disk/cdrom0c       COMPAQ     CRD-8402B        bus-1-targ-0-lun-0
   47: /dev/disk/dsk0c         COMPAQ     BD009734A3       bus-2-targ-0-lun-0
   50: /dev/disk/dsk1c         COMPAQ     BD009635C3       bus-3-targ-0-lun-0
   51: /dev/disk/dsk2c         COMPAQ     BD009635C3       bus-3-targ-1-lun-0
   52: /dev/disk/dsk3c         COMPAQ     BD009635C3       bus-3-targ-2-lun-0
   53: /dev/disk/dsk4c         COMPAQ     BD009635C3       bus-3-targ-3-lun-0
   54: /dev/disk/dsk5c         COMPAQ     BD009635C3       bus-3-targ-4-lun-0
   55: /dev/disk/dsk6c         COMPAQ     BD009635C3       bus-3-targ-5-lun-0
```

Taking the output from the "hwmgr -view device" command on both members you can see that it is slightly different. The reason for the difference is that you are seeing each member's physical view of the hardware. We used the tee(1) command to be able to save the output to a file so that we could see the differences between the two members' hardware. We will use the diff(1) command.

```
# diff hwmgr_view_device.*
4,8d3
<      4: scp                               (unknown)        (unknown)
<      5: /dev/kevm
<     35: /dev/disk/floppy0c                3.5in floppy     fdi0-unit-0
<     46: /dev/disk/cdrom0c      COMPAQ     CRD-8402B        bus-1-targ-0-lun-0
<     47: /dev/disk/dsk0c        COMPAQ     BD009734A3       bus-2-targ-0-lun-0
14a10,15
>     58: scp                               (unknown)        (unknown)
>     59: /dev/kevm
>     89: /dev/disk/floppy1c                3.5in floppy     fdi0-unit-0
>    102: /dev/disk/cdrom1c      COMPAQ     CRD-8402B        bus-0-targ-0-lun-0
>    103: /dev/disk/dsk8c        COMPAQ     BB009235B6       bus-2-targ-0-lun-0
>    104: /dev/disk/dsk9c        COMPAQ     BB009235B6       bus-2-targ-1-lun-0
```

The output that is preceded by a "<" shows the hardware that is specific to molari while the output preceded by a ">" shows sheridan's hardware.

12.3.2.1 How Can I See a Clusterwide Hardware View?

Many of the hwmgr command options provide for the ability to "focus" the command on a member or the cluster. The "-cluster" option can be used to focus on the entire cluster.

```
[sheridan]
# hwmgr -view device -cluster
 HWID: Device Name          Mfg       Model            Hostname   Location
--------------------------------------------------------------------------------
    3: /dev/dmapi/dmapi                                molari
    3: /dev/dmapi/dmapi                                sheridan
    4: scp                            (unknown)        molari     (unknown)
    5: kevm                                            molari
   35: /dev/disk/floppy0c             3.5in floppy     molari     fdi0-unit-0
   46: /dev/disk/cdrom0c    COMPAQ    CRD-8402B        molari     bus-1-targ-0-lun-0
   47: /dev/disk/dsk0c      COMPAQ    BD009734A3       molari     bus-2-targ-0-lun-0
   50: /dev/disk/dsk1c      COMPAQ    BD009635C3       molari     bus-3-targ-0-lun-0
   50: /dev/disk/dsk1c      COMPAQ    BD009635C3       sheridan   bus-3-targ-0-lun-0
   51: /dev/disk/dsk2c      COMPAQ    BD009635C3       molari     bus-3-targ-1-lun-0
   51: /dev/disk/dsk2c      COMPAQ    BD009635C3       sheridan   bus-3-targ-1-lun-0
   52: /dev/disk/dsk3c      COMPAQ    BD009635C3       molari     bus-3-targ-2-lun-0
   52: /dev/disk/dsk3c      COMPAQ    BD009635C3       sheridan   bus-3-targ-2-lun-0
   53: /dev/disk/dsk4c      COMPAQ    BD009635C3       molari     bus-3-targ-3-lun-0
   53: /dev/disk/dsk4c      COMPAQ    BD009635C3       sheridan   bus-3-targ-3-lun-0
   54: /dev/disk/dsk5c      COMPAQ    BD009635C3       molari     bus-3-targ-4-lun-0
   54: /dev/disk/dsk5c      COMPAQ    BD009635C3       sheridan   bus-3-targ-4-lun-0
   55: /dev/disk/dsk6c      COMPAQ    BD009635C3       molari     bus-3-targ-5-lun-0
   55: /dev/disk/dsk6c      COMPAQ    BD009635C3       sheridan   bus-3-targ-5-lun-0
   58: scp                            (unknown)        sheridan   (unknown)
   59: /dev/kevm                                       sheridan
   89: /dev/disk/floppy1c             3.5in floppy     sheridan   fdi0-unit-0
  102: /dev/disk/cdrom1c    COMPAQ    CRD-8402B        sheridan   bus-0-targ-0-lun-0
  103: /dev/disk/dsk8c      COMPAQ    BB009235B6       sheridan   bus-2-targ-0-lun-0
  104: /dev/disk/dsk9c      COMPAQ    BB009235B6       sheridan   bus-2-targ-1-lun-0
```

12.3.2.2 How Can I See Another Member's Hardware View?

The "-member" option can be used to focus on a particular member.

```
[sheridan]
# hwmgr -view device -member molari
 HWID: Device Name          Mfg       Model            Hostname   Location
--------------------------------------------------------------------------------
    3: /dev/dmapi/dmapi                                molari
    4: scp                            (unknown)        molari     (unknown)
    5: kevm                                            molari
   35: /dev/disk/floppy0c             3.5in floppy     molari     fdi0-unit-0
   46: /dev/disk/cdrom0c    COMPAQ    CRD-8402B        molari     bus-1-targ-0-lun-0
   47: /dev/disk/dsk0c      COMPAQ    BD009734A3       molari     bus-2-targ-0-lun-0
   50: /dev/disk/dsk1c      COMPAQ    BD009635C3       molari     bus-3-targ-0-lun-0
   51: /dev/disk/dsk2c      COMPAQ    BD009635C3       molari     bus-3-targ-1-lun-0
   52: /dev/disk/dsk3c      COMPAQ    BD009635C3       molari     bus-3-targ-2-lun-0
   53: /dev/disk/dsk4c      COMPAQ    BD009635C3       molari     bus-3-targ-3-lun-0
   54: /dev/disk/dsk5c      COMPAQ    BD009635C3       molari     bus-3-targ-4-lun-0
   55: /dev/disk/dsk6c      COMPAQ    BD009635C3       molari     bus-3-targ-5-lun-0
```

12.3.2.3 What **hwmgr** Command Options Have Focus?

The easiest way to determine whether a command option can be focused clusterwide or redirected to another member is to ask hwmgr with the "-help" option. For example, say we want to scan for new hardware but want to ensure that we perform the scan clusterwide.

```
# hwmgr -help scan
Usage: hwmgr -scan component [ -id <hardware-component-ID> ]
        [ -category <hardware-category>   ]
        [ -recurse ]
        [ -instance <member-instance-number> ]
        [ -member   <cluster-member-name> ]
        [ -cluster ]
Usage: hwmgr -scan [name] -entry <hardware-name>
        [ -member <cluster-member-name> ]
        [ -cluster (scan cluster-wide)  ]
Usage: hwmgr -scan scsi
        [ -bus <scsi-bus>                 ]
        [ -target <scsi-target>           ]
        [ -lun <scsi-lun>                 ]
        [ -member <cluster-member-name> ]
```

According to the help output, the "hwmgr -scan component" command provides a member or a cluster option, whereas the "hwmgr -scan scsi" command only provides a member option. Table 12-3 shows the various hwmgr commands and whether or not they can be directed to the cluster or an alternate member.

NOTE:

We have written a script to run the "hwmgr scan scsi" command on every member. The clu_scan_scsi script is available at the TruCluster Server Handbook website (see Appendix B for the URL).

12.3.3 The **dsfmgr(8)** Command Revisited

When using the dsfmgr command in cluster, there are a few things to keep in mind:

- When adding a device class, specify a "c" as the entry_type to indicate that the device will have a clusterwide scope.

  ```
  # dsfmgr -a class guitar c 755
  ```

See the last line of the following output for the results of the previous command.

hwmgr(8) Command Options

option	-member	-cluster	option	-member	-cluster
add name	✓	✗	scan component	✓	✓
delete component	✗	✗	name	✓	✓
name	✓	✗	scsi	✓	✗
scsi	✗	✗	set attribute	✓	✓
edit name	✓	✗	show component	✓	✓
scsi	✓	✗	name	✓	✗
get attribute	✓	✓	scsi	✓	✗
category	✗	✗	status component	✓	✗
locate	✗	✗	unconfigure	✓	✗
offline	✗	✗	unidict	✓	✗
online	✗	✗	unload name	✓	✗
power	✗	✗	view cluster	✗	✗
redirect scsi	✗	✗	devices	✓	✓
refresh component	✓	✓*	env	✗	✗
scsi	✓	✗	hierarchy	✓	✗
reload name	✓	✗	timestamps	✓	✓
remove	✓	✗	transaction	✓	✓

* - default

Table 12-3: hwmgr Command Options

- When using the "-s" option, a "c" in the scope of the Device Class Directory Default Database indicates that that class is clusterwide.

```
# dsfmgr -s | grep -p "Device Class Directory Default Database"
Device Class Directory Default Database:
     # scope mode  name
    -- ---   ----  -----------
     1  l    0755  .
     2  l    0755  none
     3  c    0755  cport
     4  c    0755  disk
     5  c    0755  rdisk
     6  c    0755  tape
     7  c    0755  ntape
     8  c    0755  changer
     9  c    0755  dmapi
    10  c    0755  guitar
```

We used the grep(1) command in order to shorten the rather lengthy output of the "dsfmgr -s" output and to save a few trees.

- The "-o" and "-O" options, used to create legacy device special file names (e.g., rz34c), cannot be used in a cluster because legacy device special files are not supported.

12.4 Event Manager (EVM) Revisited

In a cluster, you will have multiple systems generating events. Prior to *TruCluster* Server version 5.0A, events generated in a cluster were only member-specific. In other words, every member would log its own events via syslog and/or binlog, and unless the administrator set up a central logging repository, the logs also resided in each member's /var/adm directory. Troubleshooting cluster problems was often a trying experience in a cluster prior to *TruCluster* Server version 5.0A because of the compartmentalization of the members' logs. For example, to troubleshoot a problem in an eight-member cluster, the administrator would need to look at the logs from eight systems. This could mean that there were up to nine logs per system (binary.errlog, messages, and the seven logs in /var/adm/syslog.dated) or seventy-two logs in an eight-member cluster. That's a lot of logs to merge, sort, search, and analyze! As we wrote in chapter 8, EVM was designed specifically to address this type of situation.

In a cluster, events can be logged to a particular member or to the entire cluster. There is an event attribute, cluster_event, that if set to true will generate that event clusterwide. Conversely, if it is set to false, then that event is generated on a per-member basis. The majority of the EVM event templates have the cluster_event attribute set to true. Furthermore, EVM has the ability to retrieve events from any or all members in the cluster.

12.4.1 What EVM Events Are Clusterwide?

To determine whether or not an event is clusterwide, you can use the evmwatch(8) command.

```
# evmwatch -i | evmsort -A -s @cluster_event-:@name -t "@cluster_event%5 - @name"

True  - sys.unix.clu.caa.action_script
True  - sys.unix.clu.caa.app.error
True  - sys.unix.clu.caa.app.modified
True  - sys.unix.clu.caa.app.registered
...
False - sys.unix
False - sys.unix.binlog
False - sys.unix.binlog.hw.backplane_raid_ctlr
False - sys.unix.binlog.hw.console
...
```

The options for the evmwatch(8) and evmsort(8) commands can be found in their respective reference pages; however, here is an explanation of the options we used above.

evmwatch:

- -i – This option returns all loaded event templates.

We take the output and pipe it into the evmsort(8) command to sort the events first by the cluster_event and then by the name.

evmsort:

- -A – This option displays the output in ASCII format.
- -s – This option is the sort specification. In this case we are sorting the cluster_name in reverse alphabetical order, followed by the name in alphabetical order.
- -t – This option is used to define the "show template" which is set to display the cluster_event in a five-character (%5) field, followed by a space, a hyphen, a space, and the event name.

As of this writing, there are 338 events defined, and 142 of these events are clusterwide events.

```
# evmwatch -A -i -t @cluster_event | wc -l
      338
```

```
# evmwatch -A -i -t @cluster_event | grep True | wc -l
      142
```

12.4.2 How Can I Retrieve Events From a Member?

You can filter events by the member's hostname with the evmget(8), evmshow(8), and evmwatch commands and the "-f [host = *hostname*]" option.

```
# evmget -f "[host molari] AND [age < 1d]" | \
> evmshow -t " - @host_name: @name" -T "%T"
00:00:52 - molari.tcrhb.com: sys.unix.hw.net.niff.alert
00:00:57 - molari.tcrhb.com: sys.unix.hw.net.niff.alert
00:02:57 - molari.tcrhb.com: sys.unix.hw.net.niff.alert
00:03:02 - molari.tcrhb.com: sys.unix.hw.net.niff.alert
00:08:02 - molari.tcrhb.com: sys.unix.hw.net.niff.alert
00:08:07 - molari.tcrhb.com: sys.unix.hw.net.niff.alert
00:09:07 - molari.tcrhb.com: sys.unix.hw.net.niff.alert
00:09:12 - molari.tcrhb.com: sys.unix.hw.net.niff.alert
03:03:12 - molari.tcrhb.com: sys.unix.fs.advfs.fset.umount
03:03:12 - molari.tcrhb.com: sys.unix.clu.cfs.advfs.not_served
04:10:32 - molari.tcrhb.com: sys.unix.hw.net.niff.alert
04:10:37 - molari.tcrhb.com: sys.unix.hw.net.niff.alert
```

12.4.3 EVM Event Filters and Templates Revisited

When the *TruCluster* Server is installed, there are additional event templates added to the system specific to *TruCluster* Server. If you look in the /usr/share/evm/templates directory, you will discover a new clu subdirectory. Additionally, new cluster filter files are also included in the /usr/share/evm/filters directory. Figure 12-3 shows the added event filters and template files and their locations.

12.4.3.1 EVM Events Revisited

There are two cluster events on a standalone system.

```
# evmwatch -i -f @sys:clu | evmsort -A -s @name -t @name

sys.unix.clu.versw
sys.unix.clu.versw.msg.success
```

On a cluster, however, there are forty-seven cluster events.

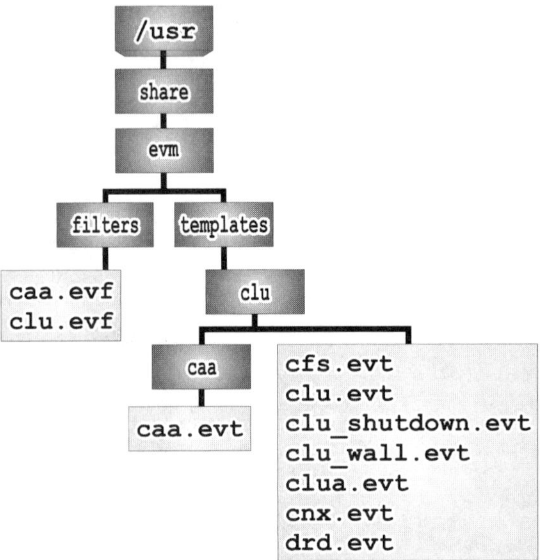

Figure 12-3: EVM Additions in a Cluster

```
# evmwatch -i -f @sys:clu | evmsort -A -s @name -t @name
sys.unix.clu.caa.action_script
sys.unix.clu.caa.app.error
sys.unix.clu.caa.app.modified
sys.unix.clu.caa.app.registered
sys.unix.clu.caa.app.running
sys.unix.clu.caa.app.stopped
sys.unix.clu.caa.app.transition
sys.unix.clu.caa.app.unregistered
sys.unix.clu.caa.cli
sys.unix.clu.caa.err
sys.unix.clu.caa.res.modified
sys.unix.clu.caa.res.registered
sys.unix.clu.caa.res.unregistered
sys.unix.clu.cfs.advfs.no_server
sys.unix.clu.cfs.advfs.not_served
sys.unix.clu.cfs.advfs.served
sys.unix.clu.cfs.fs.no_server
sys.unix.clu.cfs.fs.not_served
sys.unix.clu.cfs.fs.served
sys.unix.clu.clua.config
sys.unix.clu.clua.leave
sys.unix.clu.clua.netroute
sys.unix.clu.clua.no_gated
sys.unix.clu.clua.proxy
sys.unix.clu.clua.routeport
sys.unix.clu.clua.routerstart
sys.unix.clu.clua.routerstop
sys.unix.clu.cnx.member.join
sys.unix.clu.cnx.member.leave
sys.unix.clu.cnx.qdisk.loss
sys.unix.clu.cnx.qdisk.regain
sys.unix.clu.cnx.quorum.gain
sys.unix.clu.cnx.quorum.loss
sys.unix.clu.drd.new_accessnode
sys.unix.clu.drd.no_accessnode
sys.unix.clu.drd.server_add
sys.unix.clu.drd.server_leave
sys.unix.clu.member.add
sys.unix.clu.member.delete
sys.unix.clu.shutdown.abort
sys.unix.clu.shutdown.caa_alert
sys.unix.clu.shutdown.clean
sys.unix.clu.shutdown.private
sys.unix.clu.shutdown.start
sys.unix.clu.versw
sys.unix.clu.versw.msg.success
sys.unix.clu.wall
```

12.4.3.2 EVM Filters Revisited

The filters that were added can be seen by using the `evf(1)` script that we created. We discussed the `evf` script in chapter 8.

```
# evf -v -d /usr/share/evm/filters c[la][ua]

/usr/share/evm/filters

  caa.evf

    @caa:caa             ->  [name sys.unix.clu.caa]
    @caa:app             ->  [name sys.unix.clu.caa.app]
    @caa:cli             ->  [name sys.unix.clu.caa.cli]
    @caa:err             ->  [name sys.unix.clu.caa.err]
    @caa:res             ->  [name sys.unix.clu.caa.res]


  clu.evf

    @clu:clu             ->  [name sys.unix.clu]
    @clu:cfs             ->  [name sys.unix.clu.cfs]
    @clu:cnx             ->  [name sys.unix.clu.cnx]
    @clu:drd             ->  [name sys.unix.clu.drd]
    @clu:member          ->  [name sys.unix.clu.member]
    @clu:shutdown        ->  [name sys.unix.clu.shutdown]
    @clu:wall            ->  [name sys.unix.clu.wall]
    @clu:caa             ->  [name sys.unix.clu.caa]
    @clu:clua            ->  [name sys.unix.clu.clua]
```

12.5 NIFF Revisited

NIFF is automatically configured in a cluster because the health of a member's network interface is very important to the Cluster Alias (CLUA) subsystem as well as Cluster Application Availability (CAA) resource monitoring.

12.5.1 NIFF and the CLUA

When a cluster member enters run level 3, the `aliasd(8)` daemon is started; it in turn creates a child process known as `aliasd_niff(8)`. The `aliasd_niff` process subscribes to all NIFF events from EVM although it is really only interested in those events that signal that a network interface has been marked as up (`sys.unix.hw.net.niff.up`) or down (`sys.unix.hw.net.niff.down`). When `aliasd_niff` receives one of these events from EVM, it notifies `aliasd` so that any necessary routing changes for the cluster aliases can be addressed. For more information on NIFF, see chapter 9 as well as the `niff(7)`, `nifftmt(7)`, and `niffd(8)` reference pages. For additional information on cluster aliasing, see chapter 16 as well as the `aliasd(8)/aliasd_niff(8)` reference page.

12.5.2 NIFF and CAA

NIFF also plays a role in CAA as well. If there are any network resources registered with CAA, then the resource manager (`caad(8)`) loads a monitor (`network.so`) that subscribes to the `sys.unix.hw.net.niff.up` and `sys.unix.hw.net.niff.down` events so that CAA will know when a resource needs to be relocated due to a network interface failure. We will be covering CAA in much greater detail in chapters 23 and 24. Additional information regarding CAA can also be found in the `caa(4)` and `caad(8)` reference pages as well as the *TruCluster* Server Cluster Highly Available Applications Guide.

12.6 NetRAIN Revisited

NetRAIN is fully supported in a cluster. A cluster member can have NetRAIN configured for any set of network interfaces it has. If one member has NetRAIN configured, it does not mean that all members have to be configured for NetRAIN since network interfaces are member-specific.

Additionally, *TruCluster* Server version 5.1A includes support for Local Area Network (LAN) cluster interconnect, which can also be configured as a NetRAIN set.

For more information regarding NetRAIN, see chapter 9, the *Tru64* UNIX Network Administration Guide on V5.0A or V5.1, or the *Tru64* UNIX Network Administration: Connections Guide. For more information regarding the LAN cluster interconnect, see chapter 9 as well as the *TruCluster* Server Cluster LAN Interconnect guide for version5.1A.

12.7 Link Aggregation (LAG) Revisited

As of this writing, LAG (or trunking) can only be used on a network interface that is not associated with the LAN cluster interconnect. You must install at least the inaugural patch kit (IPK) in order for LAG to work on V5.1A. LAG did not exist on V5.0A or V5.1. For additional information, see chapter 9 and *Tru64* UNIX Network Administration: Connections Guide.

12.8 References

- The *TruCluster* Server Technical Overview Guide.
- The *TruCluster* Server Cluster Administration Guide.
- The *TruCluster* Server Cluster Highly Available Applications Guide.
- The *TruCluster* Server Cluster LAN Interconnect Guide (V5.1A).
- The *Tru64* UNIX Network Administration Guide (V5.0A & V5.1).
- The *Tru64* UNIX Network Administration: Connections Guide (V5.1A).
- Reference pages (noted within the text).

13

The Cluster File System (CFS)

In this chapter we discuss one of the truly outstanding features of Tru64 UNIX clustering: the Cluster File System. You may have heard the term "single-system image (SSI)", and while we disagree with the term "image" because it suggests using one kernel for all cluster members, the CFS does provide a common, transparent view of all file systems to all cluster members. This ability, along with the Cluster Alias subsystem (covered in chapter 16), makes up the heart and soul of Tru64 UNIX clustering.

You may be thinking, "What's so special? I can do that with NFS!" No, actually you can't. Can NFS enable every member in a cluster to share the root (`/`) file system? No. Moreover, the CFS does this transparently. No fancy mount commands, no additional configuration files. If you want to mount a file system on a cluster, you log in to **any** member in the cluster, issue a normal `mount(8)` command, and **all** members in the cluster see the same file system at the same mount point. And what happens to an NFS file system if the NFS server crashes? Bye-bye file system. The CFS does not suffer from this problem because another cluster member will transparently take over the job of serving the file system to the other cluster members. The CFS does all this and still manages to adhere to the X-Open and POSIX standards. This is really cool stuff!

The net result is that in a TruCluster Server environment you can log in to any member of the cluster and have virtually an identical view of the files on the cluster mounted file systems. We say "virtually" because some files will be member-specific, implemented as CDSLs (see discussions in chapters 6 and 12).

13.1 How Does The CFS Do That?

You may be wondering how the CFS can accomplish this, without your needing to go out and learn how to work with a new file system. The CFS is conveniently sandwiched between the Virtual File System (VFS) and the physical file systems (see Figure 13-1) and acts as a router (or traffic cop) directing I/O from the VFS to all parts physical.

A user runs a program that needs to perform file I/O. The program uses the same I/O routines it would normally use in a non-clustered environment (`open`, `read`, `write`, `fcntl`, etc.), these routines interface with the VFS, and the VFS interfaces with the CFS. It is the CFS's job to coordinate access to the physical file system by determining where in the cluster the physical file

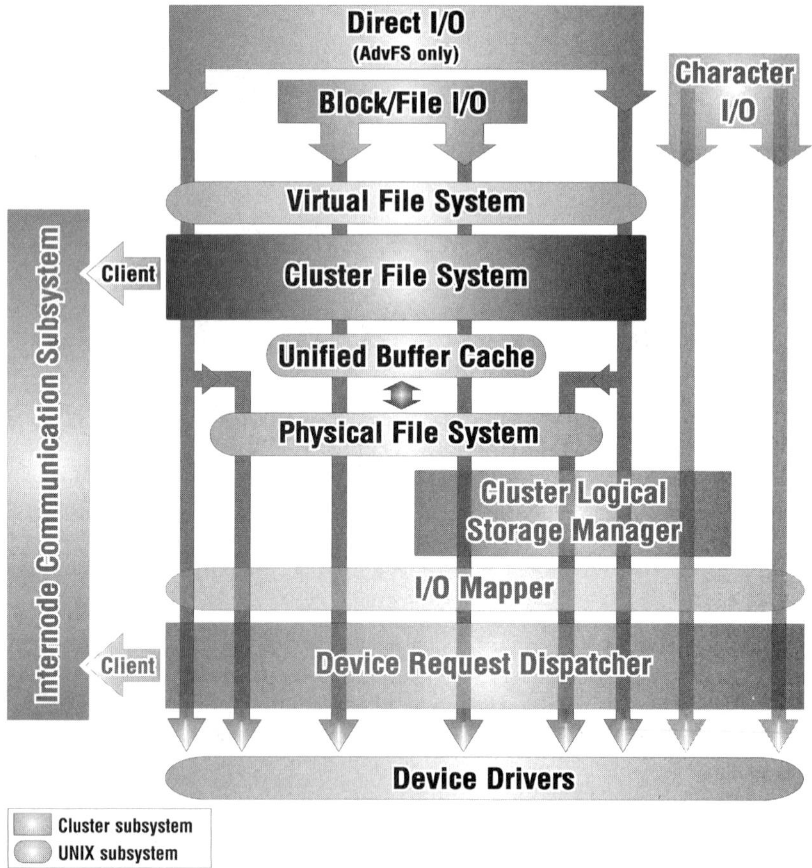

Figure 13-1: The CFS I/O Architecture

system is located and if necessary send the I/O request to the appropriate CFS server on another member in the cluster. This happens transparently from the user's perspective.

13.2 The CFS is a Client-Server Architecture

It's true – the CFS is a client-server implementation; however, the TruCluster engineers at Compaq are continually improving the CFS to reduce the amount of communication between CFS clients and the CFS servers. For example, in V5.0A, double caching at the CFS server was eliminated while read-ahead for large I/O operations and Direct I/O was added. In V5.1, Concurrent Direct I/O was introduced, allowing clients with a physical path to a device to use it, thereby reducing (but not eliminating) communication to the CFS server. And in V5.1A, Direct Access Cached Reads were introduced, increasing performance yet again. For additional information, see the following sections:

- Direct I/O 13.7
- Concurrent Direct I/O 13.7.1
- Direct Access Cached Reads 13.8

More information can also be found in the TruCluster Server Technical Overview for version 5.1 and 5.1A (section 2.2) and the TruCluster Server Cluster Administration Guide (chapter 9).

Any member in the cluster can be a CFS server, and multiple CFS servers will likely exist in any instance of a running cluster because there is a CFS server per file system (or domain).

13.2.1 Which Member is the CFS Server?

You can use the `cfsmgr(8)` command to see which member is the CFS server for each file system or domain.

```
# cfsmgr /u1 /kits

 Domain or filesystem name = /u1
 Server Name = sheridan
 Server Status : OK

 Domain or filesystem name = /kits
 Server Name = sheridan
 Server Status : OK
```

Note that you can see all the mounted file systems by using the `cfsmgr` command without any arguments.

When a cluster is first formed, the first member booted is apt to become the CFS server for all of the file systems it can see. As other members join the cluster, they will serve their member `boot_partition` file system as well as any file systems on local buses or semi-shared buses where the previously booted member(s) did not have physical access. The CFS will always choose a member with direct connectivity to a device to be the CFS server for a file system located on that device.

Here is an example showing which file systems are served (by member) on our two-member cluster:

```
# cfs
CFS Server          Mount Point                   File System                FS Type
-----------------   -------------------------     ------------------------   -------
molari              /cluster/members/member1/     root1_domain#root           AdvFS
                      boot_partition
```

```
sheridan          /cdrom                       /dev/disk/cdrom1c         CDFS
sheridan          /mnt                         /dev/disk/dsk5a            UFS
sheridan          /                            cluster_root#root        AdvFS
sheridan          /usr                         cluster_usr#usr          AdvFS
sheridan          /var                         cluster_var#var          AdvFS
sheridan          /kits                        extra#kits               AdvFS
sheridan          /u1                          home#u1                  AdvFS
sheridan          /cluster/members/member2/    root2_domain#root        AdvFS
                    boot_partition
sheridan        @ /fafrak                      tcrhb#fafrak             AdvFS
sheridan        @ /lola                        tcrhb#lola               AdvFS
```

From the output we can infer that sheridan was probably the first member booted (or that molari was rebooted at some point). In this case, sheridan was booted first.

NOTE:

The cfs command is not a Compaq-supplied command but a Perl script written for this book so that we can show the raw output from the cfsmgr command in a formatted tabular output sorted by cluster member. All of the information is gathered from the cfsmgr command with the "-F raw" and "-a server" switches.

```
# cfsmgr -F raw -a server

molari 1 2001 07 03 17 38 58
cluster_root#root AdvFS FS / sheridan 0 1
root1_domain#root AdvFS FS /cluster/members/member1/boot_partition molari 0 1
root2_domain#root AdvFS FS /cluster/members/member2/boot_partition sheridan 0 1
cluster_usr#usr AdvFS FS /usr sheridan 0 1
cluster_var#var AdvFS FS /var sheridan 0 1
home#u1 AdvFS FS /u1 sheridan 0 1
extra#kits AdvFS FS /kits sheridan 0 1
tcrhb#fafrak AdvFS FS /fafrak sheridan 0 1
tcrhb#lola AdvFS FS /lola sheridan 0 1
/dev/disk/cdrom1c CDFS FS /cdrom sheridan 0 1
/dev/disk/dsk5a UFS FS /mnt sheridan 0 1
```

You can download the cfs command from the TruCluster Server Handbook web site (See Appendix B for the URL). There are two versions of cfs:

- V5.1A, V5.1B — cfs
- V5.1 — cfs_p5.005

Tru64 UNIX version 5.1A includes Perl version 5.6.0, and the cfs command takes advantage of features specific to V5.6.0. So, if you have Perl version 5.6.0 or greater installed on your system, then use cfs; otherwise use cfs_p5.005.

13.3 File System Support

The physical file systems that are supported by the CFS are shown in Table 13-1. Note that we also list named pipes in this table even though a named pipe (or `fifo`) is not a file system, but a `fifo` is a file in a file system. Heck, we just wanted the word `fifo` in the document at least three times.

Supported File Systems

New?	File system	Read/ Write	Read Only	Local Only	Notes
	Advanced File System (advfs)	✓			The CFS Server is the member that mounts the domain. If the CFS Server fails, another member becomes the CFS Server for the domain. The CFS server is selected based on connectivity to the underlying storage.
	Network File System (nfs)				
	Server	✓			All members can be NFS Servers. NFS Clients must use the Default Cluster Alias (see chapter 16) prior to V5.1A.
	Client	✓			The CFS Server is the member that mounts the remote file system. If the member fails, the CFS Server does not relocate to another member -- the remote file system is unmounted. An automatic mount can be effected via **automount** or **autofs** for a higher availability solution.
	PC-NFS	✓			All members can be NFS Servers. NFS Clients must use the Default Cluster Alias (see chapter 16) prior to V5.1A.
V5.1A	Memory File System (mfs)	server only		✓	MFS is supported when mounted "**`-o server_only`**", and is thus available only to the member that mounts it. If the member fails, the file system does not failover to another member.
V5.1A	UNIX File System (ufs)	server only		✓	If the file system is mounted "**`-o server_only`**", the file system is available read/write to the member that mounted it, and not available to any other member. If the member fails, the file system is unmounted and does not automatically failover to another member.
			✓		If mounted cluster-wide, UFS is served read-only. The CFS Server is the member that mounts the file system. If the CFS Server fails, another member becomes the CFS Server for the domain. The CFS server is selected based on connectivity to the underlying storage.
	CD-ROM File System (cdfs)		✓		The CFS Server is the member directly connected to the CD-ROM device. Since CD-ROM devices are unsupported on a shared bus, if the serving member fails, the device becomes inaccessible.
V5.1	DVD-ROM File System (dvdfs)		✓		The CFS Server is the member directly connected to the DVD-ROM device. Since DVD-ROM devices are unsupported on a shared bus, if the serving member fails, the device becomes inaccessible.
	File Descriptor File System (fdfs)	✓		✓	Available only to the member that issues the mount command.
	File-on-file Mounting File System (ffm)	✓		✓	Available only to the member that issues the mount command.
	Named Pipes (fifo)	✓		✓	Both ends of the pipe must reside on the same member.
	Proc File System (procfs)	✓		✓	All members have their own procfs mounted locally at the `/proc` mount point. It is accessible only to that member.

Table 13-1: Supported File Systems

If a file system is mounted cluster-wide and the member serving the file system fails, as long as there is another member in the cluster with an active path to the device that contains the file system, then the CFS will automatically relocate the server function to that member. There are two exceptions to this rule:

- The file system is mounted as a partitioned file system (i.e., `mount -o server_only`). See section 13.4.
- The file system is an NFS file system.

If a cluster member is acting as the CFS server for an NFS-mounted file system (i.e., the cluster member is the NFS client) and it fails, the NFS-mounted file system is unmounted cluster-wide.

To prevent the loss of the NFS-mounted file system upon member failure, you can configure `automount` or AutoFS (`autofs`) for the NFS file systems that you want to remount.

For more information on `automount`, see the `automount(8)` reference page, the Network Administration: Services Guide for Tru64 UNIX version 5.1A, or the Network Administration Guide for Tru64 UNIX version 5.1 or version 5.0A.

For more information on `autofs`, see the `autofs(8)`, `autofsmount(8)`, and `sys_attrs_autofs(5)` reference pages as well as the Network Administration: Services Guide for Tru64 UNIX version 5.1A, or the Network Administration Guide for Tru64 UNIX version 5.1. AutoFS is not supported in V5.0A.

13.4 File System Partitioning

In the first release of the TruCluster Server product (V5.0A[1]), when you issued a mount command on any member in the cluster, all members would automatically have access to the file system at the same mount point. While this is generally considered a good thing, there might be reasons why you would not want every member in the cluster to have access to a file system. For example, you may have an application that should only run on one member at a time due to lack of synchronization built into the application. If the application was on a file system that every member has access to, then it is possible that the application could be started on more than one member at a time.

While you could set up a Cluster Application Availability (CAA) application resource to automatically start/stop/relocate the application in a cluster, you could not prevent someone from starting the application short of setting the application's permissions (which might actually create other issues). For information on CAA, see chapters 23 and 24.

The TruCluster engineers recognized the need for a mechanism to restrict a file system's scope to a member and added "Partitioned File System" support to the TruCluster Server product in V5.1. As more and more applications become cluster-aware, the usefulness of the Partitioned File System will likely fade to black – but for now, it is very useful, particularly for those customers migrating from a TruCluster Available Server Environment (ASE). For more information on migrating from ASE to TruCluster Server, see chapter 26.

---

[1] Technically the first release was V5.0, but it was a very limited release.

13.4.1 Mounting a Partitioned File System

Mounting a file system on only one member is pretty easy. All you need to do is add the "-o server_only" option to the mount(8) command. For example, the /kits mount point in our cluster is currently mounted cluster-wide. We can illustrate this by issuing a df(1) or mount command on each member in the cluster.

```
[sheridan]
# df /kits

Filesystem    512-blocks        Used    Available Capacity  Mounted on
extra#kits      13054928     4875562      8082544      38%  /kits
```

```
[molari]
# df /kits

Filesystem    512-blocks        Used    Available Capacity  Mounted on
extra#kits      13054928     4875562      8082544      38%  /kits
```

So let's unmount the file system and remount it using the "-o server_only" option. Notice that we only need to issue the umount(8) command on one member to unmount the file system cluster-wide.

```
[sheridan]
# umount /kits
```

```
[sheridan]
# mount -o server_only extra#kits /kits
```

If we now reissue the df command on each member we should see /kits mounted only on sheridan. Let's check it out:

```
[sheridan]
# df /kits

Filesystem    512-blocks        Used    Available Capacity  Mounted on
extra#kits      13054928     4875562      8082544      38%  /kits
```

```
[sheridan]
# rsh molari-ics0 df /kits

/kits: Permission denied
```

In the last example, we decided to rsh(1) to the other cluster member so that we would not need to log in. We're just being ~~lazy~~...efficient. Let's take this one step further and see what happens when we try to interact with the /kits directory on each member.

```
[sheridan]
# cd /kits ; ls

.tags                   local                   sbin
V5.1A                   perl                    usr
acrobat_v405.tar.gz     quota.group             var
cluster                 quota.user
```

```
[molari]
# ls /kits

ls: /kits: No permission
```

```
[molari]
# cd /kits

ksh: /kits: permission denied
```

Maybe you're thinking, "If it is mounted as a partitioned file system, how can I verify that fact, short of getting an error message from the `cd`, `df`, and `ls` commands?" You can use the `cfsmgr` command, although it will only show that the file system is mounted and not that it is mounted as a partitioned file system. And the `mount` command will show you that the file system it is mounted as a partitioned file system but does not indicate which system is the CFS server.

```
[molari]
# cfsmgr /kits

 Domain or filesystem name = /kits
 Server Name = sheridan
 Server Status : OK
```

You can also see what another member in the cluster sees by using the "`-h`" switch.

```
[molari]
# cfsmgr -h sheridan /kits

 Domain or filesystem name = /kits
 Server Name = sheridan
 Server Status : OK
```

You can also use the `mount` command and then `grep(1)` for "`server_only`".

```
[molari]
# mount | grep server_only

extra#kits on /kits type advfs (rw, server_only)
```

Instead of using the cfsmgr and mount commands, we recommend you use the cfs command and look for an "@" which will tell you if the file system is mounted as a partitioned file system.

```
# cfs
 .
CFS Server          Mount Point                  File System                  FS Type
-----------------   -------------------------    -------------------------    -------
molari              /cluster/members/member1/    root1_domain#root            AdvFS
                      boot_partition

sheridan            /cdrom                       /dev/disk/cdrom1c            CDFS
sheridan            /mnt                         /dev/disk/dsk5a              UFS
sheridan            /                            cluster_root#root            AdvFS
sheridan            /usr                         cluster_usr#usr              AdvFS
sheridan            /var                         cluster_var#var              AdvFS
sheridan          @ /kits                        extra#kits                   AdvFS
sheridan            /u1                          home#u1                      AdvFS
sheridan            /cluster/members/member2/    root2_domain#root            AdvFS
                      boot_partition
sheridan            /fafrak                      tcrhb#fafrak                 AdvFS
sheridan            /lola                        tcrhb#lola                   AdvFS
```

In the cfs command's output above, the /kits file system is mounted as a partitioned file system.

13.4.2 Partitioned File System Rules and Restrictions

As with most things in life, certain rules and restrictions apply. Table 13-2 shows the particular rules and restrictions that pertain to the various TruCluster Server versions.

Let's see what happens when you attempt to circumvent the rules.

13.4.2.1 Mounting an Unsupported File System "-o server_only"

We have placed an ISO-9660 formatted CD into /dev/disk/cdrom1c. According to the rules, we cannot mount this file system "-o server_only", so what happens if we try it anyway? The CD-ROM drive is located on sheridan's local bus, so we'll attempt to mount the drive "-o server_only" from sheridan. Note, even though the drive is local to sheridan, we can just as easily mount the drive from molari. In fact, due to the Device Request Dispatcher (DRD), a device located anywhere in the cluster is accessible by any member in the cluster (we will discuss the DRD in chapter 15).

File System Partitioning Rules and Restrictions

		V5.1A	V5.1	V5.0A
File Systems Supported		AdvFS, MFS, UFS	AdvFS	Unsupported
Automatic Failover?	via CFS?	No	No	
	via CAA?	Yes[1]	Yes[1]	
Manual Relocation (i.e., **`cfsmgr -a server=member`**)?		No	No	
NFS Export?		Yes[2]	No	
Mixing cluster-wide and partitioned filesets in the same domain?		No[3]	No[3]	
Mount a file system under a partitioned filesystem?		No	No	
Mount Updates (i.e., **`mount -u -o server_only`**)?		No	No	

1	Although automatic failover is not supported by the CFS, you can configure a CAA resource to unmount and mount a file system when the resource is relocated. See chapter 24 for an example.
2	In V5.1A, the restriction to where NFS clients must use the Default Cluster Alias has been lifted, so you can create a new alias, place the alias in the **`/etc/export.aliases`** file, and restrict it to the member with the mounted partitioned file system via a startup script or a CAA resource. See chapter 24 for an example. See chapter 20 for more information on the **`/etc/exports.aliases`** file.
3	The "**`-o server_only`**" option to the `mount` command applies to all filesets in a domain. In other words, if you have a fileset in a domain already mounted cluster-wide, then you cannot mount another fileset in the same domain "**`-o server_only`**" -- you will receive an error. Conversely, if you have a fileset in a domain mounted "**`-o server_only`**", any additional filesets in the domain mounted subsequently will also be mounted "**`-o server_only`**".

Table 13-2: File System Partitioning Rules and Restrictions

```
[sheridan]
# mount -o server_only /dev/disk/cdrom1c /mnt
```

```
[sheridan]
# df /mnt
Filesystem          512-blocks      Used   Available Capacity  Mounted on
/dev/disk/cdrom1c       263948    263948           0     100%  /mnt
```

Well, we did not get an error mounting it. We expect to see the `df` command succeed on the member that mounted the device, but if the file system was truly mounted "`-o server_only`", then the other member should return a "`/mnt: Permission denied`" error, but it doesn't as illustrated in the following example:

```
[molari]
# df /mnt
Filesystem          512-blocks        Used   Available Capacity  Mounted on
/dev/disk/cdrom1c       263948      263948           0    100%   /mnt
```

The moral of this story is that mounting a file system "`-o server_only`" when the file system is not allowed to be mounted as a partitioned file system yields a cluster-wide mounted file system.

13.4.2.2 No Automatic Relocation, Well Sort Of...

The CFS will not relocate a partitioned file system if the member that mounted it fails. Since only that member was using it, the other cluster members are not going to miss the file system anyway, but your users might. If the file system must be highly available and partitioned, then you should configure the file system as part of a CAA application resource. If the member running the resource fails, then the CAA subsystem will automatically choose another member to run the application (and mount the partitioned file system). We will discuss application resources and show you how to incorporate a partitioned file system within an application resource in chapters 23 and 24 – stay tuned.

13.4.2.3 Mounting Another Fileset in a Domain

According to the rules, you cannot mix cluster-wide and partitioned file system mounts in the same domain. Let's explore how the operating system handles subsequent mounts given that first fileset is mounted either cluster-wide or "`-o server_only`". We will be using a multi-fileset domain that we created for this demonstration, `tcrhb`. Let's see which filesets are in this domain.

```
# showfsets -b tcrhb
lola
fafrak
```

13.4.2.3.1 The First Fileset is Mounted Cluster-wide

Let's mount one fileset cluster-wide.

```
# mount tcrhb#fafrak /fafrak
```

Now mount the second fileset partitioned.

```
# mount -o server_only tcrhb#lola /lola
Cannot mount fileset server_only when existing domain is not.
tcrhb#lola on /lola: Function not implemented
```

The second fileset is prevented from being mounted at all. Unmount the file system so that we can mount it "-o server_only" next.

```
# umount /fafrak
```

13.4.2.3.2 *The First Fileset is Mounted "-o server_only"*

This time we will mount the first fileset partitioned.

```
# mount -o server_only tcrhb#fafrak /fafrak
```

The subsequent mounts will not fail but will also be partitioned. For example:

```
# mount tcrhb#lola /lola
WARNING: Domain is already specified server_only so this mount will be.
```

```
# mount | grep server_only
tcrhb#fafrak on /fafrak type advfs (rw, server_only)
tcrhb#lola on /lola type advfs (rw, server_only)
```

Alternatively, you could use the output of cfs command piped into the grep command – the advantage being that you can also see which member is the server of the partitioned file system.

```
# cfs | grep @
molari          @ /fafrak                    tcrhb#fafrak           AdvFS
molari          @ /lola                      tcrhb#lola             AdvFS
```

13.4.2.4 Mounting a File System Beneath a Partitioned File System's Mount Point

What happens when you attempt to mount a file system underneath a partitioned file system's mount point? You get an error – really, no kidding. Don't believe us? Okay, how about if we prove it?

```
[sheridan]
# mount -o server_only tcrhb#fafrak /fafrak
```

```
[sheridan]
# mount extra#kits /fafrak/kits
extra#kits on /fafrak/kits: Permission denied
```

13.4.2.5 Attempting a Mount Update

You cannot mount update a file system to make it "-o server_only". For example:

```
[sheridan]
# umount /fafrak
```

```
[sheridan]
# mount tcrhb#fafrak /fafrak
```

```
[sheridan]
# mount -u -o server_only /fafrak
Cannot update existing mount to be server-only.
```

If you want to change a mounted file system from a cluster-wide mount to a partitioned mount, then you must unmount the file system and mount the file system "-o server_only".

You can, however, mount update a file system from read-only mode to read-write mode. Let's remount the tcrhb#fafrak file system "-o server_only, ro", so that we can attempt to update the mount to be read-write.

```
[sheridan]
# umount /fafrak
```

```
[sheridan]
# mount -o server_only,ro tcrhb#fafrak /fafrak
```

```
[sheridan]
# mount | grep fafrak
tcrhb#fafrak on /fafrak type advfs (ro, server_only)
```

```
[sheridan]
# mount -u /fafrak
WARNING: Domain is already specified server_only so this mount will be.
```

```
[sheridan]
# mount | grep fafrak
tcrhb#fafrak on /fafrak type advfs (rw, server_only)
```

13.5 Quotas

Tru64 UNIX provides quota support on three levels:

- User
- Group
- Fileset (AdvFS-only)

The TruCluster Server has always supported fileset quotas, but user and group quota support was not added until V5.1A.

In order to keep quota support from adversely affecting the cluster file system's performance, a compromise was made in quota enforcement. The compromise is that it is possible for a user or group to exceed its quota by up to the `quota_excess_blocks` attribute in the `cfs` subsystem. By default, this value is set to 1 MB per member – so on an eight-node cluster any user or group may exceed its quota by up to 8 MB. The `quota_excess_blocks` attribute can be reconfigured while the system is running (notice the "`R`" in the "`op`" field in the following example).

```
# sysconfig -Q cfs quota_excess_blocks
cfs:
quota_excess_blocks -    type=ULONG op=CRQ min_val=0 max_val=18446744073709551615
```

The attribute value is expressed in kilobytes as you can see in the next example.

```
# sysconfig -q cfs quota_excess_blocks
cfs:
quota_excess_blocks = 1024
```

If you want to increase the value to 2 MB, for example, you can use the following command:

```
# sysconfig -r cfs quota_excess_blocks=2048
quota_excess_blocks: reconfigured
```

```
# sysconfig -q cfs quota_excess_blocks
cfs:
quota_excess_blocks = 2048
```

Note that you have only increased the value on the member you are logged into at this point. The value of the cfs:quota_excess_blocks attribute does not have to be the same on every member in the cluster.

For additional information on the cfs subsystem attributes see the sys_attrs_cfs(5) reference page.

13.6 Tokens and Cache Coherency

So the CFS Server says to a CFS client, "Here is a token of my appreciation!" But seriously, the CFS Server tends to throw in a token as a free gift when sending I/O to a CFS client. Tokens are a lightweight synchronization method used by the CFS server to guarantee that every cluster member has the same view of a file – this is known as cache coherency.

There are two token modes:

- READ – Shared. Can be held by one or more members at a time.
- READ/WRITE – Exclusive. Can be held by one member at a time.

There are three token types:

- MHOLD – Present when a file's vnode[2] is cached on a CFS client, but does not imply that the member is actually caching any data.

  The CFS server uses the MHOLD token to track where files are cached in order to notify those CFS clients when certain events occur such as the file becoming unlinked.

  The MHOLD token is never specifically requested or revoked.
- ATTR – Protects the file's cached attributes and data. Exists when a CFS client is caching file data or attributes (file size, time of last modification, etc.)
- DIOMAP – Protects the AdvFS extent map. Used for Direct I/O and Direct Access Cached Reads to cache the AdvFS extent map for the file.

  The extent map for a file indicates where the data resides on the volumes.

---

[2] A vnode (or virtual node) is the in-memory representation of the file's serial number. In UFS, the serial number is called an inode. In AdvFS, the serial number is known as a tag or bfNode (bit file node).

A token is requested by a CFS client anytime a read, write, get attribute, or set attribute operation needs to be performed. The token is held until the operation completes.

A token is granted by the CFS server as follows:

- If a CFS client requests a token for a file and no other CFS client has a token for that file, the CFS server will grant the token.
- If a CFS client requests a token mode of `READ/WRITE` for a file and another CFS client has a token in `READ/WRITE` or `READ` mode for that file, the CFS server will send a revoke request to the CFS client currently holding the token. Once the token is returned, the CFS server will grant the token to the requesting CFS client.
- If a CFS client requests a token mode of `READ` for a file and another CFS client has a token in `READ/WRITE` mode for that file, the CFS server will send a revoke request to the CFS client currently holding the token. Once the client downgrades the token to a mode of `READ` or returns the token, the CFS server will grant the token to the requesting CFS client.
- If a CFS client requests a token mode of `READ` for a file and another CFS client currently has a token in `READ` mode, the CFS server will grant the token to the requesting CFS client.

For example, members 1-3 in a four-node cluster have the file `MyDataFile` opened for read. They all hold a token with the `READ` mode set. The fourth member requests a token to write to the file opened by the other three members. The CFS server will revoke the tokens held by members 1-3, and once the tokens are returned, the CFS server will then grant the token for `MyDataFile` in `READ/WRITE` mode to `member4`. When the tokens are revoked, the information in the members' caches for `MyDataFile` is invalidated. Once the write operation is completed, `member4` will release or downgrade the token to `READ` mode, and then the remaining members can once again be granted a token in `READ` mode.

A token is currently granted on a per file basis, although greater granularity is being investigated.

IMPORTANT:

Do not confuse tokens with file locking. Tokens do not synchronize access to a file to guarantee ordered I/O as file locking does. If you want your applications to synchronize access to files, you have two choices:

- Cluster Unaware (POSIX – X/OPEN) – `fcntl(2)`, `lockf(3)`, `flock(2)`[3]
- Cluster Aware – Distributed Lock Manager (DLM)[4] Application Programming Interface (API)

---

[3] `flock` is technically not part of the POSIX or X/OPEN standard but uses the `fcntl` function (which is).

[4] See chapter 18.

Note that the term "cluster unaware" is used to indicate that this method will not make your application "aware" that it is in a cluster. In other words, it is not an API unique to the TruCluster Server. In fact, due to support for the POSIX and X/OPEN APIs in the CFS, an application written to use these standard APIs for file locking on a standalone system can move the application to the cluster and it will provide cluster-wide file locking. No special modifications are required, which is pretty cool indeed!

The job of the token is to guarantee that the members' caches do not contain different views of the file at any particular time.

Here is a simplified example (note, we do not indicate token type, only token mode). In this example, Member1 is node `sheridan` and Member2 is node `molari`.

Token Mode:	**Member1**	**Member2**
On `member1`, open a new file with your favorite editor. Write the file to disk but do not exit the editor.	`READ/WRITE`	No Token.

```
[sheridan]
# vi MyDataFile
i
La Dee Da
Yadda yadda yadda
[Esc]
:w
```

Token Mode:	**Member1**	**Member2**
On `member2`, type out the file.	Token downgraded to `READ`. Cache flushed.	`READ`

```
[molari]
# cat MyDataFile
La Dee Da
Yadda yadda yadda
```

Both members have an identical view of the file.

Token Mode:	**Member1**	**Member2**
On `member2`, append some information to the file.	Token revoked. Cache flushed & invalidated.	`READ/WRITE`

```
[molari]
# cat >> MyDataFile
toodle loo
^D
```

On both members, display the file.	Token Mode:	Member1	Member2
		READ	Token downgraded to READ. Cache flushed.

```
[molari]
# cat MyDataFile
La Dee Da
Yadda yadda yadda

toodle loo
```

```
[sheridan]
# cat MyDataFile
La Dee Da
Yadda yadda yadda

toodle loo
```

Both members still have an identical view of the file.

On member1, write the file to disk again. Remember, we're still in the editor.	Token Mode:	Member1	Member2
		READ/WRITE	Token revoked. Cache flushed & invalidated.

```
[sheridan] – still in vi

:w
```

On member2, type out the file again.	Token Mode:	Member1	Member2
		Token downgraded to READ. Cache flushed.	READ

```
[molari]
# cat MyDataFile
La Dee Da
Yadda yadda yadda
```

The behavior shown here using tokens should be familiar to you since this is exactly how a standalone system behaves without tokens. Try this example using two processes on a standalone system. The results will be the same.

To gather additional information on tokens, you can use the cfsstat(8) command. You can obtain general information and statistics for tokens by using the cfsstat command with "tokens" and "tokstats" options respectively. To retrieve specific token information for a particular file by client or server, use "clitok_log" and "svrtok_log" options respectively.

For more information, see the TruCluster Server Cluster Administration Guide and the cfsstat(8) reference page.

13.7 Direct I/O

Direct I/O was first introduced in V5.0A[5]. When a file is opened with the Direct I/O flag, all I/O performed on the file will bypass the Unified Buffer Cache (UBC). To enable Direct I/O on a file, the file must be opened with the open(2) system call using the O_DIRECTIO flag as the mode.

NOTE:

- Direct I/O can be enabled only for files on an AdvFS file system.
- Direct I/O can be enabled only on a file and not on an entire file system.
- You cannot mmap(2) a file opened with Direct I/O.

Figure 13-2 illustrates how I/O flows with Direct I/O enabled. Notice that although the I/O is "direct", the term does not imply that the I/O goes directly to disk, only that it goes directly to the CFS server (although if the CFS server is the member performing Direct I/O then the I/O will go directly to disk, bypassing the UBC).

While Direct I/O can be a performance enhancement for an application that already uses its own caching mechanism (like a database), this is generally not considered a performance enhancement and can in fact cause performance degradation because writing to a device is much slower than writing to memory.

For Direct I/O that bypasses the UBC and goes directly to disk, you want Concurrent Direct I/O.

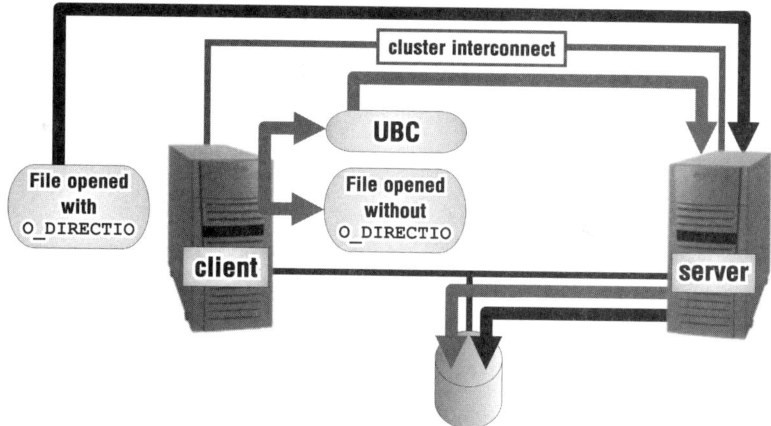

Figure 13-2: Direct I/O in V5.0A

13.7.1 Concurrent Direct I/O (CDIO)

Concurrent Direct I/O was introduced in V5.1[6] and enables members with direct access to the device where the file lives not only to bypass the UBC but also bypass the CFS server for I/O not related to log updates and metadata operations (file size changes, etc.). Those writes that allocate storage will continue to be sent to the CFS server.

It also worth noting that CDIO is truly concurrent – all members with direct physical connectivity to the shared storage devices can read and write to the file systems simultaneously.

Figure 13-3 illustrates the I/O flow using CDIO.

The cluster keeps track of Concurrent Direct I/O operations performed on the cluster, and these statistics can be retrieved using the `cfsstat` command with the "`directio`" option.

For additional information on Direct I/O, see the TruCluster Server Cluster Administration Guide and the `open(2)` reference page.

13.8 Direct Access Cached Reads

In V5.1A, when a cluster member performs a read from a file larger than 64KB and that file is on an AdvFS file system on a device physically connected to that member, then the read will be performed directly. Metadata operations and log updates will continue to go through the CFS server; writes will also go through the CFS server unless the file is also opened `O_DIRECTIO`. Figure 13-4 illustrates the I/O flow within V5.1A. By performing reads directly, traffic across the cluster interconnect can be reduced.

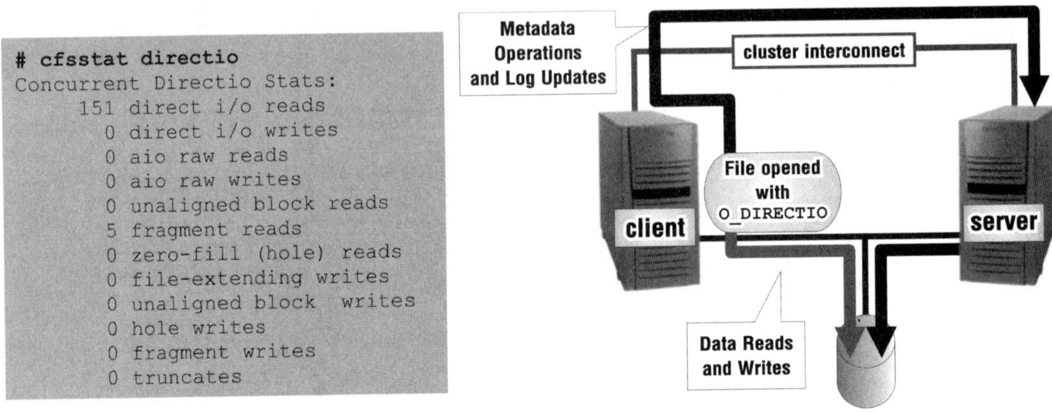

Figure 13-3: Concurrent Direct I/O

---

6 For the TruCluster Server product. Tru64 UNIX added support for CDIO in the base operating system in V5.0.

If the member does not have direct access to the device containing the AdvFS file system, reads will still be issued to the devices (and not to the CFS server) as if those devices were directly connected to the system as illustrated in Figure 13-5. It is the DRD subsystem that will send the read requests to a cluster member with direct connectivity to the storage devices containing the file system. In other words, the request will still be serviced remotely but at a lower level in the I/O subsystem hierarchy.

Direct Access Cached Reads are enabled by default, and currently there is no subsystem attribute available to modify this setting although applications that use Direct I/O will not use Direct Access Cached Reads.

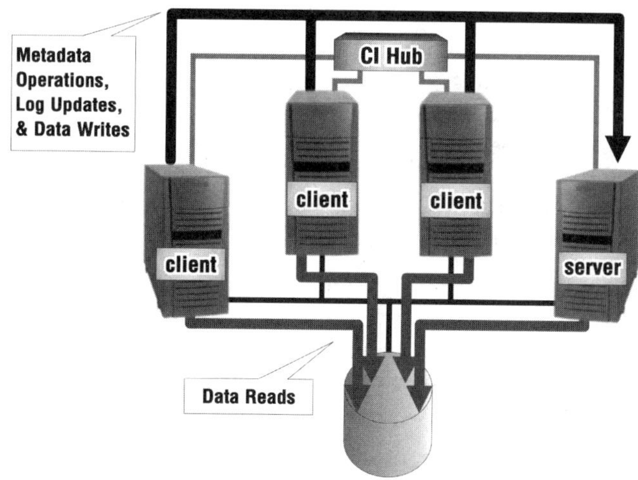

Figure 13-4: Direct Access Cached Reads

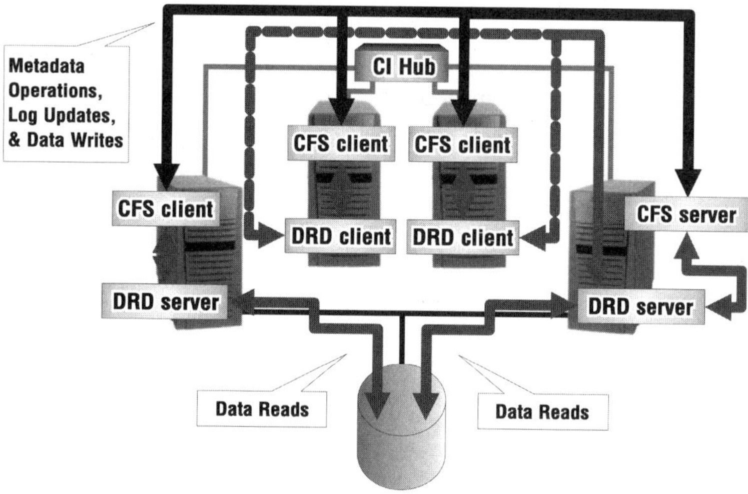

Figure 13-5: Direct Access Cached Reads – No Physical Connection

13.9 CFS Performance Optimizations

In this section we will discuss various methods for improving the performance of the CFS. Far from a definitive treatise on the subject, this is merely our attempt to give you a few places to look – and perhaps a couple of magic bullets – when performance improvements are sought. As with any discussion around performance optimizations and tuning, your mileage may vary greatly based on the road conditions, tire pressure, cycle of the moon, etc.

Performance optimizations can be sought in the following locations:

	Section
• CFS server load-balancing	13.9.1
• File system capacity issues	13.9.2
• I/O transfer size adjustments	13.9.3
• CFS memory usage adjustments	13.9.4
• Read-ahead and write-behind thread adjustments	13.9.5

Since the CFS is layered above the UBC and the physical file systems, it is important to optimize these other subsystems to obtain optimal performance for your environment.

For additional information regarding CFS performance optimizations, see the TruCluster Server Cluster Administration Guide and the `sys_attrs_cfs(5)` reference page. For additional information regarding UBC and file system optimizations, see the Tru64 UNIX File System Administration Handbook and the Tru64 UNIX System Configuration and Tuning manual.

13.9.1 CFS Server Load-Balancing

13.9.1.1 Manual Load Balancing

As we demonstrated in section 13.2.1, the first cluster member booted will likely be the CFS server for a majority of the file systems in the cluster because it will be the first member to mount the file systems on the shared buses. This can become a performance issue, and there is currently no automatic relocation of file systems to load-balance the CFS servers among cluster members.

You can manually relocate the CFS server to another member using the `cfsmgr` command with the "`-a server`" option.

For example, let's relocate the `tcrhb#fafrak` file system from server `sheridan` to server `molari`.

```
# cfsmgr /fafrak

 Domain or filesystem name = /fafrak
 Server Name = sheridan
 Server Status : OK
```

```
# cfsmgr -a server=molari /fafrak
```

You can add the "-r" switch to relocate the underlying disk storage to keep it served locally as well. This is only useful if the devices are not Direct-Access I/O (DAIO) capable. See chapter 15 for more information on DAIO devices.

Let's verify that the relocation was successful using the cfsmgr command.

```
# cfsmgr /fafrak

 Domain or filesystem name = /fafrak
 Server Name = molari
 Server Status : OK
```

NOTE:

Since there is a CFS server per AdvFS domain, relocating a file system that is a fileset of a multi-fileset domain will cause all filesets in the domain to be relocated. For example, if you recall from examples earlier in this chapter, the tcrhb domain contains two filesets: fafrak and lola. If the tcrhb#lola fileset had been mounted at the time we had done the relocation of the /fafrak file system, then the /lola file system would also have been relocated.

```
# mount tcrhb#lola /lola
```

```
# cfs | grep -E "^CFS|^-|tcrhb"
CFS Server         Mount Point                 File System                FS Type
----------------   -------------------------   ------------------------   -------
molari             /fafrak                     tcrhb#fafrak                AdvFS
molari             /lola                       tcrhb#lola                  AdvFS
```

```
# cfsmgr -a server=sheridan /fafrak
```

```
# cfs | grep -E "^CFS|^-|tcrhb"
CFS Server         Mount Point                 File System                FS Type
----------------   -------------------------   ------------------------   -------
sheridan           /fafrak                     tcrhb#fafrak                AdvFS
sheridan           /lola                       tcrhb#lola                  AdvFS
```

13.9.1.2 Automatic Load Balancing[7]

Although there is no automatic CFS server load-balancing facility, you can use a CFS server relocation script at system startup (or within a CAA application resource action script[8]) to automatically relocate file systems to specific members. The criteria you choose to determine which file systems should be served by which member is up to you, but consider the following:

- Serve the file system or domain from the member that is using it the most.
- Evenly distribute the file systems or domains among all members.
- Configure only a subset of the members as CFS servers, leaving other members to be compute servers.
- Configure file systems or domains on the same disk to the same CFS server.

Although some of these suggestions are mutually exclusive, they are meant to illustrate that there are many options when configuring your cluster. It is important that you take into account the use of the cluster and configure it based on its intended use.

13.9.1.2.1 How Do You Determine Which Member Is Using the File System the Most?

Use either the `cfsmgr` command with the "`-a statistics`" switch or our `cfs` script with the "`-s`" switch. With the `cfsmgr` command, you must run the command once for each member in the cluster to get the statistics for the specified file system. By contrast, our `cfs` command was written to accomplish this for you. In the example below, we use the `cfs` command, but we will show you the equivalent `cfsmgr` commands sans output.

For example, given the file system `tcrhb#fafrak`, let's see which member is serving the file system and then determine the statistics by member for the file system.

```
# cfs -s /fafrak

/fafrak [tcrhb#fafrak] (dsk6c,dsk5b):

                read      write    lookup    getattr   readlnk    access     other
            --------- --------- --------- --------- --------- -------- ---------
     molari:    148568    100000         2         0         0        2         3
 * sheridan:         0         0         0         0         0        0         0
      total:    148568    100000         2         0         0        2         3
```

---

[7] CFS Load Balancing is planned for V5.1B – see the `cfsd(8)` reference page for details.

[8] For additional information on CAA and action scripts, see chapter 24. See also chapter 21, section 21.4 for an example load-balancing script (`cfsldb`).

The CFS server is `sheridan` as indicated by the "*" in the first column of the output. If there is an "@" in the first column, then that member is the CFS server, and the file system is a partitioned file system (i.e., it is mounted with the "`-o server_only`" command option).

As you can see, the CFS server is not really doing any I/O to the file system, whereas the other member has done a lot more I/O.

NOTE:

The equivalent `cfsmgr` commands are:

1. Get the statistics for `member1`.
```
# cfsmgr -h molari -a statistics /fafrak
```
2. Get the statistics for `member2`.
```
# cfsmgr -h sheridan -a statistics /fafrak
```

13.9.2 File System Capacity Issues

The CFS server grants block reservations to CFS clients so that they are guaranteed available space when it comes time to write their data back to the file system.

Since the available space is reserved, the CFS clients do not have to transfer the data back to the CFS server after every write but instead can cache it locally and transfer the dirty pages back in 64K blocks in the background – potentially even after the file is closed. When a CFS client runs out of reserved space, it will request more from the CFS server. The CFS server will grant additional space, possibly revoking space reservations from other CFS clients if necessary, unless the file system free space gets too low.

A severe performance problem can occur when the free space on the file system falls below 10% or 50MB (whichever is smaller) because the CFS server reserves this space and will no longer grant block reservations to CFS clients. If a CFS client cannot get a block reservation, it must write through to the CFS server to ensure correct `ENOSPC` error handling, thereby eliminating the performance benefits of caching the data locally. See `errno(2)` reference page for details on `ENOSPC`.

The moral of the story? Do not let your file systems get too full.

13.9.3 Do Not Adjust the Block I/O Transfer Size

Documented in the TruCluster Server Cluster Administration Guide in chapter 9 is a section on tuning the block I/O transfer size. Subsequent to the release, we received a note from Compaq's CFS engineers stating that they do not recommend adjusting the block I/O transfer size.

WARNING: DO NOT ADJUST THE BLOCK I/O TRANSFER SIZE!

Adjusting the block I/O transfer size can cause adverse side effects such as headaches, dizziness, drowsiness, thinking in molasses, and general crankiness.

13.9.4 Adjusting CFS Memory Usage

If you have an application that is reporting an EMFILE error, "too many open files", you might be experiencing one of two memory-related problems:

1. The member is out of vnodes.
2. The CFS server has reached svrcfstok_max_percent.

13.9.4.1 Is the CFS Client Out of vnodes?

To see if the CFS client is out of vnodes, you can use your favorite kernel debugger and get the value for the global variables total_vnodes and free_vnodes. Then get the value of the max_vnodes attribute in the vfs subsystem using the sysconfig(8) command.

If total_vnodes is equal to vfs:max_vnodes and free_vnodes is equal to zero, then you should increase the vfs:max_vnodes value.

We wrote a Perl script to get the values and do the math so we wouldn't have to remember the rules or variable names.

```
# ./vnode

If the total (in-use) vnodes is equal to vfs:max_vnodes and
the free vnodes is equal to zero, then increase vfs:max_vnodes

vnodes in-use     vfs:max_vnodes   AND   free vnodes = zero
-------------     --------------         -----------
    6129       <       18699                  2706

This member has available vnodes.
Verify that the CFS server has not exceeded cfs:svrcfstok_max_percent
```

Using the manual approach:

```
# sysconfig -q vfs max_vnodes
vfs:
max_vnodes = 18699
```

```
# print 'printf "total_vnodes = %d, \
> free_vnodes = %d",total_vnodes,free_vnodes;quit' \
> | dbx -k /vmunix 2> /dev/null | tail -1
total_vnodes = 6129, free_vnodes = 2706
```

vfs:max_vnodes attribute values

Minimum Value	Maximum Value	Default Value	
0	1717986918	1000	If system main memory is 24MB or less
		Number of **vnodes** that can be contained in **5%** of the system's main memory.	If system main memory is greater than 24MB

Table 13-3: max_vnodes attribute values

NOTE:

The max_vnodes variable is a kernel global variable as well and can also be obtained from the kernel debugger.

The max_vnodes attribute can be reconfigured dynamically using the sysconfig command.

```
# sysconfig -r vfs max_vnodes=50000
```

The minimum, maximum, and default values of the max_vnodes attribute are shown in Table 13-3.

If the CFS client has not exceeded max_vnodes and still has free vnodes available, then you should check to see if the CFS server has reached svrcfstok_max_percent.

13.9.4.2 Has the CFS Server Reached svrcfstok_max_percent?

The CFS server must keep track of all vnodes that are cached on CFS clients – this requires approximately 1600 bytes of system memory for data structures (a token structure, AdvFS access structures, vnode structures, etc.) per cached vnode. The CFS server can use up to cfs: svrcfstok_max_percent of main memory to hold these data structures. The default for the svrcfstok_max_percent attribute is 25% but can be set from 5% to 50%.

As of this writing, in order to see if the CFS server has reached svrcfstok_max_percent, you need to use a kernel debugger to scope out the values of the svrtok_active_svrcfstok and cfs_max_svrcfstok kernel global variables.

```
# print 'printf "svrtok_active_svrcfstok = %d, \
> cfs_max_svrcfstok = %d",svrtok_active_svrcfstok,cfs_max_svrcfstok;\
> quit' | dbx -k /vmunix 2> /dev/null | tail -1
svrtok_active_svrcfstok = 4608, cfs_max_svrcfstok = 76833
```

If svrtok_active_svrcfstok is greater than or equal to cfs_max_svrcfstok, then you can try one or more of the following suggestions to get your file systems up and running again:

1. Use the cfsmgr(8) command to relocate some file systems to another cluster member. See section 13.9.1.1 for more information.
2. Increase the value of the kernel global variable cfs_max_svrcfstok using your favorite kernel debugger.

```
# dbx -k /vmunix
...
(dbx) assign cfs_max_svrcfstok=92500
92500
(dbx) pd cfs_max_svrcfstok
92500
(dbx) quit
```

3. Increase the value of cfs:svrcfstok_max_percent in /etc/sysconfigtab using the sysconfigdb(8) or dxkerneltuner(8) command and then reboot the member.

NOTE:

Never ones to shy away from a challenge, we wrote a script called cfssvrtok that checks the values of svrtok_active_svrcfstok and cfs_max_svrcfstok and then offers to modify cfs_max_svrcfstok for you.

13.9.4.3 The CFS Server is Running Out of Memory?

If a member acting as a CFS server does not have a large amount of memory, you may want to consider setting the cfs:svrcfstok_max_percent attribute's value to something lower than the 25% default. We do not recommend you do this unless you find that the member is consistently running out of memory and you cannot add additional memory.

13.9.5 Adjusting Read-Ahead and Write-Behind Threads

Sequential access of files on the CFS clients is handled by read-ahead and write-behind threads. By default, a CFS read is done in 64KB increments for remote reads (i.e., reading from the CFS server), so if the CFS detects multiple sequential reads, it uses the read-ahead thread to read the next block of data in anticipation that it too will be requested.

If you are using TruCluster Server version 5.1A, however, the CFS will use Direct Access Cached Reads (see section 13.8) so reads will be done directly from the storage devices, thus bypassing the CFS server and therefore potentially reducing the cluster interconnect traffic. Also, with Direct Access Cached Reads, I/Os can generally be larger (the preferred I/O transfer size is 128KB). Note, even with Direct Access Cached Reads, the read-ahead threads are still used.

The write-behind thread is used to write the dirty pages in the background. It attempts to find other contiguous dirty pages from the cache to consolidate the pages into larger I/O transfers to the file system.

These threads are part of the kernel idle thread and can be seen by using the following `ps(1)` command pipe to the `grep(1)` command.

```
# ps -elm | grep cfsiod_
```

By default, 32 of these read-ahead and write-behind threads exist on each cluster member. This can be easily verified by piping the previous command string into the `wc(1)` command.

```
# ps -elm | grep cfsiod_ | wc -l
        32
```

If your CFS client sequentially accesses more than 32 large files at a time, you may want to increase this number to improve performance. A good basic check to see if you need more read-ahead/write-behind threads is to check the state of the waiting threads:

```
# ps -emo state,wchan | grep cfsiod_
S    cfsiod_
S    cfsiod_
...
S    cfsiod_
S    cfsiod_
S    cfsiod_
```

If a majority of the waiting threads are in an "`S`" state (i.e., the threads have been sleeping for less than about 20 seconds) and the count of waiting threads seems to fluctuate heavily, you may need to increase the number of read-ahead and write-behind threads.

The cfs_async_biod_threads attribute in the cfs subsystem can be used to dynamically modify the number of read-ahead and write-behind threads. The cfs_async_biod_threads can have any value from 0 to 128. To modify the cfs_async_biod_threads, you can use the sysconfig command as illustrated in the following example.

Check the initial value of the cfs_async_biod_threads attribute.

```
# sysconfig -q cfs cfs_async_biod_threads
cfs:
cfs_async_biod_threads = 32
```

Reconfigure the cfs_async_biod_threads attribute, setting it to 100.

```
# sysconfig -r cfs cfs_async_biod_threads=100
cfs_async_biod_threads: reconfigured
```

Verify that the reconfiguration succeeded.

```
# sysconfig -q cfs cfs_async_biod_threads
cfs:
cfs_async_biod_threads = 100
```

You can also see that the threads have been created.

```
# ps -elm | grep cfsiod_ | wc -l
      100
```

NOTE:

This exercise was performed on a relatively idle cluster member and therefore we were able to illustrate that the number of threads was equal to the value of the cfs_async_biod_threads attribute in the cfs subsystem. It is possible that you could see a fewer number of threads than are actually configured when running:

```
# ps -elm | grep cfsiod_ | wc -l
```

This will likely indicate that the threads are currently running. The "cfsiod_" string that we are searching for is actually coming from the WCHAN, which is an address (or partial name) of the event on which the thread is waiting. In other words, if the thread is not waiting, its WCHAN will not be "cfsiod_".

According to the TruCluster Cluster Administration Guide, chapter 9, the read-ahead and write-behind threads consume few resources when not in use, so increasing the number of threads will probably not hurt your performance. If you plan to increase the number of threads, however, do it in modest increments and evaluate the effects on your system before jumping up to the maximum value. Since the attribute can be modified dynamically, if you notice any adverse effects, you can lower the value without having to reboot your system.

Once you have found an attribute value that fits your configuration, you will need to place it in your system's `/etc/sysconfigtab` file by using the `sysconfigdb` or `dxkerneltuner` command.

13.10 CFS Events

The CFS events are defined in the `/usr/share/evm/templates/clu/cfs.evt` template file. Below are the registered CFS events:

```
# evmwatch -A -i -f "[name *.cfs]" -t "[@priority] @name"

[200] sys.unix.clu.cfs.advfs.served
[200] sys.unix.clu.cfs.fs.served
[200] sys.unix.clu.cfs.advfs.not_served
[200] sys.unix.clu.cfs.fs.not_served
[300] sys.unix.clu.cfs.advfs.no_server
[300] sys.unix.clu.cfs.fs.no_server
```

13.11 References

- The TruCluster Server Technical Overview Guide.
- The TruCluster Server Cluster Administration Guide.
- The Tru64 UNIX System and Configuration Guide.
- The Tru64 UNIX File System Administration Handbook, by Steven M. Hancock, Digital Press (ISBN: 1-55558-227-3)
- Reference pages (noted within the text).

14

The Cluster Logical Storage Manager (CLSM)

The Cluster Logical Storage Manager subsystem is a cluster-aware version of the Logical Storage Manager (which is a port of the VERITAS Volume Manager[1] by Veritas Software Corporation). The CLSM allows you to use the Logical Storage Manager (LSM) in a cluster.

14.1 Introduction to the Logical Storage Manager

What follows is a brief introduction to the Logical Storage Manager. For more in depth information, see the *Tru64* UNIX Logical Storage Manager Guide as well as the *Tru64* UNIX File System Administration Handbook by Steve Hancock.

LSM is essentially RAID implemented in software. What is RAID? See Figure 14-1.

LSM manages a pool of physical storage and allows you to divide that pool in a variety of ways to create virtual devices that are presented to the operating system as logical volumes. These logical volumes can be accessed via both block and character device special files located in the `/dev/vol` and `/dev/rvol` subdirectories respectively.

The CLSM subsystem sits atop the I/O Mapper and the Device Request Dispatcher (DRD) and below the file systems layer as illustrated in Figure 14-2.

---

[1] LSM is based on version 2.3 of the Veritas Volume Manager. Additional development is also done by Compaq to enhance the product (e.g., *TruCluster* support).

14.1.1 LSM Architecture

The LSM architecture is composed of four major components:

- Physical Disk
- Subdisk
- Plex
- Volume

Figure 14-3 shows how the various components interact.

What is RAID?

RAID stands for Redundant Array of [Independent -or- Inexpensive] Disks. RAID defines certain "levels" (or a grouping of disk drives in a particular format) so that they can be combined to act as a single disk (or volume). The most common RAID Levels are:

RAID 0 – Striping
RAID 1 – Mirroring
RAID 0+1 – Striping + Mirroring
RAID 5 – Striping with parity

RAID 0

The Operating System sees the three physical disks as one large (logical) disk. However, the I/O to the device is spread evenly (striped) across all the physical disks. The stripe width is a fixed size created when the RAIDset (volume) is defined. NOTE: RAID 0 provides no redundancy.

A 24KB I/O to the volume

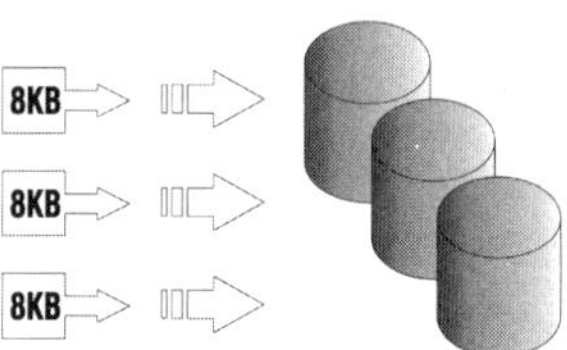

RAID 1

The Operating System sees the two physical disks as one large (logical) disk. However, writes to the device are duplicated (mirrored) to both physical disks.

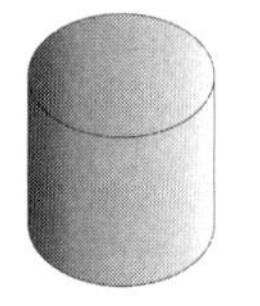

I/O to the volume

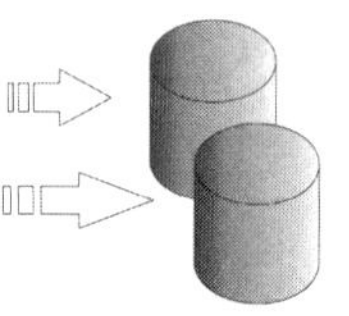

RAID 0+1

The Operating System sees the six physical disks as one large (logical) disk. However, the I/O to the device is spread evenly (striped) across pairs of mirro physical disks

A 24KB I/O to the volume

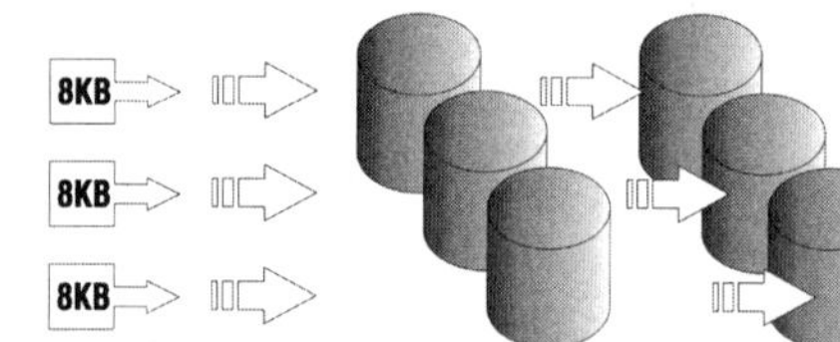

RAID 5

The Operating System sees the four physical disks as one large (logical) disk. However, the I/O to the device is spread evenly (striped) to the physical disks and an XOR (^) of each write is also written to the disks so that if a disk fails can be recreated.

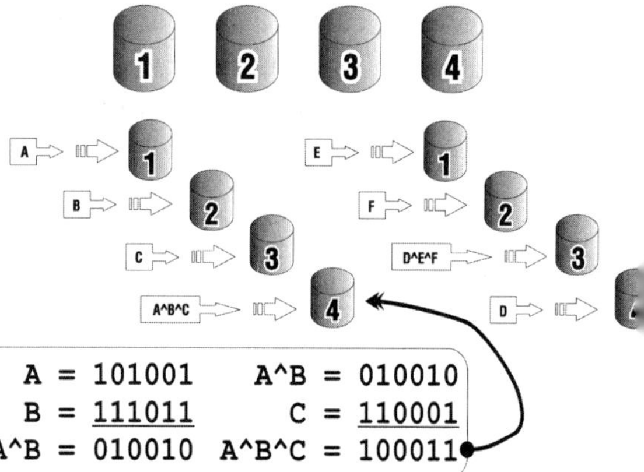

Figure 14-1: What is RAID?

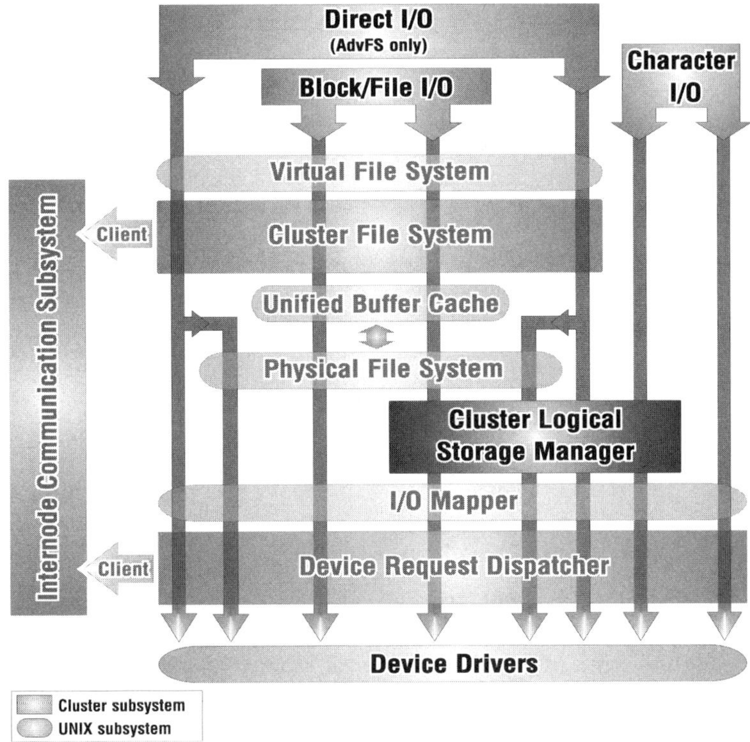

Figure 14-2: Cluster Device I/O Subsystem Relationships

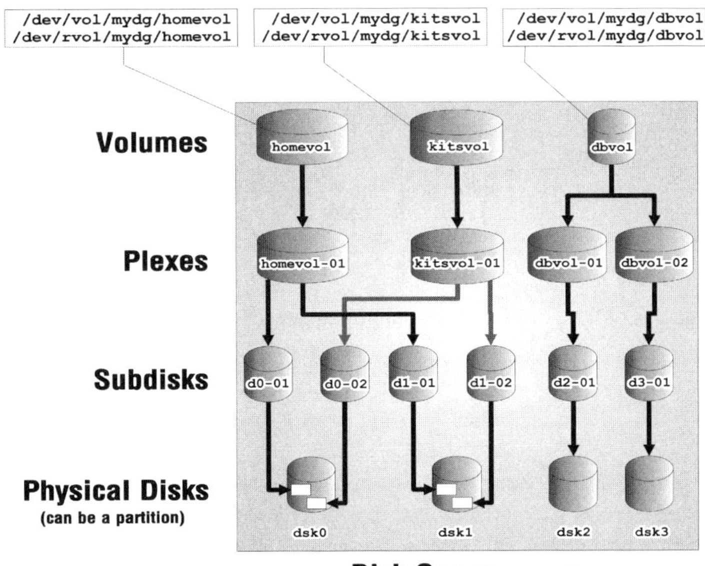

Figure 14-3: Relationship of LSM Objects

14.1.1.1 Physical Disk

Physical disks are just what you think they are: hard disk drives. However, a physical disk in LSM terms can be just a partition on a disk. One or more disks/partitions can be managed by LSM in a "pool" or disk group. A disk group is a bunch of disks/partitions grouped together, generally by their intended function (i.e., a database disk group). While you can have more than one disk group, there must be at least one disk group, the root disk group (`rootdg`). See Figure 14-4.

When a disk/partition is brought under the LSM's control, it can be treated as one of three types of LSM disks:

- `sliced` disk
- `simple` disk
- `nopriv` disk

A `sliced` disk is the default disk type that is used when an entire unused disk is brought under the LSM's control. The `sliced` disk consists of two partitions: one partition is used for private LSM metadata, and the other partition is used for user data (also known as public data). The default size for the private metadata partition is 4096 blocks.

A `simple` disk is the default disk type that is used when an unused partition of a disk is brought under the LSM's control. The `simple` disk consists of the single partition with the beginning of the partition used for private LSM metadata; the remainder of the partition is used for user data.

A `nopriv` disk is the default disk type that is used when a disk or partition that contains user data is encapsulated into LSM. The `nopriv` disk does not contain any LSM-specific data.

14.1.1.2 Subdisk

A subdisk is a set of contiguous disk blocks on a physical disk. A subdisk can be the whole disk or just a part of a disk.

14.1.1.3 Plex

A plex is composed of one or more subdisks. There are two categories of plexes:

- Data
- Log

A data plex is used to hold the volume's data and can be:

- Concatenated (writes to the subdisks are done sequentially).
- Striped (`RAID0`).
- `RAID5` plex.

A concatenated plex can be composed of subdisks of different sizes. Striped and `RAID5` plexes should be composed of subdisks that are sized in multiples of the stripe width (64K by default) to avoid splitting I/O requests unnecessarily.

Figure 14-5 illustrates the differences between a concatenated plex and striped plex.

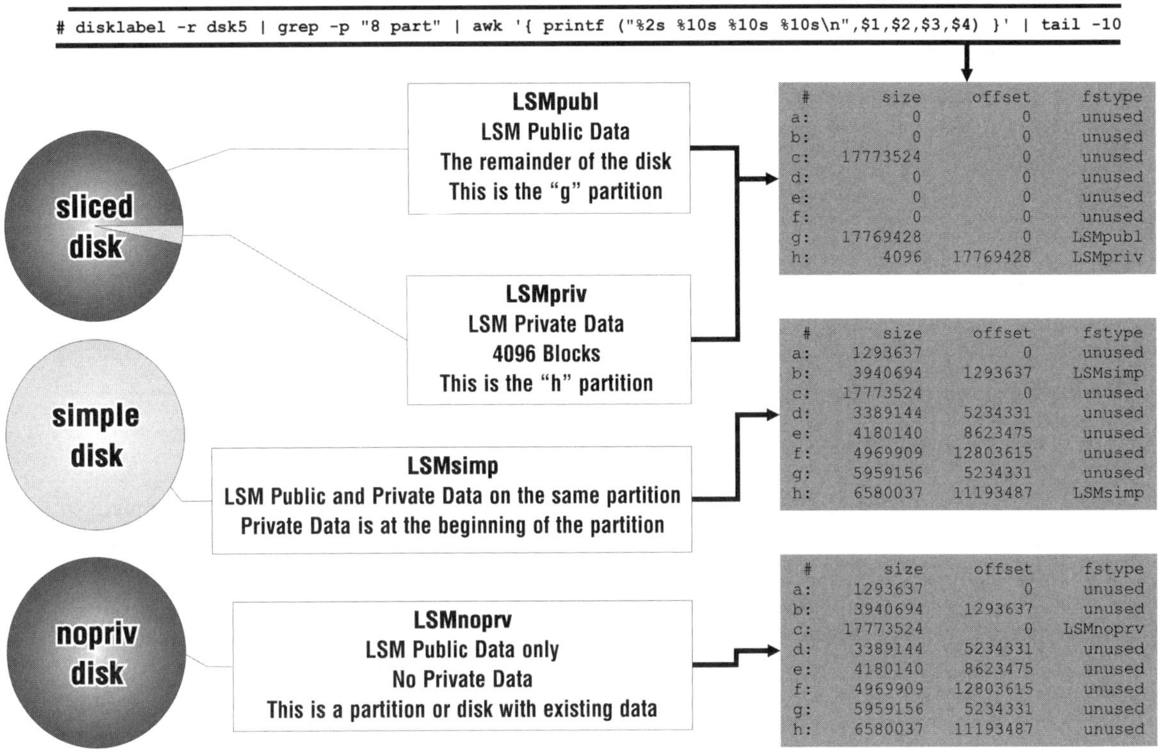

```
# disklabel -r dsk5 | grep -p "8 part" | awk '{ printf ("%2s %10s %10s %10s\n",$1,$2,$3,$4) }' | tail -10
```

sliced disk

LSMpubl
LSM Public Data
The remainder of the disk
This is the "g" partition

LSMpriv
LSM Private Data
4096 Blocks
This is the "h" partition

#	size	offset	fstype
a:	0	0	unused
b:	0	0	unused
c:	17773524	0	unused
d:	0	0	unused
e:	0	0	unused
f:	0	0	unused
g:	17769428	0	LSMpubl
h:	4096	17769428	LSMpriv

simple disk

LSMsimp
LSM Public and Private Data on the same partition
Private Data is at the beginning of the partition

#	size	offset	fstype
a:	1293637	0	unused
b:	3940694	1293637	LSMsimp
c:	17773524	0	unused
d:	3389144	5234331	unused
e:	4180140	8623475	unused
f:	4969909	12803615	unused
g:	5959156	5234331	unused
h:	6580037	11193487	LSMsimp

nopriv disk

LSMnoprv
LSM Public Data only
No Private Data
This is a partition or disk with existing data

#	size	offset	fstype
a:	1293637	0	unused
b:	3940694	1293637	unused
c:	17773524	0	LSMnoprv
d:	3389144	5234331	unused
e:	4180140	8623475	unused
f:	4969909	12803615	unused
g:	5959156	5234331	unused
h:	6580037	11193487	unused

Figure 14-4: LSM Disk Types

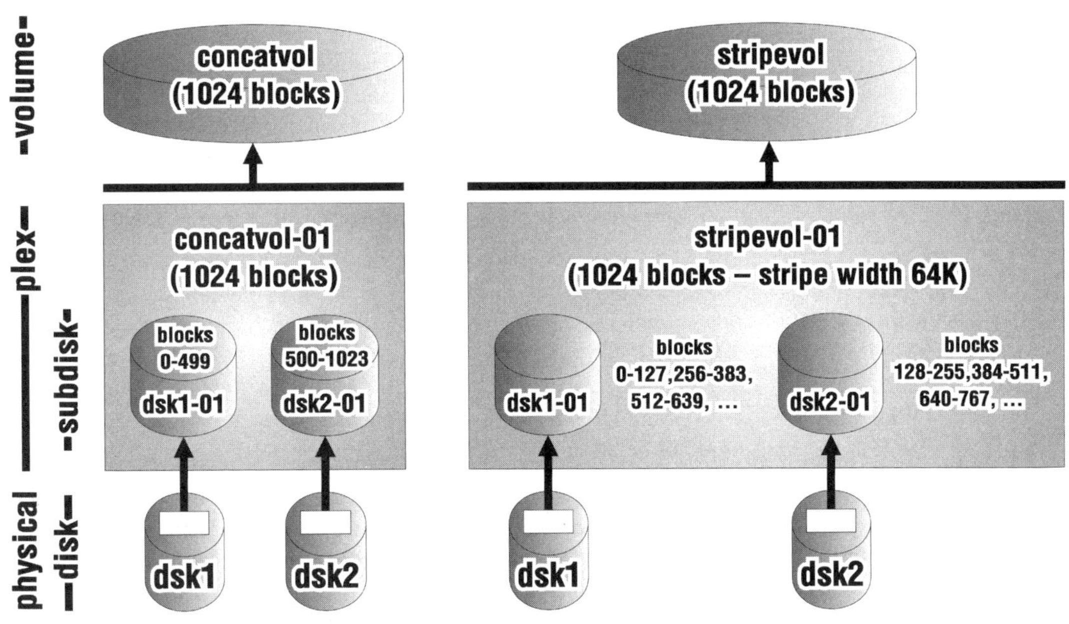

Figure 14-5: LSM Concatenated and Striped Plexes

A log plex can be a:

- Dirty Region Log (DRL) plex.
- `RAID5` log plex.

A log plex is used to track write activity on a mirrored or `RAID5` volume and is used to recover the volume's integrity after a system failure. For additional information, see the Logical Storage Manager Guide.

NOTE:

As of this writing, RAID5 plexes are not supported in a cluster.

14.1.1.4 Volume

A volume is composed of one or more plexes. If you have more than one data plex within a volume, it is a mirrored volume (i.e., data written to the volume is duplicated on each data plex). A mirrored volume that is composed of two or more concatenated data plexes is a `RAID1`-style volume, while a mirrored volume that is composed of two or more striped data plexes is a `RAID0+1`-style volume. Volumes are the logical devices that the operating system uses just like physical disks or partitions. A volume can be used as a raw device by using the volume's character device special file located in the `/dev/rvol` subdirectory. You can also create a file system on a volume which will use the volume's block device special file located in the `/dev/vol` subdirectory.

14.2 Why Do I Need LSM?

Since LSM is a software RAID implementation, it is an inexpensive alternative to hardware-based RAID. Although LSM has some limitations that prevent you from implementing a complete no-single-point-of-failure (NSPOF) solution, as we will discuss in the next section, it can still get you the redundancy you need in the most important places: your data and the cluster-common file systems. Furthermore, if you are migrating from a previous *TruCluster* configuration (V1.5 or V1.6) and it is a NSPOF cluster, then you are using LSM (it was the only way to achieve a NSPOF solution because multiple paths to storage devices were not supported until *Tru64* UNIX version 5.0).

The fact that LSM continues to be supported gives you another option for implementing redundancy. Coupled with a LAN-based cluster interconnect, you can put together an inexpensive, redundant, and highly functional cluster. Starting in *TruCluster* Server version 5.1A, you can use LSM to mirror the `cluster_root`, `cluster_usr`, `cluster_var`, `swap` partitions, and, of course, your data. What this means is you now have a low cost cluster solution. Prior to V5.1A, `cluster_root` and `swap` could not be brought into LSM.

As much as we love multiple bus, multiple switch, Fibre Channel RAID controller solutions, not everyone can afford a storage solution in that price range. So this is a welcome alternative to getting redundancy via software-based RAID. While it is not a completely redundant solution, it is close. The only pieces missing from the fully redundant pie are the quorum disk and two of the member's boot disk partitions (the `boot_partition` and `cnx` partition). Of course, one could argue that the purpose of the quorum disk is for additional redundancy, and it, in and of itself, is not a single-point-of-failure (SPOF). And the loss of one member's boot disk would not cause a cluster-wide failure, so it too is not a SPOF. Furthermore, replacing a quorum disk or member's boot disk is not a very difficult or time-consuming procedure (a process we will cover in Chapter 22).

If you already use LSM on your current pre-V5.0A cluster, then migrating any data you have on LSM volumes can be accomplished with a minimal downtime.

NOTE:

In order to enable many of the advanced LSM features (mirroring, striping, etc.), you will need to install the LSM-OA license product authorization key (PAK). This is an additional cost license, so unless you have it, you will have to contact Compaq or a reseller to get it.

14.3 CLSM Rules of the Road

Now that you know a little bit about LSM, let's discuss what you can and cannot do with LSM in a *TruCluster* Server environment. We will split this section into three parts:

	Section
• Common CLSM Notes, Rules, and Restrictions	14.3.1
• Cluster-common File Systems Rules and Restrictions	14.3.2
• Member Boot Disk Rules and Restrictions	14.3.3

14.3.1 Common CLSM Notes, Rules, and Restrictions

The following rules and restrictions apply to CLSM:

- RAID5 LSM volumes are not supported in a cluster.
- Statistics returned from the volstat(8) command apply only to the member where the command was run. As of this writing there is no cluster-wide volstat command.
- The output returned from the voldisk(8) command with the "list" switch may not be consistent from member to member with regard to devices not under LSM control.

```
[molari]
# voldisk list

DEVICE       TYPE      DISK        GROUP        STATUS
dsk0         sliced    -           -            unknown
dsk1         sliced    -           -            unknown
dsk2         sliced    -           -            unknown
dsk3         sliced    -           -            unknown
dsk4         sliced    -           -            unknown
dsk5h        simple    dsk5h       rootdg       online
dsk6         sliced    -           -            unknown
```

```
[sheridan]
# voldisk list
DEVICE       TYPE      DISK       GROUP       STATUS
dsk1         sliced    -          -           unknown
dsk2         sliced    -          -           unknown
dsk3         sliced    -          -           unknown
dsk4         sliced    -          -           unknown
dsk5h        simple    dsk5h      rootdg      online
dsk6         sliced    -          -           unknown
dsk7         sliced    -          -           unknown
dsk8         sliced    -          -           unknown
```

- There is only one root disk group (`rootdg`), and it is shared by all cluster members.

  Since there is one shared root disk group in the cluster, we recommend that the devices that are in the `rootdg` be on shared buses that are shared by all cluster members for the highest availability. Actually, this is good advice for any disk group.

- All members share a common LSM configuration.

  Like the Cluster File System (CFS)[2] that enables the sharing of all file systems and the Device Request Dispatcher (DRD)[3] that enables the sharing of all storage devices, CLSM enables the sharing of all LSM volumes to every member in the cluster.

- Dirty Region Logging (DRL) is done privately on each cluster member.

  DRL is enabled when a log plex is added to a mirrored volume. The DRL log plex divides the data plexes into a set of consecutive regions and tracks any changes to these regions as a result of writes performed on the mirrored volume. This information is used to resynchronize the plexes of a mirrored volume by recovering only those regions of the volume that have been modified, thus speeding up recovery time for mirrored volumes.

  The dirty-region log must be at least 65 blocks in size in order for DRL to be enabled on a mirrored volume. The `volassist(8)` command will automatically calculate the size of the DRL plex when a volume is added, so you needn't to be concerned about figuring out the proper size. In a *TruCluster* Server configuration, the DRL is generally 65 blocks per GB, up to a maximum of 4160 blocks, although in actuality the algorithm is a bit more complex because it rounds down any unusable space based on the actual region size.

- All disks in an LSM disk group should have the same connectivity (see Figure 14-6).

  If you have a disk group composed of disks on a bus that is private to `member1`, do not add disks from a private bus on `member2` to the same disk group.

  If you have a disk group composed of disks on multiple buses, make sure that the buses have the same connectivity within the cluster.

---

[2] See Chapter 13

[3] See Chapter 15

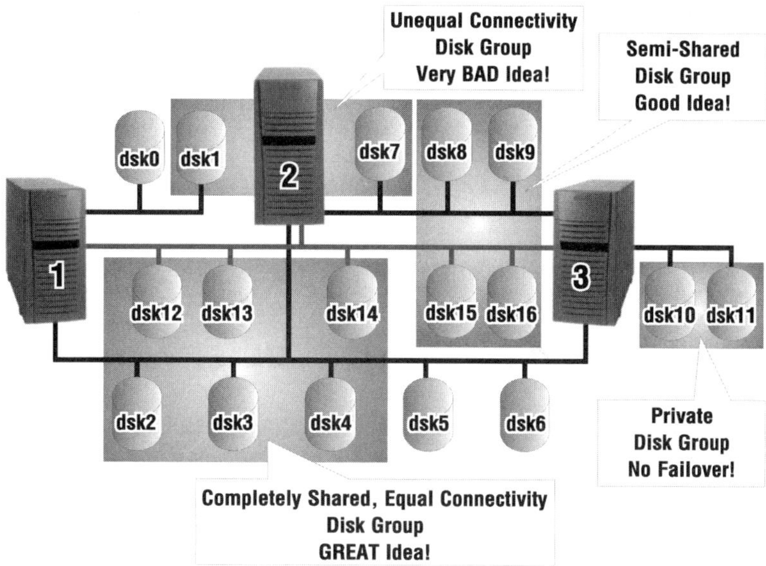

Figure 14-6: CLSM Disk Group Connectivity

14.3.2 Cluster-common File Systems Rules and Restrictions

- The `cluster_root` domain cannot be an LSM volume or have an LSM volume as one of its AdvFS volumes prior to V5.1A. In order to bring the `cluster_root` domain under LSM control, you must use the `volmigrate(8)` command. See section 14.7.1 for more information.
- The `cluster_usr` and `cluster_var` domains can be encapsulated into LSM using the `volencap(8)` command. Alternatively, in V5.1A, you can migrate these domains to LSM volumes using the `volmigrate` command. See section 14.7 for a discussion on how to decide between migration and encapsulation.
- A cluster's quorum disk cannot be an LSM volume.

14.3.3 Member Boot Disk Rules and Restrictions

- A member's `boot_partition` cannot be an LSM volume.
- A member's `cnx` partition cannot be an LSM volume.
- You cannot encapsulate a member's `swap` partitions into LSM prior to V5.1A.

  For an example on encapsulating a `swap` partition, see section 14.7.2.4.

NOTE:

In the Release Notes for *TruCluster* Server version 5.1A, section 3.7, a note states that there is a problem encapsulating the swap partition of a member with a base hostname that is greater than 24 characters in length (i.e., the "thisismyhostnameanditisreallylong" in thisismyhostnameanditisreallylong.tcrhb.com). The solution is to shorten the base hostname.

14.4 Configuring LSM in a Cluster

If you have LSM configured on your standalone system prior to creating the cluster, then LSM will be configured automatically. Once LSM is configured in a cluster, every member subsequently added to the cluster will have LSM configured.

If you did not configure LSM prior to creating the cluster, do not despair – LSM can be configured on a running cluster. In fact, it is pretty straightforward to configure LSM in a cluster. Configuring a running cluster to use LSM is only slightly different than configuring LSM on a standalone system.

1. Locate an unused disk (or partition) on a shared bus for use as the first disk in the rootdg.

   You can use the hwmgr(8) command to determine which devices are on a shared bus. Once you have found a potential device, make sure that it is not in use. There are a few things you should check to verify that you are not about to lose important data.

   - Use cfsmgr(8) command or our homegrown cfs script to see the mounted file systems and their devices. This will alert you to the devices currently in use.

     ```
     # cfs -s | grep dsk
     / [cluster_root#root] (dsk1a):
     /usr [cluster_usr#usr] (dsk1g):
     /var [cluster_var#var] (dsk1h):
     /kits [extra#kits] (dsk8h):
     /u1 [home#u1] (dsk7h):
     /cluster/members/member1/boot_partition [root1_domain#root] (dsk2a):
     /cluster/members/member2/boot_partition [root2_domain#root] (dsk3a):
     ```

   - Use the clu_quorum(8) or clu_get_info(1) command to see which device is being used as the cluster quorum disk.

     ```
     # clu_quorum | grep dsk
     Quorum disk:    dsk4h
     ```

```
# clu_get_info | grep dsk
    Quorum disk = dsk4h
```

- Check the device's disk label using the `disklabel(8)` command to see which partitions are `unused` and whether or not the partition you have in mind overlaps an "in use" partition.

```
# disklabel dsk5 | grep -p "8 part"
8 partitions:
#        size      offset    fstype  fsize  bsize   cpg  # ~Cyl values
  a:  1293637           0    4.2BSD   1024   8192    16  #      0 - 385*
  b:  3940694     1293637    unused      0      0        #    385*- 1557*
  c: 17773524           0    unused      0      0        #      0 - 5289*
  d:  3389144     5234331    unused      0      0        #   1557*- 2566*
  e:  4180140     8623475    unused      0      0        #   2566*- 3810*
  f:  4969909    12803615    unused      0      0        #   3810*- 5289*
  g:  5959156     5234331    unused      0      0        #   1557*- 3331*
  h:  6580037    11193487    unused      0      0        #   3331*- 5289*
```

- Check the `/etc/fdmns` subdirectories. These subdirectories contain symbolic links to the devices used by the AdvFS domains on the cluster. Do you remember the `fln` Korn shell function we created in chapter 6? If not, you can use an `ls(1)` command piped into the `awk(1)` command for this example or turn to chapter 6 and check it out.

```
# fln /etc/fdmns/* | sort | uniq

dsk0a -> /dev/disk/dsk0a
dsk0g -> /dev/disk/dsk0g
dsk1a -> /dev/disk/dsk1a
dsk1g -> /dev/disk/dsk1g
dsk1h -> /dev/disk/dsk1h
dsk2a -> /dev/disk/dsk2a
dsk3a -> /dev/disk/dsk3a
dsk6c -> /dev/disk/dsk6c
dsk7a -> /dev/disk/dsk7a
dsk7g -> /dev/disk/dsk7g
dsk7h -> /dev/disk/dsk7h
dsk8h -> /dev/disk/dsk8h
```

The equivalent `ls` and `awk` commands are:

```
# ls -l /etc/fdmns/* | awk '{ print $9,$10,$11 }' | sort | uniq
```

or:

```
# ls -lR /etc/fdmns | awk '/->/ { print $9,$10,$11 }' | sort
```

2. On one member in the cluster, run the `volsetup(8)` command.

```
[molari]
# volsetup dsk5h
LSM: Creating Logical Storage Manager device special files.
Checking for an existing LSM configuration

Initialize vold and the root disk group:
Add disk dsk5h to the root disk group as dsk5h:
Addition of disk dsk5h as dsk5h succeeded.
Initialization of vold and the root disk group was successful.
volwatch daemon started - mail only

You must run 'volsetup -s' on each additional node in the
cluster to initially set up LSM, unless using clu_add_member
to add additional nodes now.  The clu_add_member utility
will automatically start LSM on the new node.
```

3. On all other existing members, run the `volsetup` command with the "`-s`" switch.

```
[sheridan]
# volsetup -s
Starting LSM...
LSM: Creating Logical Storage Manager device special files.
LSM volwatch Service started - mail only
```

The "`-s`" switch is used to update the member's `/etc/inittab` file, create member-specific LSM devices, and start the LSM daemons on the member.

NOTE:

If we had not already added the second member to the cluster with the `clu_add_member(8)` command, then step 3 would have been unnecessary because any new member added to the cluster, now that LSM is configured, will be automatically configured to use LSM. You will not need to use the "`volsetup -s`" command for any newly added members, only existing members.

14.5 LSM Commands

While the intent of this chapter is not to teach you how to use LSM, but rather to show you what the differences are between LSM on a standalone system and LSM in a cluster, we thought at least to give you an idea of which commands can be used to create LSM volumes.

LSM has a whole slew of commands that accomplish various tasks. Let's look at which commands are used and when you may want to use them.

There are three interfaces that can be used with LSM:

- Graphical User Interface (GUI)[4]
- Menu-Based
- Command-line

There are two approaches that can be taken when working with LSM:

- Top-Down
- Bottom-Up

We're not referring to driving down the highway with the "top down" or chugging a beer ("bottoms up!") but rather how the commands are used to create and manipulate the various LSM components. Figure 14-7 illustrates the two approaches.

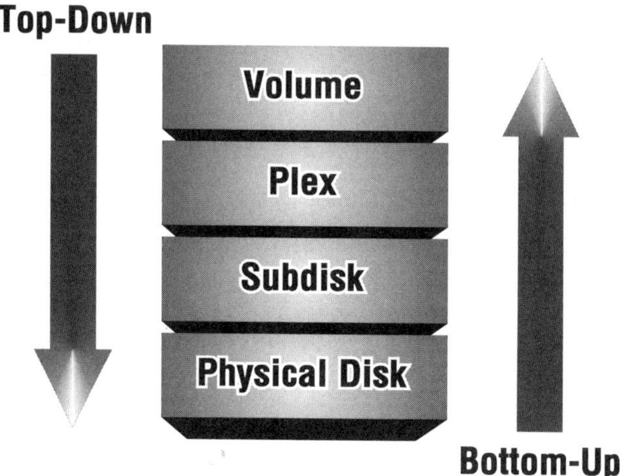

Figure 14-7: Top-Down vs. Bottom-Up

---

[4] Requires the `LSM-OA` license PAK to use.

Top-Down commands (Table 14-1) are designed to take a lot of the complexity out of working with LSM. With one command (`volassist`), you can create a volume that consists of two striped plexes.

As you become more comfortable with LSM, you may find that the Top-Down commands are a little

LSM Top-Down Commands				
Command	**Location**	**Man**	**Type**	**Description**
`volassist`	/sbin	8	binary	Program to create, mirror, back up, grow, shrink, and move LSM volumes.
`voldiskadd`	/usr/sbin	8	sh	Adds one or more disks for use within LSM.
`voldisksetup`	/usr/sbin	8	sh	Sets up a disk for use within LSM.
`volevac`	/usr/sbin	8	sh	Evacuates all volumes from a disk.
`volmirror`	/usr/sbin	8	sh	Mirrors volumes on a disk or control default mirroring.

Table 14-1: LSM Top-Down Commands

LSM Bottom-UP Commands				
Command	**Location**	**Man**	**Type**	**Description**
`voldg`	/sbin	8	binary	Manages LSM disk groups.
`voldisk`	/sbin	8	binary	Creates and manages LSM disks.
`voledit`	/sbin	8	binary	Creates, removes, and modifies LSM records.
`volmake`	/sbin	4/8	binary	Creates LSM objects. This is an advanced command that can be used to create many LSM objects quickly. It looks like a top-down command when run, but the preparation is definitely more of a bottom-up approach. Very powerful.
`volmend`	/usr/sbin	8	binary	Repairs (mends) simple problems in LSM configuration records.
`volplex`	/sbin	8	binary	Manages LSM plexes.
`volsd`	/sbin	8	binary	Manages LSM subdisks.
`volume`	/sbin	8	binary	Manages LSM volumes.

Table 14-2: LSM Bottom-Up Commands

restrictive (or perhaps too broad for a particular operation that needs to be accomplished). The Bottom-Up commands (Table 14-2) allow for more granular control.

For example, if you can create a mirrored, striped volume with one Top-Down command, how many commands would you need to accomplish the same goal with Bottom-Up commands? The answer is eight.

- `volmake(8)`
  - `volmake sd` – create a subdisk (4)
  - `volmake plex` – create a striped plex (2)
  - `volmake vol` – create a volume (1)
- `volume(8)`
  - `volume start` – initialize and start the volume (1)

Generally, you will use the Top-Down commands to add disks to LSM and add new volumes, and you will use the Bottom-Up commands to manage the LSM objects. The GUI and Menu-based programs are listed in Table 14-3.

In addition to creating and manipulating LSM objects, there are commands available to display information and statistics about the LSM configuration (Table 14-4), administrative commands and

LSM GUI and Menu-Based Programs

Command	Location	Man	Type	Description
`dxlsm`	`/usr/bin/X11`	8X	binary	Superceded by the **`lsmsa`** command.
`lsmsa`	`/usr/bin`	8	ksh	This script starts the java-based Storage Administrator program.
`lsmsad`	`/usr/sbin`	8	ksh	This script starts the java-based Storage Administrator daemon.
`voldiskadm`	`/usr/sbin`	8	sh	Menu-driven interface to manage LSM disks.

Table 14-3: LSM GUI and Menu-Based Programs

LSM Informational Commands

Command	Location	Man	Type	Description
`volinfo`	`/usr/sbin`	8	binary	Print accessibility and usability of volumes
`volnotify`	`/usr/sbin`	8	binary	Displays LSM configuration events.
`volprint`	`/sbin`	8	binary	Displays LSM configuration.
`volstat`	`/usr/sbin`	8	binary	Display LSM statistics.

Table 14-4: LSM Informational Commands

daemons (Table 14-5), as well as commands to aid in moving data to and from LSM (Table 14-6).

14.6 Importing a Disk Group

Importing a disk group where a cluster is involved differs from dealing with standalone systems.

There are a few scenarios to consider when importing disk groups in a cluster:

- Importing a disk group from a standalone system to a cluster.
- Importing a disk group from a cluster to a standalone system.
- Importing a disk group from a cluster to a cluster.

LSM Administrative Commands and Daemons

Command	Location	Man	Type	Description
`lsmbstartup`	/sbin	8	sh	Script that starts LSM during system startup.
`lsmsetup`	/usr/sbin	8	symlink	A symbolic link to the **volsetup** command.
`vold`	/sbin	8	binary	LSM volume configuration daemon.
`voldctl`	/sbin	8	binary	Controls the LSM volume configuration daemon (**vold**).
`volinstall`	/usr/sbin	8	sh	Sets up LSM after LSM installation. Creates LSM device special files, etc.
`voliod`	/sbin	8	binary	Starts, stops, and reports on LSM kernel I/O daemons.
`volrecover`	/sbin	8	binary	Performs volume recovery operations
`volrestore`	/usr/sbin	8	sh	Restores a complete or partial LSM configuration from information saved by the **volsave** command.
`volrootmir`	/usr/sbin	8	sh	Creates mirror of areas necessary for booting on a new disk. **NOT SUPPORTED IN A CLUSTER!**
`volsave`	/usr/sbin	8	sh	Saves a LSM configuration.
`volsetup`	/usr/sbin	8	sh	Initializes LSM by creating the **rootdg** disk group.
`voltrace`	/usr/sbin	8	binary	Trace operations on volumes.
`volunroot`	/usr/sbin	8	sh	Removes root and swap from LSM on a standalone system. **NOT SUPPORTED IN A CLUSTER!**
`volwatch`	/usr/sbin	8	sh	Monitors LSM for failure events and performs hot sparing.

Table 14-5: LSM Administrative Commands and Daemons

In addition to these scenarios, we must also recognize that as of *Tru64* UNIX version 5.0, a completely new version of LSM has been introduced which, among other things, changes the on-disk metadata as well as how logging is done. Due to these differences, importing disk groups from systems running *Tru64* UNIX prior to version 5.0 must be handled differently than importing a disk group from systems running *Tru64* UNIX version 5.0 or newer.

Importing a disk group is done using the `voldg(8)` command. This is the same command you would use on the standalone system. Table 14-7 shows the additional `voldg` command options based on the origin of the disk group we will be importing.

Any disk group except for `rootdg` can be deported and imported. Although you cannot deport the `rootdg`, we will show you how to import a `rootdg` from another system.

LSM Migration Commands

Command	Location	Man	Type	Description
`volencap`	`/usr/sbin`	8	binary	Encapsulates disks, disk partitions, or AdvFS domains on a single system or a cluster, or the swap devices for one or more cluster members.
`vollogcnvt`	`/usr/sbin`	8	sh	Utility to convert from pre-V5 Block Change Logging (BCL) to Dirty Region Logging (DRL).
`volmigrate`	`/usr/sbin`	8	ksh	Moves AdvFS domain storage from physical storage to LSM volumes (**`volmigrate`**) or from LSM volumes to physical storage (**`volunmigrate`**).
`volreconfig`	`/sbin`	8	sh	Used with the **`volencap`** command to complete the encapsulation process.
`volunmigrate`	`/usr/sbin`	8	symlink	See **`volmigrate`**.

Table 14-6: LSM Migration Commands

`voldg import` command options

from	to	option(s)
Tru64 UNIX version 5.0 or newer	TruCluster Server	`-o shared`
Digital UNIX version 3.2 - 4.0E Tru64 UNIX version 4.0F - 4.0G	TruCluster Server	`-o convert_old -o shared`
TruCluster Server	Tru64 UNIX version 5.0 or newer	`-o private`
TruCluster Server	Digital UNIX version 3.2 - 4.0E Tru64 UNIX version 4.0D - 4.0G	unsupported*

* = there is a scenario where it can be done, see section **14.5.2.2**

Table 14-7: The `voldg(8)` Command Import Options

14.6.1 Importing a Disk Group from a Standalone System to a Cluster

14.6.1.1 From *Tru64* UNIX Version 5.0 or Newer

To import a disk group from a standalone system to a cluster, use the following procedure:

1. Deport the disk group from LSM on the standalone system.

```
# volume -g mydg stopall
```

```
# voldg deport mydg
```

2. Disconnect the storage from the standalone system.

3. Connect the storage to the cluster.

4. Scan the SCSI bus on each cluster member.

```
[sheridan]
# hwmgr -scan scsi -bus 3
```

```
[sheridan]
# hwmgr -scan scsi -bus 3 -member molari
```

5. Create the device special files (if necessary).

```
# dsfmgr -K
```

6. Determine the new device names.

```
# hwmgr -show scsi -bus 3
```

7. Rebuild the LSM volume device nodes.

```
# voldctl enable
```

8. Import the disk group.

   - If the disk group is not the rootdg (Note: the "-f" switch may also be necessary if not every disk in the disk group is available):

   ```
   # voldg -o shared -C import mydg
   ```

   - If the disk group was the rootdg on the original system, you will need to rename the disk group because the cluster already has a rootdg.

     Before you can import the root disk group, you must determine the disk group identifier (DGID) of the standalone system's rootdg.

   ```
   # voldisk list dsk10 | grep group
   group:     name=rootdg id=999905375.1022.delenn
   ```

   Import the disk group with a new disk group name. We'll use "mydg."

   ```
   # voldg -o shared -n mydg -C import id=999905375.1022.delenn
   ```

9. Recover the volumes for the disk group in the background.

```
# volrecover -sb -g mydg
```

14.6.1.2 From *Tru64* UNIX Prior to Version 5.0

1. Save the LSM configuration.

   While saving the LSM configuration is always a good idea, it is particularly important if you are moving a disk group from a system running Digital UNIX version 3.2 through 4.0E, or *Tru64* UNIX version 4.0F through 4.0G, because you may need to move it back. Once a disk group is imported into LSM on a system running *Tru64* UNIX version 5.0 or newer, the metadata is converted to the new format and is no longer compatible with the older format. It is possible to restore the metadata to the older, pre-V5 format provided you have the older format backed up and you did not make subsequent metadata changes (e.g., detaching or moving data plexes).

```
# volsave -d /MyLSMbackupDirectory
```

2. Deport the disk group from LSM on the standalone system.

```
# volume -g mydg stopall
```

```
# voldg deport mydg
```

3. Disconnect the storage from the standalone system.

4. Connect the storage to the cluster.

5. Scan the SCSI bus on each cluster member.

```
[sheridan]
# hwmgr -scan scsi -bus 3
```

```
[sheridan]
# hwmgr -scan scsi -bus 3 -member molari
```

6. Create the device special files (if necessary).

```
# dsfmgr -K
```

7. Determine the new device names.

```
# hwmgr -show scsi -bus 3
```

8. Rebuild the LSM volume device nodes.

```
# voldctl enable
```

9. Import the disk group.

   - If the disk group is from a V3.2 through V4.0G standalone system and not the `rootdg`:

```
# voldg -o shared -o convert_old -fC import mydg
lsm:voldg: WARNING: Volume myvol: Temporarily renumbered due to conflict
```

- If the disk group is from a V3.2 through V4.0G standalone system and is the `rootdg`, you will need to rename the disk group because the cluster already has a `rootdg`. Before you can import a disk group you will be renaming, you must determine the disk group identifier (DGID) of the standalone system's `rootdg`.

```
# voldisk list dsk10 | grep group
group:      name=rootdg id=999905375.1022.delenn
```

Import the disk group with a new disk group name. We'll use "`mydg`."

```
# voldg -o shared -o convert_old -n mydg -fC import id=999905375.1022.delenn
```

10. Start the volume.

```
# volprint -Aht myvol
Disk group: mydg

V  NAME          USETYPE    KSTATE   STATE    LENGTH   READPOL   PREFPLEX
PL NAME          VOLUME     KSTATE   STATE    LENGTH   LAYOUT    NCOL/WID MODE
SD NAME          PLEX       DISK     DISKOFFS LENGTH   [COL/]OFF DEVICE   MODE

v  myvol         fsgen      DISABLED CLEAN    2097152  SELECT    -
pl myvol-01      myvol      DISABLED CLEAN    2097152  CONCAT    -        RW
sd mydg_01-01    myvol-01   mydg_01  0        2097152  0         dsk10    ENA
```

```
# volume -g mydg startall
```

For additional information, see the Logical Storage Manager manual or the `volume(8)`, `voldisk(8)`, `voldg(8)`, `volrecover(8)`, and `volsave(8)` reference pages.

14.6.2 Importing a Disk Group from a Cluster to a Standalone System

14.6.2.1 From *TruCluster* Server to a V5.0+ Standalone System

The procedure for going from a cluster to a standalone system running *Tru64* UNIX version 5.0 or newer is almost the same procedure as described in section 14.6.1.1 the only difference occurs at Step 8. Use the following command:

```
# voldg -o private -C import mydg
```

14.6.2.2 From *TruCluster* Server to a V3.2 through V4.0G Standalone System

CAUTION:

This procedure will not work if the disk group did not originate on a system that had a `volsave` performed prior to moving the data to the *TruCluster* Server environment. This procedure is really a recovery procedure and not to be used to move disk groups back and forth between the pre-V5.0 operating system environments.

If you are moving the disk group back to a standalone system running Digital UNIX version 3.2 through 4.0E, or *Tru64* UNIX version 4.0F through 4.0G, you need to restore the metadata from a backup. Replace Steps 5–10 in section 14.6.1.2 with the following procedure:

5. Scan the SCSI bus on each cluster member.

```
# scu scan edt
```

6. Restore the LSM configuration.

```
# volrestore -i -g mydg -d /MyLSMbackupDirectory
```

7. Initialize the volumes in the disk group to a `CLEAN` state (repeat as necessary).

```
# volume -g mydg init clean myCoolVolume myMultiPlex
```

8. Start all of the volumes in the disk group.

```
# volume -g mydg startall
```

For additional information, see the Logical Storage Manager Guide or the `volume(8)`, `voldg(8)`, and `volrestore(8)` reference pages.

14.6.3 Importing a Disk Group from a Cluster to a Cluster

14.6.3.1 From *TruCluster* Server to *TruCluster* Server

The procedure for going from a cluster to a cluster running *TruCluster* Server version 5.0A or newer is almost the same procedure as described in 14.6.1.1; the only difference is at Step 8. Use the following command:

```
# voldg -C import mydg
```

14.6.3.2 From *TruCluster* Version 1.5 or 1.6 to *TruCluster* Server

Importing a disk group from a cluster running *TruCluster* version 1.5 or 1.6 should be done using the `clu_migrate_*` scripts included in the `TCRMIGRATE` subset that ships with *TruCluster* Server version 5.0A (or newer). We will discuss migrating from V1.5 or V1.6 as well as those `clu_migrate_*` scripts in chapter 26.

14.7 To Migrate or Encapsulate? That is the Question

In this section, we will discuss when you may want or need to migrate versus when you may want or need to encapsulate.

- When you migrate an AdvFS domain to an LSM volume, you are actually moving your data from the storage currently associated with the domain to an LSM volume composed of different underlying storage. To migrate an AdvFS domain to LSM, use the `volmigrate` command. Conversely, to migrate from LSM to an AdvFS domain, use the `volunmigrate` command.

  Prior to *TruCluster* Server version 5.1A, the `volmigrate` and `volunmigrate` commands did not exist, so migrating an AdvFS domain would have to be done manually using one of two methods: either backing up and restoring the data from each file system in the domain to an LSM volume, or using the `addvol(8)` command to add an LSM volume to the AdvFS domain and then removing the non-LSM volume with the `rmvol(8)` command. But even these methods were not supported for the `cluster_root` file system.

  Notice that we mention only AdvFS domains with regard to migration because the `volmigrate` command only supports AdvFS domains.

  You can migrate a domain while the cluster is up and running – no reboot is required!

- When you encapsulate a disk, a disk partition, or an AdvFS domain, the underlying storage becomes LSM volumes. Unlike migration, encapsulation does not require additional storage because the current storage is simply brought under LSM control. To encapsulate a disk, a disk partition, or an AdvFS domain, use the `volencap` command.

  If you encapsulate a disk, a disk partition, or an AdvFS domain that is currently in use, encapsulation will not be completed until a reboot is performed. If, however, the device(s) are dormant, the encapsulation can be completed without a reboot.

To Migrate or Encapsulate?

Scenario: You want to use LSM to Mirror, Stripe, or Manage a disk, disk partition, or AdvFS domain that already contains data you want to keep.

Disk, Disk Partition, or AdvFS Domain	V5.1A		V5.1	V5.0A
	Migrate	Encapsulate	Encapsulate	Encapsulate
The **cluster_root** domain	✓	✗	✗	✗
The **cluster_usr** and/or **cluster_var** domain(s)	✓	✓	✓	✓
A member's **swap** partition	✗	✓	✗	✗
A member's **boot_partition**	✗	✗	✗	✗
A member's **cnx** partition	✗	✗	✗	✗
The cluster's **quorum** disk	✗	✗	✗	✗
Your application data	✓	✓	✓	✓

✓ = Supported, ✗ = Unsupported

Table 14-8: LSM Migration or Encapsulation

Table 14-8 is a comparison table we put together to help you to decide which method to use, given a particular disk, disk partition, or AdvFS domain.

If you are using V5.1A and the table indicates that you have a choice between migration and encapsulation, then your decision should be based on your site policy and/or configuration restrictions. Table 14-9 can be used to help you decide between migration and encapsulation on V5.1A.

NOTE:

The cluster-common domains (`cluster_root`, `cluster_usr`, and `cluster_var`) must be brought into the root disk group (`rootdg`).

14.7.1 Migrate Using the `volmigrate(8)` Command

If you have an AdvFS domain and additional storage, you can migrate your data to LSM volumes using the `volmigrate` command. In fact, this is the only way to get `cluster_root` into LSM.

Migration or Encapsulation Decision Tree

	Question	Yes	No
1	Is the data in an AdvFS domain?	goto 2	encapsulate
2	Is the domain **cluster_root**?	goto 3	goto 4
3	Do you have additional storage?	migrate	✘
4	Is the domain **cluster_usr** or **cluster_var**?	goto 5	goto 8
5	Do you have additional storage?	goto 6	goto 7
6	Do you want to reuse the existing storage?	goto 7	migrate
7	Can you reboot the cluster?	encapsulate	✘
8	Is the domain in use?	goto 9	goto 10
9	Can you unmount the file systems?	goto 10	goto 5
10	Do you have additional storage?	goto 11	encapsulate
11	Do you want to reuse the existing storage?	encapsulate	migrate

✘ = can't get there from here

Table 14-9: LSM Migration or Encapsulation Decision Tree for V5.1A

The advantage to performing a migration rather than an encapsulation is that a domain that is currently in use can be migrated to LSM volumes without having to reboot the cluster. The disadvantage is that you need additional unused storage and the data that you want to migrate must be in an AdvFS domain.

NOTE:

The `volmigrate` command uses the AdvFS `addvol(8)` command. You will need the `ADVFS-UTILITIES` license PAK in order to use the `addvol` command.

To migrate an AdvFS domain to one or more LSM volumes, use the following procedure:

1. Identify unused storage that is large enough to hold the AdvFS domain.

   - Find out the size of the domain with the showfdmn(8) command.

```
# showfdmn cluster_root

               Id              Date Created  LogPgs  Version  Domain Name
3acde49b.0004ec69  Fri Apr  6 11:45:31 2001     512        4  cluster_root

  Vol   512-Blks        Free  % Used  Cmode  Rblks  Wblks  Vol Name
   1L    1048576      644544     39%     on    256    256  /dev/disk/dsk1a
```

   - Locate a disk large enough to hold the domain.

     In our case, since we are looking to migrate cluster_root, we also want to find a device on the shared bus. Since we know that cluster_root is currently on a shared bus, and dsk1 is the disk that we are using for cluster_root, then let's find the bus where dsk1 is located.

```
# hwmgr -view device -dsf dsk1
 HWID: Device Name          Mfg      Model              Location
 ---------------------------------------------------------------------------
   50: /dev/disk/dsk1c      COMPAQ   BD009635C3         bus-3-targ-0-lun-0
```

```
# hwmgr -show scsi -bus 3

        SCSI                DEVICE    DEVICE  DRIVER NUM  DEVICE FIRST
 HWID:  DEVICEID HOSTNAME   TYPE      SUBTYPE OWNER  PATH FILE   VALID PATH
-------------------------------------------------------------------------
   50:  2        molari     disk      none    2      1    dsk1   [3/0/0]
   51:  3        molari     disk      none    2      1    dsk2   [3/1/0]
   52:  4        molari     disk      none    2      1    dsk3   [3/2/0]
   53:  5        molari     disk      none    2      1    dsk4   [3/3/0]
   54:  6        molari     disk      none    2      1    dsk5   [3/4/0]
   55:  7        molari     disk      none    2      1    dsk6   [3/5/0]
```

From our discussion back in section 14.4, we determined that dsk5 was the only disk we had on our cluster that was available. In fact, we already used it to configure LSM. Since we only used a partition on the disk, we will use another available partition on dsk5 to migrate our cluster_root domain. We can find an unused partition by using the disklabel command.

```
# disklabel -r dsk5 | grep -p "8 part"

8 partitions:
#          size      offset    fstype  fsize  bsize   cpg  # ~Cyl values
  a:     1293637          0    unused   1024   8192        #      0 - 385*
  b:     3940694    1293637    unused      0      0        #    385*- 1557*
  c:    17773524          0    unused      0      0        #      0 - 5289*
  d:     3389144    5234331    unused      0      0        #   1557*- 2566*
  e:     4180140    8623475    unused      0      0        #   2566*- 3810*
  f:     4969909   12803615    unused      0      0        #   3810*- 5289*
  g:     5959156    5234331    unused      0      0        #   1557*- 3331*
  h:     6580037   11193487   LSMsimp                      #   3331*- 5289*
```

Partition "a" looks large enough, so we will use it.

2. Backup the data in the domain – just in case.

3. Define the disk within LSM.

```
# voldisksetup -i dsk5a
```

4. Add the disk to the `rootdg`.

```
# voldg adddisk clu_root=dsk5a
```

5. Migrate!

```
# volmigrate cluster_root clu_root

volassist -Ucluroot make cluster_rootvol 1048576 clu_root init=active nlog=0
addvol /dev/vol/rootdg/cluster_rootvol cluster_root
rmvol /dev/disk/dsk1a cluster_root
rmvol: Removing volume '/dev/disk/dsk1a' from domain 'cluster_root'
rmvol: Removed volume '/dev/disk/dsk1a' from domain 'cluster_root'
```

6. Verify that the migration succeeded.
   - Check the `cluster_root` domain.

```
# showfdmn cluster_root

               Id              Date Created  LogPgs  Version  Domain Name
3acde49b.0004ec69  Fri Apr  6 11:45:31 2001     512        4  cluster_root

  Vol   512-Blks        Free  % Used  Cmode  Rblks  Wblks  Vol Name
   2L    1048576      644608     39%     on  65536  65536  /dev/vol/rootdg/clust
er_rootvol
```

The `cluster_root` domain is now using the LSM volume, "`cluster_rootvol`" device special file located in the `/dev/vol/rootdg` directory.

- Check LSM.

```
# volprint -Aht cluster_rootvol

Disk group: rootdg

V  NAME          USETYPE      KSTATE   STATE    LENGTH   READPOL   PREFPLEX
PL NAME          VOLUME       KSTATE   STATE    LENGTH   LAYOUT    NCOL/WID MODE
SD NAME          PLEX         DISK     DISKOFFS LENGTH   [COL/]OFF DEVICE   MODE

v  cluster_rootvol cluroot    ENABLED  ACTIVE   1048576  SELECT    -
pl cluster_rootvol-01 cluster_rootvol ENABLED ACTIVE 1048576 CONCAT -       RW
sd clu_root-01 cluster_rootvol-01 cluster_root 0 1048576 0    dsk5a    ENA
```

NOTE:

If for some reason you want to reverse your migration decision, you can use the `volunmigrate` command. In the following example, we will move the `cluster_root` domain back to the original partition.

```
# volunmigrate cluster_root dsk1a

addvol /dev/disk/dsk1a cluster_root
rmvol /dev/vol/rootdg/cluster_rootvol cluster_root
rmvol: Removing volume '/dev/vol/rootdg/cluster_rootvol' from domain 'cluster_root'
rmvol: Removed volume '/dev/vol/rootdg/cluster_rootvol' from domain 'cluster_root'
voledit -g rootdg -rf rm cluster_rootvol
```

```
# voldg rmdisk clu_root
```

```
# voldisk rm dsk5a
```

The `cluster_root` domain is back to its original device.

14.7.1.1 Migrate and Mirror the Cluster-Common File Systems

One of the main reasons for the `volmigrate` command is to provide an online process to migrate the `cluster_root` domain as we illustrated earlier in this section. Why is this important? To avoid having to shutdown the entire cluster.

Adding support for `cluster_root` (and `swap`) in V5.1A allows for lower cost cluster configurations by utilizing LSM to mirror the cluster-common domains across buses for a NSPOF failure solution.

So, we thought, if you have a cluster without a multiple-bus, dual-redundant hardware RAID controller, you might like to see an example of mirroring your cluster-common devices using LSM.

Here are the steps you will need to take:

1. Locate a disk (or disks) large enough to migrate `cluster_root`, `cluster_usr`, and `cluster_var` domains.

   Ideally, you will want the disk(s) to be on a shared bus other than the bus where the cluster-common domains are currently located. Additionally, choose the disk(s) at least the same size as the current cluster-common disk(s) so that you can reuse the original cluster-common disk(s) as the mirror.

   Our cluster-common domains are on the same disk, so we will be using another disk of the same size for the remainder of this example.

2. Save the disk label in case you want to go back to the original (non-LSM) configuration.

```
# disklabel -r dsk1 > /dsk1_noLSM.lbl
```

3. Add the disk(s) to LSM that you will be using as your destination disks.

   In this case, we will be using `dsk6`. We are going to use the entire disk and let LSM create the volumes it needs instead of splitting the disk into separate partitions for each domain.

```
# voldisksetup -i dsk6
```

4. Add the disk(s) to the root disk group.

```
# voldg adddisk dsk6
```

5. Migrate the cluster-common domains (this may take a while – be patient).

```
# volmigrate cluster_root dsk6
volassist -Ucluroot make cluster_rootvol 1048576 dsk6 init=active nlog=0
addvol /dev/vol/rootdg/cluster_rootvol cluster_root
rmvol /dev/disk/dsk1b cluster_root
rmvol: Removing volume '/dev/disk/dsk1b' from domain 'cluster_root'
rmvol: Removed volume '/dev/disk/dsk1b' from domain 'cluster_root'
```

```
# volmigrate cluster_usr dsk6

volassist -Ufsgen -g rootdg make cluster_usrvol 8389344 dsk6 init=active
addvol /dev/vol/rootdg/cluster_usrvol cluster_usr
rmvol /dev/disk/dsk1g cluster_usr
rmvol: Removing volume '/dev/disk/dsk1g' from domain 'cluster_usr'
rmvol: Removed volume '/dev/disk/dsk1g' from domain 'cluster_usr'
```

```
# volmigrate cluster_var dsk6

volassist -Ufsgen -g rootdg make cluster_varvol 8323280 dsk6 init=active
addvol /dev/vol/rootdg/cluster_varvol cluster_var
rmvol /dev/disk/dsk1h cluster_var
rmvol: Removing volume '/dev/disk/dsk1h' from domain 'cluster_var'
rmvol: Removed volume '/dev/disk/dsk1h' from domain 'cluster_var'
```

6. Verify that the migration was successful.

   You can use the `volprint` and `showfdmn` commands. Additionally, verify the disk labels with the `disklabel` command. Of course, the fact that the cluster is running is a good indication that everything went as planned.

7. Add the original cluster-common disk(s) to LSM.

```
# voldisksetup -i dsk1
```

8. Add the original cluster-common disk(s) to the root disk group.

```
# voldg adddisk dsk1
```

9. Mirror the volumes (this may take a while – be patient).

```
# volmirror dsk6 dsk1
```

10. Add a log plex for the mirrored volumes.

    We will use `dsk5h`, since it is a different physical disk within the root disk group. The `volassist(8)` reference page recommends not placing a log plex on the same physical disk as the volume data.

```
# volassist addlog cluster_rootvol dsk5h

# volassist addlog cluster_usrvol dsk5h

# volassist addlog cluster_varvol dsk5h
```

11. Verify that the mirror completed successfully.

```
# volprint cluster_rootvol cluster_usrvol cluster_varvol

Disk group: rootdg

TY NAME           ASSOC         KSTATE   LENGTH   PLOFFS  STATE    TUTIL0  PUTIL0
v  cluster_rootvol cluroot      ENABLED  1048576  -       ACTIVE   -       -
pl cluster_rootvol-02 cluster_rootvol ENABLED 1048576 - ACTIVE   -       -
sd dsk1-01        cluster_rootvol-02 ENABLED 1048576 0    -        -       -
pl cluster_rootvol-03 cluster_rootvol ENABLED LOGONLY - ACTIVE   -       -
sd dsk5-01        cluster_rootvol-03 ENABLED 65   LOG     -        -       -
pl cluster_rootvol-01 cluster_rootvol ENABLED 1048576 - ACTIVE   -       -
sd dsk6-01        cluster_rootvol-01 ENABLED 1048576 0    -        -       -

v  cluster_usrvol fsgen         ENABLED  8389344  -       ACTIVE   -       -
pl cluster_usrvol-02 cluster_usrvol ENABLED 8389344 -    ACTIVE   -       -
sd dsk1-02        cluster_usrvol-02 ENABLED 8389344 0    -        -       -
pl cluster_usrvol-03 cluster_usrvol ENABLED LOGONLY -    ACTIVE   -       -
sd dsk5-02        cluster_usrvol-03 ENABLED 195  LOG     -        -       -
pl cluster_usrvol-01 cluster_usrvol ENABLED 8389344 -    ACTIVE   -       -
sd dsk6-03        cluster_usrvol-01 ENABLED 8389344 0    -        -       -

v  cluster_varvol fsgen         ENABLED  8323280  -       ACTIVE   -       -
pl cluster_varvol-02 cluster_varvol ENABLED 8323280 -    ACTIVE   -       -
sd dsk1-03        cluster_varvol-02 ENABLED 8323280 0    -        -       -
pl cluster_varvol-03 cluster_varvol ENABLED LOGONLY -    ACTIVE   -       -
sd dsk5-03        cluster_varvol-03 ENABLED 195  LOG     -        -       -
pl cluster_varvol-01 cluster_varvol ENABLED 8323280 -    ACTIVE   -       -
sd dsk6-02        cluster_varvol-01 ENABLED 8323280 0    -        -       -
```

NOTE:

We could have reduced the number of steps taken in the previous example if we had had an extra disk so that we would not have had to reuse the original cluster-common disk. For example, with an extra disk, the approach becomes simpler. Repeat the first two steps.

3. Add the disks to LSM that you will be using as your destination disks.

```
# voldisksetup -i dsk6 dsk7
```

4. Add the disks to the root disk group.

```
# voldg adddisk dsk6
# voldg adddisk dsk7
```

5. Migrate and mirror the cluster-common domains (this may take a while – be patient).

```
# volmigrate -m 2 cluster_root dsk6 dsk7
volassist -Ucluroot make cluster_rootvol 1048576 nmirror=2 dsk6 dsk7 init=active
 nlog=0
addvol /dev/vol/rootdg/cluster_rootvol cluster_root
rmvol /dev/disk/dsk1b cluster_root
rmvol: Removing volume '/dev/disk/dsk1b' from domain 'cluster_root'
rmvol: Removed volume '/dev/disk/dsk1b' from domain 'cluster_root'
```

```
# volmigrate -m 2 cluster_usr dsk6 dsk7
volassist -Ufsgen -g rootdg make cluster_usrvol 8389344 nmirror=2 dsk6 dsk7 init
=active
addvol /dev/vol/rootdg/cluster_usrvol cluster_usr
rmvol /dev/disk/dsk1g cluster_usr
rmvol: Removing volume '/dev/disk/dsk1g' from domain 'cluster_usr'
rmvol: Removed volume '/dev/disk/dsk1g' from domain 'cluster_usr'
```

```
# volmigrate -m 2 cluster_var dsk6 dsk7
volassist -Ufsgen -g rootdg make cluster_varvol 8323280 nmirror=2 dsk6 dsk7 init
=active
addvol /dev/vol/rootdg/cluster_varvol cluster_var
rmvol /dev/disk/dsk1h cluster_var
rmvol: Removing volume '/dev/disk/dsk1h' from domain 'cluster_var'
rmvol: Removed volume '/dev/disk/dsk1h' from domain 'cluster_var'
```

6. Verify that the migration and mirroring were successful.

   You can use the `volprint` and `showfdmn` commands. Additionally, verify the disk labels with the `disklabel` command. Of course, the fact that the cluster is running is a good indication that everything went as planned.

7. Remove the log plex from `cluster_usrvol` and `cluster_varvol` because they are on the same disk that contains volume data. Add a new log plex from another disk.

   Locate the log plexes.

```
# volprint | grep LOG
pl cluster_usrvol-03 cluster_usrvol ENABLED LOGONLY -    ACTIVE   -     -
sd dsk6-03       cluster_usrvol-03 ENABLED 195   LOG      -        -     -
pl cluster_varvol-03 cluster_varvol ENABLED LOGONLY -    ACTIVE   -     -
sd dsk6-05       cluster_varvol-03 ENABLED 195   LOG      -        -     -
```

   Remove the log plexes.

```
# volplex -v cluster_usrvol dis cluster_usrvol-03
# voledit -rf rm cluster_usrvol-03
```

```
# volplex -v cluster_varvol dis cluster_varvol-03
# voledit -rf rm cluster_varvol-03
```

Add in the new log plexes from a different disk with the root disk group.

```
# volassist addlog cluster_rootvol dsk5h
# volassist addlog cluster_usrvol dsk5h
# volassist addlog cluster_varvol dsk5h
```

8. Verify that everything completed successfully.

```
# volprint cluster_rootvol cluster_usrvol cluster_varvol
Disk group: rootdg

TY NAME          ASSOC          KSTATE   LENGTH   PLOFFS   STATE    TUTIL0  PUTIL0
v  cluster_rootvol cluroot      ENABLED  1048576  -        ACTIVE   -       -
pl cluster_rootvol-01 cluster_rootvol ENABLED 1048576 - ACTIVE      -       -
sd dsk6-01       cluster_rootvol-01 ENABLED 1048576 0      -        -       -
pl cluster_rootvol-02 cluster_rootvol ENABLED 1048576 - ACTIVE      -       -
sd dsk7-01       cluster_rootvol-02 ENABLED 1048576 0      -        -       -
pl cluster_rootvol-03 cluster_rootvol ENABLED LOGONLY - ACTIVE      -       -
sd dsk5h-01      cluster_rootvol-03 ENABLED 65    LOG      -        -       -

v  cluster_usrvol fsgen         ENABLED  8389344  -        ACTIVE   -       -
pl cluster_usrvol-01 cluster_usrvol ENABLED 8389344 -      ACTIVE   -       -
sd dsk6-02       cluster_usrvol-01 ENABLED 8389344 0       -        -       -
pl cluster_usrvol-02 cluster_usrvol ENABLED 8389344 -      ACTIVE   -       -
sd dsk7-02       cluster_usrvol-02 ENABLED 8389344 0       -        -       -
pl cluster_usrvol-03 cluster_usrvol ENABLED LOGONLY -      ACTIVE   -       -
sd dsk5h-02      cluster_usrvol-03 ENABLED 195   LOG       -        -       -

v  cluster_varvol fsgen         ENABLED  8323280  -        ACTIVE   -       -
pl cluster_varvol-01 cluster_varvol ENABLED 8323280 -      ACTIVE   -       -
sd dsk7-03       cluster_varvol-01 ENABLED 8323280 0       -        -       -
pl cluster_varvol-02 cluster_varvol ENABLED 8323280 -      ACTIVE   -       -
sd dsk6-04       cluster_varvol-02 ENABLED 8323280 0       -        -       -
pl cluster_varvol-03 cluster_varvol ENABLED LOGONLY -      ACTIVE   -       -
sd dsk5h-03      cluster_varvol-03 ENABLED 195   LOG       -        -       -
```

14.7.2 Encapsulate Using the `volencap(8)` Command

When you use the `volencap` command to encapsulate an AdvFS domain, disk, or disk partition, the data that exists on the device is left unchanged. This is a good thing because if you decide to remove LSM you will not have to recreate or restore your data.

The volencap command expects as input a partition, disk, or domain:

- If you choose to have an individual disk partition encapsulated, a nopriv disk and an LSM volume are created from the disk partition.
- If you choose to have an entire disk encapsulated, a nopriv disk and an LSM volume are created for each partition on the disk that is not marked unused.
- If you choose to have an AdvFS domain encapsulated, all AdvFS volumes in the domain become LSM volumes.

The volencap command creates files in the /etc/vol/reconfig.d directory that are used by the volreconfig(8) command to create the LSM volumes, plexes, and subdisks from the devices that were input to the volencap command.

14.7.2.1 Encapsulating an AdvFS Domain

Any domain except for the cluster_root domain can be encapsulated. To place the cluster_root domain under LSM control, you must use the volmigrate command (see section 14.7.1 earlier in this chapter).

As long as the domain is not in use, encapsulation does not require a reboot. If you can, unmount the file systems in the domain you want to encapsulate so that you can avoid having to reboot the cluster.

To encapsulate a domain, do the following:

```
# volencap tcrhb

Setting up encapsulation for tcrhb.
  For AdvFS domain tcrhb:
    - Creating nopriv disk dsk6c.

The following disks are queued up for encapsulation or use by LSM:
 dsk6c

Please consult the Cluster Administration Guide for steps
that you will need to follow to complete the encapsulation.
```

You can see which devices are scheduled for encapsulation by issuing the volencap command with the “-s” switch:

```
# volencap -s

The following disks are queued up for encapsulation or use by LSM:
 dsk6c
```

In order for the encapsulation process to complete, we need to run the `volreconfig` command.

NOTE:

If you decide not to finish the encapsulation process, you cancel the encapsulation for one device by using the `volencap` command with the "`-k <diskname|partition>`" switch or cancel all queued encapsulation requests with the "`-k -a`" switch:

```
# volencap -k dsk6c
```

-OR-

```
# volencap -k -a
```

The `volreconfig` command completes the encapsulation process provided that the devices that are queued for encapsulation are not in use.

```
# volreconfig
Encapsulating dsk6c.
The following disks were encapsulated successfully:
        dsk6c
```

You can verify that the encapsulation succeeded by using the `volprint` command.

```
# volprint | grep dsk6
dm dsk6c-AdvFS  dsk6c         -       17773524 -      -      -    -
v  vol-dsk6c    fsgen         ENABLED 17773524 -      ACTIVE -    -
pl vol-dsk6c-01 vol-dsk6c     ENABLED 17773524 -      ACTIVE -    -
sd dsk6c-01     vol-dsk6c-01 ENABLED 17773524 0      -      -    -
```

You can also verify that the domain volume links were updated with the `fln` function (or you can use an "`ls -l`" command).

```
# fln /etc/fdmns/tcrhb
rootdg.vol-dsk6c -> /dev/vol/rootdg/vol-dsk6c
```

14.7.2.1.1 Encapsulating cluster_usr or cluster_var

The major difference between encapsulating any other domain and the `cluster_usr` or `cluster_var` domains is simply that `/usr` and `/var` cannot be unmounted. In other words, in order to encapsulate cluster_usr or cluster_var, you must shutdown and reboot the entire cluster!

Therefore, if you plan to bring these domains under LSM control, we recommend either running the volencap command after the cluster is first created and before any members have been added, or using the volmigrate command to migrate the domains to LSM volumes instead of encapsulating them.

14.7.2.2 Encapsulating a Disk Partition

If a partition has a UFS file system or is a raw partition (i.e., used by an application like a database), you can encapsulate one or more disk partitions as follows:

```
# volencap dsk5a dsk8h dsk12b
```

```
# volreconfig
```

Make sure that the partitions are not active or you will need to reboot before the encapsulation will be completed.

14.7.2.3 Encapsulating a Disk

Encapsulating an entire disk is similar to encapsulating a partition except that all partitions currently in use on the disk will be queued for encapsulation. To encapsulate a disk, use the disk's base name (i.e., omit the partition letter).

```
# volencap dsk5
```

```
# volreconfig
```

Make sure that the partitions are not active or you will need to reboot before the encapsulation will be completed.

14.7.2.4 Encapsulating a Swap Partition

The volencap command has a special keyword, "swap", that can be used to encapsulate a cluster member's swap devices set in the swapdevice attribute listed in the /etc/sysconfigtab file. The "swap" keyword is member-specific.

```
# volencap swap

Setting up encapsulation for dsk2b.
    - Creating simple disk dsk2f for config area (privlen=4096).
      Warning: space taken from -> dsk2b dsk2f
    - Creating nopriv disk dsk2b for molari-swap.

The following disks are queued up for encapsulation or use by LSM:
 dsk2f dsk2b

Please consult the Cluster Administration Guide for steps
that you will need to follow to complete the encapsulation.
```

```
# volreconfig
EXEC: voledit -rf rm molari-swap01
EXEC: voldg rmdisk dsk2b
EXEC: voldisk rm dsk2b
lsm:voldisk: ERROR: Failed to obtain locks:
        dsk2b: no such object in the configuration
The system will need to be rebooted in order to continue with
LSM volume encapsulation of:
 dsk2f dsk2b
```

At this point the `volreconfig` command will prompt you to reboot the system. We will give the users five minutes.

```
Would you like to either quit and defer encapsulation until later
or commence system shutdown now? Enter either 'quit' or time to be
used with the shutdown(8) command (e.g., quit, now, 1, 5): [quit] 5

Shutdown at 13:45 (in 5 minutes) [pid 525876]

#

        *** System shutdown message from root@molari.tcrhb.com ***

System going down in 5 minutes
        ... Place selected disk partitions under LSM control.

...
System going down in 2 minutes
...
System going down in 60 seconds
...
System going down in 30 seconds
...
```

You can encapsulate all cluster members' swap partitions by specifying all the devices as parameters to the `volencap` command and then issuing the `volreconfig` command on every member, but we think it is easier and less risky to simply issue the `volencap` and `volreconfig` commands on each member as follows:

```
[molari]
# /usr/sbin/volencap swap ; /sbin/volreconfig
```

```
[molari]
# rsh sheridan-ics0 "/usr/sbin/volencap swap ; /sbin/volreconfig"
```

Finish the encapsulation process by rebooting each member one at a time.

For additional information, see the *TruCluster* Server Cluster Administration Guide and the `volencap(8)` reference page.

14.7.3 Unencapsulation

There is no `volunencap` command, so the only way to unencapsulate a previously encapsulated disk, disk partition, or AdvFS domain is the hard way.

14.7.3.1 Unencapsulating an AdvFS Domain

In section 14.7.2.1 we encapsulated our `tcrhb` domain. In this section we'll remove the domain from LSM.

To remove an encapsulated AdvFS domain from LSM, follow these steps:

1. Unmount the file systems.
2. Stop the volume(s).

```
# volume stop vol-dsk6c
```

3. Remove the volume(s).

```
# voledit -rf rm vol-dsk6c
```

4. Remove the disk from the disk group.

```
# voldisk list | grep dsk6
dsk6c        nopriv    dsk6c-AdvFS  rootdg       online
```

```
# voldg rmdisk dsk6c-AdvFS
```

5. Save the disk's label.

```
# disklabel -r dsk6 > /tmp/dsk6.lbl
```

6. Remove the disk from LSM.

```
# voldisk rm dsk6c
```

7. Edit the saved label, changing the "`fstype`" from "`LSMnoprv`" back to "`AdvFS`".

```
# grep -E "LSM|AdvFS" /tmp/dsk6.lbl
  c:      17773524              0  LSMnoprv                            #       0 - 5289*
```

```
# perl -i.orig -pe 's/LSMnoprv/   AdvFS/g' /tmp/dsk6.lbl
```

There are three spaces before "`AdvFS`" in the previous example.

```
# grep -E "LSM|AdvFS" /tmp/dsk6.lbl
  c:      17773524              0     AdvFS                            #       0 - 5289*
```

8. Replace the disk's label.

```
# disklabel -rR dsk6 /tmp/dsk6.lbl
```

9. Fix the AdvFS domain's volume link(s).

```
# find /etc/fdmns -name '*dsk6*'
/etc/fdmns/tcrhb/rootdg.vol-dsk6c
```

```
# cd /etc/fdmns/tcrhb ; ln -s /dev/disk/dsk6c ; rm rootdg.vol-dsk6c ; fln
dsk6c -> /dev/disk/dsk6c
```

10. Mount the file system(s).

```
# mount tcrhb#fafrak /fafrak
```

```
# df /fafrak
Filesystem     512-blocks       Used   Available Capacity  Mounted on
tcrhb#fafrak     17773520     157782    17604000      1%    /fafrak
```

14.7.3.2 Unencapsulating a Disk or Disk Partition

Unencapsulating a disk or disk partition is similar to unencapsulating an AdvFS domain detailed in the previous section. Follow steps 1-8 replacing "AdvFS" where appropriate. For example, if the disk partition contains a UFS file system, you would replace the "fstype" with "4.2BSD".

14.7.3.3 Unencapsulating a Swap Partition

The following steps are needed to unencapsulate the swap partition from LSM. This procedure assumes that the swap partition that was previously encapsulated was on the member's boot disk.

1. Remove the LSM volume from the vm:swapdevice attribute from the member's sysconfigtab file.

   Create a stanza file for the vm:swapdevice attribute.

```
# cat > swap.stanza
vm:
^D
```

```
# sysconfigdb -l vm | grep swapdevice >> swap.stanza ; cat swap.stanza
vm:
        swapdevice = /dev/vol/rootdg/molari-swap01
```

   If you are going to remove the swap device from the member's root disk, then you will also need to remove the lsm:lsm_rootdev_is_volume and set the value to zero.

```
# sysconfigdb -l lsm >> swap.stanza ; cat swap.stanza
vm:
        swapdevice = /dev/vol/rootdg/molari-swap01

lsm:
        lsm_rootdev_is_volume = 2
```

```
# perl -i -pe 's/_volume = 2/_volume = 0/' swap.stanza ; cat swap.stanza
vm:
        swapdevice = /dev/vol/rootdg/molari-swap01

lsm:
        lsm_rootdev_is_volume = 0
```

Now that we have created the stanza file that we need, we can update the member's `sysconfigtab` file.

```
# sysconfigdb -r -f swap.stanza vm
```

```
# sysconfigdb -m -f swap.stanza lsm
Warning: duplicate attribute in lsm: was lsm_rootdev_is_volume = 2, now lsm_root
dev_is_volume = 0
```

2. Locate the swap volume's subdisk and whether or not there is a private region partition on the physical disk where the subdisk is located.

```
# volprint molari-swap01
Disk group: rootdg

TY NAME          ASSOC         KSTATE   LENGTH   PLOFFS   STATE    TUTIL0  PUTIL0
v  molari-swap01 swap          ENABLED  1568768  -        ACTIVE   -       -
pl molari-swap01-01 molari-swap01 ENABLED 1568768 -       ACTIVE   -       -
sd dsk2b-01      molari-swap01-01 ENABLED 1568768 0       -        -       -
```

It appears that the swap volume is using `/dev/disk/dsk2b`. Verify this.

```
# voldisk list | grep -E "dsk2[a-h]|^DEV"
DEVICE       TYPE      DISK         GROUP        STATUS
dsk2b        nopriv    dsk2b        rootdg       online
dsk2f        simple    dsk2f        rootdg       online
```

The output indicates that `dsk2f` is likely a private region on the disk. Before we jump to any conclusions, we can verify this as well.

```
# disklabel -r dsk2 | grep LSM
  b:      1568768       524288  LSMnoprv                    #     156*- 622*
  f:         4096      2093056   LSMsimp                    #     622*- 624*
```

The fact that the `f` partition is only 4096 sectors and it is the only other LSM partition on the disk besides the swap partition is a good indicator that `dsk2f` is a private region.

3. Remove the swap disk's private region partition.

```
# voldg rmdisk dsk2f
```

```
# voldisk rm dsk2f
```

4. Reboot the member.

```
# shutdown -sr +5 "Unencapsulating swap from LSM"
```

5. Once the member reboots, login and remove the member's swap volume from LSM.

```
# voledit -rf rm molari-swap01
```

6. Remove the swap partition from LSM.

```
# voldg rmdisk dsk2b
```

```
# voldisk rm dsk2b
```

7. Edit the member's root disk's disklabel to merge the private region (partition `f`) back into the swap partition. In this example, we will be using the `perl` command to quickly edit the label – you can just as easily use any editor you feel comfortable using in lieu of the three `perl` commands.

   Save the label.

```
# disklabel -r dsk2 | tee boot_partition.lbl | grep -p "8 part"
8 partitions:
#          size       offset    fstype  fsize  bsize   cpg  # ~Cyl values
  a:     524288            0     AdvFS                      #     0 - 156*
  b:    1568768       524288    unused      0      0        #   156*- 622*
  c:   17773524            0    unused      0      0        #     0 - 5289*
  d:          0            0    unused      0      0        #     0 - 0
  e:          0            0    unused      0      0        #     0 - 0
  f:       4096      2093056    unused      0      0        #   622*- 624*
  g:   15674324      2097152     AdvFS                      #   624*- 5289*
  h:       2048     17771476       cnx                      #  5289*- 5289*
```

Edit the label.

```
# perl -i -pe 's/1568768/1572864/' boot_partition.lbl
# perl -i -pe 's/4096/    0/' boot_partition.lbl
# perl -i -pe 's/2093056/       0/' boot_partition.lbl
```

```
# grep -p "8 part" boot_partition.lbl
8 partitions:
#          size        offset    fstype  fsize  bsize   cpg  # ~Cyl values
  a:     524288             0     AdvFS                      #      0 - 156*
  b:    1572864        524288    unused      0      0        #   156*- 622*
  c:   17773524             0    unused      0      0        #      0 - 5289*
  d:          0             0    unused      0      0        #      0 - 0
  e:          0             0    unused      0      0        #      0 - 0
  f:          0             0    unused      0      0        #   622*- 624*
  g:   15674324       2097152     AdvFS                      #   624*- 5289*
  h:       2048      17771476       cnx                      #  5289*- 5289*
```

Put the label back on the member's root disk.

```
# disklabel -rRt advfs dsk2 boot_partition.lbl
```

8. Allow the member to start using the swap partition.

```
# swapon -a /dev/disk/dsk2b
```

9. Add the `vm:swapdevice` attribute to the member's `sysconfigtab` file.

```
# cat > swap_noLSM.stanza
vm:
        swapdevice = /dev/disk/dsk2b
^D
```

```
# sysconfigdb -m -f swap_noLSM.stanza vm
```

14.8 LSM and the **dn_setup** Command

As of this writing, the dn_setup command does not recreate LSM device special files. If you use the dn_setup command with the "-clean" or "-init" options, you will need to recreate the LSM device special files using the procedure described in Chapter 7, section 7.5.2.1: "How Can I Reinitialize My /dev and /devices Directories?"

14.9 CLSM Events

While there are no events for the CLSM, there are LSM events located in the /usr/share/evm/templates/sys/lsm.volnotify.evt file.

14.10 References

- The *TruCluster* Server Technical Overview Guide.
- The *TruCluster* Server Cluster Administration Guide.
- The *Tru64* UNIX Logical Storage Manager Guide.
- The *Tru64* UNIX File System Administration Handbook, by Steven M. Hancock, Digital Press (ISBN: 1-55558-227-3).
- Reference pages (noted within the text).

15

The Device Request Dispatcher (DRD)

In this chapter we will be discussing the Device Request Dispatcher cluster subsystem. The Device Request Dispatcher, as I am sure you have probably already guessed, is the subsystem that dispatches requests to devices. Actually, it dispatches I/O requests to any storage device in the cluster (in fact there are some engineers within Compaq who prefer the name DeviceIO Request Dispatcher). The DRD also enables a cluster-wide view of all storage devices connected to any and all members of the cluster. The storage devices can be located on any bus on any system in the cluster; and not just shared buses – private buses are also handled by the DRD. The DRD does not discriminate; any storage device is fair game. And the really great thing is that the DRD does all of this transparently from the user's perspective.

You may be starting to see a trend here. Every member can see all the file systems, every member can see all the devices (even those on a private bus), and everything is accomplished transparently. Not only will your users not require special training to use the cluster, they don't even have to know that they're using a cluster! With few exceptions, the goal is for all the cluster members to cooperate such that users see the cluster as simply one system.

15.1 DRD Concepts

The primary function of the DRD is to coordinate access to the storage devices in a cluster. This coordination is accomplished by having a cluster-wide namespace for all storage devices, communication between all the DRD components of each cluster member (the DRD is a client/server implementation), and the judicious use of I/O barriers to prevent rogue nodes from corrupting data on the cluster-wide storage devices.

15.1.1 Clusterwide Device Namespace

The DRD subsystem is the mechanism that enables every member in the cluster to see every storage device in the cluster. Since devices are given a name as they are discovered, when a member is added to a cluster, its devices are given names. Device naming was covered in detail in chapter 7.

The first member in the cluster will assign names to the devices it detects in the order it detects them (see Figure 15-1).

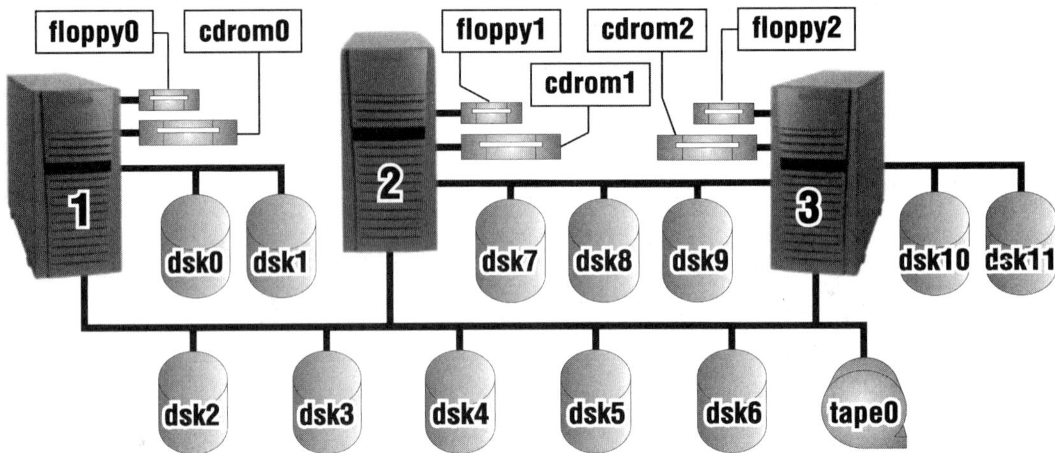

Figure 15-1: Cluster-wide Device Naming

It is important to remember that a device name is associated with the device's worldwide identifier (WWID) and not the device's location on the bus. For additional information, see the discussion on WWIDs in chapter 7. As you can see in the figure, the devices that are directly connected to `member1` have the lowest device names (i.e., `floppy0`, `cdrom0`, `dsk0-dsk6`, and `tape0`). As the second member is added to the cluster, the devices directly connected to it (and not connected directly to `member1`) are detected, and the naming continues with the next number in sequence (i.e., `floppy1`, `cdrom1`, `dsk7-dsk9`). When the third member is added to the cluster, the devices directly connected to it (and not connected directly to `member1` or `member2`) are detected and are named in sequence following those connected to `member2` (i.e., `floppy2`, `cdrom2`, `dsk10-dsk11`).

There are three instances when the DRD will look for devices:

- Boot time.

  The DRD will query the hardware management subsystem at boot time for devices it needs to manage.

- Device open.

  If the DRD does not know about a device when an open on that device is requested, it will query the hardware management subsystem for that specific device.

- Device detection.

  When a new device is added to the system, the hardware management subsystem will post an event to EVM upon detection (e.g., as a result of executing the "`hwmgr -scan scsi`" command). The DRD is a subscriber of events posted to EVM from the hardware management subsystem.

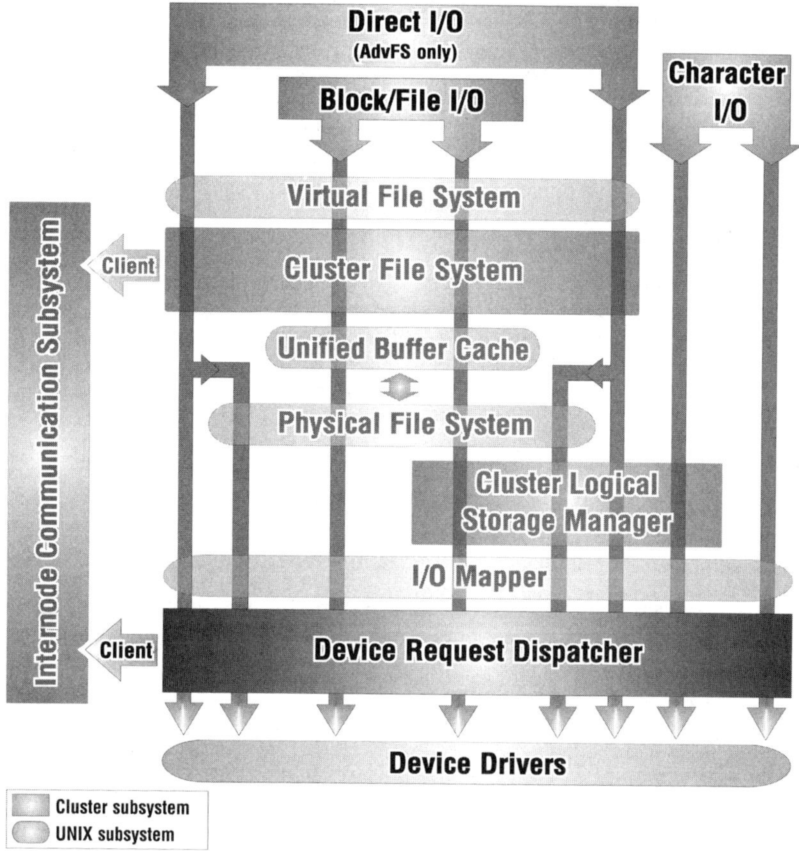

Figure 15-2: ***TruCluster*** **Server I/O Subsystems Architecture**

15.1.2 Clusterwide I/O

All I/O to a storage device in the cluster will pass through the DRD subsystem as you can see in the now familiar *TruCluster* I/O Subsystems Architecture diagram (Figure 15-2). Direct I/O (see chapter 13), character I/O, and block/file I/O eventually travel through the DRD. Even the "client" paths in the diagram are sent through the Internode Communication Subsystem (ICS) to another cluster member's DRD.

The DRD is a client/server implementation per device. And, just to make things interesting, certain devices can be served simultaneously by more than one member. So how does the DRD accomplish this feat? There are actually two approaches that the DRD can take: an indirect approach or a direct approach.

The indirect approach is handled using a client/server (or served) technique in which one cluster member acts as the DRD server for a device, and all other members are DRD clients (accessing the device through the DRD server only). This is similar to how the Distributed Raw Disk (the other DRD) component of the *TruCluster* Production Server product functions[1].

The direct approach is accomplished using devices that are Direct Access I/O (DAIO) capable. The DAIO implementation grew out of the Multi-Node Simultaneous Access (MUNSA)[2] work that was done for *TruCluster* Production Server version 1.5.

15.1.2.1 Direct Access I/O (DAIO) Device

A device can be served by more than one DRD if the device is Direct Access I/O capable. What determines whether or not a device is DAIO capable?

- The device must have hardware bad block replacement enabled.
- The device must support tagged queuing to allow command ordering from a host.
- The device must support simultaneous access from multiple initiators.

All disk devices supported by *TruCluster* Server versions 5.0A, 5.1, and 5.1A are DAIO capable.

Figure 15-3 illustrates how a DAIO device is accessed in a four-member cluster. In the figure you can see that every member in the cluster can directly access the disk. The captions for each member show a slightly modified view that you would get if you ran the `drdmgr(8)` command on each member. Since every member in the cluster has a physical connection to the bus where the disk is located, the "`number of servers`" attribute has a value of four. The servers are listed in the "`server name`" fields. The fact that all four members' "`server state`" is "`Server`" indicates that all four members can actively access this disk. Valid server states are: "`Server`" and "`Not Server`".

Although there are four active servers for this device, each member will access the disk via one server at a time. The server that the member is currently using to access the device is indicated by the "`access member name`". By default, if the member is also a server, its "`access member name`" will always be itself.

In Figure 15-3, every member has direct access because they are physically connected to the bus where the device is attached and the device supports DAIO (as indicated by the "`device type`" field). As of this writing, there are four valid device types that you will see in the output of the `drdmgr` command: "`Direct Access IO Disk`" (indicated as `DAIO` in the figure), "`Served Disk`", "`Served Tape`", and "`Served Changer`".

A device can be DAIO and yet have members in the cluster that cannot directly access the device. Although the device is capable of having more than one server, due to physical connectivity the device may have only one server. Figure 15-4 illustrates a DAIO device on a private bus. The DRD

---

[1] See chapter 2 for more information on Distributed Raw Disk and *TruCluster* Production Server.
[2] MUNSA was not part of the shipping product. It was a special patch created for a customer.

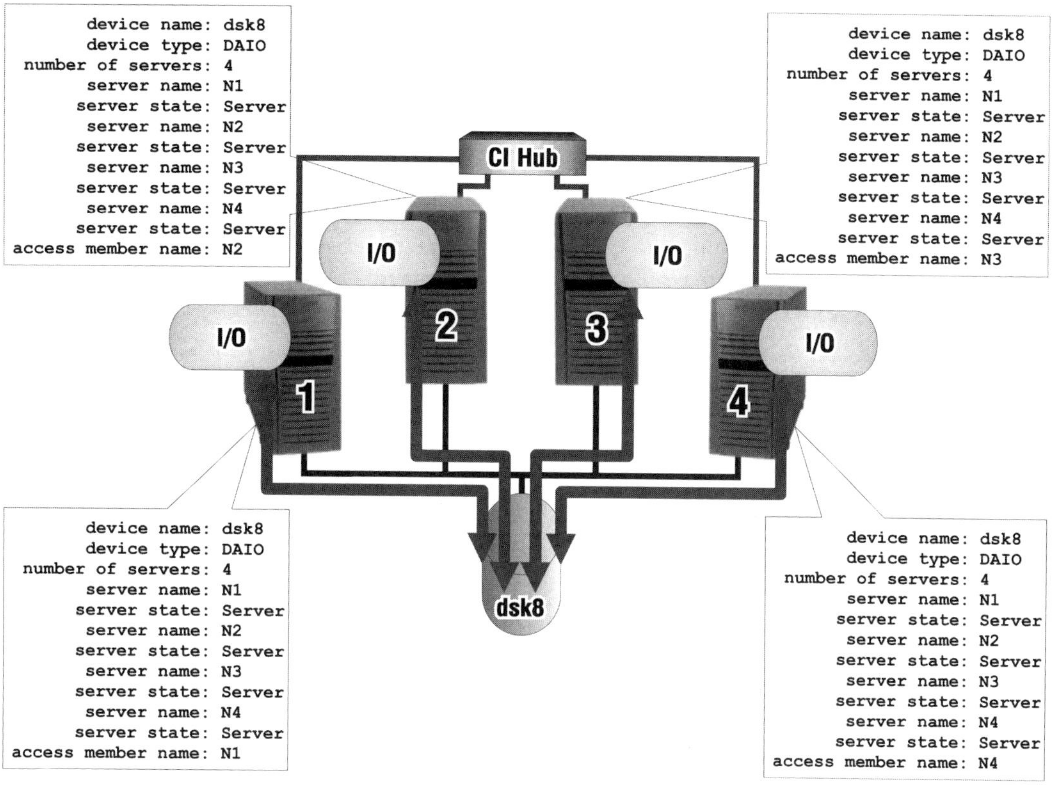

```
      device name: dsk8
      device type: DAIO
number of servers: 4
      server name: N1
     server state: Server
      server name: N2
     server state: Server
      server name: N3
     server state: Server
      server name: N4
     server state: Server
access member name: N2
```

```
      device name: dsk8
      device type: DAIO
number of servers: 4
      server name: N1
     server state: Server
      server name: N2
     server state: Server
      server name: N3
     server state: Server
      server name: N4
     server state: Server
access member name: N3
```

CI Hub

I/O 1 · I/O 2 · I/O 3 · I/O 4

dsk8

```
      device name: dsk8
      device type: DAIO
number of servers: 4
      server name: N1
     server state: Server
      server name: N2
     server state: Server
      server name: N3
     server state: Server
      server name: N4
     server state: Server
access member name: N1
```

```
      device name: dsk8
      device type: DAIO
number of servers: 4
      server name: N1
     server state: Server
      server name: N2
     server state: Server
      server name: N3
     server state: Server
      server name: N4
     server state: Server
access member name: N4
```

Figure 15-3: Direct Access I/O

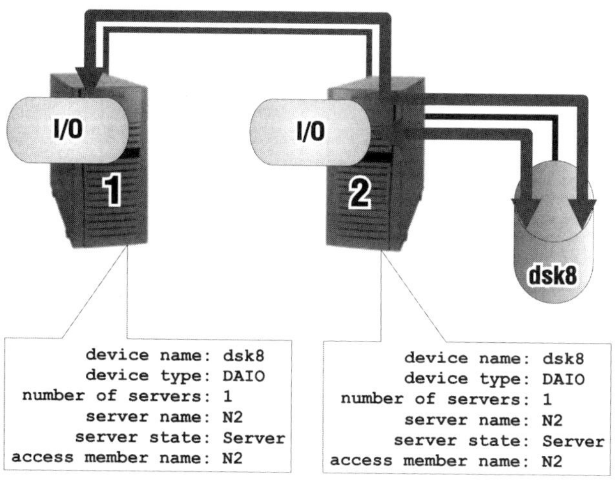

Figure 15-4: DAIO Device, Private Bus

does not really care where the device is located. If a member wants to access a device to which it is not physically connected, it dispatches the request to a DRD on a member that has a direct connection.

NOTE:

Older SCSI devices like the `RZ26`, `RZ28`, `RZ29`, and `RZ1CB-CA` do not have bad block replacement enabled by default, so if you add a device of this type, you can run the `clu_disk_install` script to enable bad block replacement. This script may take awhile to complete if you install several devices at the same time.

15.1.2.2 Served Devices

If a device is a served device, one member in the cluster actively serves the device to the other cluster members regardless of whether or not the device is accessible by more than one member via physical connection (i.e., shared bus).

Tape and changer devices as well as all CD-ROM, DVD-ROM[3], floppy disk devices, and some hard disk devices are served devices. Unlike tape and changer devices, though, CD-ROM, DVD-ROM, and floppy disk devices cannot, as of this writing, be located on a shared bus.

Figure 15-5 shows a two-member cluster with a served tape device on a shared bus. Notice that there are two potential servers, however, `member1`'s server state is "`Not Server`". This is because a tape device is not a DAIO device. In other words, even though both members can serve the device, only one device can serve the device at a time; therefore the device has a device type of "`served`" – in this case "`Served Tape`".

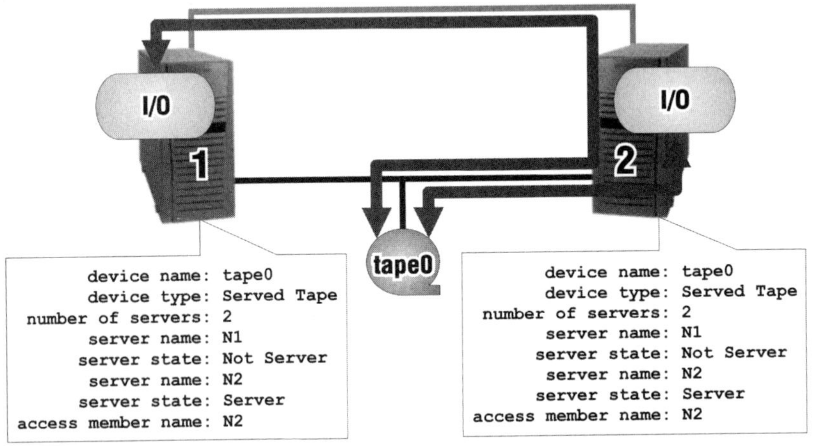

Figure 15-5: Served Device, Shared Bus

---

[3] DVD-ROM devices are supported in V5.1 and later.

15.1.3 I/O Barriers

I/O Barriers are used in a cluster to emulate how a single-system would handle I/O on shutdown or failure. In other words, when a standalone system is shutdown or crashes, any outstanding I/O will not be delivered to the device when the member reboots.

An I/O Barrier is a combination of software and hardware/firmware. On the software end, the DRD creates a barrier by blocking I/O on nodes without quorum, while on the hardware/firmware end I/O Barriers are implemented at the CAM layer using bus resets and persistent reservations.

When a cluster is running normally, all members are allowed to perform I/O to all storage devices in the cluster. Things get interesting when a member is shutdown, crashes, or becomes incommunicative (Note: the DRD also erects I/O Barriers for all devices new to the cluster as the cluster is being formed and when a member joins the cluster).

When the Connection Manager[4] (CNX) senses a member leaving the cluster, either voluntarily or otherwise, it initiates a cluster membership transition to determine which nodes are allowed to continue in the cluster and which nodes are not. When the membership transition begins, the DRD blocks and queues any new I/O while draining any I/O that was previously queued. At least that's what is supposed to happen. However, since a member may be experiencing hardware or software errors which caused the membership transition to occur in the first place, the member may not properly drain but rather continue to deliver I/O to the shared storage.

Once the cluster membership transition is complete, the CNX directs the DRD to erect an I/O Barrier around any node that is no longer a cluster member. The I/O Barrier guarantees that any I/O submitted to the DRD by a node that is no longer a member will not be committed to any cluster-wide shared storage.

For example, using the three-member cluster from Figure 15-1 earlier in the chapter, let's say that `member1` has been writing to `dsk4` when something happens to cause `member1` to shutdown. Table 15-1 shows that at time T1, all three members are able to perform I/O to any storage device in the cluster when `member1` experiences a glitch causing it to shutdown. At time T2, the cluster, as a whole, must go through a cluster membership transition, handled by the CNX on each member, to determine which members can continue to participate in the cluster. At this time, the DRD will block any new I/O and queue it to be submitted after the cluster shakeout is complete. Any I/O queued prior to the transition will be drained. After the CNX determines the new cluster membership (time T3), those members that have been voted out of the "cluster club" are locked out – in other words, I/O Barriers are erected and any Distributed Lock Manager[5] (DLM) locks are reconfigured.

You may wonder what happens when the DRD "drains" previously queued I/O. We put the question to one the *TruCluster* Server engineers who explained that pending I/O requests are processed (read from a shared storage device or written to a shared storage device). If the I/O receives an error and needs to be retried, it is re-queued. I/Os that are returned to the DRD from the shared storage devices are returned to the calling thread. When the drain is completed, no outstanding I/Os need to be processed and any new I/Os will have been queued.

---

[4] See chapter 17 for more information on the Connection Manager.
[5] See chapter 18 for more information on the Distributed Lock Manager.

Cluster Members	T1	T2		T3	T4
member1	I/O proceeds	new I/O is blocked & queued unless prevented by H/W and/or S/W error	previously queued I/O is drained unless prevented by H/W and/or S/W error	I/O Barrier	I/O rejected
member2	I/O proceeds	new I/O is blocked & queued	previously queued I/O is drained	new I/O is blocked & queued	I/O proceeds
member3	I/O proceeds	new I/O is blocked & queued	previously queued I/O is drained	new I/O is blocked & queued	I/O proceeds
	member1, member2, and member3 are cluster members. Can perform I/O to any storage device.	CNX detects a connectivity issue with member1 and starts a cluster membership transition. The DRD will block and queue new I/O until the cluster transition is complete. The DRD will drain I/O that was queued prior to the cluster state transition.		I/O Barrier is erected and any DLM locks will be reconfigured.	member1 is no longer a cluster member. Any I/O submitted from member1 after time=T2 will be rejected. I/O on **member2** and **member3** will continue.

Table 15-1: Cluster Membership Transition and the I/O Barrier

15.2 Configuring the DRD

As the DRD subsystem is designed to auto-configure it generally does not require any setup. There are a couple of things that you can do, however, to modify the configuration, such as changing a device's access member name or server and resetting a device's DRD statistics.

15.2.1 Changing the Access Member Name

Typically, the access member name of a device should not have to be modified; however, since there are a couple of instances where it might be useful, the capability is available via the `drdmgr` command. One instance when you would need to change the access member name is where you want to load balance the I/O across DRD servers in a cluster where members don't all have physical access to a device as indicated in Figure 15-6.

In Figure 15-6, `member2` and `member3` have direct access to `dsk8`, but `member1` and `member4` do not, so they will have to access the `dsk8` via `member2` or `member3`. By default, the first member booted will be the server for the other members. In Figure 15-6, `member2` was likely

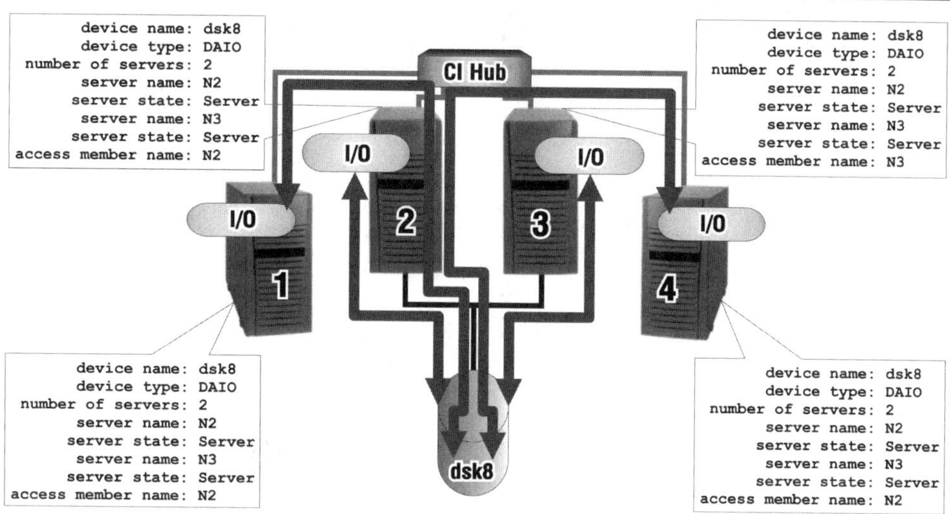

Figure 15-6: DAIO Device on a Semi-Shared Bus in a Four-Member Cluster

booted before `member3` and therefore is the "access member" for `member1`, `member4`, and itself. However, we may want to distribute the load so that `member2` is not handling all of the remote DRD requests. We can do this by modifying the access member for `member1` or `member4` using the `drdmgr` command. For example, we will change the access member on `member4` from `member2` to `member3`.

```
# drdmgr -h n4 -a accessnode=n3 dsk8
```

The result of this command is illustrated in Figure 15-7.

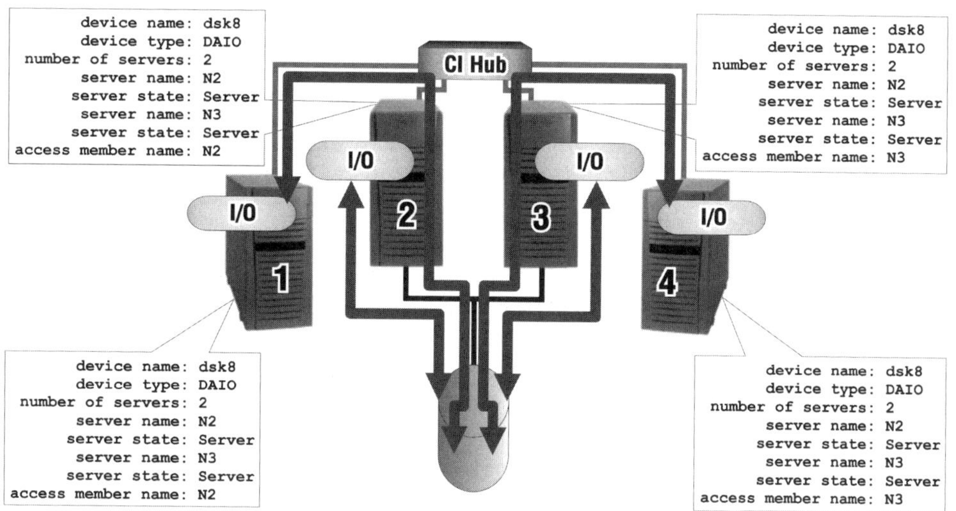

Figure 15-7: DAIO Device on a Semi-Shared Bus – After Access Node Change

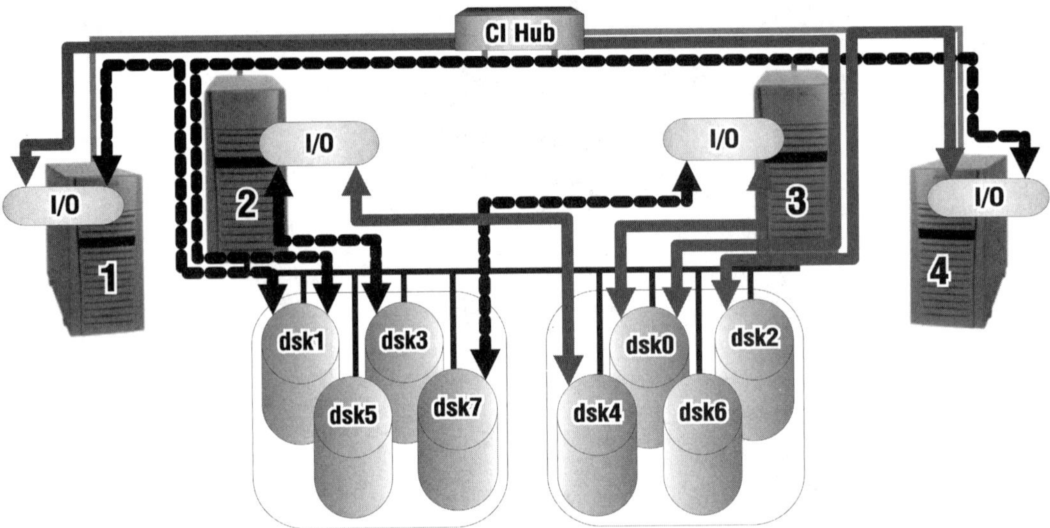

Figure 15-8: Load Balancing Multiple Devices on a Semi-Shared Bus

Notice that the configuration theoretically more balanced, but depending on the workload of `member2` and `member3`, this may not necessarily have been the best move.

Another solution might be to balance the load of several disks on the semi-shared bus between the two members as illustrated in Figure 15-8.

In this figure, `member2` serves odd numbered disks to `member1` and `member4`, while `member3` serves the even numbered disks to `member1` and `member4`. Notice that `member2` and `member3` will directly access all of the disks since they have direct access.

NOTE:

Even though we have illustrated a cluster that contains a semi-shared bus configuration, we still recommend having all buses shared by all members, if possible, as it is the highest availability solution and easiest to manage. The only situation where we are not opposed to a private bus solution is for swap, `/tmp`, and/or non-critical data where high-availability is not a priority.

15.2.2 Changing the Server

Changing the server for a device is something that you may want to do for a served device on a shared bus. If you'll recall from section 15.1.2.2, a served device cannot have more than one active server at a time, so if you want a particular member to have direct access to a served device and it is being served by another member, you'll need to change the server.

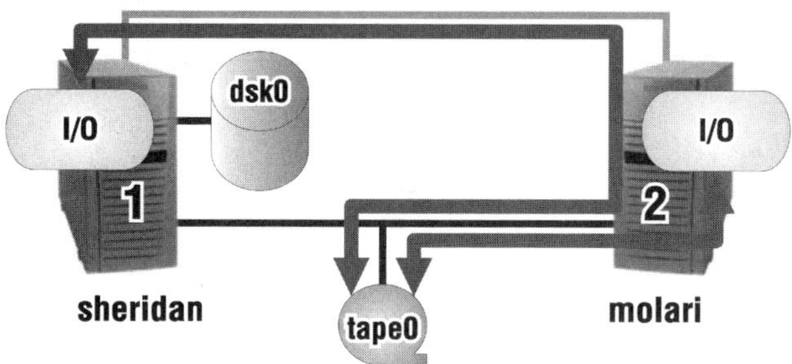

Figure 15-9: Served Device on a Shared bus in a Two-Member Cluster

Say you want to use the tape drive to backup `dsk0` (a disk that is on `member1`'s private bus) as shown in Figure 15-9. The tape drive is a "`Served Tape`" device and is currently served by `member2`. You will want to run the backup routine on `member1` (`sheridan`) since it is the only member that can directly access the disk.

The first thing you need to do is check to see who is currently serving the tape device using the `drdmgr` command.

```
# drdmgr -a server -a accessnode tape1

   View of Data from member sheridan as of 2001-05-19:23:41:54

                Device Name: tape1
                Device Type: Served Tape
              Device Status: OK
          Number of Servers: 2
                Server Name: sheridan
               Server State: Not Server
                Server Name: molari
               Server State: Server
         Access Member Name: molari
```

As you can see by the output of the `drdmgr` command, `sheridan` is not currently serving `tape1`.

It would be more efficient if `sheridan` had direct access to the tape device so that the I/O to the tape does not have to go across the cluster communications interconnect. To change the server you can use the `drdmgr` command as follows:

```
# drdmgr -a server=sheridan tape1
```

The results are shown in Figure 15-10 and verified in the following output from the `drdmgr` command.

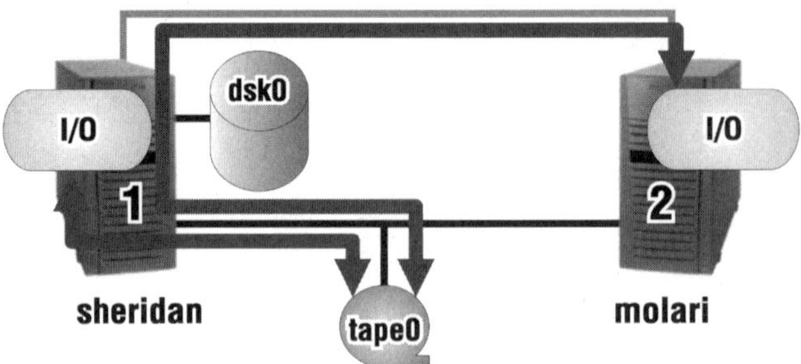

Figure 15-10: Served Device on a Shared Bus in a Two-Member Cluster after Server Relocation

```
# drdmgr -a server -a accessnode tape1
  View of Data from member sheridan as of 2001-05-19:23:49:25

                  Device Name: tape1
                  Device Type: Served Tape
                Device Status: OK
            Number of Servers: 2
                  Server Name: sheridan
                 Server State: Server
                  Server Name: molari
                 Server State: Not Server
           Access Member Name: sheridan
```

Note that you can change the server for more than one device at a time. For example, if `tape1` is one of two tape devices in a tape jukebox, you can move `tape1` as well as the changer (`mc0`) and the other tape drive (`tape2`) as follows:

```
# drdmgr -a server=sheridan tape1 tape2 mc0
```

You can then verify your results with the following `drdmgr` command (output not shown):

```
# drdmgr -a server -a accessnode tape1 tape2 mc0
```

15.2.3 Resetting the Statistics

On occasion it may be useful to reset the statistics on a device for a member to test its connectivity – in fact we'll do this in the following section. To reset the statistics for a device on the member that you are logged in to, issue the following command:

```
[sheridan]
# drdmgr -a statistics=0 dsk5
```

To reset the statistics for the same device on another member, you do not have to login to that member. Simply use the "-h" switch. Device statistics are tallied on a per-member basis.

```
[sheridan]
# drdmgr -h molari -a statistics=0 dsk5
```

15.3 DRD by Example

In this section we explore the drdmgr command in more detail and show some examples of the DAIO and served device I/O. We've discussed how I/O is supposed to work in a cluster for a DAIO device versus a served device, so let's prove it with a few examples. Another interesting thing to do here is demonstrate what happens if we create a path failure within the cluster. Sound like fun? A little bit scary? Okay, a lot scary? Well, at least our cluster is not in a production environment, so we can play around without the risk of getting fired – or so we hope.

15.3.1 DAIO Disk on a Shared Bus Examples

Let's look at how the DRD responds to I/O requests to character (/devices/rdisk/*) and block (/devices/disk/*) device special files. We discussed direct I/O and file I/O in chapter 13 so we will not show any examples here. In the following examples, we will use a two-member cluster although these examples could be done on a larger cluster.

15.3.1.1 Character I/O

We will use the dd(1) command to read and write to a spare device on the shared bus. We are not currently using dsk5, and there is no data on the disk that we cannot afford to lose. If you choose to try this exercise, we recommend that you make very, very sure that the device or partition is not in use. If you do not have a disk or partition available to write to, just read from it instead.

We have created two files, MyFile.molari and MyFile.sheridan, which contain the member's host name printed repeatedly within. Each file is between 5 and 8 MB.

Let's verify that the disk has not been recently accessed. We will get the statistics for the device using the drdmgr command.

```
[molari]
# drdmgr dsk5
   View of Data from member molari as of 2001-07-19:16:39:53

                    Device Name: dsk5
                    Device Type: Direct Access IO Disk
                  Device Status: OK
              Number of Servers: 2
                    Server Name: molari
                   Server State: Server
                    Server Name: sheridan
                   Server State: Server
             Access Member Name: molari
            Open Partition Mask: 0
   Statistics for Client Member: molari
      Number of Read Operations: 0
     Number of Write Operations: 0
           Number of Bytes Read: 0
        Number of Bytes Written: 0
```

```
[molari]
# drdmgr -h sheridan dsk5
   View of Data from member sheridan as of 2001-07-19:16:39:47


                    Device Name: dsk5
                    Device Type: Direct Access IO Disk
                  Device Status: OK
              Number of Servers: 2
                    Server Name: molari
                   Server State: Server
                    Server Name: sheridan
                   Server State: Server
             Access Member Name: sheridan
            Open Partition Mask: 0
   Statistics for Client Member: sheridan
      Number of Read Operations: 0
     Number of Write Operations: 15822
           Number of Bytes Read: 0
        Number of Bytes Written: 8912310
```

Notice that the second drdmgr command uses the "-h" switch to get the statistics for member sheridan from member molari. The device is a DAIO device and each member is a server. Also note that each member's access member name is itself.

Since the statistics for sheridan are not zero, we will set them to zero before we begin.

```
[molari]
# drdmgr -a statistics=0 -h sheridan dsk5
```

```
[molari]
# drdmgr -a statistics -h sheridan dsk5

   View of Data from member sheridan as of 2001-07-19:16:46:55

                    Device Name: dsk5
  Statistics for Client Member: sheridan
     Number of Read Operations: 0
    Number of Write Operations: 0
          Number of Bytes Read: 0
       Number of Bytes Written: 0
```

Let's write each member's "MyFile" to the "h" partition of dsk5 using the character device special file. We will write from molari and wait until the write is complete before starting to write from sheridan.

```
[molari]
# dd if=MyFile.molari of=/dev/rdisk/dsk5h
11718+1 records in
11718+1 records out
```

```
[molari]
# drdmgr -a statistics dsk5

   View of Data from member molari as of 2001-07-19:16:55:19

                    Device Name: dsk5
  Statistics for Client Member: molari
     Number of Read Operations: 0
    Number of Write Operations: 11719
          Number of Bytes Read: 0
       Number of Bytes Written: 6000000
```

```
[molari]
# drdmgr -a statistics -h sheridan dsk5

   View of Data from member sheridan as of 2001-07-19:16:55:25

                    Device Name: dsk5
  Statistics for Client Member: sheridan
     Number of Read Operations: 0
    Number of Write Operations: 0
          Number of Bytes Read: 0
       Number of Bytes Written: 0
```

Notice that the statistics on sheridan are still zero.

```
[sheridan]
# dd if=MyFile.sheridan of=/dev/rdisk/dsk5h
15625+0 records in
15625+0 records out
```

```
[sheridan]
# drdmgr -a statistics dsk5
   View of Data from member sheridan as of 2001-07-19:17:00:01

                    Device Name: dsk5
  Statistics for Client Member: sheridan
     Number of Read Operations: 0
    Number of Write Operations: 15625
          Number of Bytes Read: 0
       Number of Bytes Written: 8000000
```

```
[sheridan]
# drdmgr -a statistics -h molari dsk5
   View of Data from member molari as of 2001-07-19:17:00:09

                    Device Name: dsk5
  Statistics for Client Member: molari
     Number of Read Operations: 0
    Number of Write Operations: 11719
          Number of Bytes Read: 0
       Number of Bytes Written: 6000000
```

Since the device supports DAIO and each member has physical access to the device, each member is able to write to the device independently without passing the data across the cluster interconnect.

15.3.1.2 Block I/O

Performing block I/O (i.e., reading from and writing to the block device special file) is handled at the Cluster File System (CFS) layer prior to being sent to the DRD. Since the CFS is implemented in a client/server fashion, even though the device may support DAIO and be on a shared bus directly accessible by the members performing the I/O, the DRD will not get involved on those members that are CFS clients (unless the Direct I/O or Direct Access Cached Reads are invoked [see chapter 13]). The block device special files are located in the `/devices` directory hierarchy and are therefore served by the CFS server for the `cluster_root` domain.

So, let's demonstrate how block I/O is performed in a cluster. We will once again use the `dd` command, but this time we will use the block device special file for `dsk5`.

The first thing that we need to do is find out which member is the CFS server for the `cluster_root` domain. For this we will use the `cfsmgr(8)` command.

```
# cfsmgr -d cluster_root

 Domain or filesystem name = cluster_root
 Server Name = sheridan
 Server Status : OK
```

The node sheridan is the CFS server.

Let's reset the statistics on both members before we do any I/O.

```
[molari]

# drdmgr -a statistics=0 dsk5
```

```
[molari]

# drdmgr -a statistics=0 -h sheridan dsk5
```

We will issue the dd command on molari to illustrate that the DRD on sheridan will do the actual work. The request for I/O will go to the CFS server for the root (/) file system. The CFS server will dispatch the I/O request to the physical file system layer. The I/O will then be dispatched to the I/O mapper subsystem and then down to the DRD on the same member. The I/O architecture was illustrated in Figure 15-2.

```
[molari]
# dd if=MyFile.molari of=/dev/disk/dsk5h

11718+1 records in
11718+1 records out
```

Notice that we are using the block device special file (/dev/disk/dsk5h) and not the character device special file (/dev/rdisk/dsk5h). Let's see what the DRD statistics for dsk5 tell us from molari.

```
[molari]
# drdmgr -a statistics dsk5

   View of Data from member molari as of 2001-07-19:22:30:12

                    Device Name: dsk5
  Statistics for Client Member: molari
     Number of Read Operations: 0
    Number of Write Operations: 0
          Number of Bytes Read: 0
       Number of Bytes Written: 0
```

As you can see, the DRD on molari never saw any I/O. The DRD on sheridan, however, was rather busy.

```
[molari]
# drdmgr -a statistics -h sheridan dsk5

   View of Data from member sheridan as of 2001-07-19:22:34:01

                    Device Name: dsk5
  Statistics for Client Member: sheridan
     Number of Read Operations: 2930
    Number of Write Operations: 11719
          Number of Bytes Read: 6000640
       Number of Bytes Written: 24000512
```

15.3.2 DAIO Disk on a Private Bus Examples

When any disk is on a private bus, all I/O requests will be funneled to the member with direct physical access to the disk. This also means that if the only member with access to a device is down, then the device will not be accessible.

For example, dsk8 is on a bus that is local only to sheridan. How do we know? The most straightforward way to determine this is to use the hwmgr(8) command as follows:

```
[molari]
# hwmgr -view devices -dsf dsk8

hwmgr: No such hardware ID or category.
```

```
[molari]
# hwmgr -view devices -dsf dsk8 -m sheridan

 HWID: Device Name          Mfg      Model             Hostname   Location
---------------------------------------------------------------------------------
  103: /dev/disk/dsk8c      COMPAQ   BB009235B6        sheridan   bus-2-targ-1-lun-0
```

The device does not exist on molari, but it does exist on sheridan. To take this one step further, we can check the bus.

```
[molari]
# hwmgr -show scsi -bus 2

       SCSI                 DEVICE    DEVICE  DRIVER NUM  DEVICE FIRST
 HWID: DEVICEID HOSTNAME    TYPE      SUBTYPE OWNER  PATH FILE   VALID PATH
-------------------------------------------------------------------------
   47: 1        molari      disk      none    0      1    dsk0   [2/0/0]
```

```
[molari]
# hwmgr -show scsi -bus 2 -m sheridan

       SCSI                 DEVICE    DEVICE  DRIVER NUM  DEVICE FIRST
 HWID: DEVICEID HOSTNAME    TYPE      SUBTYPE OWNER  PATH FILE   VALID PATH
-------------------------------------------------------------------------
  102: 1        sheridan    disk      none    2      1    dsk7   [2/0/0]
  103: 2        sheridan    disk      none    2      1    dsk8   [2/1/0]
```

The fact that each member has a bus-2 is not as interesting as the fact that each member has devices on bus-2 that are different. That storage devices are unique in a cluster proves that this is a private bus. For more information on the hwmgr command, see chapter 7 as well as the hwmgr(8) reference page.

You can use the drdmgr command to check the path to a device, but this will only tell you if there is an active path to a device and not if the device is on a private bus.

Looking at the output from the drdmgr command from molari, you will see that it does not even include statistics, because the DRD on molari for dsk8 is a client only. Notice that the output, as seen from sheridan, includes statistics for both members, but molari's statistics are zero.

```
[molari]
# drdmgr dsk8

  View of Data from member molari as of 2001-07-19:23:00:56

                Device Name: dsk8
                Device Type: Direct Access IO Disk
              Device Status: OK
          Number of Servers: 1
                Server Name: sheridan
               Server State: Server
         Access Member Name: sheridan
        Open Partition Mask: 0x80 < h >
```

```
[molari]
# drdmgr -h sheridan dsk8

  View of Data from member sheridan as of 2001-07-19:23:33:52

                Device Name: dsk8
                Device Type: Direct Access IO Disk
              Device Status: OK
          Number of Servers: 1
                Server Name: sheridan
               Server State: Server
         Access Member Name: sheridan
        Open Partition Mask: 0x80 < h >
 Statistics for Client Member: molari
    Number of Read Operations: 0
   Number of Write Operations: 0
         Number of Bytes Read: 0
      Number of Bytes Written: 0
 Statistics for Client Member: sheridan
    Number of Read Operations: 20319
   Number of Write Operations: 12819
         Number of Bytes Read: 153012224
      Number of Bytes Written: 56055808
```

You can see that there has already been quite a bit of I/O on dsk8. This is primarily because of the "h" partition (as indicated in the "Open Partition Mask"). This partition contains the /kits file system (extra#kits).

```
# cfsmgr -a devices -d extra
*************************************************************
          List of Devices Used for extra

  Number of Devices = 1

      1   -    dsk8h
*************************************************************
```

All I/O to `dsk8` goes through the DRD on `sheridan`.

If we write to the "a" partition on `dsk8` (which we know is unused) from `molari` and then query the DRD statistics, you will see that the statistics on `molari` will remain zero, yet the statistics for `sheridan` will increase.

```
[molari]
# drdmgr -a statistics=0 -h sheridan dsk8
```

```
[molari]
# dd if=MyFile.molari of=/dev/disk/dsk8a
11718+1 records in
11718+1 records out
```

```
[molari]
# drdmgr -a statistics -h sheridan dsk8
   View of Data from member sheridan as of 2001-07-19:23:50:25

                   Device Name: dsk8
  Statistics for Client Member: molari
     Number of Read Operations: 0
    Number of Write Operations: 0
          Number of Bytes Read: 0
       Number of Bytes Written: 0
  Statistics for Client Member: sheridan
     Number of Read Operations: 2933
    Number of Write Operations: 11719
          Number of Bytes Read: 6006784
       Number of Bytes Written: 24000512
```

15.3.3 Served Device Examples

When a device is a served device, only one server can access it. If the served device is on a shared bus, any member connected to the bus can be the server for the device, but only one member will be the server at any point in time. We illustrated this back in Figure 15-9. In this section, we'll show how the I/O flows when accessing a served tape device.

On our two-member cluster, we have a tape device on a shared bus. As we stated in section 15.1.2.2, a tape device is not a DAIO device. Before showing how the I/O flows through the DRD for our served tape device, let's see which member is currently serving it.

```
[sheridan]
# drdmgr tape0

  View of Data from member sheridan as of 2001-07-24:14:34:56
                    Device Name: tape0
                    Device Type: Served Tape
                  Device Status: OK
              Number of Servers: 2
                    Server Name: sheridan
                   Server State: Not Server
                    Server Name: molari
                   Server State: Server
             Access Member Name: molari
            Open Partition Mask: 0
  Statistics for Client Member: sheridan
     Number of Read Operations: 0
    Number of Write Operations: 0
          Number of Bytes Read: 0
       Number of Bytes Written: 0
  Statistics for Client Member: molari
     Number of Read Operations: 0
    Number of Write Operations: 0
          Number of Bytes Read: 0
       Number of Bytes Written: 0
```

```
[sheridan]
# drdmgr -h molari tape0

  View of Data from member molari as of 2001-07-24:14:35:24
                    Device Name: tape0
                    Device Type: Served Tape
                  Device Status: OK
              Number of Servers: 2
                    Server Name: sheridan
                   Server State: Not Server
                    Server Name: molari
                   Server State: Server
             Access Member Name: molari
            Open Partition Mask: 0
  Statistics for Client Member: sheridan
     Number of Read Operations: 0
    Number of Write Operations: 0
          Number of Bytes Read: 0
       Number of Bytes Written: 0
```

As we can see from the output above, `molari` is the server. Since the statistics on the device are currently zero for both members, we will not need to reset the statistics before starting our example. If you're playing along with the home version (i.e., you are doing these examples on your cluster), however, your device might have counters greater than zero, so you may want to reset them before continuing. Okay, let's do some I/O.

```
[sheridan]
# tar -cvf /dev/tape/tape0 ./someCool.txtFile
a ./someCool.txtFile 50 Blocks
```

```
[sheridan]
# tar -tvf /dev/tape/tape0
blocksize = 20
-rw-------     0/0    25157 Jul 24 14:13:41 2001 ./someCool.txtFile
```

Since molari is the server and sheridan is where we ran the tar(1) command, if everything works the way we would expect, then the I/O counters should increase on molari, but not on sheridan.

```
[sheridan]
# drdmgr -a statistics tape0
   View of Data from member sheridan as of 2001-07-24:14:38:20
                    Device Name: tape0
  Statistics for Client Member: sheridan
     Number of Read Operations: 0
    Number of Write Operations: 0
          Number of Bytes Read: 0
       Number of Bytes Written: 0
  Statistics for Client Member: molari
     Number of Read Operations: 0
    Number of Write Operations: 0
          Number of Bytes Read: 0
       Number of Bytes Written: 0
```

```
[sheridan]
# drdmgr -h molari -a statistics tape0
   View of Data from member molari as of 2001-07-24:14:38:50
                    Device Name: tape0
  Statistics for Client Member: sheridan
     Number of Read Operations: 3
    Number of Write Operations: 3
          Number of Bytes Read: 151552
       Number of Bytes Written: 30720
```

Let's change servers and verify that the change succeeded.

```
[sheridan]
# drdmgr -a server=sheridan tape0
```

```
[sheridan]
# drdmgr -a server tape0

   View of Data from member sheridan as of 2001-07-24:14:39:48
                   Device Name: tape0
                   Device Type: Served Tape
                 Device Status: OK
             Number of Servers: 2
                   Server Name: sheridan
                  Server State: Server
                   Server Name: molari
                  Server State: Not Server
```

Now that sheridan is acting as the server, let's reset the statistics and do some I/O from molari and sheridan this time.

```
[molari]
# drdmgr -a statistics=0 tape4
```

```
[molari]
# drdmgr -h sheridan -a statistics=0 tape4
```

```
[molari]
# tar -cvf /dev/tape/tape0 ./someCool.txtFile

a ./someCool.txtFile 50 Blocks
```

```
[molari]
# tar -tvf /dev/tape/tape0

blocksize = 20
-rw-------     0/0    25157 Jul 24 14:13:41 2001 ./someCool.txtFile
```

```
[sheridan]
# tar -cvf /dev/tape/tape0 ./someCool.txtFile

a ./someCool.txtFile 50 Blocks
```

```
[sheridan]
# tar -tvf /dev/tape/tape0

blocksize = 20
-rw-------     0/0    25157 Jul 24 14:13:41 2001 ./someCool.txtFile
```

The I/O should now be tallied on sheridan this time.

```
[sheridan]
# drdmgr -a statistics tape0

   View of Data from member sheridan as of 2001-07-24:14:44:23
                   Device Name: tape0
  Statistics for Client Member: sheridan
     Number of Read Operations: 3
    Number of Write Operations: 3
          Number of Bytes Read: 151552
       Number of Bytes Written: 30720
  Statistics for Client Member: molari
     Number of Read Operations: 3
    Number of Write Operations: 3
          Number of Bytes Read: 151552
       Number of Bytes Written: 30720
```

```
[sheridan]
# drdmgr -h molari -a statistics tape0

   View of Data from member molari as of 2001-07-24:14:44:47
                   Device Name: tape0
  Statistics for Client Member: sheridan
     Number of Read Operations: 0
    Number of Write Operations: 0
          Number of Bytes Read: 0
       Number of Bytes Written: 0
```

15.3.4 DRD Path Failure Response

What happens if sheridan loses its direct physical access to a device? Let's find out.

In this example, we are going to simulate a path failure by pulling the SCSI cable out from one of sheridan's SCSI adapters. Specifically, we will pull the cable connected to the shared bus. "The shared bus? No, not the shared bus! You can't pull the cable on the shared bus because sheridan's boot_partition is on the shared bus! The cluster-common partitions are on the shared bus!" you exclaim. As we stated earlier in the chapter, our cluster is a test cluster, so we have nothing to lose. Will sheridan crash? Will sheridan hang? Let's find out but first let's see which disks are on the shared bus.

```
[sheridan]
# hwmgr -show scsi -bus 3

        SCSI                DEVICE    DEVICE  DRIVER NUM  DEVICE FIRST
 HWID:  DEVICEID HOSTNAME   TYPE      SUBTYPE OWNER  PATH FILE   VALID PATH
-------------------------------------------------------------------------
   50:  3        sheridan   disk      none    2      1    dsk1   [3/0/0]
   51:  4        sheridan   disk      none    2      1    dsk2   [3/1/0]
   52:  5        sheridan   disk      none    2      1    dsk3   [3/2/0]
   53:  6        sheridan   disk      none    2      1    dsk4   [3/3/0]
   54:  7        sheridan   disk      none    2      1    dsk5   [3/4/0]
   55:  8        sheridan   disk      none    2      1    dsk6   [3/5/0]
```

The shared bus for both sheridan and molari is bus 3, and there are six disks (dsk1-dsk6) on the bus. Using the cfs script that we introduced in chapter 13, we'll see which file systems are using which disks so that we can watch what happens when we pull the cable. You can also obtain this information by using the "cfsmgr -a devices" command, which we previously demonstrated in section 15.3.2.

```
[sheridan]
# cfs -s | grep dsk

/ [cluster_root#root] (dsk1a):
/usr [cluster_usr#usr] (dsk1g):
/var [cluster_var#var] (dsk1h):
/kits [extra#kits] (dsk8h):
/u1 [home#u1] (dsk7h):
/cluster/members/member1/boot_partition [root1_domain#root] (dsk2a):
/cluster/members/member2/boot_partition [root2_domain#root] (dsk3a):
/fafrak [tcrhb#fafrak] (dsk6c):
```

Next, let's see which file systems sheridan is serving:

```
[sheridan]
# cfs -h sheridan

CFS Server       Mount Point                 File System               FS Type
---------------- -------------------------   ------------------------  -------
sheridan         /                           cluster_root#root          AdvFS
sheridan         /usr                        cluster_usr#usr            AdvFS
sheridan         /var                        cluster_var#var            AdvFS
sheridan         /kits                       extra#kits                 AdvFS
sheridan         /u1                         home#u1                    AdvFS
sheridan         /cluster/members/member2/   root2_domain#root          AdvFS
                    boot_partition
```

From the output of the cfs script, it appears that sheridan is the CFS server for the cluster-common file systems and its own boot_partition.

In our cluster configuration, dsk1 is the disk that holds cluster_root, cluster_usr, and cluster_var while dsk3 holds sheridan's boot_partition. So, let's see what information the DRD has for dsk1 and dsk3.

```
[sheridan]
# drdmgr -a server -a accessnode dsk1 dsk3

   View of Data from member sheridan as of 2001-07-23:23:53:46

                  Device Name: dsk1
                  Device Type: Direct Access IO Disk
                Device Status: OK
            Number of Servers: 2
                  Server Name: molari
                 Server State: Server
                  Server Name: sheridan
                 Server State: Server
           Access Member Name: sheridan

                  Device Name: dsk3
                  Device Type: Direct Access IO Disk
                Device Status: OK
            Number of Servers: 2
                  Server Name: molari
                 Server State: Server
                  Server Name: sheridan
                 Server State: Server
           Access Member Name: sheridan
```

Now that we know which disks are on the shared bus, which file systems are using those disks, which file systems `sheridan` is acting as CFS server for, and how the DRD is configured on `sheridan`, let's get ready to pull the plug (or cable in this case).

On `molari` and `sheridan`, let's monitor EVM for events so that we can see what the cluster sees when the cable is disconnected. We'll use the following commands:

```
# export EVM_SHOW_TEMPLATE="@member_id [@priority] @name"

# evmwatch -A -f "[name *.scsi]|[name *.drd]|[name *.cfs]"
```

We pulled the plug; let's see what happened. We will look at the output from `molari`:

```
[molari]
# export EVM_SHOW_TEMPLATE="@member_id [@priority] @name"

[molari]
# evmwatch -A -f "[name *.scsi]|[name *.drd]|[name *.cfs]"

2 [200] sys.unix.clu.drd.server_leave._hwid.50
2 [200] sys.unix.clu.drd.server_leave._hwid.53
2 [200] sys.unix.clu.drd.server_add._hwid.50
2 [200] sys.unix.clu.drd.new_accessnode._hwid.50
2 [200] sys.unix.clu.drd.new_accessnode._hwid.50
2 [200] sys.unix.clu.drd.server_leave._hwid.52
2 [200] sys.unix.clu.drd.server_add._hwid.53
2 [200] sys.unix.clu.drd.new_accessnode._hwid.53
2 [200] sys.unix.clu.drd.new_accessnode._hwid.53
2 [200] sys.unix.clu.drd.server_add._hwid.52
2 [200] sys.unix.clu.drd.new_accessnode._hwid.52
2 [200] sys.unix.clu.drd.new_accessnode._hwid.52
```

It looks like the DRD on sheridan (member2) detected a problem. We only see a small number of events on molari as compared to what was seen from sheridan. "Do you mean that sheridan did not hang or crash?" you ask. That's correct, sheridan is still running. In fact, here is what sheridan saw when we pulled the cable:

```
[sheridan]
# export EVM_SHOW_TEMPLATE="@member_id [@priority] @name"

[sheridan]
# evmwatch -A -f "[name *.scsi]|[name *.drd]|[name *.cfs]"
2 [200] sys.unix.clu.drd.server_leave._hwid.50
2 [200] sys.unix.clu.drd.server_leave._hwid.53
2 [200] sys.unix.clu.drd.server_add._hwid.50
2 [200] sys.unix.clu.drd.new_accessnode._hwid.50
2 [200] sys.unix.clu.drd.new_accessnode._hwid.50
2 [200] sys.unix.clu.drd.server_leave._hwid.52
2 [200] sys.unix.binlog.hw.scsi._hwid.50
…
2 [700] sys.unix.binlog.hw.scsi
2 [400] sys.unix.binlog.hw.scsi
…
2 [400] sys.unix.binlog.hw.scsi._hwid.51
2 [200] sys.unix.binlog.hw.scsi._hwid.51
2 [400] sys.unix.binlog.hw.scsi._hwid.52
2 [200] sys.unix.binlog.hw.scsi._hwid.52
2 [200] sys.unix.binlog.hw.scsi._hwid.53
2 [400] sys.unix.binlog.hw.scsi._hwid.54
2 [200] sys.unix.binlog.hw.scsi._hwid.54
2 [400] sys.unix.binlog.hw.scsi._hwid.55
2 [200] sys.unix.binlog.hw.scsi._hwid.55
…
2 [200] sys.unix.clu.drd.server_add._hwid.53
2 [200] sys.unix.clu.drd.new_accessnode._hwid.53
2 [200] sys.unix.clu.drd.new_accessnode._hwid.53
2 [200] sys.unix.binlog.hw.scsi._hwid.50
2 [200] sys.unix.clu.drd.server_add._hwid.52
2 [200] sys.unix.clu.drd.new_accessnode._hwid.52
2 [200] sys.unix.clu.drd.new_accessnode._hwid.52
2 [200] sys.unix.binlog.hw.scsi._hwid.51
…
```

We truncated the output to save a page or two, but as you can see, in addition to DRD events, sheridan also saw SCSI Hardware events. This is not a big surprise considering it can no longer see several disks.

How is it that sheridan is still running? Let's find out. Using the hwmgr command, let's see which devices we can still see:

```
[sheridan]
# hwmgr -show scsi -bus 3

        SCSI                  DEVICE     DEVICE  DRIVER NUM  DEVICE FIRST
 HWID:  DEVICEID HOSTNAME     TYPE       SUBTYPE OWNER  PATH FILE   VALID PATH
---------------------------------------------------------------------------
   50:  3        sheridan     disk       none    0      1    dsk1
   51:  4        sheridan     disk       none    2      1    dsk2
   52:  5        sheridan     disk       none    0      1    dsk3
   53:  6        sheridan     disk       none    0      1    dsk4
   54:  7        sheridan     disk       none    2      1    dsk5
   55:  8        sheridan     disk       none    2      1    dsk6
```

If you compare this output to the output from the hwmgr command we received before disconnecting the cable, you can see that we no longer have any valid paths to the devices.

What does the DRD on sheridan see? We can use the same drdmgr command we used before to find out:

```
[sheridan]
# drdmgr -a server -a accessnode dsk1 dsk3

   View of Data from member sheridan as of 2001-07-24:00:27:02

                Device Name: dsk1
                Device Type: Direct Access IO Disk
              Device Status: OK
          Number of Servers: 1
                Server Name: molari
               Server State: Server
         Access Member Name: molari

                Device Name: dsk3
                Device Type: Direct Access IO Disk
              Device Status: OK
          Number of Servers: 1
                Server Name: molari
               Server State: Server
         Access Member Name: molari
```

You can see by the output above that molari is now serving the data to sheridan.

Okay, now for the real tough question, "Which member is the CFS server for cluster_root, cluster_usr, cluster_var, and sheridan's boot_partition?" Well, we did not see any CFS events. Can sheridan still serve the file systems despite no longer having direct access to the devices? You bet.

```
[sheridan]
# cfs

CFS Server        Mount Point                  File System               FS Type
----------------  -------------------------    ------------------------  -------
molari            /cluster/members/member1/    root1_domain#root          AdvFS
                     boot_partition
molari            /fafrak                      tcrhb#fafrak               AdvFS

sheridan          /                            cluster_root#root          AdvFS
sheridan          /usr                         cluster_usr#usr            AdvFS
sheridan          /var                         cluster_var#var            AdvFS
sheridan          /kits                        extra#kits                 AdvFS
sheridan          /u1                          home#u1                    AdvFS
sheridan          /cluster/members/member2/    root2_domain#root          AdvFS
                     boot_partition
```

How can this be? Well, the CFS server sends I/O requests to the DRD. The CFS never sees an error because the DRD handled the problem by automatically rerouting where it dispatched the request. The DRD sensed that it could no longer use the access member it was using, so it got a new access member from the list of servers for the device.

After we reattached the cable, the DRD almost immediately noticed the devices again. Checking the path to one of the devices, we see:

```
[sheridan]
# drdmgr -a check_path dsk1

   View of Data from member sheridan as of 2001-07-24:00:42:42

                    Device Name: dsk1
              Local Device Path: Exists
```

The path has returned. The DRD on sheridan is also once again serving the disks locally.

```
[sheridan]
# drdmgr -a server -a accessnode dsk1 dsk3

   View of Data from member sheridan as of 2001-07-24:00:42:53

                    Device Name: dsk1
                    Device Type: Direct Access IO Disk
                  Device Status: OK
              Number of Servers: 2
                    Server Name: molari
                   Server State: Server
                    Server Name: sheridan
                   Server State: Server
             Access Member Name: sheridan
```

```
            Device Name: dsk3
            Device Type: Direct Access IO Disk
          Device Status: OK
      Number of Servers: 2
            Server Name: molari
           Server State: Server
            Server Name: sheridan
           Server State: Server
     Access Member Name: sheridan
```

All we did was reattach the cable – the DRD did the rest, automatically and transparently. This is incredible stuff!

15.4 DRD Events

The DRD events are defined in the `/usr/share/evm/templates/clu/drd.evt` template file. Below are the registered DRD events.

```
# evmwatch -A -i -f "[name *.drd]" -t "[@priority] @name"

[200] sys.unix.clu.drd.server_add
[200] sys.unix.clu.drd.server_leave
[200] sys.unix.clu.drd.new_accessnode
[300] sys.unix.clu.drd.no_accessnode
```

15.5 References

- The *TruCluster* Server Technical Overview Guide.
- The *TruCluster* Server Cluster Administration Guide.
- Reference pages (noted within the text).

16

The Cluster Alias Subsystem (CLUA)

At first glance, the notion of a cluster alias seems straightforward. Simply conjure up a name and address to be used in the network that represents the cluster as a whole. What's the big deal? For starters, let's take a few steps back and remind ourselves why the nodes in a network are given names in the first place.

16.1 Network Node Names

The alternative to having names for network locations is to always use 32 bit (soon to be 128 bit with IPV6) IP addresses to refer to targets. Once you get used to them, IP addresses are not that difficult to remember, right? Which would be easier for you to remember, "`frodo`" or `192.128.168.34`? Except for die-hard propeller heads, we'll assume most people find that names are easier to use and remember than IP addresses. At your site, you are probably using a Domain Name Service (DNS), specifically the Berkeley Internet Name Domain (BIND) service, to help with node name to IP address (and vice versa) translations. BIND supports the frequently used `whatz.ting.ugot.com` style of naming.

16.2 Cluster Alias IP Address

So it sounds like all we have to do is establish a name as an alias for the cluster, associate it with an IP address, and there you have it ladies and gents – the cluster alias. But what IP address do we associate with the cluster alias? All of the cluster members have network interfaces, and all of the interfaces have IP addresses associated with them. Which of those IP addresses do we associate with the cluster alias? If you select one of the existing IP addresses that represents a member's network interface (imagine that each member has a single network interface for now), all of the client traffic (`telnet(1)`, `ftp(1)`, `nfs(4)`, etc.) will be directed to that single cluster member. Doesn't that defeat the purpose of having the cluster (and the cluster alias)?

The cluster alias name will have to be associated with an IP address that is not tied to a single network interface on a single member of the cluster; otherwise, the bulk of the cluster network services will be executing on one (potentially overloaded) cluster member. Sounds like we should associate the cluster alias with an IP address that is not in use by a particular network interface on a cluster member. Okay, let's go with that and see how it might work.

Most folks figure that IP addresses are used to locate a target machine in a network. That is true to a certain degree, but a few points must be brought out now in order to get a grip on the complexities of the Cluster Alias (CLUA) subsystem. An IP address is associated with a network interface, not a machine. So when you present an alleged node name to a utility (like `ping(8)`, `telnet`, `ftp`, etc.), you are actually identifying a network interface, and only indirectly the machine. Since a machine can have multiple network interfaces, it can have multiple IP addresses.

16.2.1 MAC Address

You should also keep in mind that an IP address is usually associated with a 48-bit Media Access Control (MAC) address (looks like `08-00-2b-12-34-56`). The MAC addresses are "burned" onto a PROM chip on the network device (think Ethernet device) in order to uniquely identify each device. When an IP address is assigned to the network device, the MAC address is associated with the IP address.

Somehow, we have to take an IP address that is not associated with any particular interface, nor directly associated with any cluster member, and associate it with a MAC address so that network clients can use the services in the cluster without overburdening a particular cluster member. Sounds like maximum smoke and mirror action will be necessary to make this work.

When a client in a network connects to a server, it does so by running an application (identified by a port number) on the client that needs network access and identifies the server by a "node name". The "node name" is translated into an IP address by the contents of the `/etc/hosts` file, or by BIND, NIS, or some other mechanism. The IP address is translated into a MAC address by finding the IP address in the Address Resolution Protocol (ARP) cache in the client's memory. If the IP address is not found in the ARP cache (the cache information decays after about 20 minutes), the client uses the ARP, which broadcasts a request, to find out who has the IP address that the client is trying to access. A single (hopefully) network node responds with its MAC address (sometimes called an ARP address or a hardware address), which is cached on the client for subsequent use. Finally, the request is put out on the wire using the MAC address as the target for the datagram. When the datagram arrives at the appropriate interface, it is presented to the IP software for processing. (Note that we are only discussing IP here. Other network protocols would follow a similar series of steps.) The IP software checks to see if the destination IP address is indeed an interface on this network node. If so, the packet is presented to either the Transmission Control Protocol (TCP) software or the User Datagram Protocol (UDP) software. If not, IP checks to see if this node has forwarding (routing) responsibilities. If so, it checks its in-memory routing table to see how to route the datagram toward its destination. These transport layer protocols (TCP and UDP) then pass the payload to the target application, which is identified by a 16-bit port number.

We mention all of this to prepare you for the beauty and beast that is CLUA.

16.3 The CLUA Subsystem – Beauty and Beast

We have established that we should create a cluster alias. We will associate it with an IP address that is not in use by any cluster members (nor can it be in use by any other nodes in the network or subnet within which the cluster resides). We now need to associate the newly selected cluster alias IP address with a MAC address. Unfortunately, we cannot just fabricate a MAC address (more on this later), but we can associate multiple IP addresses with an individual network device. This sets up an IP alias for the interface. Sounds like all we have to do is set up an IP alias using the selected IP address through the `ifconfig(8)` command, and we will be ready to have clients use the cluster alias.

Once again, it sounds like we are back to causing the selected cluster member to be potentially overloaded with network services, since all of the requests from clients will be using the cluster alias IP address, which will be translated into the MAC address for an interface on the selected cluster member.

NOTE:

Do not confuse the cluster alias with an IP interface alias. The concepts are similar. See the `ifconfig(8)` reference page for information on the creation of an IP alias for the interface.

16.4 Proxy ARP

In order to avoid the problem of overloading the member on which the device using the MAC address physically resides, we deem the selected cluster member as the "proxy ARP master" for the cluster. The proxy ARP master cluster member will be responsible for handling incoming requests for access to the cluster alias and routing the requests to other cluster members where appropriate (see Figure 16-1). Only one cluster member at a time will function as the proxy ARP master,

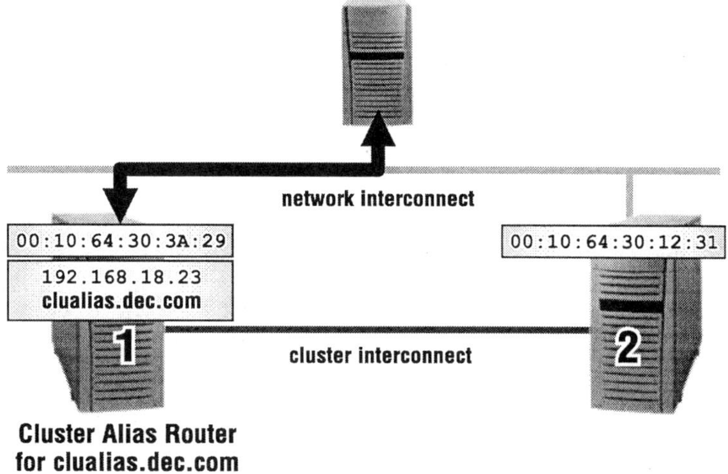

Figure 16-1: Cluster Alias IP to MAC

although any member of the cluster may take over this responsibility if the current master fails or is removed from the cluster.

When a new proxy ARP master is selected, the MAC address that will be sent back in the case of an ARP request from a network client will be different than it was prior to the proxy master change. The clients will not send out an ARP request if the IP address to MAC translation is already present in the client's ARP cache. The ARP cache on a client can potentially be holding the wrong MAC address for the ~20 minutes it takes for the ARP cache to decay. Therefore, a client could be sending datagrams to a non-existent MAC address for a relatively long time before it figures out that the MAC information in its cache is incorrect (see Figure 16-2). Not a good thing.

16.4.1 Gratuitous ARP

The cluster software tries to compensate for this by sending out a gratuitous ARP broadcast to inform all network nodes that they need to replace an entry in their ARP cache. This eliminates the potential havoc caused by the client ARP cache being behind the times.

The following example illustrates gratuitous ARP. All output is generated from a client node. Note how the hardware address associated with `babylon5` changes as the current proxy ARP server in the cluster is shutdown.

Note that cluster member `sheridan`'s `tu0` interface MAC address ends in "`3a:29`", while cluster member `molari`'s `tu0` interface MAC address ends in "`12:31`".

```
# rsh sheridan /usr/sbin/netstat -I tu0

Name  Mtu   Network      Address             Ipkts Ierrs    Opkts Oerrs  Coll
tu0   1500  <Link>       0:10:64:30:3a:29   452512     0   267120     2     0
tu0   1500  DLI          none               452512     0   267120     2     0
tu0   1500  192.168.0    sheridan           452512     0   267120     2     0
```

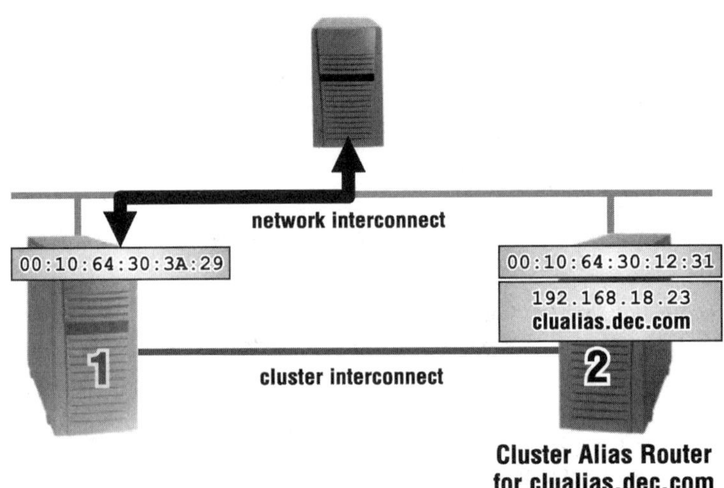

Figure 16-2: Gratuitous ARP Ignored or Denied

```
# rsh molari /usr/sbin/netstat -I tu0
Name  Mtu   Network      Address              Ipkts Ierrs    Opkts Oerrs  Coll
tu0   1500  <Link>       0:10:64:30:12:31   1244810     0   595031     3     0
tu0   1500  DLI          none               1244810     0   595031     3     0
tu0   1500  192.168.0    molari             1244810     0   595031     3     0
```

```
# ping clualias
PING clualias.dec.com (192.168.18.23): 56 data bytes
64 bytes from 192.168.18.23: icmp_seq=0 ttl=64 time=1 ms
64 bytes from 192.168.18.23: icmp_seq=1 ttl=64 time=0 ms

----clualias.dec.com PING Statistics----
2 packets transmitted, 2 packets received, 0% packet loss
round-trip (ms)  min/avg/max = 0/0/1 ms
```

Before shutting down sheridan (the current proxy ARP master), the client has the “3a:29” address in its ARP cache.

```
# arp clualias
clualias (192.168.18.23) at 00-10-64-30-3a-29
```

Shutdown sheridan!

After shutting down sheridan, the client sees the “12:31” address in its ARP cache.

```
# arp clualias
clualias (192.168.18.23) at 00-10-64-30-12-31
```

Client access still works seamlessly.

```
# ping clualias
PING clualias.dec.com (192.168.18.23): 56 data bytes
64 bytes from 192.168.18.23: icmp_seq=0 ttl=64 time=0 ms
64 bytes from 192.168.18.23: icmp_seq=1 ttl=64 time=0 ms

----clualias.dec.com PING Statistics----
2 packets transmitted, 2 packets received, 0% packet loss
round-trip (ms)  min/avg/max = 0/0/0 ms
```

Can’t get to sheridan anymore (member is down).

```
# rsh sheridan /usr/sbin/netstat -I tu0
sheridan: Connection timed out
```

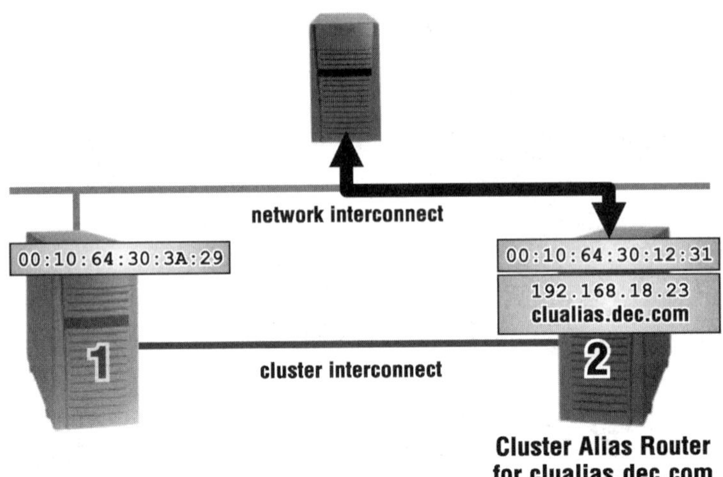

Figure 16-3: Client ARP Cache Refreshed through Gratuitous ARP

Confirming `molari`'s accessibility and MAC address.

```
# rsh molari /usr/sbin/netstat -I tu0
Name  Mtu   Network     Address              Ipkts Ierrs    Opkts Oerrs  Coll
tu0   1500  <Link>      0:10:64:30:12:31   1245087     0   595328     3     0
tu0   1500  DLI         none               1245087     0   595328     3     0
tu0   1500  192.168.0   molari             1245087     0   595328     3     0
```

However, it is possible that the client node will be running an IP software package that ignores gratuitous ARP broadcasts. If this is the situation at your site, you will need to set up a phony MAC address that does not change if the proxy ARP master changes. This is, in effect, a virtual (or fake) MAC address. Thus this very important option is referred to as Virtual MAC or vMAC.

16.4.2 Virtual MAC (vMAC)

The goal of vMAC is to allow client systems to reference an IP address that resolves to a MAC address that does not change as the proxy ARP mastering responsibilities move from one cluster member to another over the life of the cluster (see Figure 16-4). This allows clients whose IP software is designed to ignore gratuitous ARP requests to interact with the cluster using the standard cluster alias mechanisms. This requires no special efforts from the client. But the cluster members must have certain vMAC variables set in `/etc/rc.config.common` file.

Before we take a look at how to set up vMAC, it's important to realize that your Ethernet device is not as simple as you may have thought. Earlier we described the device as having a "burned on" MAC address that ends up in a client system's ARP cache associated with the IP address assigned to the interface. While this is essentially true, the capabilities go beyond that. You may be aware that you can set up an interface with more than one IP address (called an IP alias – not to be confused with a cluster alias, mentioned earlier in this chapter). The interface can also be assigned an additional MAC address using the "physaddr" or "vphysaddr" options to the ifconfig(8) command (see the ifconfig(8) reference page for more information).

You can probably see where we are taking you at this point. In order to support vMAC, the current proxy ARP master will have its network interface configured with a MAC alias that will be associated with the cluster alias IP address. If the proxy ARP master cluster member fails, a surviving member will automatically be selected as the new proxy ARP master for the cluster alias **using the same vMAC address**. This means that the clients will not need to change anything in their ARP caches. The MAC address they currently have will still be correct. Completely transparently to the clients, the proxy ARP master on the cluster has changed.

All cluster members will be configured identically to support vMAC by setting VMAC_ENABLED to "yes" in their /etc/rc.config.common file.

```
# rcmgr -c set VMAC_ENABLED yes
```

By default, the vMAC address will be formed as follows: Take the cluster alias IP address and convert it to hex. (192.168.18.23 becomes C0:A8:12:17). Then prepend the default vMAC prefix, which is AA:01, yielding the entire vMAC address of AA:01:C0:A8:12:17. If desired, the vMAC prefix value (AA:01) can be altered by setting VMAC_PREFIX to some other value in the /etc/rc.config.common file.

```
# rcmgr -c set VMAC_PREFIX "BB:02"
```

When a client tries to ping 192.168.18.23, and there is no current translation for this address in the client's ARP cache, the client sends out an ARP request broadcast asking "who has" 192.168.18.23. The current proxy ARP master on the cluster will respond with the vMAC address. The client will stash that information in its ARP cache for future use. The client forms a datagram with the destination MAC address of AA:01:C0:A8:12:17, which is picked up by the

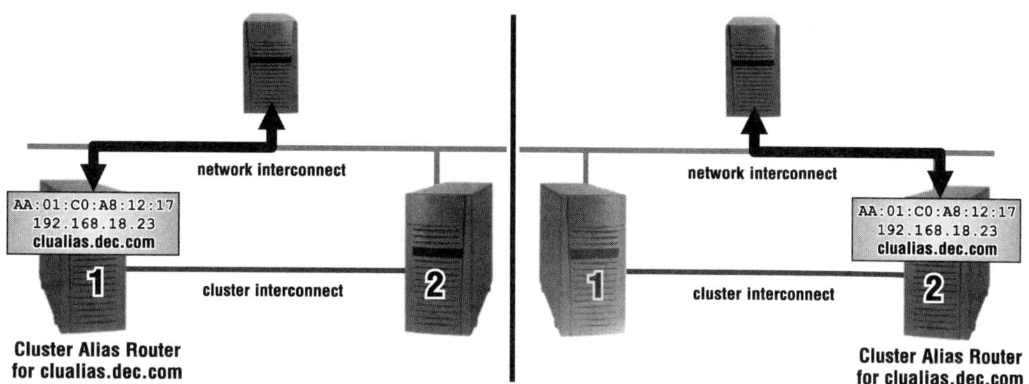

Figure 16-4: vMAC in Action

current proxy ARP master in the cluster. The proxy ARP master may service the request itself, or may route the request to another cluster member.

The routing decisions will be discussed in the next section.

The following example shows vMAC being enabled in a two-member cluster using the "`cluamgr -r vmac`" command. The proxy serving member is then shut down. Note that the client sees no change in its ARP information.

The following `rcmgr` command will ensure that vMAC is enabled as the system boots. The "`-c`" option causes an entry to be placed in cluster-wide `/etc/rc.config.common` file.

```
[molari]
# rcmgr -c set VMAC_ENABLED yes
```

```
[molari]
# rcmgr -c get VMAC_ENABLED
VMAC_ENABLED="yes"
```

The `clu_alias` script (available at the BRUDEN or Digital Press website – see Appendix B) enables vMAC on all cluster members by running the "`/usr/sbin/cluamgr -r vmac`" command on each system in the cluster.

```
# clu_alias -r vmac
member1: (molari) "/usr/sbin/cluamgr -r vmac"
member2: (sheridan) "/usr/sbin/cluamgr -r vmac" - accessing via sheridan-ics0"
```

In the following sequence, the client successfully pings the cluster alias (`babylon5`) and caches the vMAC address.

```
# ping babylon5
PING babylon5.dec.com (192.168.0.70): 56 data bytes
64 bytes from 192.168.0.70: icmp_seq=0 ttl=64 time=1 ms
64 bytes from 192.168.0.70: icmp_seq=1 ttl=64 time=0 ms
```

```
# arp babylon5
babylon5 (192.168.0.70) at aa-01-c0-a8-00-46
```

The following sequence shows that the cluster member `molari` is the current proxy ARP master.

```
[molari]
# /sbin/arp babylon5
babylon5 (192.168.0.70) at aa-01-c0-a8-00-46 permanent published
```

```
[sheridan]
# /sbin/arp babylon5

babylon5 (19.168.0.70) -- no entry
```

Shut Down molari (the current proxy ARP server)! As you would expect, cluster member sheridan becomes the new proxy ARP server. However, this time there is no change in the client's ARP cache since the aa-01-c0-a8-00-46 address is a vMAC address.

```
# ./clu_arp babylon5
==============================================================================
member1: (molari) "/sbin/arp babylon5" - accessing via molari-ics0
------------------------------------------------------------------------------

babylon5 (192.168.0.70) at aa-01-c0-a8-00-46 permanent published
==============================================================================
member2: (sheridan) "/sbin/arp babylon5"
------------------------------------------------------------------------------

babylon5 (192.168.0.70) -- no entry
```

Now, back on the client, note that it has no knowledge of the upheaval that has just occurred in the cluster. The ARP information is the same as it was when molari was the proxy ARP master.

```
# arp babylon5
babylon5 (192.168.0.70) at aa-01-c0-a8-00-46
```

All is well from the client's perspective.

```
# ping babylon5
PING babylon5.dec.com (192.168.0.70): 56 data bytes
64 bytes from 192.168.0.70: icmp_seq=0 ttl=64 time=0 ms
64 bytes from 192.168.0.70: icmp_seq=1 ttl=64 time=0 ms

----babylon5.dec.com PING Statistics----
2 packets transmitted, 2 packets received, 0% packet loss
round-trip (ms)  min/avg/max = 0/0/0 ms
```

16.5 Cluster Alias Routing

So a datagram has arrived at the proxy ARP master for the cluster. The next step is to deliver that datagram to the appropriate member of the cluster for final handling. The IP software on the proxy ARP master can see that the destination IP address (the IP address associated with the cluster alias) is one of the IP addresses that it really owns. If the request is for a new TCP or UDP connection, it uses a weighted and potentially round robin list of eligible target members to decide to whom to forward the request. If it is a pre-existing TCP/IP connection, it forwards to the appropriate member.

Note that it is the IP software that makes routing decisions based on the contents of the in-memory routing table. A common misperception is that the routing daemons (`routed(8)` and `gated(8)`) make the routing decisions and implement routing. The job of the routing daemons is to populate the routing table. This means that a system can potentially be configured as a router and not have a routing daemon running. Once again, the act of routing entails forwarding packets that arrive at a system but are not ultimately destined for that system. Therefore, they must be sent back out through an interface that will move the packet closer to its destination. Within the cluster, the act of forwarding packets over the CI to a target cluster member is sometimes referred to as "tunneling".

16.5.1 Alias Routing vs. IP Routing

In a cluster, the routing decisions will primarily involve cluster alias routing, not the standard IP routing. We recommend that you use a routing device or a non-clustered system to perform standard IP routing. (This will separate the two types of routing for the sake of management simplicity. See Chapter 20 for more discussion of standard IP routing.) Cluster alias routing provides a mechanism whereby the handling of incoming network service requests (`telnet`, `ftp`, NFS, etc.) can be spread across the cluster members if desired. The forwarding of packets from the proxy ARP master to other cluster members will use the CI (Cluster Interconnect), which may be a Memory Channel or LAN-based connection.

16.5.1.1 Volunteering to Do Alias Routing

The cluster member issuing the following command has volunteered for the responsibility of routing for the cluster alias named "`clua_den`". It has not volunteered to actually service any requests from clients for "`clua_den`". Note that the string "`clua_den`" will have to be resolvable to an IP address through the `/etc/hosts` file, BIND, NIS, or another mechanism in order for this sequence to work. The `/etc/hosts` file is the best alternative on the cluster itself, while BIND or NIS may be preferred for ease of client use. (A less attractive alternative is to use an IP address instead of a cluster alias name.)

```
# cluamgr -a alias=clua_den
```

Cluster members can indicate a willingness to handle routing responsibilities, and/or join in on the service handling responsibilities (i.e., become a member of the cluster alias). Note that after volunteering for routing responsibilities (and, in this case, creating the alias), no additional information has been placed in the routing table.

```
# netstat -rn | wc -l
      14
```

16.5.1.2 Volunteering to Service (Join) an Alias

So you figure that naturally something will be added to the routing table after the cluster member asks to "join" in the service responsibilities (see the following series of commands).

```
# netstat -rn | wc -l
      14
```

```
# cluamgr -a alias=clua_den,join
```

Still no change in the routing tables. The cluster alias daemon (aliasd(8)) has not been informed of the need to start processing activities for the new alias.

```
# netstat -rn | wc -l
      14
```

The next output shows that once the daemon has been informed (through the "cluamgr -r start" command), it adds a new route to the routing table.

```
# cluamgr -r start
```

```
# netstat -rn | wc -l
      15
```

```
# netstat -r | grep clua_den
clua_den          localhost         UH        0        0  lo0
```

16.5.1.3 Proxy ARP Master

Note also that the cluster member that created the alias has a special ARP entry in its cache indicating that the entry is permanent (won't be eliminated from the cache after 20 minutes) and published (supported by gratuitous ARP). This member will serve as the proxy ARP master for this alias.

```
# arp clua_den
clua_den (192.168.0.129) at 00-10-64-30-12-31 permanent published
```

16.5.1.4 Alias Status and Statistics

The following output displays information and statistics about all aliases known to this cluster member. The first entry is for the default cluster alias (babylon5 in this example), and the second entry is for the newly created clua_den alias.

```
[molari]
# cluamgr -s all

Status of Cluster Alias: babylon5.dec.com

netmask: 0.0.0.0
aliasid: 1
flags: 7<ENABLED,DEFAULT,IP_V4>
connections rcvd from net: 5
connections forwarded: 2
connections rcvd within cluster: 7
data packets received from network: 1373
data packets forwarded within cluster: 1289
datagrams received from network: 180
datagrams forwarded within cluster: 180
datagrams received within cluster: 6
fragments received from network: 0
fragments forwarded within cluster: 0
fragments received within cluster: 0
Member Attributes:
memberid: 1, selw=3, selp=1, rpri=1 flags=11<JOINED,ENABLED>
memberid: 2, selw=3, selp=1, rpri=1 flags=11<JOINED,ENABLED>

Status of Cluster Alias: clua_den

netmask: 0.0.0.0
aliasid: 2
flags: 5<ENABLED,IP_V4>
connections rcvd from net: 0
connections forwarded: 0
connections rcvd within cluster: 0
data packets received from network: 0
data packets forwarded within cluster: 0
datagrams received from network: 0
datagrams forwarded within cluster: 0
datagrams received within cluster: 0
fragments received from network: 0
fragments forwarded within cluster: 0
fragments received within cluster: 0
Member Attributes:
memberid: 1, selw=1, selp=1, rpri=1 flags=11<JOINED,ENABLED>
```

The member attributes section of this output indicates that two members (of this two member cluster) have joined in on the responsibilities of servicing client requests destined for the default cluster alias (babylon5). In addition, both members have been enabled to handle routing responsibilities (although only one member will be doing the routing for a particular alias at any one time). See the selected portion of the "cluamgr -s" command below. Note that only one member is involved with the new alias (clua_den).

```
# cluamgr -s all | grep -E "^Status|^[Mm]ember|^$" | uniq

Status of Cluster Alias: babylon5.dec.com

Member Attributes:
memberid: 1, selw=3, selp=1, rpri=1 flags=11<JOINED,ENABLED>
memberid: 2, selw=3, selp=1, rpri=1 flags=11<JOINED,ENABLED>

Status of Cluster Alias: clua_den

Member Attributes:
memberid: 1, selw=1, selp=1, rpri=1 flags=11<JOINED,ENABLED>
```

The following output is from the other cluster member. Note that the only cluster alias of which it is aware is the default cluster alias (babylon5).

```
[sheridan]
# cluamgr -s all

Status of Cluster Alias: babylon5.dec.com

netmask: 0.0.0.0
aliasid: 1
flags: 7<ENABLED,DEFAULT,IP_V4>
connections rcvd from net: 6
connections forwarded: 5
connections rcvd within cluster: 3
data packets received from network: 2929
data packets forwarded within cluster: 332
datagrams received from network: 99860
datagrams forwarded within cluster: 6
datagrams received within cluster: 99558
fragments received from network: 0
fragments forwarded within cluster: 0
fragments received within cluster: 0
Member Attributes:
memberid: 1, selw=3, selp=1, rpri=1 flags=11<JOINED,ENABLED>
memberid: 2, selw=3, selp=1, rpri=1 flags=11<JOINED,ENABLED>
```

The following cluamgr command makes the issuing member a router for the clua_den cluster alias.

```
[sheridan]
# cluamgr -a alias=clua_den
```

Nothing is evident in the routing table since aliasd has not been asked to refresh its cached information.

```
[sheridan]
# netstat -r | grep clua_den
```

The following command adds service responsibilities to this member for the alias clua_den. Note: still no routing table changes.

```
[sheridan]
# cluamgr -a alias=clua_den,join
```

```
[sheridan]
# netstat -r | grep clua_den
```

The `clua_den` alias is now reflected as being joined and enabled on both cluster members.

```
# cluamgr -s clua_den | grep -E "^Status|^[Mm]ember|^$" | uniq

Status of Cluster Alias: clua_den

Member Attributes:
memberid: 1, selw=1, selp=1, rpri=1 flags=11<JOINED,ENABLED>
memberid: 2, selw=1, selp=1, rpri=1 flags=11<JOINED,ENABLED>
```

After the routing table information is refreshed through the "`cluamgr -r start`" command, the routing tables will have been updated to reflect the handling of traffic directed to the `clua_den` alias. The routing table indicates that traffic for `clua_den` can be handled by the "`localhost`", which is this member. Note that the routing responsibilities will not be handled on this member (at least for now), as indicated by the absence of the "permanent and published" entry in the ARP table on this member.

```
[sheridan]
# cluamgr -r start
```

```
[sheridan]
# netstat -r | grep clua_den

clua_den          localhost          UH          0          0  lo0
```

```
[sheridan]
# arp clua_den

arp: clua_den: Unknown host
```

16.5.1.5 Making Aliases

Remember the last time you watched a duck glide serenely across the surface of a pond? Beneath the surface, those little webbed feet were paddling like crazy! That's the way we view cluster aliases. You have to admit that cluster aliases seem simple on the surface, but are in fact quite complex (and we have yet to grasp the full truth about the cadence of the paddling). Before we move into deeper waters with cluster aliases, we thought it might be time to step back and examine the usefulness of this cluster feature.

16.5.1.5.1 Why Use Additional Aliases?

The cluster software creates a default cluster alias whether you want one or not. The client nodes can use the default cluster alias to access the services available within the cluster. Sounds terrific, wouldn't you say? If it's so terrific, why would we ever need to create additional cluster aliases?

If your configuration will include applications whose resources involve a subset of cluster members, it makes sense to set up a separate alias that is "joined" by selected cluster members only. Or, if your clients expect to use the cluster as an NFS server, but not all cluster members can access the NFS served storage with equal performance, it may be best to set up another alias. This alias would include selected cluster members, or include all cluster members but have different selection weight (`selw`) values to help load balance or otherwise determine which members are used for the bulk of the NFS serving activities. Note that it may still be best to include all cluster members in the new alias, just in case the preferred members go down. Slow access is much better than no access.

Additional aliases are created and managed by the `cluamgr` command. Note that the contents of the `/etc/clua_alias.config` file will be a series (well, at least one) of `cluamgr` commands. The entry to create the default cluster alias is shown in the next section. The following example creates an alias, called `clua_den`, and arranges for the issuing cluster member to "join" the alias, and route for the alias if necessary. This command would have to be issued on other cluster members in order for them to recognize the alias also. As shown in section 16.5.1.4, the "`cluamgr -s all`" command provides statistics and status reports on cluster alias use.

```
# cluamgr -a alias=clua_den,join
```

16.5.1.6 Making Aliases Permanent

Any changes made using the `cluamgr` command at the command line prompt do not survive a reboot. In order to make your alias permanent, you must add entries to the `/etc/clu_alias.config` file. This file is a CDSL, thus allowing each member to manage its own suite of aliases. The contents of this file will be `cluamgr` commands. The following example shows a `/etc/clu_alias.config` file with just the default cluster alias being defined.

```
# cat /etc/clu_alias.config
/usr/sbin/cluamgr -a selw=3,selp=1,join,alias=DEFAULTALIAS
```

This file is executed as a script from within the `/sbin/init.d/clu_alias` script at boot time. The following is an excerpt from the `/sbin/init.d/clu_alias` script.

The "`test -s`" syntax checks to see if the file exists and has a non-zero size.

```
if test -s "/etc/clu_alias.config"
then
    /etc/clu_alias.config
fi
```

For more information, see the clu_alias.config(4) reference page.

16.5.1.7 Eliminating an Alias

If a cluster member needs to change its responsibilities relative to an alias that it has previously "joined", the member may "leave" the alias. This would eliminate the member's responsibility for servicing client requests through the alias but will not eliminate alias routing responsibilities. The following example shows cluster members leaving an alias.

```
[molari]
# cluamgr -s clua_den | grep -E "^Status|^[Mm]ember|^$" | uniq

Status of Cluster Alias: clua_den

Member Attributes:
memberid: 1, selw=1, selp=1, rpri=1 flags=11<JOINED,ENABLED>
memberid: 2, selw=1, selp=1, rpri=1 flags=11<JOINED,ENABLED>
```

The next command shows cluster member molari requesting to "leave" the cluster alias clua_den.

```
[molari]
# cluamgr -a alias=clua_den,leave
```

```
[molari]
# cluamgr -s clua_den | grep -E "^Status|^[Mm]ember|^$" | uniq

Status of Cluster Alias: clua_den

Member Attributes:
memberid: 1, selw=1, selp=1, rpri=1 flags=11<JOINED,ENABLED>
memberid: 2, selw=1, selp=1, rpri=1 flags=10<ENABLED>
```

The following rsh command requests that sheridan "leave" the clua_den cluster alias as well.

```
# rsh sheridan /usr/sbin/cluamgr -a alias=clua_den,leave
```

Note that the alias still exists and both members are still potential routers for the alias. In order to stop routing, the cluamgr -r stop command must be issued (this stops routing for all cluster aliases), or the rpri attribute must be set to zero (this stops routing for an individual alias).

```
# cluamgr -s clua_den | grep -E "^Status|^[Mm]ember|^$" | uniq

Status of Cluster Alias: clua_den

Member Attributes:
memberid: 1, selw=1, selp=1, rpri=1 flags=10<ENABLED>
memberid: 2, selw=1, selp=1, rpri=1 flags=10<ENABLED>
```

Based on our testing, setting the rpri value to 0 on all members for a particular alias (and then restarting the routing activities with a "cluamgr -r start" command) will leave the cluster without a designated proxy ARP master for that alias. This is contrary to the following excerpt from the cluamgr(8) reference page.

```
A value of 0 is a special case. If you set rpri=0 for an alias on a member system,
that system will not route cluster alias traffic into the cluster unless two
conditions are met: all active members of that alias have rpri=0, and that system is
elected to provide the proxy ARP response for the alias.
```

Engineering has informed us that the implementation has changed (as we pointed out above), and that the reference page is currently (V5.1a) incorrect but will be corrected in the future. The part that needs to be forced is the election of the new proxy ARP master. This will certainly happen after a reboot, but you may want to force the action by manually resetting rpri to a non- zero value on the cluster member that you would like to be the new proxy ARP master and then restarting the routing activities with the "cluamgr -r start" command.

16.5.1.8 Dynamic Routing of Cluster Aliases

Now that we have all of this terrific alias information under our belts, it's time to refine our understanding of the interactions between the network clients and the cluster itself. We have discussed the role of the ARP protocol in discerning the actual target cluster member to which the request for service is sent prior to being routed within the cluster to its ultimate destination. How, though, does a request from a client that is not on the same subnet as the cluster (assuming the cluster network interfaces are on one subnet) get resolved?

Suppose a network client resides several hops away (think of a hop as a visit to a network router) from the cluster. Our wonderful MAC magic does us no good once we are off the local area network. There has to be a mechanism whereby the cluster can advertise what it has in its routing table to other routers in the local area network. Once a router picks up the advertisement, that router, in turn, advertises (through broadcasts out each of its network interfaces) what it has in its routing table, and so forth.

16.5.1.9 Dynamic Routing Daemons

In this way, the existence of routes to cluster aliases is propagated between routers. The protocol that is used is called the Routing Information Protocol (RIP). The advertisements are sent and heard by daemon processes running the RIP protocol. In a cluster, the recommended dynamic routing daemon is gated (pronounced gate-dee), although in V5.1B (or V5.1A with appropriate patch kits installed), there is support for the use of both routed (pronounced route-dee) and static routing. Thus, a client many hops away can be directed to use the appropriate network interface to send the datagram on its way toward the cluster. Once the datagram gets to a router within the same network (or subnet) as the cluster, the MAC-level activities discussed earlier in the chapter take place.

Earlier, we saw that a new entry was placed in the routing table after a "cluamgr -r start" command was issued. The cluamgr command interacts with the aliasd daemon. The aliasd daemon maintains a special version of the traditional /etc/gated.conf file called /etc/gated.conf.member*n* where the "*n*" is the cluster member's ID. Note that this file (/etc/gated.conf.member*n*) is not a CDSL, but yet is member-specific as indicated by the naming convention. This allows members to offer to route for a subset of the cluster's aliases. Do not edit the /etc/gated.conf.member*n* file by hand. It is managed automatically by aliasd.

Normally, the /sbin/init.d/clu_alias file will be used for cluster alias subsystem initiation. This boot time script executes the /etc/clu_alias.config file which contains one or more cluamgr commands to set up the default cluster alias (and potentially others).

```
# cat /etc/clu_alias.config
/usr/sbin/cluamgr -a selw=3,selp=1,join,alias=DEFAULTALIAS
```

Use of the cluamgr command is normally limited to troubleshooting situations but is also useful for managing temporary aliases, getting alias status and statistics, restarting routing, and causing the /etc/clua_services file to be re-read. It is used in this chapter primarily for demonstration purposes.

16.5.1.10 The gated.conf.member*n* File

When cluster alias routing is started on a member (or restarted using "cluamgr -r start"), the gated process is started using the special cluster version of gated.conf (/etc/gated.conf.member*n*), which contains RIP information describing a host route to the cluster alias. Note the command line argument passed to gated on a cluster member.

```
# ps -A | grep gated | grep -v grep
1051031 ??       S          0:00.13 /usr/sbin/gated -f /etc/gated.conf.member2
```

The gated process sends broadcasts out all of the system's configured network interfaces advertising a route to any cluster aliases that it is aware of and has routing responsibilities. Remember that an alias can be "joined," in which case the cluster member is willing to provide the service represented by the alias, or the alias can be routed, or both. Use the gdc(8) command to dump gated's current state into a file if you are interested in more details on gated's function (See the gdc(8) reference page for more information.)

```
# cat /etc/gated.conf.member2
# This file created automatically by "aliasd", DO NOT EDIT!
#

# Set up a trace file in /usr/tmp
traceoptions "/usr/tmp/gated.log" replace size 1000k files 2 general;

# any dead interfaces will be entered here with a high (i.e. undesireable)
# preference, so that gated will be compelled to put a better route
# in the kernel forwarding table
#
```

```
interfaces {
    interface all passive;
};

# broadcast routes with RIP if at least one interface is healthy
#
# make a default route through the cluster interconnect look expensive
#
# If an interface has been marked as "dead" by NIFF then we
# will also exclude RIP routes via the affected interface.
# This closes a hole where gated doesn't qualify the interfaces
# over which it hears broadcasts, and will possibly install a route
# through a dead interface.
#
# Lastly, we place a catch-all "all nripin noripout" here so that
# if an interface is brought on-line after aliasd has started, it
# won't automatically get used by gated.
#
rip yes {
    broadcast;
    interface ics0 ripin ripout metricout 10;
    interface tu0 ripin ripout;
    interface all noripin noripout;
};

# one "host" or network number per alias
#
# aliasd will also reroute direct routes for interfaces
# marked as "dead" by NIFF by inserting a new gateway
# for that route here
#
static {
    host 192.168.0.70 interface 127.0.0.1;
};

# arrange to export alias host/network routes:
#
# o don't publish routes learned through RIP
# o publish the "static" routes given above, except for
#   orphaned networks that we're routing around
# o publish direct routes for virtual subnets which have real
#   interfaces attached to them
#
# this default may have been learned from RIP (proto rip)
# or it may have been statically configured (proto kernel)
# we give a slight advanatge to a default route via RIP
#
export proto rip interface 10.0.0.2 {
    proto rip {
        default;
    };
    proto kernel {
        default metric 3;
    };
};

export proto rip interface 192.168.0.69 {
    proto rip restrict;
};
```

The following example uses the `clu_ps` script available through the websites associated with this book.

```
# clu_ps "=-Ao pid,command" | grep -E 'PID|gated|^[-=]|^member' | grep -v grep

================================================================================
member2 (sheridan)          ps -Ao pid,command
--------------------------------------------------------------------------------
   PID COMMAND
1051031 /usr/sbin/gated -f /etc/gated.conf.member2
================================================================================
member1 (molari)          ps -Ao pid,command
--------------------------------------------------------------------------------
   PID COMMAND
539007 /usr/sbin/gated -f /etc/gated.conf.member1
================================================================================
```

Host routes take the highest priority in a routing table. Therefore, if a router has information about a host route (a route to a specific host), a network route (a route to the network), and a default route (a route to use when there is nothing else useful in the routing table), all in the same routing table, it will always give precedence to the host route. This information becomes significant if you decide to create a cluster alias using a virtual subnet rather than the standard common subnet (see section 16.8 for an example using a virtual subnet).

16.6 Alias Attributes

Notice how gracefully we slipped by the other alias attributes. Only professional authors and technical bullet dodgers can get away with that kind of move. Since we know you are curious, let's discuss some routing and alias issues that have been avoided so far.

16.6.1 The `rpri` Alias Attribute

If multiple cluster members are willing to route for an alias, how does the cluster determine which member actually pulls the packet off the wire and makes the subsequent routing decisions? Each member can apply a routing priority (`rpri`) to an alias. The higher the `rpri` number (the range is 0-100), the more likely the member will be the one selected to do the routing activities.

NOTE:

An `rpri` value of zero indicates that the member does not want to volunteer for routing duties unless every other member is also trying to dodge the bullet too. This would effectively eliminate the member as an alias router under normal circumstances. An `rpri` value of 100 is a special case while the normal `rpri` values (1-99) cause an entry to be placed in the routing table with a cost metric of 14. If you set `rpri` to 100, the same routing table information appears but with a cost metric of 10. The RIP clients will prefer the lower cost route.

If multiple members set up the same routing priority for an alias (as seen in the example output below), the alias router will be the first member to boot (if the clients were already up at the time of the cluster booting). If the cluster boots before the clients, the alias router will be the member that has the highest `rpri` and sent out the most recent routing information to the client's dynamic routing daemon.

```
Member Attributes:
memberid: 1, selw=1, selp=1, rpri=1 flags=11<JOINED,ENABLED>
memberid: 2, selw=1, selp=1, rpri=1 flags=11<JOINED,ENABLED>
```

16.6.2 The `selw` and `selp` Alias Attributes

To determine to which member the request for service is routed within the cluster, two attributes are used: selection weight (`selw`) and selection priority (`selp`). The `selp` number determines which node(s) are asked to perform the service (`telnet`, `ftp`, `ping`, etc.). Only a member with the highest selection priority will provide the service. If more than one member has the highest selection priority, they all will share the service load. Remember that if a member has a `selp` that is not the highest in the cluster, the member will not provide the service at all, until the other cluster members (with higher `selp`) are removed or fail (or change their `selp`).

In the case of a tie `selp` value, the members will provide the service in a round robin fashion based on the value of the selection weight (`selw`) attribute. The selection weight dictates how many services requested through the alias will be handled by the first member with the highest `selp` value before switching over to the next member with the exact same `selp` value. The `selw` value provides a mechanism whereby some members may handle more instances of the service than others, despite having the same `selp` value.

If `member1` (`molari`) has an alias with `selp`=6 and `selw`=3, while `member2` (`sheridan`) has the same alias with `selp`=6 and `selw`=1, the first member will handle the first three requests for service through the alias. The other member will then handle one request before we go back to the first member for the next three requests and so on.

```
# rsh babylon5 hostname
molari.dec.com

# rsh babylon5 hostname
molari.dec.com

# rsh babylon5 hostname
molari.dec.com

# rsh babylon5 hostname
sheridan.dec.com

# rsh babylon5 hostname
molari.dec.com
```

`member1` receives the first three requests.

`member2` gets one request.

The cycle starts again. This is the "weighted" round robin member selection process.

16.7 Alias Subsystem Attributes

You must have IP addresses available to create your aliases. If you don't have any IP addresses available, we will show you how to maneuver around the problem in section 16.8 of this chapter. Let's assume you have extra IP addresses to use for your cluster aliases. How many can you create and why would you want to create more aliases? By default, you are limited to creating 8 (7 plus the default cluster alias). If you need more than that, you must alter the `max_aliasid` attribute in the `clua` subsystem. This is a dynamic attribute, but be sure to alter it consistently on all cluster members. The last time we checked, the maximum number of cluster aliases was in the range of 102k. That ought to do, don't you think? The following output documents the `clua` subsystem attributes. Note that `max_aliasid` is the only one of the `clua` attributes that you may change without a recommendation from HP engineering.

Aliases in addition to the cluster default alias may be useful for refining the target to a subset of the members of the cluster, or may simply be a different mnemonic that is more meaningful for certain applications. Additional aliases may also be used to off-load routing or service responsibilities from less powerful cluster members.

```
# sysconfig -q clua max_aliasid
clua:
max_aliasid = 8
```

```
# sysconfig -Q clua max_aliasid
clua:
max_aliasid -    type=INT op=CRQ min_val=2 max_val=102400
```

The following is an extract from the `sys_attrs_clua` reference page.

```
max_aliasid
    Determines the maximum number of cluster aliases allowed. Although the
    theoretical maximum is 102,400 aliases, the practical upper limit is
    memory-restricted. There are no known issues with the use of 100 or so
    aliases.

    When increasing the value of this attribute, be sure to increase it
    consistently on all cluster members before using the additional
    aliases.
```

16.8 Virtual vs. Common Subnets

If an IP address in a real subnet containing interfaces in one or more cluster members is used, the subnet is referred to as a "common" subnet. Client nodes will view a cluster alias from a common subnet as if it were an actual node on the network. The primary means for clients to locate the cluster alias when using a common subnet is through proxy ARP. Any routing within the cluster

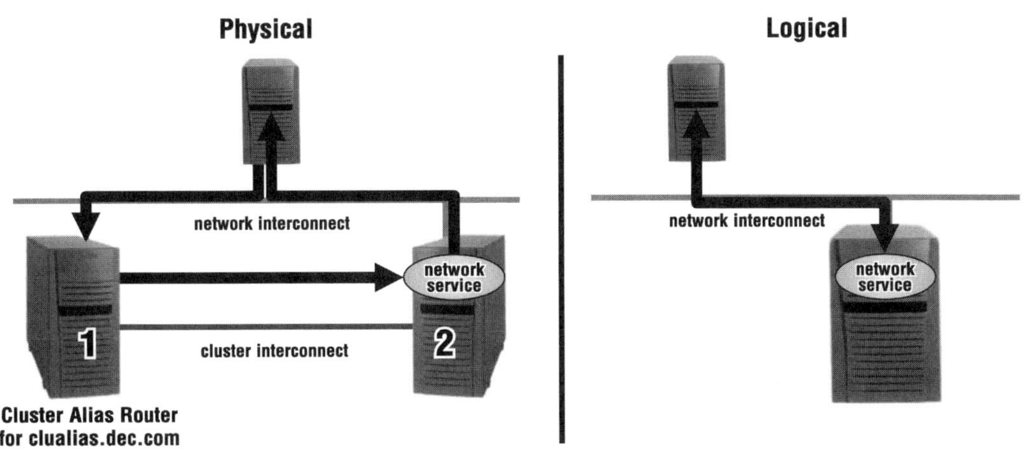

Figure 16-5: Common Subnet: Physical vs. Logical View

will be transparent to the clients. Routing beyond the local network will involve host routes only (no network routes).

Suppose you have no spare IP addresses at your site. Does this mean that you cannot use cluster aliases? That sad situation would eliminate one of the more important capabilities within the cluster. The solution is to use an IP address from within a "virtual subnet." A "virtual subnet" is made up of IP addresses that are not associated with any real interfaces. Clients will access the IP addresses in the virtual subnet (used by the cluster aliases, naturally) through the cluster member serving as the router for that alias. When dealing with high traffic, a common subnet is likely to provide better performance than a virtual subnet, although a virtual subnet provides much more flexibility.

One notable difference when dealing with virtual subnets is that the route advertised by `gated` will be both a network route and a host route (a common subnet would advertise the host route only).

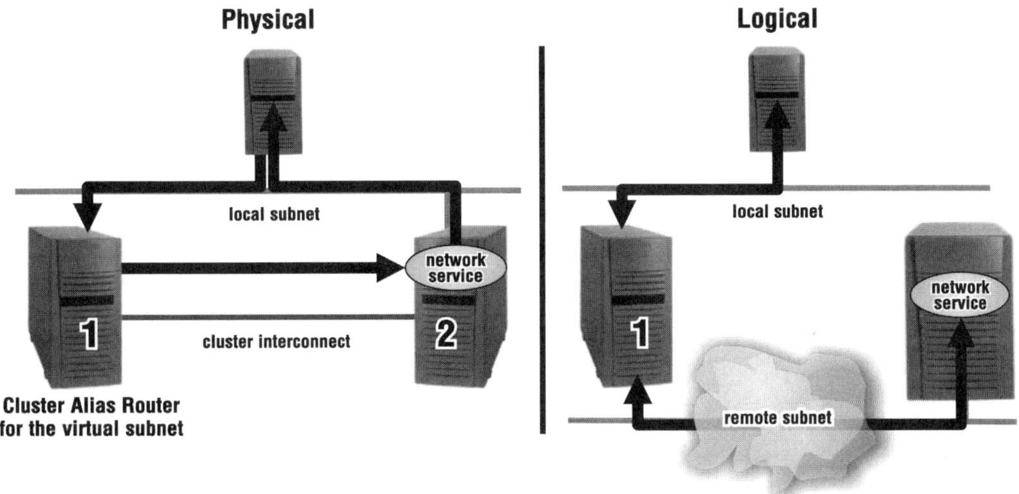

Figure 16-6: Virtual Subnet: Physical vs. Logical View

The network route should be advertised once per member, even if there is more than one alias assigned to the subnet.

CAUTION:

You may not use an address from within the subnet used by the cluster interconnect. This is true for the common subnet aliases as well. Moreover, an address in the virtual subnet cannot be in use on the network. If you choose a virtual subnet that is a real subnet somewhere in the world, the general-purpose router should not route this subnet externally.

Use the `cluamgr` command to set the virtual option on a subnet.

```
# cluamgr -a alias=clua_den,virtual
```

The following output shows a cluster member creating a cluster alias using a virtual subnet. Note that the IP address must not be associated with a real interface.

```
# grep clua_den_virt /etc/hosts
192.206.126.99  clua_den_virt
```

```
# cluamgr -a alias=clua_den_virt,mask=255.255.255.0,join,virtual=t
```

```
# cluamgr -s clua_den_virt
Status of Cluster Alias: clua_den_virt
netmask: ffffff
...
Member Attributes:
memberid: 20, selw=1, selp=1, rpri=1 flags=31<JOINED,ENABLED,VIRTUAL>
```

The cluster alias routing has not been restarted yet. Note that there are 15 entries in the routing table and nothing pertaining to the alias in the ARP cache.

```
# netstat -r | wc -l
      15
```

```
# arp clua_den_virt
clua_den_virt (192.206.126.99) -- no entry
```

After restarting routing on the current cluster member, the routing table has added two entries. The ARP table shows no additional data because virtual subnetting does not rely directly on proxy ARP as common subnet routing does.

```
# cluamgr -r start
```

```
# arp clua_den_virt
clua_den_virt (192.206.126.99) -- no entry
```

```
# netstat -r | wc -l
      17
```

```
# netstat -r
...
192.206.126      localhost        UG          0       0  lo0
clua_den_virt    localhost        UH          0       0  lo0
...
```

The following output is from a client node. We ran the `routed` daemon and specified that it run silently (`-q` no outgoing route advertising) and display a trace of its activities (`-t`). The `routed` daemon understands the RIP protocol just as the `gated` daemon. Therefore, it is legitimate to mix `routed` and `gated` daemons in a network as long as both do not run in the same network node. The first part of the output is standard `routed` startup sequence where it sends a broadcast (`192.168.0.255`) to announce its presence and hears back from itself on port 520 (`192.168.0.104.520`). So far, no excitement.

```
# routed -q -t

Tracing packets started Wed Sep 18 20:04:53 2002


Wed Sep 18 20:04:53:
ADD dst 127.0.0.0, router 127.0.0.1, metric 1,
       flags UP state PASSIVE|INTERFACE|CHANGED|EXTERNAL timer 0
ADD dst 192.168.0.0, router 192.168.0.104, metric 1,
       flags UP state INTERFACE|CHANGED timer 0
SIOCADDRT: File exists
REQUEST to 192.168.0.255.0 Wed Sep 18 20:04:53:
REQUEST from 192.168.0.104.520 Wed Sep 18 20:04:53:
```

The `routed` trace after this point happened just after the "`cluamgr -r start`" command was issued on the cluster member. The `gated` daemon on the cluster (at address `192.168.0.69`) advertised two items to the client, one network route that identifies a router with which to communicate when attempting to access a node on network `192.206.126`, and one host route that identifies a router with which to communicate when attempting to access the interface at address `192.206.126.99`. These items were added to the current information in the client's routing table.

```
REQUEST from 192.168.0.69.520 Wed Sep 18 20:19:04:
RESPONSE from 192.168.0.69.520 Wed Sep 18 20:19:09:

Wed Sep 18 20:19:09:
ADD dst 192.206.126.99, router 192.168.0.69, metric 15,
        flags UP|GATEWAY|HOST state CHANGED timer 0
ADD dst 192.206.126.0, router 192.168.0.69, metric 2,
        flags UP|GATEWAY state CHANGED timer 0
```

We stopped routed and restarted it in the background using the "routed -q" command to eliminate repetitive trace output. The client node's routing table contained the following entries sent to it by the gated running on the cluster member that had defined the clua_den_virt alias. Both entries indicate that sheridan (a cluster member) is the way to get where they want to go. The first entry is the network entry; the second entry is the host entry.

```
# netstat -r
...
192.206.126       sheridan.dec.com  UG         0         0  tu0
clua_den_virt     sheridan.dec.com  UGH        0         0  tu0
...
```

In the following sequence, the host-specific entry in the routing table on the client shows traffic, but the network counter has not budged. Host routes take precedence over network routes.

```
# rsh clua_den_virt hostname
sheridan.dec.com
# rsh clua_den_virt hostname
sheridan.dec.com
```

```
# netstat -r
...
192.206.126       sheridan.dec.com  UG         0         0  tu0
clua_den_virt     sheridan.dec.com  UGH        2        13  tu0
...
```

The network route would get used in situations where the client attempts to access another node on the virtual subnet that is not currently reflected with a host route in the client routing table. This may be useful to summarize a series of cluster aliases on a virtual subnet in the cluster with one network advertisement.

```
# ping 192.206.126.98
PING 192.206.126.98 (192.206.126.98): 56 data bytes

----192.206.126.98 PING Statistics----
6 packets transmitted, 0 packets received, 100% packet loss
```

```
# netstat -r
...
192.206.126      sheridan.dec.com  UG          0        6  tu0
clua_den_virt    sheridan.dec.com  UGH         0       13  tu0
...
```

Back on the cluster, we can see the appropriate counters increasing. If another cluster member were the ultimate destination of the client request, the "forward" counts would increase, indicating that cluster routing (forwarding) is happening.

```
# cluamgr -s clua_den_virt

Status of Cluster Alias: clua_den_virt

netmask: ffffff
aliasid: 3
flags: 5<ENABLED,IP_V4>
connections rcvd from net: 4
connections forwarded: 0
connections rcvd within cluster: 4
data packets received from network: 22
data packets forwarded within cluster: 0
datagrams received from network: 0
datagrams forwarded within cluster: 0
datagrams received within cluster: 0
fragments received from network: 0
fragments forwarded within cluster: 0
fragments received within cluster: 0
Member Attributes:
memberid: 2, selw=1, selp=1, rpri=1 flags=31<JOINED,ENABLED,VIRTUAL>
```

16.8.1 Not Common, Kinda' Virtual

If you look up the word "virtual" in a Merriam-Webster dictionary, you'll find the following definition, "being in essence or in effect though not formally recognized or admitted". Or you could condense the definition and simply say that "virtual" means "fake". So when we talk about a virtual subnet, we are really talking about a "fake" subnet. Fake in that it does not really have any interfaces defined on the subnet. Suppose we only wanted to use a few addresses from a virtual subnet for aliases?

According to the previous section, we can create an alias using an address in a virtual subnet by attaching the syntax "`virtual`" or "`virtual=t`" in our `cluamgr` command, such as:

```
# cluamgr -a alias=clua_den_virt,mask=255.255.255.0,join,virtual=t
```

The alias `clua_den_virt` equates to an IP address (`192.206.126.99`) on a subnet that has no real interfaces on it. Consider what it would mean if we used the exact same syntax but left off the "`virtual=t`". Wouldn't the alias still be in a "fake" subnet? Indeed it would, but there would be no advertisement for the network route to the subnet. There would only be an advertisement for the host route.

The following syntax creates an alias in a virtual subnet but does not advertise the network route to the virtual subnet (it still advertises the host route). Note that the only thing in this syntax that identifies the alias as being in a virtual subnet (as opposed to a common subnet) is the fact that the IP address for the alias is in a subnet with no real interfaces.

```
# cluamgr -a alias=clua_den_virt,mask=255.255.255.0,join
```

This technique may be useful if you have multiple clusters and would like to create aliases on multiple clusters using IP addresses from the same virtual subnet. If the "virtual=t" option were used in creating the aliases, the external routers would be informed of a network route to the subnet that may direct traffic to the wrong cluster. This would only be an issue when you have multiple clusters and need to use only one virtual subnet between the multiple clusters.

We recommend (for sanity reasons) that you use a separate virtual subnet for each of your clusters if possible.

16.9 Reserved Addresses

Request For Comment (RFC) 1918 lists three areas of IP addresses that are "private." Private addresses are essentially non-routable and as such are available for use within a network without officially owning the addresses. The only potential problem is that if you use one of these three suites of addresses, gated is smart enough to not advertise them. This is not a problem if your clients are within the local area network. But if you have a more complex arrangement of networks, gated has to be specifically instructed to advertise these "private" addresses that you may have assigned to your cluster aliases. Use the "cluamgr -r resvok" command to inform aliasd and indirectly gated of your wishes. The reserved private address ranges are as follows:

```
   10.0.0.0  –  10.255.255.255
 172.16.0.0  –  172.31.255.255
192.168.0.0  –  192.168.255.255
```

This option should be used with caution. Setting any of these addresses as routable could potentially have major repercussions in a wide area network. While experimenting, we inadvertently managed to get access to a cluster member in Australia (from a machine in Georgia). Upon review, the cluster administrator had used this option without fully understanding its implications. His dynamic routers (on the same LAN as his cluster) were advertising access to several of the private addresses in the table above.

16.10 CLUA and IP Ports

So far, the bulk of this chapter has been focused on aliases, IP addresses, ARP, and various activities and attributes related to cluster alias routing. An important piece is still missing from the CLUA puzzle. How are client requests directed to the appropriate server process? Not to the appropriate server, but to the appropriate server process on the actual serving member. You should already understand how the request arrives at the appropriate cluster member, but that cluster member can be running many different applications, any of which may be the target of the client request, or the target process may need to be started by `inetd`. It's like being dropped off in a neighborhood without any clue of how to arrive at the correct house.

If we can forget clusters for a minute, and focus on typical network client-server activities, you may recall that the notion of a socket can represent many things in the mind of a network administrator or network programmer. It can represent a system call (see the `socket(2)` reference page), data structure, file, end point in network communication, or combination of a 32-bit IP address and a 16-bit port number. Consider, for a moment, the power of being able to identify a process anywhere on the Internet using 48 bits of information (32-bit IP address plus the 16-bit port number). Pretty impressive, isn't it?

16.10.1 The Services File

The port number is a 16-bit integer assigned to represent an application. Two of the more well-known port numbers are 21 for `ftp` and 23 for `telnet`. Port numbers can be viewed in the cluster shared `/etc/services` file. Note that there are 64k port numbers available for TCP services, and another 64k port numbers available for UDP services.

```
# cat /etc/services
...

#
# Description:  The services file lists the sockets and protocols used for
#               Internet services.
#
# Syntax:  ServiceName PortNumber/ProtocolName [alias_1,...,alias_n] [#comments]
#
# ServiceName    official Internet service name
# PortNumber     the socket port number used for the service
# ProtocolName   the transport protocol used for the service
# alias                 unofficial service names
# #comments             text following the comment character (#) is ignored
#
echo            7/tcp
echo            7/udp
discard         9/tcp           sink null
discard         9/udp           sink null
systat          11/tcp          users
daytime         13/tcp
daytime         13/udp
netstat         15/tcp
quote           17/udp          text
chargen         19/tcp          ttytst
chargen         19/udp          ttytst
ftp             21/tcp
telnet          23/tcp
smtp            25/tcp          mail
...
(lots more)
...
rdg             10403/tcp
rdg             10403/udp
wnn4            22273/tcp               # Wnn Ver 4.1
AdvFS           30000/tcp       advfs   # AdvFS GUI/daemon communications
gii             616/tcp         # GateD Interactive Interface
```

16.10.2 Viewing Port and Socket Use

The current use of ports and sockets on a cluster member (or any system) can be displayed using the "`netstat -a`" command. The local address and foreign address columns in the output below display the port numbers as the number or mnemonic after the final dot (the port number in "`molari.dec.com.4035`" is `4035`).

```
# netstat -a

Active Internet connections (including servers)
Proto Recv-Q Send-Q  Local Address              Foreign Address          (state)
tcp        0      0  molari.dec.com.4035        dns5.dec.com.domain      TIME_WAIT
tcp        0    217  molari.dec.com.telnet      laptop2.dec.com.1184     ESTABLISHED
tcp        0      0  babylon5.dec.com.domain    *.*                      LISTEN
tcp        0      0  molari.dec.com.domain      *.*                      LISTEN
tcp        0      0  localhost.domain           *.*                      LISTEN
tcp        0      0  molari-ics0.domain         *.*                      LISTEN
tcp        0      0  *.596                      *.*                      LISTEN
...
(lots more)
...
tcp        0      0  molari.dec.com.1153        *.*                      LISTEN
tcp        0      0  localhost.1153             *.*                      LISTEN
tcp        0      0  molari-ics0.1153           *.*                      LISTEN
tcp        0      0  molari.dec.com.1152        *.*                      LISTEN
tcp        0      0  localhost.1152             *.*                      LISTEN
tcp        0      0  molari-ics0.1152           *.*                      LISTEN
tcp        0      0  *.830                      *.*                      LISTEN
tcp        0      0  *.2049                     *.*                      LISTEN
tcp        0      0  *.1022                     *.*                      LISTEN
tcp        0      0  *.gii                      *.*                      LISTEN
tcp        0      0  *.111                      *.*                      LISTEN
udp        0      0  *.2049                     *.*
udp        0      0  *.time                     *.*
udp        0      0  babylon5.dec.com.domain    *.*
udp        0      0  molari.dec.com.domain      *.*
udp        0      0  localhost.domain           *.*
udp        0      0  molari-ics0.domain         *.*
udp        0      0  *.111                      *.*
udp        0      0  *.1139                     *.*
udp        0      0  *.1144                     *.*
udp        0      0  *.1145                     *.*
udp        0      0  *.1146                     *.*
udp        0      0  babylon5.dec.com.ntp       *.*
udp        0      0  molari.dec.com.ntp         *.*
udp        0      0  localhost.ntp              *.*
...
(lots more)
...
```

The raw port numbers can more easily be discerned by adding the "`-n`" option to the previous `netstat` command. Once again, the number following the rightmost dot is the port number.

```
# netstat -an

Active Internet connections (including servers)
Proto Recv-Q Send-Q  Local Address          Foreign Address        (state)
tcp        0      0  192.168.0.69.4034      192.168.0.2.53         TIME_WAIT
tcp        0      0  192.168.0.69.4035      192.168.0.2.53         TIME_WAIT
tcp        0    301  192.168.0.69.23        192.168.0.2.1184       ESTABLISHED
tcp        0      0  192.168.0.70.53        *.*                    LISTEN
tcp        0      0  192.168.0.69.53        *.*                    LISTEN
tcp        0      0  127.0.0.1.53           *.*                    LISTEN
tcp        0      0  10.0.0.2.53            *.*                    LISTEN
tcp        0      0  *.596                  *.*                    LISTEN
…
(lots more)
…
tcp        0      0  192.168.0.69.1153      *.*                    LISTEN
tcp        0      0  127.0.0.1.1153         *.*                    LISTEN
tcp        0      0  10.0.0.2.1153          *.*                    LISTEN
tcp        0      0  192.168.0.69.1152      *.*                    LISTEN
tcp        0      0  127.0.0.1.1152         *.*                    LISTEN
tcp        0      0  10.0.0.2.1152          *.*                    LISTEN
tcp        0      0  *.830                  *.*                    LISTEN
tcp        0      0  *.2049                 *.*                    LISTEN
tcp        0      0  *.1022                 *.*                    LISTEN
tcp        0      0  *.616                  *.*                    LISTEN
tcp        0      0  *.111                  *.*                    LISTEN
udp        0      0  *.2049                 *.*
udp        0      0  *.37                   *.*
udp        0      0  192.168.0.70.53        *.*
udp        0      0  192.168.0.69.53        *.*
udp        0      0  127.0.0.1.53           *.*
udp        0      0  10.0.0.2.53            *.*
udp        0      0  *.111                  *.*
udp        0      0  *.1139                 *.*
udp        0      0  *.1144                 *.*
udp        0      0  *.1145                 *.*
udp        0      0  *.1146                 *.*
udp        0      0  192.168.0.70.123       *.*
udp        0      0  192.168.0.69.123       *.*
udp        0      0  127.0.0.1.123          *.*
…
(lots more)
…
```

16.10.3 Dynamically Assigned Port Numbers

The port numbers can be associated with an actual application by examining the `/etc/services` file (see section 16.10.1). Note that not all port numbers are found in this file. For example, examining the `/etc/services` file for a `telnet` entry shows that `telnet` is associated with TCP port number 23. But there are two sides to a connection. What port number is used for the other side of the `telnet` connection? The server side (running `telnetd`) will be associated with port number 23. The client side will have allocated a port that is reserved for user requests.

These client side ports are dynamically chosen by the networking software in the kernel. Since the clients are usually not cluster members, there tend to be plenty of these "ephemeral" ports for the clients to use. But have we ever said that a cluster cannot be a client?

16.10.4 The Cluster as a Client

What happens with respect to these dynamically allocated ports when the cluster member is the client? The dynamic port numbers must be unique to the cluster in order to distinguish an application in a particular cluster member from the same application running in another cluster member, and we know that the cluster can have 8 members maximum (at the present time). How many of these dynamic ports are available for use in typical client/server network activities?

The number of available dynamic ports can be discerned by calculating the difference between two `inet` subsystem attributes – `ipport_userreserved` (default is 5000) and `ipport_userreservedmin` (default is 1024). The difference is 3976. Using the default values, this number indicates how many concurrent client activities can be executing within the cluster at any one time. While the 3976 number may be plenty for a single node machine, it is potentially a bottleneck for a multi-member cluster.

HP recommends that the `ipport_userreserved` attribute be increased to its maximum (65535) on clusters with more than two members. This will provide approximately 63k ports for concurrent use spread across the cluster members. See section 19.3.7.3 for an example modifying `ipport_userreserved`.

16.10.5 The `inetd.conf` File

The server side of network applications such as `telnet` and `ftp` (`telnetd` or `ftpd`) is not started until the client has requested access (through the `telnet` or `ftp` commands). The server daemons are started up (upon client request) by the `inetd` daemon, which is responsible for handling the startup of any services listed in the `/etc/inetd.conf` file. Below is a sample of an `inetd.conf` file.

```
# cat /etc/inetd.conf
...
######################################################################
#
# Internet server configuration database
#
# Description:  The inetd.conf file is the first file that the inetd
#               daemon reads for information on how to handle Internet
#               service requests.  It contains global services that
#               can be run on all members in a cluster.
#
# Precedence:   Entries in inetd.conf.local will override entries in
#               inetd.conf because it is read after inetd.conf.
#
# Syntax:  ServiceName  SocketType  ProtocolName  Wait/NoWait  UserName \
#          ServerPath  ServerArgs
#
# ServiceName     name of an Internet service defined in the /etc/services file
# SockettType     type of socket used by the service, either stream or dgram
# ProtocolName    name of an internet protocol defined in the /etc/protocols
#                 file
```

```
# Wait/NoWait        determines whether the inetd daemon waits for
#                    a datagram server to release the socket before continuing
#                    to listen at the socket
# UserName           the login that inetd should use to start the server
# ServerPath         full pathname of the server
# ServerArgs         optional command line arguments that inetd should use to
#                    execute the server
#
ftp     stream  tcp     nowait  root    /usr/sbin/ftpd          ftpd
telnet  stream  tcp     nowait  root    /usr/sbin/telnetd       telnetd
shell   stream  tcp     nowait  root    /usr/sbin/rshd          rshd
login   stream  tcp     nowait  root    /usr/sbin/rlogind       rlogind
exec    stream  tcp     nowait  root    /usr/sbin/rexecd        rexecd
# Run as user "uucp" if you don't want uucpd's wtmp entries.
#uucp   stream  tcp     nowait  root    /usr/sbin/uucpd         uucpd
#finger  stream  tcp     nowait  root   /usr/sbin/fingerd       fingerd
#tftp   dgram   udp     wait    root    /usr/sbin/tftpd         tftpd /tmp
comsat  dgram   udp     wait    root    /usr/sbin/comsat        comsat
#talk    dgram   udp     wait    root   /usr/sbin/talkd         talkd
ntalk   dgram   udp     wait    root    /usr/sbin/ntalkd        ntalkd
# Please note that bootp functionality has been subsumed by the
# DHCP daemon (joind).  Please refer to the joind(8) man page
#bootps dgram   udp     wait    root    /usr/sbin/bootpd        bootpd
#bootps dgram   udp     wait    root    /usr/sbin/joind         joind
#time   stream  tcp     nowait  root    internal                time
time    dgram   udp     wait    root    internal                time
#daytime stream tcp     nowait  root    internal                daytime
…
```

The /etc/inetd.conf file is not a CDSL and thus is shared by all cluster members. Suppose you need to disallow certain server-side applications from executing on a subset of your cluster members? For instance, suppose you only wanted one cluster member to execute the ftp service (or substitute any network-oriented service where we mention ftp). This is not resolved by cooking up a cluster alias and having only certain members "join" that alias. That would simply limit the cluster routing and/or serving activities for a particular alias. It says nothing about the particular services offered by the members of the cluster alias. It's like buying a ticket in order to watch the lion tamer at the circus, but the ticket gets you a seat where you can watch the clowns, trapeze artists, elephants, or anything you want.

If you make an alias called clu_ftp_den that you would like used to access ftp service delivered by a single cluster member, but a client issues the "telnet clu_ftp_den" command, there is nothing built into the cluster alias that says it should only be used for accessing ftp service. The alias name is just a name. If all clients follow the convention implicit in the name (clu_ftp_den is supposed to be used for ftp only), then the scheme will work. But the scheme relies on the convention being followed by all clients.

The following example shows the creation of the clu_ftp_den alias that is "joined" by one member of the cluster. The alias is then used to ping and telnet to the cluster member proving that the alias has no direct control over the service it is used to activate.

The client uses the non-existent alias in an unsuccessful ping attempt. At this point, the client's /etc/hosts file already contains the alias name and IP address, but the alias does not exist in the cluster.

```
# hostname
climach4
```

```
# ping clu_ftp_den
PING clu_ftp_den (192.168.0.171): 56 data bytes

----clu_ftp_den PING Statistics----
3 packets transmitted, 0 packets received, 100% packet loss
```

```
# grep den /etc/hosts
192.168.0.171    clu_ftp_den
```

The cluster member also has the alias name and IP address reflected in the /etc/hosts file.

```
[molari]
# grep den /etc/hosts
192.168.0.171    clu_ftp_den
```

Create the alias on cluster member molari.

```
[molari]
# /usr/sbin/cluamgr -a alias=clu_ftp_den
```

```
[molari]
# /usr/sbin/cluamgr -s clu_ftp_den

Status of Cluster Alias: clu_ftp_den

netmask: 0
aliasid: 2
flags: 5<ENABLED,IP_V4>
connections rcvd from net: 0
connections forwarded: 0
connections rcvd within cluster: 0
data packets received from network: 0
data packets forwarded within cluster: 0
datagrams received from network: 0
datagrams forwarded within cluster: 0
datagrams received within cluster: 0
fragments received from network: 0
fragments forwarded within cluster: 0
fragments received within cluster: 0
Member Attributes:
memberid: 2, selw=1, selp=1, rpri=1 flags=10<ENABLED>
```

The alias has not been joined, and aliasd is not yet aware of the new alias. Let's correct that situation.

```
[molari]
# /usr/sbin/cluamgr -a alias=clu_ftp_den,join
```

```
[molari]
# /usr/sbin/cluamgr -s clu_ftp_den

Status of Cluster Alias: clu_ftp_den

netmask: 0
aliasid: 2
flags: 5<ENABLED,IP_V4>
connections rcvd from net: 0
connections forwarded: 0
connections rcvd within cluster: 0
data packets received from network: 0
data packets forwarded within cluster: 0
datagrams received from network: 0
datagrams forwarded within cluster: 0
datagrams received within cluster: 0
fragments received from network: 0
fragments forwarded within cluster: 0
fragments received within cluster: 0
Member Attributes:
memberid: 2, selw=1, selp=1, rpri=1 flags=11<JOINED,ENABLED>
```

```
[molari]
# /usr/sbin/cluamgr -r start
```

From the client system:

```
# ping clu_ftp_den

PING clu_ftp_den (192.168.0.171): 56 data bytes
64 bytes from 192.168.0.171: icmp_seq=0 ttl=64 time=1 ms
64 bytes from 192.168.0.171: icmp_seq=1 ttl=64 time=0 ms


----clu_ftp_den PING Statistics----
2 packets transmitted, 2 packets received, 0% packet loss
round-trip (ms)  min/avg/max = 0/0/1 ms
```

```
# telnet clu_ftp_den

Trying 192.168.0.171...
Connected to clu_ftp_den.
Escape character is '^]'.


Compaq Tru64 UNIX V5.1A (Rev. 1885) (molari.dec.com) (pts/1)

login: root
…

# exit

Connection closed by foreign host.
```

Cluster member sheridan is not aware of the clu_ftp_den alias.

```
[sheridan]
# /usr/sbin/cluamgr -s all

Status of Cluster Alias: babylon5.dec.com

netmask: 0
aliasid: 1
flags: 7<ENABLED,DEFAULT,IP_V4>
connections rcvd from net: 5
connections forwarded: 5
connections rcvd within cluster: 0
data packets received from network: 1277
data packets forwarded within cluster: 174
datagrams received from network: 28
datagrams forwarded within cluster: 0
datagrams received within cluster: 28
fragments received from network: 0
fragments forwarded within cluster: 0
fragments received within cluster: 0
Member Attributes:
memberid: 1, selw=3, selp=1, rpri=1 flags=11<JOINED,ENABLED>
memberid: 2, selw=3, selp=1, rpri=1 flags=11<JOINED,ENABLED>
```

For another example, suppose you make an alias and have only three members of a four-member cluster actually join the alias. When a client requests telnet/ftp/other network services using the cluster alias, there is nothing inherent in the alias itself that would limit its use to a particular subset of the network services. The cluster alias simply determines a list of cluster members that will potentially respond when the alias (which is after all an IP address) is used by a client node on the network.

Figure 16-7 documents some of the decisions made by the cluster alias subsystem. Note that the last thing that is checked is port (application) availability. The only way a port is unavailable is through manipulation of /etc/inetd.conf or /etc/inted.conf.local or /etc/services or /etc/clua_services.

16.10.6 The inetd.conf.local File

In order to provide a more granular approach to network services offered by the cluster, there is a member-specific version of the /etc/inetd.conf file called /etc/inetd.conf.local. The /etc/inetd.conf.local file provides a mechanism whereby an individual member of the cluster may effectively "turn off" its ability to respond to a request for a particular service. (This can also be thought of in the reverse – that is, you can disable all services cluster wide, but then turn on selected services in appropriate members' /etc/inetd.conf.local file(s).) The member-specific local file is read after the cluster-wide /etc/inetd.conf file. By default, the contents of the /etc/inetd.conf.local file is nothing but comments (see the following example).

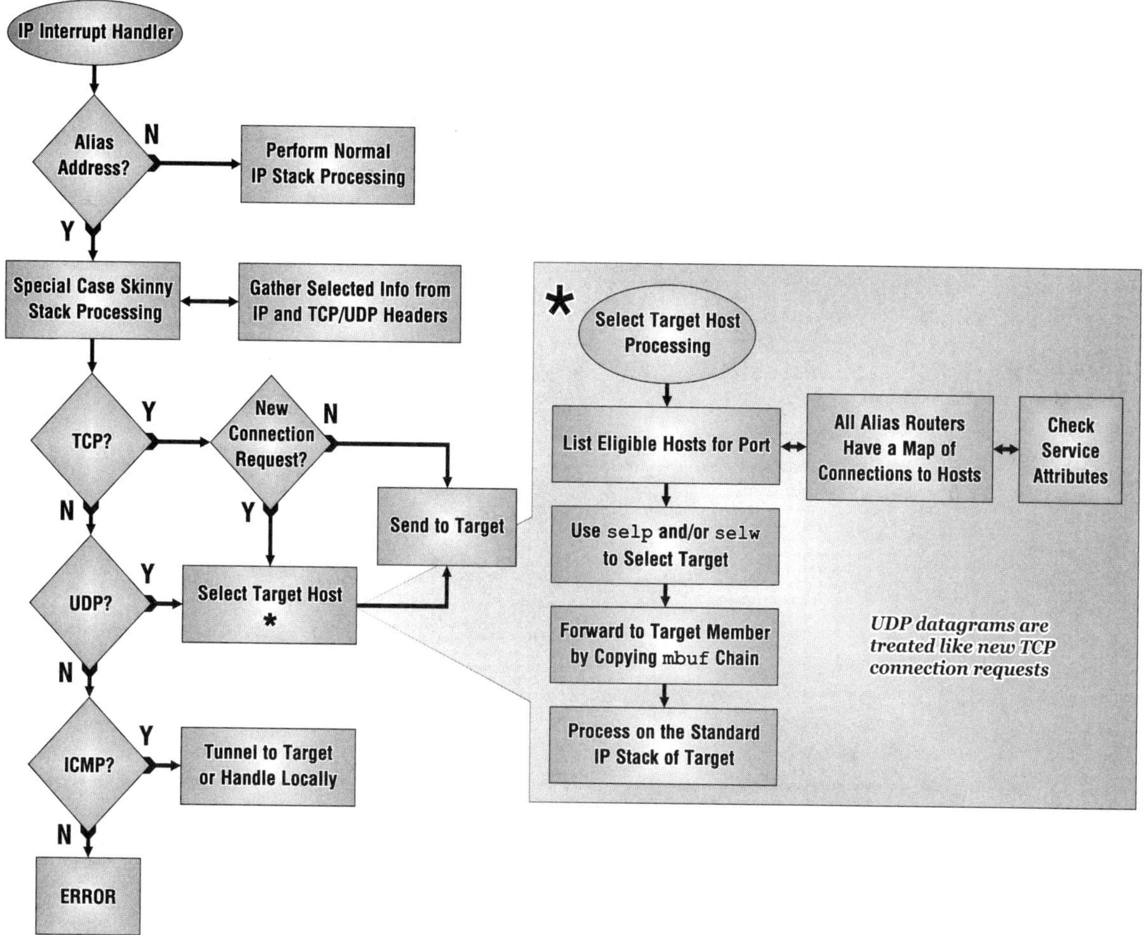

Figure 16-7: Cluster Alias Connection Decision Tree

```
# cat /etc/inetd.conf.local
...
#
##########################################################################
#
# Internet server configuration database
#
# Description:   The inetd.conf.local file is the second file that the inetd
#                daemon reads for information on how to handle Internet service
#                requests.  It contains local services that can only
#                be run on this member, and not other members, in a cluster.
#                It can also be used to disable a service for this member
#                by using 'disable' in the ServerPath field of a service.
#
# Precedence:    Entries in inetd.conf.local will override entries in
#                inetd.conf because it is read after inetd.conf.
```

```
#
# Syntax:  ServiceName  SocketType  ProtocolName  Wait/NoWait  UserName \
#           ServerPath  ServerArgs
#
# ServiceName      name of an Internet service defined in the /etc/services file
# SockettType      type of socket used by the service, either stream or dgram
# ProtocolName     name of an internet protocol defined in the /etc/protocols
#                  file
# Wait/NoWait      determines whether the inetd daemon waits for
#                  a datagram server to release the socket before continuing
#                  to listen at the socket
# UserName         the login that inetd should use to start the server
# ServerPath       full pathname of the server
# ServerArgs       optional command line arguments that inetd should use to
#                  execute the server
```

If we add the following to this file, the cluster member owning this file would be disallowed from satisfying a client request for the `telnet` (or whatever) service.

```
telnet stream tcp nowait root disable telnetd
```

The key syntax in the above line is "`disable,`" which will be read by the `inetd` after it has read the contents of `/etc/inetd.conf`, thus enabling `telnet` service on all cluster members except members that include the "`disable`" syntax in their member-specific `/etc/inetd.conf.local` file.

NOTE:

This feature does not work in V5.0A or V5.1. It does work in V5.1A and beyond, but the V5.1A release notes incorrectly state that it is broken. (The release notes will probably be corrected by the time you read this.) If you are still using V5.0A or V5.1, the way around this problem is to disable the service completely from the cluster-wide `/etc/inetd.conf` file, and then enable it in the appropriate member-specific `/etc/inetd.conf.local` file(s).

The key point to remember is that the cluster alias determines which members can service client requests that use the alias, but aliases have no control over which services are available on particular members. The `/etc/inetd.conf.local` file provides the ability to further determine which services are available from individual cluster members.

This extra level of service granularity does not come for free. There will be extra CLUA effort involved in assuring that the client's request ends up being delivered to a cluster member that is able to fully respond. For instance, suppose the `selp` attribute indicates that `member1` should handle a client request for `telnet` service. Further suppose that the client used a cluster alias to identify the target as the cluster (or a subset of the cluster). The CLUA subsystem would select `member1` to handle the activity based on `member1` having the highest `selp` attribute, but suppose `member1` has "`telnet stream tcp nowait root disable telnetd`" in its

/etc/inetd.conf.local file. This would ultimately cause the CLUA subsystem to select the next best member based on selp.

These decisions will cost extra CPU cycles. However, once the TCP connection has been made, it will not be necessary to repeat the CLUA discovery and routing process. Note that for UDP, there will be a need for some repetition of the CLUA decision-making process due to the connectionless nature of UDP.

The following output depicts a normal round robin use of cluster members as network servers based on default selp and selw values.

From the client system:

```
# rsh clua_den /usr/sbin/cluamgr -s clua_den | grep -E "^Status|^[Mm]ember" | more
Status of Cluster Alias: clua_den

Member Attributes:
memberid: 1, selw=1, selp=1, rpri=1 flags=11<JOINED,ENABLED>
memberid: 2, selw=1, selp=1, rpri=1 flags=31<JOINED,ENABLED,VIRTUAL>
```

```
# rsh clua_den hostname
molari.dec.com

# rsh clua_den hostname
sheridan.dec.com

# rsh clua_den hostname
molari.dec.com

# rsh clua_den hostname
sheridan.dec.com
```

If we change the selp attribute on one of the members (molari), the member with the highest selp value will always be selected to handle the service request from the client as shown in the following example.

```
[molari]
# cluamgr -a alias=clua_den,selp=2

[molari]
# cluamgr -s clua_den | grep -E "^Status|^[Mm]ember" | uniq
Status of Cluster Alias: clua_den
Member Attributes:
memberid: 1, selw=1, selp=1, rpri=1 flags=11<JOINED,ENABLED>
memberid: 2, selw=1, selp=2, rpri=1 flags=31<JOINED,ENABLED,VIRTUAL>
```

On the client, the behavior now favors the member with the highest selp value (molari).

From the client system:

```
# rsh clua_den hostname
molari.dec.com

# rsh clua_den hostname
molari.dec.com

# rsh clua_den hostname
molari.dec.com
```

But if the service is disabled in the member's /etc/inetd.conf.local file, the selp dominance is meaningless as shown by member sheridan getting the request in the following example. The "kill -HUP" command informs the inetd that there has been a change to the configuration file.

```
[molari]
# grep rshd /etc/inetd.conf.local
shell   stream  tcp     nowait  root  disable  /usr/sbin/rshd          rshd
```

```
# kill -HUP 1049621
```

From the client system:

```
# rsh clua_den hostname
sheridan.dec.com

# rsh clua_den hostname
sheridan.dec.com

# rsh clua_den hostname
sheridan.dec.com
```

16.10.7 The clua_services File

Starting to feel like you've got a grip on the relationship between CLUA and various network services? Fasten your seatbelt – there's more. Remember the nice and simple /etc/services file presented earlier in the chapter? The truth is that in a cluster, the CLUA subsystem uses the /etc/clua_services file. This file has almost the same look and feel as the /etc/services file, but it allows the use of several new cluster attributes that can be associated with various services. The cluster attributes are described by the comments at the beginning of the file.

```
# cat /etc/clua_services
...
# Description:  The services file lists the properties of
#               Internet sockets and protocols used with
#               TruCluster Alias.
#
# Syntax: ServiceName PortNumber/ProtocolName [opt_1,...,opt_n] [#comments]
#
# ServiceName           official Internet service name (informational only)
# PortNumber            the socket port number used for the service
# ProtocolName          the transport protocol used for the service
# opt_n         options, one or more of the following:
#
#       < the following options are mutually exclusive >
#
#       in_multi        may act as a server on multiple nodes
#       in_single       may act as a server on one node, with transparent
#                       failover to an instance of the service on another node
#               (default for both TCP and UDP)
#       in_noalias      this port will not receive inbound alias messages
#
#       < the following options may be used with any option above >
#
#       out_alias       if this port is used as a destination, the default
#               cluster alias will be used as the source address
#       in_nolocal      connections to non-alias addresses will not be
#                       honored
#       static  this port may not be assigned as a dynamic port
#               (e.g. as an ephemeral port or through bindresvport)
#               Should be set for any ports above 512 used by an
#               active daemon (e.g. those in inetd.conf)
#
# #comments             text following the comment character (#) is ignored
#
#
echo            7/tcp           in_multi
echo            7/udp           in_multi
discard         9/tcp           in_multi
discard         9/udp           in_multi
daytime         13/tcp          in_multi
daytime         13/udp          in_multi
netstat         15/tcp          in_single
quote           17/udp          in_multi
chargen         19/tcp          in_multi
chargen         19/udp          in_multi
ftp             21/tcp          in_multi
telnet          23/tcp          in_multi,out_alias
...
bootps          67/udp          in_single,out_alias
tftp            69/udp          in_single
finger          79/tcp          in_noalias
...
(lots more)
```

In the following sections, we will be changing entries in the /etc/clua_services file for various services. The changes will not take effect until the cluster alias subsystem is made aware of the changes through the "cluamgr -f" command. Furthermore, if the service is started by inetd, the inetd daemon must be informed of the change as well. This can be achieved by issuing the "kill -HUP" command on the inetd child process. See the following output, which uses the clu_alias script supplied at the Digital Press and BRUDEN websites (see Appendix B for the URL).

```
[sheridan]
# ./clu_alias -f

member1: (molari) "/usr/sbin/cluamgr -f" - accessing via molari-ics0"

member2: (sheridan) "/usr/sbin/cluamgr -f"
```

```
[sheridan]
# kill -HUP $(cat /var/run/inetd.pid)
```

```
[sheridan]
# kill -HUP $(cat /var/cluster/members/member1/run/inetd.pid)
```

The same result can be achieved more succinctly by using the following syntax:

```
# kill -HUP $(cat /var/cluster/members/member[12]/run/inetd.pid)
```

The kill command is not a cluster-wide command prior to V5.1A. If you are using V5.0A or V5.1, you will need to use the rsh command.

```
# rsh hostname 'kill -HUP $(cat /var/run/inetd.pid)'
```

This is shown in the example in section 16.10.7.1.

16.10.7.1 The in_single Attribute

By default, each service has the in_single attribute associated with it. This attribute indicates that incoming traffic destined for the service should only be delivered on one cluster member at a time. It does not mandate that there be only one active instance of the service running. It indicates that if a second active instance of the service needs to be started, it will be started on the same cluster member as the first instance, if the first instance is still functioning. This usually results in the service running on the member with the oldest inetd running.

If the member on which the first instance was running has gone down, the CLUA software will select another eligible cluster member to serve the requests. But at no time will there be more than one active instance running on more than one cluster member (active means accepting incoming communications). There may be inactive instances of the application in existence on other cluster members, but once again, active instances will be executing on one cluster member at a time.

The following example sets up the cluster to be a tftp server. The attribute associated with tftp is in_single, so we should see all tftpd server instances executing on one cluster member.

```
[molari]
# grep tftp /etc/clua_services
tftp            69/udp            in_single
```

Make a directory to be used for tftp experiments.

```
# mkdir /tftp
```

Make a file with a decent size so that a tftp request takes some time to execute.

```
# dd if=/dev/zero of=/tftp/big1 bs=64k count=100k
3494+0 records in
3493+0 records out
```

Allow access to all requesters.

```
# chmod a+rwx /tftp/big1
```

```
# ls -l /tftp/big1
-rwxrwxrwx   1 root     system   228982784 Sep  2 16:29 /tftp/big1
```

Alter the /etc/inetd.conf entry for tftp such that it allows tftp access to files in the /tftp directory. Currently, it supports access to files in /tmp only.

```
# grep tftp /etc/inetd.conf
#tftp   dgram   udp    wait    root    /usr/sbin/tftpd         tftpd /tmp
```

This amusing sed command searches for lines that start with "tftp", replaces the string "/tmp" with the string "/tftp", and places the altered file in /etc/inetd.conf.tmp. Then it is used to replace the original file.

```
# sed -e 's/^#tftp/tftp/' -e 's/tmp/tftp' /etc/inetd.conf > /etc/inetd.conf.temp
```

```
# mv /etc/inetd.conf.temp /etc/inetd.conf
```

```
# grep tftp /etc/inetd.conf
tftp    dgram    udp      wait     root      /usr/sbin/tftpd           tftpd /tftp
```

```
# cat /var/run/inetd.pid
1049621
```

```
# kill -HUP $(cat /var/run/inetd.pid)
# rsh sheridan-ics0 'kill -HUP $(cat /var/run/inetd.pid)'
```

or

```
# kill -HUP $(cat /var/cluster/members/member[12]/run/inetd.pid)
```

On the client, after issuing two `tftp` commands for execution in the background, both of the `tftpd` servers are running on the same cluster member. This would be true no matter how many `tftp` commands were issued. They would all be served by daemons running on the same cluster member because of the `in_single` service attribute. Think of `in_single` as meaning incoming requests are serviced on a single cluster member.

From the client system:

```
# tftp babylon5 -get /tftp/big1 /dev/null &
[1]     29390
```

```
# tftp babylon5 -get /tftp/big1 /dev/null &
[2]     29392
```

From the cluster members:

```
[molari]
# ps -A | grep tftp | grep -v grep
 1049590 ??        S         0:02.01 tftpd /tftp
 1049598 ??        S         0:01.25 tftpd /tftp
```

```
[sheridan]
# ps -A | grep tftp | grep -v grep
<no output>
```

16.10.7.2 The in_multi Attribute

The most common alternative to in_single is in_multi. This attribute indicates that if a service is already running on one cluster member, and a client requests a second instance, the service may run on a different cluster member if warranted. Thus, the service can potentially be running on multiple cluster members simultaneously. The cluster member(s) chosen to run the server will be determined by the highest selp cluster alias attribute. If there are multiple members with the same selp value, the members will be used selw times before switching to the next cluster member with equal selp. Cluster members with lower selp values will not be used unless all members with higher selp are down or otherwise unavailable.

The following example replaces the in_single service attribute with the in_multi service attribute. Thus we can see the tftpd daemons running on both members. The example uses the default cluster alias (babylon5). By default, the selw for the default cluster alias is 3. For this example, it is changed to 1, in order to see the results of the in_multi service attribute more easily.

```
[molari]
# cluamgr -s babylon5 | grep selw

memberid: 1, selw=3, selp=1, rpri=1 flags=11<JOINED,ENABLED>
memberid: 2, selw=3, selp=1, rpri=1 flags=11<JOINED,ENABLED>
```

```
[molari]
# cluamgr -a alias=babylon5,selw=1
```

```
[molari]
# cluamgr -s babylon5 | grep selw

memberid: 1, selw=3, selp=1, rpri=1 flags=11<JOINED,ENABLED>
memberid: 2, selw=1, selp=1, rpri=1 flags=11<JOINED,ENABLED>
```

```
[sheridan]
# cluamgr -a alias=babylon5,selw=1
```

```
[sheridan]
# cluamgr -s babylon5 | grep selw

memberid: 1, selw=1, selp=1, rpri=1 flags=11<JOINED,ENABLED>
memberid: 2, selw=1, selp=1, rpri=1 flags=11<JOINED,ENABLED>
```

Next we change the service to in_multi.

```
[molari]
# grep tftp /etc/clua_services

tftp            69/udp          in_single
```

```
[molari]
# sed 's/single/multi/' /etc/clua_services > /etc/clua_services.temp
```

```
[molari]
# mv /etc/clua_services.temp /etc/clua_services
```

```
[molari]
# grep tftp /etc/clua_services
tftp            69/udp          in_multi
```

On the client, we run a few `tftp` commands and see which cluster members do the serving. It turns out that both cluster members are running an instance of the `tftpd` server. This is allowed because of the `in_multi` service attribute applied to the `tftp` service. Think of `in_multi` as meaning incoming requests can be handled on multiple members.

From the client system:

```
# rsh molari ps -A | grep tftp | grep -v grep

# rsh sheridan ps -A | grep tftp | grep -v grep
```

```
# tftp babylon5 -get /tftp/big1 /dev/null &
[1]     5039
```

```
# tftp babylon5 -get /tftp/big1 /dev/null &
[2]     5040
```

```
# rsh molari ps -A | grep tftp | grep -v grep
1049590 ??      S       0:02.01 tftpd /tftp
```

```
# rsh sheridan ps -A | grep tftp | grep -v grep
525680 ??       S       0:05.13 tftpd /tftp
```

16.10.7.3 The `in_noalias` Attribute

Another alternative attribute is `in_noalias`. Setting this attribute on a service indicates that the service is not available to clients if they request the service using the cluster alias. Note that `in_single`, `in_multi`, and `in_noalias` are mutually exclusive attributes. This means that only one of these three attributes will be applied to a particular service. If you happen to set up a service with incompatible attributes, the "`cluamgr -f`" command will reject the attribute and issue an error message. The following example shows what happens if you make the mistake of trying to apply the incompatible combination of `in_noalias` and `in_multi`.

```
# grep tftp /etc/clua_services
tftp              69/udp            in_noalias,in_multi
```

```
# cluamgr -f

Illegal option supplied
service file entry: tftp                    69/udp          in_noalias,in_multi
```

The following example shows that the result of applying the `in_noalias` service attribute to the `tftp` service prevents the `tftpd` server daemon from running when requested from a client that is using a cluster alias to access the service. The `in_noalias` attribute has no effect if the client requests the service using an actual member name instead of an alias.

From the client system:

```
# rsh molari grep tftp /etc/clua_services
tftp              69/udp            in_noalias
```

No current `tftp` activity on either cluster member.

```
# rsh molari ps -A | grep tftp | grep -v grep

# rsh sheridan ps -A | grep tftp | grep -v grep
```

Try to get some `tftp` activity going using the cluster alias.

```
# tftp babylon5 -get /tftp/big1 /dev/null &
[1]     5118
```

```
# tftp babylon5 -get /tftp/big1 /dev/null &
[2]     5119
```

No luck because of the `in_noalias` service attribute.

```
# rsh molari ps -A | grep tftp | grep -v grep

# rsh sheridan ps -A | grep tftp | grep -v grep
```

Now try to get some `tftp` activity going using the actual cluster member names (not an alias).

```
# tftp molari -get /tftp/big1 /dev/null &
[1]     5139
```

The `tftpd` daemon started on `molari` because we used the actual member name. Our request, therefore, was not affected by the `in_noalias` attribute.

```
# rsh molari ps -A | grep tftp | grep -v grep
1049745 ??        S           0:01.70 tftpd /tftp
```

16.10.7.4 The `in_nolocal` Attribute

As you (hopefully) recall, a cluster alias provides an additional IP address through which access to cluster services may be gained. You may want to restrict access to a service such that the clients must use a cluster alias to get access to the service. Attaching the `in_nolocal` attribute to a service indicates that there should be no access to the service unless the alias is used. This means that use of any of the member's local IP interface addresses (or node names) will not provide access to any service with the `in_nolocal` attribute.

The following example first shows successful client access to a service using a cluster alias, and then shows an unsuccessful attempt due to the `in_nolocal` attribute having been applied to the `tftp` service.

From the client system:

```
# rsh sheridan grep tftp /etc/clua_services
tftp            69/udp          in_multi,in_nolocal
```

Get some `tftp` activity going using the cluster alias. Works like a charm.

```
# tftp babylon5 -get /tftp/big1 /dev/null &
[1]     5182
```

```
# rsh molari ps -A | grep tftp | grep -v grep
1049867 ??        S           0:00.00 tftpd /tftp
```

Try to get some `tftp` activity going using a member name. No luck because of the `in_nolocal` attribute.

```
# tftp sheridan -get /tftp/big1 /dev/null &
[1]     5202
```

```
# rsh sheridan ps -A | grep tftp | grep -v grep
```

16.10.7.5 The `out_alias` Attribute

When communication takes place between nodes in a network, the nodes will identify themselves in the IP header with an IP address that is in use on the sending node. This would normally be the IP address associated with a local interface and not the IP address associated with a cluster alias. In the case where various authentication mechanisms may be in place, these mechanisms may function better if the sending node's (actually a cluster member's) IP address is the IP address associated with a cluster alias rather than a somewhat unpredictable, interface-based IP address that, in some cases, may come from different cluster members at varying points in the communication. It is better to have the IP address identifying the sending node be consistent and predictable. It also buries the fact that the response (or request) is from the cluster. This is achieved by applying the out_alias attribute to a service.

This service attribute is particularly useful for the rlogin, rsh, and rcp services that allow the creation of a trust between accounts on multiple nodes in the network using the /etc/hosts.equiv or ~/.rhosts files. Rather than having to place an entry for each cluster member in these files, the server (non-cluster member) can place one entry in the file. The single entry would contain the cluster alias.

The following example uses the login service as an example of a service using the out_alias attribute. After the attribute is removed, the rlogin activity requires a password. Prior to removing the out_alias attribute, the trust between the systems provided a convenient login with no password required. Needless to say, you probably do not want this trust enabled in a highly secure computing environment.

```
[sheridan]
# grep login /etc/clua_services
login           513/tcp         in_multi,out_alias,static
```

Remove out_alias from the login line and issue a "cluamgr -f" command to inform the CLUA software of the change.

```
[sheridan]
# grep login /etc/clua_services
login           513/tcp         in_multi,static
```

```
# cluamgr -f
```

Login using the cluster alias. Notice no password was requested. This usually indicates that there is a trust enabled between the client and server through the /etc/hosts.equiv file or the ~/.rhosts file. See the reference pages for hosts.equiv or rhosts for more information on these files.

From the client system:

```
# rlogin babylon5
Last login: Tue Sep  3 00:41:34 EDT 2002 from babylon5.dec.com
...
```

```
# hostname
sheridan.dec.com
```

Notice that when the login request is handled by molari, there is a prompt for password information. As you will see below, the information in the /etc/hosts.equiv file and/or the

~/.rhosts file consisted of the cluster alias and not the individual cluster member names. This works fine as long as the out_alias attribute is applied to the login service in the /etc/clua_services file.

From the client system:

```
# rlogin babylon5
Password:
Last login: Tue Sep  3 00:46:19 EDT 2002 from babylon5.dec.com
…
```

```
# hostname
molari.dec.com
```

In order to achieve the convenient trust that was enabled prior to removing the out_alias attribute from the /etc/clua_services file, we will have to enter a line for each individual cluster member in the /.rhosts file.

```
[molari]
# cat /.rhosts
babylon5.dec.com
sheridan-ics0
molari-ics0
climach4
climach3
```

```
[molari]
# cat >> /.rhosts
molari
sheridan
```

```
[molari]
# cat /.rhosts
babylon5.dec.com
sheridan-ics0
molari-ics0
climach4
climach3
molari
sheridan
```

Now the login works without a password required.

From the client system:

```
# rlogin babylon5
Last login: Tue Sep  3 00:48:42 EDT 2002 from sheridan.dec.com
```

You can take the out_alias attribute to mean that outgoing traffic will use the alias IP address to identify the sending node on the network.

16.10.7.6 The **static** Attribute

The final flag, static, makes services associated with port numbers higher than 512 be statically associated with their assigned port numbers. The port numbers will not be assigned as dynamic ports. For example, once port 540 is associated with uucp (started by inetd), that is the only service that will be associated with port 540.

As mentioned earlier, if you make a change to the /etc/clua_services file, you will have to force the file to be re-read through the "cluamgr -f" command (on each member). If the change involves a service started by inetd, the inetd must be restarted (on each member) as well using a "kill -HUP" command.

16.11 CAA vs. CLUA

So far, this chapter has explained what happens when services are started as necessary by the inetd daemon. There are other network services that are started at boot time such as NFS, DNS/BIND, and NIS. These services are usually controlled though the CAA subsystem (See Chapter 24 for CAA examples). CAA is designed to manage applications that run on a single cluster member at a time. Contrast that with the CLUA subsystem, which is tasked with the routing of client connection requests addressed to cluster aliases. Sometimes the concepts of CAA and CLUA seem to blur, but if you remember that CLUA involves cluster alias routing decisions, and CAA involves starting, managing, and failing over applications, the distinctions should become clear.

CAA will be most useful on applications with the in_single CLUA attribute. CAA will be responsible for starting applications under its control, failing over applications when necessary, and monitoring the availability of any resources necessary for the CAA controlled application to run. See Chapters 23 and 24 for more information on CAA.

16.12 NFS and Aliases

NFS is an example of a network service that is started at boot time. As such, it is not under the control of the inetd daemon. Typical use of NFS in a cluster is as a highly available NFS server. Recall that NFS is a software mechanism for allowing file systems (or directories) to be accessible to client nodes in the network through remote mounting. Should we worry about which member of the cluster actually functions as the NFS server?

Under normal circumstances, where the storage to be served is on a bus shared by all cluster members, it makes little difference which member serves the data. But imagine the overhead involved with a member of the cluster having been chosen to do the NFS serving that does not have direct access to the storage to be served. This would require excess traffic over the CI in order to access the CFS server for the data to be served out over NFS. Yikes! What a waste of system resources.

16.12.1 The `exports.aliases` File

In this case, a solution would be to define a cluster alias that includes the member(s) with direct access to the storage, and then have the clients use that cluster alias when doing their remote mounts. The problem is that the `mountd` will not work unless it is requested using the default cluster alias – or if the alias is reflected in the `/etc/exports.aliases` file (new for V5.1A). This simple file consists of a list of cluster aliases that may be used by clients in their remote mount requests. This file does not associate aliases with particular file systems. See Chapter 20, or the contents of the `/etc/exports.aliases` file, or the `exports.aliases(4)` reference page for more information.

16.13 CLUA Components

Throughout this chapter we have discussed many facets of CLUA. What seems to be a fairly straightforward concept turns out to present many "what ifs." The result is a cluster subsystem that consists of many components including processes (`aliasd` and `aliasd_niff`), files (`/etc/clu_alias.config`, `/sbin/init.d/clu_alias`, `/etc/gated.conf`, `/etc/gated.conf.member`*n*, `/etc/clua_services`, `/etc/exports.aliases`), a utility (`cluamgr`), an API (`clua_isalias(3)` and others – not discussed in this book), a kernel subsystem (`clua`), and various other kernel components (also not discussed in this book – see the *TruCluster* Cluster Technical Overview for more information on kernel activities to support CLUA).

16.14 References

- *TruCluster* Server Cluster Administration Guide.
- *TruCluster* Server Cluster Technical Overview.
- HP *TruCluster* Server Internals Course Materials.
- HP *TruCluster* Server Configuration and Management Course Materials
- *Tru64* UNIX Reference Pages (noted within the text).

17

The Connection Manager

"We must all hang together, or assuredly we shall all hang separately."

– Benjamin Franklin

In the previous sixteen chapters, we have discussed what a cluster is; why you would want to have a cluster as your computing platform; how to plan, install, and configure a cluster; and some of the components that make a cluster work. What we haven't touched on yet is how a cluster is formed and how individual systems become members.

A cluster is formed when there are a sufficient number of voting members to reach a quorum. Quorum is defined as a simple majority. A quorum must be present in order for a cluster to be formed. Similarly, a quorum must be present for an existing cluster to continue performing useful work, or when a member shuts down or leaves the cluster.

The first step in determining a quorum is calculating the cluster's expected votes. The cluster's expected votes value is the maximum number of votes that would be available if every voting member were up and the quorum disk[1], if configured with a vote, were available. In a cluster that consists of five members, the cluster's expected votes value would be equal to five, assuming that each member has one vote. As of this writing, members can have one vote or zero votes.

Once a cluster's expected votes value is determined, the number of votes required for quorum is calculated. If the cluster has enough votes to meet or exceed the quorum vote value, the cluster is formed.

The kernel subsystem responsible for determining whether or not a cluster has reached quorum is the Connection Manager (CNX).

In this chapter, we will cover the Connection Manager cluster component, voting and quorum strategies, and the quorum disk. Additionally, we will cover what occurs as a system boots, which subsystems are configured, the boot messages that you can expect to see, how a cluster is formed, and how a system becomes a member of an existing cluster.

---

[1] We will cover the quorum disk in more detail in sections 17.2.4 and 17.8.3.

17.1 What is the Connection Manager?

The simple answer is that the Connection Manager dynamically collects data reflecting the connectivity and communications between cluster members and uses this data to make cluster membership decisions. In order for a cluster to form (or for a node to join an established cluster), all members must be able to fully communicate with one another.

The more complex answer is that the Connection Manager is a distributed, multi-threaded kernel component that performs the following tasks:

- Forms a cluster.
- Maintains the cluster membership list and insures that each active member has the same list.
- Adds members to the cluster.
- Removes members from the cluster.
- Detects and handles member failures.
- Notifies registered kernel subsystems when CNX events occur.
- Reconfigures the cluster when members join or leave the cluster (also known as a cluster state transition).
- Detects a potential cluster partition and ensures that at most one side of that partition remains active as the cluster.

17.2 The CNX Architecture

The CNX Architecture is composed of several components:

- The CNX kernel threads.
- The Cluster System Block (CSB).
- The Quorum Disk (which includes a `cnx` partition).
- A `cnx` partition on each member's boot disk.
- The `clubase` and `cnx` subsystems.
- The `sysconfigtab` and `sysconfigtab.cluster` files where the `clubase` attribute values are stored.

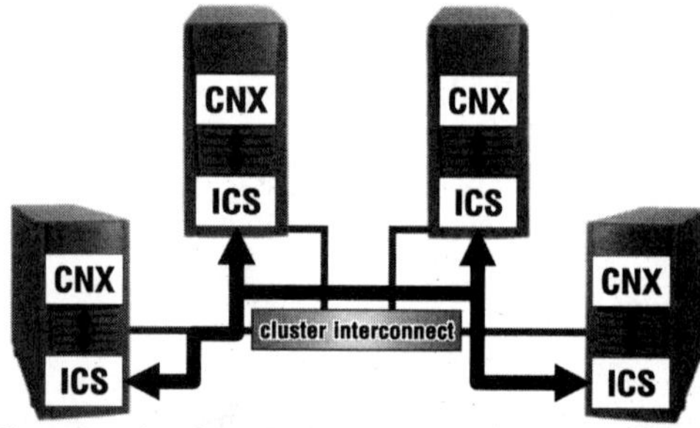

Figure 17-1: CNX - ICS Communication

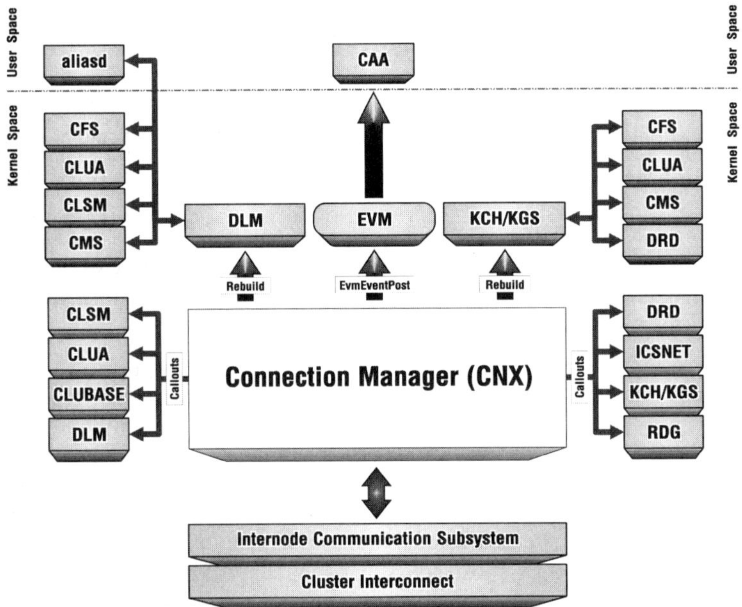

Figure 17-2: CNX Cluster Subsystem Communication

We will begin this section with an overview of how the CNX communication takes place in a cluster.

17.2.1 CNX Communication

Every system configured to be a cluster member has a CNX that communicates (or attempts to communicate) to the CNX of any other systems connected to the cluster interconnect. The CNX uses the Internode Communication Subsystem (ICS)[2] as the communications interface to other members' CNX as shown in Figure 17-1.

In addition to communicating to the CNX on other systems, the CNX is also responsible for communicating to other cluster subsystems. The CNX uses three primary methods:

- Posting events using the Event Manager (EVM).
- Dispatching callouts to those cluster subsystems that registered routines with the CNX.
- Rebuilding the Distributed Lock Manager (DLM)[2] and Kernel Group Services (KGS)[3].

Figure 17-2 illustrates the communication flow from the CNX to the various cluster subsystems.

---

[2] See Chapter 18 for a discussion on ICS, DLM, and KCH/KGS.

[3] Also known as the Kernel Cat Herder (KCH); see Chapter 18 for more details.

The CNX notifies the Cluster Application Availability (CAA) daemon via EVM events. The CAA daemon (`caad(8)`) subscribes to four specific CNX events:

- Member has joined the cluster `sys.unix.clu.cnx.member.join`
- Member has left the cluster `sys.unix.clu.cnx.member.leave`
- Quorum has been gained `sys.unix.clu.cnx.quorum.gain`
- Quorum has been lost `sys.unix.clu.cnx.quorum.loss`

The CNX is also event driven and transaction oriented. In fact, the purpose of the main CNX thread is to handle CNX-related events that will often result in a three-phase transaction to complete the necessary action cluster-wide.

A CNX transaction is needed to form the cluster; to allow a member to join the cluster; to reconfigure the cluster; and to adjust the cluster's expected votes, a member's vote value, or quorum disk's vote value.

Additionally, certain events will occur that will cause the CNX to dispatch callouts to those cluster subsystems that have registered routines with the CNX when the subsystems were configured. Although we will not detail the specific events that the CNX handles, Table 17-1 lists the events that cause the CNX to dispatch callouts to those subsystems that have registered.

CNX Callout Events

Callout Event	Description	Subsystems
Add Node	This callout is triggered when the CNX handles a "Node Up" event. The "Node Up" event is set when a node becomes a member.	drd, icsnet
Remove Node	This callout is triggered when the "Grim Reaper" thread removes a member from the cluster.	drd, icsnet, rdg
Quorum Gain	This callout is triggered when enough votes are added to the cluster to gain quorum.	clua, clubase, dlm, drd, kch
Quorum Loss	This callout is triggered when enough votes are removed from the cluster to lose quorum.	clua, dlm, drd, kch
Cluster Reconfiguration Pending	This callout is triggered when a member is removed from the cluster or if the cluster detects a partition or a communication error.	clsm, dlm, drd, kch
Start Cluster Rebuild	This callout is triggered when a cluster membership change has occurred.	clsm, drd
Quorum Disk Loss	This callout is triggered when the quorum disk becomes unavailable due to an error.	none as of this writing
Quorum Disk Regain	This callout is triggered once the cluster can once again read from the quorum disk following a quorum disk loss.	none as of this writing

Table 17-1: CNX Callout Events

When a member is added to, or removed from, the cluster, the CNX must inform the DLM and KGS. This is known as a cluster rebuild.

Both the DLM and KGS are used to synchronize resources in a cluster so it is important that these components are made aware of any changes in cluster membership.

Figure 17-3 summarizes the CNX interaction with the other cluster subsystems during a cluster rebuild as well as the callout events.

We have intentionally not provided too much detail here because most of the inner workings of the CNX will not be visible. We did, however, want to show the importance of the CNX in keeping the cluster functioning. Since the CNX is in charge of which systems can or cannot become cluster members, it must also communicate to the various cluster subsystems so that resources and data can stay synchronized and corruption can be prevented.

As an example, consider the Device Request Dispatcher (DRD). The DRD makes all storage devices anywhere in a cluster available to all members of the cluster. When a "Cluster Reconfiguration Pending" callout event occurs, the CNX is about to remove one or more members from the cluster. In order to prevent those systems that will no longer be part of the cluster from performing any further I/O to cluster storage devices, the DRD must erect I/O barriers. It is the responsibility of the CNX to inform the DRD when to put I/O barriers in place. For more information on DRD and I/O barriers, see Chapter 15.

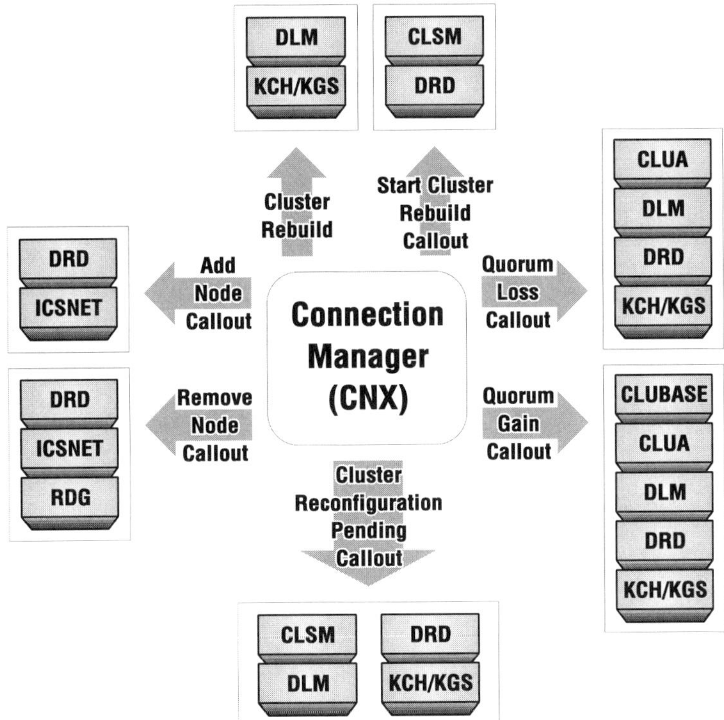

Figure 17-3: CNX Rebuild and Callouts

17.2.2 CNX Threads

As stated earlier, the CNX is multi-threaded; the exact number of threads can vary depending on the cluster's state and whether or not a quorum disk is configured. For example, here is a script that we wrote that displays the CNX threads on one of the members of our cluster.

```
# ./cnxthreads -p

                                WCHAN
                                -------
[ 1] "wait for rbld"          - e616e8
[ 2] "wait for rbld"          - e61728
[ 3] "csb event thread"       - csb eve
[ 4] "wait for csb"           - e60fe0
[ 5] "wait for csb"           - e60ff8
[ 6] "wait for csb"           - e61010
[ 7] "wait for csb"           - e61028
[ 8] "wait for csb"           - e61040
[ 9] "wait for csb"           - e61058
[10] "wait for csb"           - e61070
[11] "cnx grim reaper"        - cnx gri
[12] "qdisk tick delay"       - qdisk t

USER     %CPU PRI SCNT WCHAN         USER       SYSTEM COMMAND            PID
root      0.0  38    0 *          0:00.00     1:28.27 [kernel idle]   1048576
          0.0  38    0 e616e8     0:00.00     0:00.00
          0.0  38    0 e61728     0:00.00     0:00.00
          0.0  38    0 csb eve    0:00.00     0:00.00
          0.0  38    0 e60fe0     0:00.00     0:00.00
          0.0  38    0 e60ff8     0:00.00     0:00.00
          0.0  38    0 e61010     0:00.00     0:00.00
          0.0  38    0 e61028     0:00.00     0:00.00
          0.0  38    0 e61040     0:00.00     0:00.00
          0.0  38    0 e61058     0:00.00     0:00.00
          0.0  38    0 e61070     0:00.00     0:00.00
          0.0  38    0 cnx gri    0:00.00     0:00.00
          0.0  38    0 qdisk t    0:00.00     0:01.66
```

On our member we have twelve threads. Our script shows the actual "wait message" for the thread but also shows what the wait channel (`WCHAN`) field would be if you used the `ps(8)` command. The "`-p`" option runs a "`ps -emo THREAD,command,pid`" command and displays the CNX threads. Another interesting point to note is that these threads are part of the `[kernel idle]` task.

Table 17-2 shows the threads that make up the CNX and their various tasks.

17.2.3 The Cluster System Block (CSB)

As you might have noticed by looking at the names of some of the threads in the previous section, the CNX seems to be interested in something known as the CSB. The CSB (or cluster system block) is actually a data structure that contains information about a cluster member. In fact every member

Connection Manager Threads			
Thread	# of threads	Wait Message	Comments
CNX Transaction Thread	1	`csb event thread`	This is the main CNX thread. It sleeps until there is some CNX event that needs to be handled. When a CNX event is queued, this thread wakes up, handles the event, and then goes back to sleep until more events need attention.
Pinger Thread	1	`cnx pinger` `cnx pinger thread`	This thread broadcasts the node's information on the ICS boot channel so that other nodes will know about this node. If there is an existing cluster then communication channels are established with this node. Once the node becomes a cluster member the pinger thread kills itself.
Grim Reaper Thread	1	`cnx grim reaper`	The grim reaper sleeps until a member needs to be removed from the cluster. This thread performs the necessary clean up tasks to remove a member from the cluster.
Qdisk Thread	1	`qdisk tick delay`	If a quorum disk is configured, this thread reads from the disk and writes to the disk at a set interval (currently every 5 seconds).
Rebuild Manager Thread	2	`1st rbld` `wait for rbld`	These threads are used to rebuild the DLM and KCH/KGS when a CNX event occurs that requires a cluster rebuild. They sleep until a rebuild is requested.
Remote Communications Thread	7	`wait for csb` `remote csb event thread`	These threads wait for remote nodes to send them a CSB. Once the CSB is sent, this thread is awakened and sets up an ICS communication channel to the remote node. Also handles certain CNX events.

Table 17-2: CNX Threads

has a CSB for itself and a CSB for each and every other node that the member has received an announcement from and has been able to establish a communication channel with. So the CNX is not exactly driven by the CSB but actually handles events stored in the CSB.

A member uses its list of CSBs to keep track of the state of the nodes as well as other information including the node's name, member ID, votes, expected votes, quorum disk configuration, incarnation, cluster system identification number (`csid`), connectivity topology, etc. This information is vital to determining whether or not a node can be a cluster member.

17.2.3.1 The Incarnation Number

The incarnation number (or `incarn`) is a pseudo-random number that uniquely identifies the current existing cluster and member instances. The `incarn` can be retrieved using the `clu_get_info(8)` command with the "`-full`" option.

```
# clu_get_info -full | grep incarn
    Cluster incarnation = 0x923f8
```

17.2.3.2 The Cluster System Identification Number (csid)

Every member has a `csid` to identify the cluster member to the cluster. The `csid` is composed of an index number into a `csid` vector (essentially it indicates the order that the member joined the cluster) and the number of times that the member has joined the cluster since it was formed. For example a `csid` of `0x30001` would indicate that the first member to join the cluster has (re)joined the cluster three times since it was formed.

You can see the `csid` by using the `clu_get_info` command with the "`-full`" or "`-raw`" options. It is also the `node_csid` attribute in the `cnx` subsystem.

Here's an example from a two-member cluster where the `memberid` and `csid` vector index match.

```
# clu_get_info -raw | awk '/^M/ { FS=":" ; print "memberid: "$2", csid: "$12 }'
memberid: 1, csid: 0x30001
memberid: 2, csid: 0x10002
```

Here's an example from an eight-member cluster where the `memberid` and `csid` vector index do not match.

```
# clu_get_info -raw | awk '/^M/ { FS=":" ; print "memberid: "$2", csid: "$12 }'
memberid: 1, csid: 0x10003
memberid: 2, csid: 0x20008
memberid: 3, csid: 0x10002
memberid: 4, csid: 0x10006
memberid: 5, csid: 0x10007
memberid: 6, csid: 0x20005
memberid: 7, csid: 0x10001
memberid: 8, csid: 0x20004
```

17.2.4 The Quorum Disk

The quorum disk can be thought of as a virtual cluster member in that it can add an additional vote to a cluster with an even number of members to increase the cluster's availability. In order for a disk to be used as a quorum disk, the following conditions must be met:

- The disk must be unused because the quorum disk is dedicated for use by the CNX.
- It is highly recommended that the disk be on a shared bus that is connected to all voting cluster members.
- There can be only one quorum disk in a cluster.

The quorum disk can be used to contribute one vote or zero votes to a cluster.

We will cover the quorum disk in greater detail in section 17.8.3.

17.2.5 The `cnx` Partition

The quorum disk contains a `cnx` partition, 1 MB (2048 sectors) in size, located on the "`h`" partition. In fact, this is the only partition that can be used on the entire disk! Due to the small amount of space that is used on the disk, we recommend using the smallest disk possible.

Every member's boot disk also has a `cnx` partition that is located on the "`h`" partition.

Although both types of disks contain `cnx` partitions, they use different portions of the partition (as we will learn in section 17.8.5.1).

The following series of Korn shell commands displays the `cnx` partition information from the disk label of our cluster's disks.

```
# for i in dsk2 dsk3 dsk4
> do
>   echo ; echo "[${i}] \c"
>   disklabel -r ${i} | \
>     awk '/label:/ { printf ("%11s - ",$2) } \
>          / h:/ { printf ("partition: h, type: %s, size: %s sectors\n",$4,$2) }'
> done

[dsk2] clu_member1 - partition: h, type: cnx, size: 2048 sectors

[dsk3] clu_member2 - partition: h, type: cnx, size: 2048 sectors

[dsk4]      Quorum - partition: h, type: cnx, size: 2048 sectors
```

In section 17.8.5 we will discuss how to manage the `cnx` partition.

17.2.6 The `clubase` Subsystem

The configuration information that is required to form (or join) a cluster is stored in the Cluster Base (clubase) subsystem in the member-specific sysconfigtab file located in the /cluster/members/{memb}/boot_partition/etc directory. You can see the attributes and values for the clubase subsystem contained in a member's sysconfigtab file by using the sysconfigdb(8) command with "-l" option.

```
# sysconfigdb -l clubase

clubase:
        cluster_qdisk_major = 19
        cluster_qdisk_minor = 272
        cluster_qdisk_votes = 1
        cluster_expected_votes = 3
        cluster_node_votes = 1
        cluster_name = babylon5
        cluster_node_name = molari
        cluster_node_inter_name = molari-ics0
        cluster_interconnect = mct
        cluster_seqdisk_major = 19
        cluster_seqdisk_minor = 80
```

The cluster_expected_votes attribute is also stored in the cluster-wide sysconfigtab.cluster file located in the /etc directory. The subsystem attributes are described in Table 17-3.

```
# sysconfigdb -t /etc/sysconfigtab.cluster -l clubase

clubase:
        cluster_expected_votes = 3
```

The sysconfigtab.cluster file is used to keep subsystem attribute values that should be identical in every member's sysconfigtab file in synch upon reboot. When a member reaches run level 3, the clu_min script is called to propagate entries in the sysconfigtab.cluster file to the member's sysconfigtab file.

For more information on the clubase subsystem, see the sys_attrs_clubase(4) reference page.

17.3 Quorum and Voting

Quorum is a simple majority. A cluster will not form without quorum. If a cluster is running and loses too many votes, then quorum is lost, and the cluster will suspend.

When a cluster is suspended, all access to cluster managed storage, all process activity, and any network operations are suspended. The only exception is that the CNX and DRD subsystems continue to function so that they can:

clubase subsystem attributes	
cluster_expected_votes	This attribute contains the maximum number of votes that the cluster expects to have if every voting member is up. Note that this value also includes the vote for the quorum disk if it is configured and is assigned a vote. The **cluster_expected_votes** attribute value should be the same on **all** cluster members.
cluster_interconnect	This attribute contains the cluster interconnect type. As of this writing, this value can be: ▪ **mct** – Memory Channel Transport ▪ **tcp** – LAN Interconnect
cluster_name	The **cluster_name** attribute contains the name of the cluster. All members must have the same **cluster_name**. The attribute is used as the name of the Default Cluster Alias as well. For more information on cluster aliasing, see Chapter 16.
cluster_node_inter_name	This attribute contains the node name for the virtual cluster interconnect (**ics0**).
cluster_node_name	This attribute contains the node name of the cluster member.
cluster_node_votes	This attribute contains the number of votes this member will contribute toward quorum. As of this writing, this value can be 0 or 1.
cluster_qdisk_major, **cluster_qdisk_minor**	This is the major and minor number of the quorum disk's "**h**" partition. This partition is the **cnx** partition and is discussed in section 17.4.
cluster_qdisk_votes	This attribute contains the number of votes that the quorum disk will contribute toward quorum. As of this writing this value can be 0 or 1.
cluster_seqdisk_major, **cluster_seqdisk_minor**	This is the major and minor number of the member boot disk's "**h**" partition. This partition is the **cnx** partition and is discussed in section 17.4.

Table 17-3: The clubase subsystem attributes

- Quiesce the cluster.
- Drain any outstanding I/O in process.
- Continue to access the cnx partition on the cluster member and quorum disks.
- Attempt to reform the cluster from surviving members.

Note: the cluster may continue to function for a period of time after quorum is lost; however, all application I/O directed at cluster storage will be suspended.

The cluster will appear hung, but it's not hung. If you check the console, you will see output similar to the following:

```
CNX MGR: quorum lost, suspending cluster operations.
```

The Connection Manager continues to function, attempting to accumulate enough votes to regain quorum so that the cluster can resume operation.

```
CNX MGR: quorum (re)gained, (re)starting cluster operations.
```

Every system that is added to the cluster can be a voting member or a non-voting member. Furthermore, a quorum disk[4] can be added to the cluster to increase availability and act as a tiebreaker in the event of a cluster partition. Currently, a system can have one vote or zero votes (the same is true for the quorum disk).

Every member (or potential member) determines what quorum is based on the "Quorum Algorithm."

17.3.1 The Quorum Algorithm

The CNX calculates the number of votes needed for quorum based on the number of votes it expects to see in the cluster if all voting members (and the quorum disk if configured and assigned a vote) are up.

The first thing that the CNX needs to do is determine the maximum number of booting nodes that are fully connected (meaning that each node can communicate with every other node).

Secondly, the CNX will determine the Cluster's Expected Votes (CEV) from the set of "fully connected" nodes.

The CEV is defined as the maximum number of votes from the following:

- The previous CEV.

  The previous CEV only applies if the cluster is going through a membership transition and not when the cluster is first forming (as the CEV from a previous cluster incarnation is not stored).

---

[4] For more information on the quorum disk, see section 17.8.3.

- The highest member-specific `cluster_expected_votes` attribute value.

  This is the `clubase:cluster_expected_votes` attributes from each member's `sysconfigtab` file in the `/.local../boot_partition/etc` directory.

  Normally this value should be the same for all members.

- The sum of node votes (`cluster_node_votes`) and quorum disk votes (`cluster_qdisk_votes`).

  The `cluster_node_votes` and `cluster_qdisk_votes` are located in the clubase subsystem. The specific values are defined in each member's `sysconfigtab` file in the `/.local../boot_partition/etc` directory.

Finally, the CNX will determine the number of votes required to reach quorum.

The quorum votes (QV) value is calculated as follows:

`QV = round_down ((CEV + 2)/2)`

Here's another way of looking at this, especially if you're a programmer:

`QV = (CEV >> 1) + 1`

For example, in a three-member cluster where each member has one vote, every member should have a `cluster_expected_votes` value of 3.

If the `CEV` is `3`:

```
QV = (3 + 2) / 2
QV = 5 / 2
QV = 2.5
QV = 2
```

So in order to form a cluster, at least two systems must be booted.

Here's a little one line Perl script to calculate quorum.

`# perl -e 'printf("%d\n", (CEV >> 1) + 1);'`

```
# perl -e 'printf("%d\n", (3 >> 1) + 1);'
2
```

Let's consider that the cluster is fully up, and we add a fourth member using the clu_add_member(8) command. The "BEFORE" values are what the CNX will be using prior to the clu_add_member command. The "AFTER" values are what the CNX will be using after the clu_add_member command but before booting the newly added member. And the "BOOT" values are what the CNX will use after the new member has been booted and attempts to join the cluster.

	BEFORE	AFTER	BOOT
CEV	3	3	4
QV	2	2	3
Current Votes	3	3	4
Member-Specific cluster_expected_votes	3	4	4

The cluster's previous expected votes value was 3. However, when the new member is added, each member's expected votes value will be modified in their sysconfigtab file to 4. Since 3 members are up, the current number of votes is 3.

Once the new member is booted, the CEV will be recalculated to 4, which would increase the QV to 3.

If QV = 3, then 3 out of 4 cluster members would have to be booted in order for a cluster to form. At this point adding a quorum disk to the cluster would increase the cluster's availability.

	BEFORE	AFTER
CEV	4	5
QV	**3**	**3**
Current Votes	4	5
Member-Specific cluster_expected_votes	4	5

By adding the quorum disk, the QV value does not change, but the number of potential votes has increased by 1 thus decreasing the number of members required to reach quorum.

Table 17-4 shows the number of votes required to form a cluster as well as recommendations on when to configure in a quorum disk.

17.4 Cluster Partition

When communication failures occur, it is the connection manager's job to make sure that only one cluster is formed (or maintained). If a cluster were to "partition" into more than one active cluster, nasty things like data corruption could occur. This, of course, would be a very bad thing!

To prevent this situation from occurring, the connection manager will detect the problem and reconfigure the cluster to remove any member without complete communications connectivity to the other cluster members. Any member that cannot fully communicate with the other cluster members will be prevented from joining the cluster, and, in many cases, it will panic.

Votes Required For Quorum QV = (CEV >> 1) + 1					
# of Members with 1 Vote	Quorum Disk with 1 Vote	Expected Votes (CEV)	Votes Required for Quorum (QV)	% of Voting Members Required for Quorum	Recommendation
2	×	2	2	100%	Bad Idea
2	✓	3	2	67%	Highly Recommended
3	×	3	2	67%	Highly Recommended
3	✓	4	3	75%	Bad Idea
4	×	4	3	75%	Bad Idea
4	✓	5	3	60%	Highly Recommended
5	×	5	3	60%	Highly Recommended
5	✓	6	4	67%	Bad Idea
6	×	6	4	67%	Okay
6	✓	7	4	57%	Recommended
7	×	7	4	57%	Highly Recommended
7	✓	8	5	63%	Bad Idea
8	×	8	5	63%	Okay
8	✓	9	5	56%	Recommended

Table 17-4: Votes Required for Quorum

Below are the possible panic strings that could be seen as a result of a cluster partition:

- `"CNX MGR: partition action"`
- `"CNX MGR: this node removed from cluster"`
- `"CNX MGR: phase1 form: cluster already formed"`
- `"CNX MGR: restart requested to resynchronize with cluster with quorum"`
- `"CNX MGR: rcnx_status: restart requested to resynchronize with cluster with quorum"`
- `"CNX QDISK: configuration error. Qdisk in use by cluster of different name."`
- `"CNX QDISK: configuration error. Qdisk written by cluster of different name."`
- `"CNX QDISK: Yielding to foreign owner without quorum."`
- `"CNX QDISK: Yielding to foreign owner with provisional quorum."`
- `"CNX QDISK: Yielding to foreign owner with quorum."`

An example of a situation where a cluster partition might occur would be in the case where there was a break in the cable for the CI of a two-member cluster with a quorum disk configured as shown in Figure 17-4.

Since each member would be unable to communicate with the other via the CI, and since they both have enough votes to attain quorum, a partition is possible. In other words, since `member1` has a CEV value of 3, that would mean 2 votes are needed to attain quorum. Well, `member1` has 2 votes

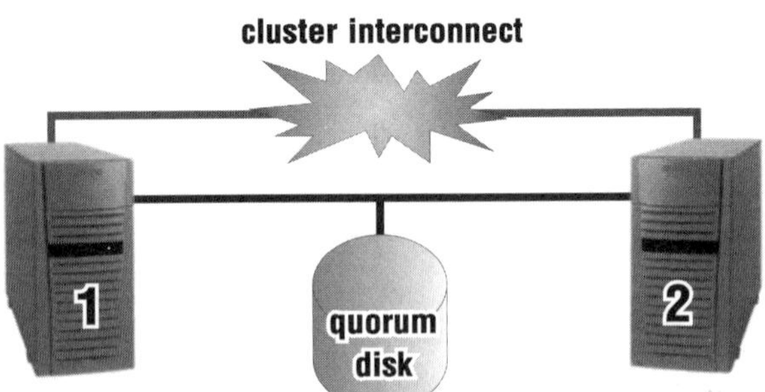

Figure 17-4: Cluster Partition

(1 for itself and 1 because it can claim the quorum disk). The same situation holds true for member2. So if both members could come up with enough votes to reach quorum, we have a problem. Fortunately, the CNX is ready for this type of scenario, and as a result one member will panic, probably with one of the last two panic strings listed above. The member that has claimed the quorum disk will continue to function.

17.5 The Boot Sequence

To see how a cluster is formed (or for that matter how a node becomes a member), let's see what happens when you boot a node in a cluster.

When the "boot" command is issued from the console of a node that's part of a cluster configuration that node will boot off of its member boot disk. Contained on the boot disk at logical block number (LBN) zero is the boot block.

```
CPU 0 booting

(boot dkb100.1.0.3.2 -flags A)
block 0 of dkb100.1.0.3.2 is a valid boot block
```

17.5.1 From the Boot Block to the Kernel

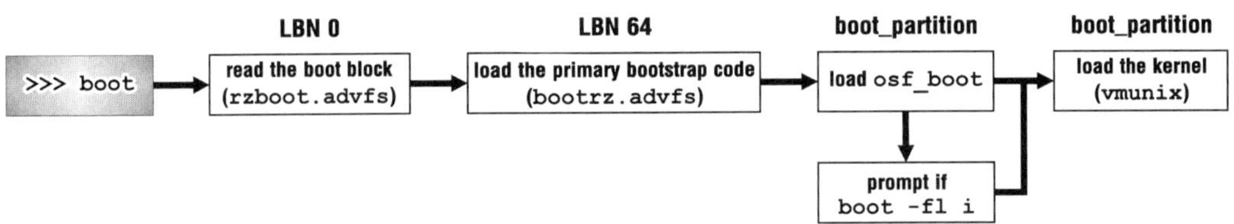

The boot block code points to the primary bootstrap code at LBN 64.

```
reading 19 blocks from dkb100.1.0.3.2
bootstrap code read in
Building FRU table
base = 200000, image_start = 0, image_bytes = 2600
initializing HWRPB at 2000
initializing page table at 1f2000
initializing machine state
setting affinity to the primary CPU
jumping to bootstrap code
```

The primary bootstrap code loads the osf_boot program, located on the boot_partition (partition "a") of the boot disk. It is the osf_boot program that handles prompting for the kernel and subsystem attributes during an interactive boot (i.e., boot -fl i). The osf_boot program is also responsible for loading the kernel.

```
UNIX boot - Wednesday August 01, 2001

Loading vmunix ...
Loading at 0xfffffc0000230000

Sizes:
text =  8624320
data =  1778320
bss  =  3908272
Starting at 0xfffffc0000242360
```

Once the kernel is loaded and starts to execute, many things happen prior to single-user mode including cluster formation! So, please turn your hymnals to "The Ballad of V. M. Unix" and follow along. Please feel free to shout out or sing along if the muse strikes you.

17.5.2 Loading the Kernel to Subsystem Configuration

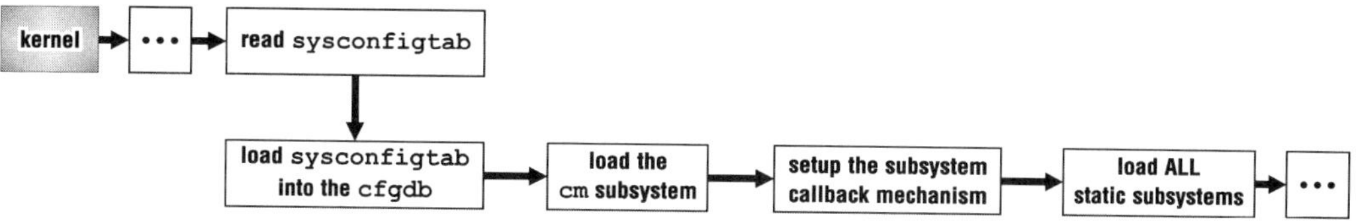

While we don't intend to walk through every step in the kernel boot sequence, we want to point out a few steps to help in understanding how a cluster is formed.

One of the kernel's earliest tasks is to read the sysconfigtab file. This is the reason why the sysconfigtab file is located in the etc directory on the boot_partition. Once the sysconfigtab file is read, the kernel loads the attributes into the configuration management database (cfgdb), loads the Configuration Manager (cm) subsystem, and sets up the subsystem callback mechanism. After the callback mechanism is loaded, the kernel configures all the static kernel subsystems.

If you are curious about how the kernel knows which subsystems to configure, take a look at the conf.c file in any member's /sys/*HOSTNAME* directory.

```
# cd /usr/sys/MOLARI ; grep -p static_subsys_list conf.c \
> | grep CFG_STATE_LOADED | cut -d, -f2 | cut -d\" -f2 | tee /tmp/conf_c

...
rm
rmvm
rdg
clubase
kevm_clu
drd
cnx
kch
dlm
mcs
clua
ics_hl
ics_ll_tcp
ics_ll_mct
cfs
cms
token
icsnet
clsm
...
```

The conf.c file is created by the config(8) program which is run by the doconfig(8) script.

Of course, once a system is up and running it is usually much more straightforward to query the configuration manager using the sysconfig program to see which subsystems are statically loaded.

```
# sysconfig -m | grep static | cut -d: -f1 | tee /tmp/sysconfig
```

Using the diff(1) command on the two files we created in the previous two examples, we can see that there are no differences.

```
# diff /tmp/conf_c /tmp/sysconfig
<no output>
```

There are approximately 97 static subsystems loaded into the kernel. Of course this number can vary depending on your configuration and the options chosen.

```
# wc -l /tmp/sysconfig /tmp/conf_c
        97 /tmp/sysconfig
        97 /tmp/conf_c
       194 total
```

17.5.3 Interactive Boot Subsystem Attribute Overrides

Getting back to our boot discussion…

```
Loading vmunix symbol table ... [2188944 bytes]
Alpha boot: available memory from 0x10c8000 to 0xff3e000
```

Between "`Loading vmunix symbol table ... [2188944 bytes]`" and the very next line ("`Alpha boot: available memory from 0x10c8000 to 0xff3e000`"), the `sysconfigtab` file is read, the static subsystems are configured, and any subsystem attribute values that were entered on the command-line via an interactive boot are retrieved and used to override the values read from `sysconfigtab`.

By booting interactively, attribute values in `sysconfigtab` can be superseded. Remember this little piece of information because we'll take advantage of this feature in section 17.8.5.

CAUTION:

Unlike a standalone system, a cluster member cannot be booted without a `sysconfigtab` file (i.e., `boot -fl c`) as there are some very important cluster base (`clubase`) subsystem attributes that are needed in order for the system to form or join a cluster.

Here is an example of what happens when you boot without a `sysconfigtab` file.

```
>>> boot -fl c
...
TruCluster Server V5.1A  (Rev. 1312); 08/14/01 10:35
panic (cpu 0): clubase_cfg: no cluster name in /etc/sysconfigtab


trap: invalid memory ifetch access from kernel mode

    faulting virtual address:     0x0000000000000000
    pc of faulting instruction:   0x0000000000000000
    ra contents at time of fault: 0xfffffc0000799414
    sp contents at time of fault: 0xfffffe0413427920

DUMP: A dump found in memory will tie up 2605056 bytes until released.
...
```

17.5.4 Subsystem Callback Dispatch Points

When a static subsystem is configured, it may register callback routines to complete its configuration at a later time in the boot process. Think of this as a wakeup call for the subsystem. In fact, since a subsystem can register more than one callback and the callbacks can be registered for different points along the boot process, think of it as both a wakeup call and a snooze button. To illustrate, here's how one author's wife gets up for work in the morning:

She sets the alarm for 5:30 AM. When the alarm goes off, she hits the snooze button deciding to cuddle for 15 minutes (callback number 1). At 5:45 AM, callback number 2 is reached; she rolls over and hits the snooze button again for a 15-minute pre-shower-power-nap. Finally, at 6:00 AM, the last callback is triggered as the alarm sounds to indicate it's time to get on with the day.

Callback routines are triggered when particular dispatch points are reached. Additionally, some subsystems must be configured before or after other subsystems at the same dispatch point, so callback routines can also be registered at a specified priority to insure that callbacks are called in the proper order. When a dispatch point is reached, all subsystem callbacks, registered for that dispatch point, will be executed in order of priority. Callback dispatch points are defined in the `sysconfig.h` file located in the `/sys/include/sys` directory.

We will not discuss what happens at each and every dispatch point but instead, in Table 17-5 we will show you the boot messages you will likely see (if any) as the various cluster and cluster-related subsystems are configured. These messages will appear on the system's console as well as the `messages` file in the `/var/adm` directory.

For more information regarding a particular subsystem, you can consult the `sys_attrs_`*`subsystem`* reference page.

17.6 Configuring the Connection Manager

When a system that has been configured to run in a cluster is booted, it will perform the following steps when the Connection Manager is configured.

- Initialize data structures including the cluster membership list.
- Create the main CNX transaction thread ("`csb event thread`").
  - Set a wakeup call for 10 seconds. Try to form a cluster when timeout is reached.
- Create the remote communication threads ("`wait for csb`"). There are currently 7 threads.
- Create the grim reaper thread ("`cnx grim reaper`").
- Create the CNX pinger thread ("`cnx pinger`").
- If a quorum disk is configured, start the quorum disk thread ("`qdisk tick delay`").

As you can see, at this point the CNX has several threads running and theoretically doing things simultaneously. However, certain things (more or less) need to occur in a sequential order.

Cluster Subsystem Boot Messages

dispatch point	subsys	ics	boot messages
CFG_PT_LOCK_AVAIL CFG_PT_PRECONFIG	mchan	mct	mchan0: Module revision = 35 mchan0: jumpered as VH0 configuration mchan0 at pci0 slot 16
CFG_PT_TOPOLOGY_CONF	kevm_clu		
CFG_PT_OLD_CONF_ALL CFG_PT_POSTCONFIG	rm	mct	rm primary: mchan0, hubslot = 0, phys_rail 0 (size 512 MB) rm primary: log_rail 0 (size 512 MB), phys_rail 0 (mchan0)
	rmvm		
	rdg	mct	Configuring RDG to use Memory Channel
		tcp	Configuring RDG to use TCP
	clubase		TruCluster Server V5.1A (Rev. 1312); 08/14/01 10:35
CFG_PT_CLU_CONF	clubase		TNC kproc_creator_daemon: Initialized and Ready clubase: configured
	ics_ll_mct	mct	ics_mct: icsinfo set for node 1 ics_mct: Declaring this node up 1
	ics_ll_tcp	tcp	ics_ll_tcp: cluster network interface started: rendezvous port is 900 ics_tcp_init: Declaring this_node up 1
	ics_hl	mct	ics_hl: Configuring memory channel as transport.
		tcp	ics_hl: Configuring TCP as transport.
	cnx		
	icsnet		icsnet: configured
	drd		drd configured 0
	kch		kch: configured
	dlm		dlm: configured
	clubase		Starting CFS daemons
	cfs		Registering CFS Services Initializing CFSREC ICS Service Registering CFSMSFS remote syscall interface
	cms		Registering CMS Services
	token		
	clua		cluster alias subsystem enabled
	clsm		clsm: checking for peer configurations clsm: initialized clsm: loading root configuration
	cnx		CNX MGR: insufficient votes to form cluster: have 1 need 2 CNX QDISK: Adding 1 quorum disk vote toward formation. CNX MGR: Cluster babylon5 incarnation 0x910e6 has been formed CNX MGR: Founding node id is 1 csid is 0x10001 CNX MGR: membership configuration index: 1 (1 additions, 0 removals) CNX MGR: Node molari 1 incarn 0x910e6 csid 0x10001 has been added to the cluster
	clubase		

Table 17-5: Cluster Subsystem Boot Messages

17.6.1 The Node Announcement

The CNX pinger thread repeatedly sends out an announcement message until the system becomes a cluster member. Once the system becomes a cluster member the CNX pinger thread kills itself.

Essentially what happens here is the CNX pinger thread broadcasts an announcement message across the cluster interconnect using the ICS BOOT channel[5]. If there are any other systems that are up to receive the announcement message, they will respond by exchanging information with the booting system. Included in the node announcement is the cluster name, node name, incarnation, member ID, version, and how it can be reached via ICS.

You may observe a message similar to the following:

```
CNX MGR: Node molari id 1 incarn 0x914b6 attempting to form or join cluster babylon5
```

Figure 17-5 illustrates the node announcement communication flow.

When the announcement message is received by a cluster member (or potential member), the systems establish a communication channel to each other and exchange more information to flesh out each other's CSB information.

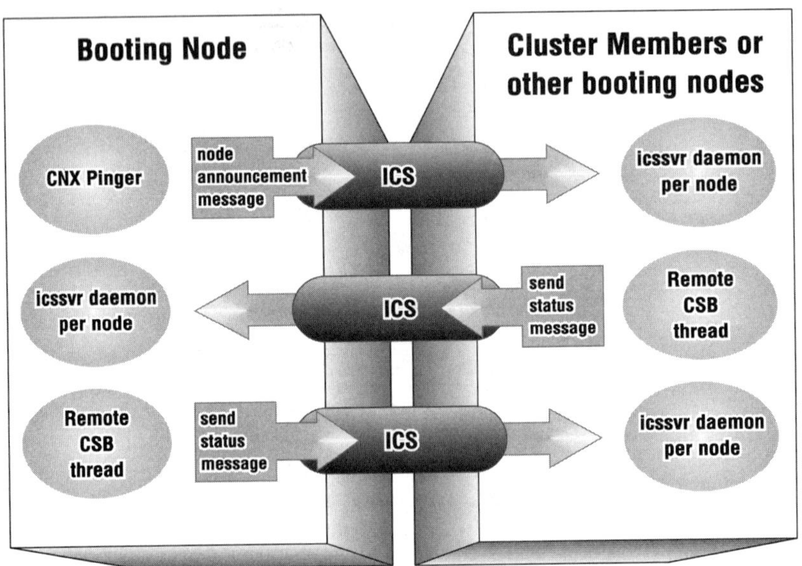

Figure 17-5: CNX Node Announcement

---

[5] See Chapter 18 for more information on the ICS subsystem.

Note that each system contains its own list of cluster members (or potential members) that is used to determine what systems it can communicate with and to calculate the expected vote value and ultimately the quorum vote value.

Since we have been asked many times, "What are all those ICS Server threads use for?," we chose to include Figure 17-5 to illustrate the interaction between the various CNX threads and the ICS threads. As you can see, this remote procedure call (RPC) communication between members in a cluster is done using the ICS. The ICS Server threads are kernel threads that are used to send and receive communication to and from many of the cluster subsystems.

For more information on the ICS, see Chapter 18.

17.6.2 Cluster Formation

After ten seconds, if the node has not heard from a cluster, it will attempt to form a cluster.

```
CNX MGR: insufficient votes to form cluster: have 1 need 2
```

As you can see by the console output, the node initially counts its own vote toward forming the cluster. The system will effectively loop here until enough votes are attained to reach quorum.

If there is a quorum disk configured, then you will see a message similar to the following:

```
CNX QDISK: Adding 1 quorum disk vote toward formation.
```

In the last two lines of output, you can see that enough votes have been added to attain quorum because the first message stated, "`have 1 need 2`". In other words, the CNX has determined that it needs 2 votes to reach quorum. When the quorum disk's vote is added, the CNX will have the necessary second vote.

Once enough votes have been added to reach quorum, the cluster will form as shown in the output below.

```
CNX MGR: Cluster babylon5 incarnation 0x94a1e has been formed
CNX MGR: Founding node id is 1 csid is 0x10001
CNX MGR: membership configuration index: 1 (1 additions, 0 removals)
CNX MGR: quorum (re)gained, (re)starting cluster operations.
CNX MGR: Node molari 1 incarn 0x94a1e csid 0x10001 has been added to the cluster
```

17.6.2.1 Cluster Formation – The Details

You want additional details? Hold on tight.

When a system decides to form a cluster, it does the following:

- From the list of nodes the system has established communication with, it determines which ones are potential members.
  - If a node in the list is already a cluster member:
    - Verify this system has the same quorum disk (if configured) or panic.

```
CNX MGR: quorum disk doesn't match cluster member
```

    - Send a "Join Request" – see section 17.6.3.
  - If a node on the list is a potential member, but the quorum disk doesn't match, the cluster will not form and will loop with the following message until the node(s) that don't match are halted.

```
CNX MGR: cannot form: existing nodes disagree on quorum disk.
```

    This should only occur if a cluster administrator (or someone with super-user access) modified a member's `sysconfigtab` incorrectly. Administrative changes regarding voting and the quorum disk should **only** be done with `clu_quorum(8)` command.
  - If a node on the list is a potential member with a vote:
    - Count up the number of votes from these potential members.
    - Determine the maximum expected votes count.
- If the quorum disk is configured, make sure it's not in use by another system or cluster.
  - If the quorum disk is not in use, add its vote to the count of potential votes.
  - If the quorum disk is in use, there is likely a communication problem.

```
CNX MGR: cannot form: quorum disk is in use.  Unable to establish contact
with members using disk.
```

    Do not try to form.
- Check to see that there are enough votes to reach quorum.
  - If not, you will see the following message:

```
CNX MGR: insufficient votes to form cluster: have 1 need 2
```

- Become the "Coordinator" for this CNX transaction.

  Any member can be the coordinator for any particular CNX transaction, but there can be only one coordinator at a time. The coordinator calls the shots during a CNX transaction so that it is done in an orderly (or coordinated) manner.

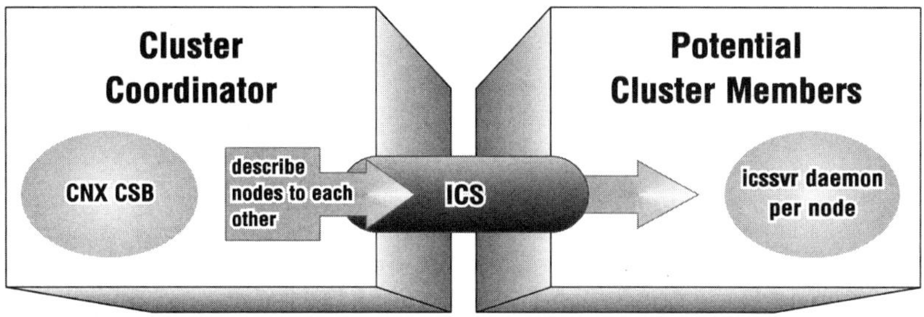

Figure 17-6: Describe Nodes

- Allocate a CSID for each node that has been selected as a potential member.
- Describe the nodes to each other (see Figure 17-6) and prepare a connectivity matrix (or topology).

  Think of the matrix as a topology bitmap that shows node connectivity. The goal is to determine the best-connected (or fully connected) cluster. This is done to prevent a cluster partition.

  If every member is communicating with every other member, then the matrix will be identical for all members. This is the normal operating environment.

  When there is a communication problem, this matrix may not be the same. The CNX will determine the best-connected cluster from the topology bitmap. Systems not communicating will hang or panic. The systems in the matrix will continue as the cluster.

  Figure 17-7 shows an example of a connectivity matrix with a communication problem. Every member can communicate with the quorum disk, but `member3` and `member5` cannot communicate with other members. Since the CNX will detect this problem, `member3` and `member5` will not be allowed to join the cluster.

- Determine the best-connected cluster from the connectivity matrix and clear nodes from the

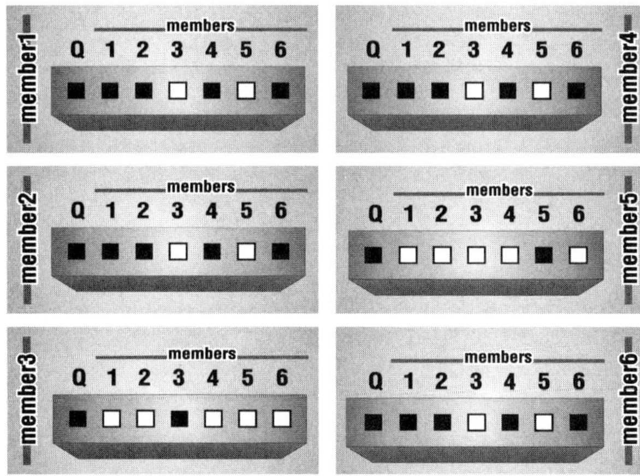

Figure 17-7: Connectivity Matrix (aka Topology Bitmap)

connectivity matrix that are not selected to be part of the cluster.

- Calculate quorum from the maximum expected votes value from the best-connected cluster configuration.
- If there are enough votes to attain quorum, form the cluster.

  Committing the transaction in three phases forms the cluster. If all nodes in the best-connected cluster list agree to the proposed cluster, then each node will acknowledge the proposal (phase 1), prepare to commit the transaction (phase 2), and commit the transaction (phase 3). The reason for three phases is to make sure that every node agrees and, as an additional failsafe, to detect any communication problems not previously detected (see Figure 17-8).

17.6.3 Joining a Cluster

As we learned in section 17.6.1, when the CNX is configured one of the first things to happen is that the CNX pinger thread sends an announcement message. If the system has established communication channels with members of an existing cluster, it will send a request to join the

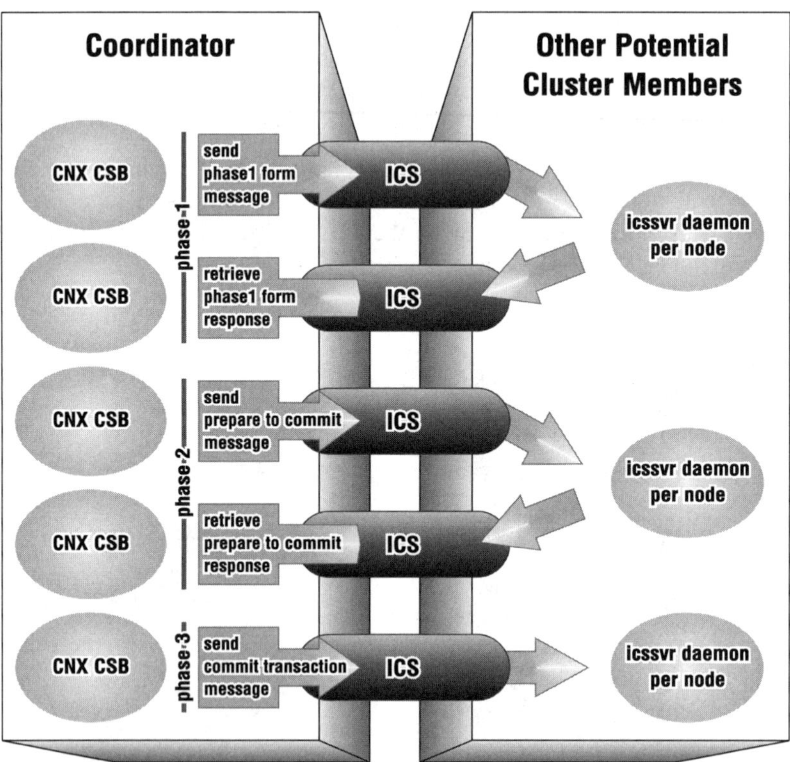

Figure 17-8: Cluster Formation Transaction

cluster instead of trying to form a cluster.

The boot process for a system joining a cluster is pretty much the same as it is for systems forming a cluster except that once the system becomes aware that there is a cluster, it sends a join request to the existing cluster members as was shown in Figure 17-9.

Once the join request is sent, one of the cluster members will temporarily take charge of responding to this request by becoming the "Cluster Coordinator" for the cluster. The job of the coordinator is as follows:

- Determine whether or not the node requesting to join would cause the cluster to lose quorum. If this is true, then the node cannot be allowed to join the cluster.

```
CNX MGR: join request rejected: adding node would cause cluster to lose quorum
...
CNX MGR: halting join rejected 20 times
```

- Allocate a CSID for the node and proceed to describe the requestor to each cluster member and describe each cluster member to the requestor (see Figure 17-10). Since each member should already have a CSB allocated for the requestor and the requestor should already have a CSB for each cluster member, this step really involves verification of the CSB and passing along the CSID.
- Describe the cluster to the new node (see Figure 17-10). This involves passing the requestor the current cluster's information including the incarnation number, the founder, CSIDs of every member, etc.
- Calculate Quorum based on the requestor's addition to the cluster.
- Prepare a connectivity matrix (or topology).

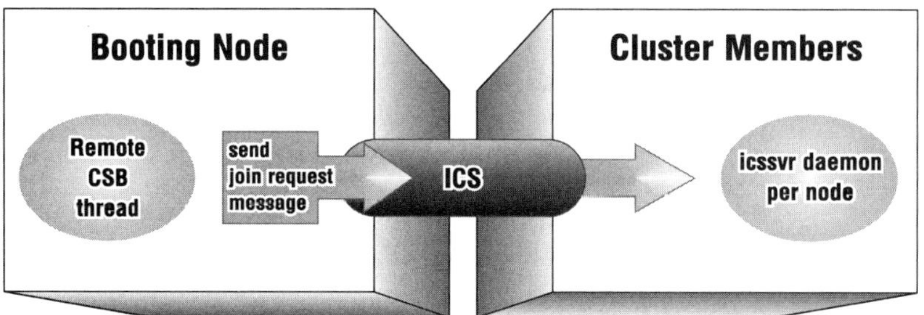

Figure 17-9: Send a Join Request

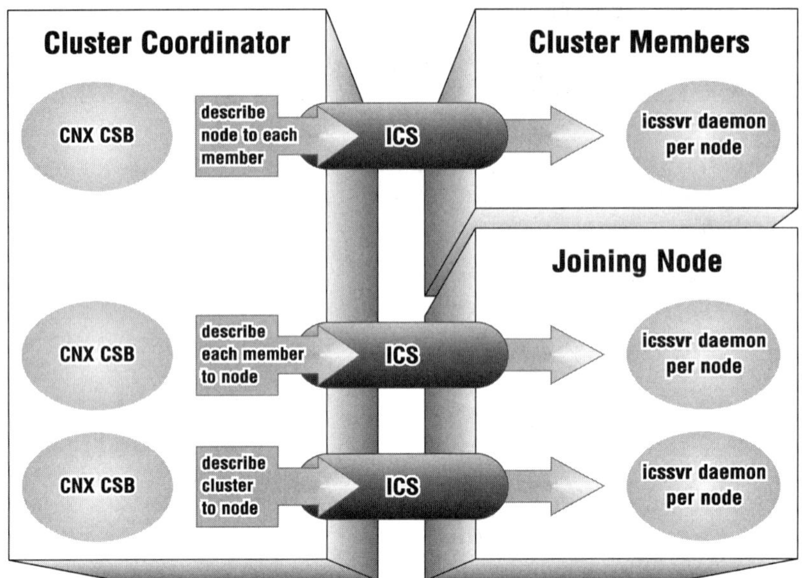

Figure 17-10: Describe Member & Cluster

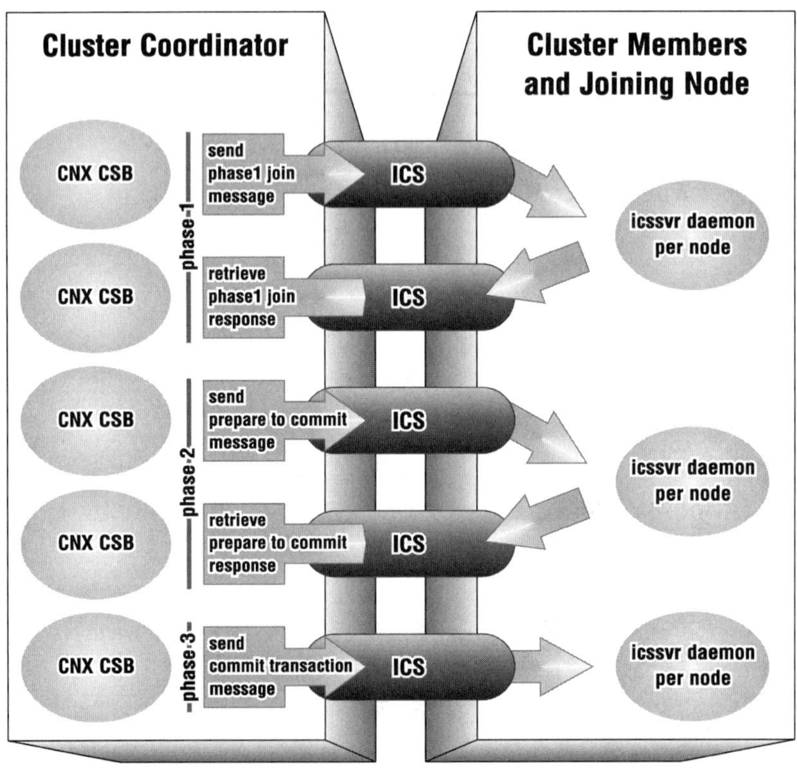

Figure 17-11: Member Join Transaction

- Initiate a three-phase transaction to add the requestor to the cluster (see Figure 17-11). If all members and the requestor agree to the proposal, then each node will acknowledge the proposal (phase 1), prepare to commit the transaction (phase 2), and commit the transaction (phase 3).

17.7 Quorum and Voting Strategies

Some system administrators have questioned the wisdom of needing quorum to be able to form a cluster, especially in large cluster configurations due to the number of nodes that would need to be up simultaneously. We do not see this as a problem because one of the purposes of a cluster is high availability – the point is to keep as many members participating in the cluster as possible.

The questions that inevitably follow:

- "Well, what if I want to take half of my systems down for maintenance?"
- "What if I need to take several systems out of the cluster for a while to use on a development project?"
- "What if half my systems crash?"

While we wonder why someone would break apart their production cluster, extenuating and unforeseen circumstances do occur which often require creative solutions, so…

You should plan your cluster for maximum availability at all times even when some members will be unavailable. Here are a few tips:

- If you have a cluster with an even number of members, configure a quorum disk. See section 17.8.3.1.
- If you have a cluster with an odd number of members, do not configure a quorum disk (or configure the quorum disk with zero votes – see section 17.8.3.1.1).
- Only members with a direct, physical connection to the `cluster_root`, `cluster_usr`, and `cluster_var` file systems should be voting members.
- If a member will be down for a planned but extended period of time, set the member's votes to zero (i.e., a non-voting member). See section 17.8.2.1.
- If you lose several members unexpectedly such that one more failure will cause the cluster to lose quorum, adjust the cluster's expected votes until the members are once again added to the cluster. See section 17.8.2.2.

Both expected votes and member votes can be administratively modified, so it is no big deal to modify the votes within the cluster so that it requires fewer votes to form or continue. In the following sections we will discuss managing quorum in a cluster.

17.8 Managing Quorum

As you add members to your cluster using the clu_add_member(8) command or remove members from your cluster using the clu_delete_member(8) command, votes are automatically adjusted to maintain quorum. Generally, this will suffice; however, there may be times when you will need to alter your cluster's expected votes or a member's votes (for example, if you need to remove several members from your cluster for preventative maintenance). In the event that you do need to modify votes administratively, you should use the clu_quorum(8) command.

17.8.1 Viewing Quorum Status

The easiest way to know if you have quorum is to see if you can login to the system (or if you are logged in, see if the system responds when you type in a command). Barring the obvious, you may be curious to see your cluster's current voting and quorum status. You can use the clu_quorum command without any command options.

```
# clu_quorum

 Cluster Quorum Data for: babylon5 as of Thu Jan 10 03:37:04 EST 2002

Cluster Common Quorum Data
Quorum disk:   dsk4h
File:          /etc/sysconfigtab.cluster

Attribute                                    File Value
expected votes                                        3

Member 1 Quorum Data
Host name:     molari.tcrhb.com                Status:                UP
File:          /cluster/members/member1/boot_partition/etc/sysconfigtab

Attribute                Running Value       File Value
current votes                        3              N/A
quorum votes                         2              N/A
expected votes                       3                3
node votes                           1                1
qdisk votes                          1                1
qdisk major                         19               19
qdisk minor                        112              112

Member 2 Quorum Data
Host name:     sheridan.tcrhb.com              Status:                UP
File:          /cluster/members/member2/boot_partition/etc/sysconfigtab

Attribute                Running Value       File Value
current votes                        3              N/A
quorum votes                         2              N/A
expected votes                       3                3
node votes                           1                1
qdisk votes                          1                1
qdisk major                         19               19
qdisk minor                        112              112
```

From the output of the clu_quorum command, you can see that our cluster has a quorum disk configured. Additionally, you can see the values that the cluster is currently using ("Running Value") as well as the values that members will use the next time they are booted ("File Value").

The clu_quorum command gets the "File Value" information from the member's sysconfigtab file as it clearly denotes, but where does the "Running Value" come from? This information is stored in the Connection Manager (cnx) kernel subsystem.

17.8.1.1 The **cnx** Subsystem

The cnx subsystem contains the attributes that the system is currently using.

```
# sysconfig -q cnx

cnx:
name = Connection Manager
version = 1
cluster_name = babylon5
cluster_founder_csid = 65537
node_cnt = 2
has_quorum = 1
qdisk_trusted = 1
member_cnt = 2
current_votes = 3
expected_votes = 3
quorum_votes = 2
qdisk_major = 19
qdisk_minor = 112
qdisk_votes = 1
mem_seq = 2
add_seq = 2
rem_seq = 0
node_id = 2
node_name = sheridan
node_csid = 65537
node_votes = 1
node_expected_votes = 3
msg_level = 1
```

As you can see from the output, all the attributes (and more) from the clu_quorum command's "Running Value" are represented.

For more information on the cnx subsystem, see the sys_attrs_cnx(5) reference page.

17.8.1.2 The **sysconfigtab** File and the **clubase** Subsystem

The cluster base (clubase) subsystem contains the attributes that define the cluster as mentioned in section 17.2.6. These attributes are loaded from the system's sysconfigtab file when the system is booted. Although the attribute values may be modified in a member's sysconfigtab file, they will not be reflected in the clubase subsystem until the system is rebooted. This is not a big deal, though, because these attributes are only used to configure or join the cluster. The running values for the system are stored in the cnx subsystem as we discussed in the previous section.

Here is an example to show how the sysconfigtab file can differ from what the clubase subsystem can see. We have booted a one-member cluster. The system's sysconfigtab file shows that no quorum disk is configured and that the cluster_expected_votes value is 1.

```
# sysconfigdb -l clubase

clubase:
        cluster_expected_votes = 1
        cluster_quorum_conf_active = 0
        cluster_qdisk_major = 0
        cluster_qdisk_minor = 0
        cluster_qdisk_votes = 0
        cluster_name = babylon5
        cluster_node_name = molari
        cluster_node_inter_name = molari-ics0
        cluster_node_votes = 1
        cluster_interconnect = mct
        cluster_seqdisk_major = 19
        cluster_seqdisk_minor = 96
```

The clubase subsystem on the system confirms these values.

```
# sysconfig -q clubase cluster_expected_votes \
> cluster_qdisk_major cluster_qdisk_minor cluster_qdisk_votes

clubase:
cluster_expected_votes = 1
cluster_qdisk_major = 0
cluster_qdisk_minor = 0
cluster_qdisk_votes = 0
```

We will now add a second member to the cluster as well as a quorum disk. To add a second member we will use the clu_add_member(8) command as we discussed in Chapter 11. We will discuss how to add a quorum disk in section 17.8.3.1. To save a tree, we will not show the output here but instead illustrate how these actions affect the cluster.

Looking at the clubase subsystem on our member after the quorum disk and member have been added, you can see that nothing has changed.

```
# sysconfig -q clubase cluster_expected_votes \
> cluster_qdisk_major cluster_qdisk_minor cluster_qdisk_votes

clubase:
cluster_expected_votes = 1
cluster_qdisk_major = 0
cluster_qdisk_minor = 0
cluster_qdisk_votes = 0
```

The sysconfigtab file, however, does reflect the recent changes.

```
# sysconfigdb -l clubase | grep -E "expected|_qdisk"

        cluster_expected_votes = 3
        cluster_qdisk_major = 19
        cluster_qdisk_minor = 112
        cluster_qdisk_votes = 1
```

CAUTION:

Do not modify a member's sysconfigtab file to adjust votes. Use the clu_quorum command. The clu_quorum command contains logic to insure that you do not attempt to set a value that would cause the cluster to lose quorum. Furthermore it makes sure that each member's cluster_expected_votes value is the same.

Another important point is that the cluster_expected_votes attribute is also stored in a cluster-common file, /etc/sysconfigtab.cluster. The clu_quorum command also ensures that this file is properly updated.

You can also use the clu_quorum command with the "-v" option to see the clubase subsystem values. They are under the "Booted Value" field. See Figure 17-12.

When molari was booted, cluster_expected_votes was 1 and no quorum disk was configured. After the clu_add_member command, you can see that sheridan's cluster_expected_votes value was 2. Finally, we added the quorum disk after sheridan was booted. We know this because both the "Running Value" and "File Value" indicate that a quorum disk is configured but neither member's "Booted Value" shows a quorum disk.

NOTE:

The clu_quorum command logs changes to the clu_quorum.log file located in the /cluster/admin directory.

17.8.2 Modifying Votes

It may be necessary on occasion to change a member's status from a voting member (i.e., a member with 1 vote), to a non-voting member (i.e., a member with zero votes).

Why would you want to change a member to non-voting member? Anytime a system will be removed from the cluster for a temporary, but extended, period of time, it is a good idea to adjust the number of votes required to form and maintain the cluster. You could use the clu_delete_member(8) command to remove the member, but this would be overkill. By making the member a non-voting member, the cluster's expected votes will be lowered by one as well.

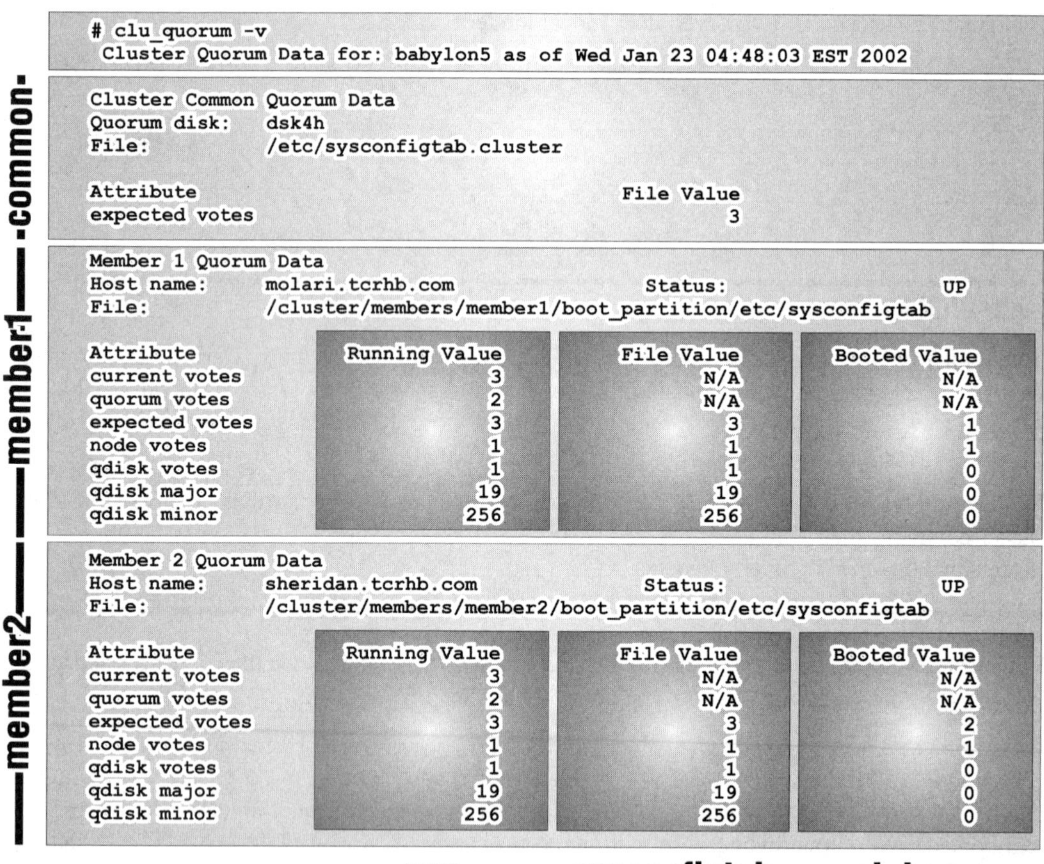

```
# clu_quorum -v
 Cluster Quorum Data for: babylon5 as of Wed Jan 23 04:48:03 EST 2002

Cluster Common Quorum Data
Quorum disk:    dsk4h
File:           /etc/sysconfigtab.cluster

Attribute                                            File Value
expected votes                                                3

Member 1 Quorum Data
Host name:      molari.tcrhb.com                  Status:              UP
File:           /cluster/members/member1/boot_partition/etc/sysconfigtab

Attribute                Running Value       File Value      Booted Value
current votes                        3              N/A               N/A
quorum votes                         2              N/A               N/A
expected votes                       3                3                 1
node votes                           1                1                 1
qdisk votes                          1                1                 0
qdisk major                         19               19                 0
qdisk minor                        256              256                 0

Member 2 Quorum Data
Host name:      sheridan.tcrhb.com                Status:              UP
File:           /cluster/members/member2/boot_partition/etc/sysconfigtab

Attribute                Running Value       File Value      Booted Value
current votes                        3              N/A               N/A
quorum votes                         2              N/A               N/A
expected votes                       3                3                 2
node votes                           1                1                 1
qdisk votes                          1                1                 0
qdisk major                         19               19                 0
qdisk minor                        256              256                 0
```


Figure 17-12: "`clu_quorum -v`" explained

IMPORTANT:

If turning a member into a non-voting member gives you a cluster with an odd number of voting members, you should also adjust the quorum disk vote to zero (or temporarily remove the quorum disk from the cluster). See section 17.8.3 for more information on managing the quorum disk.

17.8.2.1 How to Adjust a Member's Votes

You can adjust the number of votes a member can contribute by using the `clu_quorum` command with the "`-m`" option.

`clu_quorum -m` *`member_name #votes`*

The only two acceptable values for the *`#votes`* parameter as of this writing are 0 or 1.

```
# clu_quorum -m molari 0
Collecting quorum data for Member(s): 1 2

Member votes successfully adjusted.
```

To verify that the votes were changed, you can issue the following command:

```
# clu_get_info -m 1 -full | grep -E "Hostname|votes"
    Hostname = molari.tcrhb.com
    Member votes = 0
```

The "-m 1" option to clu_get_info(8) command gets member1's information. Notice the slight difference in the "-m" option between the two commands – clu_quorum uses the member's name whereas clu_get_info uses the memberid. Due to this inconsistency, it may be easier to stick with the clu_quorum command sans options.

```
# clu_quorum | grep -E "^Host|^node|Running"
Host name:      molari.tcrhb.com               Status:                  UP
Attribute              Running Value         File Value
node votes                         0                  0
Host name:      sheridan.tcrhb.com             Status:                  UP
Attribute              Running Value         File Value
node votes                         1                  1
```

In order to adjust a member's votes, the cluster must have access to the member's boot_partition. If the member is down, however, the boot_partition will be unmounted. If the member is down, but at least one of the cluster members has physical access to the member's boot disk, you can add the "-f" option to the clu_quorum command to "force" the operation. The "-f" option mounts the member's boot_partition, modifies the sysconfigtab file, and unmounts the member's boot_partition. This is a good reason why member boot disks should be accessible by multiple cluster members. If the member is down, the clu_quorum command will notify you.

```
# clu_quorum -m molari 1
Collecting quorum data for Member(s): 1 2

*** Error ***
One or more cluster members are DOWN. You may use the -f option to force the
quorum operation.
```

By adding the "-f" option, the clu_quorum command completes successfully.

```
# clu_quorum -f -m molari 1
Collecting quorum data for Member(s): 1 2


Member votes successfully adjusted.
```

You can also use "-f" option to see a down system's sysconfigtab values.

```
# clu_quorum -f | grep -E "^Host|^node|Value" | tail -6
Host name:      molari.tcrhb.com                 Status:              DOWN
Attribute                                      File Value
node votes                                              0
Host name:      sheridan.tcrhb.com               Status:                UP
Attribute              Running Value           File Value
node votes                          1                   1
```

17.8.2.2 How to Adjust the Cluster's Expected Votes

It is the cluster's expected votes (CEV) value that is used to determine the cluster's quorum votes (the number of votes that are required to form a cluster and keep the cluster running).

The CEV value will not be lowered once the cluster is formed if a member joins or leaves the cluster. Remember that the CEV value is equal to the maximum of the following:

- The previous CEV value. This is the CEV value that was calculated the last time a state transition occurred in the current cluster incarnation.
- The largest cluster_expected_votes value of all members. This value **should** be the same on every member.
- The sum of all cluster_node_votes, plus the cluster_qdisk_votes (if the quorum disk is configured and assigned a vote).

So what would happen if enough cluster members were to fail such that one more failure would cause the cluster to lose quorum?

There are only two methods to lower a CEV value. You can delete a member using the clu_delete_member command or use the clu_quorum command with the "-e" option.

For example, say a lightning storm hits a building containing a cluster causing 50% of the cluster members to crash. Due to the severity of the storm, the power transformer that provides power to these members stops functioning, causing the members to be down for an indeterminate period of time.

The cluster contains eight voting members and is configured with a one-vote quorum disk. Given this configuration, the CEV value would be 9, which means that the number of votes required for quorum would be 5. Since 50% of the cluster members crashed, the cluster's current votes value is 5 (4 voting members and the quorum disk).

If there were one more failure, the cluster would lose quorum. Since the members that are down will not have power for a while, we will want to adjust the CEV value to increase the cluster's availability by lowering the number of members required to form the cluster.

You can adjust the `cluster_expected_votes` attribute (and the cluster's current expected votes value) by using the `clu_quorum` command with the "`-e`" option.

`clu_quorum -e` *`#votes`*

The *`#votes`* parameter cannot be set to any value that will cause the cluster to lose quorum.

```
# clu_quorum -e 12

*** Error ***
The requested expected vote adjustment would result in an
expected votes value of '12'. This value would cause all members of the
current cluster configuration to lose quorum.
```

The *`#votes`* parameter cannot be set to any value lower than the current votes value minus one. This would increase the potential to partition the cluster, which is not good.

In our example, the current votes value is 5, so anything lower than 4 is illegal.

```
# clu_quorum -e 3

*** Error ***
The requested expected vote adjustment would result in an illegal
expected votes value of '3'. This value is too low.
```

The *`#votes`* parameter cannot be set to a value of zero.

```
# clu_quorum -e 0

*** Error ***
Expected Votes cannot be set to 0 (Zero).
```

The *`#votes`* parameter can generally be set to +1/-1 of the current votes, provided that quorum would not be lost. We will set expected votes to the current votes value.

```
# clu_quorum -e 5

Collecting quorum data for Member(s): 1 2 3 4 5 6 7 8

*** Error ***
One or more cluster members are DOWN. You may use the -f option to force the
quorum operation.
```

Since some members are down, we will need to use the "-f" option.

```
# clu_quorum -f -e 5

Collecting quorum data for Member(s): 1 2 3 4 5 6 7 8

Expected vote successfully adjusted.
```

As previously noted, the clu_quorum command modifies the cluster_expected_votes value in each member's sysconfigtab file as well as the /etc/sysconfigtab.cluster file (a cluster-common file).

17.8.3 Managing the Quorum Disk

We've mentioned previously that adding a quorum disk is a way to increase the availability of your cluster by adding a vote to the cluster's current votes value. We also mentioned that the quorum disk should be used only in a cluster that has an even number of members.

How does this increase the cluster's availability? Let's see. Figure 17-13 shows a four-member cluster that is configured without a quorum disk.

If we were to lose a member, would we lose quorum? Since a picture is worth a thousand words, let's see what Figure 17-14 has to say.

So far, so good. One member is down, but since the current votes is equal to the quorum votes, the cluster will continue. Now, let's take another member down.

We have lost quorum, and therefore the cluster is suspended (See Figure 17-15).

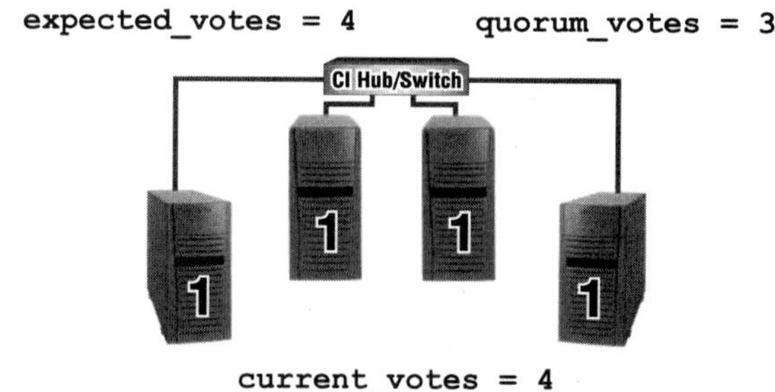

Figure 17-13: Four-Member Cluster without a Quorum Disk

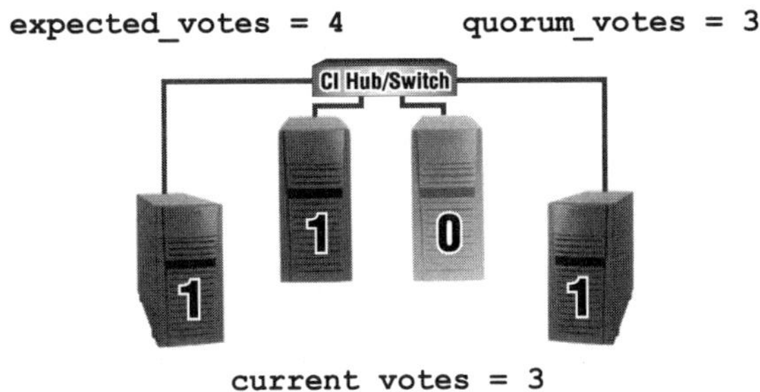

Figure 17-14: Four-Member Cluster without a Quorum Disk – One Member Down

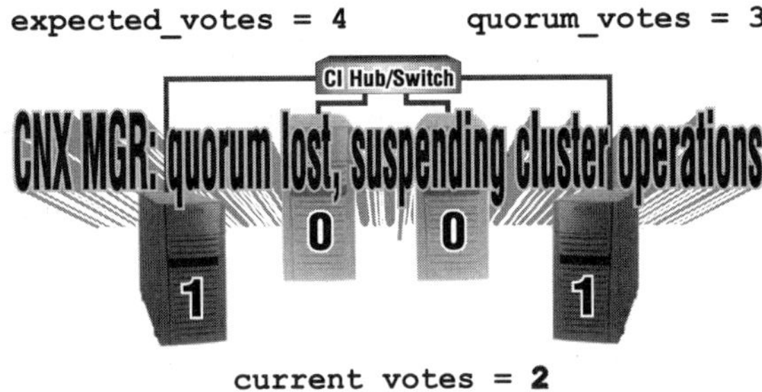

Figure 17-15: Four-Member Cluster without a Quorum Disk – Two Members Down

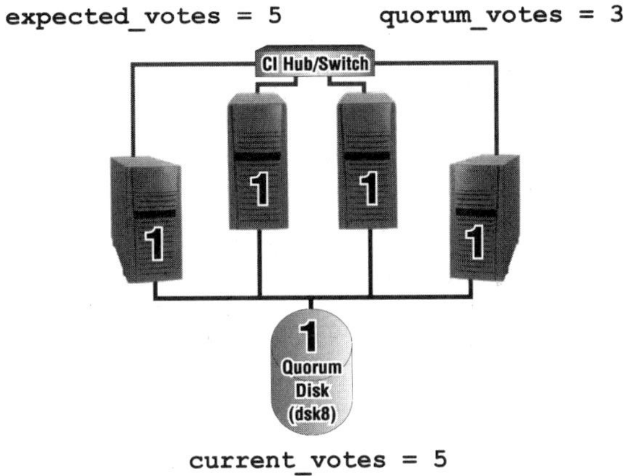

Figure 17-16: Four-Member Cluster with a Quorum Disk

Okay, so let's try this again, this time with a quorum disk. We'll start with Figure 17-16.

What's the difference? Well, both the cluster's expected votes as well as the current votes have increased, but the quorum votes remain the same. You can probably see where this is going. Let's fast-forward to the same scenario that we had before – two-members down. Will we lose quorum this time? We submit Figure 17-17 for your perusal.

A cluster with an even number of members with a quorum disk has higher availability.

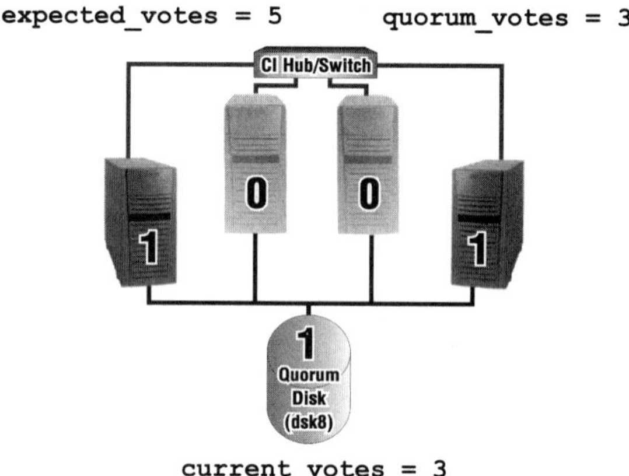

Figure 17-17: Four-Member Cluster with a Quorum Disk – Two Members Down

Besides the quorum disk's adding another vote to a cluster with an even number of members, it also acts as a tiebreaker to prevent a cluster partition (see section 17.4) in the event that there is a cluster interconnect communication failure.

It is also interesting to note that due to the type of information contained on the `cnx` partition of the quorum disk (see section 17.8.5.1), and the way the CNX identifies and manages the quorum disk, various cluster interconnect communication failures can be diagnosed because cluster members can "sense" something wrong from the markings etched into the mysterious qdisk idol by our cluster's nemesis, the split-brained, anti-cluster from the depths of… scratch that – for some reason the author thought that he was writing a new sci-fi-adventure-mystery novel for a brief moment. Medication has been administered. We now return you to "Managing the Quorum Disk", already in progress…

…various cluster interconnect communication failures can be diagnosed because cluster members can "sense" something wrong by the data written on the quorum disk by some other cluster.

Before the cluster can add the quorum disk's vote to the total current votes toward quorum, the quorum disk must be trusted.

A quorum disk is trusted if all the following conditions are true:

- The member attempting to claim the disk for the cluster has direct physical access to the disk.

  Note: this is an important reason why the quorum disk should be a disk on a bus that is accessible directly by every member in the cluster.

- The member can read from and write to the disk.
- The member can either claim ownership of the quorum disk, or is a member of a cluster that has already claimed the quorum disk.

You can determine whether or not the quorum disk is trusted from any given member by examining the `cnx:qdisk_trusted` attribute on that member.

```
[sheridan]
# sysconfig -q cnx qdisk_trusted
cnx:
qdisk_trusted = 1
```

As the previous output demonstrates, `sheridan` trusts the quorum disk.

Any member can claim the quorum disk for the cluster, but only one member will claim it at a time. If a CNX event occurs that causes a cluster state transition to happen, the quorum disk will be reclaimed, which could result in a different member claiming the disk for the cluster.

Approximately every five seconds, every cluster member's qdisk thread will read from and write to the quorum disk to make sure the quorum disk is still accessible and functioning as a quorum disk for this cluster.

Despite the fact that the CNX uses a very small portion of the quorum disk (exactly 1MB located on the "`h`" partition), this disk should not contain any data on it that you wish to keep. No I/O barriers are placed on the quorum disk; therefore any node can write to the disk. Consequently, it is possible that the data on the disk could be corrupted.

For more information on I/O barriers, see section 15.1.3.

17.8.3.1 How to Add the Quorum Disk

You can add a quorum disk to the cluster using the `clu_quorum` command with the "`-d add`" option.

`clu_quorum -d add` *`disk_name #votes`*

The arguments are the disk's device special file name and the number of votes. You can only input 0 or 1 as the *`#votes`* value.

```
# clu_quorum -d add dsk4 1
Collecting quorum data for Member(s): 1 2

  Initializing cnx partition on quorum disk : dsk4h

Quorum disk successfully created.
```

Once the quorum disk is added to the cluster, the CNX quorum disk thread is started.

```
# cnxthreads | grep qdisk
[12] "qdisk tick delay" - qdisk t
```

NOTE:

The disk does not need to have a disk label on it, since the `clu_quorum` command will label the disk. The `clu_quorum` command will let you know there is no label but will continue without a problem.

```
*** Info ***
Disk available but has no label: dsk4
```

17.8.3.1.1 Adding a Quorum Disk with Zero Votes

You may be wondering why you would want to add a quorum disk without a vote. One reason is to reserve the disk for use as a quorum disk before actually using it. If you currently have a cluster with an odd number of members, adding a quorum disk with a vote would not be a good idea, so to avoid creating a situation where the quorum disk could hurt instead of help, you can add it with a 0 vote value.

How can it hurt? Consider a three-member cluster. The cluster's expected votes value is 3, which would make quorum votes equal to 2. How many members can fail and still maintain quorum? Only one.

If you add a quorum disk with 1 vote to the three-member cluster, expected votes is increased to 4, which will increase quorum votes to 3. How many members can fail now? Only one. So, how have we hurt ourselves? By adding another potential point of failure.

17.8.3.1.2 Adding a Quorum Disk without Equal Connectivity

If you try to add a quorum disk using a disk that does not have equal connectivity to all members, the `clu_quorum` command will warn you that this action can lead to madness (or at least quorum loss).

```
# clu_quorum -d add dsk4 1
Collecting quorum data for Member(s): 1 2

All members do not have direct access to the specified quorum disk: dsk4
Members without direct access to the quorum disk may be more likely to
lose quorum than those members with direct access to the quorum disk.
Do you want to continue with this operation? [yes]:
```

Despite the fact that the *TruCluster* Server Cluster Administration Guide merely states that the quorum disk **should** be located on a shared bus, we believe that placing the quorum disk anywhere but on a shared bus that is connected to all members is not a good idea at all!

17.8.3.1.3 *Adding a Quorum Disk with Existing Data*

As of this writing, adding a quorum disk (with existing data) to a cluster is not supported. As stated earlier, no I/O barriers are placed on the quorum disk, and therefore the data on the disk could be overwritten or corrupted. As a safety mechanism, the `clu_quorum` command will return an error if you attempt to add a disk that has an existing in-use partition.

If the proposed quorum disk contains an AdvFS file system on a partition, the `clu_quorum` command will return the following error (even if the fileset is not mounted):

```
# clu_quorum -d add dsk6 1

*** Error ***
Disk 'dsk6' has a least one partition that is in use.
The partition in use is open as an Advfs Domain.

*** Error ***
Cannot configure quorum disk.
```

If the proposed quorum disk contains an LSM partition and LSM is configured, the `clu_quorum` command will return the following error:

```
# clu_quorum -d add dsk6 1

*** Error ***
Disk 'dsk6' has a least one partition that is in use.
The partition in use is open as an LSM volume.

*** Error ***
Cannot configure quorum disk.
```

WARNING:

If LSM is not in use on the cluster, the `clu_quorum` command will add the disk as the quorum disk. It will replace the existing disk label with a new one, and no error will be given.

If the proposed quorum disk contains a UFS file system on a partition, and the file system is mounted, the `clu_quorum` command will return the following error:

```
# clu_quorum -d add dsk6 1

*** Error ***
Disk 'dsk6' has a least one partition that is in use.
The partition in use is open as a UFS Filesystem.

*** Error ***
Cannot configure quorum disk.
```

WARNING:

If the UFS file system is not mounted, the clu_quorum command will add the disk as the quorum disk. It will replace the existing disk label with a new one, and no error will be given.

17.8.3.2 How to Remove the Quorum Disk

If you have a quorum disk but wish to remove it, the clu_quorum command with the "-d remove" option should do the trick.

```
# clu_quorum -d remove
Collecting quorum data for Member(s): 1 2


Quorum disk successfully removed.
```

What reason could you have for removing the quorum disk? If you add or remove a member from the cluster resulting in an odd number of members, you should remove the quorum disk or at least adjust its votes to a value of zero.

Once the quorum disk is removed from the cluster, the CNX quorum disk thread is stopped. We can verify this by running the cnxthreads program we wrote and grep for "qdisk". No output should be displayed.

```
# cnxthreads | grep qdisk
```

17.8.3.3 How to Adjust the Quorum Disk Votes

If you have a quorum disk and need to shutdown a member of the cluster for an extended period of time but do not want to remove the quorum disk, you can use the clu_quorum command with the "-d adjust" option.

clu_quorum -d adjust *#votes*

Set the *#votes* value to zero.

```
# clu_quorum -d adjust 0
Collecting quorum data for Member(s): 1 2


Quorum disk votes successfully adjusted.
```

Once the member is returned to the cluster, you can adjust the quorum disk vote by repeating the command and changing *#votes* value from 0 to 1.

```
# clu_quorum -d adjust 1
Collecting quorum data for Member(s): 1 2

Quorum disk votes successfully adjusted.
```

17.8.3.4 How to Replace a Failed Quorum Disk

Replacement of a failed quorum disk is covered in Chapter 22, section 22.6.

17.8.4 Using the clu_quorum Command When a Member Is Unavailable

Since the clu_quorum command modifies every member's sysconfigtab file, which is located in /.local../boot_partition/etc, it stands to reason that every member's boot_partition needs to be mounted so that the clubase subsystem attributes can be modified. This is just one important reason why member boot disks should be on a bus that is directly accessible by all members.

For example, if you use the clu_quorum command to modify votes or add/remove the quorum disk, you will receive an error if a member is down.

```
# clu_quorum -d add dsk4 1
Collecting quorum data for Member(s): 1
*** Warning ***
Cannot access member 1's member specific /etc/sysconfigtab file.
2

*** Error ***
One or more cluster members are DOWN. You may use the -f option to force the
quorum operation.
```

If the disk is on a shared bus, then you can use the "-f" option.

```
# clu_quorum -f -d add dsk4 1
Collecting quorum data for Member(s): 1 2

  Initializing cnx partition on quorum disk : dsk4h

Adding the quorum disk could cause a temporary loss
of quorum until the disk becomes trusted.
Do you want to continue with this operation? [yes]:

Quorum disk successfully created.
```

If the down node's boot disk is not on a bus that a cluster member can mount, then the previous command will fail even with the "-f" switch.

17.8.5 Managing the cnx Partition

The cnx partition can be managed with the Cluster Boot Disk Manager (clu_bdmgr(8)) command although this should rarely be needed.

When a volume is added to the cluster_root domain, the cluster_root domain is brought under LSM control; and when the quorum disk is added or removed, the cnx partition updates automatically. In fact, the only time that the system administrator needs to take direct action to manage a cnx partition is when a member boot disk fails.

The clu_bdmgr command with the "-c" option can be used to prepare a boot disk. The command will create an AdvFS file system on the "a" partition. It will also create a cnx partition on the "h" partition but it will not configure it.

```
# clu_bdmgr -c dsk6 2

Error: Disk 'dsk6' has at least one partition that is in use.
The partition in use is open as an Advfs Domain.
Domain root2_domain already exists for member 2. If you continue this
domain will be removed and a new domain, of the same name, will
be created.

Do you want to continue creating this boot disk? [yes]:
rmfdmn: domain root2_domain removed.

Creating AdvFS domains:
  Creating AdvFS domain 'root2_domain#root' on partition '/dev/disk/dsk6a'.
```

As you can see by the previous output, the file system is made. The cnx partition is also created but not configured (evidenced by the disklabel(8) and the clu_bdmgr commands). The clu_bdmgr command with the "-d" option is used the retrieve the configuration information from a cnx partition.

```
# disklabel -r dsk6 | grep cnx
  h:          2048      17771476          cnx                    #    5289*- 5289*
```

```
# clu_bdmgr -d dsk6
Bad magic number for ADVFS

*** Error ***
Cannot produce cnx configuration file for device /dev/disk/dsk6h
Failure to process request
```

If a member boot disk fails, the cnx partition must be restored. The good news is that the cnx partition configuration is saved to a file on the boot_partition every time the member boots. The clu_max startup script, which is executed at runlevel 3, calls the clu_bdmgr command with the "-b" option to save the cnx partition configuration information to the /.local../boot_partition/etc/clu_bdmgr.conf file.

To restore the cnx partition from the configuration file, use the clu_bdmgr command with the "-h" option.

```
# clu_bdmgr -h dsk6 /.local../boot_partition/etc/clu_bdmgr.conf
```

Since the cnx partition on every member's boot disk is identical (as of this writing), we used the clu_bdmgr.conf file from the member that we're logged into to restore the cnx partition instead of using the member's restored boot_partition.

Once the cnx partition is restored, the "clu_bdmgr -d" command will return the configuration information.

```
# clu_bdmgr -d dsk6

# clu_bdmgr configuration file
# DO NOT EDIT THIS FILE
::TYP:m:CFS:/dev/vol/cluster_rootvol:LSM:30,/dev/disk/dsk5h|simp,/dev/disk/dsk6g
|simp,/dev/disk/dsk5g|simp::
```

The output from "clu_bdmgr -d" shows the four field identifiers that are defined in the clupt.h file in /sys/include/sys.

```
# grep -E "[A-Z] field id" /sys/include/sys/clupt.h

#define CLUP_TYP_NAME     "TYP:"   /* TYP field identifier+separator      */
#define CLUP_LSM_NAME     "LSM:"   /* LSM field identifier+separator      */
#define CLUP_CFS_NAME     "CFS:"   /* CFS field identifier+separator      */
#define CLUP_CNX_NAME     "CNX:"   /* CNX field identifier+separator      */
```

The "TYP" field indicates that this is a member boot disk as indicated by the "m" (a "q" represents a quorum disk). The "CFS" field indicates the volumes in the cluster_root domain. The last field is the "LSM" field, which lists the sequence number (30), the devices, and their LSM disk type (/dev/disk/dsk5h|simp, /dev/disk/dsk6g|simp, and /dev/disk/dsk5g|simp).

NOTE:

The clu_quorum command stores the quorum disk's cnx partition configuration information in the clu_quorum_qdisk file in the /cluster/admin directory.

We will cover how to restore a member's boot disk in much more detail in Chapter 22. For additional information on the clu_bdmgr command, see the clu_bdmgr(8) reference page.

17.8.5.1 What's on the `cnx` Partition?

Before digging into the depths of the cnx partition, it should be noted that not much documentation exists on the subject. This is by design because most of the information is not generally useful to managing your cluster on a daily basis, although it is has been brought to our attention that in rare instances it can be useful in troubleshooting some cluster problems related to quorum. Finally, you should be aware that the information presented here is only valid as of this writing since the cluster engineers could choose to modify the layout of the cnx partition in a future *TruCluster* Server release.

So, why bother presenting the information at all? Well, many, many system administrators, students, and support personnel have requested more information about the cnx partition.

According to the `clupt.h` header file located in the `/sys/include/sys` directory, the cnx partition is currently split into three sections:

0	256K	512K
Quorum Division	Member Division	Unused Division

Both the quorum and member divisions are divided into five segments:

Quorum Division (0 - 255K)

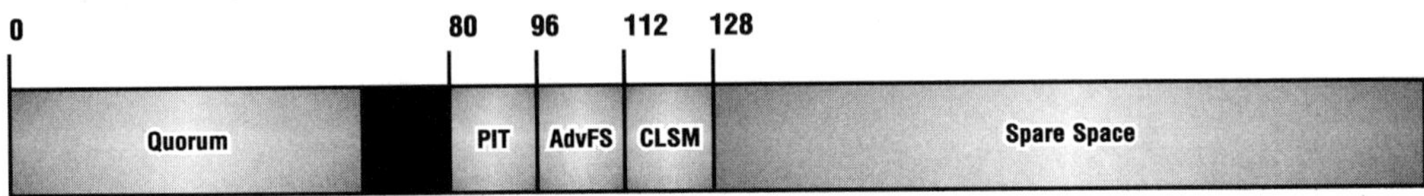

Member Division (256K - 511K)

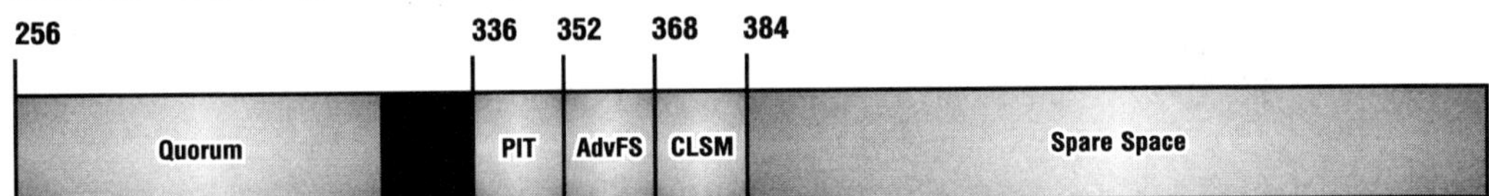

Quorum	–	**64K Quorum segment**
PIT	–	**16K Partition in Time (PIT) segment**
AdvFS	–	**16K AdvFS `cluster_root` devices segment**
CLSM	–	**16K Cluster Logical Storage Manager (CLSM) `cluster_root` devices segment**
Spare Space	–	**128K Spare Space segment**

The quorum division is used only on a quorum disk while the member division is used only on a member disk. The quorum segment is not used on the member division. The PIT section does not appear to be used in either division as of this writing.

We wrote a little program (`cnxread`) to check out the information contained on the `cnx` partition to see what information is actually stored on the disk. We will use it to illustrate the content of the `cnx` partition on both the quorum and member disks.

17.8.5.1.1 The Quorum Segment

The quorum segment contains two sections:

- Cluster and Owner Information Section
- Activity Section

The Cluster and Owner Information Section contains information regarding the cluster and member currently claiming ownership of the quorum disk. This information includes:

- Cluster Information
  - The cluster's name
  - The cluster incarnation number
  - The cluster founder's CSID
  - The number of members in the cluster
  - The number of votes the quorum disk has
  - The current number of votes the cluster has
  - The number of votes required for the cluster to reach quorum
  - A flag indicating whether or not the cluster has quorum

- Owner Information
  - The owner's CSID
  - The owner's incarnation
  - The owner's name
  - The owner's member ID
  - The time that the node claimed ownership of the disk

The Activity Section contains information regarding the last time the quorum disk was accessed and by which member. The information contained in the Activity Section includes:

- The writer's CSID
- The writer's incarnation
- The writer's name
- The writer's member ID
- The activity count
- The time the last write was performed

The quorum disk thread on each member attempts to access the quorum disk approximately every five seconds.

Let's see what's on our quorum disk.

```
# cnxread dsk4

The CNX Partition info for /dev/rdisk/dsk4h.  This is the quorum disk.

Quorum Section Information:

  babylon5 (CSID: 0x10001, incarn: 0x6478c)

  # Members   -   Current Votes   -   Quorum Votes   -   Qdisk Votes
  ---------       -------------       ------------       -----------
      2                 3                  2                  1

  Qdisk claimed on 20020110 at 01:20:19 by member:
    sheridan (CSID: 0x10002, incarn: 0x7bd63, memberid: 2)

  Qdisk written on 20020110 at 04:41:04 by member:
    molari (CSID: 0x20001, incarn: 0x92f6a, memberid: 1)

  Activity count = 3883
```

Notice that sheridan claimed the quorum disk but molari was the last member to write to the disk. If we rerun the program, there is an equal chance that either member may be the last writer as all members write to the quorum disk. For example, here is the output from another run of the program where sheridan is the writer.

```
# cnxread dsk4

The CNX Partition info for /dev/rdisk/dsk4h.  This is the quorum disk.

Quorum Section Information:

  babylon5 (CSID: 0x10001, incarn: 0x6478c)

  # Members   -   Current Votes   -   Quorum Votes   -   Qdisk Votes
  ---------       -------------       ------------       -----------
      2                 3                  2                  1

  Qdisk claimed on 20020110 at 01:20:19 by member:
    sheridan (CSID: 0x10002, incarn: 0x7bd63, memberid: 2)

  Qdisk written on 20020110 at 04:41:09 by member:
    sheridan (CSID: 0x10002, incarn: 0x7bd63, memberid: 2)

  Activity count = 3884
```

We will now use cnxread to dump the quorum section on molari's member disk's cnx partition. By default, the cnxread program will not show the quorum section since a member disk's quorum section is not used, but if we use the "-q" option, we can instruct the program to output the quorum section.

```
# cnxread -q dsk2
The CNX Partition info for /dev/rdisk/dsk2h.  This is a member boot disk.

Quorum Section Information:

  nada (CSID: 0, incarn: 0)

  # Members   -  Current Votes  -  Quorum Votes  -  Qdisk Votes
  ---------      -------------     ------------     -----------
      0               0                 0                0

  Qdisk claimed on 19691232 at 19:00:00 by member:
    nobody (CSID: 0, incarn: 0, memberid: 0)

  Qdisk written on 19691232 at 19:00:00 by member:
    nobody (CSID: 0, incarn: 0, memberid: 0)

  Activity count = 0
...
```

The quorum section contains nothing of interest on a member disk.

17.8.5.1.2 Partition in Time (PIT) Segment

As of this writing, the PIT segment has been reserved for future use.

17.8.5.1.3 AdvFS `cluster_root` Devices Segment

This segment is defined in the `clupt.h` file as containing the following information:

- A magic number
- A data sequence number
- The number of devices in the `cluster_root` domain
- An array of device IDs

Using the `cnxread` program to look at a member's boot disk `cnx` partition, we can see that the `cluster_root` domain has only one device.

```
# cnxread dsk2
The CNX Partition info for /dev/rdisk/dsk2h.  This is a member boot disk.

Cluster Root Filesystem (AdvFS) Segment Information

  Magic #: 0x42534, Sequence #: 88

                maj,min
                --- ---
  Devices: [  1]: 19, 52
```

We can quickly determine what device has major/minor number of "19, 52" by using the following command:

```
# ls -l /dev/disk/* | grep "19, 52"
brw-------    1 root      system     19, 52 Nov 27 03:59 /dev/disk/dsk1b
```

Let's temporarily add a device to the `cluster_root` domain.

```
# addvol /dev/disk/dsk6g cluster_root
```

```
# cnxread dsk2

The CNX Partition info for /dev/rdisk/dsk2h.  This is a member boot disk.

Cluster Root Filesystem (AdvFS) Segment Information

  Magic #: 0x42534, Sequence #: 90

                 maj,min
                 --- ---
  Devices: [  1]: 19,142
           [  2]: 19, 52
```

The second device is also shown.

17.8.5.1.4 CLSM `cluster_root` Devices Segment

The CLSM segment is similar to the AdvFS segment in that it contains device information. This segment contains:

- A magic number
- A sequence number
- The LSM (or Veritas) version number
- Number of devices
- An array of device information (device name, type, ID)

Here's the output of a member boot disk's `cnx` partition using an LSM volume for the `cluster_root` device. For more information on using LSM in a cluster, see Chapter 14.

```
# cnxread -l dsk2

The CNX Partition info for /dev/rdisk/dsk2h.  This is a member boot disk.

Cluster Root Filesystem (AdvFS) Segment Information

  Magic #: 0x42534, Sequence #: 116

                 maj,min
                 --- ---
  Devices: [  1]: 40,  5

CLSM Segment Information

  Magic #: 0x46185, Sequence #: 22, Version 3.1

                 maj,min
                 --- ---
  Devices: [  1]: 19,128   dsk5h (simp)
           [  2]: 19,142   dsk6g (simp)
           [  3]: 19,126   dsk5g (simp)
```

In our cluster, dsk5g and dsk6g are the two plexes in a mirrored volume that are used for cluster_root. The first device listed (dsk5h) is the private region disk in the rootdg. We are not exactly sure why it shows up because it is not in the cluster_root volume, but it does appear that any device in the rootdg will show up in the output.

```
# volprint -g rootdg
TY NAME         ASSOC        KSTATE   LENGTH   PLOFFS   STATE    TUTIL0  PUTIL0
dg rootdg       rootdg       -        -        -        -        -       -

dm clu_mroot    dsk5g        -        8686058  -        -        -       -
dm clu_root     dsk6g        -        8686058  -        -        -       -
dm dsk5h        dsk5h        -        8686058  -        -        -       -

v  cluster_rootvol cluroot   ENABLED  1048576  -        ACTIVE   -       -
pl cluster_rootvol-01 cluster_rootvol ENABLED 1048576 - ACTIVE   -       -
sd clu_mroot-01 cluster_rootvol-01 ENABLED 1048576 0    -        -       -
pl cluster_rootvol-02 cluster_rootvol ENABLED 1048576 - ACTIVE   -       -
sd clu_root-01  cluster_rootvol-02 ENABLED 1048576 0    -        -       -
```

17.9 How to Regain Quorum

In the event that you lose quorum, and it cannot be regained by booting additional members, there are ways to rectify the problem without having to rebuild the cluster.

For example, let's say we have a six-member cluster without a quorum disk and three members crash for some reason (hit by cosmic rays or something). The three remaining members would not have enough votes to keep the cluster running. Since we have lost quorum, we cannot use the `clu_quorum` command to adjust the cluster's expected votes. What should we do?

We can halt one of the suspended cluster members and boot it interactively to adjust the cluster's expected votes. The `cluster_adjust_expected_votes` attribute in the `clubase` subsystem, when set to zero, will cause the cluster to adjust expected votes to the number of votes that it can currently see.

You boot a system interactively by using an "`i`" to the "`-flags`" boot option. Note: the "a" indicates that the system should not stop in single-user mode but come all the way up.

```
>>> boot -fl ai

(boot dkb100.1.0.3.2 -flags ai)
block 0 of dke100.1.0.3.2 is a valid boot block
reading 19 blocks from dke100.1.0.3.2
bootstrap code read in
Building FRU table
base = 200000, image_start = 0, image_bytes = 2600
initializing HWRPB at 2000
initializing page table at 1f2000
initializing machine state
setting affinity to the primary CPU
jumping to bootstrap code

UNIX boot - Wednesday August 01, 2001


Enter: <kernel_name> [option_1 ... option_n]
  or: ls [name]['help'] or: 'quit' to return to console
Press Return to boot 'vmunix'
#
```

The boot process will stop at the "#" prompt and wait for input. At this point, enter the kernel name followed by any number of white space delimited "`subsystem:attribute=value`" strings. In our case, the kernel is `vmunix`, the subsystem is `clubase`, the attribute is `cluster_adjust_expected_votes`, and the value is 0.

```
# vmunix clubase:cluster_adjust_expected_votes=0
```

At this point the node will continue to boot. Once the Connection Manager gets started, the cluster will adjust expected votes based on the number of votes currently available.

```
Loading vmunix ...
Loading at 0xfffffc0000230000

Sizes:
text =  8624320
data =  1778320
bss  =  3908272
Starting at 0xfffffc0000242360

Loading vmunix symbol table ... [2188944 bytes]
Kernel argument clubase:cluster_adjust_expected_votes=0
Alpha boot: available memory from 0x1c78000 to 0x1fffc000
...
CNX MGR: after joining the cluster, expected votesCNX MGR: Join operation complete
CNX MGR: membership configuration index: 4 (3 additions, 1 removals)
CNX MGR: cannot adjust expected votes, cluster busy.
CNX MGR: Node molari 1 incarn 0xdf41e csid 0x10001 has been added to the cluster
CNX MGR: cannot adjust expected votes, cluster busy.
ics_mct: Declaring this node up 1
CNX MGR: Node sheridan 2 incarn 0x4c644 csid 0x50002 has been added to the cluster
CNX MGR: Node delenn 3 incarn 0xec4fc csid 0x30003 has been added to the cluster
CNX MGR: cannot adjust expected votes, cannot become coordinator.
CNX MGR: cannot adjust expected votes, cannot become coordinator.
CNX MGR: Using current votes (3) for expected votes.
CNX MGR: Adjust expected votes operation completed with quorum.
CNX MGR: quorum (re)gained, (re)starting cluster operations.
```

CAUTION:

You can only use "`clubase:cluster_adjust_expected_votes=0`" to regain quorum of a formed cluster. It cannot be used to form a cluster.

Furthermore, the `cluster_adjust_expected_votes` attribute only affects the expected votes value of the currently formed cluster. In other words, this will get your cluster running but does not permanently change the `cluster_expected_votes` value in each member's `sysconfigtab` file. If you need to make the change permanent, use the `clu_quorum` command with the "`-e`" or "`-m`" option once the cluster regains quorum.

As of this writing, the `cluster_adjust_expected_votes` attribute is not documented in the `sys_attrs_clubase(5)` reference page but is documented in the *TruCluster* Server Cluster Administration Guide.

17.10 Forming a Cluster without Enough Votes

What if your cluster is down and you are unable to boot enough members to form a cluster? If you have insufficient votes to form a cluster, you can boot the systems interactively and set `cluster_expected_votes` to a value that will allow the cluster to form.

If we consider our six-member cluster configuration again, let's assume that all the members came down but only three can be rebooted. Since we can boot three systems, we should set the `cluster_expected_votes` value to 3.

Boot each member as follows:

```
>>> boot -fl ai

(boot dkb100.1.0.3.2 -flags ai)
block 0 of dke100.1.0.3.2 is a valid boot block
reading 19 blocks from dke100.1.0.3.2
bootstrap code read in
Building FRU table
base = 200000, image_start = 0, image_bytes = 2600
initializing HWRPB at 2000
initializing page table at 1f2000
initializing machine state
setting affinity to the primary CPU
jumping to bootstrap code

UNIX boot - Wednesday August 01, 2001


Enter: <kernel_name> [option_1 ... option_n]
  or: ls [name]['help'] or: 'quit' to return to console
Press Return to boot 'vmunix'
#
```

At the prompt enter the following:

```
# vmunix clubase:cluster_expected_votes=3
```

Once two of the members configure the Connection Manager, the cluster will have 2 votes, which is sufficient for quorum and the cluster will form. As with the example in section 17.8.5, the change will not survive a reboot.

To make a more permanent change, once you can login, use the `clu_quorum` command to adjust the votes on the members that will be unavailable for an extended period of time using the "`-m`" option or adjust the cluster's expected votes value using the "`-e`" option. And remember, do not edit a member's `sysconfigtab` file manually!

17.10.1 Forming a Cluster without Enough Votes and/or a Failed Quorum Disk

If we modify our previous scenario to include a quorum disk that failed, can we boot interactively by simply using the `cluster_expected_votes` value alone? Yes and no. While you can boot a cluster with a failed quorum disk, the quorum disk thread will attempt to retry the disk for some time before finally giving up. Prior to V5.1A, this would delay the boot process. As an alternative, at the interactive boot prompt, add a second attribute, `cluster_qdisk_votes`.

```
# vmunix clubase:cluster_expected_votes=3 clubase:cluster_qdisk_votes=0
```

Another option would be to add the `cluster_qdisk_major` and `cluster_qdisk_minor` attributes to the interactive boot prompt so that the `cnx` will not load the `qdisk` attributes at all.

```
# vmunix clubase:cluster_expected_votes=2 clubase:cluster_qdisk_votes=0 clubase:
cluster_qdisk_major=0 clubase:cluster_qdisk_minor=0
```

CAUTION:

The interactive boot prompt line must be one continuous line. Do not put in a "\" to continue onto the next line; it will not work. Also, be extremely careful to type everything correctly. Typos are generally ignored by the subsystem. This, unfortunately, will not give you the desired effect since you will not have successfully overridden the attribute value(s).

17.11 References

- The *TruCluster* Server Technical Overview Guide.
- The *TruCluster* Server Cluster Administration Guide.
- The *TruCluster* Server Internals Course Material.
- Reference pages (noted within the text).

18

Miscellaneous Subsystems

You get up in the morning and drive your car to work. Normally you don't pay special attention to the roads, streetlights, stop signs, car engine, or buildings. They're just there. However, consider the difficulty of driving to work if there were no roads, or maybe there are roads but no stoplights and other traffic controls. A nightmare scenario, wouldn't you say? This chapter takes the standard drive to work in the morning and exposes the critical infrastructure of the traffic control system and roads. The Internode Communication Services (ICS – the roads upon which cluster communication travels), Distributed Lock Manager (DLM – the traffic controls), Kernel Group Services (KGS – providing for car pool membership and decisions during cluster communication), and the Reliable Datagram (RDG – providing messaging between applications on a cluster – horn honking and turn signals) mechanisms are described in this chapter. We also look at the Cluster Mount Subsystem (CMS) and the Token subsystem to round out our discussion of miscellaneous subsystems.

These components are essential to the lower level functioning of the cluster, and these miscellaneous subsystems provide the critical infrastructure for all the components discussed previously in this book.

18.1 Internode Communication Services (ICS)

The internode communications subsystem (ICS) supports communication between members within a cluster. It provides the roads and traffic control infrastructure mentioned in the chapter introduction. In V1.X releases of *TruCluster*, there was no need for a flexible cluster communications component such as ICS because only Memory Channel was supported for the Cluster Interconnect (CI). The use of the Ethernet as a communications medium between cluster members introduced an additional option for the cluster transport. Basically, the cluster software must support the ability to choose between MC and LAN for your communications medium (like choosing between the interstate or travel local roads). The development of ICS was not an afterthought to support LAN but a plan to seamlessly prepare for future cluster interconnects and remove the dependencies that were in the earlier *TruCluster* software.

ICS provides the means to carry communication between cluster members. It is organized as a layer of abstraction, meaning that it will not have to change radically as the underlying hardware technology changes over time. ICS is divided into two levels: the lower level handles the details of

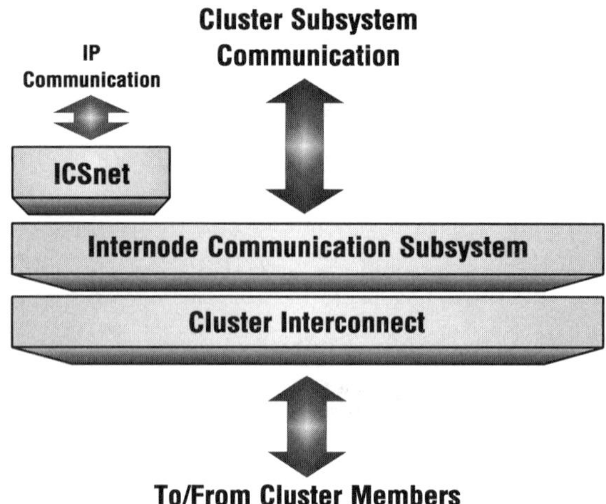

Figure 18-1: ICS Cluster Subsystem Communication

transporting the data, and the upper level provides a hardware independent interface to the services that rely on ICS.

Thus cluster software components (cluster services – such as CFS, CLSM, CNX, CLUA, DLM, DRD, and others in the future) are built currently, and can be built in the future, to communicate with the high level of ICS, eliminating the necessity of grappling with the complexities of the underlying hardware technology and providing a more hierarchical relationship between components. The high level ICS code communicates with the appropriate low level ICS software on behalf of the service. Figure 18-1 shows how the ICS subsystem fits into the cluster subsystem component hierarchy. It is above the actual communications hardware and below such critical components as the CFS, CNX, DLM, and DRD. Below the ICS will be whatever software constitutes a device driver for the hardware (Memory Channel, Ethernet, others).

There are two layers of software within ICS:

- High-level ICS (`ics_hl`)
    - Used by cluster subsystems (CFS, CLSM, CNX, DRD, DLM, CLUA).
    - Provides hardware-independent support for component initialization (used by DRD).
    - Provides information supporting cluster membership changes (used by CNX).
    - Provides high-level server control code (used by DLM).
    - Provides generic transport of data across the interconnect (used by CFS).
- Low-level ICS (`ics_ll_mct` or `ics_ll_tcp`)
    - Provides the transport-specific (not hardware independent) component.
    - Handles the actual transmission and reception of data across the cluster interconnect.
    - Detects communication failures.
    - Low-level ICS software is called solely by routines in the High-Level ICS.

Figure 18-2 illustrates the structure of ICS.

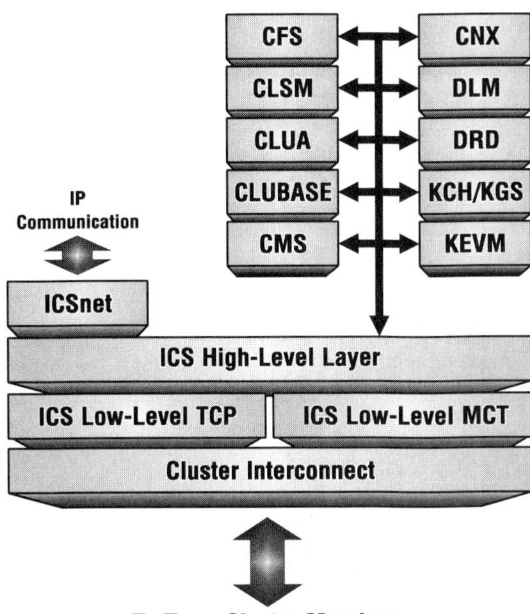

Figure 18-2: ICS Cluster Subsystem Communication – Detailed

```
# sman all sys_attrs_ics

Section   Reference Page               Description
-------   -------------------------    -----------------------------------------

   5      sys_attrs_ics_hl             ics_hl subsystem attributes

   5      sys_attrs_ics_ll_tcp         ics-ll-tcp subsystem attributes

   5      sys_attrs_icsnet             icsnet subsystem attributes
```

18.1.1 ICSNET

ICSNET is another service that interfaces with the ICS high-level software. ICSNET is essentially a network driver that puts TCP/IP (or UDP/IP) headers and data on the CI encapsulated in an Ethernet format (despite that fact the data may not be sent over the Ethernet). Consider the situation where information is picked up from the network and needs to be delivered to a cluster member other than the one that received the data. Let's say that this cluster uses the Memory Channel for its CI. The Ethernet device physically connected to the cluster member receiving the network transmission will issue an interrupt and cause the Ethernet driver's Interrupt Service Routine to execute.

Eventually the `netisr_thread` kernel thread will execute to handle the mid-layer IP protocol stack decisions. The data will be stored in message buffer structures (called mbufs). So far, this is normal processing of network activity. The problem, at this point, is that the processing of the data may be taking place on the wrong cluster member. (We are assuming that the receiving member is not the member to whom the data is ultimately being sent.) The data should be forwarded to the target member and fully processed by the receiving application on the target cluster member. The data (in the mbufs) must be sent through the CI (think Memory Channel in this case) to the correct cluster member, but the Memory Channel is accessible through ICS (see Figure 18-2). Control will be transferred to the `netisr_thread` software as is customary when processing the data through the IP stack, but the ICSNET software will be called by the `netisr_thread` to pass the data to the target cluster member over the Memory Channel (or Ethernet in the case of a LAN-based cluster).

The ICS Network driver (ICSNET) is used during steady state operation of the cluster to channel messages across the CI that emanate from cluster applications (as opposed to cluster kernel services). The cluster kernel services interface directly with ICS as pictured in Figure 18-2.

18.1.2 ICS Implementation

ICS is implemented using client-server strategies. A request begins execution within a client service (such as CFS, CLSM, DRD, CLUA, DLM, etc.); it is then transported to the ICS server for execution (using Remote Procedure Calls). See Figure 18-2. The ICS server software is implemented as a potentially dynamic number of daemons. The daemons contain one or more threads, which provide the context within which to execute the server side of the RPCs issued by the ICS clients. The number of daemons supporting the client requests can be static or dynamic depending on the necessities of the individual client request.

The ICS subsystem may request the creation of more daemons depending on the workload and the nature of the service. For instance, the count of server side ICS daemons created for DLM will not be dynamic since processing should be performed in the order that the requests are received. The count of daemons for DRD, on the other hand, will be drawn from a pool that grows and shrinks based on the amount of DRD activity requested. The following output shows some of the daemons supporting ICS.

```
# ps -eo pid,command | grep ics

524291 [icssvr_nomem_dae]
524292 [icssvr_throttle_]
524293 [icssvr_daemon_fr]
524294 [icssvr_daemon_fr]
524295 [icssvr_nanny]
524296 [icscli_throttle_]
524298 [icssvr_daemon_fr]
524299 [icssvr_daemon_fr]
524300 [icssvr_daemon_fr]
524301 [icssvr_daemon_fr]
524302 [icssvr_daemon_fr]
524303 [icssvr_daemon_pe]
524304 [icssvr_daemon_pe]
524305 [icssvr_daemon_pe]
524306 [icssvr_daemon_pe]
524307 [icssvr_daemon_pe]
```

```
524308 [icssvr_daemon_pe]
524309 [icssvr_daemon_fr]
524310 [icssvr_daemon_fr]
524311 [icssvr_daemon_fr]
524312 [icssvr_daemon_fr]
524328 [icssvr_daemon_pe]
524929 [icssvr_daemon_pe]
524946 [icssvr_daemon_pe]
524947 [icssvr_daemon_pe]
525602 [icssvr_daemon_fr]
525603 [icssvr_daemon_fr]
```

The following output is from a Memory Channel-based cluster. The program will be available on the BRUDEN or Digital Press web site (see Appendix B for the URLs).

```
# ./kernel_idle_threads | grep ics
 55:0x0fffffc000f09c380:0x0fffffc0000ef0758:"ics_mct_thread"
 59:0x0fffffc000f09d180:0x0fffffc0000ef03d8:"ics_mct_recv_nohandle"
118:0x0fffffc000e9eaa80:0x0fffffc00008a2888:"ics_mct_heapwalker_main
```

The following output was generated on a LAN-based cluster. It shows 16 ICS kernel threads.

```
# ./kernel_idle_threads | grep ics
116:0x0fffffc001db0b500:0x0fffffc001db1800a:"ics_chan_listen"
117:0x0fffffc001db0b880:0x0fffffc001db1838a:"ics_chan_listen"
118:0x0fffffc001db0bc00:0x0fffffc001db1870a:"ics_chan_listen"
119:0x0fffffc001db10000:0x0fffffc001db18a8a:"ics_chan_listen"
120:0x0fffffc001db10380:0x0fffffc001db18e0a:"ics_chan_listen"
121:0x0fffffc001db10700:0x0fffffc001db1918a:"ics_chan_listen"
122:0x0fffffc001db10a80:0x0fffffc001db1950a:"ics_chan_listen"
123:0x0fffffc001db10e00:0x0fffffc001db1988a:"ics_chan_listen"
124:0x0fffffc001db11180:0x0fffffc001db19c0a:"ics_chan_listen"
125:0x0fffffc001db11500:0x0fffffc001db1a00a:"ics_chan_listen"
126:0x0fffffc001db11880:0x0fffffc001db1a38a:"ics_chan_listen"
127:0x0fffffc001db11c00:0x0fffffc001db1a70a:"ics_chan_listen"
128:0x0fffffc001db12000:0x0fffffc001db1aa8a:"ics_chan_listen"
129:0x0fffffc001db12380:0x0fffffc001db1ae0a:"ics_chan_listen"
130:0x0fffffc001db12700:0x0fffffc001db1b18a:"ics_chan_listen"
131:0x0fffffc001db12a80:0x0fffffc001db1b50a:"ics_chan_listen"
```

```
# ps -lmp 524288 | grep ics | wc -l
      16
```

The following sections further describe selected ICS server processes.

18.1.2.1 ICS Server Daemon from Pool [icssvr_daemon_fr]

Some services are able to share a pool of daemons available to satisfy their processing needs dynamically. Services that use this pool of daemons include CFS, CLSM, DRD, and KGS. The activity level of these services can vary greatly over the life of the cluster. Thus, it makes sense to handle their ICS requests such that the system will dynamically create more of these daemons during bursts of activity.

Note that the count of daemons also has downward flexibility so that at one point you may see N of these daemons, and at another point you may see N-2.

18.1.2.2 ICS Server Daemon Per Node [icssvr_daemon_pe]

Some services require a more predictable server environment. The predictability is based on a server daemon per node. It's like having a multi-lane highway with each lane taking you to exactly one location. Technically these lanes are called "channels". (At least you don't have to worry about the exit number, or keeping up with traffic while traveling in these lanes.) Services requiring this kind of server environment include CLUA, CNX, DLM, Memory Channel Transport (MCT), and others.

18.1.2.3 Miscellaneous ICS Server Daemons

Two more ICS server daemons exist to handle special case situations. The `icssvr_nomem_daemon` is used when kernel level memory allocation fails and a thread context is needed in order to wait for memory to be deallocated. This daemon should rarely be required.

The `icssvr_throttle_daemon` should also be rarely used. It is awakened to handle client activities that have been throttled due to lack of memory. This daemon will be responsible for waking any throttled clients once their channel or memory issue is resolved.

18.1.2.4 ICS Channels

The traffic between cluster members using ICS goes through channels. Each channel can handle zero or more services. Think of our multi-lane highway example from the previous section, and put the Distributed Lock Manager service from one cluster member on one end of the lane (channel) and the Distributed Lock Manager service from another cluster member on the other end. Placing data on the channel guarantees delivery to the target service and the order of delivery. For a service like DLM, these guarantees are critical to ensure fair access to locked resources.

Now imagine a lane on a super-highway where multiple services use the same lane. This would require some dispatching on the receiving end to make sure that the message gets to the proper service on the target member. This strategy is used on a channel traveled by CFS, AdvFS, and CMS. They all share a channel. It works out well since these services are all file related anyway. Section 18.1.4 shows channel statistics generated by the `cfsstat(8)` command.

Table 18-1 relates various services and their associated channels.

ICS Services per ICS Channel

Channel	#	Services	Cluster Subsystem	# of Services	ICS Server Daemon
BOOT	0	CNX	cnx	3	per node
		(CLUSTER_PANIC)	ics_hl		custom
		SIGNAL	ics_hl		from pool
PRI0	1	none	n/a	0	n/a
PRI1	2	none	n/a	0	n/a
CFS	3	ADVFS, CFS, FS	cfs	4	from pool
		CMS	cms		from pool
NET	4	CLUMGT	clubase	2	from pool
		ICSNET	icsnet		custom
CLSM	5	CLSM	clsm	1	from pool
DRD	6	DRDV1, DRDV2	drd	2	from pool
TUNL	7	TUNNEL	clua	1	per node
CLUA	8	CLUA	clua	1	per node
KEVM	9	KEVM	kevm_clu	1	per node
CFSR	10	CFSREC	cfs	1	from pool
RBLD	11	RBLD	cnx	2	from pool
		SSN	n/a		from pool
KCH	12	KCH	kch	1	from pool
DLM	13	DLM	dlm	1	per node
TEST	14	(TEST), (TEST1), (TEST2), (TEST3), (TEST4), (TEST5), (TEST6), (TEST7)	n/a	7	varies
PBT	15	MCTCTL_SVC	ics_ll_mct	1	per node

Table 18-1: ICS Services per ICS Channel

18.1.2.5 ICS Server Nanny Process [icssvr_nanny]

So who's in charge of all these hale and hearty ICS server processes? When you were young, you may have had a nanny looking after you (or maybe you just had your older brother, or a neighbor, or weird old Hal from down the street); similarly, the ICS server processes are watched over by the "nanny" process. It will cause the creation of the pool-based processes when needed and will cause the creation of the per-node based processes as members come and go from the cluster.

If you were a really rambunctious kid, and you had lots of siblings, you may have needed a second nanny. Similarly, when the ICS server nanny is overstressed, it may be joined by other nannies.(We guess they just call for backup assistance when necessary.) Note that, as of this writing, it would be unusual to see more than one nanny.

18.1.3 ICS Attributes

The following output provides information on the `sysconfig` attributes supporting ICS.

NOTE:

A typical cluster member will use `ics_ll_tcp` or `ics_ll_mct` attributes but not both, although both sets of attributes will be visible. Also, note that the low-level attributes are undocumented and should not be altered unless you are directed to change them by HP engineering. We include them here to show the existence of software levels within the ICS subsystem.

```
# for i in $(sysconfig -m | grep ics | cut -d: -f1)
> do
>    print
>    sysconfig -q $i
> done

ics_hl:
ics_hl_debug = 1
Module_Config_Name = attribute does not allow this operation
ics_hl_verbose = 2
ics_idle_daemons_lwm = 4
ics_idle_daemons_hwm = 15

ics_ll_tcp:
Module_Config_Name = attribute does not allow this operation
ics_tcp_rendezvous_port = 0
ics_tcp_ports[0] = 0
...
ics_tcp_ports[15] = 0
ics_tcp_inetaddr0 =
ics_tcp_netmask0 =
ics_tcp_adapter0 =
ics_tcp_ipmtu0 = 1500
ics_tcp_nr0[0] =
...
ics_tcp_nr0[7] =
```

← ICS High-Level Attributes.

← ICS Low-Level TCP Attributes.

```
ics_ll_mct:
ics_mct_debug_flags = 0
ics_mct_fsw_timeout = 4096
ics_mct_rsw_timeout = 4096
ics_mct_old_vers = 1
ics_mct_new_vers = 1
ics_mct_heap_timeout = 30
ics_mct_small_bucket = 512
ics_mct_medium_bucket = 2048
ics_mct_large_bucket = 8192
ics_mct_frag_freelim = 32
ics_mct_nodedown_timeout = 100
ics_mct_nodedown_paniclimit = 0
ics_mct_enabled = 1
ics_mct_auto_oolbucket_up = 0
ics_mct_hb_disable = 0
ics_mct_yield_ticks = 10
Module_Config_Name = attribute does not allow this operation

icsnet:

hdwr_addr = 42:00:00:00:00:01
verbose = 0
icsnet_mtu = 7000
```

← ICS Low-Level Memory Channel Transport Attributes.

← Network Interface Communication Attributes.

← Internally managed MAC address

In order to quickly handle spikes of activity from ICS client services requesting unordered activities (such as CFS and DRD), a pool of idle processes is kept ready. The `ics_hl` subsystem attribute `ics_idle_daemons_lwm` sets the low water mark for this pool. The process count may grow up to `ics_idle_daemons_hwm` and even grow beyond it to handle heavy bursts of activity.

```
# sysconfig -q ics_hl ics_idle_daemons_hwm

ics_hl:
ics_idle_daemons_hwm = 15
```

```
# ps aux | grep icssvr_daemon_fr | wc -l

      18
```

Once the process count has been increased, it will never fall back below the high water mark, and it won't decrease at all if it stays less than the high water mark. The previous output shows the attribute values and then counts the current number of processes. In this case, the count exceeds the high water mark. If this situation arises consistently, the `ics_idle_daemons_hwm` may need to be raised since it could indicate a constant creation and deletion of the ICS daemon processes. If the kernel process creator daemon shows noticeable CPU time, you should raise the high water mark.

```
# ps -eo user,pid,time,command | awk '/^USER|kproc/ { print $0 }'

USER        PID        TIME COMMAND
root     524290     0:00.05 [kproc_creator_da]
```

The CPU time column in the above output shows no measurable CPU time, so there is no need to alter the `ics_hl` subsystem attributes.

18.1.4 ICS Statistics

The "`ics`" option in the `cfsstat` command provides statistics on ICS activities. Despite the command's name, it provides a wealth of ICS statistics. It can be issued with an interval option providing excellent insights into ongoing ICS activities.

Note that there are many options within `cfsstat` that focus on various ICS statistics as shown in Table 18-2.

ICS Options to **`cfsstat(8)`**

Option	V5.1B V5.1A	V5.1 V5.0A	Description
ics	✓	✓	Displays all ICS statistics
icsstat	✓	✓	Displays ICS client/server statistics
icschan	✓	✓	Displays ICS channel statistics (same as icschanbytes)
icssvc	✓	✓	Displays ICS service statistics (same as icssvcbytes)
icschanbps	✓	✗	Displays ICS channel statistics (byte per second mode)
icschanops	✓	✗	Displays ICS channel statistics (ops per second mode)
icschanbytes	✓	✗	Displays ICS channel statistics (byte mode)
icschancounts	✓	✗	Displays ICS channel statistics (count mode)
icssvcbytes	✓	✗	Displays ICS service statistics (byte mode)
icssvccounts	✓	✗	Displays ICS service statistics (count mode)
icschanhist	✓	✗	ICS channel transfer size histograms (total table)
icschanhisttot	✓	✗	ICS channel transfer size histograms (total table)
icschanhistcli	✓	✗	ICS channel transfer size histograms (client table)
icschanhistsvr	✓	✗	ICS channel transfer size histograms (server table)
icschanhistclisend	✓	✗	ICS channel transfer size histograms (cli send table)
icschanhistclirecv	✓	✗	ICS channel transfer size histograms (cli recv table)
icschanhistsvrrecv	✓	✗	ICS channel transfer size histograms (svr recv table)
icschanhistsvrsend	✓	✗	ICS channel transfer size histograms (svr send table)
icschanhistall	✓	✗	ICS channel transfer size histograms (all tables)
icslog	✓	✓	Displays last 200 message sent/received by ICS -- Available only in DEBUG kernels

Table 18-2: ICS options to the `cfsstat(8)` command

The following output displays ICS statistics per channel.

```
# cfsstat -i 5 icschanbps

 TOTL BOOT PRI0 PRI1  CFS  NET CLSM  DRD TUNL CLUA KEVM CFSR RBLD  KCH  DLM TEST
 680m  15k  90m   9k 282m   1m 520  265m  17k  32m   6m    0    0 316k   2m    0
 136m    0    0    0    0    0    0    0    0  808    0    0    0    0    0    0
   3k    0    0    0    0    0    0    0    0   3k    0    0    0    0  350    0
   2k    0   1k    0  284    0    0    0    0  808    0    0    0    0  175    0
   7k    0    0    0   7k    0    0    0    0    0    0    0    0    0    0    0
```

The following output gives you an idea of the spectacular quantity of statistics available from `cfsstat`. The "`-S`" option requests that the display be sorted from largest to smallest and eliminates any zero statistics.

```
# cfsstat -S ics | more

ICS static stats:
      16 total number of channels (istat_num_chans)
       3 total number of priority channels (istat_num_prios)
      64 maximum number of services (istat_max_svcs)
      27 number of elements per histogram (istat_hist_num_elems)
       4 histogram element size (istat_hist_elem_size)

ICS client stats:
   31544 number of sync rpcs sent (istat_clirpc)
    8404 number of async rpcs sent (istat_climsg)
      11 signals forwarded (istat_clisigforward)
      11 signal forward retries (istat_clisigforward_retry)

ICS server stats:
     319 number allocated handles (istat_svrhand_create)
     319 number of handles in use (istat_svrhand)
  110854 number of sync rpcs recvd (istat_svrrpc)
   11849 number of async rpcs recvd (istat_svrmsg)
       1 handle allocs deferred due to no memory (istat_svrhand_nomem)
      13 number of daemons created (istat_svrdaemon_create)
      13 number of waiting daemons (istat_svrdaemon)

ICS Channel Stats: Total bytes per interval: 403219489 (cli:  8% svr: 91%)
Channel Svcs Usage        CliSend        CliRecv        SvrRecv        SvrSend
_______ ____ _____ ______________ ______________ ______________ ______________
6   DRD    2   70%           7796          21096        2661844      280235728
3   CFS    4   22%        6984632       16638304       37480556       29464584
1  PRI0    0    4%        2298888          67800       14105516         188824
8  CLUA    1    1%        3821840           1208        2545200            928
9  KEVM    1    1%        2169040              0        2111344              0
13  DLM    1    0%         716276              0         685032              0
12  KCH    1    0%         123911          72644         134066          62348
5  CLSM    1    0%         235564              4              0              0
4   NET    2    0%         118208              0         116964              0
7  TUNL    1    0%           2184              0         110080              0
0  BOOT    3    0%          10800             72          10316             32
15  PBT    1    0%           4912           1640           5196           1736
2  PRI1    0    0%            900            456            452            232
10 CFSR    1    0%            216             36             72             12
11 RBLD    1    0%              0              0              0              0
```

```
ICS Service Stats: Total bytes per interval: 403219569 (cli:  8% svr: 91%)
Service    Ch #Pr Usage         CliSend          CliRecv          SvrRecv          SvrSend
_________  __ ___ _____  ______________  _______________  _______________  _______________
16  DRDV1   6   7   70%            5276             1560          2633064        280202392
12     FS   3  53   20%         6936472         10096108         37396624         27511744
9     CFS   3  15    6%         2219684          6473128         13979868          1886716
18   CLUA   8   2    1%         3821840             1208          2545200              928
19   KEVM   9   1    1%         2169040                0          2111344                0
23    DLM  13   6    0%          716280                8           685036                8
26  ADVFS   3  36    0%           59224           135364            82272           253480
22    KCH  12   2    0%          123911            72644           134066            62348
25   CLSM   5  13    0%          235564                4                0                0
14 ICSNET   4   2    0%          118208                0           116964                0
20 CFSREC  10   5    0%           65940               68           123300               72
17 TUNNEL   7   2    0%            2184                0           110160                0
27  DRDV2   6   7    0%            2520            19536            32732            34584
0     CNX   0  25    0%           10800               72            10316               32
24 MCTCTL  15   8    0%            4912             1640             5196             1736
10    CMS   3   9    0%            2032             1424              128              160
21   RBLD  11   1    0%             896              448              448              224
7  SIGNAL   0   3    0%             384               48                0                0

Total:

     BOOT PRI0 PRI1  CFS  NET CLSM  DRD TUNL CLUA KEVM CFSR RBLD  KCH  DLM TEST
   0    0    0    0    0    0    0    0    0    0    0    0    0    0    0    0
   1    0    0    0    0    0    0    0    0    0    0    0    0    0    0    0
   2    0    0    0    0    0    0    0    0    0    0    0    0    0    0    0
   4    0   1k    2    0    0    1    0    0  534    0   12    0    0    0    0
   8   17    4   86    0    0    0  125    0    0    0    0    0    0    0    0
  16    1    4   84    0    0    0  175    0    0    0   12    0    0    0    0
  32    4  813    0  39k   82    0  530    0    0    0    0    0  299    0    0
  64    3   2k    0   5k   2k    0   5k   1k    0    0    0    0  387    0    0
 128    0   2k    0 120k   11    0  159   25    0  127    0    0   78    0    0
 256   77   1k    0  90k    0    0  153    0    0   9k    0    0  109   4k    0
 512    0   84    0   2k    0    0   23    0    0   24    0    0  311    0    0
  1k    0  169    0  226    0    0   12    0    0    0    0    0    0    0    0
  2k    0  330    0  124    0    0    0    0   1k    0    0    0   12    0    0
  4k    0  305    0   82    0    0    0    0    0    0    0    0    9    0    0
  8k    0   1k    0   2k    0    0   1k    0    0    0    0    0    0    0    0
 16k    0  138    0  118    0    0  126    0    0    0    0    0    3    0    0
 32k    0    3    0   70    0    0  584    0    0    0    0    0    0    0    0
 64k    0    0    0   16    0    0   3k    0    0    0    0    0    0    0    0
128k    0    0    0    0    0    1  212    0    0    0    0    0    0    0    0
256k    0    0    0    0    0    0    0    0    0    0    0    0    0    0    0
512k    0    0    0    0    0    0    0    0    0    0    0    0    0    0    0
  1m    0    0    0    0    0    0    0    0    0    0    0    0    0    0    0
  2m    0    0    0    0    0    0    0    0    0    0    0    0    0    0    0
  4m    0    0    0    0    0    0    0    0    0    0    0    0    0    0    0
  8m    0    0    0    0    0    0    0    0    0    0    0    0    0    0    0
 16m    0    0    0    0    0    0    0    0    0    0    0    0    0    0    0
more    0    0    0    0    0    0    0    0    0    0    0    0    0    0    0
```

18.2 Distributed Lock Manager (DLM)

Most system administrators have a working knowledge of locking mechanisms available to applications. Some of the more common functions used by applications to achieve a form of mutual exclusion are `flock(2)`, `fcntl(2)`, and `lockf(3)`. As you probably expected, the introduction of clustering adds a level of complexity to the locking scenarios. The kernel data structures supporting traditional locking are found in the physical memory of a particular system. This raises legitimate concerns over the effectiveness of asking for UNIX (POSIX) locks in a *TruCluster* Server cluster. Have no fear. CFS is POSIX compliant and is prepared to deal with all lock requests.

But traditional UNIX locks are not as sophisticated as needed for many components and applications functioning in a cluster environment. The *TruCluster* Server Distributed Lock Manager (DLM) component provides a form of distributed (cluster-wide) locking that goes well beyond traditional locks by providing:

- More than just exclusive and shared access locks (see the excerpt from the `dlm(4)` reference page below)
- Asynchronous notification of lock holder that a lock being held is currently blocking another application's request for the lock
- Asynchronous lock grant notification
- Lock conversion capability (synchronous and asynchronous)
- Application created resource names representing the contested resource
- A per-resource lock value block for communication between contending applications
- Deadlock detection and notification mechanisms
- DLM API to create cluster-aware applications

The following is an excerpt from the `dlm(4)` reference page showing the available lock types.

```
DLM_NLMODE
          Null mode (NL). This mode grants no access to the resource; it
          serves as a placeholder and indicator of future interest in the
          resource. The null mode does not inhibit locking at other lock
          modes; further, it prevents the deletion of the resource and lock
          value block, which would otherwise occur if the locks held at the
          other lock modes were dequeued.
```

```
DLM_CRMODE
          Concurrent Read (CR). This mode grants the caller read access to
          the resource and permits write access to the resource by other
          users. This mode is used to read data from a resource in an
          unprotected manner, because other users can modify that data as
          it is being read. This mode is typically used when additional
          locking is being performed at a finer granularity with sublocks.

DLM_CWMODE
          Concurrent Write (CW). This mode grants the caller write access
          to the resource and permits write access to the resource by other
          users. This mode is used to write data to a resource in an unpro-
          tected fashion, because other users can simultaneously write data
          to the resource. This mode is typically used when additional
          locking is being performed at a finer granularity with sublocks.

DLM_PRMODE
          Protected Read (PR). This mode grants only read access to the
          resource by the caller and other users. Write access is not
          allowed. This is the traditional share lock.

DLM_PWMODE
          Protected Write (PW). This mode grants the caller write access to
          the resource and permits only read access to the resource by
          other users; the other users must have specified concurrent read
          mode access. No other writers are allowed access to the resource.
          This is the traditional update lock.

DLM_EXMODE
          Exclusive (EX). The exclusive mode grants the caller write access
          to the resource and permits no access to the resource by other
          users. This is the traditional exclusive lock.
```

How is DLM used? Which *TruCluster* Server components use it and which resource names do they use? Can user applications use DLM? DLM is used to coordinate cluster-wide activities. It is **not** restricted to file locking. DLM locks the access to a resource name, which represents a system resource. The resources can be real (device, data structure, alias, etc.) or ephemeral (user-defined or system-defined resource name representing anything -- or nothing).

A homegrown resource name, shown in the following examples, is "`den`". This resource name represents nothing but a figment of our imagination, although we can use it in a communication scenario where an application running on `member1` needs to know if a companion application is running on `member2` (within the same cluster). If the first application takes out an Exclusive lock on the resource named "`den`", then when the second application tries to get the Exclusive lock on the resource named "`den`", it is refused. It gets an unsuccessful status returned. At that time it knows that the companion application is up and running. If it gets a success status back, it knows that it is the first of the companion apps running and that the other is not currently running.

What did these applications lock? Nothing at which we can point a finger. They locked a resource name representing something that had meaning to them and had no meaning to any other applications in the cluster. The following is a truncated display of the system attributes (approximately 60 in total) pertaining to DLM.

```
# sysconfig -q dlm
dlm:
dlm_name                = Distributed Lock Manager - V2.0
dlm_lkbs_allocated      = 36
dlm_rsbs_allocated      = 36
dlm_tot_lkids           = 8191
dlm_lkids_inuse         = 36
dlm_ddlckq_len          = 0
dlm_timeoutq_len        = 0
...
```

Note that the following is a `kdbx(8)` command. It displays many of the Resource Block (RSB) resource names supporting the cluster components, as well as the one supporting our "`den`" resource (array element 2605). This command takes a while to complete and this particular run was stopped before it finished. It would be interesting to run this command on both members in a two-member cluster to see if the per member lock databases are the same. Remember that this component is called the **Distributed** Lock Manager because portions of the in-memory lock database can be distributed across the members of the cluster. However, if the locking can be accomplished using one member only, then the other members need little or no knowledge of the locking activities.

But what happens if another cluster member asks for a lock that is currently in use on only one member of the cluster? How will the member that is new in the locking scenario become aware that the resource he wants to lock is already locked on another member? One solution would be to **really** distribute the lock database (in its entirety) in the memory of all cluster members. This solution wastes memory and causes traffic between members each time a lock is created, tested, deleted, or accessed in any way.

The actual solution distributes a lock mastering table, which will be exactly the same on each cluster member. When access to a lock is requested, the resource name (representing the lock) is passed through a hashing algorithm that ultimately generates an offset into the lock mastering table (called the `lock directory vector` table). The appropriate entry in the table will identify the cluster member who is the director for the lock traffic involving this particular resource. All requests for new locks for a particular resource are funneled to the same director cluster member, who will be responsible for directing the lock traffic to the cluster member who is mastering the lock structures for this resource (see Figure 18-3 & Figure 18-4). Note that once a requesting member is told where

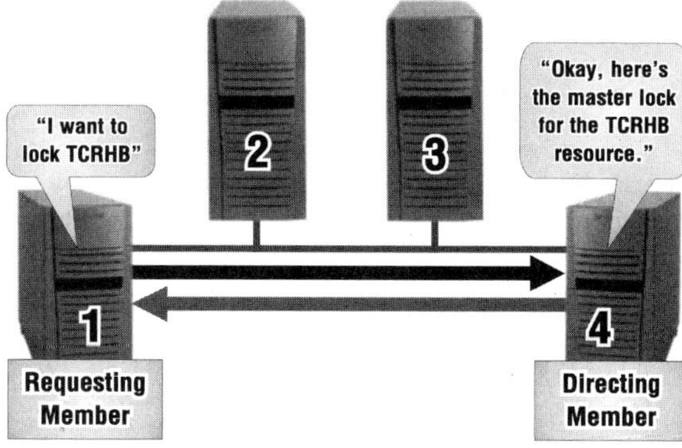

Figure 18-3: DLM – Create a Lock

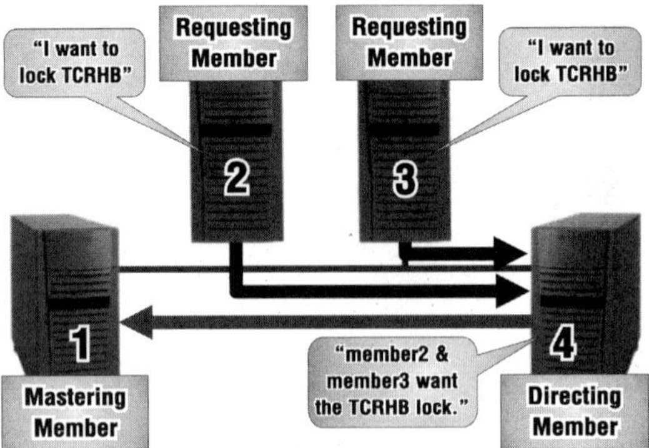

Figure 18-4: DLM – Directing Lock Request to the Lock Master

the mastering member is for a particular lock, subsequent lock activities for the same lock go directly to the mastering member.

This seems like a double indirect without much payback, but in fact, it allows the `lock directory vector` table to remain constant as long as cluster membership does not change. Meanwhile, the directing member will direct traffic to the mastering member. The mastering member will have the master copy of the lock database for this particular resource. Other cluster members may be the master for other locks. Thus the lock database (and its associated processing responsibilities) is distributed across the cluster.

If a member is requesting a brand new lock (such as "`den`" in our example), the string "`den`" will be hashed down to a number between zero and one less than the cluster member count. The derived number will be used as an offset into the `lock directory vector` table to figure out which member is the director for this resource. The director member is queried to find out which member is the master member for the resource "`den`". The director responds that it currently has no knowledge of the resource "`den`" and so deems that the master will be the requesting member. (You asked for it, you deal with it.) The director member keeps track of the fact that the new master for "`den`" is the requesting member, so that any subsequent requests from any cluster member will be directed to the appropriate member for lock mastering information.

When a member leaves the cluster, the DLM database has to be rebuilt. This may require the selection of a new master for a resource and will cause the directory vector to be recreated and distributed to all remaining members.

Discussing the internals of *TruCluster* Server is beyond the scope of this book, but you may find it enlightening to scan through the resource names in the following output and see if you can recognize some of the cluster components and services that use DLM for cluster-wide synchronization. Also, note that not all cluster components use DLM.

```
# kdbx -k /vmunix
...
(kdbx) array_action "rhash_tbl_entry_t *" 8191 &rhash_tbl[0] -cond %c.chain!=0 p %i,
(char *)(%c.chain).rsbdom.resnam
134 0xfffffc001d4c9878 = "cfs_devt:swap:19_83"
209 0xfffffc00024995f8 = "rootdg"
249 0xfffffc001ba9c838 = "clua_si_616_0"
347 0xfffffc001a235c38 = "/etc/exports\377^C"
515 0xfffffc000dd07238 = "cluster_lockd^C"
527 0xfffffc001d59f738 = "cfs_devt:19_198"
626 0xfffffc00098f4bf8 = "clua_si_1126_1"
639 0xfffffc0003443738 = "clua_doorbell"
727 0xfffffc000b0f7eb8 = "00000080-PR-DBP815000000-MM-DBP8^B"
790 0xfffffc0006cc6fb8 = "clua_si_1484_0"
841 0xfffffc000ebc81f8 = "clua_si_2301_0"
917 0xfffffc001a2354b8 = "RPC100005.17^A"
981 0xfffffc00077bf238 = "clua_si_1142_1"
1056 0xfffffc001e98d378 = "clua_si_2793_1"
1070 0xfffffc0006cc61f8 = "clua_si_765_1"
1100 0xfffffc00195aad38 = "clua_si_619_1"
1337 0xfffffc0003442e78 = "clua_pm_16.85.0.35"
1464 0xfffffc000bcd0838 = "clua_si_1198_0"
1492 0xfffffc001e98deb8 = "clua_si_111_1"
1563 0xfffffc001a2341f8 = "clua_si_1137_0"
1576 0xfffffc0019246978 = "clua_si_965_1"
1637 0xfffffc000b5bb9b8 = "clua_si_316_1"
1782 0xfffffc000d12d378 = "00000000-PR-DBP815000000-MM-DBP8^B"
2141 0xfffffc001d59ebf8 = "cfs_devt:19_126"
2508 0xfffffc001e98dc38 = "596"
2539 0xfffffc001d59eab8 = "cfs_devt:19_114"
2570 0xfffffc00195ab5f8 = "clua_si_842_0"
2605 0xfffffc000a5d95f8 = "den"
2656 0xfffffc001a2345b8 = "clua_si_618_0"
2845 0xfffffc001d59f9b8 = "cfs_devt:19_128"
2851 0xfffffc00029a6ab8 = "clua_si_1143_1"
2852 0xfffffc000e24cab8 = "00000001-PR-DAALL_DB0000-MM-DAAL^B"
2884 0xfffffc001d59e0b8 = "lock_dg"
3258 0xfffffc0005e670f8 = "00000000-MN-DAALL_DB"
3370 0xfffffc001d59e838 = "clua_si_3354_1"
3576 0xfffffc00034421f8 = "clua_si_1149_0"
3755 0xfffffc001ce38ab8 = "clua_si_1122_0"
3863 0xfffffc0004f55c38 = "clua_si_1124_0"
3874 0xfffffc001d59e6f8 = "cfs_devt:40_5"
4061 0xfffffc001ba9d0f8 = "RPC100005.6"
4397 0xfffffc001ce39738 = "00000081-PR-DBP815000000-MM-DBP8^B"
4536 0xfffffc000e60d378 = "00000000-MS-DBP815"
4539 0xfffffc0019247eb8 = "clua_si_967_0"
4585 0xfffffc000a3e7d78 = "00000001-MP-DBP815"
4610 0xfffffc00032015f8 = "00000001-MN-DBP815"
4769 0xfffffc000b5baab8 = "clua_si_177_0"
5136 0xfffffc000dd06e78 = "clua_si_1022_1"
5239 0xfffffc0004f554b8 = "clua_si_1123_0"
...
```

Figure 18-5 shows the position of DLM in the component hierarchy.

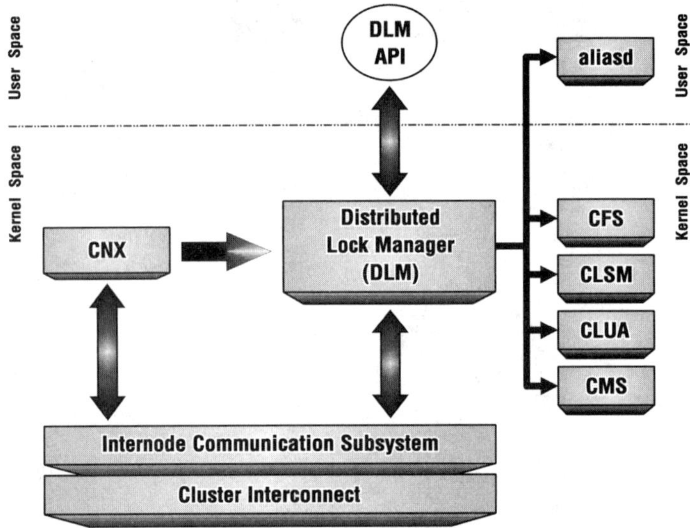

Figure 18-5: DLM Cluster Subsystem Communication

Additional information on DLM is available in Appendix B.

18.3 Reliable Datagram (RDG)

Reliable Datagrams provide messaging between applications in a cluster. We described this function in the chapter introduction as "horn honking and turn signals." Some cluster applications require a low latency, high bandwidth messaging system. When you honk your horn, it is usually to indicate a significant event to other drivers. Traditionally, datagrams are an unreliable mechanism for communication (your horn may not be heard). Datagrams are usually connectionless, meaning that a datagram is sent to a target without any guarantees of delivery. The benefit of traditional datagram messaging is that it is low overhead and usually faster than a connection-based mechanism.

The Reliable Datagram service provides a mechanism whereby a cluster-aware application can reliably send messages to other applications in the cluster (arrangements are made so that your horn will definitely be heard), yet still maintain the high speed and low latency associated with traditional datagrams.

Two basic usage models are provided for application developers interested in RDG: endpoints and buffers.

- Endpoints
    - The Receiver calls RDG to create an endpoint.
    - Port number is chosen by the system or specified.
    - The Receiver prequeues receive addresses.
    - The Sender sends to the receiver's endpoint (node number, port).
    - Node numbers are mapped to IP addresses.

- Buffers
  - The Receiver address space buffer is mapped for receiving data.
  - The buffer ID is chosen by the system or specified.
  - The Receiver prequeues regions to hold messages.
  - The Sender writes by specifying target node number and buffer ID.

Statistics pertaining to RDG activities can be viewed by using the lightly documented (no reference page) `rdgstats` command. The `rdgstats` command displays a subset of the statistics from the "`sysconfig -q rdg`" command output. By default, it displays statistics since the system booted. You can get a snapshot of statistics over a span of time using the "`-d`" option. For instance, "`rdgstats -d 20`" gathers statistics for 20 seconds before displaying them. You may also want to zero out the RDG statistics before running the `rdgstats` command by using "`sysconfig -r rdg stats_zero=1`".

```
# sysconfig -r rdg stats_zero=1
stats_zero: reconfigured
```

```
# find / -name '*rdg*'
/usr/sbin/rdginit
/usr/sbin/rdgstats                          ← Note the command
/usr/shlib/librdg.so                        ← RDG shared library
/usr/ccs/lib/librdg.a                       ← RDG object library
/usr/opt/TruCluster/sys/rdg.mod             ← RDG kernel module
/usr/share/man/man5/sys_attrs_rdg.5         ← RDG man page for attributes
/usr/sys/include/sys/rdg.h                  ← RDG header file
/usr/sys/XPNINE/rdg.mod
/usr/sys/XPNINE/rdg.h
```

```
# sysconfig -q rdg
rdg:
version                 = 39
ident                   = RDG V39.46
max_objs                = 1024
msg_q_size              = 32
msg_size                = 16384
stats_collect           = 1
stats_zero              = 0
assertions              = 0
...                                          ← Lots of attributes (mostly statistics)
rdg_tcp_interface       = tu0
```

The following output shows maximums and minimums pertaining to RDG.

```
# sysconfig -Q rdg
rdg:
version -       type=INT      op=Q   min_val=1      max_val=10000
ident -         type=STRING   op=Q   min_len=1      max_len=256
max_objs -      type=INT      op=CQ  min_val=0      max_val=50000
msg_q_size -    type=INT      op=CQ  min_val=0      max_val=10000
msg_size -      type=INT      op=CQ  min_val=0      max_val=1048576
stats_collect - type=INT      op=CRQ min_val=0      max_val=1
stats_zero -    type=INT      op=CRQ min_val=0      max_val=1
assertions -    type=INT      op=CRQ min_val=0      max_val=1
...
```

The following output would be of more use in a cluster running applications built using the RDG API (such as some database products).

```
# rdgstats
Cluster membership status of node molari-ics0 is MEMBER

RDG statistics - time duration: 0
molari-ics0:
        snd_msg_attempts = 0
        snd_buf_attempts = 0
        snd_blocks = 0
        snd_msg_successes = 0
        snd_buf_successes = 0
        snd_thread_wakeups = 0
        snd_kernel_queued_local = 0
        snd_kernel_queued_remote = 0
        rcv_msg_attempts = 0
        rcv_blocks = 0
        rcv_msg_successes = 0
        rcv_thread_wakeups = 0
        bytes_sent = 0
        bytes_rcvd = 0


Aggregate sends: 0
Aggregate receives: 0
```

The following performance comments are approximations only.

If the "`Aggregate sends`" divided by the count of Memory Channel rails approaches 300-400 MB/s, the cluster may perform better by adding another Memory Channel rail. Additionally, for each system, sum the "`bytes_sent`" and "`bytes_rcvd`" attributes and divide the sum by the number of Memory Channel rails. If the total for each system is greater than 60 MB/s, adding an additional rail may provide benefit. Contact your HP representative for more details on RDG performance and statistics.

In order to utilize RDG in your cluster-aware application, you will call RDG routines from the RDG library. This is commonly done by database software. The following extracts some function names from the RDG shared library. Once again, this API is not published, so further information should come from your HP representative.

```
# odump -Dt /usr/shlib/librdg.so | grep Rdg
[    14] RdgInit
[    15] RdgShutdown
[    16] RdgNodeLookup
[    17] RdgClusterIncarn
[    18] RdgEpLookup
[    19] RdgBufLookup
[    20] RdgBufCreate
[    21] RdgBufDestroy
[    22] RdgEpCreate
[    23] RdgEpDestroy
[    24] RdgIoPost
[    25] RdgIoPoll
[    26] RdgIoCancel
```

18.4 Kernel Group Services (KGS a.k.a. KCH)

Kernel Group Services, as described in the chapter introduction, provides for "car pool membership and decisions during cluster communication." A cluster, by its nature, can change dynamically. Members can be added and removed, applications can come and go, services can change, and so forth. If one person in the car pool wants to go to the local donut shop, do we just drop him off, or do we all go? In order to keep track of all these comings and goings, and to provide a mechanism to moderate decisions during changes, KGS is in place.

Rumor has it that as this software was being developed, it had a name that indicates the difficulty of its control and moderator duties. They called it the Kernel Cat Herder (KCH). As you can see in the following sample outputs, the old acronym still has validity. So you will notice references to KGS and KCH. Both terms refer to the same functionality. Figure 18-6 shows the position of KGS in the component hierarchy.

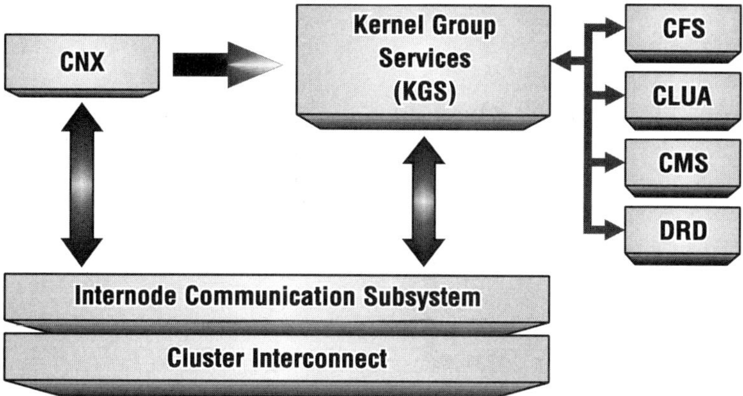

Figure 18-6: KGS Cluster Subsystem Communication

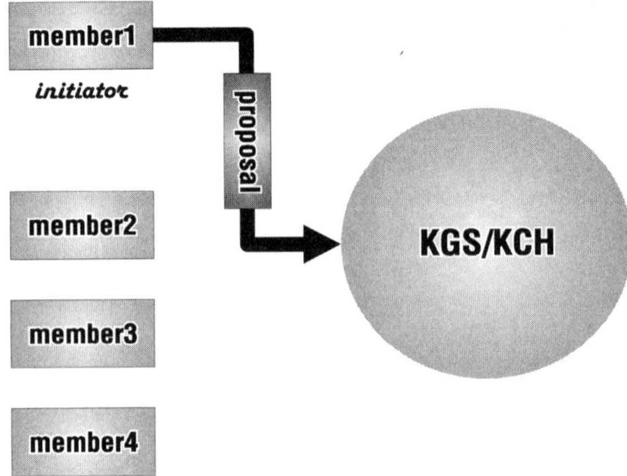

Figure 18-7: KGS – "I feel the need for a donut."

The basic idea was to hide the details of the dynamic activities happening within the cluster from the clients. KGS is used by the CFS, CLUA, CMS, and DRD and may be used by other components. In order to be informed of cluster events pertaining to a particular service, the services would ask KGS to allow them to join a "set". (This set is like a herd of cats. Imagine how difficult it would be to get a bunch of cats to move in the same direction. If you've ever spent time with cats, you know what it means.) If a set member (the initiator) senses a change about which the other members should be informed, it sends this information to KGS in the form of a "proposal" (i.e., "I feel the need for a donut" – Figure 18-7).

Other members of the set are notified by KGS of the proposed change ("Let's all go to the Donut Shop" – Figure 18-8).

The members "vote" on whether to "accept" the proposal ("How many of you want to go?" – Figure 18-9).

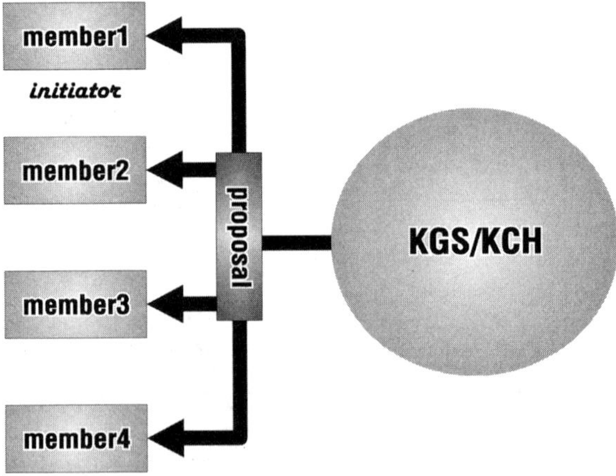

Figure 18-8: KGS – "Let's all go to the Donut Shop."

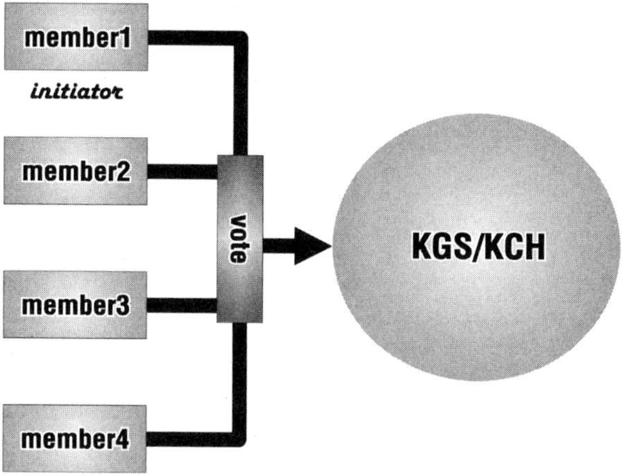

Figure 18-9: KGS – "How many of you want to go?"

If any member "rejects" the proposal, it is not "committed" (the change is not recognized – somebody in the car pool needed to get to work or is on a diet). Otherwise, the change is committed ("We're going for donuts" – Figure 18-10).

KGS is the moderator during the decision making process. An example would be as follows: if a system tries to run a software product that is potentially incompatible with software running in an existing cluster, the system trying to "join" in the existing software set could report to KGS concerning the version of the software that it is running. If it is not compatible with the software running on current members of the cluster, there will be a "rejection," and the requesting member's software activities could be excluded from the cluster or otherwise disallowed from running the incompatible software. This unfortunate event would be reported to the applicant by KGS. This example would require that the software be built using the KGS mechanisms (usually reserved for kernel components). Another example of the use of KGS is presented in section 18.5 (Cluster Mount Services).

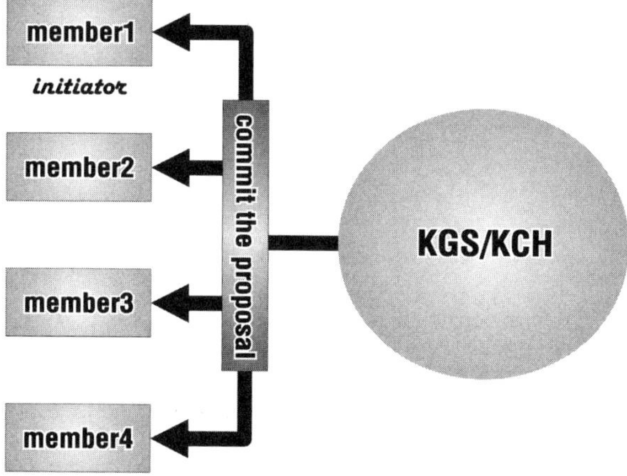

Figure 18-10: KGS – "We're going for donuts."

There is no reference page to support the sub-system attributes shown in the output below. We are presenting our best estimation of the meaning of the attributes. Before examining them, here are some additional terms and concepts.

The first member to initiate a "set" will be the "synchronizer" member (think of the director in the lock manager – it uses a similar strategy). Other references to the set are resolved by hashing the set name into a number, using the number as an offset into a directory weight table containing cluster system IDs (`csids`). The `csid` found at the calculated offset in the hash table will be the ID of the director to the synchronizer member for that set. Note that the director member may also be the synchronizer. The director member (found through the directory weight table) checks its "set" information to see if it knows which member is the "synchronizer" for the requested set. The "director" responds to the "initiator" and indicates who the "synchronizer" member is. Subsequent requests for that set are sent directly to the synchronizer. The idea is to distribute the KGS activities over the members of the cluster. If you have a member of the cluster with much more capacity than the others, you may improve its odds of being chosen as a "synchronizer" by increasing the `kch_dirwt` attribute below (maximum value is 4). Note that as of this writing, the `kch_dirwt` value is fixed at 1.

CAUTION:

These attributes should not be altered unless directed to do so by HP engineering.

```
# sysconfig -q kch

kch:
kch_enabled = 1                      ← Service enabled (1=yes)
kch_sets_allocated = 25              ← Existing set count
kch_mbrs_allocated = 25              ← Members are active set participants
kch_lstnrs_allocated = 0             ← Listeners are nonvoting members of a set
kch_dirwt = 1                        ← Directory table weight factor
kch_set_tbl_hash_size = 8192         ← Hash table size
```

```
# sysconfig -Q kch

kch:
kch_enabled            -  type=INT   op=CQ  min_val=0     max_val=1
kch_sets_allocated     -  type=UINT  op=Q   min_val=0     max_val=4294967295
kch_mbrs_allocated     -  type=UINT  op=Q   min_val=0     max_val=4294967295
kch_lstnrs_allocated   -  type=UINT  op=Q   min_val=0     max_val=4294967295
kch_dirwt              -  type=INT   op=Q   min_val=0     max_val=4
kch_set_tbl_hash_size  -  type=UINT  op=CQ  min_val=8192  max_val=32768
```

18.5 Cluster Mount Services (CMS)

By now you're probably aware that there are many behind-the-scenes components of a cluster all struggling to make the entire operation of a very complex environment as transparent as possible. One component that quietly does its job is the Cluster Mount Services (CMS). Somehow, magically, when you `mount` a file system on one member of the cluster, all the other members can see the mount point. Not that we're trying to turn this into an internals discussion, but every mounted file system is supported by a `mount` structure in the kernel. No big deal, right? Consider the fact that this activity was instigated on one cluster member but ended up writing into kernel address space on all cluster members! A very impressive deed requiring synchronization among all cluster members (and yes, it does involve DLM to achieve some of the synchronization – but you were already thinking that weren't you?).

The following output displays CMS subsystem attributes that limit the number of cluster-wide mounts available per file system type.

```
# sysconfig -q cms

cms:
cmsdbg_flags = 0
cfs_advfs_mount_limit = 4096
cfs_cdfs_mount_limit = 512
cfs_dvdfs_mount_limit = 512
cfs_nfs_mount_limit = 8192
cfs_ufs_mount_limit = 512
cfs_mfs_mount_limit = 512
```

```
# sysconfig -Q cms

cms:
cmsdbg_flags -  type=ULONG op=CRQ min_val=0 max_val=18446744073709551615
cfs_advfs_mount_limit -         type=INT op=CRQ min_val=0 max_val=2147483647
cfs_cdfs_mount_limit -  type=INT op=CRQ min_val=0 max_val=2147483647
cfs_dvdfs_mount_limit -         type=INT op=CRQ min_val=0 max_val=2147483647
cfs_nfs_mount_limit -   type=INT op=CRQ min_val=0 max_val=2147483647
cfs_ufs_mount_limit -   type=INT op=CRQ min_val=0 max_val=2147483647
cfs_mfs_mount_limit -   type=INT op=CRQ min_val=0 max_val=2147483647
```

The mount activity starts with a local mount command that involves CFS and is ultimately propagated to other cluster members through RPCs. The CMS activity heavily involves KGS (section 18.4). In fact, we can say that CMS is a client of KGS. CMS receives mount proposals (and membership change information) from KGS. The mounting member may be told (through KGS) that the file system has already been mounted by another member. In that case, CMS simply "joins" the KGS set. If it has not been mounted by another member, the member proposes that other members "join" the new KGS set representing the file system.

KGS is at the heart of CMS and uses DLM for synchronization.

18.6 Token Subsystem

Now that we have the file system mounted up, our users can start doing I/Os to it. But how do we coordinate the software running on various cluster members as they access the file? File locking is completely supported in a cluster, so any application level locking will work just fine. Think a little lower in the food chain (closer to the belly of the beast – the kernel). The following output shows the only system attribute that supports the token subsystem.

```
# sysconfig -q token

token:
svrtok_hash_size = 3183
```

```
# man sys_attrs_token

(...)
  svrtok_hash_size
      Determines the size of the svrcfstok hash table.

      On a CFS server, the svrcfstok hash table manages data structures that
      represent each active file in the cluster.

      For better hashing performance, the value you assign should be an odd
      number. Because of this, if you set svrtok_hash_size to an even value,
      the software automatically adds a 1 to it.

      On a system that is strictly a CFS client, you can set svrcfstok to its
      minimum value, 64.

      Supported operations: Query; Configure at boot time

      Default value: 797

      Minimum value: 64

      Maximum value: 16384
```

Apparently, these tokens are important enough to merit a hash table so the system can quickly locate token information. Note that the CFS server will have a much larger hash table to promote quicker access to the token data. There are usually fewer tokens needed on a CFS client.

Doesn't the kernel cache file system data in the Unified Buffer Cache (UBC)? And doesn't each member have a UBC? The answer to both questions is yes, and therein lies some of the complexity. How does the system know that file system data that is currently cached in the local memory (UBC) is still synchronized with data from the disk (or in other members' caches)? Note that cache coherency is discussed in Chapter 13 on CFS.

This issue is dealt with through the token subsystem. Bottom line: if the token representing file system data is held by the CFS client, then the cached data is OK. If the token is not held by the client, the client will request the token from the CFS server, and the data will be acquired from the CFS server's cache (if possible) or from the CFS server's disk.

You're thinking, "What if another CFS client currently holds the token?" In that case, the CFS server notifies all clients that the tokens have been "revoked," so if any client requests the data again, they know that they have to check in with the CFS server. The sequence of events is covered in Chapter 13.

The following output provides some statistics on the use of tokens in a cluster (more examples are found in Chapter 13).

```
# cfsstat -S tokstats | more

Total CFS messages processed: 1736541
            token messages: 97978 ( 5%)
tok_rets        tok_grants        tok_reqs        tok_revs
87777 89%       3672  3%          3672  3%        2857  2%
```

```
# cfsstat -S tokens | more

Client token stats:
Request stats:
    3647            total number of otw requests (requests_sent)
Request hold failures:
    3647            ( 0%) holds causing otw requests (tok_hold_reqsent)
Release stats:
    14              release with revokes waiting (tok_release_revoke)
    14              delayed releases (tok_release_delayed)
Grant stats:
    3647            total number of grants received (grants_received)
    3647            (100%) total number of grants processed (tok_grants)
Installs stats:
    179931          total number of installs received (tok_installs)
Revoke stats:
    2606            total revokes received (revokes_received)
    739             (28%) total revokes processed (tok_revokes)
    173901                total returns sent (returns_sent)
    206             ( 7%) revoke failure due to no cnode. (fhtovp_nocp)
    13              ( 0%) revoke failure due to hold count (tok_revokes_hcnt)
```

```
Server token stats:
Return stats:
    426758          total number of returns received (returns_received)
Requests stats:
    5720            total number of requests received (reqs_recvd)
    297960          (5209%) total number of requests processed (tok_reqs)
    5720            (100%) total number of grants sent (grants_sent)
    889             (15%) requests granted w/out revoking (tok_reqs_grants)
    4831            (84%) requests causing revokes (tok_reqs_revoke)
Installs stats:
    636490          total number of installs tried (tok_insts)
    259014          (40%) number of successful installs (tok_insts_grants)
revoke stats:
    4831            total number of revokes sent (revokes_sent)
Miscellaneous Stats

Server token processing stats:
    10551           messages queued to client
           5720            (54%) grants (msg_queued[1][0])
           4831            (45%) revokes (msg_queued[1][1])
    10551           messages sent to client
           5720            (54%) grants (msg_processed[1][0])
           4831            (45%) revokes (msg_processed[1][1]
Client token processing stats:
    6253            messages queued to server
           3647            (58%) requests (msg_queued[0][0])
           2606            (41%) returns (msg_queued[0][1])
    6253            messages sent to server
           3647            (58%) requests
           2606            (41%) returns
    2606            total returns processed
```

18.7 References

- *TruCluster* Server Cluster Administration Guide.
- *TruCluster* Server Technical Overview.
- HP *TruCluster* Server Internals Course Materials.
- *Tru64* UNIX Reference Pages (noted within the text).

19

System Administration Tasks

The typical day of a typical system administrator consists of handling many tasks such as responding to user requests, responding to management requests, attending meetings pertaining to the response to management and user requests, adding and maintaining accounts, maintaining file systems, maintaining disks and other devices, assisting the network administration team, handling performance, network, and hardware problems, and managing various other ad hoc responsibilities boiling down to firefighting.

This chapter will help you to understand the differences (and similarities) in the life of a system administrator once your cluster is up. The following chapter (Chapter 20) will focus on how network administration differs in a clustered environment, and finally, in Chapter 21, we will present tools for administering the cluster itself (as opposed to administering a system in a cluster).

19.1 System Administration in a Cluster

Unfortunately, there is precious little help that a cluster can provide that will minimize the time you spend in meetings or holding a user's hand. Despite the fact that human interaction can consume a significant chunk of an administrator's time, we propose no solutions in these pages for that part of the job. HP would probably sell a million clusters in a week if it could guarantee a reduction in the amount of time spent dealing with human interactions in administering a system.

One way to imagine your administrative situation is that the meetings with the bean counters have already taken place. You have decided to purchase a *TruCluster* Server from HP, and you are reading this book to help understand and properly use the system. Notice that we refer to the cluster as "the system." In many ways, the cluster should be thought of as a single system. We know the facts. A cluster is a closely coupled series of machines sharing a common management interface and common resources.

What's that? A common management interface? As part of their marketing efforts, Compaq/HP has always referred to the existence of a single management interface to the members in a cluster. Sounds like it's right up our alley for this chapter. Let's take a look and see what needs to be considered in this "common" management interface.

19.1.1 Common Management Interface (SysMan)

Managing a *Tru64* UNIX system is commonly done by a fairly experienced UNIX person who has grown up with some flavor of UNIX, and who primarily uses the command-line interface to make changes and requests of the system. This semi-fictitious person knows every option of every command available and is prepared to handle all configuration, installation, monitoring, and performance issues within two seconds of notification. – Not! In reality, many system administrators have had the job thrust upon them. They may have started out as an engineer, programmer, support person, or some other kind of technical person. Then one day the "real" system administrator ups and leaves (or is asked to up and leave), leaving you holding the proverbial *Tru64* UNIX admin bag.

Tru64 UNIX provides several options for system administration tasks. Most of them have come into existence in an attempt to standardize, homogenize, or otherwise improve the life of a system administrator. We recently had a conversation with a frazzled and overworked administrator who was responsible for over 400 systems! They were not all Tru64 UNIX and she did have some help, but far from enough. Clearly, anything that HP can do to make her life as a system administrator easier would be very welcome. Compaq/HP has been making strides to simplify the task of managing *Tru64* UNIX systems, and this effort has resulted in the creation of the `sysman(8)` utility (and many options within it) as well as the Insight Manager.

Most folks assume that `sysman` is just another GUI tool that gives a point-and-click interface to an administrator for the bulk of the commonly needed administrative activities. It actually is more than that. We mention all of this because the `sysman` utility can be given a "focus" that is member-specific, cluster-wide, or both. Therefore, the `sysman` activities that you may have been using to manage a standalone system will most likely also serve you well in a cluster.

The `sysman` suite actually consists of three tools: "`sysman -menu`", "`sysman -station`" (can be executed with the `sms` command), and "`sysman`" on the command-line. All three of these options lead to the same capabilities (for the most part). Note that more information on `sysman` is available in Chapter 5.

The difference in the three options is in how they can be invoked. For instance, the "`sysman`" command with the "`-menu`" option can be invoked from a cluster member, PC, or the web using the Insight Manager. This requires that the tool be able to function in various environments including the X Window System, Java, Java Applet, and character cell.

Figure 19-1 shows the cluster portion of the `sysman` command. Note the *TruCluster*-specific portion of the screen.

For additional coverage of SysMan, see section 4.2 of the *Tru64* UNIX Administrator's Guide; Cheek, Fafrak, Hancock, Moore, Yates; Digital Press, ISBN 1-55558-255-9; or Chapter 1 of the *Tru64 UNIX System Administrator's Guide*.

The bulk of our future discussions will focus on various commands, but you may feel more comfortable at first managing your cluster the way you have managed your standalone system. As you will see in subsequent chapters, there are approximately 30 commands that have been created to function specifically in a cluster (out of approximately 600 administrative commands in *Tru64* UNIX).

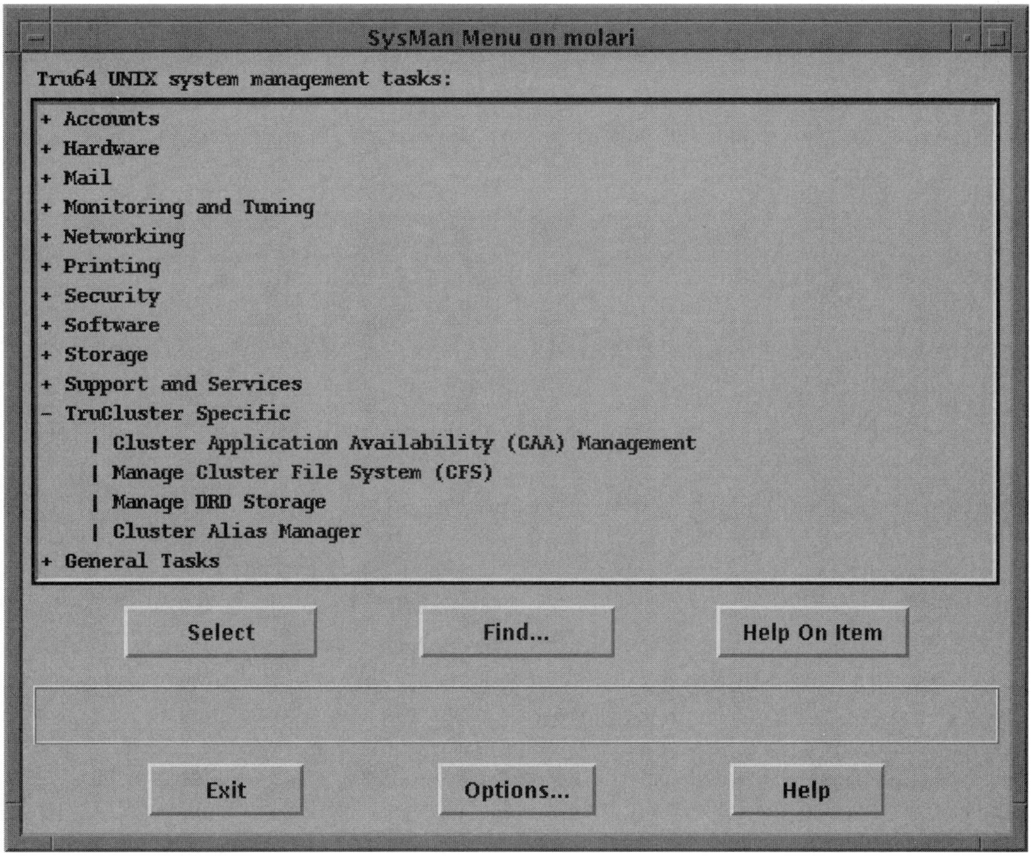

Figure 19-1: SysMan Menu

19.2 Commands in a Cluster

Now that you know there are some menu-oriented tools available for system administration, let's dig a little deeper and see how *Tru64* UNIX commands have been tweaked to handle cluster-wide activities. You will see cluster only commands in Chapter 21. Keep in mind that we are working in a SSI (single system image) environment, so we really shouldn't be too worried about each individual command. We'll mention a few commands while we're in the mood. OK?

19.2.1 Administration Commands

Pick your favorite administration command or system database file (`ps(1)`, `disklabel(8)`, `df(1)`, `du(1)`, `vmstat(1)`, `sysman`, `passwd(4)`, `adduser(8)`, `fuser(8)`, `hwmgr(8)`, `mount(8)`, etc.). The list is nearly endless, isn't it? When you run a command on a cluster member, it can either produce the same output no matter which cluster member you are using to run it, or it can produce member-specific results. Likewise, the files that you access (`vmunix`, printcap(4), inittab(4), rc.config(8), etc.) can be member-specific or cluster-wide. Note that rc.config and init(8) are discussed in Chapter 6.

Tru64 UNIX provides both mechanisms in order to present a single system interface to the application. Note that some commands have been modified to support cluster-wide requests. The following display shows output from a command (wall(1)) that has a cluster-specific option added to it (-c).

```
[molari]
# wall -c

test
^D
```

```
[molari]
#

Broadcast Message from obrien@molari.dec.com (pts/3) at 16:28 ...

test
```

Out of curiosity, we checked to see if we could figure out what the wall command uses to get messages to other cluster members. The following output shows that the traditional wall command has been altered to use a non-traditional program called /usr/sbin/clu_wall. We can assume that most other commands that have cluster-specific options have been altered in some way to handle their responsibilities cluster wide.

```
# strings $(which wall) | grep sbin/clu | sort | uniq
/usr/sbin/clu_wall
```

19.2.2 Shutdown Command

The shutdown command is another example of a command that has been altered to handle cluster-wide activities. Note the "-c" option causes special actions to take place to handle user login attempts (/etc/nologin and /etc/nologin_hostname) while a shutdown is in progress. To prevent new members from joining a cluster that is being shut down, the /cluster/admin/.clu_shutdown_file is created and an entry is made in the file describing the member requesting the shutdown and the time (see example below). This file is also checked before starting a cluster-wide shutdown, thus preventing multiple simultaneous shutdown requests from occurring. The /cluster/admin/.clu_shutdown_log file does what the name implies. It logs information about cluster shutdowns (see the following example). Note also that init, halt(8), and reboot(8) have been modified to no longer unmount file systems.

```
# cd /cluster/admin && ls -l .clu_shut*
-rw-------    1 root     system       149 Jul  4 01:54 .clu_shutdown_file
-rw-r--r--    1 root     system      3572 Jul  4 01:54 .clu_shutdown_log
```

```
# cat /cluster/admin/.clu_shutdown_file
BEGIN_ENTRY
HOST=molari
TIME=Sat Aug 17 14:25:50 2001
CMND=shutdown now
MEMBER_SHUTDOWN_SEQUENCE=molari-ics0
END_ENTRY
```

```
# date
Sat Aug 17 15:22:13 EDT 2001
```

```
# shutdown -c now
```

After the cluster is booted, let's login and check the shutdown file once again. Note that the log file tracks the history of cluster shutdowns, while the shutdown file tracks the last shutdown.

```
# cat /cluster/admin/.clu_shutdown_file
BEGIN_ENTRY
HOST=molari
TIME=Sat Aug 17 15:22:47 2001
CMND=shutdown now
MEMBER_SHUTDOWN_SEQUENCE=molari-ics0
END_ENTRY
```

```
# cat .clu_shutdown_log
BEGIN_ENTRY
HOST=molari
TIME=Sat Aug 17 12:38:54 2001
CMND=shutdown now
MEMBER_SHUTDOWN_SEQUENCE=molari-ics0
END_ENTRY
```

```
BEGIN_ENTRY
HOST=molari
TIME=Sat Aug 17 14:25:50 2001
CMND=shutdown now
MEMBER_SHUTDOWN_SEQUENCE=molari-ics0
END_ENTRY

BEGIN_ENTRY
HOST=molari
TIME=Sat Aug 17 15:22:47 2001
CMND=shutdown now
MEMBER_SHUTDOWN_SEQUENCE=molari-ics0
END_ENTRY
```

```
# date
Sat Aug 17 15:56:39 EDT 2001
```

19.2.3 File System Manipulation Commands

Other commands seem to work properly in a cluster without any special options. Consider the purpose of file manipulation commands such as `showfdmn(8)`, `mkfdmn(8)`, `mount(8)`, etc. The CFS makes their actions inherently cluster-wide. Therefore you will see no special cluster options in file system oriented commands. Some commands (such as the `passwd(1)` command) use cluster-wide database files and thus become cluster-oriented indirectly.

Back up and restore activities in a cluster are similar to a standalone system's backup and restore, but since members share the file systems (for the most part) you only have to backup the cluster once and not once per member. CDSLs are treated as any other symbolic link would be treated.

19.2.4 Kill Command

The `kill(1)` command will work properly and signal the target process even if that process is running on another cluster member. You are probably a step ahead of me in figuring out how this could possibly work given that Process Identifiers (PIDs) are specific to a system. There has been a change in the meaning of several bits in the PID. If you ever find yourself yearning for the good old days when you could conveniently understand PIDs, the following script may help.

```
# ps -Ao pid,comm | grep init

524289 init
525353 rdginit
```

```
# ./cvtpid 524289
1
cluster pid = 524289; standalone pid = 1
```

```
# ./cvtpid 525353
1065
cluster pid = 525353; standalone pid = 1065
```

```
# cat cvtpid
#! /usr/bin/ksh

if [[ $# != 1 ]]
then
  print "USAGE: $0 <pid_to_convert>"
  exit 1
fi

sapid=$(print "$1 % (2 ^ 19 )" | bc )
print cluster pid = $1\; standalone pid = $sapid
```

Let's start a process on cluster member `sheridan`. Note the PID of 1067727.

```
[sheridan]
# cat &
[1]     1067727
```

On `molari`, let's see if we can see the process. No. Nothing appears except my `grep` command itself.

```
[molari]
# ps -Ao pid,comm | grep 1067727
532818 grep 1067727
```

Or use our home cooked cluster-wide `ps` command called "`clu_ps`" (discussed later in this chapter).

```
# clu_ps "=-efp 1067727"
=============================================================================
member2 (sheridan)          ps -efp 1067727
-----------------------------------------------------------------------------
UID         PID    PPID    C STIME    TTY           TIME CMD
root     1067727 1067722  0.0 03:31:28 pts/1       0:00.01 cat

=============================================================================
```

The process is not on `molari`, but then again we already knew that. However, this will not prevent us from killing the process running on `sheridan` from `molari`.

```
[molari]
# kill 1067727
```

It is gone!

```
[sheridan]
# ps -Ao pid,comm | grep 1067727

532818 grep 1067727
```

```
[sheridan]
# jobs -l

[1] + 1067727   Terminated                    cat &
```

Tru64 UNIX has altered the format of the PIDs beginning in V5.0 such that they include a cluster member identifier in bits 19:26 (See Chapter 6, section 6.5). This allows commands (such as the `kill` command) that reference a PID to indirectly use ICS to figure out on which member the target process lives.

Note that using the `kill` command on PID 1 sends a signal to the `init` process on the issuing member only.

Also note that a standalone system (not in a cluster) will be assigned member identifier zero. Recall that you can discern your system's cluster `memberid` through the following `sysconfig` command:

```
# sysconfig -q generic memberid

generic:
memberid = 1
```

In a cluster, the lowest member identifier will be one. The `ps` command is an example of a command that will only display information that is specific to the member on which it is running. While we all wait expectantly for a cluster-wide version of `ps`, below is some output from a home cooked script that does the cluster-wide `ps` job. So in the meantime, this script is available from the Digital Press web site and from the BRUDEN web site (See Appendix B for the URLs). To get a "`ps`" from `member2` using our `clu_ps` script:

```
# ./clu_ps -m2

===========================================================================
member2 (sheridan)           ps -ef
---------------------------------------------------------------------------
UID          PID   PPID    C STIME    TTY             TIME CMD
root     1048576      0  0.0  Jul 04 ??         0:44.66 [kernel idle]
root     1048577 1048576  0.0  Jul 04 ??        0:00.19 /sbin/init -a
root     1048578 1048576  0.0  Jul 04 ??        0:00.00 [kproc_creator_da]
root     1048579 1048578  0.0  Jul 04 ??        0:00.00 [icssvr_nomem_dae]
...
```

There are other options in this useful script. Here is the usage message to give you an idea of what it can do.

```
# ./clu_ps -h

Usage: ./clu_ps [-m memberid] ["=ps_command_options"]

  Example:

    ./clu_ps                        -- runs "ps -ef" on all members
    ./clu_ps -m 1 "=-elfm"          -- runs "ps -elfm" on member1
    ./clu_ps "=-eo pid,command"     -- runs "ps -eo pid,command" on all members
    ./clu_ps "=aux"                 -- runs "ps aux" on all members
```

We wanted to show at least one run of the script where it acquired information from more than one member. The following uses the "-p" option of the ps command to retrieve some process information from both members of a two-member cluster. Enjoy!

```
# ./clu_ps "=ap '524288,1048576'"

===========================================================================
member1 (molari)           ps ap '524288,1048576'
---------------------------------------------------------------------------
   PID TTY      S           TIME CMD
524288 ??       R <      1:04.73 [kernel idle]

===========================================================================
member2 (sheridan)           ps ap '524288,1048576'
---------------------------------------------------------------------------
   PID TTY      S           TIME CMD
1048576 ??       R <      0:45.09 [kernel idle]

===========================================================================
```

19.3 Common Files

Cluster-wide files are a distinguishing feature of the *TruCluster* Server product. Having common administration files is one of those good news, bad news situations, however. Sit back and consider whether you would like to have a cluster common `/etc/rc.config` file for example. You can quickly see that there are configuration items (such as `HOSTNAME`) that should not be shared among members. Yet the sharing of files such as `/etc/passwd` provides the good news of having the cluster appear to the users as a single system.

19.3.1 The `passwd` and `group` Files

Adding a new user account is an example of a typical system administration activity that is made easier (or at least no harder) by the existence of cluster common files. The `/etc/passwd` file and the `/etc/group` file are both shared by all cluster members. Therefore any information added to these files through "`sysman accounts`", `adduser`, or `dxaccounts(8)` is immediately accessible to all cluster members. So rather than having to repeat the operation on each cluster member, do it once and you're done. Any activities served by a database file in a common directory will function similarly.

19.3.2 Mounting File Systems

If you create and mount a file system, all cluster members immediately see it. Once again, if you think of the cluster as a single system, it makes sense that all members should see essentially the same files except for some configuration and support files. Needless to say, the `/etc/fstab` file is shared by all cluster members.

19.3.3 Swap Space

What about swap space? That's not allocated from a file system so it can't be handled by CFS activities. Swap space is allocated from one or more raw partitions. Since we are being coached to think of the cluster as a single system, does that mean that all systems are served by a single swap space? The answer is that the swap partition is indicated by the `swapdevice` entry in the `vm subsystem` portion of `sysconfigtab(4)`. The `/etc/sysconfigtab` file is a CDSL and thus is member-specific. So each member will have its own swap space. Note that if you are in the habit of reflecting your swap space in `/etc/fstab`, change your habit. It is no longer meaningful in that file. Also be aware that if you use the `swapon(8)` command to add more swap space on the fly, the addition will be member-specific.

If you are concerned with performance, HP recommends that the swap partition be on a disk local to the member that uses it. This offloads some of the traffic on the shared bus where your swap partition would normally be. We suggest that you think this over carefully. Everybody wants to squeeze the last possible drop of performance from his or her system. But in this case the performance gain comes at the cost of your reliability. If your non-shared bus adapter fails, your system can no longer access swap space and will hang or crash. If the swap partition is on a shared bus, and one adapter fails, access should still be available. Furthermore, the typical *Tru64* UNIX system in the 21st century is usually chock full of memory. If this describes your system, you probably don't get into paging out or swapping activities anyway, so why not keep the swap space on the shared bus in that case? Note that either way the swap space is still member-specific.

Another reason to keep your swap space on a shared bus is that it may be useful after a member crashes and cannot come back up for some reason. In order to find out anything about the nasty event that caused the member's seemingly permanent demise, we'll need access to the crash dump. But the crash dump is written to the swap partition until the system comes back up, at which point it is copied (by the `savecore(8)` program) into `/var/adm/crash` (a CDSL and therefore member-specific). So we are between a rock and a hard place in the case where the swap partition is on a non-shared bus. But if the swap partition is on a shared bus, another cluster member can run `savecore` (and `crashdc(8)` also to create the `crash-data.`*n* file) and either examine the crash in-house or `ftp` it to the HP Customer Support Center.

19.3.4 Command Directories

Speaking of commands, isn't the code for `ps` (and all other commands) in a file system somewhere on disk? As you may have guessed, they are comfortably ensconced in some famous directories such as `/usr/bin`, `/sbin`, and others. Are these directories and files duplicated on each system in a cluster? Ask yourself if we need multiple copies of the code for `ps` (or any other command). No matter where we are in the cluster, the command code will be the same, so why waste the disk space making copies of common code? This section briefly discusses CFS and CDSLs, which are thoroughly covered in Chapters 13 and 6 respectively.

As you know, the Cluster File System (CFS) handles common code very nicely since it provides a single view of all storage to all cluster members. Even file systems on local (non-shared) disks can be seen by each cluster member. Incidentally, a feature of CFS is that a software product installation is usually necessary only once per cluster, instead of once per cluster member.

You may be thinking that you would prefer to have multiple copies of the commands (and other files) in case one of the disks goes bad or the system goes down. Several RAID options are available to help with your concerns, including CLSM (discussed in Chapter 14). If you are convinced that it makes sense for the commands to exist in one place on the cluster, can't we apply the same thinking to some of the system's configuration files as well?

19.3.5 Device and Kernel Files

But what about `/vmunix`? What about the `/dev` directory? What about `/etc/sysconfigtab` and all of the boot sequence files? When we boot a cluster member, we'll still be issuing the boot command from the system console, won't we? If so, then the console will look to the boot device and start working from there to bring up the system. If this device is not accessible because the device is not local, and this member is the first member being booted, it will be impossible for the member to finish booting until the cluster-wide root file system has been mounted. Note that device directories are discussed in Chapters 7, 12, and 15, and the boot sequence is examined more closely in Chapter 17.

So how does the cluster provide a single cluster-wide view of the directory hierarchy from root on down while still providing each system access to a member-specific version of the vmunix file (and others)? The answer is Context Dependent Symbolic Links (CDSLs). The `vmunix` file is a CDSL in a cluster that points to `/.local../boot_partition/vmunix` and thus is a member-specific file.

19.3.6 CDSLs

Remember learning about symbolic links when you got into UNIX? They are usually thought of as pretty impressive stuff. We remember using a symbolic link to free up space on a packed disk by simply moving a bunch of files to a less packed disk. We then created a symbolic link from the original directory over to the location of the files on a different disk so as not to foul up the software that was expecting the files to be in their original location. CDSLs take that capability to another level. They provide a mechanism where a reference to a symbolic link (context dependent) will be translated into a location in a member-specific directory (CDSLs were covered in Chapters 6 and 12). Keep in mind that CDSLs are not the only mechanism used by the cluster to create member-specific files. Sometimes the file name itself indicates which member owns and uses the file (for example `/etc/gated.conf.member*`). The Virtual File System software (part of the *Tru64* UNIX kernel) will insert the string "`member`" with the member's own cluster `memberid` into the "`{memb}`" location providing completely transparent access to files that must contain member-specific information.

19.3.7 System Startup

CDSLs play a prominent role during system startup. This topic is covered more fully in Chapter 17, but we visit it here to remind you of its importance. As the system comes up, it starts the `init` process (formerly PID #1, now some larger PID but with the rightmost 19 bits containing a 1. See the `cvtpid` script in section 19.2.4). The `init` process runs the `init` daemon, which reads the contents of the `/etc/inittab` file to get its marching orders.

19.3.7.1 The `inittab` File

The `inittab` file will contain entries to start `getty(8)` processes, if necessary, and to execute the `rc0(8)`, `rc2(8)`, and `rc3(8)` scripts (among other things). Since each system may want to start up in a different manner, the `/etc/inittab` file is a CDSL. It is very likely, however, that the member-specific `inittab` files will be pretty much the same. How much of the `init` part of system startup will vary from system to system? If a particular member has a unique local device (non-storage oriented), then certainly its processes, daemons, or other supporting software need only to be started on that particular member. If software needs to be forced to run on only one member without failover, then use a restricted CAA placement policy. If software needs to run on only one member at a time, with failover, then use CAA. Basically, unless the software can run on every member it should not be in `rc?.d`, unless you make the decision to start based on a variable in `rc.config`.

Furthermore, the `/sbin/rc0`, `rc2`, and `rc3` scripts are all cluster common, as is the `/sbin/init` program itself (why would we need more than one copy of the `init` program?) The system administration implication is that if an administrator were to put something into the `rc3` script that starts a particular piece of software, the software would ultimately be started on all members since the `rc3.d` and `rc3` files are cluster common.

It is important to note that if you have an application that installs its startup information in `init.d/rc?.d`, and that application cannot run more than one copy at a time, then the link from the `rc?.d` directory should be removed and the application should be managed by CAA. See Chapters 23 and 24 for more information on CAA.

19.3.7.2 The `rc.config` Scripts

While executing the startup scripts, the `rc.config` script will be run. Most people are not aware that `rc.config` is a script. The common misconception is that it is a file with a series of attributes that apply to various startup activities. It is actually a Bourne shell script that creates a series of exported variables. The exported variables stay in existence beyond the script within which they are created. Therefore the variables are available for subsequent scripts such as those run by the `rc` scripts.

```
# fln /etc/rc.config
/etc/rc.config -> ../cluster/members/{memb}/etc/rc.config
```

Note: the `fln` Korn shell function was defined in Chapter 6.

```
# ls -lL /etc/rc.config
-rwxr-xr-x   1 bin      bin          5252 Oct 31  2001 /etc/rc.config
```

```
# cat /etc/rc.config
#!/bin/sh
...
# Read in the cluster attributes before overriding them with the member
# specific options.
#
. /etc/rc.config.common
#
#
...
CLU_BOOT_FILESYSTEM="root1_domain#root"
export CLU_BOOT_FILESYSTEM
...
```

Notice that rc.config is a CDSL and thus is member-specific. Also notice that rc.config requests the execution of a cluster common script named rc.config.common (approximately five lines down, bolded, in the above file). Thus systems in a cluster can be fed a variety of system-specific configuration items through /etc/rc.config as well as cluster common attributes through /etc/rc.config.common. (Details can be found in Chapter 6).

So when would we use this new rc.config.common file, and how do we add entries to it and otherwise interact with it? Traditionally, rc.config was altered through the rcmgr command. Yeah, we know. You probably just used vi(1) on the rc.config file. Technically you should be using the rcmgr command. This is especially important now that the file has been broken up into the cluster common and the member-specific parts. The rcmgr command has options that allow you to designate whether the changes are to be applied cluster wide (rc.config.common) or to a specific system (rc.config). The command options are "-c" (cluster wide) and "-h" (host specific). There is a third option on the rcmgr command that designates a site-specific rc.config file (rc.config.site). This file may contain variables describing characteristics of site-specific software.

19.3.7.3 The **sysconfigtab** File

There are other system configuration options that need to be addressed as well. *Tru64* UNIX reads the contents of the /etc/sysconfigtab file to access system attributes and driver characteristics. This file is member-specific so that each member of the cluster may be tweaked as appropriate for the applications it will be running. Just as with rc.config, there will also be a cluster-wide version of sysconfigtab called /etc/sysconfigtab.cluster. So if all cluster members are exactly the same, the bulk of the system attributes can be reflected in the /etc/sysconfigtab.cluster file. Most system attributes placed in the cluster-wide file get merged into the member-specific /etc/sysconfigtab file upon boot (see /sbin/init.d/clu_min).

```
# fln /etc/sysconfigtab
/etc/sysconfigtab -> ../cluster/members/{memb}/boot_partition/etc/sysconfigtab
```

```
# ls -Ll /etc/sysconfigtab
-rwxr-xr-x   1 bin      bin        22756 Dec 31 20:18 /etc/sysconfigtab
```

```
# sysconfigdb -l clubase ics_ll_tcp

clubase:
 cluster_expected_votes=2
 cluster_name=babylon5
 cluster_node_name=molari
 cluster_node_inter_name=molari-ics0
 cluster_node_votes=1
 cluster_interconnect=tcp
 cluster_seqdisk_major=19
 cluster_seqdisk_minor=47
 cluster_qdisk_major=19
 cluster_qdisk_minor=63
 cluster_qdisk_votes=1

ics_ll_tcp:
 ics_tcp_inetaddr0=10.1.0.1
 ics_tcp_netmask0=255.255.255.0
 ics_tcp_adapter0=tu0
```

```
# ls -l /etc/sysconfigtab.cluster

-rw-r--r--   1 root     system        38 Nov 15  2001 /etc/sysconfigtab.cluster
```

```
# sysconfigdb -t /etc/sysconfigtab.cluster -l clubase
clubase:

        cluster_expected_votes = 2
```

Upon booting into a cluster, a script is run (/sbin/init.d/clu_min) that checks for differences between the member-specific /etc/sysconfigtab file and the cluster-wide /etc/sysconfigtab.cluster file. If differences exist, the member-specific file is made to match any cluster-wide entries that differ. (This is not a copy of the common file; it is an analysis of the entries themselves.) Note that the /etc/sysconfigtab.cluster file is managed by utilities such as clu_quorum(8) but can also be used by an administrator to make cluster-wide additions to the member-specific sysconfigtab files. Sound contradictory? The following example shows how you can use this mechanism without having to issue individual sysconfigdb commands on each cluster member.

```
# sysconfigdb -t /etc/sysconfigtab.cluster -l inet

inet: Entry not found in /etc/sysconfigtab.cluster
```

```
# sysconfigdb -t /etc/sysconfigtab.cluster -m -f inet.stanza inet

<no output>
```

```
# sysconfigdb -t /etc/sysconfigtab.cluster -l inet

inet:
        ipport_userreserved = 65535
```

The next output shows that the cluster members' /etc/sysconfigtab files do not reflect the inet entry.

```
# for i in 1 2
> do
>   print "\nmember$i's sysconfigtab:"
>   sysconfigdb -t /.local../../member$i/boot_partition/etc/sysconfigtab -l inet
> done

member1's sysconfigtab:
inet: Entry not found in /cluster/members/member1/boot_partition/etc/sysconfigtab


member2's sysconfigtab:
inet: Entry not found in /cluster/members/member2/boot_partition/etc/sysconfigtab
```

The next output shows the undocumented (no reference page) /usr/sbin/clu_update_sysconfig command that actually forces the dispersal of changes found in the /etc/sysconfigtab.cluster file to the member-specific /etc/sysconfigtab files and then uses a "for" loop to display the sysconfigtab files on each member.

```
# /usr/sbin/clu_update_sysconfig /etc/sysconfigtab.cluster
<no output>
```

```
# for i in 1 2
> do
>   print "\nmember$i's sysconfigtab:"
>   sysconfigdb -t /.local../../member$i/boot_partition/etc/sysconfigtab -l inet
> done


member1's sysconfigtab:

inet:
        ipport_userreserved = 65535

member2's sysconfigtab:

inet:
        ipport_userreserved = 65535
```

Be aware that an unpatched V5.1A system would disallow the use of the sysconfigdb command that used /etc/sysconfigtab.cluster as the target file.

19.4 General Administration Differences

The following chart lists administrative components and indicates whether they are cluster wide or member specific.

Certain commands are member-specific and return information only for the member on which the command executes (such as fuser, volstat(8), ps, mailstats(8), uptime(1), vmstat, who(1), etc.). Details are available in the reference pages and in the *TruCluster* Server Cluster Administration Guide as well as the *Tru64* UNIX System Administration Guide.

Other commands are limited but yield interesting information that goes beyond the member on which the command is issued (iostat(1) can show disk statistics on local disks and on disks on a shared bus; however, statistics will be pertinent to traffic generated to and from the local member only).

Still others have had new options added (such as "-c") to indicate that the command should function cluster wide (such as "hwmgr view device -cluster" and "shutdown -c") or have cluster-wide information in their output such as "dsfmgr -s" which indicates a local or cluster-wide visibility for devices with the 'scope' column (shown below).

```
# dsfmgr -s
dsfmgr: show all datum for system at /

Device Class Directory Default Database:
     # scope mode  name
    -- ---   ----  -----------
     1  l    0755  .
     2  l    0755  none
     3  c    0755  cport
     4  c    0755  disk
     5  c    0755  rdisk
     6  c    0755  tape
     7  c    0755  ntape
     8  c    0755  changer
     9  c    0755  dmapix
...
```

The "c" in the "scope" field indicates the Device Class Directory is cluster-wide.

System Administration Tasks

Task	Cluster-Wide	Member-Specific	Chapter or Section	Notes
Accounting	✗	✓	19	Enable on a specific host. `rcmgr -h 3 set ACCOUNTING YES` Enable cluster-wide. `rcmgr -c set ACCOUNTING YES`
Auditing	✓	✗	19.4.4.1	Cluster-wide Configuration, Member-Specific Audit Logs.
Backups	✓	✗	22	CDSLs are normal symbolic links.
Cron	✗	✓	21	**/usr/spool/cron** is a CDSL
Dumps	✗	✓	A	Use **dumpsys** to force dumps on each member.
EVM Events	✓	✓	8, 12	**cluster_event** attribute forces posting to all members
File Systems	✓	✓	6, 13	CFS allows cluster-wide file systems
Kernel Builds	✗	✓	12	Kernel configuration files are located in **cluster_usr**, and can be built on any member, but the kernel itself is member-specific.
Licensing	✗	✓	4, 5, 10, 11	Every cluster member must be individually licensed.
Loading Software	✓	✗	10, 19	Installed once, supported by CAA
LSM	✓	✓	14	Cannot be used for member boot partition
Non-Storage Devices	✗	✓	19	Member-specific
O/S Install/Updates	✓	✗	5, 11, 19, 26	Rolling Upgrade Supported
Performance	✓	✓	19, 21, A	Cluster-Wide for Cluster Services, Member-Specific for Local Services
Printing	✓	✗	19.4.3	New "**on**" printcap attribute
Processes and Scheduling	✗	✓	6, 19.2.4	PIDs cluster-wide, Scheduling member-specific
Shutdown	✓	✓	19.2.2	Cluster-wide shutdown is supported
Startup	✗	✓	17	Member-specific startup files
Storage Devices	✓	✗	7, 12, 15	Supported through DRD and CFS
System Time	✗	✓	20	Must be Synchronized
User Accounts	✓	✗	19.3.1	The **passwd** and **group** files are cluster-wide

Table 19-1: System Administration Tasks

```
# hwmgr  -view devices -cluster
HWID: Device Name           Mfg      Model           Hostname   Location
-------------------------------------------------------------------------------
   3: /dev/dmapi/dmapi                               molari
   3: /dev/dmapi/dmapi                               sheridan
   4: /dev/scp_scsi                                  molari
   5: /dev/kevm                                      molari
  35: /dev/disk/floppy0c             3.5in floppy    molari     fdi0-unit-0
  46: /dev/disk/cdrom0c     COMPAQ   CRD-8402B       molari     bus-1-targ-0-lun-0
  47: /dev/disk/dsk0c       COMPAQ   BD009734A3      molari     bus-2-targ-0-lun-0
  50: /dev/disk/dsk1c       COMPAQ   BD009635C3      molari     bus-3-targ-0-lun-0
  50: /dev/disk/dsk1c       COMPAQ   BD009635C3      sheridan   bus-3-targ-0-lun-0
  51: /dev/disk/dsk2c       COMPAQ   BD009635C3      molari     bus-3-targ-1-lun-0
  51: /dev/disk/dsk2c       COMPAQ   BD009635C3      sheridan   bus-3-targ-1-lun-0
  52: /dev/disk/dsk3c       COMPAQ   BD009635C3      molari     bus-3-targ-2-lun-0
  52: /dev/disk/dsk3c       COMPAQ   BD009635C3      sheridan   bus-3-targ-2-lun-0
  54: /dev/disk/dsk5c       COMPAQ   BD009635C3      molari     bus-3-targ-4-lun-0
  54: /dev/disk/dsk5c       COMPAQ   BD009635C3      sheridan   bus-3-targ-4-lun-0
  55: /dev/disk/dsk6c       COMPAQ   BD009635C3      molari     bus-3-targ-5-lun-0
  55: /dev/disk/dsk6c       COMPAQ   BD009635C3      sheridan   bus-3-targ-5-lun-0
  58: scp                                            sheridan
  59: kevm                                           sheridan
  89: /dev/disk/floppy1c             3.5in floppy    sheridan   fdi0-unit-0
 102: /dev/disk/cdrom1c     COMPAQ   CRD-8402B       sheridan   bus-0-targ-0-lun-0
 103: /dev/disk/dsk8c       COMPAQ   BB009235B6      sheridan   bus-2-targ-0-lun-0
 104: /dev/disk/dsk9c       COMPAQ   BB009235B6      sheridan   bus-2-targ-1-lun-0
 108: /dev/disk/dsk4c       COMPAQ   BD009635C3      molari     bus-3-targ-3-lun-0
 108: /dev/disk/dsk4c       COMPAQ   BD009635C3      sheridan   bus-3-targ-3-lun-0
```

The hwmgr command has several other cluster-oriented options such as "-member" that allows a command to be focused on a particular cluster member, or "-cluster" that forces the command to act cluster wide. The default action is that the command works from the perspective of the issuing member.

See Chapters 7 and 12 for more information on hwmgr and dsfmgr.

19.4.1 AdvFS

The Advanced File System (AdvFS) has grown in importance over the years. At first it was plagued with problems. Slowly but surely the problems were resolved so that the current release of AdvFS (version 4) is very robust. In fact, it is the default file system for *Tru64* UNIX starting with version 5.0. Prior to that, the default file system was UFS.

In a cluster environment, AdvFS can be used to expand the cluster_root domain. Big deal, you say? Well normally, the root domain cannot be expanded, so it is a big deal! Generally, we discourage the use of multi-volume domains, but it sure is convenient to add a bigger volume to an AdvFS domain if and when necessary and then remove the smaller volume. Note that adding and removing volumes requires the ADVANCED-UTILITIES license.

Fileset quotas are available within AdvFS in a cluster as are user and group quotas. Note that user and group quotas within AdvFS in a cluster became available as of V5.1A (see Chapter 13 for more information).

The verify(8) utility can run on active domains using the "-a" option. This allows checking the cluster_root domain while it is up and running. This is big news because typically verify would be run on a domain with no mounted filesets. The following example shows the verify command being run on the cluster_root domain (an active domain). Note that there will be some extraneous errors (bolded in the output below) reported since the domain is currently active.

CAUTION:

The "verify -a" command should only be run on the member that is the CFS server for the domain.

The CFS server for a domain can be discerned from the output of the cfsmgr(8) command.

```
# cfsmgr /

 Domain or filesystem name = /
 Server Name = molari
 Server Status : OK
```

```
# showfdmn cluster_root

               Id              Date Created  LogPgs  Version  Domain Name
3be01cb1.000be1e0  Wed Oct 31 10:45:53 2001     512        4  cluster_root

  Vol   512-Blks        Free  % Used  Cmode  Rblks  Wblks  Vol Name
   1L     401408      165040     59%     on    256    256  /dev/disk/dsk3b
```

```
# df /

Filesystem           512-blocks       Used   Available Capacity  Mounted on
cluster_root#root        401408     215962      165040      57%    /
```

```
# /sbin/advfs/verify -a cluster_root
+++ Domain verification +++

Domain Id 3be01cb1.000be1e0

Checking disks ...

Checking storage allocated on disk /dev/disk/dsk3b

Checking mcell list ...

Checking that all in-use mcells are attached to a file's metadata mcell chain...

Checking tag directories ...

Found 2 references to files that cannot be found in any directory.
Most likely this is from file activity on the active domain.


+++ Fileset verification +++

  +++++ Fileset root +++++

Checking frag file headers ...

Checking frag file type lists ...

Scanning directories and files ...
     100
Scanned 175 directories.

Scanning tags ...
    2100
Scanned a total of 2146 tags.

Searching for lost files ...
Creating //lost+found
    2100
Found 4 lost files out of 2146 checked.
Most likely this is from file activity on the active domain.
```

In the unlikely event that a cluster member fails while the `verify` command is active, leaving the filesets in an unmountable state, don't despair. Check for temporary mount points found under `/etc/fdmns/domain_name/fset[0-9]_verify_identifier`, where "identifier" is a unique id chosen by the `verify` utility. Unmount and delete these mount points and you should be in good shape again. These strange mount points were left behind because `verify` was interrupted in the middle of its operations and its temporary mounts were failed over to another member. (This will not happen on a standalone system.)

When a formerly standalone node is being added to an existing cluster, there is no magical way to get its domains recognized and its file systems mounted. Well, maybe the mechanism is a bit magical. It is always amazing to consider the jobs accomplished by commands such as `verify`, `defragment(8)`, `salvage(8)`, `advscan(8)`, `fixfdmn(8)`, and other effort saving (sometimes job saving) utilities. The new member's AdvFS file systems must be reflected in the

/etc/fstab file, which is shared by all cluster members. Getting the domains recognized can be done in either of two ways: by manually creating a directory entry under /etc/fdmns matching the new domain name and then creating the symbolic links pointing to the domain's volumes; or by using the (somewhat magical) advscan command, which searches for AdvFS partitions and creates entries in /etc/fdmns if appropriate.

The cluster_root domain is treated in a special way by the verify utility. As we discussed, the utility can examine the integrity of the root file system while it is mounted if invoked using the "-a" option. But the powerful fix-it-up "-f" and "-d" options are not available when using the "-a" option. So here you are with a wonderful report from verify indicating several metadata errors and you would like to have the utility (which is smart enough to figure out that there are problems with the domain's metadata) take the next step and do its darnedest to fix the problems. Under normal circumstances this is not a big deal because the target domain will have no file systems mounted, so verify can have its unabashed way with the metadata. But when cluster_root is the problem domain, we have a sticky situation because the cluster_root file system is mounted and can't be dismounted without losing access to just about everything including the verify command itself.

In this case you will have to boot the "emergency repair" disk, which can be the system disk of the initial cluster member. Once booted, you can give verify a shot at repairing the cluster_root domain or restore the domain from backup storage.

19.4.2 Event Manager

The Event Manager (EVM) supports cluster-wide events. Certain events will have a "cluster_event" attribute. If that attribute is set to "false", the event will only be posted on the member generating the event; otherwise it is posted on all cluster members. The CAA, CFS, CLUA, CNX, and DRD cluster subsystems have EVM templates.

The Event Manager is discussed in Chapter 8, and the cluster_event attribute is covered in Chapter 12.

19.4.3 Printing

A printer that is connected to a cluster member may be accessed by the other cluster members.

When using lprsetup(8), there will be an additional "on" attribute, which is used to indicate which cluster member has the physical connection to the printer. The /etc/printcap file is not a CDSL, so it is shared by all cluster members. The following output shows the new "on" printcap option in use and then displays information available from within lprsetup by typing the "?" when prompted for the "on" string.

```
# grep ':on' /etc/printcap
        :on=molari:\
```

```
# lprsetup

Tru64 UNIX Printer Setup Program

Command  < add modify delete exit view quit help >: m
```

```
Modifying a printer entry, type '?' for help.

Enter printer name to modify (or view to view printcap file): lp0
```

```
Enter the name of the symbol you wish to change.
Enter 'p' to print the current values, 'l' to list
 all printcap values or 'q' to quit.

Enter symbol name:  on
```

```
There is 1 node in the babylon5 cluster.

Do you want a list of cluster-member nodenames (y|[n])? y
```

```
Member ID  Member Hostname
---------  ---------------
1           molari
2           sheridan
3           ivanova


Enter a new value for symbol 'on'?  [molari] ? [Enter]
```

```
The 'on' parameter specifies the on-list, which is the list of
one or more cluster member nodenames which are authorized to
run the queue-daemon for the spool queue.  The format of the on-list
string is illustrated by the following examples:

                :on=localhost: \
                :on=node1: \
                :on=node1,node2,nodeN: \

If this parameter is not specified, 'localhost' is assumed
by default.

The order of the nodes in the on-list, from left to right, specifies
the priority from highest to lowest which the member-node parent print
daemons will use to determine which member-node will run the queue-daemon.

If localhost is specified, all member-nodes will be authorized to
run the queue-daemon.  Which node will actually run it is determined
by the first node that submits a job to the queue while it is empty.

In a cluster, localhost or no value should be specified only for
printers that are connected using tcp.

Printers that are connected to a device specified in the /dev/
directory must specify an on-list if the device is connected to
a node that is part of a multi-node cluster. It is recommended that
an on-list be specified if the cluster only contains one node.

For non-clustered, stand-alone hosts, use of an on-list specifying
the local hostname or 'localhost' is optional.

Enter a new value, or press RETURN to use the default.

Enter a new value for symbol 'on'?  [molari] [Enter]
...
```

There is also a new lock file used to coordinate `lpd(8)` activities from cluster members. The following is an excerpt from the `lpd(8)` reference page.

```
/usr/spool/lpd/lpd.lock
      On clustered systems, this transient file is created to contain the
      daemon status.  Note that the /usr/spool/lpd directory is a Context
      Dependent Symbolic Link (CDSL) and should not be manually created or
      destroyed.
```

Note that the `/usr/spool/lpd` directory is a CDSL, so the spooling directory is member-specific. The `/usr/spool/lpd/lpd.lock` file is used to synchronize activities from the `lpd` daemons running on each cluster member. The printer's log file (usually found in `/usr/adm/lp0err` – or a similar file name) is not a symbolic link, so all cluster members will log printing activities to the same file. The reference pages warn that the `lpd` does not purge its log files, so you may want to monitor their size periodically using a `crontab` entry (see existing entries under `/usr/var/spool/cron/crontabs`).

19.4.4 Security

Security is treated as a cluster-wide choice. Either all of the systems are running with enhanced security enabled, or none of the members are running with enhanced security enabled. Therefore, the cluster is treated as a single security domain. HP recommends that Enhanced Security be enabled before the creation of a cluster. Otherwise, the entire cluster will have to be shutdown and rebooted as part of the enhanced security configuration process. So much for high availability!! We recommend that you evaluate your site's security needs before leaping into the installation and configuration of your first cluster member. If security is set up on the first member, it will automatically be ready to function on all subsequently added cluster members.

19.4.4.1 ACLs

Given the existence of CFS, yielding cluster-wide file systems, any file with an Access Control List (ACL) associated with it will be protected by its ACL cluster wide.

19.4.4.2 Auditing

If you are using auditing, there will be an `auditd(8)` daemon running on each member. The `auditd` daemon will write to a member-specific audit log file. The audit log file is the only security related file that is member-specific. Administrators using auditing are usually paranoid about something (and sometimes for good reason). Rest assured that if a cluster member goes down, auditing continues on the remaining systems. Note that auditing is enabled or disabled on a cluster-wide basis, but it actually runs independently on each cluster member.

19.4.4.3 The `.rhosts` and `hosts.equiv` Files

If the culture at your site is such that your users are inclined to use the "`r`" commands (`rlogin(1)`, `rcp(1)`, `rsh(1)`), you should be aware that the outgoing request will be identified as emanating from the cluster alias name (not the individual cluster member's name). This may have repercussions on any "trusts" set up between machines on your network using the `/etc/hosts.equiv` file or the `~/.rhosts` files.

CAUTION:

The cluster software currently uses `rsh` across the cluster interconnect. Thus there will be a `.rhosts` file in your root directory and a `/etc/hosts.equiv` file in existence whether you want them or not. The files will contain an entry listing the cluster alias as well as several names created by the cluster software itself (i.e., `hostname-ics0` and `member1-icstcp0`). In V5.1B of *Tru64* UNIX, there will be an `ssh` command (currently non-existent) for communications providing a more robust internode communication mechanism for the cluster software utilities with less reliance on the `/.rhosts` and `/etc/hosts.equiv` files.

19.5 References

- *TruCluster* Server Cluster Administration Guide.
- *Tru64* UNIX System Administration Guide.
- *Tru64* UNIX Reference Pages.
- *Tru64 UNIX System Administrator's Guide* – Cheek, Fafrak, Hancock, Moore, Yates (Digital Press, ISBN: 1-55558-255-9).

20

Network Administration Tasks

Network administration can be even more of a black art than traditional system administration. Most people tend to lump the two functions under one common heading, "system administration." For our purposes, we will consider them separately. This chapter addresses network administration issues as they pertain to the world of clusters.

Last time we checked, the network administration team just stampeded down the hall to track down a routing/NFS/NIS/hardware/BIND/some_other_arcane_network problem. Imagine the team's reaction when we introduce clustered machines into their already bubbling over cauldron of responsibilities! In the previous chapter on System Administration Tasks, we saw that some commands worked unchanged in a cluster and were common to all members, some worked with slight changes, and others were specific to cluster members. Here too some of the network-oriented services will be common, others will be member-specific, and a few will not be recommended.

20.1 Routing

An article appeared in *SysAdmin* magazine a few years ago in which the author was discussing routing and subnet masks. Just a few columns were enough to convince us that several misconceptions were being presented. Considering that the article was written by someone who thought he understood the concept of routing well enough to be published in a magazine, it's fair to say that routing is one of the least understood and most error prone aspects of network administration. The *TruCluster* Server Cluster Administration Guide suggests that the cluster not be configured as a router. This doesn't mean that it can't function as a router; they just don't recommend it. In a way, this is good news for you.

Go out and buy a piece of hardware/software to deal with routing. Why waste the beauty of the cluster on the narrowly focused job of forwarding IP packets from one network to another? Your cluster has much more important processing to do.

20.1.1 Cluster Alias Routing

During the cluster alias discussion in Chapter 16, we mentioned some details on the responsibility of dealing with routing incoming requests for access to the cluster alias. This activity involves routing within the cluster. Indeed the necessity of routing within the cluster is the reason that the engineers suggest that the cluster not be used as a full-fledged IP router. The cluster already has a routing responsibility involving the routing of cluster alias traffic to an appropriate target member in the cluster. Each member in the cluster usually runs the `gated` dynamic routing daemon and references a special version of the `gated.conf` file named `/etc/gated.conf.membern` where "*n*" is the member number. This file is created and maintained by `aliasd` and is not to be directly edited by anyone. There is altogether too great a chance that an attempt to alter the `gated.conf(4)` file for your own purposes will end up preventing the cluster alias subsystem from doing its job. The member-specific `gated.conf.membern` file will provide the `gated` daemon the information necessary to establish the default cluster alias route and also request that the `gated` daemon advertise this route using the Routing Information Protocol (RIP).

20.1.2 Routing Options

Up until Patch Kit 1(PK1) for V5.1A, the `gated(8)` dynamic routing daemon was the only dynamic routing daemon supported. Several changes were implemented in PK1. Neither the other popular routing daemon, `routed(8)`, nor support for static routes reflected in the `/etc/routes` file were compatible with the cluster alias subsystem and `aliasd(8)`. The improved `aliasd`, while still optimized for `gated`, will work with `routed` or `gated` (not both concurrently) running on the member. In fact, `aliasd` will even run with neither `routed` nor `gated` running on the member. This would require the configuration of static routing. Don't lose sight of the fact that the dynamic routing daemons (`routed` and `gated`) have a job to do. Strange as it may seem, their job is not to do routing. Their job is to populate the in-memory routing table with correct information about routes so that the act of routing can happen in an intelligent and efficient manner.

20.1.3 Routing Information Protocol and `gated`

In a cluster, `gated` has always been implemented using the Routing Information Protocol (RIP). The RIP allows the convenient periodic (every 30 seconds) publicizing of information currently in a member's routing table and the acceptance of routing table information from other dynamic routing daemons if appropriate. The goal of the routing daemon is to keep the routing table information that exists in all network routers and end nodes as accurate as possible. HP suggests in the Release Notes that "configuring a cluster to perform non-standard routing tasks should only be configured by an experienced network administrator." For that reason, we will focus the rest of this chapter on the standard cluster routing configuration using the `gated` dynamic routing daemon.

20.1.4 Configuration Files for gated

As mentioned earlier, each member's aliasd daemon (part of the cluster alias component discussed in Chapter 16) will create a member-specific gated.conf file (not a CDSL) named /etc/gated.conf.member*n* (with the "*n*" replaced by a member number). The following example shows the member-specific gated.conf file. (For more information on the syntax of this file, see the following reference pages: gated.conf(4), gated.control(4), gated.proto(4), gated_intro(4)).

```
# cd /etc && file gated*

gated.conf:      symbolic link to ../cluster/members/{memb}/etc/gated.conf
gated.conf.default:      c program text
gated.conf.member1:      c program text
gated.conf.member2:      c program text
```

```
# cat /etc/gated.conf.member1

# This file created automatically by "aliasd", DO NOT EDIT!
#

traceoptions "/usr/tmp/gated.log" replace size 1000k files 2 general;

# any dead interfaces will be entered here with a high (i.e. undesireable)
# preference, so that gated will be compelled to put a better route
# in the kernel forwarding table
#
interfaces {
    interface all passive;
};

# broadcast routes with RIP if at least one interface is healthy
#
# make a default route through the cluster interconnect look expensive
#
# If an interface has been marked as "dead" by NIFF then we
# will also exclude RIP routes via the affected interface.
# This closes a hole where gated doesn't qualify the interfaces
# over which it hears broadcasts, and will possibly install a route
# through a dead interface.
#
# Lastly, we place a catch-all "all nripin noripout" here so that
# if an interface is brought on-line after aliasd has started, it
# won't automatically get used by gated.
#
rip yes {
    broadcast;
    interface ics0 ripin ripout metricout 10;
    interface tu0 ripin ripout metricout 10;
    interface tu1 ripin ripout;
    interface all noripin noripout;
};
```

```
# one "host" or network number per alias
#
# aliasd will also reroute direct routes for interfaces
# marked as "dead" by NIFF by inserting a new gateway
# for that route here
#
```

Note, the next few lines describe the default cluster alias.

```
static {
    host 192.168.0.70 interface 127.0.0.1;
};

# arrange to export alias host/network routes:
#
# o don't publish routes learned through RIP
# o publish the "static" routes given above, except for
#   orphaned networks that we're routing around
# o publish direct routes for virtual subnets which have real
#   interfaces attached to them
#
# for the cluster interconnect, arrange to broadcast a
# high-cost default route over it
#
# this default may have been learned from RIP (proto rip)
# or it may have been statically configured (proto kernel)
# we give a slight advantage to a default route via RIP
#
```

Note, the next few lines describe the Cluster Interconnect (CI) virtual address.

```
export proto rip interface 10.0.0.1 {
    proto rip {
        default;
    };
    proto kernel {
        default metric 3;
    };
};
```

Note, the next few lines describe the LAN interconnect.

```
export proto rip interface 10.1.0.1 {
    proto rip {
        default;
    };
    proto kernel {
        default metric 3;
    };
};

export proto rip interface 192.168.0.68 {
    proto rip restrict;
};
```

Pretty ugly, huh? You are probably starting to see why HP recommends not setting up your system as an IP router unless you are very experienced with `gated` and network administration in general. (See the first line of the `gated.conf.membern` file: "`# This file created automatically by "aliasd", DO NOT EDIT!`")

Still want to give it a whirl? Then follow these steps according to the *TruCluster* Server Cluster Administration Guide in the documentation set (Chapter 6): If `gated` is running, stop it with the following command:

```
# /sbin/init.d/gateway stop
```

1. Enter the following command:

   ```
   # cluamgr -r start,nogated
   ```

2. Modify `gated.conf` (to the name that you are using for the configuration file).

   Use the version of `/etc/gated.conf.membern` that was created by the "`cluamgr -r nogated,start`" command as the basis for edits to a customized `gated` configuration file. You will need to correctly merge the cluster alias information from the `/etc/gated.conf.membern` file into your customized configuration file.

3. Start `gated` with the following command:

   ```
   # /sbin/init.d/gateway start
   ```

In this special case, you will be providing a non-standard configuration file for `gated` to use (perhaps requesting Open Shortest Path First (OSPF) instead of RIP); therefore, you will need to enter the string "`nogated`" for `CLUA_ROUTE_ARGS` in `/etc/rc.config.common` in order to prevent `aliasd` from restarting `gated` using the `gated.conf.membern` file upon reboot.

Retrieve the `CLUA_ROUTE_ARGS` from the `rc.config.common` file. We do this to verify that there is not any previous attribute value (and to merge the contents if necessary).

```
# rcmgr -c get CLUA_ROUTE_ARGS
```

Add in the new value for the `CLUA_ROUTE_ARGS` environment variable.

```
# rcmgr -c set CLUA_ROUTE_ARGS "nogated"
```

NOTE:

Do not place the `CLUA_ROUTE_ARGS` environment variable in a member-specific `rc.config` file.

20.2 BIND (DNS) in a Cluster

One of the most recognizable components of TCP/IP (or the Internet in general) is the Domain Name System (DNS). The most common DNS option in use today is the ubiquitous Berkeley Internet Name Domain (BIND). You will see it everywhere you turn due to the common World Wide Web identifiers in many advertisements today (i.e., www.bruden.com). As you may know, BIND is just a scalable scheme to provide the ability to translate node names (whatz.ting.ugot.com) into IP addresses (`193.12.23.45`) or vice versa. To make a very long story very short, BIND is implemented through a series of servers that provide addressing information to other servers and ultimately to a client.

Your cluster can be configured to run as a BIND server, a BIND client, or both. If you configure the cluster as a BIND server, only one member actually does the serving (the first server will typically be the member on which you ran the `bindconfig(8)` or "`sysman dns`" command). This will be the only member running the BIND server daemon (appropriately named `named(8)`). The `named` daemon is implemented as a CAA resource; so in the case of member failure, another member will take over the server responsibilities. Remember, only one member at a time is actually doing the serving.

```
# caa_stat -t named
Name          Type          Target    State     Host
------------------------------------------------------------
named         application   ONLINE    ONLINE    molari
```

The other BIND servers (and clients) should reference the default cluster alias to identify the name of the BIND server in their `/etc/resolv.conf` file (which is cluster-wide).

20.3 DHCP in a Cluster

The Dynamic Host Configuration Protocol (DHCP) provides a mechanism whereby a system can be presented with an IP address dynamically. This is usually (but not necessarily) done at boot time. If you have a DSL connection to the Network, you are probably getting an IP address through DHCP sent to your PC as you boot it. The address is probably different each time you boot.

The cluster **cannot** function as a DHCP client because clusters require static addresses, but it can function as a DHCP server. The server will have access to a database that identifies the pool of IP addresses to be loaned out and identifies the legitimate clients. The cluster will function as a DHCP server and also provide failover capabilities through CAA.

```
# caa_stat -t dhcp
Name          Type          Target    State     Host
------------------------------------------------------------
dhcp          application   ONLINE    ONLINE    sheridan
```

Since the DHCP database will be available to all members of the cluster through the magic of CFS, it is relatively easy for CAA to handle the failover if necessary.

All DHCP clients must request access to the DHCP server using the default cluster alias in order to avoid having to reconfigure the DHCP software each time the serving member leaves the cluster.

20.4 NFS in a Cluster

NFS is a very heavily used mechanism for allowing transparent remote access to file systems. It requires a cooperative effort between the client system (doing the remote mount request) and the server system (providing the remote access).

20.4.1 NFS Client

Setting up a cluster member as an NFS client means that any NFS file systems mounted by the client member will be accessible to the other members of the cluster through the mounting member. Other members can also be NFS clients, but only one member can mount a particular NFS exported file system at a time. NFS clients will remotely mount file systems (or access directories) that actually exist on another system in the network. Given what we know about CFS, it is reasonable to expect that a file system that is mounted on one member will be visible to all members. This is indeed true for NFS mounted file systems as well. In truth, one member will request the remote mount, but all other members will get access to the remotely mounted file system through the member that actually did the mount. The member requesting the NFS mount automatically becomes the CFS server for that file system (see Figure 20-1).

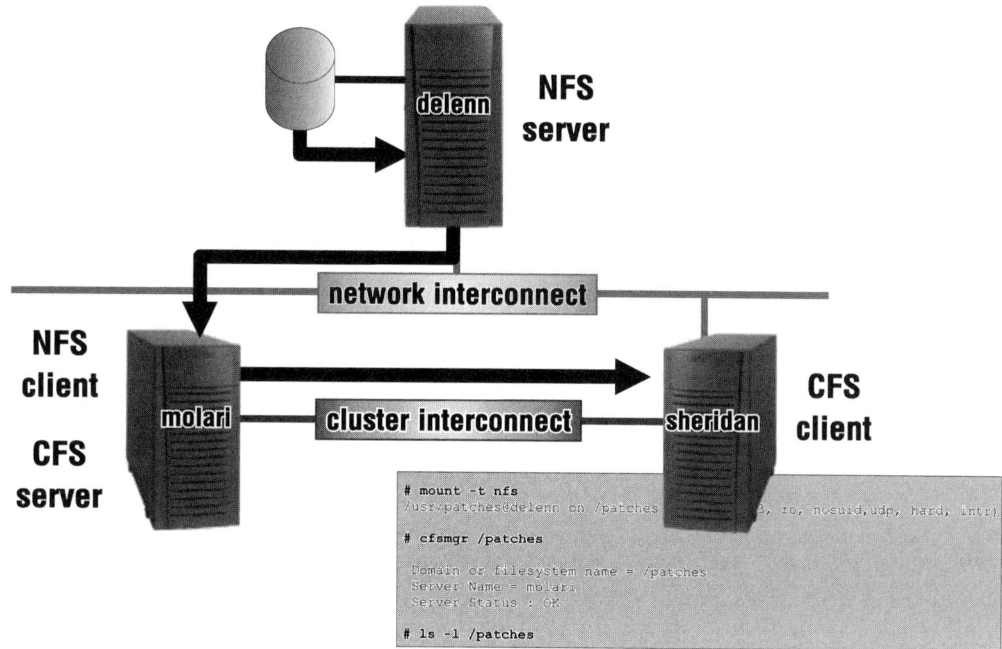

Figure 20-1: NFS Client – CFS Server

NOTE:

If the mounting member fails, the NFS mount disappears and another member will not automatically become the new NFS client/CFS server unless `automount(8)` (V5.0A-V5.1A) or `autofs(8)` (V5.1-V5.1B) is configured.

```
# mount -t nfs
/usr/patches@delenn on /patches type nfs (v3, ro, nosuid,udp, hard, intr)
```

```
# cfsmgr /patches

 Domain or filesystem name = /patches
 Server Name = molari
 Server Status : OK
```

```
# ls -l /patches
T64V51AB01AS0001-20020116.tar.gz
T64V51AB02AS0002-20020513.tar.gz
```

20.4.1.1 AutoFS

Note that the failure of a client member that has mounted a remote file system and is providing access (through CFS) to the remote file system to all other cluster members causes all members to lose access to the remote file system. AutoFS became available in *Tru64* UNIX version 5.1 as a higher availability option to the `automount` command. HP recommends using AutoFS as an "`automount`" mechanism whereby remote file systems are automatically mounted upon reference. More importantly, if AutoFS is configured in a cluster, it will be configured (using CAA) such that automatic failover of the mounted file system can be arranged.

```
# caa_stat -t autofs
Name           Type           Target     State      Host
-------------------------------------------------------------
autofs         application    ONLINE     ONLINE     molari
```

Note that this is based on client side activities (NFS mounting is done only on the client). For more information on AutoFS, see the *Tru64* UNIX Network Administration Guide: Services (the Network Administration Guide was split into two books in V5.1A) in the documentation set.

An interesting alternative to `autofs` exists. It involves creating a CDSL (which will be cluster-wide) and using the CDSL as the NFS mount point. The advantage to this is that there will be a form of "virtual client failover" since the CFS serving part of the NFS client responsibilities (don't forget that the member that does the NFS client mount is also going to function as the CFS server) can now be accomplished by any cluster member (because the CDSL can be seen cluster wide). The disadvantage of this technique is that all coherency issues are the responsibility of NFS, which is less sophisticated in this area than CFS. The *TruCluster* Server Configuration Guide suggests the following three steps:

- Create the mount point if one does not already exist.

```
# mkdir /mountpoint
```

- Use the "mkcdsl -a" command to convert the directory into a CDSL. This will copy an existing directory to a member-specific area on all members.

```
# mkcdsl -a /mountpoint
```

- Using the same NFS server, mount the NFS file system on each cluster member.

```
# mount server:/filesystem  /mountpoint
```

20.4.2 NFS Server

The cluster can also be configured as an NFS server. The typical arrangement is such that the entire cluster is treated as the NFS server.

20.4.2.1 Exporting File Systems Containing CDSLs

We suggest that you consider the contents of the file systems that you export. If the exported file system contains CDSLs, you would think that the client should receive access to the member-specific file pointed to by the CDSL. At first glance this seems to be an acceptable arrangement. But consider what happens when a system (any system – even a non-clustered system) accesses a file using a CDSL. Recall that the CDSLs exist in a standalone system (such as our NFS client), but they resolve to `/cluster/member/member0` locations (as opposed to `/cluster/member/member1`, or `/cluster/member/member2`, ...). Therefore an NFS client system that resolves a file reference to a CDSL on the NFS server actually resolves the CDSL on the NFS client! Oops – definitely not what we had in mind. The more you think about it, the more it makes sense. Any time a system references a CDSL, it resolves it to a location on the system that is referencing the CDSL, which is the NFS client in this case. The lesson here is to export file systems that do not have CDSLs, or at least design the client-side applications so that they do not access the CDSLs without being aware of the repercussions. The following example shows some notable behavior when accessing CDSLs from an NFS client. As odd as this behavior may seem, it is reasonable. But it serves to emphasize that CDSLs can potentially be a problem in an exported file system.

```
# file /etc/rc.config
/etc/rc.config: symbolic link to ../cluster/members/{memb}/etc/rc.config
```

```
# grep "HOSTNAME=" /cluster/members/member?/etc/rc.config
/cluster/members/member0/etc/rc.config:HOSTNAME="molari.dec.com"
/cluster/members/member1/etc/rc.config:HOSTNAME="molari.dec.com"
/cluster/members/member2/etc/rc.config:HOSTNAME="sheridan.dec.com"
```

From a client system, mount the cluster's `/etc` directory.

```
# mount babylon5:/etc /mnt
```

```
# grep "HOSTNAME=" /mnt/rc.config
HOSTNAME="delenn.dec.com"
```

20.4.2.2 Excluding Members from NFS Server Responsibilities

If desired, some members may be excluded from the duties of NFS serving using the "`sysman`" with the "`-focus`" option (see the *TruCluster* Server Cluster Administration Guide for more information). By focusing the configuration utility (`sysman` or `nfsconfig`) on a particular member, it will override the cluster-wide configuration. So you can configure the cluster as an NFS server but then exclude certain members if you prefer. The following output shows that the NFS serving variables are normally reflected in the `/etc/rc.config.common` file, but if the member is reconfigured as a member-specific NFS server, the variables appear in the member-specific `/etc/rc.config` file.

```
# grep -i NFS /etc/rc.config /etc/rc.config.common
/etc/rc.config.common:NUM_NFSIOD="7"
/etc/rc.config.common:export NUM_NFSIOD
/etc/rc.config.common:NFS_CONFIGURED="1"
/etc/rc.config.common:export NFS_CONFIGURED
/etc/rc.config.common:NFSSERVING="1"
/etc/rc.config.common:export NFSSERVING
/etc/rc.config.common:NFSLOCKING="1"
/etc/rc.config.common:export NFSLOCKING
/etc/rc.config.common:PCNFSD="0"
/etc/rc.config.common:export PCNFSD
```

```
# nfsconfig -ui cui -focus molari
```

De-configure the member and then reconfigure it as a member-specific NFS server.

```
# grep -i NFS /etc/rc.config /etc/rc.config.common

/etc/rc.config:NFS_CONFIGURED="1"
/etc/rc.config:export NFS_CONFIGURED
/etc/rc.config:NFSSERVING="1"
/etc/rc.config:export NFSSERVING
/etc/rc.config:NFSLOCKING="1"
/etc/rc.config:export NFSLOCKING
/etc/rc.config:PCNFSD="0"
/etc/rc.config:export PCNFSD
…
```

Alternatively, you could leave the NFS values in `rc.config.common` so that all members are configured and then set `NFS_CONFIGURED` to "0" in the `rc.config` file of the member that you do not want configured. The `rc.config` file overrides the values in `rc.config.common`.

20.4.2.3 The `exports.aliases` File

Note that the NFS clients must reference the default cluster alias (or an alias that has been established in the `/etc/exports.aliases` file – new in V5.1A) in order to enable the cluster to transparently provide some NFS server failover capabilities. The following output shows an attempt to do an NFS `mount` using a member name rather than the default cluster alias. The successful `mount` uses the cluster alias to identify the server.

```
# showmount -e babylon5

Exports list on babylon5:
/etc                                    Everyone
/usr/den                                Everyone
```

```
# showmount -e molari

Can't do Exports rpc: RPC: Program unavailable
```

```
# mount molari:/etc /mnt

Can't access molari:/etc: Connection refused
```

```
# mount babylon5:/etc /mnt
```

```
# df -t nfs

Filesystem                  512-blocks        Used   Available Capacity  Mounted on
babylon5:/etc                 1002864       185468      805728     19%     /mnt
```

Essentially, if the member currently serving out access to the exported file systems fails, another cluster member should pick up the flag and keep on serving.

The NFS client and server daemons can be running simultaneously on multiple cluster members. Currently, there's no way to restrict a particular mount point to be exported to a particular alias. But by using the `/etc/exports.aliases` file, an alias name (joined by particular cluster members only) can be used by a client's `mount` command yielding a situation where only selected members of the cluster (members of the alias) will do NFS serving for the requesting client.

The following is an important excerpt from `the /etc/exports.aliases` file:

```
# *** You must be very careful to ensure that for each file system
#     being exported to NFS clients, the CFS server of the file system
#     is a member of the cluster alias being used by the clients.
#     Otherwise performance will be severely degraded for NFS over UDP
#     mounts.  This is because an attempt is always made to tunnel NFS
#     over UDP packets to the CFS server for the file system.  If the
#     server is not a member of the cluster alias being used, then
#     each packet is randomly assigned to a node that is a member of
#     the alias by the cluster alias round robin algorithm.  Having IO
#     requests for the same file handled by different CFS clients will
#     severely degrade performance.
```

For more information, see the `exports.aliases(4)` reference page.

NFS can be configured using `nfsconfig` or `sysman`. Using `sysman` without specifying a focus indicates that the configuration should take place cluster wide. Therefore any configuration information will be placed in `/etc/rc.config.common`.

20.4.3 NFS Locking

Your applications may need file locking during their dealings with NFS mounted file systems. If so, the client copy of the `rpc.lockd(8)` and `rpc.statd(8)` daemons must be running on the client members. The server versions of these lock daemons will run on one member of the cluster at a time. In your cluster, these daemons are run as a highly available application resource (`cluster_lockd`) managed by CAA.

```
# caa_stat -t cluster_lockd

Name            Type           Target     State      Host
------------------------------------------------------------
cluster_lockd   application    ONLINE     ONLINE     molari
```

For more information on CAA, see Chapters 23 and 24. For more information on NFS locking, see the `rpc.lockd(8)` and `rpc.statd(8)` reference pages as well as the *Tru64* UNIX Network Administration Guide (V5.0A and V5.1) and the *Tru64* UNIX Network Administration: Services Guide (V5.1A and newer).

20.5 NIS in a Cluster

Network Information Service (NIS) is another client/server-based mechanism whereby data can be effectively distributed among network nodes. One common use of NIS is to distribute the `/etc/passwd` file among multiple network nodes so that a password changed on one node is effectively distributed to all nodes. The master server will be responsible for distributing copies of the database files (think password file) to the slave servers (if any). The NIS clients request information from the servers and are fed the data as they request it. The clients do not have copies of the database files. The slave servers have a copy of the file sent down to them from the master server.

A cluster can be an NIS client, NIS slave server, or an NIS master server. This service does not have the same level of flexibility as NFS in a cluster. You cannot have some members serving and others functioning as clients. All members must use the same NIS domain name. This means that you can't set up NIS such that half the cluster serves one domain, and the other half serves another domain. If NIS was configured at the time of cluster creation, the cluster will come up with NIS functioning. You can also configure NIS after the cluster is up using `nissetup(8)`. On other members, use "`/sbin/init.d/nis start`". For master server, slave server, or client, the general sequence to configure NIS is to use `nissetup` on one member and then manually start up NIS on all other members.

The NIS server map transfer daemon (`ypxfrd(8)`) controls activities where the master server sends information to the slave servers (`yppush(8)`), or where the slave servers request data from the master server (`ypxfr(8)`). The `ypxfrd(8)` is multi-instance and active on all members. The `rpc.yppasswdd(8)` also exists on all members of a master server cluster but is single-instance. In other words, only one instance of `rpc.yppasswdd` is functioning at a time in the cluster but not implemented as a CAA.

20.6 Miscellaneous Services

This section provides summary information on several other services that you may use in your cluster.

20.6.1 The Internet Server Daemon (`inetd`)

The internet daemon (`inetd(8)`) is responsible for starting many other server daemons in response to incoming network requests. The `inetd`'s configuration file (`/etc/inetd.conf`) is a cluster-wide file. It provides a mechanism for requesting daemon-based services that should run identically on every member. In a cluster, there is another configuration file (`/etc/inetd.conf.local`) that is used to configure services that are per member. To disable a service on a particular member in the cluster, alter the "local" configuration file such that it reflects "disable" in the "ServerPath" field in the /etc/inetd.conf.local file.

CAUTION:

In V5.0A and V5.1, the "disable" does not work. This fact is clearly stated in the release notes. In V5.1A, it does work, but the Release Notes still state that it is broken.

20.6.2 Mail

All cluster members running a mail utility must have the same mail configuration and use the same protocols. For instance, if SMTP is used on one cluster member, it must be used on all cluster members. SMTP is a cluster-aware protocol and will use the default cluster alias. Other mail protocols (MTS, UUCP, X.25, DecNET Phase IV, DecNET Phase V) will treat cluster members as standalone systems. The mailstats(8) utility will return member-specific results because it references the member-specific /usr/adm/sendmail/sendmail.st file. Caution, the mailstats command will not work in an unpatched V5.1A system. The command works in V5.1B.

Cluster alias selection priority and selection weight can be used to load balance mail activities over the cluster members if desired (see Chapter 16 for more information). Configure mail with mailconfig(8) or mailsetup(8) but do not switch between utilities since they use different configuration file formats.

20.6.3 NIFF - NetRAIN

The Network Interface Failure Finder daemon (niffd(8)) must run on every member in order to monitor network connectivity. NIFF is also used in conjunction with the cluster alias subsystem. The aliasd forks a child (aliasd_niff) that is used to subscribe the niff-related EVM events and notify aliasd when an interface goes down so that alias routing can be adjusted.

The NIFF daemon can be used to monitor a NetRAIN pseudo device, if desired. NetRAIN identifies a series of physical network devices as one virtual network device. If the active interface in the set fails, the NetRAIN software fails over to another network interface in the set using the same IP address.

NIFF and NetRAIN are covered in Chapters 9 and 12. Also see the *Tru64* UNIX Network Administration manuals in the documentation set for further information on these options.

20.6.4 The `ifaccess.conf` File

In order to prevent the great unwashed from deciding to masquerade as a member of your cluster and get access to all of your precious data, the system provides an interface access filter file (`/etc/ifaccess.conf`). This file provides a mechanism whereby an interface can define and limit access to the interface from various networks or subnets. If your cluster uses a LAN interface, each member must provide an `/etc/ifaccess.conf` file with an entry for the virtual network address (typically 10.0.0.1) and an entry for the network address for each physical interface. (The Memory Channel does not require the physical address entries but does require an entry for the virtual network interface address.)

On each cluster member other than the first member, you must manually edit the `/etc/ifaccess.conf` file and add a line for the physical network addresses for each network interface. The following output shows the contents of the `/etc/ifaccess.conf` file:

```
#              Interface Access Filtering Configuration File
#
# Description:  The ifaccess.conf file contains the permit/deny mode for
#               one or more interfaces running the Internet Protocol.
#
# Syntax:      interface-name  address  mask  action
#
# Comment lines begin with number sign (#).
#
# Example:
#
# ln0 16.1.0.0 255.255.255.0 permit     # permit net 16.1.0 on ln0
# ln0 16.0.0.0 255.0.0.0 denylog        # deny and log net 16 on ln0
# tu1 192.15.32.0 255.255.255.0 deny    # deny net 192.15.32 on tu1
#
# Refer to the ifaccess.conf(4) man page for further explanation.
#
sl0 10.0.0.0 255.255.255.0 deny
tu0 10.0.0.0 255.255.255.0 deny
tu1 10.0.0.0 255.255.255.0 deny
tu2 10.0.0.0 255.255.255.0 deny
```

For extra security, be sure to run the `ifconfig` command and specify the "`filter`" parameter after adding information to the `ifaccess.conf` file. As of this writing, the filtering must be turned on by hand.

```
# ifconfig tu0 filter
```

20.6.5 NTP

In order to keep all cluster members in virtual synchronization with respect to time, the Network Time Protocol (NTP) is used. NTP uses a time stratum strategy whereby time can be considered to be more accurate when delivered from one NTP server as compared with another. The most accurate time is delivered from a "stratum 1" server that has an accurate time derived from some highly reliable source (see www.ntp.org for a list of public servers). If a member serves out time that was acquired from a stratum 1 server, the time value served out by that member is treated as if it came from a stratum 2 server and so forth. If an NTP client receives time from several NTP servers, it simply selects the time from the lowest stratum rated server.

According to the *Tru64* UNIX Cluster Installation manual, NTP is automatically configured on the first member of your cluster when you issue the `clu_create(8)` command. However, as of V5.1A, the `clu_create` script simply checks to see if you have NTP configured, and if not, it errors out. Therefore, we recommend installing NTP prior to installing the first cluster member. If you will be using one or more external time sources, it is imperative to install NTP as described above because when/if the software catches up with the documentation, the `clu_create` and `clu_add_member` commands will set up the members as NTP peers of each other.

Additional cluster members have NTP automatically configured as they are added to the cluster. All members in the cluster are configured as NTP peers. This allows all cluster members to provide their version of time to other cluster members. This mechanism usually provides synchronization within ten thousandths of a second. Note that two members that are out of time sync will gradually (as opposed to instantaneously) be brought back in sync. This avoids the potential for software repercussions if time changes too drastically and too quickly.

To avoid the blind leading the blind, we would recommend configuring NTP on your initial system such that it is synched to an accurate external source; although for starters, you may want to have one member synch to `127.127.0.1` (the local reference clock – for more information see the `ntp_manual_setup(7)` and `ntp.conf(4)` reference pages).

20.7 Summary Chart

Table 20-1 yields handy information concerning network management tasks in a cluster.

Service		Configuration	Cluster Aware	CAA	Notes
Network Services					
DHCP	client	✗	✗	✗	Not Allowed. Static addresses only.
	server	common	✗	✓	Implemented as a single-instance, highly-available CAA application resource (**dhcp**). Clients should use the default cluster alias.
DNS/BIND	client	common	✗	✗	**/etc/resolv.conf** is a cluster-common file.
	server	common	✗	✓	Implemented as a single-instance, highly-available CAA application resource (**named**).
NFS	client	common	✗	✗	By default, the NFS is configured and enabled on all members.
	server	common	✓	✗	The NFS server implementation is cluster-aware. By default, the NFS is configured and enabled on all members. Clients must use the default cluster alias prior to V5.1A. As of V5.1A, alternate aliases can be defined in **/etc/exports.aliases**.
			✗	✓	Server versions of **rpc.statd** & **rpc.lockd** are implemented as a single-instance, highly-available CAA application resource (**cluster_lockd**).
	autofs	common	✗	✓	Implemented as a single-instance, highly-available CAA application resource (**autofs**).
NIS	client	common	✗	✗	By default, the NFS is configured and enabled on all members.
	master server	common	✓	✗	If configured on one member, it is configured the same on all members. **ypxfrd** is multi-instance, and is active on all the members. Although **rpc.yppasswdd** runs on every node, it is single-instance; only one daemon is actually active at a time. Clients should use the default cluster alias.
	slave server	common	✗	✗	By default, the NFS is configured and enabled on all members.
NTP		member-specific	✗	✗	Time must be synchronized. Members are configured as peers.
Routing		member-specific	✗	✗	Must be enabled prior to V5.1A PK1.
	gated	common	✗	✗	Member-specific routing information added and maintained by CLUA (**aliasd**).

Table 20-1: Network Services Summary

20.8 Internet Express

Since we're in a networking kind of mood, we figured we should mention a useful package of network administration tools that you may want to explore. Most of these utilities have been modified to work in a cluster. The following is an excerpt from Compaq/HP's product description:

"Internet Express is a collection of popular open source Internet software and administration software developed by Compaq/HP. Customers are encouraged to purchase a service contract for Internet Express that entitles them to receive upgrades to Internet Express, which is released approximately every four months.

The Internet Express product provides the following features and benefits:

- A collection of open source Internet software (binaries and sources), tested and qualified on *Tru64* UNIX
- Automatic installation and configuration of Internet software
- Web-based Internet Express Administration utility to manage Internet services and tune kernel attributes for Internet service performance
- Internet Monitor (Web-based Quality of Service monitor)
- LDAP Module for System Authentication
- Compaq Secure Web Server based on Apache with SSL capability
- iPlanet (Netscape) Directory Server (limited by license to 200,000 entries)
- Netscape LDAP Software Development Kit
- FireScreen (basic firewall based on `screend`)
- Support for *TruCluster* Server – All services are configured to run on *TruCluster* Server providing a true high availability environment
- IPv6 support in some components:
  - UW-IMAP, Pine (IMAP client), POP3, `procmail`, `sendmail`, TCP wrapper, IRC (chat client and server)
  - Apache 2.0 Early Adopter's Kit.
  - Mozilla 0.9.8 Web Client evaluation kit

You can access the Internet Express Administration utility through any graphical Web browser that supports JavaScript. Online help is provided through links to the *Administration Guide* (in HTML format)."

The URL is:

```
http://www.tru64unix.compaq.com/internet/osis.htm
```

20.9 References

- *TruCluster* Server Cluster Administration Guide
- *TruCluster* Server Technical Overview
- *Tru64* UNIX System Administration Guide
- *Tru64* UNIX Network Administration Guide (V5.0A and V5.1)
- *Tru64* UNIX Network Administration Guide: Services (V5.1A)
- *Tru64* UNIX V5.1A Cluster Release Notes
- *Tru64* UNIX 5.1A and *TruCluster* Server 5.1A: Patch Summary and Release Notes for Patch Kit-0001
- *Tru64* UNIX Reference Pages (noted within the text).
- *Tru64 UNIX System Administrator's Guide* – Cheek, Fafrak, Hancock, Moore, Yates (Digital Press, ISBN: 1-55558-255-9).

21

Cluster Administration Tasks

After your cluster is built, certain administration tasks need to be implemented to ensure that the systems will operate smoothly. Some of these tasks deal with monitoring how the cluster behaves; others are more involved and relate to changing the behavior of the cluster. It's also just good to know the behavior of daemons that are the system administrator's friends so you know which ones to check and keep running.

In this chapter, we will cover the following:

	Section
• Cluster Administration GUIs	21.1
• Moving the `/tmp` File System	21.2
• Moving Swap to a Local Disk	21.3
• Load-balancing CFS Servers	21.4
• Configuration Variables	21.5
• Cluster-wide `cron`	21.6
• Essential Services Monitor Daemon	21.7
• Important Files and Information to Have and to Hold	21.8
• Cluster Command Summary	21.9

21.1 Cluster Administration GUIs

There is a nice Graphical User Interface (GUI) that the system administrator can use to monitor and manage the cluster. These types of tools are especially useful in a cluster because they present a picture and layout of the various cluster components, whether we're talking about hardware, file systems, or other cluster pieces. Starting this GUI is rather simple. Start SysMan from a graphics-capable display device.

```
# sysman -station
```

Or

```
# sms
```

This starts a set of windows that look something like this:

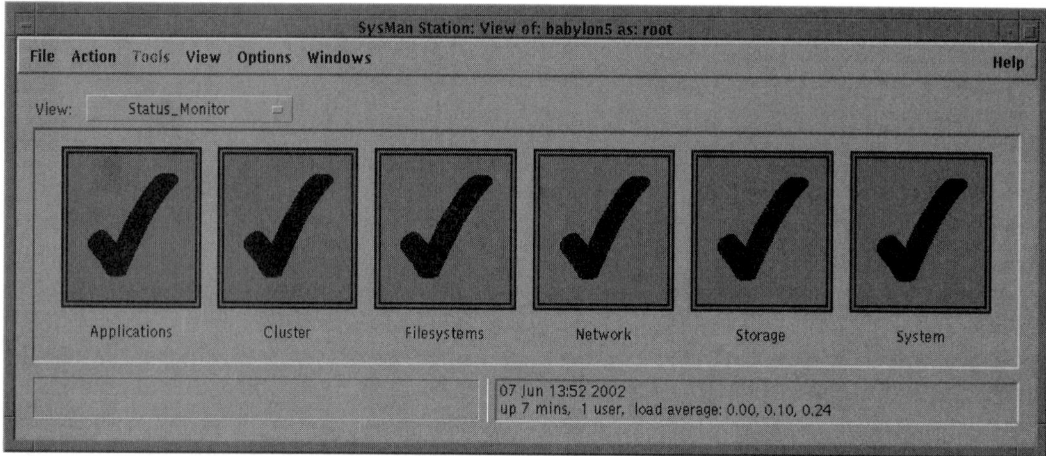

Figure 21-1: SysMan Station – Main Screen

As Figure 21-1 demonstrates, you get a quick "up or down" on the main categories of the cluster. If one of the categories is something other than a green box with a checkmark, you can double-click on that icon and see why it's yellow or red.

Since this book is not in color, Figure 21-2 describes the three possible icons that you might see while looking at the SysMan Station main screen.

Figure 21-3 is particularly helpful, especially in a large cluster because you can see each member and how the cluster is put together. This display also allows you to look for errors on a particular component or manage a component. For example, by selecting a disk, you can modify the disklabel, create an AdvFS domain, or fire up the Event Viewer to see if there are any events that relate to that disk as seen in Figure 21-4.

	GREEN	This indicates that everything is okay.
	YELLOW	This indicates a potential problem, an event has occurred.
	RED	This indicates a serious problem has occurred.

Figure 21-2: SysMan Station – Color/Icon Descriptions

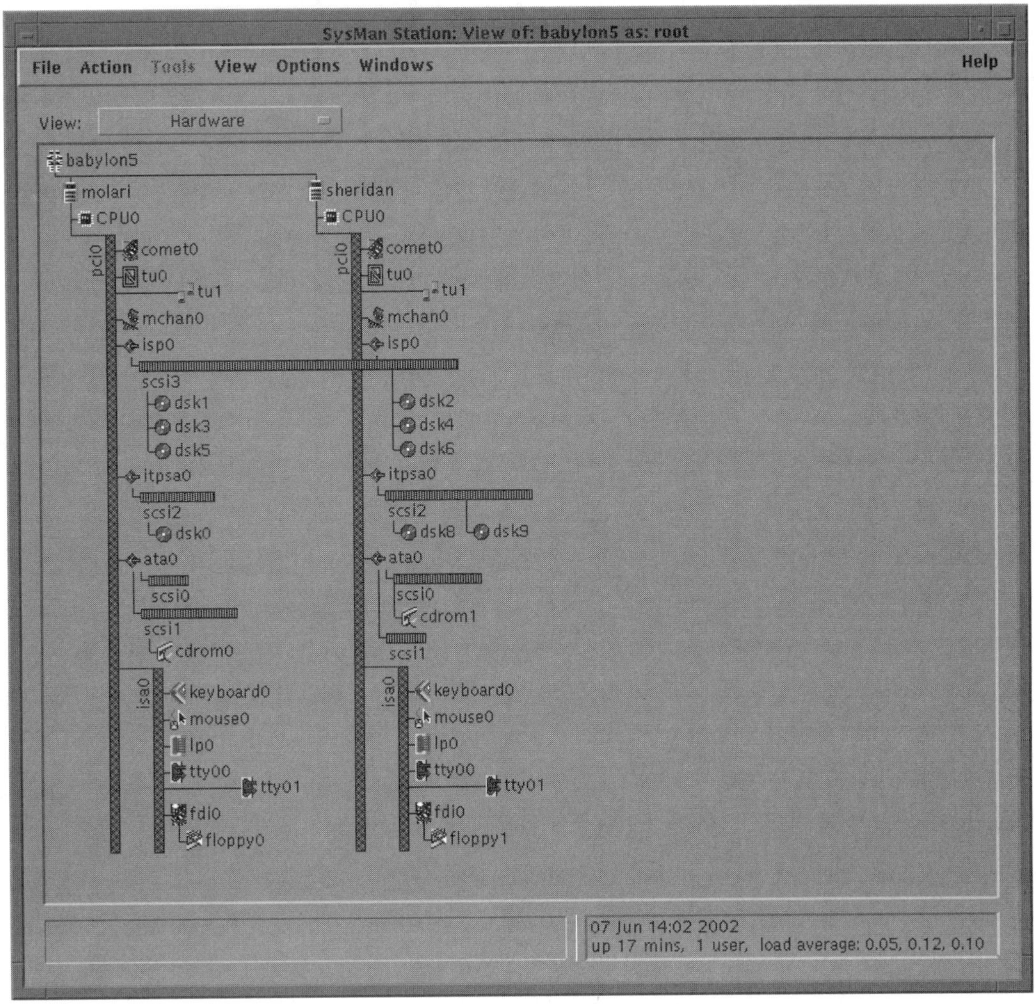

Figure 21-3: SysMan Station – Hardware View

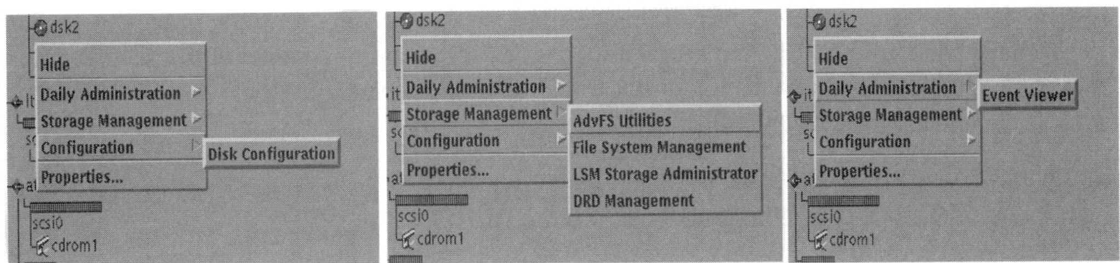

Figure 21-4: SysMan Menu Popups

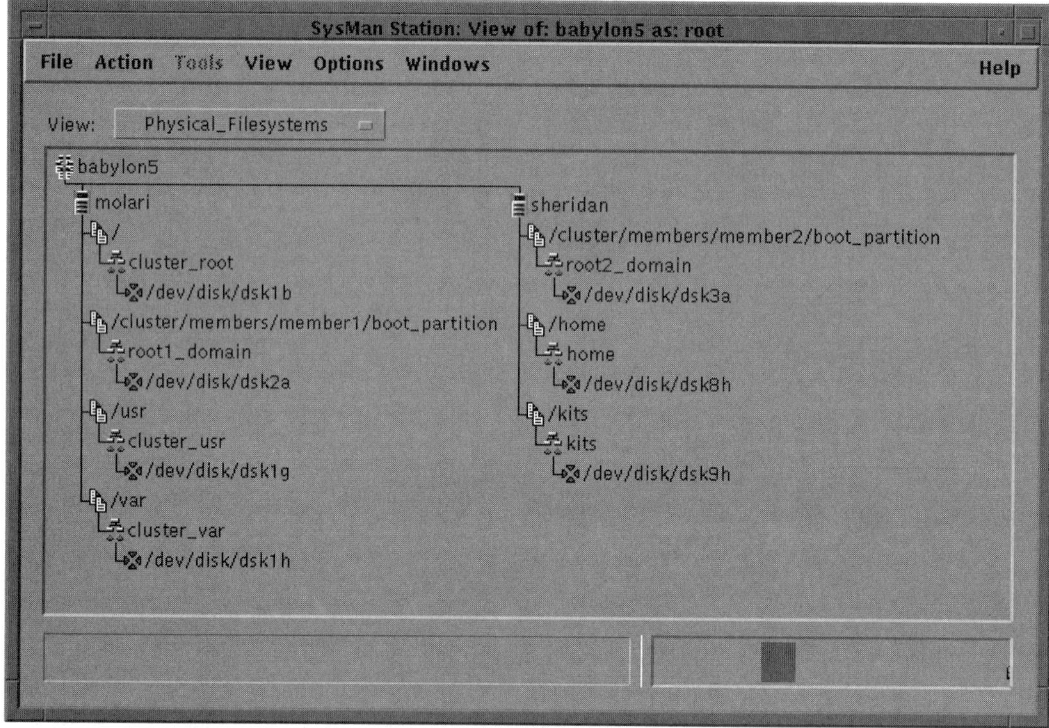

Figure 21-5: SysMan Station -- Physical File System View

There are several views that can be displayed by SysMan Station, and as you have probably guessed, the hardware view is one of the most useful. We won't look at every view, but one more that's particularly good is the physical_filesystems view as seen in Figure 21-5.

This view lists the various systems and the CFS-serving relationship for each mounted file system. If you want to manage the CFS configuration, you can start the CFS manager from this display and change the CFS server for a file system. Additionally you may wish to keep this view active to monitor how and if the CFS relationships change throughout the life of the cluster.

21.2 Moving the `/tmp` File System

A system manager will frequently want to move the `/tmp` file system to either a drive local to a cluster member or to another disk to improve file system performance. Another reason to move /tmp is because a user could potentially fill up the root file system by writing to `/tmp`. Making it a separate file system eliminates that possibility.

21.2.1 Creating `/tmp` on a Local Disk

First create an AdvFS domain and fileset on the desired disk/partition.

```
# mkfdmn /dev/disk/dsk21c gilligan_tmp
```

```
# mkfset gilligan_tmp tmp
```

Then modify the /etc/fstab file to include this mount.

```
gilligan_tmp#tmp        /cluster/members/member2/tmp    advfs rw 0 0
```

You can verify that gilligan is indeed member2 by issuing the clu_get_info(8) command.

```
[gilligan]
# clu_get_info -m 2

    Cluster memberid = 2
    Hostname = gilligan.alf.cpqcorp.net
    Cluster interconnect IP name = gilligan-mc0
    Member state = UP
```

Now when gilligan boots, since it has access to dsk21, it will be able to mount the file system. Any other member will fail to mount the file system, but that's perfectly okay.

21.2.2 Creating /tmp on a Shared Bus Disk

Another possibility is to create /tmp on a disk that happens to be on the shared bus. Again make the domain and fileset and add an entry to the /etc/fstab file as above. If you prefer having /tmp accessible only to the member that is using it, you can mount the file system with the mount(8) command using "-o server_only". This isn't necessary but may be desirable and will behave like the local bus example even though the file system is on a shared resource.

21.3 Moving Swap to a Local Disk

Just as moving /tmp to a local or alternate location is a rather simple operation, so is moving swap. The only thing you have to do is modify the /etc/sysconfigtab file to list your intended swap partitions:

```
vm:
 swapdevice=/dev/disk/dsk15b,/dev/disk/dsk3b
```

Then execute "swapon -a" if you are adding additional swap space. If you are replacing the primary swap space, you will need to reboot for this change to take effect since you cannot yank a swap partition away from the OS. It should be noted that moving the swap space to a local disk is good for performance and reduces I/O to the shared bus, but it also makes that swap partition more vulnerable to a controller problem. If swap is moved to a local partition and there is a failure on that path, it could cause the system to hang or panic. If the swap partition is on a shared disk, you won't face this problem if at least one member maintains access to the disk. Another benefit of having swap on a shared bus is if that member crashes and for some reason is not bootable, the crash dump can be processed by another cluster member and crash analysis can begin before the original member is even booted. For example, if we know that dsk6b is the other member's swap partition and that the partition is large enough to hold the crash dump, we can process the dump and create the requisite vmunix.0 and vmzcore.0 files (and from those create crash-data.0 if we're so inclined).

```
# /sbin/savecore -d /dev/disk/dsk6b .

System went down at Thu Jun 27 23:11:13 2002
Saving 23949312 bytes of image in vmzcore.0
```

```
# /usr/bin/crashdc vmunix.0 vmzcore.0 > crash-data.0
```

```
# ls

crash-data.0      vmunix.0       vmzcore.0
```

To see how swap is currently configured, issue the "swapon -s" command:

```
# swapon -s

Swap partition /dev/disk/dsk16b (default swap):
    Allocated space:        211639 pages (1.61GB)
    In-use space:              129 pages (  0%)
    Free space:             211510 pages ( 99%)

Swap partition /dev/disk/dsk4b:
    Allocated space:        124063 pages (969MB)
    In-use space:              129 pages (  0%)
    Free space:             123934 pages ( 99%)


Total swap allocation:
    Allocated space:        335702 pages (2.56GB)
    Reserved space:          11873 pages (  3%)
    In-use space:              258 pages (  0%)
    Available space:        323829 pages ( 96%)
```

In this example there are two swap partitions.

21.4 Load-balancing CFS Servers

In the next release of *TruCluster* Server (V5.1B), tools will be included with the clustering software that automatically manage load balancing the CFS activity, but until then, we will provide tips and examples of how to manage this load-balancing act.

The reason we even care to try and balance the CFS activity is that if the member that's performing the I/O is not the CFS server, file system traffic has to go across the cluster interconnect, whether that's MEMORY CHANNEL or Ethernet. And if you get too many unfavorable combinations of cross-member I/O, or a single member with more than its fair share of CFS serving, you can wind up with a performance problem. That doesn't mean that CFS is bad, but there is a tradeoff: a little performance for the sizable benefit of the Single System Image.

To see the current CFS layout, you can use our `cfs` command:

```
# cfs
CFS Server         Mount Point                  File System                FS Type
----------------   --------------------------   -------------------------  -------
battra             /cluster/members/member4/    battra_usr#tmp              AdvFS
                      tmp
battra             /cluster/members/member4/    root4_domain#root           AdvFS
                      boot_partition

gamera             /archive                     archive#archive             AdvFS
gamera             /usr/dec                     dec#dec                     AdvFS
gamera             /var/spool/ftp               ftp#ftp                     AdvFS
gamera             /cluster/members/member3/    gamera_usr#tmp              AdvFS
                      tmp
gamera             /var/spool/mail              mail#mail                   AdvFS
gamera             /cluster/members/member3/    root3_domain#root           AdvFS
                      boot_partition
gamera             /usr/staff                   staff#staff                 AdvFS

mothra             /                            cluster_root#root           AdvFS
mothra             /usr                         cluster_usr#usr             AdvFS
mothra             /var                         cluster_var#var             AdvFS
mothra             /cluster/members/member2/    mothra_usr#tmp              AdvFS
                      tmp
mothra             /cluster/members/member2/    root2_domain#root           AdvFS
                      boot_partition
rodan              /usr/ris                     ris#ris                     AdvFS
rodan              /cluster/members/member1/    root1_domain#root           AdvFS
                      boot_partition
rodan              /usr/src                     src#src                     AdvFS
rodan              /cluster/members/member1/    usr_domain#tmp              AdvFS
                      tmp
```

Notice that this four-member cluster is configured with local `/tmp`.

Your CFS management could be as simple as watching the CFS serving, as displayed by SysMan Station, and manually relocating the file systems to balance out the number of file systems per member. Or you might watch the CFS statistics with something like our custom `cfs` command and balance them based on the cross-member file system traffic. For example, look at this output and see if, based on the recent past, the `/usr/staff` file system should be relocated and if so to which member.

```
# cfs -s /usr/staff
/usr/staff [staff#staff] (dsk13c):
               read     write    lookup   getattr  readlnk   access    other
            --------- --------- --------- --------- --------- -------- ---------
    battra:         0         0        26         0         0        1         5
*   gamera:         0         0        26        27         0        1         5
   mothra:        13        40        47         0         0       20        51
     rodan:       225     12880        63         3         0       21        31
     total:       238     12920       162        30         0       43        92
```

As we can see, member rodan is the heaviest reader and writer to the `/usr/staff` file system and it may be beneficial to relocate it from gamera to `rodan` (the "*" shows that gamera is the CFS server in the above `cfs` output). This is a good idea if you believe that past behavior is an indicator of future behavior, but as most stockbrokers will tell you, don't bet the farm on it. Make these CFS tweaks based on your knowledge of your cluster and buttressed by statistics such as those above.

Now, let's move on to the example script. Until the HP delivered solution appears, this script should make managing the CFS a little easier. The `cfsldb` script, provided at the book's website (see Appendix B), reads the CFSSVR configuration variable from the member-specific `rc.config` file. The script will relocate file systems based on what the `CFSSVR` variable contains. `CFSSVR` is a white-space delimited list of mount points the member should serve. If the file system is already served by the member, it skips it. The script also writes a log in `/cluster/admin` called `cfsldb_<hostname>.log` which is overwritten each time the program is run.

For example, to have a member serve root, `/usr`, and `/var`:

```
# rcmgr set CFSSVR "/ /usr /var"
```

```
# ./cfsldb start
cfsldb: Relocating / from sheridan to molari...done!
cfsldb: Relocating /usr from sheridan to molari...done!
cfsldb: Relocating /var from sheridan to molari...done!
```

The log will look like:

```
# more /cluster/admin/cfsldb_molari.log
Mon Jun  3 03:35:49 EDT 2002

cfsldb:  Attempting to relocate / from sheridan to molari
cfsldb:    Relocation succeeded

cfsldb:  Attempting to relocate /usr from sheridan to molari
cfsldb:    Relocation succeeded

cfsldb:  Attempting to relocate /var from sheridan to molari
cfsldb:    Relocation succeeded

 Domain or filesystem name = /var
 Server Name = molari
 Server Status : OK

 Domain or filesystem name = /usr
 Server Name = molari
 Server Status : OK

 Domain or filesystem name = /
 Server Name = molari
 Server Status : OK
```

If you attempt to relocate a file system that cannot be relocated, you will receive an error in the log. For example, what happens if we add a file system that is on a private bus?

```
# rcmgr set CFSSVR "/ /usr /var /home"
```

```
# ./cfsldb start
cfsldb: Relocating /home from sheridan to molari...failed!!!
cfsldb: One or more file systems failed to relocate
        See the /cluster/admin/cfsldb_molari.log for more information
```

```
# more /cluster/admin/cfsldb_molari.log

Mon Jun  3 03:49:05 EDT 2002

cfsldb:  molari is already the CFS server for /
cfsldb:  molari is already the CFS server for /usr
cfsldb:  molari is already the CFS server for /var
cfsldb:  Attempting to relocate /home from sheridan to molari
cfsmgr:  The server for /home filesystem should not be relocated to molari
cfsmgr:  Use  -f flag for force relocation

 Domain or filesystem name = /home
 Server Name = sheridan
 Server Status : OK
```

Note, the other file systems don't relocate, because they are already in the right location. This is the sort of output you'll see in `/var/adm/messages`:

```
Jun  3 03:54:44 molari vmunix: Recovering filesystem mounted at / to this node (
member id 1)
Jun  3 03:54:44 molari vmunix: Recovery to this node (member id 1) complete for
filesystem mounted at /
Jun  3 03:54:47 molari vmunix: Recovering filesystem mounted at /usr to this nod
e (member id 1)
Jun  3 03:54:48 molari vmunix: Recovery to this node (member id 1) complete for
filesystem mounted at /usr
Jun  3 03:54:51 molari vmunix: Recovering filesystem mounted at /var to this nod
e (member id 1)
Jun  3 03:54:52 molari vmunix: Recovery to this node (member id 1) complete for
filesystem mounted at /var
```

Make sure you understand your environment before implementing a script such as this because it could lead to undesired effects such as extra cluster interconnect traffic, which would reduce file system performance if you have I/O from multiple nodes (especially if that I/O pattern changes from time to time).

21.5 Configuration Variables (`rc.config`, `rc.config.common`)

Prior to version 5.0 of *Tru64* UNIX (and the V5.X *TruCluster* Server software that came along with it), all the configuration variables were stored in the `rc.config` file and managed by the `rcmgr(8)` utility. With version 5.0A of *TruCluster* Server, a few of the variables are member-specific but others are actually common throughout the cluster, thus the split in `rc.config`. As you may remember from Chapter 6, the `rc.config` file is a CDSL and contains the member-specific variables. Here's some of what you'll see in `rc.config` that is cluster-related:

```
[gilligan]
# grep -E "CLU|TCR" /etc/rc.config

CLU_BOOT_FILESYSTEM="root2_domain#root"
export CLU_BOOT_FILESYSTEM
CLUSTER_NET="gilligan-mc0"
export CLUSTER_NET
TCR_INSTALL="TCR"
export TCR_INSTALL
TCR_PACKAGE="TCR"
export TCR_PACKAGE
CLU_NEW_MEMBER="0"
export CLU_NEW_MEMBER
CLU_VERSION="TruCluster Server V5.1 (Rev. 389)"
export CLU_VERSION
```

NOTE:

An `rc.config.site` file is supported but *Tru64* UNIX doesn't ship this file by default and the system administrator would have to create and maintain it.

Let's also take a quick peek at `rc.config.common` to see the sorts of variables defined there.

```
...
NUM_NFSIOD="7"
export NUM_NFSIOD
NFS_CONFIGURED="1"
export NFS_CONFIGURED
NFSSERVING="1"
export NFSSERVING
...
NIS_DOMAIN="BRAVO"
export NIS_DOMAIN
NIS_ARGS="-s -S OSD,fathom.abc.net,reverse.abc.net"
export NIS_ARGS
NIS_SERVERARGS=""
export NIS_SERVERARGS
SECURITY="BASE"
export SECURITY
...
```

Things like security settings, NIS setup, NFS, etc. are common to the cluster, and it makes sense that they would be in a cluster-common variable definition file. The important point here is that there are two files to keep in mind when setting and checking variable definitions.

For more on rc.config, check back to Chapters 6 and 12.

21.6 Clusterwide `cron`

One area of cluster confusion involves the `cron(8)` daemon. The `crontab` files for each member (found in `/var/spool/cron/crontabs`) are member-specific – `/var/spool/cron` is a CDSL.

```
# fln /var/spool/cron
/var/spool/cron -> ../cluster/members/{memb}/spool/cron
```

Not only are the `crontab` files member-specific, but the `cron` daemon is also not cluster-aware.

```
# clu_ps | grep -E "^member|^=|^-|cron" | grep -v grep
================================================================================
member1 (molari)          ps -ef
--------------------------------------------------------------------------------
root      525300 524289  0.0 13:47:26 ??          0:00.02 /usr/sbin/cron
================================================================================
member2 (sheridan)          ps -ef
--------------------------------------------------------------------------------
root      1049553 1048577  0.0 13:47:25 ??          0:00.01 /usr/sbin/cron
================================================================================
```

This means that on each member, cron acts independently from all the other members, and that a cron job to backup a data directory would run on the same file systems at the same times on all members in the cluster. Obviously not a good arrangement!

This problem is solved in one of the Best Practices documents that can be found on HP's Best Practices website:

http://www.tru64unix.compaq.com/docs/best_practices/clus_bps.html

This Best Practices document shows you how to set up a CAA service to handle cron jobs that need to be addressed in a cluster-aware fashion.

For more on setting up CAA, refer to Chapters 23 and 24.

21.7 Essential Services Monitor Daemon (esmd)[1]

Sometimes a cluster will stop behaving properly because one of the critical daemons has died, for one reason or another. This should be a rare situation, but if it happens, it's up to the system administrator to identify the problem, figure out what went wrong, and correct it. To eliminate some of this problem, there is a new feature implemented in what is called the Essential Services Monitor daemon (esmd). This daemon watches certain essential daemons/services (thus its name) and will automatically restart them if they terminate. But "who watches the watchers?," you ask. The init process starts esmd and will restart it automatically if it terminates. So what are these "essential services" anyway? At least for now, it's the Event Manager daemon and the CAA daemon (if in a cluster). If you have an "essential service," you should implement it as a CAA resource. For more on CAA resources, please refer to Chapters 23 and 24.

Since all state changes and restart failures are logged through syslogd (to the daemon.log) or to the console (when syslogd is not running), you can see what the esmd is doing. If esmd is unable to restart a daemon, it will send a high priority message via syslogd. If this happens, the system administrator should investigate the problem, fix it, and manually restart the daemon since esmd will not try to restart a daemon once it fails to do so. After a failed attempt is corrected by the system administrator and the daemon is running again, esmd will again monitor that daemon and

[1] This functionality is available in V5.1A Patch Kit 2 and later.

attempt to restart it if it terminates. You can verify that `esmd` has resumed monitoring the daemon by checking the `syslogd` log.

For more information about `esmd`, see the `esmd(8)` reference page.

21.8 Important Files and Information to Have and to Hold

As the Boy Scouts say, "Be Prepared." So, in planning for the worst, it's a good idea to have certain files on hand—either in electronic form, hardcopy, or both. We'll talk about some of these files and/or command outputs that are invaluable if you are rebuilding a broken cluster, especially if you weren't the mastermind behind the original setup.

First, let's look at command output (hardcopy):

- `/etc/rc.config*`

  Lists the configuration variables (both cluster and non-cluster specific).

- `hwmgr -view hierarchy`

  Shows the entire hardware database list.

- `hwmgr -view devices`

  Shows all devices, especially disks.

- `clu_check_config`

  Displays configuration data.

- `clu_get_info -full`

  Lists important cluster configuration data including member numbers, versions, etc.

- `cluamgr -s all`

  Displays the cluster aliases, including their selection priorities, weights, and router priorities.

- `caa_stat -t -v`

  Displays the CAA services and their states and where they're running.

- `volprint -Aht`

  Lists all of the LSM volumes including their make-up (plexes, subdisks, disks).

- File system layout drawing

  Record cluster root, `/usr`, `/var`, quorum disk, and member disks at least.

- Storage map (really important if a SAN, need a picture)

  This picture that you provide should include the controllers, switches, storage controllers, and which ports are used and for what.

Now for the files either backed up onto tape or otherwise accessible when booted from the installation CD:

- volsave

  Can be used to help recreate the LSM configuration.

- sys_check's escalate.tar

  Contains a great deal of useful configuration information.

- /etc/*

  Contains lots of system configuration files and is relatively small.

- /var/cluster/caa/

  The CAA profiles and configuration.

- /cluster/admin

  Cluster log files and configuration information.

- Configuration data from the boot disk CNX partition.

  Save a copy of the clu_bdmgr.conf file which is located in the /cluster/members/member<ID>/boot_partition/etc directory.

- Inventory of site-specific CDSLs.

  Save a copy of the /var/adm/cdsl_admin.inv file.

- Store the makeup of your AdvFS domains.

```
# ls -lR /etc/fdmns > etc_fdmns_links
```

- Store the all-important LSM volumes makeup in a file.

```
# volprint -Aht > lsm_volumes
```

- Save the license PAKs

  In the Korn shell:

```
# for i in $( lmf list | awk '/^[A-Z0-9][A-Z0-9].*/ { print $1 }')
do
  lmf issue \
  /.root/PAKS/${i}.pak $i lmf register - < \
  /.root/PAKS/${i}.pak
done
```

```
# lmf reset
```

In case you have to re-register the licenses.

- Save the disk labels

  In the Korn shell:

```
# for i in $( hwmgr view devices \
| awk '/dsk/ { print $2 }' \
| cut -d/ -f4 )
do
i=${i%c}
disklabel -r $i > $i.lbl
done
```

  In case you have to replace disks.

- /var/adm/patch/log

  If patches are installed, the log directory is useful to know which patch kit is installed.

- /var/evm/adm

  If site-defined EVM templates, channels, and filters were created.

- /etc/dt

  If CDE customization has been done.

- /sbin/init.d

  If there are site-defined startup scripts.

- Initial disk used to create the cluster

  Could be used in recovery.

Note the sys_check(8) utility places some good data in /var/recover/sys_check. This data can also be useful to repair a damaged system, and you should consider adding this to the list of files/directories to backup.

```
# ls

apply.ksh    devls       etcfiles     lmf         vfs.stanza
clufiles     devlsL      hsz          map
consolevars  disklabels  inet.stanza  proc.stanza
```

Finally a complete set of backups for cluster root, /usr, /var, each member boot disk, and, of course, your data. These backups might be necessary if the problem was particularly severe but in most cases will not be required.

21.9 Cluster Command Summary

Let's review some key cluster commands and utilities and catalog them here. We'll start with the standard utilities shipped with the cluster software or base operating system as shown in Table 21-1 and Table 21-2.

Command	Description	Chapter Reference
arp(8)	Display the address resolution protocol table.	16
caa*(8)	Cluster Application Availability commands.	23, 24
cdslinvchk(8)	Check the current CDSL inventory.	6, 12
cfsmgr(8)	Manage the Cluster File System.	10, 13, 15
cfsstat(8)	Display Cluster File System statistics.	13, 18
cleanPR	Remove the Persistent Reservations from disks. **Undocumented.**	22
clu_add_member(8)	Add a member to an existing cluster.	11
clu_bdmgr(8)	Manage the cluster boot disks.	17, 22
clu_check_config(8)	Check overall configuration of the cluster.	10
clu_create(8)	Create a cluster.	10
clu_delete_member(8)	Delete a member from an existing cluster.	11
clu_disk_install	Allow a disk to function as a direct-access I/O device.	22
clu_get_info(8)	Display detailed information about the cluster members.	10, 17
clu_quorum(8)	Display detailed quorum information and manage quorum.	10, 11, 17, 22
clu_update_sysconfig	Update member-specific subsystem configuration database for each member. **Undocumented.**	19
clu_upgrade(8)	Used in performing cluster rolling upgrade.	25
cluamgr(8)	Manage the Cluster Alias.	10, 16
dbx(1)	Kernel debugger	13
diskconfig(8)	GUI to display and modify the disk partition layout.	4
disklabel(8)	Display and modify the disk partition layout.	4, 14
dn_setup	Script that uses **dsfmgr** to create or recreate devices depending on the use.	7
drdmgr(8)	Manage the Device Request Dispatcher (DRD).	10, 15
dsfmgr(8)	Manage device special files.	7, 12, 19
dupatch(8)	Manage patches on a *Tru64* UNIX system or cluster.	25

Table 21-1: Cluster Commands – Part 1

Command	Description	Chapter Reference
evm*	Event Management utilities.	8, 12
hwmgr(8)	Display hardware device information.	7, 12, 14, 15, 19, 22
ifconfig(8)	Configure network interface.	9
installupdate(8)	Perform update installation.	25
lagconfig(8)	Configure a Link Aggregation Group.	9
mc_cable	Memory channel diagnostic command. SRM Console.	4
mc_diag	Memory channel diagnostic command. SRM Console.	4
mkcdsl(8)	Create CDSLs.	6, 12
mount(8)	Mount a file system.	13
mv(1)	Destroyer of CDSLs.	6
netstat(1)	Display network statistics.	9, 16
nfsconfig(8)	Configure the NFS system.	20
niffconfig(8)	Configure Network Interface Failure Finder (NIFF).	9
rcmgr(8)	Get and set configuration variables.	6
rdgstats	Displays various RDG statistics. **Undocumented.**	18
scu(8)	SCSI CAM Utility.	14, 22
shutdown(8)	Shut down a system or entire cluster.	19
sysconfig(8)	Display subsystem configuration database.	13
sysconfigdb(8)	Update subsystem configuration database.	14, 19
sysman(8)	System management interface.	19
verify(8)	Check an AdvFS domain.	19
vol*(8)	LSM configuration commands.	14
wwidmgr	View and make viewable storage in a Fibre Channel fabric. SRM Console.	4

Table 21-2: Cluster Commands – Part 2

In addition to the standard utilities, there are a few custom commands you get only from us. Table 21-3 lists these commands with a brief description and reference for each.

Command	Description	Chapter Reference
`cfs`	Displays Cluster File System information in a tabular format.	13, 15, 21
`cfsldb`	CFS auto-relocation script.	21
`cfssvrtok`	"Tuning helper" for **`cfs_max_svrcfstok`**.	18
`clu_alias`	Cluster-wide **`cluamgr(8)`** command.	16
`clu_arp`	Cluster-wide **`arp`** command.	16
`clu_exec`	Runs any command cluster-wide.	unused
`clu_ps`	Shows cluster-wide "**`ps`**" output.	16, 19, 21
`clu_scan_scsi`	Cluster-wide "**`hwmgr scan scsi`**" command.	7, 8
`clu_w`	Cluster-wide "**`w`**" command.	unused
`cnxread`	Display information about the **`cnx`** partition.	17
`cnxthreads`	Display the Connection Manager threads on a member.	17
`cvtpid`	Decode a cluster process ID (PID).	19
`evf`	Script to see what EVM filters are available in a filter file.	8, 12, 23
`fln`	Display the target of a CDSL. (Korn shell function.)	6, 12, 14, 19, 21
`kernel_idle_threads`	Displays details about the threads in the **`[kernel_idle]`** process.	18
`sman`	Section-based "**`man -k`**".	18, 23, 28
`vnode`	Utility to help see if certain vnode tuning is required	13
`wwid_decoder`	Decodes the worldwide ID header.	7

Table 21-3: Custom Cluster Commands

21.10 References

- Cluster Administration Guide.
- Compaq *TruCluster* Server Configuration and Management Class.
- Using `cron` in a *TruCluster* Server Cluster Best Practice.
- Reference pages (noted within the text).

22

Cluster Maintenance and Recovery

Clusters are great when things are working well. Clusters are great even when things aren't working so well since some of the benefits of a cluster are its high availability and robustness, but we need to be prepared for some possible bad situations. For example, what do you do if you lose an entire member boot disk (which only affects a single member) or `cluster_root`, `cluster_usr`, and `cluster_var`? Or what if something happens to your data file system(s)? These types of problems should be extremely rare if you've followed our advice and the advice given in the *TruCluster* Server documentation and built your cluster with no single point of failure. But sometimes bad things still happen. For example, an errant "`rm *`" at the wrong place will cause extensive damage that may only be repaired by a restore of the affected file system(s). We'll tackle some of these types of problems and show you how to work your way out of a few tight situations. In addition we'll show how to change some of the characteristics of your cluster such as the IP address and the cluster interconnect.

We will cover the following:

	Section
• Backup and Restore of Critical Cluster File Systems	22.1
• Replacing HBA and/or HSx Controllers	22.2
• Installing Customer Specific Patches	22.3
• Multi-Path Storage	22.4
• I/O Barriers and the `cleanPR` Command	22.5
• How to Replace a Failed Quorum Disk	22.6
• Migrating from MC to LAN Cluster Interconnect (and vice versa)	22.7
• Name and Address Changes	22.8
• References	22.9

22.1 Backup and Restore of Critical Cluster File Systems

First of all, after your cluster is built you must put together a regimen of cluster backups. Backing up your cluster includes saving each member's boot disk, `cluster_root`, `cluster_usr`, and cluster_var. While you may use an enterprise-wide backup package to backup your data, we recommend something simple (and something that's on the Operating System CD-ROM) like vdump(8)/vrestore(8) to handle these critical operating system-specific file systems. Otherwise you have to do a full operating system installation and then install the enterprise package and probably index a few tapes to finally get to the point where you can recover anything. With a simple solution like vdump/vrestore, you just boot the OS CD or a base OS standalone disk and begin recovering right away.

22.1.1 Backup of Member Boot Disk and Cluster-Common File Systems

Let's remember what the member boot disk contains: on partition "a" is the file system that holds /vmunix, sysconfigtab and a few other important files; partition "b" is swap; and partition "h" is the CNX partition. Regarding the CNX partition, each time the system boots, it automatically saves a copy of the configuration file that can be used to rebuild the CNX partition as /.local../boot_partition/etc/clu_bdmgr.conf. See sections 17.2.5 and 17.8.5 for more information about the CNX partition.

Given a current copy of this file, the CNX partition of any of the cluster boot disks can be restored using clu_bdmgr(8). For example, given member gilligan's clu_bdmgr.conf file, you can repair member skipper's CNX partition (which is on dsk3) with this command.

```
[gilligan]
# clu_bdmgr -h dsk3 /.local../boot_partition/etc/clu_bdmgr.conf
```

Now that we've taken care of the CNX partition, it's a simple vdump command to produce backup tapes of the AdvFS file systems on each key partition.

For example, to create a vdump tape of member3's boot partition, you can use the following command:

```
# vdump 0f /dev/ntape/tape2 /cluster/members/member3/boot_partition
```

Repeat this or your favorite variation of the 0-level vdump for each of the file systems we mentioned above. In most environments there will be both 0-level vdumps as well as incremental vdumps. Just be sure to apply all of the incremental vdumps if you have to perform a restoration of any particular file system.

Once you have a good backup scheme in place, you will be prepared to restore each member boot disk, cluster_root, cluster_usr, and cluster_var.

As a final note on member boot disk backups, because of their limited size, you can fairly easily fit them in one of the cluster-common OS file systems (especially if they are gzip'd) so that you could rebuild an entire boot disk in mere moments (as opposed to restoring from tapes or resorting to clu_delete_member and clu_add_member).

```
[/var/bd_backups]
root@molari # ls -l
total 42312
-rw-r--r--   1 root     system   21627236 May 28 00:28 molari_bd_vdump.gz
-rw-r--r--   1 root     system   21688542 May 28 00:27 sheridan_bd_vdump.gz
```

22.1.2 Restoring the Cluster Root

Let's say that critical files on your cluster_root file system have been deleted, and after some investigation you determine that the problem is widespread (and to make things more interesting, cluster_usr and cluster_var are also affected and are on the same disk) and you decide that you need to restore the file systems. There is no need to destroy the file system that is currently known as the cluster_root, since keeping that file system around will allow you to troubleshoot the original problem when the heat is off. Don't panic! Since you have the backups (we will assume vdump tapes), you can restore the cluster either onto a disk already known to the cluster (the preferred option) or to a disk new to the cluster.

22.1.2.1 Restoring Cluster Root to an Existing Disk

The least complicated scenario for restoring the cluster_root file system is to restore it to a disk that is already known to the cluster.

To perform the restore, we need a disk on a shared bus that is accessible to all members of the cluster, that was known to the cluster before the problem with cluster_root, and that was known to the cluster prior to the cluster_root backup. The restoring member must have access to the Emergency Repair (ER) disk (or equivalent), and this OS disk must be at the same operating system version and patch kit as the cluster. See section 22.1.3 for more discussion about the ER disk.

In this scenario:

- Original cluster root was dsk5.
- Bootable standalone (ER) disk is dsk13 .
- Disk to which cluster_root is restored is dsk11 .

1. Ensure all members are halted.
2. Boot the ER disk or equivalent.

```
>>> boot DKB100
```

`DKB100` corresponds to `dsk13` in this cluster.

WARNING:

Once booted from the ER disk you may have a different view of the storage, namely the device special file names.

3. Determine if the device name for the new `cluster_root` is the same while booted from the ER disk as it is while booted from the cluster.

```
# hwmgr -view device
```

Verify by checking the Bus/Target/LUN **and** the disk name. If the target device doesn't have the same device special file name, rename it so that it does. This will avoid confusion later.

```
# dsfmgr -m dsk55 dsk11
```

4. Partition the new `cluster_root` disk (using saved `disklabel` information per Chapter 21, probably the hardcopy version of the saved disklabels).

```
# disklabel -e dsk11
```

5. Create the new `cluster_root`, `cluster_usr`, and `cluster_var` domains and filesets (they all reside on the same disk in our example, but this may not always be true). If you are using the ER disk, the `/etc/fdmns/cluster_*` directories will already exist, so remove those before attempting to create the new domains.

```
# cd /etc/fdmns
# rm -r cluster_root cluster_usr cluster_var
```

Now create the domains.

```
# mkfdmn /dev/disk/dsk11a cluster_root
# mkfset cluster_root root
```

```
# mkfdmn /dev/disk/dsk11g cluster_usr
# mkfset cluster_usr usr
```

```
# mkfdmn /dev/disk/dsk11h cluster_var
# mkfset cluster_var var
```

NOTE:

If you need the extra file system space, you can add up to two additional volumes to cluster_root at this point. Just remember to account for them in steps 10, 11, and 12. See Chapter 11 of the *TruCluster* Server Cluster Administration manual for more details.

```
# addvol /dev/disk/dsk70c cluster_root
```

6. Mount cluster_root.

```
# mount cluster_root#root /mnt
```

7. Restore cluster_root from backup.

```
# vrestore -xf /dev/tape/tape2 -D /mnt
# umount /mnt
```

8. Restore cluster_usr and cluster_var by repeating steps 6 and 7 but for the cluster_usr#usr and cluster_var#var filesets. (Or you could leave cluster_root mounted and mount these filesets at /mnt/usr and /mnt/var respectively and restore them.)

9. Re-mount cluster_root if you unmounted it in step 7.

```
# mount cluster_root#root /mnt
```

10. Fix the restored /etc/fdmns/cluster_root device linkage to reflect the new device name. (Also update cluster_usr and cluster_var if those file systems were also restored.)

```
# cd /mnt/etc/fdmns/cluster_root
# rm *
# ln -s /dev/disk/dsk11a
```

11. Take note of the major and minor numbers of the new cluster_root device.

```
# file /dev/disk/dsk11a
/dev/disk/dsk11a:        block special (19/97)
```

12. Boot the member boot disk interactively specifying the major and minor numbers (above) for the newly restored cluster_root.

```
>>> boot -flags "ia"
...
Enter: <kernel_name> [option_1 ... option_n]
  or: ls [name]['help'] or: 'quit' to return to console
Press Return to boot 'vmunix'
# vmunix cfs:cluster_root_dev1_maj=19 cfs:cluster_root_dev1_min=97
```

NOTE:

In cluster_root_dev#_maj and cluster_root_dev#_min, the "#" can range from 1 to 3, meaning that you can have from 1 to 3 AdvFS volumes in cluster_root.

13. Boot each cluster member one at a time.

22.1.2.2 Restoring Cluster Root to a New Disk

This procedure is more involved, as you'll see, so only choose this option if there is no disk already available on a shared bus. In fact, you might even configure a "hot spare" disk for such an emergency.

In this scenario:

- Original cluster_root was dsk5.
- Member boot disk is dsk6 .
- Bootable standalone (ER) disk is dsk13 .
- Disk to which cluster_root is restored is dsk21 .

1. Ensure all members are halted.
2. Boot the ER disk or equivalent.

```
>>> boot DKB100
```

DKB100 corresponds to dsk13 in this cluster.

WARNING:

Once booted from the ER disk you may have a different view of the storage, namely the device special file names.

3. Note the device name and Bus/Target/LUN of the disk that will be the new `cluster_root`.

```
# hwmgr -view device
```

4. Partition the new `cluster_root` disk (using saved `disklabel` information per Chapter 21, probably the hardcopy version of the saved disklabels).

```
# disklabel -e dsk21
```

5. Create the new `cluster_root`, `cluster_usr`, and `cluster_var` domains and filesets (they all reside on the same disk in our example, but this may not always be true).

   If you are using the ER disk, the `/etc/fdmns/cluster_*` directories will already exist, so remove those before attempting to create the new domains.

```
# cd /etc/fdmns

# rm -r cluster_root cluster_usr cluster_var
```

   Now create the domains and filesets.

```
# mkfdmn /dev/disk/dsk21a cluster_root
# mkfset cluster_root root
```

```
# mkfdmn /dev/disk/dsk21g cluster_usr
# mkfset cluster_usr usr
```

```
# mkfdmn /dev/disk/dsk21h cluster_var
# mkfset cluster_var var
```

NOTE:

If you need the extra file system space, you can add up to two additional volumes to `new_root` at this point. Just remember to account for them in steps 21, 27, and 28. See Chapter 11 of the *TruCluster* Server Cluster Administration manual for more details.

```
# addvol /dev/disk/dsk70c cluster_root
```

6. Mount `cluster_root`.

```
# mount cluster_root#root /mnt
```

7. Restore `cluster_root` from backup.

```
# vrestore -xf /dev/tape/tape2 -D /mnt
# umount /mnt
```

8. Restore `cluster_usr` and `cluster_var` by repeating steps 6 and 7 but for the `cluster_usr#usr` and `cluster_var#var` filesets. (Or you could leave `cluster_root` mounted and mount these filesets at `/mnt/usr` and `/mnt/var` respectively and restore them.)

9. Re-mount `cluster_root` if you unmounted it in step 7.

```
# mount cluster_root#root /mnt
```

10. Copy the restored cluster databases and member-specific databases to `/etc` on the ER disk so that when you reboot from the ER disk you will have the proper (cluster) view of storage.

```
# cd /mnt/etc
# cp dec_unid_db dec_hwc_cdb dfsc.dat /etc
# cd /mnt/cluster/members/member1/etc
# cp dfsl.dat /etc
```

11. Create the links in `/etc/fdmns` for the member boot disk if you don't already have them.

```
# cd /etc/fdmns
# mkdir root1_domain
# cd root1_domain
# ln -s /dev/disk/dsk6a
```

12. Mount the member boot partition.

```
# cd /
# umount /mnt
# mount root1_domain#root /mnt
```

13. Copy the databases from the member boot partition to `/etc` on the ER disk so that when you reboot from the ER disk you will have the proper (cluster) view of storage.

```
# cd /mnt/etc
# cp dec_devsw_db dec_hw_db dec_hwc_ldb dec_scsi_db /etc
```

14. Unmount the member boot partition.

```
# cd /
# umount /mnt
```

15. Create the .bak (backup) database files.

```
# cd /etc
# for i in dec_*db
> do
>   cp $i $i.bak
> done
```

16. Reboot to single-user mode using the ER disk as the boot device. The system will now boot with the same hardware configuration that the cluster previously had.

```
>>> boot -fl s DKB100
```

17. Scan the SCSI buses.

```
# hwmgr -scan scsi
```

18. Mount the root file system as read/write.

```
# mount -u /
```

19. Verify and update the device database.

```
# dsfmgr -v -F
```

20. Display and note the current device layout.

```
# hwmgr -view devices
```

21. Fix the local file domains, if necessary, by removing and remaking the correct links in the /etc/fdmns directory. Examine usr_domain, root1_domain, and cluster_root to see if any changes are necessary based on the output from step 20. If you need to make changes follow this example:

```
# cd /etc/fdmns/cluster_root
# rm *
# ln -s /dev/disk/dsk21a
```

22. Mount the local file systems.

```
# bcheckrc
```

23. Copy the updated cluster database files to `cluster_root` so that when you reboot with the new cluster disk, you will have the proper (cluster) view of storage.

```
# mount cluster_root#root /mnt
# cd /etc
# cp dec_unid_db* dec_hwc_cdb* dfsc.dat /mnt/etc
# cp dfsl.dat /mnt/cluster/members/member1/etc
```

24. Fix `/etc/fdmns/cluster_root` on the `cluster_root`.

```
# rm /mnt/etc/fdmns/cluster_root/*
# cd /etc/fdmns/cluster_root
# tar cf - * | (cd /mnt/etc/fdmns/cluster_root && tar xf -)
```

25. Fix `/etc/fdmns/cluster_usr` and `/etc/fdmns/cluster_var` on the `cluster_root` as in the previous step. (This step is only necessary if `cluster_usr` and `cluster_var` are on the same disk as `cluster_root`.)

```
# rm /mnt/etc/fdmns/cluster_usr/*
# cd /etc/fdmns/cluster_usr
# tar cf - * | (cd /mnt/etc/fdmns/cluster_usr && tar xf -)
# rm /mnt/etc/fdmns/cluster_var/*
# cd /etc/fdmns/cluster_var
# tar cf - * | (cd /mnt/etc/fdmns/cluster_var && tar xf -)
```

26. Copy the updated cluster database files to the member boot disk.

```
# cd /
# umount /mnt
# mount root1_domain#root /mnt
# cd /etc
# cp dec_devsw_db* dec_hw_db* dec_hwc_ldb* dec_scsi_db* /mnt/etc
```

27. Take note of the major and minor numbers of the new cluster_root device.

```
# file /dev/disk/dsk21a
/dev/disk/dsk21a:        block special (19/467)
```

28. Boot the member boot disk interactively specifying the major and minor numbers (above) for the newly restored cluster_root.

```
>>> boot -flags "ia"
...
Enter: <kernel_name> [option_1 ... option_n]
  or: ls [name]['help'] or: 'quit' to return to console
Press Return to boot 'vmunix'
```

```
# vmunix cfs:cluster_root_dev1_maj=19 cfs:cluster_root_dev1_min=467
```

NOTE:

In cluster_root_dev#_maj and cluster_root_dev#_min, the "#" can range from 1 to 3, meaning that you can have from 1 to 3 AdvFS volumes in cluster_root.

29. Boot each cluster member one at a time.

22.1.3 Emergency Repair Disk

As mentioned in the previous section, to restore cluster_root you must have a bootable non-clustered operating system disk at the same operating system version and patch level as the current cluster. Our recommendation is that when you install a patch kit on your cluster, you always copy the patch kit tar(1) file to a file system on the Emergency Repair (ER) disk; that way you'll have it if you need it. What is the Emergency Repair disk you ask? It's the disk that you originally used to build the operating system and from which you ran clu_create(8). We recommend keeping this disk and the operating system file systems intact after installation.

22.1.4 Replacing a Member Disk

If you need to replace only a member disk and you have a vdump of the "a" partition, you can restore that disk or restore the data to a new disk. In the procedure that follows, you can skip any steps that "correct" for the fact that we are restoring to a different disk already known to the cluster (those steps will be marked with a "†"). Please see section 7.4.4 for more on adding disks to a system. Our original configuration had molari's (member1) member boot disk as dsk2 and its replacement disk is dsk10. Unless otherwise stated, all steps take place on a booted member of the cluster.

1. Make sure that the member with the failed boot disk is down.

```
# clu_get_info -m 1
```

2. Setup dsk10 as the boot disk for member 1.

```
# /usr/sbin/clu_bdmgr -c dsk10 1
```

If dsk10 is not the original boot disk for molari, you will get a warning message and will see instructions to change the /etc/sysconfigtab file to reflect this change†. Write down these changes. They will look something like this:

```
The new member's disk, dsk10, is not the same name as the original disk
configured for domain root1_domain.  If you continue the following
changes will be required in member1's /etc/sysconfigtab file:
        vm:
        swapdevice=/dev/disk/dsk10b
        clubase:
        cluster_seqdisk_major=19
        cluster_seqdisk_minor=195
```

3. Mount molari's new boot disk root domain. (The clu_bdmgr command created the domain and fileset.)

```
# mount root1_domain#root /mnt
```

4. Restore the member's boot_partition.

```
# vrestore -xf /dev/tape/tape0 -D /mnt
```

5. Modify the /etc/sysconfigtab to reflect the new disk (dsk10) per the earlier instructions in step 2. Extract the existing member's clubase and vm sections into a stanza file:

```
# sysconfigdb -t /mnt/etc/sysconfigtab -l clubase vm > /tmp/bd_mod.stanza
```

Edit the stanza file:

```
# vi /tmp/bd_mod.stanza
```

Make it so:

```
# sysconfigdb -t /mnt/etc/sysconfigtab -m -f /tmp/bd_mod.stanza vm
# sysconfigdb -t /mnt/etc/sysconfigtab -m -f /tmp/bd_mod.stanza clubase
```

6. Restore the "h" partition (cnx).

```
# /usr/sbin/clu_bdmgr -h dsk10
```

7. Unmount the member's boot_partition.

```
# umount /mnt
```

8. Adjust the bootdef_dev console variable on molari's console to reflect the change.

```
>>> set bootdef_dev DKB202
```

   The device DKB202 is the appropriate console device name that corresponds to dsk10 in UNIX.

9. Boot molari.

```
>>> boot
```

22.1.5 Restoring a Critical Data File System

Just as losing a file system critical to the operating system can be a problem for your cluster, so can losing a critical data file system. Restoring a data or non-OS file system is really no different in a cluster than in a standalone *Tru64* UNIX system. For example, if your backups are made with vdump, you can restore them quite easily with this vrestore command:

```
# vrestore -xf /dev/tape/tape0 -D /data
```

If restoring to a new disk, you will, of course, have to disklabel it and create a new file system (either AdvFS or UFS) before restoring and either rename the device special file or adjust any references to the device name (like in /etc/fdmns) to point to the new device. The point here is that it isn't special because it's a cluster.

22.2 Replacing HBA and/or HSx Controllers

During the life of your cluster, you could have certain hardware failures, which in and of themselves are no big deal since you have your cluster configured with No Single Point of Failure (NSPOF). Handling these maintenance items usually requires a small dose of thought and then the cluster continues to hum merrily along.

22.2.1 Replacing an HSG80 Controller

In most cases, if you have a storage controller failure such as an HSG80, only one of the dual pair will fail at a time. In that case, the prospect of the `WWID` changing is not a problem; it's taken up by the remaining controller and survives the failed controller's replacement. If you should have a dual failure or some other failure where the `WWID` is destroyed, however, you must be able to reset the `WWID` on the HSG80. You do this with a single command at the HSG80 console.

```
HSG80> set this node=5000-1FE1-0000-9630 YO
```

In this case, "`5000-1FE1-000-9630`" is the `WWID` and "`YO`" is the checksum. You can get both of these values from the HSG80 controller. The values are on the device, not on the replaceable controllers themselves but on the more permanent part of the HSG80 enclosure.

22.2.2 Replacing an HSZ70 Controller

If your controller is a dual (either transparent failover or multibus failover) HSZ70, and you have a single failure, you'll be okay as long as you replace the failed controller before there is a problem with the other one. If you happen to have a dual failure (which is extremely rare), then you will have to do some work with `dsfmgr(8)` to return your disk names to their previous state. This is one reason that we recommend keeping on hand the files and command output we mentioned in Chapter 21. In addition, it is very important that you have the latest, patched HSOF software. For this procedure to work properly, your HSZx0 should be at least at these patch levels:

- HSZ40: V37Z-1.
- HSZ50: V57Z-1.
- HSZ70: V77Z-1.

Become familiar with these HSOF commands before proceeding. They can result in data loss if used incorrectly.

- `set nofailover`
- `set failover copy=this`
- `set multibus_failover copy=this`

22.2.2.1 HSZ70 in Transparent Failover Mode

This procedure works for the HSZ70 but also works for the HSZ40 and HSZ50 controller when configured in transparent failover mode. The operating system must be booted to handle the controller change. If not already booted, you must at least boot to single-user mode.

1. Begin with the running operating system (the devices on the impacted HSZx0 should be present and seen).

2. Issue the "`set nofailover`" command at the HSZx0 while connected to the functioning controller.

3. When the green LED status light is no longer blinking, remove failed controller.

4. Scan the bus with "`hwmgr -scan scsi -bus N`" (where "N" is the bus number associated with that HSZx0) on each member or use our `clu_scan_scsi` script (this will allow us to notice the change from dual controller to single controller).

   You may see several "was dual, now single" messages on the HSZx0 console.

   Even though the prompt returns rather quickly after the "`hwmgr`" command, the scan was only initiated. Give the scan about a minute to complete before proceeding to the next step.

5. Replace failed controller.

6. Scan the bus with "`hwmgr -scan scsi -bus N`" again.

7. Issue "`set failover copy=this`" command (while connected to the original good controller).

   You should see several "upgraded to dual" messages on the HSZx0 console.

8. Scan the bus a final time with "`hwmgr -scan scsi -bus N`" or `clu_scan_scsi` (this will allow us to notice the change from single controller back to the new dual redundant pair).

22.2.2.2 HSZ70 in Multibus Failover Mode

This procedure requires either a patch to *TruCluster* Server version 5.1A or version 5.1B. As of this writing, the patch is not yet part of an aggregate patch kit.

This procedure works for the HSZ70 when configured in multibus failover mode. The operating system must be booted to handle the controller change. If not already booted, you must at least boot to single-user mode.

NOTE:

Avoid applying this procedure during heavy I/O periods as you may get "phantom" devices. Eliminate I/O to the controller and/or refer to the HSZ70 documentation concerning port quiescence.

1. Begin with the running operating system (the devices on the impacted HSZ70 should be present and seen).

2. From the *Tru64* UNIX host, issue the "`sysconfig -r cam_disk rec_use_alt_params=1`" command to switch to alternate recovery timing (required for this type of procedure).

3. Issue the "`set nofailover`" command at the HSZ70 while connected to the functioning controller.

   You may see several "was dual, now single" messages on the HSZx0 console.

4. When the green LED status light is no longer blinking, remove failed controller.

5. Scan the bus with "`hwmgr -scan scsi -bus N`" (where "N" is the bus number associated with that HSZx0) on each member or use our `clu_scan_scsi` script (this will allow us to notice the change from dual controller to single controller).

   Even though the prompt returns rather quickly after the "`hwmgr`" command, the scan was only initiated. Give the scan about a minute to complete before proceeding to the next step.

6. Replace failed controller.

7. Scan the bus with "`hwmgr -scan scsi -bus N`" again.

8. Issue "`set multibus_failover copy=this`" command (while connected to the original good controller).

   You should see several "upgraded to dual" messages on the HSZ70 console.

9. Issue the "`sysconfig -r cam_disk rec_use_alt_params=0`" command to return to the default recovery timing.

10. Scan the bus a final time with "`hwmgr -scan scsi -bus N`" or `clu_scan_scsi` (this will allow us to notice the change from single controller back to the new multibus failover pair).

22.2.3 Replacing a Fiber Channel HBA

When you replace a failed KGPSA in *Tru64* UNIX version 5, you don't need to do anything special to preserve the existing (disk) device names. However, the new KGPSA will have a new WWID and therefore will have new connections at the HSG80 (or other FC storage box) that need to be addressed especially if you are implementing Selective Storage Presentation to allow only certain systems to access certain storage. Also the SAN zones may need to be adjusted to account for the new connections. For more on SAN storage, refer to Chapter 4.

22.2.4 Replacing a Shared SCSI HBA

To replace a KZPBA, KZPSA, or other shared storage HBA you should make sure that you keep the same SCSI ID and ensure proper bus termination. For more details about storage setup, see Chapter 4.

22.3 Installing Customer Specific Patches

Sometimes your system will need a patch that does not exist as part of a current aggregate patch kit. It could be that you reported a problem to HP Support, and they provided a Customer Specific Patch (CSP) for you to install to correct whatever problem you were having. Alternatively, there may already be an Early Release Patch that was on the `ftp(1)` server but not in the currently shipping patch kit. Usually with these patches you can either install them "manually" or by using the rolling upgrade method. Let's look at installing this patch manually. For more on rolling upgrades see Chapter 25.

Let's take this fictitious patch as an example. You may have gotten this patch by way of HP Services or maybe you found it on the *Tru64* UNIX `ftp` patch site:

`http://ftp.support.compaq.com/public/unix/v5.1a/`

The first step after copying the file down with `ftp` is to verify the checksum of the patch `tar` file. There are `sum(1)` and `cksum(1)` checksums listed in the `README` file in addition to more complex "checksums" MD5 and SHA1 results. Here is how to check this checksum (`sum`):

```
# sum TCV51AB1-C0000000-11111-M-20020521.tar
60146   2810 TCV51AB1-C0000000-11111-M-20020521.tar
```

The reason we want to verify the file (checksum or one of the other verification methods) is that we want to be reasonably sure that we don't have a truncated tar file. Nothing can waste a system administrator's time like chasing a problem that only exists because of a file transfer problem. Once we've verified that the file is good, we'll create an install directory and untar the kit and run the installation script.

```
# mkdir -p /tmp/CSPkit1
# cd /tmp/CSPkit1
# tar -xvpf TCV51AB1-C0000000-11111-M-20020521.tar
# cd patch_kit/TruCluster_V5.1A/ManualKit
# ./TCRPATC0000000520.install.sh
```

After running the script, the patched files (which usually contain "`.mod`" files that are used to deliver kernel changes) are moved into place, and if a kernel rebuild is required you are prompted to perform the kernel build. Don't forget to do this on each member in the cluster and then to `cp(1)`, **not** `mv(1)`, the new kernel into place. To save space, you can then remove the kernel in `/sys/HOSTNAME`. For more on kernel building and cleanup see section 12.2.1.

Now all that is required is a cluster-wide reboot[1] for the patches to take effect.

22.4 Multi-Path Storage

Storage Area Networks (SANs) are being implemented in many of the clusters that we see being built. This is fabulous for performance and flexibility, but can be a source of headaches when trying to track down disk statistics. One particular such statistic is "cross-RAD I/O". This happens in GS-series AlphaServers where the disk I/O originates in one QBB[2] (or RAD[3]) but travels to another RAD to be written to disk. This is to be avoided if possible by spreading enough I/O controllers amongst the QBBs, but unfortunately may not be possible to eliminate completely due to architectural restrictions (i.e., not enough PCI bus slots). To see how much of this sort of I/O is happening, you can use `hwmgr` to check:

```
# hwmgr -get attribute current | grep -E "dev_base_name|cross_rad|path_xfer"
```

The output will look like this:

```
  dev_base_name = kevm
  dev_base_name = dsk0
  path_xfer_0 = 186
  cross_rad_iocnt = 19
  cross_rad_initiated_iocnt = 15
  dev_base_name = dsk1
  path_xfer_1 = 43
  path_xfer_1 = 0
  path_xfer_1 = 0
  path_xfer_1 = 0
  cross_rad_iocnt = 0
  cross_rad_initiated_iocnt = 0
...
  dev_base_name = dsk2
  path_xfer_1 = 167
  cross_rad_iocnt = 9
  cross_rad_initiated_iocnt = 9
...
```

---

1 Currently you cannot automatically reboot the entire cluster. You will need to shutdown the entire cluster (i.e., "`shutdown -c now`") and boot each member.

2 Quad Building Block

3 Resource Affinity Domain

```
dev_base_name = dsk3
cross_rad_iocnt = 8
cross_rad_initiated_iocnt = 8
dev_base_name = dsk4
cross_rad_iocnt = 14
cross_rad_initiated_iocnt = 14
dev_base_name = dsk5
path_xfer_1 = 0
path_xfer_1 = 119
cross_rad_iocnt = 5
cross_rad_initiated_iocnt = 5
dev_base_name = dsk6
path_xfer_1 = 123
cross_rad_iocnt = 8
cross_rad_initiated_iocnt = 8
dev_base_name = dsk7
path_xfer_1 = 43
path_xfer_1 = 0
cross_rad_iocnt = 0
cross_rad_initiated_iocnt = 0
dev_base_name = cdrom0
path_xfer_2 = 2
cross_rad_iocnt = 0
cross_rad_initiated_iocnt = 0
dev_base_name = dsk8
path_xfer_4 = 159639
cross_rad_iocnt = 8093
cross_rad_initiated_iocnt = 5253
dev_base_name = dsk9
path_xfer_4 = 364
cross_rad_iocnt = 99
cross_rad_initiated_iocnt = 99
dev_base_name = dsk10
path_xfer_4 = 619
cross_rad_iocnt = 315
cross_rad_initiated_iocnt = 306
dev_base_name = dsk11
path_xfer_6 = 747
cross_rad_iocnt = 248
cross_rad_initiated_iocnt = 239
dev_base_name = cdrom1
path_xfer_7 = 2
cross_rad_iocnt = 0
cross_rad_initiated_iocnt = 0
dev_base_name = mc0
path_xfer_1 = 0
path_xfer_1 = 0
dev_base_name = tape0
path_xfer_1 = 0
dev_base_name = tape1
dev_base_name = scp0
path_xfer_1 = 0
path_xfer_1 = 0
path_xfer_1 = 0
path_xfer_1 = 0
```

From the highlighted output above you can see that dsk8 has the most cross-RAD I/O. You can avoid some cross-RAD I/O by configuring each QBB with an HBA to the shared storage, but if you see lop-sided cross-RAD I/O, you may need to specify that certain I/O intensive applications run on particular QBBs or RADs using the `runon(1)` command. Further I/O tuning of this sort is beyond the scope of this book.

22.5 I/O Barriers and the `cleanPR` Command

I/O Barriers are used in *TruCluster* Server version 5 to ensure data integrity in the cluster. For systems to be allowed to access storage, the member must be a part of the cluster and the cluster must have quorum. Barriers come into play when certain abnormal conditions occur such as member panics or member hangs or "normal" conditions like issuing a halt command, pushing the halt button, or pulling a system's plug. In these situations, CNX requests DRD to impose barriers against writes to most disk units. Note that certain devices (listed below) do not have barriers erected around them and thus are not suitable for critical data, since the integrity of that data cannot be ensured without the barrier(s). Devices that are excluded from the barrier list are: swap devices, quorum disks, boot devices, and tape drives.

The SCSI-3 Persistent Reserve command set can be used by the *TruCluster* Server barrier mechanism for many disks (i.e., HSZ80, HSG80, and HSV110 storage) but in some isolated cases can cause a problem since the reservations persist (this is only a problem in cases where the disks are moved from a cluster to a standalone system, when performing cluster recovery, or when reinstalling). For example, if an HSG80's disks were re-allocated away from a cluster and to a standalone system, that standalone system may not be able to access the disks because of a persistent reservation on those devices.

You can see the persistent reservations by using the "`cleanPR show`" command.

```
# cleanPR show

      cleanPR Version: 1.5
...
 Checking device 5 1 100
                         Key Entry 0: 0x30001
                         Key Entry 1: 0x30002
                         Key Entry 1: 0x30002
                         Key Entry 3: 0x30001
                         Key Entry 6: 0x30001
                         Key Entry 6: 0x30002
                         Key Entry 6: 0x30001
                         Key Entry 6: 0x30002
...
Total of 5 devices found w/Persistent Reservations
Total of 0 devices cleared of Persistent Reservations
```

Or if you're more curious, you can check the unit, for example, on an HSG80 to see if there is a persistent reservation on it.

```
HSG80> show d100
   LUN                                          Uses              Used by
------------------------------------------------------------------------------

  D100                                          DISK30100
        LUN ID:       6000-1FE1-000B-1A40-0009-0361-3888-0062
        NOIDENTIFIER
        Switches:
          RUN                    NOWRITE_PROTECT        READ_CACHE
          READAHEAD_CACHE        WRITEBACK_CACHE
          MAX_READ_CACHED_TRANSFER_SIZE = 32
          MAX_WRITE_CACHED_TRANSFER_SIZE = 32
        Access:
              ALL
        State:
          ONLINE to this controller
          Persistent reserved
          NOPREFERRED_PATH
        Size:             17769177 blocks
        Geometry (C/H/S): ( 5258 / 20 / 169 )
```

Did you notice the "`Persistent reserved`" under "`State`"? That tells us that unit `D100` has a PR. Let's continue to track this particular unit down and see who set the PR. We happen to know that unit `D100` on the HSG80 is `dsk108` on our cluster (if we didn't know this, we could track it down based on the WWID).

```
# hwmgr -show scsi -full |grep -E "dsk|6000-1fe1-000b-1a40-0009-0361-3888-0062"
  272:  22        skipper    disk       none     2       4     dsk105 [5/1/105]
  274:  18        skipper    disk       none     2       8     dsk106 [5/1/62]
  563:  11        skipper    disk       none     0       8     dsk108 [5/1/100]
      WWID:01000010:6000-1fe1-000b-1a40-0009-0361-3888-0062
   64:  0         skipper    disk       none     2       1     dsk9   [0/0/0]
   67:  3         skipper    disk       none     2       4     dsk1   [5/1/1]
   68:  4         skipper    disk       none     2       4     dsk2   [5/1/2]
   69:  5         skipper    disk       none     0       5     dsk3   [5/2/3]
   74:  8         skipper    disk       none     0       4     dsk15  [5/1/9]
   75:  9         skipper    disk       none     0       4     dsk8   [5/1/8]
  151:  23        skipper    disk       none     2       4     dsk20  [5/1/20]
```

```
# hwmgr -show scsi -full -id 563 | more

        SCSI                       DEVICE     DEVICE  DRIVER NUM  DEVICE FIRST
 HWID:  DEVICEID HOSTNAME   TYPE       SUBTYPE OWNER  PATH FILE   VALID PATH
-------------------------------------------------------------------------
  563:  18        gilligan   disk       none     0       8     dsk108 [5/1/100]

      WWID:01000010:6000-1fe1-000b-1a40-0009-0361-3888-0062

      BUS   TARGET  LUN   PATH STATE
      ------------------------------
      5     1       100   valid
      5     2       100   valid
      5     3       100   valid
      5     4       100   valid
```

```
    6     1       100   valid
    6     4       100   valid
    6     3       100   valid
    6     2       100   valid
```

And by using `scu(8)` we can see what reservation keys are being used (just as `cleanPR show` indicated).

```
# scu
scu> set nexus bus 5 target 1 lun 100
Device: HSG80, Bus: 5, Target: 1, Lun: 100, Type: Direct Access
```

```
scu> show reservations
Persistent Reservation Header:

                 Generation Value: 28
                Additional Length: 144

Reservation Descriptors:

                  Reservation Key: 0x30001
           Scope-Specific Address: 0
                 Reservation Type: 0x5 (Write Exclusive Registrants Only)
                Reservation Scope: 0 (LU - full logical unit)
                    Extent Length: 0
                  Reservation Key: 0x30002
           Scope-Specific Address: 0
                 Reservation Type: 0x5 (Write Exclusive Registrants Only)
                Reservation Scope: 0 (LU - full logical unit)
                    Extent Length: 0
                  Reservation Key: 0x30002
           Scope-Specific Address: 0
                 Reservation Type: 0x5 (Write Exclusive Registrants Only)
                Reservation Scope: 0 (LU - full logical unit)
                    Extent Length: 0
                  Reservation Key: 0x30001
           Scope-Specific Address: 0
                 Reservation Type: 0x5 (Write Exclusive Registrants Only)
                Reservation Scope: 0 (LU - full logical unit)
                    Extent Length: 0
                  Reservation Key: 0x30001
           Scope-Specific Address: 0
                 Reservation Type: 0x5 (Write Exclusive Registrants Only)
                Reservation Scope: 0 (LU - full logical unit)
                    Extent Length: 0
                  Reservation Key: 0x30002
           Scope-Specific Address: 0
                 Reservation Type: 0x5 (Write Exclusive Registrants Only)
                Reservation Scope: 0 (LU - full logical unit)
                    Extent Length: 0
                  Reservation Key: 0x30001
```

```
         Scope-Specific Address: 0
               Reservation Type: 0x5 (Write Exclusive Registrants Only)
              Reservation Scope: 0 (LU - full logical unit)
                  Extent Length: 0
                Reservation Key: 0x30002
         Scope-Specific Address: 0
               Reservation Type: 0x5 (Write Exclusive Registrants Only)
              Reservation Scope: 0 (LU - full logical unit)
                  Extent Length: 0
```

The reservation keys are based on the CSID (cluster system id); in our case, 0x30001 and 0x30002. For more on the CSID, see section 17.2.3.2.

```
# clu_get_info -full | grep -E "Hostname|csid"

    Hostname = skipper.dec.com
    csid = 0x30001
    Hostname = gilligan.dec.com
    csid = 0x30002
```

If the storage in question is **not** part of a cluster but the base OS system still cannot access the storage, the cleanPR command may be used to clear the persistent reservation (issued from a standalone system).

```
# cleanPR clean

                        cleanPR Version: 1.5

                                WARNING

        This shell script will clear all Persistent Reservations
        from the HSX80 devices attached to this system.

                                WARNING

Do you wish to proceed ? <y/n> [n]: y

        Removing Persistent Reservations from all HSX80 devices...

 Checking HSG80 at /dev/rdisk/dsk108a (SCSI #5 (SCSI ID #2) (SCSI LUN #100))
 Checking HSG80 at /dev/rdisk/dsk6a (SCSI #5 (SCSI ID #9) (SCSI LUN #15))

Total of 0 devices found w/Persistent Reservations
Total of 0 devices cleared of Persistent Reservations
```

WARNING:

Never use cleanPR clean in a live cluster! Doing so compromises the existing I/O Barriers and could lead to data corruption.

22.6 Replacing a Failed Quorum Disk

If the quorum disk fails when the cluster is up, you can replace it online as long as the loss of the disk does not cause the cluster to lose quorum.

Since we do not have a quorum disk that is about to break, we will physically remove the quorum disk to illustrate how to replace it. In case you're interested in the errors that the cluster will see when it detects a problem with the quorum disk, we will monitor the action with the `evmwatch(8)` command. Additionally, to save space we will filter by one member – both members will log the events so you would see the same event for each member. And some duplicated events have been trimmed.

```
# export EVM_SHOW_TEMPLATE=" (@host) @name\n@@\n"
# evmwatch -f "[host molari]" | evmshow -T "[%T]"
[08:44:53] (molari) sys.unix.binlog.hw.scsi._hwid.106
SCSI event
...
[08:44:59] (molari) sys.unix.hw.state_change.unavailable.disk._hwcomp
onent.SCSIWWID0c00000800000e1100189f1f._hwid.106
Component State Change: Component "SCSI-WWID:0c000008:0000-0e11-0018-9f1f" is in
 the unavailable state (HWID=106)

[08:44:59] (molari) sys.unix.hw.no_connections.disk._hwid.106
Connectivity has been lost for device (HWID=106 lid=5 btl=3/3/0)
...
[08:45:09] (molari) sys.unix.binlog.hw.scsi._hwid.106
SCSI event
...
[08:45:14] (molari) sys.unix.clu.cnx.qdisk.loss
CNX MGR: Cluster quorum disk 19,240 has become unavailable due to a read error (
status 5)

[08:45:14] (molari) sys.unix.clu.drd.server_leave._hwid.106
DRD: Removed (unmapped) DRD server molari
...
[08:45:14] (molari) sys.unix.syslog.kern
vmunix: CNX QDISK: Cluster quorum disk 19,240 has become unavailable due to a re
ad error (status 5).

[08:45:15] (molari) sys.unix.clu.drd.server_add._hwid.106
DRD: Added (mapped) DRD server sheridan

[08:45:15] (molari) sys.unix.clu.drd.new_accessnode._hwid.106
DRD: Server sheridan selected for device 106

[08:45:15] (molari) sys.unix.clu.drd.new_accessnode._hwid.106
DRD: Server sheridan selected for device 106

[08:45:15] (molari) sys.unix.binlog.hw.scsi._hwid.106
SCSI event

[08:45:15] (molari) sys.unix.syslog.kern
vmunix: CNX QDISK: Quorum disk lost, removing 1 vote.
...
[08:45:16] (molari) sys.unix.clu.drd.no_accessnode._hwid.106
DRD: No server found for device 106
```

1. Remove the quorum disk.

```
# clu_quorum -d remove
Collecting quorum data for Member(s): 1 2

Quorum disk successfully removed.
```

EVM should note that this happened.

```
[08:46:10] (molari) sys.unix.syslog.kern
vmunix: CNX QDISK: Bad close status (6) on device 19, 240.

[08:46:10] (molari) sys.unix.syslog.kern
vmunix: CNX MGR: Delete quorum disk operation completed with quorum.
```

2. Verify that the quorum disk has been removed.

```
# clu_quorum | grep "Quorum disk"
Quorum disk:   Not Configured
```

3. Locate the HWID of the failed device.

   The EVM events will have noted the failing component, but it can also be found using the hwmgr(8) command.

```
# hwmgr view device -dsf dsk4
 HWID: Device Name          Mfg      Model            Location
 ----------------------------------------------------------------------------
  106: /dev/disk/dsk4c      COMPAQ   BD009635C3       bus-3-targ-3-lun-0
```

4. Remove the failed component.

```
# hwmgr del -id 106
hwmgr: Delete operation was successful
```

The EVM will see this as:

```
[08:46:59] (molari) sys.unix.hw.deregistered.undefined._hwid.106
A hardware component has been de-registered (HWID=106)

[08:46:59] (sheridan) sys.unix.hw.deregistered.undefined._hwid.106
A hardware component has been de-registered (HWID=106)

[08:46:59] (molari) sys.unix.syslog.kern
vmunix: drd_delete_device: received status 16 when attempting to delete hwid 106.
```

```
[08:47:01] (molari) sys.unix.syslog.daemon
syslog: hotswapd: subsystem hwc may have successfully run the command '/sbin/dsfmgr
-Z rm_cluster_hwid 106 4611977471623797587'

[08:47:02] (molari) sys.unix.syslog.daemon
syslog: hotswapd: subsystem hwc may have successfully run the command '/sbin/dsfmgr
-Z rm_local_hwid 106 4612241719486683987'
```

5. Replace the disk.

   You can either physically replace the disk at this point, or identify another disk that you can use as the quorum disk. In this example, we will go plug our disk back in.

6. Scan for the new component.

   Use the `hwmgr` command to identify the new device.

```
# hwmgr scan component -category disk -cluster

hwmgr: Scan request successfully initiated
hwmgr: Scan request successfully initiated
```

The EVM will see events similar to the list below.

```
[08:48:29] (sheridan) sys.unix.hw.scan_completed.platform._hwid.56
A hardware scan has just completed

[08:48:30] (molari) sys.unix.hw.scan_completed.platform._hwid.1
A hardware scan has just completed

[08:48:46] (molari) sys.unix.binlog.hw.scsi
SCSI event

[08:48:46] (molari) sys.unix.hw.registered.disk._hwid.107
A hardware component has been registered (HWID=107)

[08:48:46] (molari) sys.unix.sysman.station.update.MEMBER
SysMan Station: daemon on host molari.fafrak.com has written new serialization f
iles. These files allow the daemons to communicate state and topology changes.

[08:48:47] (sheridan) sys.unix.hw.registered.disk._hwid.107
A hardware component has been registered (HWID=107)

[08:48:49] (molari) sys.unix.hw.cluster_attribute_change.disk._hwid.107
A change has occurred in a cluster attribute for device (HWID=107 lid=5)

[08:48:50] (sheridan) sys.unix.hw.cluster_attribute_change.disk._hwid.107
A change has occurred in a cluster attribute for device (HWID=107 lid=6)

[08:48:51] (molari) sys.unix.hw.dev_base_name_changed.disk._hwid.107
Device base name changed from "unknown" to "dsk12" (HWID=107)

[08:48:51] (sheridan) sys.unix.hw.dev_base_name_changed.disk._hwid.107
Device base name changed from "unknown" to "dsk12" (HWID=107)

[08:48:54] (molari) sys.unix.syslog.daemon
syslog: hotswapd: subsystem hwc may have successfully run the command '/sbin/dsf
mgr -Z cr_new  4612491815432330179'
```

An alternative method to scan for the new hardware:

```
# for i in molari sheridan
> do
>    hwmgr scan scsi -member $i
> done

hwmgr: Scan request successfully initiated
hwmgr: Scan request successfully initiated
```

Or you can use the `clu_scan_scsi` script we wrote which essentially does the same thing.

7. If the new disk is an RZ26, RZ28, RZ29, or RZ1CB-CA that is not located behind a RAID controller (e.g., an HSZ or HSG controller), run the `clu_disk_install` command.

   The `clu_disk_install` script runs the `scu(8)` program to enable bad block replacement for the disk, which allows the device to function as a Direct-Access I/O (DAIO) device. This command can take awhile to complete, so be patient.

```
# clu_disk_install
```

NOTE:

If the disk is present at boot time, `clu_disk_install` automatically runs and finds it.

8. Locate the new device.

```
# hwmgr -show scsi

          SCSI                 DEVICE    DEVICE  DRIVER NUM  DEVICE FIRST
  HWID:   DEVICEID HOSTNAME    TYPE      SUBTYPE OWNER  PATH FILE   VALID PATH
-------------------------------------------------------------------------
     50:  3        sheridan    disk      none    2      1    dsk1   [3/0/0]
     51:  4        sheridan    disk      none    2      1    dsk2   [3/1/0]
     52:  5        sheridan    disk      none    2      1    dsk3   [3/2/0]
     54:  7        sheridan    disk      none    2      1    dsk5   [3/4/0]
     55:  8        sheridan    disk      none    0      1    dsk6   [3/5/0]
    102:  0        sheridan    cdrom     none    0      1    cdrom1 [0/0/0]
    103:  1        sheridan    disk      none    2      1    dsk8   [2/0/0]
    104:  2        sheridan    disk      none    2      1    dsk9   [2/1/0]
    107:  6        sheridan    disk      none    0      1    dsk10  [3/3/0]
```

The new device is `dsk10`. Note that on V5.1, the device name is not always assigned. You may see something like:

```
    107:  6        sheridan    disk      none    0      1    (null) [3/3/0]
```

If this happens, use the dsfmgr(8) command with the "-K" option to assign a device special file name. Output is not shown.

```
# dsfmgr -K
```

9. Rename the device special file name back to the old device special file name (optional).

```
# dsfmgr -m dsk10 dsk4
  dsk10a=>dsk4a  dsk10b=>dsk4b  dsk10c=>dsk4c  dsk10d=>dsk4d  dsk10e=>dsk4e  dsk
10f=>dsk4f  dsk10g=>dsk4g  dsk10h=>dsk4h  dsk10a=>dsk4a  dsk10b=>dsk4b  dsk10c=>
dsk4c  dsk10d=>dsk4d  dsk10e=>dsk4e  dsk10f=>dsk4f  dsk10g=>dsk4g  dsk10h=>dsk4h
```

The EVM will see the following event.

```
[08:49:44] (molari) sys.unix.hw.dev_base_name_changed.disk._hwid.107
Device base name changed from "dsk10" to "dsk4" (HWID=107)

[08:49:44] (sheridan) sys.unix.hw.dev_base_name_changed.disk._hwid.107
Device base name changed from "dsk10" to "dsk4" (HWID=107)

[08:49:58] (molari) sys.unix.hw.disk_label_memory_written.disk._hwid.107
Base hardware event

[08:49:58] (molari) sys.unix.hw.disk_label_disk_written.disk._hwid.107
Base hardware event

[08:49:58] (molari) sys.unix.hw.disk_label_disk_written.disk._hwid.107
Base hardware event
```

If you receive the following message, see section 7.5.1.4.

```
dsfmgr: ERROR: second device status is active: dsk4a
```

10. Add the new disk as the quorum disk.

```
# clu_quorum -d add dsk4 1
Collecting quorum data for Member(s): 1 2
  Initializing cnx partition on quorum disk : dsk4h
Quorum disk successfully created.
```

The EVM will see the following events.

```
[08:50:02] (molari) sys.unix.syslog.kern
vmunix: CNX MGR: Add quorum disk operation completed with quorum.

[08:50:22] (molari) sys.unix.syslog.kern
vmunix: CNX QDISK: Successfully claimed quorum disk, adding 1 vote.
```

22.7 Migrating from MC to LAN Cluster Interconnect (and vice versa)

One of the exciting new features of *TruCluster* Server version 5.1A is the LAN Cluster Interconnect. This functionality opens up far more systems to clustering and the benefits of Single System Image management (which means, for starters, that you only have to install the OS once, applications once, etc.). We'll show the steps required to migrate from a MEMORY CHANNEL Cluster Interconnect (CI) to a LAN CI. But first, let's review a few requirements.

The Cluster Interconnect LAN:

- Must be private to the cluster members alone.
- Can be direct or configured with hubs or switches but not both.
- Must disable Spanning Tree Protocol on switch ports that connect to cluster members
- Must configure the switches in a "fully redundant LAN cluster interconnect" so that there is no packet forwarding between them.
- Must be 100Mbps or 1000Mbps full duplex throughout the configuration (including switches/hubs). Using the half-duplex option (hubs) is not recommended because of the limited performance of hub technology.
- Must be configured such that there is at least one point-to-point path between each member.
- Must not be configured with Link Aggregation (LAG).
- Must not be configured with more than two switches between any two members.

22.7.1 Moving from MEMORY CHANNEL to LAN Cluster Interconnect

Say that you built your cluster at a pre-V5.1A version, upgraded to V5.1A, and now want to try out the LAN CI that you've heard so much about. The first thing you should do is take out the *TruCluster* Server Cluster LAN Interconnect manual provided by HP and look in Chapter 4 for the directions. These steps are covered thoroughly in the manual but we'll go over them briefly here.

To perform this switch from MC to LAN Interconnect, we obviously have to schedule some down time because we're making a radical change to the medium that the cluster uses to do a whole suite of communicating and in order to install and/or remove hardware:.

1. Shut down and power off each member.
2. Install the network adapters for the private CI LAN if they aren't already installed and set the NIC's mode at the console prompt. For example:

```
>>> set ewa1_mode FastFD
```

3. Configure any switches or hubs to be used.

4. Power up and boot each member using the generic kernel (`genvmunix`). (It will boot with MEMORY CHANNEL as the cluster interconnect.)

5. Build a new kernel with `doconfig(8)` on each member.

6. Copy (don't `mv`!) the new kernel into `/` on each member. See Chapter 12, section 12.2.1 for more information about copying in the new kernel.

7. Configure the network using `ifconfig(8)` as a private subnet (cluster members only) and test it to make sure it works before trying to use it as the cluster interconnect. (Don't configure the network using any of the network setup tools or by modifying `/etc/rc.config` because the test network configuration must not survive a reboot.)

8. Save a copy of each member's `/etc/sysconfigtab` and `/etc/rc.config`.

```
# for i in 1 2
> do
>    cp /.local../../member${i}/boot_partition/etc/sysconfigtab \
>       /.local../../member${i}/boot_partition/etc/sysconfigtab.ni
>    cp /.local../../member${i}/etc/rc.config \
>       /.local../../member${i}/etc/rc.config.ni
> done
```

9. Inspect each member's `/etc/rc.config` checking NETDEV_* and NRDEV_*. If either of these environment variables is associated with the LAN device to be used for the CI, you must edit these variables manually so that there is no interference with the LAN CI configuration during boot. (This step will probably be an issue only if you are reconfiguring NICs that the system had been using.)

10. Modify or add the `clubase` and `ics_ll_tcp` kernel subsystems similar to the following on each member:

```
clubase:
cluster_interconnect = tcp
```

```
ics_ll_tcp:
ics_tcp_adapter0 = nr0
ics_tcp_nr0[0] = ee0
ics_tcp_nr0[1] = ee1
ics_tcp_inetaddr0 = 10.1.0.1
ics_tcp_netmask0 = 255.255.255.0
```

If you are not using NetRAIN for the CI, you obviously will set the `ics_tcp_adapter0` attribute to the value of "`ee0`", for example, and not include the `ics_tcp_nr*` entries. Refer to section 19.3.7.3 for details on modifying sysconfigtab.

11. Check the clubase:cluster_node_inter_name attribute.

    If this was a cluster that was upgraded from an earlier version, the node name may contain "mc0"; if it does, change this to "ics0".

    For example, change molari-mc0 to molari-ics0.

12. Edit the /etc/hosts file to reflect the new IP names and addresses of the LAN CI devices. Again, if this cluster was upgraded from an earlier release, you may have to change the "mc0" entries to "ics0" entries.

13. Change the CLUSTER_NET configuration variable to reflect the "ics0" name as well if it was upgraded from an earlier release. Use "rcmgr get CLUSTER_NET" to check it and "rcmgr set CLUSTER_NET <node>_ics0" to change it.

14. Shut down all members.

15. Boot each member.

22.7.2 Moving from LAN to MEMORY CHANNEL Cluster Interconnect

To convert your cluster from a LAN CI to a MEMORY CHANNEL CI, the process is similar but not quite as involved.

1. Shut down and power off each member.

2. Install the MEMORY CHANNEL hardware (including hubs if using hubs).

3. Power up and boot each member using the generic kernel (genvmunix). (It will boot with the LAN as the cluster interconnect.) Note that you could simply add the entry "config_driver mchan" to the kernel configuration file in the proper location (in /sys/conf/<HOSTNAME>) and rebuild the kernel instead of booting the generic kernel in this step.

4. Build a new kernel with doconfig on each member.

5. Copy (don't mv!) the new kernel into / on each member. See Chapter 12, section 12.2.1 for more information about copying the new kernel.

6. Save a copy of each member's /etc/sysconfigtab.

```
# for i in 1 2
> do
>   cp /.local../../member${i}/boot_partition/etc/sysconfigtab \
>      /.local../../member${i}/boot_partition/etc/sysconfigtab.ni
> done
```

7. Modify the clubase kernel subsystem on each member, changing the cluster_interconnect attribute to "mct", and remove the ics_ll_tcp subsystem from sysconfigtab.

8. Shut down all members.

9. Boot each member.

22.8 Name and Address Changes

After building your cluster, you may want or need to change its identity. For example, you may need to change the IP address or the name of the cluster or cluster members. These changes are discussed in Best Practices documents and the *TruCluster* Server Cluster Administration Guide, Chapter 5, so we won't go into great detail here other than to briefly outline the steps required to make these changes.

22.8.1 Changing the Cluster Name

For the cluster name change to take effect, the entire cluster must be shut down and restarted after the changes are complete.

1. Create a stanza file that contains the name change attributes: clubase:cluster_name.

```
# cat > clubase-cluster_name.stanza
clubase:
        cluster_name=jetsons
^d
```

2. Merge the stanza file into the sysconfigtab file on each member.

```
# sysconfigdb -t /etc/sysconfigtab.cluster -m -f \
  clubase-cluster_name.stanza clubase
```

```
# /usr/sbin/clu_update_sysconfig /etc/sysconfigtab.cluster
```

3. Change the cluster name in both /etc/hosts and /etc/hosts.equiv.

   In /etc/hosts

```
192.168.0.159     minnow.dec.com  minnow  # Global cluster alias
```

   becomes

```
192.168.0.159     jetsons.dec.com  jetsons  # Global cluster alias
```

and in /etc/hosts.equiv

```
minnow.dec.com
```

becomes

```
jetsons.dec.com
```

4. Add the new cluster name to the /.rhosts file and leave the old cluster name until the system has rebooted. Note that any other .rhosts files that reference the old cluster name will need to be updated as well.

```
jetsons.dec.com
```

5. Shut the entire cluster down and reboot.

```
# shutdown -c +5 "Changing the cluster name."
```

6. Verify the change (this is also a good time to remove the old cluster name from /.rhosts).

```
# clu_get_info
```

If you see the new cluster name listed at the beginning of this output, you were successful in changing the cluster name. If not, go back and make sure each step was followed completely.

22.8.2 Changing the Cluster IP Address

Changing the cluster's IP address is a little less complicated and doesn't require a cluster reboot. It **does**, however, require a reboot of each cluster member, but you should retain quorum and therefore the cluster will continue to operate for the duration of the changes.

1. Change the cluster's IP address in the /etc/hosts file.

```
192.168.0.159      minnow.dec.com  minnow  # Global cluster alias
```

becomes

```
192.168.0.160      minnow.dec.com  minnow  # Global cluster alias
```

2. Shut down and reboot one member at a time until all members have been rebooted.

3. Verify the change with a `ping(8)` command, preferably from a client outside of the cluster. (This assumes that either the client `/etc/hosts` file or whatever network name database, such as DNS, has been updated to reflect the new name/IP address.)

```
# ping minnow.dec.com
PING minnow.dec.com (192.168.0.160): 56 data bytes
64 bytes from 192.168.0.160: icmp_seq=0 ttl=64 time=5 ms
```

The `ping` output should reflect the new cluster name and report successful pings.

22.8.3 Changing a Member Name, Member IP Address, or Interconnect Address

If you need to change the member name, member IP address, or a member's cluster interconnect address, you have to remove that member from the cluster and re-add it with the appropriate change.

1. Shut down just the member.
2. Remove the member from the cluster using one of the remaining cluster members.

```
# clu_delete_member -m <memberid>
```

3. Add the member back to the cluster using one of the remaining cluster members.

```
# clu_add_member
```

When adding the member back in, use the new name, IP address, and/or interconnect address.

22.9 References

- The *TruCluster* Server Technical Overview manual.
- The *TruCluster* Server Cluster Administration manual.
- The *TruCluster* Server Cluster LAN Interconnect manual.
- Early Release Patch Documentation.
- *Tru64* UNIX Hardware Management (V5.1B).
- Reference pages (noted within the text).

23

Cluster Application Availability (CAA)

In this chapter we will be discussing the Cluster Application Availability (CAA) framework. CAA is used to make an application that would normally be restricted to running on only one member in a cluster capable of automatically relocating to another cluster member in the event that the member where it is running were to fail or is shutdown for maintenance. In other words, CAA can make an application highly available.

Many applications can only run on one member in a cluster at any given time, due to the way they're written. An application that writes to a file, without first locking it, is just one example. In fact, many applications (known as single-instance applications) are written without any thought to concurrency. These are candidates for CAA.

Another example is an application that performs its synchronization using interprocess communication (IPC). This type of application can run multiple processes (or instances) that coordinate access to shared resources. However, since the coordination is done in memory, all instances are restricted to running on a single member and are therefore candidates for CAA if high availability is a requirement.

23.1 Single-Instance Applications

A single-instance application is an application that is/was not designed to run more than one copy (or instance) on any cluster member at a time. This is due to lack of synchronization built into the application. As stated above in the introduction, an application that writes to a file without coordinating access to the file must be a single-instance application, because running more than one copy of the application at a time would cause unpredictable results (usually data corruption).

A simple example of this scenario can be illustrated using the `cat(1)` command to write to a file on both members of our two-member cluster at the exact same time.

member1

```
# cat > /usr/aRandomFile

yadda yadda yadda
^D
```

member2

```
# cat > /usr/aRandomFile

la dee da
^D
```

When you type out the file after the writes complete, however, the result is not what you might expect.

```
# cat /usr/aRandomFile
la dee da
a yadda
```

This is not a good thing.

A single-instance application is not very highly available either – also not a good thing. So, we need a way to take our single-instance applications and make them highly available – precisely what CAA is designed to do. CAA will allow us to take our single-instance application and make it a highly available single-instance application.

What about multi-instance applications? Can we use CAA with multi-instance applications?

23.2 Multi-Instance Applications

A multi-instance application is an application that is designed to run multiple copies at the same time.

What makes an application a multi-instance application?

- If an application does not write to a common data file without synchronization, it could be a multi-instance application. For example, a web server[1].
- If an application uses POSIX file locking for synchronization, it could be a multi-instance application.
- If an application is multi-threaded and synchronizes access with mutexes and conditionals, it could be considered a multi-instance application.
- If an application uses IPC, it could be a multi-instance application.
- If an application uses named pipes, it could be a multi-instance application.

If an application is a multi-instance application, then we must determine if what makes it multi-instance also restricts it to a single system. To assist in this, we have put together a decision tree (Table 23-1). If your application is restricted to a single system, then in order to make the application highly available it must be monitored by CAA.

Notice that there are a few instances where applications can be deployed cluster wide. If an application does not require synchronization or if the application uses file locking, then it can be deployed simultaneously on any number of cluster members. If an application uses the Distributed Lock Manager (DLM) API (or equivalent), then the application is said to be a cluster-aware application. Cluster-aware (also known as distributed) applications are designed to run throughout the cluster.

---

[1] Although a web server can be used to run CGI scripts (or programs) that perform write operations to files, the web server itself primarily serves pages and does not write data.

Multi-Instance Application Deployment

If your application...	CAA	Cluster-Wide
Does Not Require Synchronization	✓	✓
Is Multithreaded	✓	✗
Message Queues	✓	✗
Semaphores	✓	✗
Shared Memory	✓	✗
Uses Named Pipes (fifo)	✓	✗
Uses Pipes (pipe)	✓	✗
Uses Posix File Locking	✓	✓
Uses the DLM	✓*	✓

* - an instance of a cluster-aware application can be monitored by CAA so that the application can be automatically restarted.

Table 23-1: Multi-Instance Decision Tree

An example of a cluster-aware application that uses the DLM is the Advanced Server for UNIX (ASU). ASU can be installed as a distributed (or cluster-aware) application, or a single-instance application that uses CAA for failover. An example of a cluster-aware application that does not use the DLM is Oracle Corporation's Oracle Parallel Server (OPS). The OPS application uses a proprietary locking mechanism that enables multiple instances to run in parallel on any number of cluster members.

NOTE:

CAA has the capability to check the status of an application at a predefined interval and restart it if it is not running. Many cluster architects have come to appreciate this "auto-restart" functionality and are using CAA to monitor instances of cluster-aware applications as well.

We will discuss this in more detail in section 23.6.4 and provide an example in section 24.7.

An example of a cluster-unaware application, that can run multi-instance across multiple cluster members, is a web server (such as the Compaq Secure Web Server). Web Servers do not write to files except for log files, so by making the log files member-specific using a CDSL, web servers can be deployed cluster wide. It is important to keep in mind, however, that not all web servers are used only to serve pages. Many web servers act as application servers, so it is important to consider the synchronization capability, if any, of the applications (or CGI scripts) before choosing to make your web server multi-instance. If the CGI script writes to a common file without synchronizing access to the file then there is the potential for data corruption to occur if there were multiple-instances deployed throughout the cluster.

Applications that use the POSIX or X/Open API for file locking can be run multi-instance across the cluster. The file locking calls that can be used are `fcntl(2)`, `flock(2)`, and `lockf(3)`; although `fcntl` is the only call technically listed in the POSIX standard.

All multi-instance applications that are limited to running on one system at a time should use CAA for high availability (unless of course they have some other mechanism to provide for high availability).

23.3 What is Cluster Application Availability?

The Cluster Application Availability facility is a framework to manage and monitor an application to make it highly available. If an application would normally be restricted to running on one cluster member at a time, CAA can be used to relocate the application from one cluster member to another in order to keep the application running within the cluster at all times.

For example, if you have an application called "NaHA-Widget[2]", that is restricted to running on `member1`, and `member1` is shutdown (or crashes), what would happen to "NaHA-Widget"? It would no longer be available to your users.

If, however, the application was placed under the control of CAA, and `member1` is shutdown (or crashes), then the "NaHA-Widget[3]" would automatically start up on another cluster member.

CAA monitors and manages resources. Resources can be applications, network interfaces, tape and media changer devices. A resource is defined by creating a profile. Once the profile is created, it must be registered with the CAA Resource Manager (`caad(8)`) before it can be managed.

23.3.1 CAA Architecture

Figure 23-1 shows the CAA architecture.

---

[2] Not a Highly-Available Widget

[3] Now a Highly-Available Widget ☺

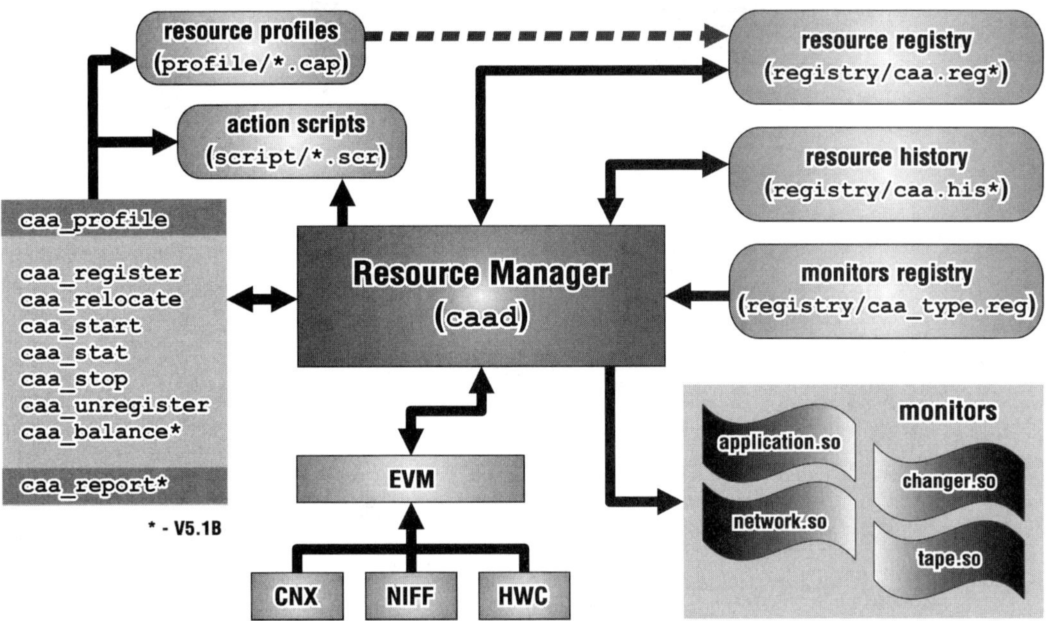

Figure 23-1: The CAA Architecture

23.3.2 The Resource Manager (caad)

Each member has a Resource Manager that communicates to the other cluster members' resource managers. The Resource Manager monitors the various resource types and manages (starts, stops, relocates) the application resources when certain events occur or other criteria are met. Events can be those received from EVM (see Table 23-2) or by direct intervention from the cluster administrator (e.g., running a `caa_*` command – see section 23.3.6). The term "other criteria" is used to indicate when an attribute value, defined within a resource's profile, is reached, causing the Resource Manager to take action. We will discuss this further in the following sections.

The Resource Manager only monitors and manages those resources that are in the CAA registry (`/var/cluster/caa/registry/caa.reg*`). In other words, once you create (or modify) a resource, you must register the resource with CAA.

For more information on the CAA Resource Manager, see the `caad(8)` reference page.

23.3.3 Resource Monitors

Resource Monitors are shared library plug-ins that the Resource Manager uses to monitor and control a particular resource type. Since CAA supports four resource types (as of this writing), the `/var/cluster/caa/monitors` directory contains four requisite resource monitors.

EVM Event Subscriptions	
Attribute	**Event**
CAA	clu.cnx.member.leave
	clu.cnx.member.join
	clu.cnx.quorum.loss
	clu.cnx.quorum.gain
	clu.member.add
	clu.member.delete
	hw.net.down
	hw.net.up
Changer Resource	hw.state_change.media_changer
	hw.state_change.media_changer._hwid.*
	hw.deregistered.media_changer._hwid.*
Network Resource	hw.net.niff.down
	hw.net.niff.up
Tape Resource	hw.state_change.available
	hw.state_change.unavailable

Table 23-2: CAA Components EVM Event Subscription

Note that as of V5.1A, there exists a resource monitor registry (`caa_type.reg`) where resource monitors are registered with the resource manager. This registry is a text file but do not attempt to edit it.

The resource monitor registry does contain non-printable characters within it, so to see what resource monitors are within the `caa_type.reg` file, we recommend using the `strings(1)` command.

```
# strings /var/cluster/caa/registry/caa_type.reg

application application.so SCRIPTPATH=/var/cluster/caa/script
network network.so NONE
tape tape.so NONE
changer changer.so NONE
```

The changer, tape, and network resource monitors subscribe to EVM events in order to know when the monitored hardware component has failed or has become available (see Table 23-2).

23.3.4 Resource Registry Database

The resource registry database is located in the `/var/cluster/caa/registry` directory. The file name may differ depending on the version of the *TruCluster* Server software that is installed but starts with "`caa.reg`".

NOTE:

We have seen two file names as of this writing:

- `caa.reg` – V5.0A, V5.1, V5.1A (unpatched)
- `caa.reg.binaryDB` – V5.1A (IPK and above), V5.1B

The resource registry database contains all of the information that the Resource Manager needs to monitor and manage the registered resources. The resource registry database must be updated whenever a resource's profile is modified. If a resource has not been added to the resource registry database, CAA will not know about it.

The resource registry database is a binary file, therefore the information contained within it cannot be easily gleaned simply by using the `cat(1)` command or your favorite editor. You could of course get some information by using the `strings` command, but this would not dump all of the information contained therein.

The easiest way to get information from the resource registry database is to use the `caa_stat(1)` command.

```
# caa_stat -t

Name           Type          Target    State     Host
------------------------------------------------------------
autofs         application   OFFLINE   OFFLINE
cluster_lockd  application   ONLINE    ONLINE    sheridan
clustercron    application   ONLINE    ONLINE    sheridan
dhcp           application   OFFLINE   OFFLINE
named          application   OFFLINE   OFFLINE
```

You can get more in-depth information about a registered resource's attributes by using the "`-p`" option.

```
# caa_stat -p clustercron

NAME=clustercron
TYPE=application
ACTION_SCRIPT=clustercron.scr
ACTIVE_PLACEMENT=0
AUTO_START=1
CHECK_INTERVAL=60
DESCRIPTION=clustercron
FAILOVER_DELAY=0
FAILURE_INTERVAL=0
FAILURE_THRESHOLD=0
HOSTING_MEMBERS=
OPTIONAL_RESOURCES=
PLACEMENT=balanced
REBALANCE=
REQUIRED_RESOURCES=
RESTART_ATTEMPTS=1
SCRIPT_TIMEOUT=60
```

We will discuss resource attributes in section 23.4.4; so don't be concerned if none of this makes sense at this stage. Our intent is to show you how to get to the information, not how to interpret it – that will come later in the chapter.

If you are a senior-level-cluster-guru-type-dude (a.k.a., Chief Troubleshooter in *TruCluster* Server Snoopology (CT^2S^2)) and would like to dump the raw contents of the resource registry database, you can use a relatively unknown (currently undocumented and hence unsupported) tool located in the `/usr/sbin/cluster` directory known as `caa_dbConvert`.

Here is an example of dumping the resource registry database (`caa.reg.binaryDB`) to a text file (`caa.reg.txt`) in the `/tmp` directory.

```
# cd /var/cluster/caa/registry
# /usr/sbin/cluster/caa_dbConvert DUMP caa.reg.binaryDB /tmp/caa.reg.txt
```

Although we have not shown the contents of the `/tmp/caa.reg.txt`, it does contain quite a bit of interesting information.

NOTE:

If you see the following error when using the above-mentioned command, use the full pathname to indicate the resource registry database (or change your directory location as we did in the previous example).

```
mmapFile::mapFile, caa.reg.binaryDB, open error
```

For example:

```
# caa_dbConvert DUMP /var/cluster/caa/registry/caa.reg.binaryDB /tmp/caa.reg.txt
```

23.3.4.1 Resource Registry History Database

The resource registry history database is also located in the `/var/cluster/caa/registry` directory. As with the resource registry database, the file name may differ depending on which version of the *TruCluster* Server software is installed but starts with "`caa.his`".

NOTE:

We have seen two file names as of this writing:

- `caa.his` – V5.0A, V5.1, V5.1A (unpatched)
- `caa.his.binaryDB` – V5.1A (IPK and above), V5.1B

The resource registry history database is used to track the failure history of a resource. This database, like the resource registry database, is binary in format, so the best approach to getting information from the database is to use the caa_stat command. Resource failure history can be retrieved using the "-v" option.

```
# caa_stat -v nicUP
NAME=nicUP
TYPE=network
FAILURE_THRESHOLD=2
FAILURE_COUNT=0 on molari
FAILURE_COUNT=0 on sheridan
TARGET=ONLINE on molari
TARGET=ONLINE on sheridan
STATE=ONLINE on molari
STATE=ONLINE on Sheridan
```

As with the resource registry database (if you're a CT^2S^2 that is), you can dump the resource registry history database using the caa_dbConvert command.

```
# /usr/sbin/cluster/caa_dbConvert DUMP caa.his.binaryDB /tmp/caa.his.txt
```

Here is an excerpt of the convert database showing the information for the nicUP resource.

```
...
__RESOURCE__,nicUP
2_FAILURE_HISTORY,1018678401 1018682922
...
```

You can see that the last two times the nicUP resource failed as follows:

```
# perl -e 'foreach $i (1018678401,1018682922)
> { printf ("%s\n", scalar localtime $i) };'
Sat Apr 13 02:13:21 2002
Sat Apr 13 03:28:42 2002
```

23.3.5 Directory Layout

Figure 23-2 shows the various locations where the majority of CAA-related directories and files are located. Note that we have not included each and every file or directory location. For an exhaustive list you can use the find(1) command.

```
# find / -name '*[Cc][Aa][Aa]*'
```

If you happen to have a cluster that is running a patched version of V5.1A, you will see a hybrid directory layout containing some of the files seen in V5.1B. This is due to the work that was done by the CAA Engineering group in support of the "Compaq Database Utility with Oracle9*i* Real Application Clusters".

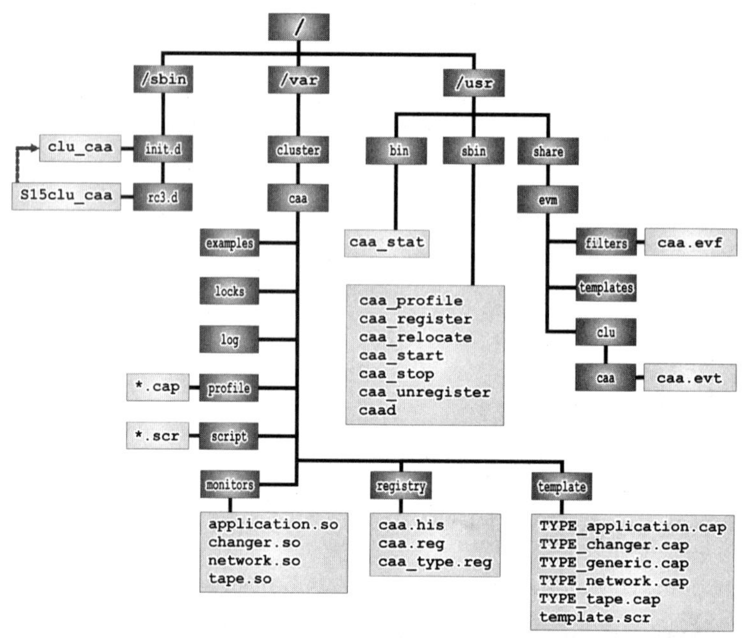

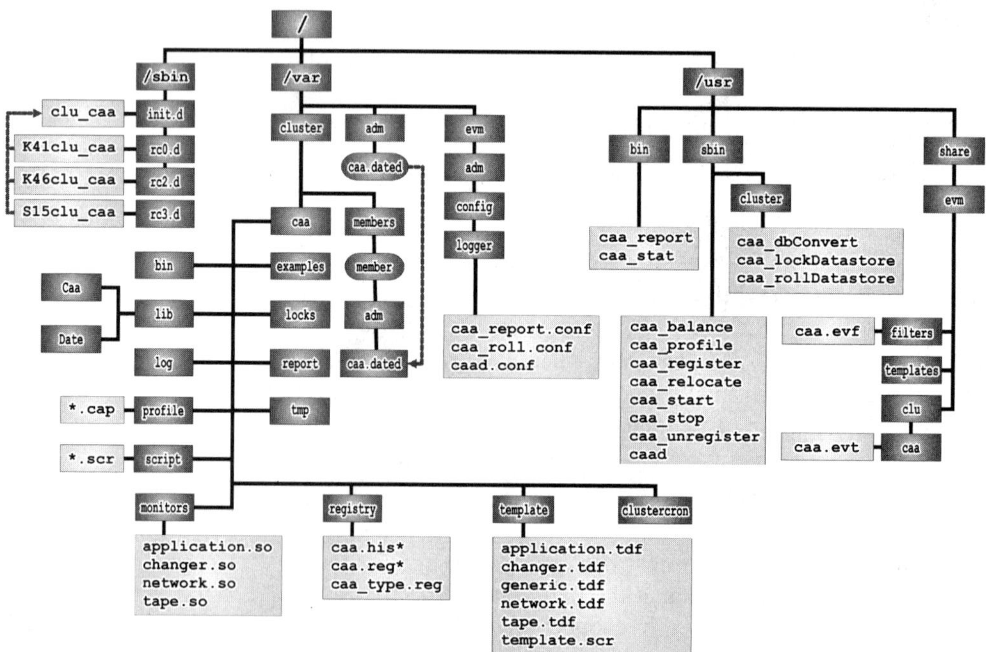

Figure 23-2: CAA Directories and Files

Note that the log subdirectory under /var/cluster/caa is obsolete and should no longer be used.

23.3.6 CAA Commands

CAA has a command-line interface as well as a graphical user interface (GUI). The easiest way to determine what CAA commands are available (or really what CAA information is available), you can simply use the man(1) command with the "-k" option (or the apropos(1) command).

```
# man -k caa
```

Another option is to use the sman script that we wrote. The sman command is essentially a section-based "man -k" command that also formats the output. The advantage of sman is that you can narrow your search criteria to only the sections in which you are interested. For example, if you only want commands, you can limit your search to sections 1 and 8.

```
# sman [18] caa

Section   Reference Page              Description
-------   -------------------------   --------------------------------------------

   8      caa_balance                 Finds the optimal member for an
                                      application resource and relocates the
                                      resource to that member if it is not
                                      currently placed there.

   8      caa_profile                 Creates, validates, deletes, and updates
                                      a Cluster Application Availability (CAA)
                                      resource profile

   8      caa_register                Registers a resource with Cluster
                                      Application Availability (CAA)

   8      caa_relocate                Relocates an application resource from
                                      one cluster member to another

   1      caa_report                  reports availability statistics for
                                      application resources

   8      caa_start                   Starts resources that have been
                                      registered with Cluster Application
                                      Availability (CAA).

   1      caa_stat                    Provides status on Cluster Application
                                      Availability (CAA) resources within a
                                      cluster.

   8      caa_stop                    Stops a Cluster Application Availability
                                      (CAA) application resource

   8      caa_unregister              Unregisters a Cluster Application
                                      Availability (CAA) resource.

   8      caad                        Cluster Application Availability (CAA)
                                      daemon
```

Using the "all" keyword will search all man sections.

```
# sman all caa

Section   Reference Page              Description
-------   ------------------------    ----------------------------------------

   4      caa                         Cluster Application Availability (CAA)
                                      information
...
```

The good news with CAA is that the commands you will be using all start with "caa_". All you need to remember is the action you want to perform.

Note that the GUI does not show up in the output of "man -k" or "sman". This is because the GUI is a sysman(8) application plug-in. Use the "sysman -list" command to find the list of sysman accelerators.

```
# sysman -list | grep -i caa
    | Cluster Application Availability (CAA) Management [caa]
```

To manage CAA with sysman using the "caa" accelerator.

```
# sysman caa
```

NOTE:

The caa_balance(8) and caa_report(1) commands were added in V5.1B.

23.4 Resources

Think of a resource as something that CAA manages and monitors. If you are familiar with earlier versions of *TruCluster* (ASE and Production Server (PS)), we referred to resources as services. In fact, ASE had four service types: Disk, NFS, Tape, and User-Defined. Production Server added a fifth service, the Distributed Raw Disk (the old DRD) service.

TruCluster Server has four types of CAA resources as of this writing: Application, Changer, Network, and Tape.

Can we draw a parallel between the old ASE and Production Server services and CAA resources? Yes and no, but we have not lost any capability. In fact, as you will soon see, the CAA resource (along with the CFS, the new DRD, and Cluster Alias subsystem) adds more flexibility and capability.

In ASE and PS, the service was responsible for a lot more than starting and stopping an application. For example, a disk service was used to manage storage, optionally add and remove IP aliases, optionally import and deport LSM disk groups, and mount and unmount file systems. With

TruCluster Server, the DRD manages the storage, the CLSM manages the disk groups, the CFS manages the file systems, and the CLUA manages the aliases.

So what does CAA manage? Resources.

What types of resources exist?

23.4.1 Resource Types

As of this writing, CAA supports four resource types:

- Application
- Changer
- Network
- Tape

Application resources must have a resource profile (see section 23.4.3) and an action script (see section 23.4.5).

Non-application resources must have a resource profile (of course, configured and functioning hardware is also important ☺).

23.4.2 Resource States

Table 23-3 shows what states the resources can have and a description of each state as it relates to each resource. Note, each resource will have a `TARGET` state and a current `STATE`.

23.4.3 Resource Profile

The profile for a resource contains the attributes that define the resource. The resource profile is an ASCII file so it can be edited using your favorite editor, although you may find it convenient to create it using the `caa_profile` command or using `sysman` with the "`caa`" keyword accelerator.

A resource profile is required for all resource types. Creating a resource is not the last step along the way. Once a profile has been created (and any time it is modified), it must be registered with the resource manager.

In the following sections we will show you the attributes that can, and must, be used for each resource type. We will also show you how to register a resource, update the registration when a profile is modified, and unregister a resource that is no longer needed.

Let's start by defining the resource attributes.

23.4.4 Resource Attributes

As of this writing there are four resource types. Each resource type uses certain attributes. Some attributes are required while others are optional. Some attributes are common to all resource types.

In the following sections, we will list each attribute, state whether or not it is required, identify its default value, and describe how it is used.

Resource Attribute Category	Section
• Common	23.4.4.1
• Application	23.4.4.2
• Network	23.4.4.3
• Tape and Media Changer	23.4.4.4

For the most up-to-date resource attribute information, see the `caa(4)` reference page.

Resource States

Resource	State	Description: STATE*	Description: TARGET*
Application	**ONLINE**	The application started by the resource is running.	The resource has been set to start (i.e., **caa_start** was executed).
Application	**OFFLINE**	The application started by the resource is not running or the resource has been administratively stopped.	The resource has been set to stop (i.e., **caa_stop** was executed).
Application	**UNKNOWN**	The stop entry point within the action script failed or reached the **SCRIPT_TIMEOUT**. To set the state back to **OFFLINE**, use "**caa_stop -f *resource_name***".	Not Applicable.
Network	**ONLINE**	The network interface is functioning.	The network interface has not failed.
Network	**OFFLINE**	The network interface has failed or is misconfigured.	The network resource has reached the **FAILURE_THRESHOLD**. Once the problem is resolved the **TARGET** can be set **ONLINE** using the **caa_start** command.
Tape & Changer	**ONLINE**	A direct connection to the device (via the SCSI or Fibre Channel bus) exists.	A direct connection to the device (via the SCSI or Fibre Channel bus) exists.
Tape & Changer	**OFFLINE**	No direct connection to the device exists. This can be due to a path failure or simply because the cluster member does not have a direct connection to the bus where the device is connected (e.g., a private or semi-shared bus).	The changer or tape resource has reached the **FAILURE_THRESHOLD**. Once the problem is resolved **TARGET** can be set **ONLINE** using the **caa_start** command.

* - the **STATE** and **TARGET** can be seen using the **caa_stat(1)** or "**sysman caa**" commands

Table 23-3: CAA Resource States

23.4.4.1 Common Resource Attributes

Table 23-4 lists the resource attributes that are common to each resource type.

23.4.4.2 Application Resource Attributes

Table 23-5 and Table 23-6 list the resource attributes specific to an Application resource.

Common Resource Attributes

Required?	Attribute	Default	Description
✓	`TYPE =` ***resource-type***	none	The ***resource-type*** can be either: • **`application`** • **`changer`** • **`network`** • **`tape`**
✓	`NAME =` ***resource-name***	none	The ***resource-name***: • Must be a unique, user-defined name containing any alphanumeric character, a period, a comma, or an underscore. • Cannot start with a period. • **Must** be the same name as the prefix of the profile file.
✗	`DESCRIPTION =` ***description***	none	The ***description*** is a user-defined string that describes the resource.
✗	`FAILURE_THRESHOLD =` ***value***	0	The ***value*** is the number of times that a resource may fail to start within a period of time (see **`FAILURE_INTERVAL`**), before CAA will mark the resource as **`UNAVAILABLE`** and discontinue monitoring it. Both the **`FAILURE_THRESHOLD`** and the **`FAILURE_INTERVAL`** must be non-zero for monitoring to occur. A ***value*** of 0 (zero) disables failure threshold monitoring.
✗	`FAILURE_INTERVAL =` ***value***	0	The ***value*** is the time (in seconds) that the **`FAILURE_THRESHOLD`** is tallied and applied. Both the **`FAILURE_THRESHOLD`** and the **`FAILURE_INTERVAL`** must be non-zero for monitoring to occur. A ***value*** of 0 (zero) disables failure threshold monitoring.

Table 23-4: CAA Common Resource Attributes

Application Resource Attributes

Required?	Attribute	Default	Description
✓	`ACTION_SCRIPT = `*script*	none	• The ***script*** is the name of the shell script that CAA will call when starting, stopping, and (optionally) checking the application resource. • The ***script*** is typically the same name as was used in the NAME attribute (*see Common Resource Attributes*) with a "**`.scr`**" extension. • Unless the script is located in the **`/var/cluster/caa/script`** directory the full pathname must be used. The action script must include a `start` and `stop` entry point.
✗	`CHECK_INTERVAL = `*seconds*	**60**	The number of ***seconds*** that will elapse before CAA calls the action script's check entry point. A value of 0 (zero) indicates no check will be performed.
✗	`SCRIPT_TIMEOUT = `*seconds*	**60**	The maximum number of ***seconds*** that an action script may take to complete before CAA returns an error status.
✗	`PLACEMENT = `*policy*	`balanced`	The ***policy*** can be either: **`balanced`** – Place the resource such that the number of resources across the cluster is as balanced as possible (subject to dependency restrictions). **`favored`** – Start the resource on a member listed in the **`HOSTING_MEMBERS`** attribute. If no members listed in **`HOSTING_MEMBERS`** are available, start on any available cluster member. **`restricted`** – Start the resource on a member listed in the **`HOSTING_MEMBERS`** attribute. If no members listed in **`HOSTING_MEMBERS`** are available, do not start.
Varies. See item description	`HOSTING_MEMBERS = `*members*	none	Where ***members*** is a white-space delimited list of members where the resource can or must run (see **`PLACEMENT`**). If **`PLACEMENT`** is **`balanced`**, then **`HOSTING_MEMBERS`** is not used.
✗	`ACTIVE_PLACEMENT = `*value*	**0**	If ***value*** is set to **1**, then the placement of the resource is reevaluated per the **`PLACEMENT`** attribute when a cluster member rejoins the cluster. See section 23.6.3.

Table 23-5: CAA Application Resource Attributes – Part 1

Application Resource Attributes (continued)

Required?	Attribute	Default	Description
✘	`OPTIONAL_RESOURCES = `***reslist***	none	Where ***reslist*** is a white-space delimited list of resources that a member should have available if possible. If some or even all of the listed resources are not available on the member, the resource will still start unless there is a member with a greater set of these optional resources available. The maximum number of resources in ***reslist*** is currently limited to 58.
✘	`REQUIRED_RESOURCES = `***reslist***	none	Where ***reslist*** is a white-space delimited list of resources that a member must have available in order for this resource to start.
✘	`REBALANCE = `*time*	none	Where ***time*** is in the form **t:day:hour:min** when reevaluation is to occur. **day** day of the week (0 - 6) where 0 = Sunday **hour** hour of the day (0 - 23) **min** minute of the day (0 - 59) An asterisk (*) can be used as a wildcard to specify every day and/or every hour.
✘	`AUTO_START = `***value***	**0**	If ***value*** is set to **1**, then start the application resource automatically after a member reboot, regardless of the state of the resource prior to the reboot. If ***value*** is set to **0** (zero), then start the application resource *only* if it was `ONLINE` before the reboot.
✘	`RESTART_ATTEMPTS = `***value***	**1**	The ***value*** is the number of times that the resource manager will attempt to restart the resource on the member before attempting to relocate the resource.
✘	`FAILOVER_DELAY = `***seconds***	**0**	The number of ***seconds*** that the resource manager will wait before attempting to relocate the application resource after it failed.

Table 23-6: CAA Application Resource Attributes – Part 2

Required?	Attribute	Description
✓	SUBNET = *xxx.xxx.xxx.xxx*	The ***xxx.xxx.xxx.xxx*** is the network subnet. The network subnet is the bitwise AND of the IP address and the netmask. IP Address = 18. 32. 64. 121 & netmask = 255. 255. 255. 0 subnet = 18. 32. 64. 0

Table 23-7: CAA Network Resource Attribute

Tape/Media Changer Resource Attributes

Required?	Attribute	Description
✓	DEVICE_NAME = *device-name*	The ***device-name*** is the tape or media changer device-special file name. You can specify either the full path or only the device-special file name. /dev/tape/tape0 — tape0 /dev/changer/mc0 — mc0

Table 23-8: CAA Tape and Media Changer Resource Attribute

23.4.4.3 Network Resource Attributes

Table 23-7 lists the one attribute that is specific to the Network resource type.

23.4.4.4 Tape and Media Changer Resource Attribute

Table 23-8 lists the one attribute that is specific to both the Tape and Media Changer resources.

23.4.5 Type Definition File

Starting with *TruCluster* Server version 5.1A-IPK the `TYPE_*.cap` files in the `/var/cluster/caa/template` directory have been replaced with a new file format, the type definition file (`*.tdf`). This change was made primarily to facilitate ease of customization in adding user-defined attributes to application resources.

The type definition file defines the attributes for a resource. The following entries define a resource attribute.

- `attribute` – The name of the attribute.
- `switch` – This is the `caa_profile` command switch to assign a value to this attribute.
- `type` – The data type of the attribute. Valid data types include: `boolean`, `file`, `internet_address`, `name_list`, `name_string`, `positive_integer`, `string`.
- `default` – The default value of the attribute.
- `required` – Whether or not the attribute is required.

For example, here is an excerpt from the application resource type definition file (`application.tdf`) that defines the `AUTO_START` attribute.

```
# grep -p AUTO_START application.tdf
#!==========================
attribute: AUTO_START
type: boolean
switch: -o as
default: 0
required: no
```

The "`AUTO_START`" resource attribute is not a required attribute. The value of the resource is expected to be a Boolean with a default value of 0. The "`-o as`" switch is the command option that passes the `AUTO_START` attribute value to the `caa_profile(8)` command (see section 23.4.6 for more information).

Additionally, user-defined attributes can be added to the application resource type definition file. We will cover this topic in section 23.5.3.3.

23.4.6 Creating a Resource Profile

There are several ways that a resource profile can be created.

- Use the `caa_profile` command.
- Use the "`sysman caa`" command (see section 23.5.2 for an example).
- Create a profile with your favorite editor.
- Use a combination of the previous options.

This section will explore the first option.

The `caa_profile` command can be used to create a resource from the default profile template, located in `/var/cluster/caa/template`, or with the "`-I`" option to use a template located elsewhere.

The caa_profile(8) Command's Primary Options

Option	Description
-create	Create a resource profile
-delete	Delete a resource profile
-update	Modify a resource profile
-template	Create a resource profile template
-print	Print a resource profile
-validate	Validate a resource profile to determine there are no typos.

Table 23-9: CAA Profile Primary Options

There are many, many options to the caa_profile command, but they are logically categorized by primary, secondary, and tertiary options. The primary options are shown in Table 23-9.

There are many additional options to "-create" switch that directly correlate to the resource attributes that were shown in section 23.4.4. We put together a chart to illustrate the parallels (see Table 23-10).

Note, that *resource_name* will become the value of the NAME resource attribute, while the string following the "-t" option will become the value of the TYPE resource attribute.

Also of note is the "-B" option that is used to indicate the name of the program (or application) that is to be managed by CAA. If starting your application happens to be more complex than executing one program, it would probably be easier to edit the generated script (or write your own) and not use the "-B" option.

NOTE:

A resource is not managed or monitored by CAA until it is registered. See section 23.4.11 for more information.

23.4.7 Validating a Resource Profile

Using the caa_profile command or "sysman caa" instead of editing the profile manually can help you to avoid typos in the resource attribute names.

To validate a resource profile, use the caa_profile command with the "-validate" option.

```
# caa_profile -validate memberUP
```

caa_profile -create *resource_name* -t application

Option		Resource Attribute
-B		*executable application*
-a		ACTION_SCRIPT
-d		DESCRIPTION
-h		HOSTING_MEMBERS
-l		OPTIONAL_RESOURCES
-p		PLACEMENT
-r		REQUIRED_RESOURCES
-o	ap	ACTIVE_PLACEMENT
	as	AUTO_START
	bt	REBALANCE
	ci	CHECK_INTERVAL
	fd	FAILOVER_DELAY
	fi	FAILURE_INTERVAL
	ft	FAILURE_THRESHOLD
	ra	RESTART_ATTEMPTS
	st	SCRIPT_TIMEOUT

caa_profile -create *resource_name* -t network

Option		Resource Attribute
-s		SUBNET
-d		DESCRIPTION
-o	fi	FAILURE_INTERVAL
	ft	FAILURE_THRESHOLD

caa_profile -create *resource_name* -t [changer | tape]

Option		Resource Attribute
-n		DEVICE_NAME
-d		DESCRIPTION
-o	fi	FAILURE_INTERVAL
	ft	FAILURE_THRESHOLD

options that apply to all "-create" versions

Option	Description	Option	Description
-f	forces the creation of a profile if a previous profile exists.	-q	run in "quiet" mode -- no output is displayed.

Table 23-10: CAA Profile Create Options to Resource Attributes

What is validated? Table 23-11 illustrates the attributes that are validated.

23.4.8 Updating a Resource Profile

Use the caa_profile command with the "-update" option (or use sysman – see section 23.5.2) to modify a resource profile. You also have the option of editing the profile using your favorite editor.

```
# caa_profile -h | grep update
    caa_profile -update resource_name [option ...] [-o option,...] [-q]
```

CAA Resource Profile Validation

Attribute	Description	Error Message
NAME	Must match the profile name exactly sans the **.cap** extension.	NAME attribute must be the same as filename
	Must not be greater than 128 characters, empty, or start with a period (.)	Improper Name: .memberUP
TYPE	Must be a validate resource type. Valid types are: **application, changer, network, tape**. This attribute is case sensitive.	Invalid Type: guitar
PLACEMENT	Must be a valid placement policy. Valid placement policy can be: **balanced**, **favored**, **restricted**. This attribute is case sensitive.	PLACEMENT invalid: restrict
HOSTING_MEMBERS	If the placement policy is not **balanced** then this attribute must exist.	HOSTING_MEMBERS is required for: favored placement policy HOSTING_MEMBERS is required for: restricted placement policy
	If the placement policy is **balanced** then this attribute must not exist.	No HOSTING_MEMBERS is needed for balanced placement policy
ACTION_SCRIPT	If the profile is for an **application** then the profile must contain this attribute.	The ACTION_SCRIPT attribute of the resource profile must be set
SUBNET	If the profile is for a **network** resource then the profile must contain this attribute. The actual subnet or hardware is not validated although it does check that the subnet number is in correct format.	Invalid subset setting for network resource
DEVICE_NAME	If the profile is for a **changer** or **tape** resource then the profile must contain this attribute. The hardware is not checked to see if exists.	DEVICE_NAME must be set for changer DEVICE_NAME must be set for tape
AUTO_START CHECK_INTERVAL FAILURE_DELAY FAILURE_INTERVAL FAILURE_THRESHOLD RESTART_ATTEMPTS	If the the profile is for an **application** resource these attributes are checked. The attribute value must be a number but not a negative. However, the maximum value is not checked.	AUTO_START out of range: -1 FAILURE_INTERVAL out of range: 10 widgets
OPTIONAL_RESOURCES REQUIRED_RESOURCES	Attribute value must not contain a colon (:), semicolon (;), or a comma (,). However, the value is not checked to be a list of existing resources.	OPTIONAL_RESOURCES syntax error: nicUP;tapeDrive REQUIRED_RESOURCES syntax error: nicUP,tapeDrive

Table 23-11: CAA Profile Validation

You can use the majority of the options listed in Table 23-9. See the `caa_profile(8)` reference page for more information.

NOTE:

Any time a resource profile is modified the resource registry database must be updated. See section 23.4.12 for more information.

23.4.9 Printing a Resource Profile

Printing a profile can be accomplished in three ways.

- Use the `cat(1)` or `more(1)` command.
- Use the Details... button in "`sysman caa`" (see section 23.5.2).
- Use the `caa_profile` command with the "`-print`" option.

```
# caa_profile -h | grep print
        caa_profile -print [resource_name [...]] [-q]
```

```
# caa_profile -print nicUP
NAME=nicUP
TYPE=network
DESCRIPTION=nicUP
FAILURE_INTERVAL=0
FAILURE_THRESHOLD=0
SUBNET=192.168.0.0
```

23.4.10 Deleting a Resource Profile

Deleting a profile can be accomplished in three ways:

- Use the `rm(1)` command to delete the profile.
- Use the Delete... button in "`sysman caa`" (see section 23.5.2).
- Use the `caa_profile` command with the "`-delete`" option.

```
# caa_profile -delete nicUP
```

NOTE:

You cannot delete a profile that is associated with a registered resource. You'll receive the following error:

```
Can not delete profile for resource nicUP as it is currently registered.
```

See section 23.4.13 for more information on unregistering a resource.

CAUTION:

Prior to V5.1B, using `caa_profile` with the "`-delete`" option to remove an application resource's profile will also delete the resource's action script! Note, "`sysman`" will do the same thing.

```
# caa_profile -delete memberUP
```

```
# ls /var/cluster/caa/script/memberUP.scr
ls: /var/cluster/caa/script/memberUP.scr not found
```

For more information on the `caa_profile` command, see the `caa_profile(8)` reference page.

23.4.11 Registering a Resource

Once you have created and edited a resource profile, the resource must be registered with CAA before it can be managed or monitored.

NOTE:

Before registering a resource with CAA you should always do the following:

- Validate the profile (see section 23.4.7).
- If it is an Application Resource, see the "scripting tips" in section 23.5.1.
- If it is a non-application resource make sure that it is configured.

You can register a profile using the `caa_register` command.

```
# caa_register myResource
```

For more information on registering resources, see the `caa_register(8)` reference page.

23.4.12 Updating a Registered Resource

Any time that modifications are made to a resource profile, CAA must be notified. Registered profiles are stored in the caa.reg database in /var/cluster/caa/registry and not read from the profile directory.

If the profile is for an application resource, the profile can be updated using the caa_register command with the "-u" option.

```
# caa_register -u myApplicationResource
```

NOTE:

Prior to V5.1B, if the resource is a non-application resource, then the resource must be unregistered and then registered. Since non-application resources are only used as a dependency for an application resource, this presents a bit of an inconvenience in that the application resource must also be unregistered and then registered.

For example, say we have a network resource (nicUP) that is a REQUIRED_RESOURCE for an application resource (memberUP). When we attempt to unregister the profile we receive an error.

```
# caa_unregister nicUP
Can't unregister `nicUP` because it is required by other resources.
Could not unregister resource nicUP.
```

So we must unregister every resource that depends on nicUP.

1. Find the resources that require the nicUP resource.

   ```
   # grep nicUP *.cap | grep -v nicUP.cap
   memberUP.cap:REQUIRED_RESOURCES=nicUP
   ```

2. If the resource is running, stop it.

   ```
   # caa_stat -a memberUP -r && caa_stop memberUP
   Attempting to stop `memberUP` on member `molari`
   Stop of `memberUP` on member `molari` succeeded.
   ```

   Note that we used the "-r" option with the "-a" option to the caa_stat command to see if the resource was running.

3. If the resource is registered, unregister it.

   ```
   # caa_stat -a memberUP -g && caa_unregister memberUP
   ```

   Note that we used the "-g" option with the "-a" option to the caa_stat command to see if the resource was registered.

4. Unregister and register the non-application resource.

```
# caa_unregister nicUP && caa_register nicUP
```

5. Register and start the application resource.

```
# caa_register memberUP && caa_start memberUP

Attempting to start `nicUP` on member `molari`
Start of `nicUP` on member `molari` succeeded.
Attempting to start `memberUP` on member `molari`
Start of `memberUP` on member `molari` succeeded.
```

For more information on updating the resource registry, see the `caa_register(8)` reference page.

23.4.13 Unregistering a Resource

If a resource is no longer needed, it can be unregistered so that CAA will no longer manage or monitor the resource. To unregister, use the `caa_unregister` command.

```
# caa_unregister myResource
```

Note that the resource must be **stopped** before it can be unregistered.

```
# caa_unregister myResource
Could not unregister resource myResource.
```

Also note that this does not remove the profile or the action script from the `/var/cluster/caa` subdirectories; it merely removes the profile from the CAA registry database (`caa.reg`).

For more information on unregistering resources, see the `caa_unregister(8)` reference page.

23.4.14 Starting a Resource

Once you have registered a resource it must be started. When an application resource is started, the "`start`" entry point in the action script is called to start the application. To start a resource, use the `caa_start` command.

```
# caa_start memberUP
```

You can start a resource on a particular member using the "`-c`" option.

```
# caa_start -c sheridan memberUP
```

You can start all registered resources using the "-all" option.

```
# caa_start -all
```

You can modify user-defined resource attributes when starting a resource as well.

```
# caa_start USR_ALIAS_IP=16.60.45.10 aliasAPP
```

See section 23.5.3.3 for more information on user-defined resource attributes.

If you receive the following error, the "start" entry point failed (i.e., a non-zero value was returned), but the "stop" entry point ran successfully. Note, when the "start" entry point fails, the "stop" entry point is automatically called.

```
# caa_start memberUP
Attempting to start `memberUP` on member `molari`
Start of `memberUP` on member `molari` failed.
Attempting to start `memberUP` on member `sheridan`
Start of `memberUP` on member `sheridan` failed.
No more members to consider
Could not start resource memberUP.
```

Note that the target state remains ONLINE, yet the current state is OFFLINE.

```
# caa_stat -t -v memberUP
Name           Type           R/RA   F/FT   Target    State     Host
---------------------------------------------------------------------
memberUP       application    0/1    0/0    ONLINE    OFFLINE
```

If you receive the following error, both the "start" and "stop" entry points failed.

```
# caa_start memberUP
Attempting to start `memberUP` on member `molari`
`memberUP` on member `molari` has experienced an unrecoverable failure.
Human intervention required to resume its availability.
Could not start resource memberUP.
```

Note that in this case since the "stop" entry point also failed. CAA no longer knows the state of the resource.

```
# caa_stat -t -v memberUP
Name           Type           R/RA   F/FT   Target    State     Host
---------------------------------------------------------------------
memberUP       application    0/1    0/0    ONLINE    UNKNOWN   molari
```

A resource cannot be started from an UNKNOWN state. It must be forcefully stopped first (see section 23.4.15).

One final note on starting resources: non-application resources typically do not need to be started in order for them to be ONLINE. However, if a non-application resource reaches its FAILURE_THRESHOLD, its target state will be set to OFFLINE. If a non-application resource is in an OFFLINE target state, it can be set to an ONLINE target state using the caa_start command. Note, however, that you will need to correct the problem that forced the resource to an OFFLINE state in the first place before it will go ONLINE.

For example, we have a network resource (nicUP) that is currently ONLINE.

```
# caa_stat -t -v nicUP
Name             Type            R/RA   F/FT   Target    State     Host
---------------------------------------------------------------------------
nicUP            network          -     0/2    ONLINE    ONLINE    molari
nicUP            network          -     1/2    ONLINE    ONLINE    sheridan
```

We have set the FAILURE_THRESHOLD to 2 and the FAILURE_INTERVAL to 600. In other words, nicUP cannot fail more than twice in a ten minute period or its target state will be set to OFFLINE.

```
# caa_stat -p nicUP
NAME=nicUP
TYPE=network
DESCRIPTION=nicUP
FAILURE_INTERVAL=600
FAILURE_THRESHOLD=2
SUBNET=192.168.0.0
```

We will literally pull the plug on the network associated to nicUP (which is our tu0 interface on sheridan).

```
# ifconfig tu0
tu0: flags=c63<UP,BROADCAST,NOTRAILERS,RUNNING,MULTICAST,SIMPLEX>
     inet 192.168.0.69 netmask ffffff00 broadcast 192.168.0.255 ipmtu 1500
```

Note that the tu0 inet address is 192.168.0.69, and the network subnet nicUP is configured to use is 192.168.0.0.

The plug is pulled.

```
# caa_stat -t -v nicUP
Name             Type            R/RA   F/FT   Target    State     Host
---------------------------------------------------------------------------
nicUP            network          -     0/2    ONLINE    ONLINE    molari
nicUP            network          -     1/2    ONLINE    OFFLINE   sheridan
```

Failure #1 has occurred. We plug the interface back in and wait for the state to return ONLINE.

```
# caa_stat -t -v nicUP
Name            Type            R/RA   F/FT   Target    State     Host
----------------------------------------------------------------------
nicUP           network         -      0/2    ONLINE    ONLINE    molari
nicUP           network         -      1/2    ONLINE    ONLINE    sheridan
```

Okay, pull the plug again. This will induce the second failure within the FAILURE_INTERVAL, which will force the target state to OFFLINE.

```
# caa_stat -t -v nicUP
Name            Type            R/RA   F/FT   Target    State     Host
----------------------------------------------------------------------
nicUP           network         -      0/2    ONLINE    ONLINE    molari
nicUP           network         -      2/2    OFFLINE   OFFLINE   sheridan
```

Plug the interface back in. Note that the target state remains OFFLINE.

```
# caa_stat -t -v nicUP
Name            Type            R/RA   F/FT   Target    State     Host
----------------------------------------------------------------------
nicUP           network         -      0/2    ONLINE    ONLINE    molari
nicUP           network         -      0/2    OFFLINE   ONLINE    sheridan
```

If we now attempt to start a resource that has a dependency on nicUP, note the results.

```
# caa_start memberUP
molari : Resource memberUP (application) cannot run on molari
sheridan : Resource nicUP (network) is not available on sheridan

Resource memberUP has placement error.
```

The reason for the first error message is that we restricted memberUP to run only on sheridan. We did this purely to illustrate that a resource that is dependent upon a REQUIRED_RESOURCE will be unable to start if the target state of the REQUIRED_RESOURCE is set to OFFLINE, which is illustrated by the second error message.

Here is a look at the pertinent entries in the memberUP profile:

```
# caa_profile -print memberUP | grep -E "^REQ|^HOST|^PLACE"
HOSTING_MEMBERS=sheridan
PLACEMENT=restricted
REQUIRED_RESOURCES=nicUP
```

To solve this problem, simply set the target state of the nicUP resource to ONLINE by using the caa_start command.

```
# caa_start nicUP memberUP

`nicUP` re-enabled on member `sheridan`
Attempting to start `nicUP` on member `sheridan`
Start of `nicUP` on member `sheridan` succeeded.
Attempting to start `memberUP` on member `sheridan`
Start of `memberUP` on member `sheridan` succeeded.
```

```
# caa_stat -t -v nicUP memberUP

Name            Type           R/RA   F/FT   Target    State     Host
------------------------------------------------------------------------
memberUP        application    0/1    0/0    ONLINE    ONLINE    sheridan
nicUP           network         -     0/2    ONLINE    ONLINE    molari
nicUP           network         -     0/2    ONLINE    ONLINE    sheridan
```

NOTE:

When a dependency comes ONLINE, any dependents that have their TARGET set to ONLINE will also be started.

For additional information regarding starting a resource, see the caa_start(8) reference page.

23.4.15 Stopping a Resource

Unless an application resource is in an UNKNOWN state, you can stop it using the caa_stop command. Note, only application resources can be stopped.

```
# caa_stop memberUP

Attempting to stop `memberUP` on member `sheridan`
Stop of `memberUP` on member `sheridan` succeeded.
```

If the "stop" entry fails, the resource is placed in an UNKNOWN state. In order to get the resource state back to OFFLINE, the resource must be forcefully stopped using the "-f" option.

Here's an example where we hacked the "stop" entry point to immediately exit with status of 1 (anything except a status of zero is considered a failure).

```
# caa_stop memberUP

Attempting to stop `memberUP` on member `sheridan`
`memberUP` on member `sheridan` has experienced an unrecoverable failure.
Human intervention required to resume its availability.
```

```
# caa_stat -t memberUP
Name           Type           Target     State      Host
------------------------------------------------------------
memberUP       application    OFFLINE    UNKNOWN    sheridan
```

The "Human intervention required" means that you will need to determine the cause of the failure (and may need to stop your application manually). Additionally, you may want to modify the action script to automatically handle (if possible) the situation that caused the failure to occur in the first place so that "human intervention" will not be required in the future.

Once the cause of the failure is addressed, you must use the `caa_stop` command with the "`-f`" option to get the resource state set to `OFFLINE`.

```
# caa_stop -f memberUP && caa_stat -t memberUP
Attempting to stop `memberUP` on member `sheridan`
Stop of `memberUP` on member `sheridan` succeeded.
Name           Type           Target     State      Host
------------------------------------------------------------
memberUP       application    OFFLINE    OFFLINE
```

You can now start the resource using the `caa_start` command (see section 23.4.14).

You can modify user-defined resource attributes when stopping a resource as well.

```
# caa_stop USR_STOP_CODE=Because memberUP
```

See section 23.5.3.3 for more information on user-defined resource attributes.

For more information on stopping a resource, see the `caa_stop(8)` reference page.

23.4.16 Relocating a Resource

An application resource will automatically relocate to an available cluster member if the member where it is running fails. However there may be an occasion when you would like to relocate the resource. An application resource can be relocated to another member (including a non-favored member). This can be accomplished by using the `caa_relocate` command.

```
# caa_relocate memberUP
Attempting to stop `memberUP` on member `sheridan`
Stop of `memberUP` on member `sheridan` succeeded.
Attempting to start `nicUP` on member `molari`
Start of `nicUP` on member `molari` succeeded.
Attempting to start `memberUP` on member `molari`
Start of `memberUP` on member `molari` succeeded.
```

Note only application resources can be relocated.

If you want to relocate the application resource to a specific member, you can use the "-c" option (output not shown).

```
# caa_relocate -c sheridan memberUP
```

You can modify user-defined resource attributes when relocating a resource.

```
# caa_relocate USR_ALIAS_IP=192.168.0.74 aliasAPP
```

See section 23.5.3.3 for more information on user-defined resource attributes.

If an application resource's PLACEMENT is set to "restricted" and there are no other HOSTING_MEMBERS available, you will see the following error.

```
# caa_relocate memberUP
molari : Resource memberUP (application) cannot run on molari
Resource memberUP has placement error.
```

The resource will continue running on the member where it is currently placed.

A final note regarding relocation: you can use "-s" option to relocate all the resources currently running on that member to another member.

```
# caa_relocate -s molari
Attempting to stop `memberUP` on member `molari`
Stop of `memberUP` on member `molari` succeeded.
Attempting to start `nicUP` on member `sheridan`
Start of `nicUP` on member `sheridan` succeeded.
Attempting to start `memberUP` on member `sheridan`
Start of `memberUP` on member `sheridan` succeeded.
Attempting to stop `cluster_lockd` on member `molari`
Stop of `cluster_lockd` on member `molari` succeeded.
Attempting to start `cluster_lockd` on member `sheridan`
Start of `cluster_lockd` on member `sheridan` succeeded.
```

Note, resources with a PLACEMENT of "restricted" will not relocate unless another member in the HOSTING_MEMBER attribute is available. Also, a resource's REQUIRED_RESOURCES must be available on the target member in order for the relocation to succeed.

For more information regarding resource relocation, see the caa_relocate(8) reference page.

23.4.17 Load-Balancing Resources

Placement of an application resource, based on the load of a particular cluster member, can be accomplished using one of methods shown in Table 23-12.

Application Resource Placement and Load-Balancing

		Approach	V5.1B	V5.1A	V5.1	V5.0A
command	`caa_start`	The Cluster Administrator runs the **`caa_start`** command and the resource is optimally placed based on its **`PLACEMENT`** while modified by optional (**`OPTIONAL_RESOURCES`**) and/or required (**`REQUIRED_RESOURCES`**) dependencies.	✓	✓	✓	✓
command	`caa_relocate`	The Cluster Administrator runs the **`caa_relocate`** command and the resource is optimally placed based on its **`PLACEMENT`** while modified by optional (**`OPTIONAL_RESOURCES`**) and/or required (**`REQUIRED_RESOURCES`**) dependencies.	✓	✓	✓	✓
command	`caa_balance`	The Cluster Administrator runs the **`caa_balance`** command and the placement of resources are reevaluated by the Resource Manager. Load-balancing can be reevaluated for the set of application resources listed, by the application resources on the member listed, or by all application resources in the cluster.	✓	✗	✗	✗
cluster	**formation**	When the cluster is formed, all resources with a **`TARGET`** state of **`ONLINE`**, or a **`TARGET`** state of **`OFFLINE`** and **`AUTO_START`** set to 1 will be started and optimally placed based on its **`PLACEMENT`** while modified by optional (**`OPTIONAL_RESOURCES`**) and/or required (**`REQUIRED_RESOURCES`**) dependencies.	✓	✓	✓	✓
cluster	**member join**	When a member joins the cluster any resource with an **`ACTIVE_PLACEMENT`** value of 1 will be reevaluated based on its **`PLACEMENT`** while modified by optional (**`OPTIONAL_RESOURCES`**) and/or required (**`REQUIRED_RESOURCES`**) dependencies and possibly relocated. Note that **`AUTO_START`** is also evaluated (see **formation**)	✓	✓	✓	✓
cluster	**member leave**	When a member leaves the cluster any resource that was running on that member will be optimally placed on another member based on the resource's **`PLACEMENT`** while modified by optional (**`OPTIONAL_RESOURCES`**) and/or required (**`REQUIRED_RESOURCES`**) dependencies. This can result in a resource not relocating to another, but rather, stopped.	✓	✓	✓	✓
time		An application resource's placement is reevaluated for optimal placement at the time set in the **`REBALANCE`** attribute, if set.	✓	✗	✗	✗

Table 23-12: Application Resource Load-Balancing Options

23.4.17.1 Command-Initiated

There are three commands that cause CAA to evaluate the placement and balance of application resources:

- The `caa_balance` command.
- The `caa_start` command (covered in section 23.4.14).
- The `caa_relocate` command (covered in section 23.4.16).

Starting in V5.1B, the `caa_balance` command can be used at any time to reevaluate the placement of application resources within the cluster.

- Reevaluate all application resources in the cluster.

```
# caa_balance -all
Attempting to stop `cluster_lockd` on member `alph11`
Stop of `cluster_lockd` on member `alph11` succeeded.
Attempting to start `cluster_lockd` on member `alph12`
Start of `cluster_lockd` on member `alph12` succeeded.
Resource clustercron is already well placed
Resource memberUP is already well placed
Resource powerUP is already well placed
clustercron is placed optimally. No relocation is needed.
memberUP is placed optimally. No relocation is needed.
powerUP is placed optimally. No relocation is needed.
```

- Reevaluate the resources on a particular cluster member.

```
# caa_balance -s molari
Attempting to stop `cluster_lockd` on member `alph12`
Stop of `cluster_lockd` on member `alph12` succeeded.
Attempting to start `cluster_lockd` on member `alph11`
Start of `cluster_lockd` on member `alph11` succeeded.
Resource memberUP is already well placed
Resource powerUP is already well placed
memberUP is placed optimally. No relocation is needed.
powerUP is placed optimally. No relocation is needed.
```

- Reevaluate specific application resources.

```
# caa_balance memberUP powerUP
Resource memberUP is already well placed
Attempting to stop `powerUP` on member `alph11`
Stop of `powerUP` on member `alph11` succeeded.
Attempting to start `powerUP` on member `alph12`
Start of `powerUP` on member `alph12` succeeded.
memberUP is placed optimally. No relocation is needed.
```

For more information on application resource load-balancing, see the `caa_balance(8)` reference page as well as the *TruCluster* Server Cluster Highly Available Applications guide.

23.4.17.2 Cluster-Initiated

When the cluster is formed, or a member joins or leaves the cluster, CAA will balance the application resource's load based on the following criteria:

- When the cluster is formed, resources are started and load-balanced based on:
  - The AUTO_START attribute.
  - The ACTIVE_PLACEMENT attribute.
  - The PLACEMENT and HOSTING_MEMBERS attributes.
  - The REQUIRED_RESOURCES and OPTIONAL_RESOURCES attributes.

- If a member joins the cluster, resources are load-balanced based on:
  - The ACTIVE_PLACEMENT attribute.
  - The PLACEMENT and HOSTING_MEMBERS attributes.
  - The REQUIRED_RESOURCES and OPTIONAL_RESOURCES attributes.

- If a member leaves the cluster, resources failover (and load-balanced) based on:
  - The PLACEMENT and HOSTING_MEMBERS attributes.
  - The REQUIRED_RESOURCES and OPTIONAL_RESOURCES attributes.

23.4.17.2.1 Resource Placement and Load Balance at Cluster Formation

CAA determines which resources to start as follows:

- If a resource's TARGET state is ONLINE, start the resource.
- If a resource's TARGET start is OFFLINE, but AUTO_START is set to 1, start the resource.

When CAA starts resources, it must place the resource on a member that meets the criteria set forth in the resource's profile, and the number of resources currently running in the cluster.

Determine the PLACEMENT of the resource. If PLACEMENT is "favored" or "restricted", then determine what HOSTING_MEMBERS are available.

- PLACEMENT is "balanced"
  - No Dependencies

    Place the resource on the member with the fewest number of online resources.
  - OPTIONAL_RESOURCES

    Place the resource on the member that has the requisite resource(s) available AND has the fewest number of resources running. If there are no members that have the requisite resource(s) available, start on the member running the least number of resources.

- `REQUIRED_RESOURCES`

  Place the resource on the member that has the requisite resource(s) available AND has the fewest number of resources running. If no members have the requisite resource(s) available, do not start.

- `PLACEMENT` is "`favored`"

  - No Dependencies

    Place the resource on the favored member with the fewest number of online resources. If there are no favored members available, place the resource on the non-favored member with the fewest number of online resources.

  - `OPTIONAL_RESOURCES`

    Place the resource on the favored member that has the requisite resource(s) available AND has the fewest number of resources running.

    If there are no favored members available, but there is a non-favored member with the requisite resource(s), then start the resource on the non-favored member.

    If there are no members with the requisite resource(s) available, start the resource on a favored member anyway.

    If there are no favored members available AND no non-favored members available with the requisite resource(s) available, start the resource on a non-favored member anyway.

  - `REQUIRED_RESOURCES`

    Place the resource on the favored member that has the requisite resource(s) available AND has the fewest number of resources running. If there are no favored members with the requisite resource(s) available, but there is a non-favored member with the requisite resource(s), then start the resource on the non-favored member. If no members have the requisite resource(s) available, do not start.

- `PLACEMENT` is "`restricted`"

  - No Dependencies

    Place the resource on the restricted member with the fewest number of online resources. If there are no restricted members available, do not start.

  - `OPTIONAL_RESOURCES`

    Place the resource on the restricted member that has the requisite resource(s) available AND has the fewest number of resources running. If no restricted members have the requisite resource(s) available, start on a restricted member anyway.

  - `REQUIRED_RESOURCES`

    Place the resource on the restricted member that has the requisite resource(s) available AND has the fewest number of resources running. If no restricted members have the requisite resource(s) available, do not start.

23.4.17.2.2 Resource Placement and Load Balancing When a Member Joins the Cluster

Placement and load balancing will only take place if there are resources that are currently ONLINE that have an ACTIVE_PLACEMENT set to 1.

If a resource has the ACTIVE_PLACEMENT attribute set to 1, then the resource might relocate to the joining member. Whether or not the resource will actually relocate to the joining member is determined by CAA based on the resource's PLACEMENT, HOSTING_MEMBERS, OPTIONAL_RESOURCES, and REQUIRED_RESOURCES attributes as discussed in section 23.4.17.2.1.

23.4.17.2.3 Resource Placement and Load Balancing When a Member Leaves the Cluster

This is the classic resource failover scenario. A resource will locate to another cluster member as long as the placement policy for the resource is satisfied and dependencies for the resource are available on another cluster member. The placement policy and dependency determination were discussed in section 23.4.17.2.1.

23.4.17.3 Time-Initiated

Also starting in V5.1B, the REBALANCE attribute was added to the application resource profile. The REBALANCE attribute contains a time specification denoting when the application resource should have its placement reevaluated. The time specification value has the following format:

t:day:hour:minute

day	=	0-6 (where Sunday = 0)
hour	=	0-23
minute	=	0-59

An asterisk (*) can be used to designate every day, hour, or minute.
Multiple values can be comma delimited, although a range cannot be specified as of this writing.

For example, to have an application resource's placement reevaluated every Monday @ 2:10PM:

```
REBALANCE=t:1:14:10
```

To have an application resource's placement reevaluated every day @ 20 minutes after every hour:

```
REBALANCE=t:*:*:20
```

Here's an example where we actually set the memberUP resource's REBALANCE attribute and update its registration.

1. Set the REBALANCE attribute to reevaluate every Monday, Wednesday, and Friday at Midnight and Noon.

```
# caa_profile -update memberUP -o bt="t:1,3,5:00,12:00"
```

2. Update the registration.

```
# caa_register -u memberUP
REBALANCE entries will be added to clustercron
```

3. Verify the change has taken place.

```
# caa_stat -p memberUP | grep REBALANCE
REBALANCE=t:1,3,5:00,12:00
```

NOTE:

Application resource load balancing is accomplished using a cluster-wide cron(8) application resource (clustercron), which was introduced in V5.1B.

A similar solution is documented in the "Using cron in a *TruCluster* Server Cluster" Best Practice, September, 2001. However, the clustercron application resource implementation we are discussing here is strictly for use by CAA and should not be used as a general-purpose cluster-wide cron.

Essentially, clustercron is implemented as a single-instance, high-availability application. Its job is to ensure that certain cluster-related tasks are run from cron. Whatever member clustercron is running on will have its root crontab file modified to run those cluster-related tasks.

For example, when we updated memberUP's registration, the following message was displayed:

```
REBALANCE entries will be added to clustercron
```

An entry was placed in the crontab of the member where clustercron is running, which instructs cron to execute the "caa_balance memberUP" command every Monday, Wednesday, and Friday at Midnight and Noon.

Let's prove it. First, see where clustercron is running.

```
# caa_stat -t clustercron
Name            Type           Target     State      Host
------------------------------------------------------------
clustercron     application    ONLINE     ONLINE     molari
```

Since clustercron is running on node molari, we'll search its crontab file for the memberUP application resource.

```
[molari]
# /usr/bin/crontab -l | grep memberUP
00 00,12 * * 1,3,5 /usr/sbin/caa_balance memberUP     #clustercronData
```

For information on how to create your own cluster-wide cron solution, see the Best Practice, "Using cron in a *TruCluster* Server Cluster," available at:

http://www.tru64unix.compaq.com/docs/best_practices.

23.4.18 Resource Availability Statistics

In V5.1B, a resource's availability can be obtained using the caa_report command. You can see the statistics of every resource by using the command without any switches, or, by using the "-a" switch, you can choose which resources to return statistics on.

```
# caa_report -a "memberUP powerUP"
Time report for period from earliest known begin-date to Wed Jul 3 00:02:10 2002

        Application Availability Report for babylon5

Applications            starting/ending              uptime
---------------------------------------------------------------
memberUP                Tue Jul  2 23:40:44 2002     99.61 %
                        Wed Jul  3 00:02:10 2002

powerUP                 Tue Jul  2 23:41:06 2002     99.05 %
                        Wed Jul  3 00:02:10 2002
```

The caa_report command can return only those resources that have non-zero statistics by using the "-o" switch. Additionally, using the caa_report command with the "-s" switch will return all resources where statistics exist.

An application's availability for a particular time period can be obtained using the "-b *time*" and "-e *time*" switches for a beginning and end time range respectively, where *time* is in the form of *mm/dd/yy:hh:mm*.

To see that memberUP is available from June 15, 2002 at Midnight to the present, you can use the following command:

```
# caa_report -a memberUP -s 6/15/02:00:00
```

For more information, see the caa_report(1) reference page.

23.4.19 Resource Status

As you have probably noticed by now, a resource's status can be determined by using the caa_stat command. There are two primary forms of output generated by the caa_stat command: list output (multiple lines per resource) and tabular output (one-line per resource).

List output is the default, whereas tabular output is achieved by using the "-t" switch. Note, there is an "-l" (lowercase "L") switch to the caa_stat command that can be used for list output, although it is implied.

Most of the output you have seen in this chapter has been in tabular form, primarily because the output is more compact.

Here is an example of the list output showing the following forms of output for the caa_stat command:

- Default output.
- Verbose output (the "-v" switch).
- The in-memory profile (or currently registered attribute values) obtained using the "-p" switch.
- Full output obtained using the "-f" switch (a combination of the "-p" and "-v" switches).

Default	Verbose	Currently Registered Attribute Values	Full (Verbose + CRAV)
# caa_stat ARes NAME=ARes TYPE=application TARGET=ONLINE STATE=ONLINE on molari	**# caa_stat -v ARes** NAME=ARes TYPE=application RESTART_ATTEMPTS=1 RESTART_COUNT=0 REBALANCE=t:*:1:0 FAILURE_THRESHOLD=0 FAILURE_COUNT=0 TARGET=ONLINE STATE=ONLINE on molari	**# caa_stat -p ARes** NAME=ARes TYPE=application ACTION_SCRIPT=ARes.scr ACTIVE_PLACEMENT=0 AUTO_START=0 CHECK_INTERVAL=60 DESCRIPTION=ARes FAILOVER_DELAY=0 FAILURE_INTERVAL=0 FAILURE_THRESHOLD=0 HOSTING_MEMBERS= OPTIONAL_RESOURCES= PLACEMENT=balanced REBALANCE=t:*:1:0 REQUIRED_RESOURCES= RESTART_ATTEMPTS=1 SCRIPT_TIMEOUT=60	**# caa_stat -f ARes** NAME=ARes TYPE=application ACTION_SCRIPT=ARes.scr ACTIVE_PLACEMENT=0 AUTO_START=0 CHECK_INTERVAL=60 RESTART_ATTEMPTS=1 RESTART_COUNT=0 DESCRIPTION=ARes FAILOVER_DELAY=0 FAILURE_INTERVAL=0 HOSTING_MEMBERS= OPTIONAL_RESOURCES= PLACEMENT=balanced REBALANCE=t:*:1:0 REQUIRED_RESOURCES= SCRIPT_TIMEOUT=60 FAILURE_THRESHOLD=0 FAILURE_COUNT=0 TARGET=ONLINE STATE=ONLINE on molari

Table 23-13: caa_stat Output

23.4.19.1 How Can I Determine If a Resource is Registered?

There are a couple of ways to determine whether or not a resource is registered. You can use the caa_stat command followed by the resource name. If the resource is not registered you will receive an error.

```
# caa_stat aNonRegisteredResource
Could not find resource aNonRegisteredResource.
```

However, if you're writing a script, it would be much easier to be able to check the return status of the caa_stat command by using the "-g" switch with the "-a *resource*" switch.

```
# caa_stat -g -a memberUP ; echo $?
0
```

If the resource is registered, a zero is returned.

```
# caa_stat -g -a aNonRegisteredResource ; echo $?
1
```

If the resource is not registered, a value of "1" is returned.

23.4.19.2 How Can I Determine If a Resource is Running?

You can use the caa_stat command followed by the resource name. If the resource's STATE is ONLINE, it's running.

You can use the caa_stat command with the "-r -a *resource*" switches to check the return status. This is particularly useful if you're writing a script.

```
# caa_stat -r -a memberUP ; echo $?
0
```

If the resource is running, a zero is returned. Conversely, if the resource is not running, a "1" is returned.

```
# caa_stop memberUP
Attempting to stop `memberUP` on member `alph12`
Stop of `memberUP` on member `alph12` succeeded.
```

```
# caa_stat -r -a memberUP ; echo $?
1
```

23.4.19.3 How Can I Determine Which Attribute Values are Registered For a Given Resource?

You can use the caa_stat command with "-p" switch to see the currently registered attribute values for a given resource. Note, this can be particularly useful in determining whether you remembered to update the registration of a resource after modifying its profile.

Note, that what is actually registered may be different from what is in your profile.

Currently Registered (In Memory):

```
# caa_stat -p nicUP

NAME=nicUP
TYPE=network
DESCRIPTION=nicUP
FAILURE_INTERVAL=600
FAILURE_THRESHOLD=2
SUBNET=192.168.0.0
```

In Profile:

```
# caa_profile -print nicUP

NAME=nicUP
TYPE=network
DESCRIPTION=nicUP
FAILURE_INTERVAL=0
FAILURE_THRESHOLD=0
SUBNET=192.168.0.0
```

Remember to update your registration when you modify your profile (see section 23.4.12).

23.4.19.4 How Can I See Which Resources are Running On a Particular Cluster Member?

The caa_stat command with the "-c *hostname*" switch can be used to retrieve resource status for a particular cluster member.

```
# caa_stat -t -c molari

Name          Type          Target    State     Host
------------------------------------------------------------
clustercron   application   ONLINE    ONLINE    molari
memberUP      application   ONLINE    ONLINE    molari
nicUP         network       ONLINE    ONLINE    molari
```

For more information, see the caa_stat(1) reference page.

23.5 The Action Script

Every Application resource must have an action script. The action script starts and stops the application resource as well as optionally checking the status of the application resource.

The action script can be written in any language. The only requirement is that the script accept a "start", "stop", and (optionally) "check" arguments on the command line.

- myAppResource.scr start – Starts myAppResource
- myAppResource.scr stop – Stops myAppResource
- myAppResource.scr check – Checks the status of myAppResource

The *TruCluster* Server software includes a `template.scr` that the `caa_profile` command uses to create an application resource. The `template.scr` script, which is located in the `/var/cluster/caa/template` directory, includes all three entry points.

NOTE:

The `template.scr` script is different in nearly every *TruCluster* Server release we've seen to date. Therefore, the output in this book that pertains to this script may differ from that on your cluster.

23.5.1 Application Resource Action Script Tips

This section contains suggestions for what to think about when writing an action script.

1. Completely test your script before registering your application resource.
2. The action script should be named in the form of `AppResourceName.scr`.

   If your application resource is named "`guitar`", then it is a good idea to name the action script `guitar.scr`. This is not a requirement, but we recommend keeping things consistent and simple to avoid confusion.
3. Make sure that your script is located in the `/var/cluster/caa/script` directory and that you edit the `ACTION_SCRIPT` attribute in the application resource's profile to be the name of the script. If you choose to place the action script in an alternate directory, make sure it is on a disk physically shared by all members in the cluster and not mounted as a partitioned file system. Partitioned file systems were covered in Chapter 13. If the action script is located in an alternate directory, then the `ACTION_SCRIPT` attribute must contain the full pathname.

   If the action script is…

   in `/var/cluster/caa/script` – `ACTION_SCRIPT = guitar.scr`

   not in `/var/cluster/caa/script` – `ACTION_SCRIPT = /altScrDir/guitar.scr`

   We recommend keeping all action scripts in the `/var/cluster/caa/script` directory.
4. Add environment variables that the action script may need to properly execute.

   The action script will not be running with the benefit of the environment variables that are in a user's `.profile`, `.kshrc`, or `.login` scripts. For example, if the application were an X Window System application, the `DISPLAY` environment variable would need to be set.
5. Verify that the action script has the execute permission bit set.
6. Verify that the action script is owned by `root`, and that only `root` has permission to write to the script.
7. The exit status is defined as:

   0 (zero) – Success
   !0 (not zero) – Failure

8. If your application is designed to run in the foreground, make sure to put it in the background otherwise your action script will timeout (see SCRIPT_TIMEOUT above), which is considered a failure by caad.

9. Remember to redirect stdin, stdout, and stderr if necessary.

23.5.2 Redirecting Action Script Output

By default an action script does not open stdin, stdout, and stderr. So, if you need your action script to receive input and/or write output, you will need to handle this explicitly.

For example, within the action script for the memberUP resource, we placed "print" statements within the start and stop entry points. We did not redirect the output.

```
# grep print memberUP.scr

    print "Entering the 'start' entry point for $_CAA_NAME..."
    print "Entering the 'stop' entry point for $_CAA_NAME..."
```

We will start the memberUP resource.

```
# caa_start memberUP

Attempting to start `memberUP` on member `sheridan`
Start of `memberUP` on member `sheridan` succeeded.
```

Note that the output does not include our print statement.

There are a couple of methods of getting information from your action script:

- Redirect stdin, stdout, and stderr as you would within any script.

  ```
  $START_APPCMD > $tmpfile 2>&1
  ```

- Set the _CAA_UI_FMT environment variable, which was introduced in V5.1A-IPK, to redirect output of an action script to your stdout when using the caa_start, caa_stop, and caa_relocate commands.

  Valid values for the _CAA_UI_FMT environment variable are:

  - v – Verbose

    ```
    sheridan:memberUP:Entering the 'start' entry point for memberUP...
    ```

  - vs – Verbose, but suppress the "member:resource:" information

    ```
    Entering the 'start' entry point for memberUP...
    ```

  Set the environment as you would any shell environment variable.

To complete the example we started at the beginning of this section, let's set the environment variable and then stop the memberUP resource.

```
# export _CAA_UI_FMT=v
```

```
# caa_stop memberUP
Attempting to stop `memberUP` on member `sheridan`
Stop of `memberUP` on member `sheridan` succeeded.
sheridan:memberUP:Entering the 'stop' entry point for memberUP...
```

You can see by the previous output, stdout was redirected as expected.

23.5.3 CAA Action Script Environment Variables

Introduced in V5.1-IPK, an application resource action script is able to access a number of environment variables in the following categories:

- Profile Attributes
- Reason Codes
- User-Defined Attributes
- Locale Information

23.5.3.1 Profile Attribute Environment Variables

Any profile attribute can be accessed within an application resource's action script by adding the "_CAA_" prefix to the attribute name.

To see the resource's SCRIPT_TIMEOUT value, use the _CAA_SCRIPT_TIMEOUT environment variable for example.

Here is a short and extremely simple code snippet (in Korn shell) illustrating how you can make decisions based on the value of a particular attribute value.

```
# grep -p ARG memberUP.scr
if [[ $_CAA_REQUIRED_RESOURCES != "" ]]     ← If there are any Required Resources...
then
  ARG="REQ"                                 ← Set ARG to "REQ"
fi

if [[ $_CAA_OPTIONAL_RESOURCES != "" ]]     ← If there are any Optional Resources...
then
  ARG="${ARG}OPT"                           ← Set ARG to the current value of ARG plus
fi                                            the string "OPT".

START_APPCMD="/code/caa/xhostname $ARG"
```

In this example, the action script checks to see if the resource has any required or optional resources that it depends upon. If it does, an additional parameter is passed to the program that the resource will start.

The REQUIRED_RESOURCES and OPTIONAL_RESOURCES are shown in the following output.

```
# caa_stat -p memberUP | grep _RESOURCE

OPTIONAL_RESOURCES=nicUP
REQUIRED_RESOURCES=powerUP
```

So the START_APPCMD would be set to "/code/caa/xhostname REQOPT".

23.5.3.2 Reason Code Environment Variable

When an application resource's action script is called, the _CAA_REASON environment variable is set to the reason the script was called. Valid reasons are shown in Table 23-14.

23.5.3.3 User-Defined Attributes and Environment Variables

User-defined attributes can be added to application resources by defining the new attribute in the application.tdf file that is located in the /var/cluster/caa/template directory. Once defined, the user-defined attributes can be used from within an application resource profile and action script.

Note, user-defined resource attributes should always start with "USR_" so that your attribute names do not conflict with CAA resource attributes that exist (or may exist in a future release).

Furthermore, the caa_start, caa_stop, and caa_relocate commands have been modified to be able to override user-defined attributes that are defined in an application resource profile when starting, stopping, or relocating the resource. This action is not permanent – it does not modify the resource profile. It merely overrides the value for the running (or soon to be non-running) instance and is designed to be used to modify the behavior of the action script.

23.5.3.3.1 Creating a User-Defined Attribute

Defining a user-defined attribute simply involves defining the attribute in the application.tdf file.

1. Save the original application.tdf file.

```
# cd /var/cluster/caa/template
```

```
# cp application.tdf application.tdf.orig
```

CAA Reason Codes

Reason	Description
`user`	The action script was invoked by user action. The cluster administrator ran a **`caa_*`** command.
`failure`	The action script was invoked from the result of a failure condition. This reason is usually set as a result of failure in the "**`check`**" entry point.
`dependency`	The action script was invoked as a result of being a dependency of another resource. For example, if the **`powerUP`** resource is a dependent of the **`memberUP`** resource, and both resources are **`OFFLINE`**, then if the **`memberUP`** resource is started, the **`powerUP`** resource would also be started. This value would be set in the **`_CAA_REASON`** environment variable for **`powerUP`**.
`boot`	The action script was invoked when the cluster was booted. The resource was running prior to cluster shutdown.
`autostart`	The action script was invoked when the cluster was booted. The resource's **`AUTO_START`** attribute was set to **`1`** and the resource was **`OFFLINE`** prior to cluster shutdown.
`system`	The action script was invoked by the system during normal maintenance.
`unknown`	If the **`_CAA_REASON`** is set to this state the action script was invoked when the internal state was unknown. If this value is set, record the state of the application and the cluster, then contact the HP Customer Support Center.

Table 23-14: CAA Reason Codes

2. Add the attribute.

   We decided to add two attributes to be used to manage a cluster alias from our application resource.

```
# grep -p ALIAS application.tdf

#!==========================
attribute: USR_ALIAS_NAME
type: name_string
switch: -o an
default:
required: no

#!==========================
attribute: USR_ALIAS_IP
type: internet_address
switch: -o aa
default:
required: no
```

3. You can now use the attribute.

   For example, we will create a new application resource using the new attributes.

```
# caa_profile -create aliasAPP -t application -B /code/caa/aliasAPP \
> -o an=caa_alias,aa=192.168.1.71
```

   We can verify that the resource was created by printing the resource profile using the `caa_profile` command. Note the output has been trimmed.

```
# caa_profile -print aliasAPP | grep -E "NAME|ALIAS"

NAME=aliasAPP
USR_ALIAS_IP=192.168.1.71
USR_ALIAS_NAME=caa_alias
```

23.5.3.3.2 Using a User-Defined Attribute in an Action Script

User-defined attributes can be accessed within an application resource's action script by adding an underscore prefix to the attribute name.

For example, we added two `print` statements to the action script of the `aliasAPP` resource we created in the previous section.

```
# grep print aliasAPP.scr

print "_USR_ALIAS_NAME = \"$_USR_ALIAS_NAME\""
print "   _USR_ALIAS_IP = \"$_USR_ALIAS_IP\""
```

We still have the `_CAA_UI_FMT` environment variable set from section 23.5.2, so all we need to do is register and start the resource (of course, we had to modify the action script and test it too).

```
# caa_register aliasAPP
```

```
# caa_start aliasAPP

Attempting to start `aliasAPP` on member `sheridan`
Start of `aliasAPP` on member `sheridan` succeeded.
_USR_ALIAS_NAME = "caa_alias"
   _USR_ALIAS_IP = "192.168.1.71"
```

As you see by the output, our user-defined attributes are accessible from the action script.

23.5.3.3.3 Modifying a User-Defined Attribute Value Temporarily

You can temporarily modify a user-defined attribute using the `caa_start`, `caa_stop`, and `caa_relocate` commands.

For example, we will relocate aliasAPP and change the USR_ALIAS_NAME and USR_ALIAS_IP using the caa_relocate command.

```
# caa_relocate USR_ALIAS_NAME=clu_faf USR_ALIAS_IP=192.168.1.77 aliasAPP

Attempting to stop `aliasAPP` on member `molari`
Stop of `aliasAPP` on member `molari` succeeded.
Attempting to start `aliasAPP` on member `sheridan`
Start of `aliasAPP` on member `sheridan` succeeded.
sheridan:aliasAPP:_USR_ALIAS_NAME = "clu_faf"
sheridan:aliasAPP:   _USR_ALIAS_IP = "192.168.1.77"
molari:aliasAPP:_USR_ALIAS_NAME = "clu_faf"
molari:aliasAPP:   _USR_ALIAS_IP = "192.168.1.77"
Start of `aliasAPP` on member `molari` succeeded.
```

Note the values were modified. Let's relocate it back to the other member. This time we will not modify the attribute values.

```
# caa_relocate aliasAPP

Attempting to stop `aliasAPP` on member `molari`
Stop of `aliasAPP` on member `molari` succeeded.
Attempting to start `aliasAPP` on member `sheridan`
Start of `aliasAPP` on member `sheridan` succeeded.
molari:aliasAPP:_USR_ALIAS_NAME = "caa_alias"
molari:aliasAPP:   _USR_ALIAS_IP = "192.168.1.71"
sheridan:aliasAPP:_USR_ALIAS_NAME = "caa_alias"
sheridan:aliasAPP:   _USR_ALIAS_IP = "192.168.1.71"
```

The attribute values are returned to those defined in the resource profile.

23.5.3.4 Locale Information Environment Variable

The _CAA_CLIENT_LOCALE environment variable contains a whitespace delimited list of the current locale where the action script is invoked.

The locale information contained in the list is in the following order:

LC_ALL, LC_CTYPE, LC_MONETARY, LC_NUMERIC, LC_TIME, LC_MESSAGES

Here is an example output from an application resource when we started it in the cluster.

```
# grep _CAA_CLIENT_LOCALE /var/cluster/caa/script/powerUP.scr
  print "_CAA_CLIENT_LOCALE = \"$_CAA_CLIENT_LOCALE\""
```

Since we still have the _CAA_UI_FMT environment variable set from section 23.5.2, we will start the powerUP resource but grep(1) for only the _CAA_CLIENT_LOCALE output.

```
# caa_start powerUP | grep _CAA_CLIENT_LOCALE
_CAA_CLIENT_LOCALE = "C C C C C C"
```

For more information on locales, see the `locales(5)`, `locale(1)`, and `setlocale(3)` reference pages.

23.6 Resource Attributes Revisited

We were thinking about resource attributes, considering the tables presented earlier in the chapter (see section 23.4.4), and several interesting questions popped into our collective mind. What questions exactly? Read on.

In the following examples, the dependent resource is `memberUP`, the supporting cast of resources is `nicUP` (a network resource) and `powerUP` (an application resource).

23.6.1 Dependencies – Optional or Required?

- If a resource is dependent on another resource, what happens if the resource it is depending on goes away or relocates?

  To answer this question, let's consider two scenarios:

  1. `powerUP` is an `OPTIONAL_RESOURCE` of `memberUP`.

```
# caa_stat -t -v memberUP powerUP

Name              Type             R/RA    F/FT    Target     State      Host
-------------------------------------------------------------------------------
memberUP          application      0/1     0/0     OFFLINE    OFFLINE
powerUP           application      0/1     0/0     ONLINE     ONLINE     molari
```

Update memberUP's profile so that powerUP is an OPTIONAL_RESOURCE.

```
# caa_profile -update memberUP -l powerUP
```

Update the CAA registry with the updated `memberUP` profile and start `memberUP`.

```
# caa_register -u memberUP && caa_start memberUP

Attempting to start `memberUP` on member `molari`
Start of `memberUP` on member `molari` succeeded.
```

Okay, both resources are running on `molari`. Let's stop `powerUP`.

```
# caa_stop powerUP

Attempting to stop `powerUP` on member `molari`
Stop of `powerUP` on member `molari` succeeded.
```

Did this adversely affect `memberUP`?

```
# caa_stat -t -v memberUP powerUP

Name            Type            R/RA    F/FT    Target    State     Host
------------------------------------------------------------------------
memberUP        application     0/1     0/0     ONLINE    ONLINE    molari
powerUP         application     0/1     0/0     OFFLINE   OFFLINE
```

Should it have? No, powerUP is only "optional"; therefore, memberUP will not stop (or even relocate). If powerUP were "required" however…

2. powerUP is a REQUIRED_RESOURCE of memberUP.

   The first thing we need to do here is modify memberUP's profile, stop memberUP, and update the registry.

```
# caa_profile -update memberUP -l "" -r powerUP ; caa_stop memberUP

Attempting to stop `memberUP` on member `molari`
Stop of `memberUP` on member `molari` succeeded.
```

```
# caa_register -u memberUP ; caa_start memberUP

Attempting to start `powerUP` on member `molari`
Start of `powerUP` on member `molari` succeeded.
Attempting to start `memberUP` on member `molari`
Start of `memberUP` on member `molari` succeeded.
```

Note that powerUP started as well. This is due to the fact that memberUP now requires powerUP to be running on the same member. Let's see what happens if we attempt to relocate or stop powerUP.

```
# caa_relocate powerUP

sheridan : Resource memberUP (application) is running on molari

Resource powerUP has placement error.
```

```
# caa_stop powerUP

Resources depending on powerUP are running
Resource powerUP has placement error.
```

No joy. Can we force powerUP to relocate or stop? The "-f" option to the caa_relocate (or caa_start) command allows CAA to stop and/or start those resources, upon which the application resource depends, to enable the task to succeed. For example, since we want to relocate memberUP to molari, but memberUP requires powerUP (which is currently on sheridan), stop powerUP as well as memberUP and start them both on molari.

```
# caa_relocate powerUP -f

Attempting to stop `memberUP` on member `molari`
Stop of `memberUP` on member `molari` succeeded.
Attempting to stop `powerUP` on member `molari`
Stop of `powerUP` on member `molari` succeeded.
Attempting to start `powerUP` on member `sheridan`
Start of `powerUP` on member `sheridan` succeeded.
Attempting to start `memberUP` on member `sheridan`
Start of `memberUP` on member `sheridan` succeeded.
```

```
# caa_stat -t -v memberUP powerUP

Name           Type          R/RA   F/FT   Target    State     Host
----------------------------------------------------------------------
memberUP       application   0/1    0/0    ONLINE    ONLINE    sheridan
powerUP        application   0/1    0/0    ONLINE    ONLINE    sheridan
```

```
# caa_stop powerUP -f

Attempting to stop `memberUP` on member `sheridan`
Stop of `memberUP` on member `sheridan` succeeded.
Attempting to stop `powerUP` on member `sheridan`
Stop of `powerUP` on member `sheridan` succeeded.
```

```
# caa_stat -t -v memberUP powerUP

Name           Type          R/RA   F/FT   Target    State     Host
----------------------------------------------------------------------
memberUP       application   0/1    0/0    OFFLINE   OFFLINE
powerUP        application   0/1    0/0    OFFLINE   OFFLINE
```

So we were able to successfully relocate and stop `powerUP` forcefully; however, `memberUP` was also relocated and stopped.

Finally, to complete our answer to the first question, let's add `nicUP` as a `REQUIRED_RESOURCE`, update the CAA registration database, start `memberUP`, and then unplug the network associated with `nicUP`.

```
# caa_profile -update memberUP -l "" -r "powerUP nicUP"
```

```
# caa_register -u memberUP ; caa_start memberUP

Attempting to start `powerUP` on member `sheridan`
Start of `powerUP` on member `sheridan` succeeded.
Attempting to start `nicUP` on member `sheridan`
Start of `nicUP` on member `sheridan` succeeded.
Attempting to start `memberUP` on member `sheridan`
Start of `memberUP` on member `sheridan` succeeded.
```

Prior to unplugging the network, you may want to start `evmwatch(1)` to monitor the failover activity.

```
# evmwatch -A -t "@name [@priority]\n@@\n"
```

Note that use of the "\n" in the "-t" option was introduced in V5.1A.

As there will be many events generated, the output is not shown. NIFF will mark the network interface as down and this will generate an event (sys.unix.hw.net.niff.down). In Table 23-2 we listed the EVM events that CAA subscribes to – note that sys.unix.hw.net.niff.down is one of the events that network resource monitor is interested in. As a result, CAA initiates a relocation of memberUP and powerUP.

```
# caa_stat -t -v memberUP powerUP nicUP

Name           Type           R/RA   F/FT   Target    State     Host
-----------------------------------------------------------------------
memberUP       application    0/1    0/0    ONLINE    ONLINE    molari
nicUP          network         -     0/2    ONLINE    ONLINE    molari
nicUP          network         -     0/2    ONLINE    OFFLINE   sheridan
powerUP        application    0/1    0/0    ONLINE    ONLINE    molari
```

- If you have a resource that is depending on multiple resources, what happens if these resources are not all running on the same members? Where does the dependent resource start?

  This is merely an extension of our last example. Let's stop memberUP, relocate powerUP to sheridan, and then start memberUP and see what happens.

```
# caa_stop memberUP ; caa_relocate powerUP -c sheridan

Attempting to stop `memberUP` on member `molari`
Stop of `memberUP` on member `molari` succeeded.
Attempting to stop `powerUP` on member `molari`
Stop of `powerUP` on member `molari` succeeded.
Attempting to start `powerUP` on member `sheridan`
Start of `powerUP` on member `sheridan` succeeded.
```

```
# caa_start memberUP

molari : Resource powerUP (application) is already running on sheridan
sheridan : Resource nicUP (network) is not available on sheridan

Resource memberUP has placement error.
```

We get an error. Okay, let's try to force it.

```
# caa_start memberUP -f

Attempting to stop `powerUP` on member `sheridan`
Stop of `powerUP` on member `sheridan` succeeded.
Attempting to start `powerUP` on member `molari`
Start of `powerUP` on member `molari` succeeded.
Attempting to start `nicUP` on member `molari`
Start of `nicUP` on member `molari` succeeded.
Attempting to start `memberUP` on member `molari`
Start of `memberUP` on member `molari` succeeded.
```

That works. What if the resources were not required but optional? Then memberUP would start on the member with the most optional resources available.

23.6.2 Dependencies Versus Placement Policy

- If a resource is favored to a member, but the resource it depends on is running on a non-favored member, where does dependent resource start?

  If the resource has its placement policy set to "favored", but the optional resources are on a non-favored member, the resource will start on the favored member. Below is a list of commands you can use to verify this assertion. No output is shown.

```
# caa_stop memberUP
# caa_profile -update memberUP -p favored -h sheridan -r "" -l "powerUP nicUP"
# caa_register -u memberUP
# caa_start memberUP
# caa_stat -t -v memberUP powerUP nicUP
```

  If the resource has its placement policy set to "favored", but the required resources are on a non-favored member, the resource will start on the non-favored member. You can use the same list of commands from the previous example — just swap the "-l" and "-r" options in the caa_profile command (although you will not need the "-p" or "-h" since these do not need to be modified a second time).

```
# caa_profile -update memberUP -l "" -r "powerUP nicUP"
```

- If a resource is restricted to a member, but the resource it depends on is running on a member that is not in the HOSTING_MEMBERS list, where does the dependent resource start?

  This is a slight modification to our previous example. If the resource has its placement policy set to "restricted", but the optional resources are on a member not in the HOSTING_MEMBERS list, the resource will start on a restricted member.

```
# caa_stop memberUP
# caa_profile -update memberUP -p restricted -h sheridan -r "" -l "powerUP nicUP"
# caa_register -u memberUP
# caa_start memberUP
# caa_stat -t -v memberUP powerUP nicUP
```

  If the resource has its placement policy set to "restricted", but the required resources are on a member not in the HOSTING_MEMBERS list, let's see what happens.

Stop memberUP. Modify memberUP's profile as follows:

- PLACEMENT=restricted
- HOSTING_MEMBERS=sheridan
- REQUIRED_RESOURCES=powerUP nicUP

```
# caa_stop memberUP

# caa_profile -update memberUP -p restricted -h sheridan -l "" -r "powerUP nicUP"
```

Update the CAA registry with memberUP's modified profile and start memberUP. Note the required resources are currently running on molari, but memberUP is now restricted to sheridan.

```
# caa_register -u memberUP ; caa_start memberUP

molari : Resource memberUP (application) cannot run on molari
sheridan : Resource powerUP (application) is already running on molari

Resource memberUP has placement error.
```

Can it be forcefully started? No.

```
# caa_start memberUP -f

molari : Resource memberUP (application) cannot run on molari
sheridan : Resource nicUP (network) is not available on sheridan

Resource memberUP has placement error.
```

Can it be forcefully started if we plug our network cable back in so that nicUP will go ONLINE? Yes.

```
# caa_start memberUP -f

Attempting to stop `powerUP` on member `molari`
Stop of `powerUP` on member `molari` succeeded.
Attempting to start `powerUP` on member `sheridan`
Start of `powerUP` on member `sheridan` succeeded.
Attempting to start `nicUP` on member `sheridan`
Start of `nicUP` on member `sheridan` succeeded.
Attempting to start `memberUP` on member `sheridan`
Start of `memberUP` on member `sheridan` succeeded.
```

```
# caa_stat -t -v memberUP powerUP nicUP

Name           Type           R/RA   F/FT   Target    State     Host
----------------------------------------------------------------------------
memberUP       application    0/1    0/0    ONLINE    ONLINE    sheridan
nicUP          network         -     0/2    ONLINE    ONLINE    molari
nicUP          network         -     0/2    ONLINE    ONLINE    sheridan
powerUP        application    0/1    0/0    ONLINE    ONLINE    sheridan
```

Note, though, that if we unplug the cable again, nicUP will be set to OFFLINE and memberUP will be stopped.

```
caa_stat -t -v memberUP nicUP powerUP

Name            Type          R/RA    F/FT    Target     State      Host
----------------------------------------------------------------------
memberUP        application   0/1     0/0     ONLINE     OFFLINE
nicUP           network       -       0/2     ONLINE     ONLINE     molari
nicUP           network       -       1/2     ONLINE     OFFLINE    sheridan
powerUP         application   0/1     0/0     ONLINE     ONLINE     sheridan
```

Will memberUP automatically start if the cable is plugged in again? Since the target state remains ONLINE, yes. Plug in the cable.

```
# caa_stat -t -v memberUP powerUP nicUP

Name            Type          R/RA    F/FT    Target     State      Host
----------------------------------------------------------------------
memberUP        application   0/1     0/0     ONLINE     ONLINE     sheridan
nicUP           network       -       0/2     ONLINE     ONLINE     molari
nicUP           network       -       0/2     ONLINE     ONLINE     sheridan
powerUP         application   0/1     0/0     ONLINE     ONLINE     sheridan
```

23.6.3 Active Placement

Use the ACTIVE_PLACEMENT attribute **only** if the application resource should be relocated immediately when a more favored member becomes available. This attribute should be used with caution as it can cause your users to be disrupted more often than necessary.

For example, consider that you have a two-member cluster where an application resource is favored to member1. If member1 were to become unavailable for whatever reason, the application resource would relocate to member2. Restarting the application resource on member2 will take at least a few seconds (but could take up to several minutes), thus disrupting your user's ability to get work accomplished.

The good news is that the application resource will be restarted automatically. The bad news is that it is not necessarily transparent.

If ACTIVE_PLACEMENT is set to the value of 1, when member1 reboots, CAA will automatically relocate the application resource back to member1 (the favored member). This means that the users would once again be disrupted.

What would happen if member1 experienced a problem that caused it to go down again and again? Your users would be continuously disrupted as the machine crashed and rebooted.

An alternative to setting the ACTIVE_PLACEMENT attribute to 1 is to have the cluster administrator relocate the application resource to the favored member at a time when the relocation will cause the least disruption. The REBALANCE attribute exists specifically to address this scenario.

23.6.4 Polling an Application Resource

One of the optional functions of the Resource Manager is its ability to check the status of an application resource every CHECK_INTERVAL seconds. In order to take advantage of this feature, the action script must have a "check" entry point written to check the application's status. If the check is unsuccessful, the application is not running; therefore, CAA will run the action script with the "start" entry point to restart the application.

This "check" entry point can be as simple as performing a ps(1) and searching for the command name or PID or as complex as contacting the application and performing some function to determine its status. The exact implementation is left to the cluster administrator or developer in charge of writing the action script.

Note the template.scr script in the /var/cluster/caa/template directory performs a simple check using the ps and grep commands. This is the default script used by the caa_profile and "sysman caa" commands.

NOTE:

Although the "check" that is performed in the template.scr is simple, it is inefficient and does not handle the scenario where the application is hung. Therefore, we strongly recommend that you rewrite your action script's "check" entry point to probe the application to verify that it is actually running.

23.7 CAA Events

CAA events are defined in the /usr/share/evm/templates/clu/caa/caa.evt template file. Below are the registered CAA events.

```
# evmwatch -i -f "[name *.caa]" | \
> evmsort -A -s "@priority:@name" -t "[@priority] @name"

[200] sys.unix.clu.caa.action_script
[200] sys.unix.clu.caa.app.trigger                  ← added in V5.1A IPK
[200] sys.unix.clu.caa.cli
[200] sys.unix.clu.caa.err
[300] sys.unix.clu.caa.app.registered
[300] sys.unix.clu.caa.app.running
[300] sys.unix.clu.caa.app.stopped
[300] sys.unix.clu.caa.app.transition
[300] sys.unix.clu.caa.app.unregistered
[300] sys.unix.clu.caa.res.profile.create           ← added in V5.1A IPK
[300] sys.unix.clu.caa.res.profile.delete           ← added in V5.1A IPK
[300] sys.unix.clu.caa.res.profile.update           ← added in V5.1A IPK
```

```
[500] sys.unix.clu.caa.app.error
[500] sys.unix.clu.caa.app.modified          ← priority 300 in V5.1B
[500] sys.unix.clu.caa.res.modified          ← removed in V5.1B
[500] sys.unix.clu.caa.res.registered        ← removed in V5.1B
[500] sys.unix.clu.caa.res.unregistered      ← removed in V5.1B
```

CAA also has the following predefined event filters.

```
# evf -vd /usr/share/evm/filters caa clu \
> | awk '/evf|^\// { print "\n",$1 ; next } /caa/ { print }'

/usr/share/evm/filters

caa.evf
    @caa:caa              ->  [name sys.unix.clu.caa]
    @caa:app              ->  [name sys.unix.clu.caa.app]
    @caa:cli              ->  [name sys.unix.clu.caa.cli]
    @caa:err              ->  [name sys.unix.clu.caa.err]
    @caa:res              ->  [name sys.unix.clu.caa.res]

clu.evf
    @clu:caa              ->  [name sys.unix.clu.caa]
```

Incidentally, the following command is sufficient. We added the awk line to make the output more compact and to filter out any filters not specifically CAA-related.

```
# evf -vd /usr/share/evm/filters clu caa
```

The evf(1) command was written for the *TruCluster* Server Handbook and is not part of the *TruCluster* Server or *Tru64* UNIX software distribution. See the book's website to download – Appendix B contains the URL.

23.8 References

- The *TruCluster* Server Cluster Technical Overview.
- The *TruCluster* Server Cluster Highly Available Applications.
- Reference pages (noted within the text).

24

CAA by Example

In the last chapter we discussed the details of how CAA works. In this chapter we will discuss how to implement application resources for some common tasks.

	Section
• A simple highly available resource	24.2
• A highly available resource with dependencies	24.3
• A highly available resource with CFS Server Relocation	24.4
• A highly available resource that requires privately-mounted file systems	24.5
• A highly available resource that requires managing its own cluster alias	24.6
• A non-highly available resource that is used to automatically (re)start an application	24.7
• Mutually exclusive resources	24.8
• Creating a resource using SysMan	24.9

24.1 Creating a Resource – Step by Step

Once you have determined that you need a resource in order to achieve a highly available application, here are the steps that you must take to create, register, and start a resource.

	Section
1. Create a Resource Profile	23.4.5
2. If you created an Application Resource, create an Action Script	23.4.1.5
3. Test your Action Script	23.5.1
4. Validate the Resource Profile	23.4.8
5. Register the Resource with CAA	23.4.12
6. Start the Resource	23.4.15

24.2 Simple, Highly Available Resource

A simple, highly available resource can be defined as an application resource that manages one application.

24.2.1 Creating the Application

For illustrative purposes we created a simple Tcl/Tk[1] script. You will probably already have an application or two identified for this task.

Create the script.

```
# cat > xhostname
#!/usr/bin/wish

set hname [exec hostname -s]
set clarg [lindex $argv 0]

wm minsize . 350 30
wm title   . "$argv0 on $hname $clarg"

button .hostname -font helvb24 -text $hname -command { exit }
pack   .hostname -padx 10 -pady 10

^D
```

Change the permission bits so that the program can execute.

```
# chmod u+x ./xhostname
```

Change the ownership and group to `root` and `system` respectively.

```
# chown root:system ./xhostname
```

Test the script.

```
[molari]
# ./xhostname
```

Figure 24-1 shows the `xhostname` script in action.

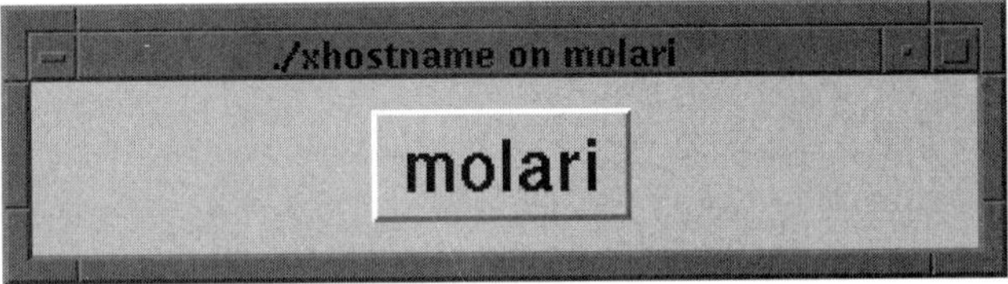

Figure 24-1: The `xhostname` Tcl/Tk Script

[1] Tcl is a general-purpose scripting language written by Dr. John K. Ousterhout. Tk is an X Windows System toolkit based on Tcl. For more information, see the Tcl Developer's Site at http://dev.scriptics.com/.

24.2.2 Create the Application Resource

Using the caa_profile(8) command we can create an application to manage the xhostname script. Note, use the full pathname of the application.

```
# caa_profile -create myFirstCAA_app -t application -B /code/caa/xhostname
```

The caa_profile command will create two files: a profile and an action script.

```
# ls /var/cluster/caa/*/myFirstCAA_app*
/var/cluster/caa/profile/myFirstCAA_app.cap
/var/cluster/caa/script/myFirstCAA_app.scr
```

Since the xhostname script is designed to display in an X Window System environment and run in the foreground, we will need to modify the action script (myFirstCAA_app.scr).

Locate the main case statement and add the DISPLAY environment variable before it.

Find these lines:

```
case $1 in
'start')
```

Add a line above:

To display on a specific system:

```
export DISPLAY="yourSystemNameHere:0"
```

To display on the member where the resource is running:

```
export DISPLAY="$(/sbin/hostname -s):0"
```

Then locate the line in the script where the command is executed. It will be a few lines below the main case statement, in the 'start' case.

	Line	Original	Proposed Modification
V5.0A	– 361:	`$START_APPCMD >> ${LOG}`	`$START_APPCMD >> ${LOG} &`
V5.1 V5.1A	– 320:	``out=`$START_APPCMD` ``	`out=$($START_APPCMD) &`
V5.1B	– 322:	`$START_APPCMD >$tmpfile 2>&1`	`$START_APPCMD >$tmpfile 2>&1 &`

24.2.3 Test the Application Resource

Make sure the action script works. In this case, if the action script successfully starts the xhostname script as shown in Figure 24-1 and exits successfully, the action script does what we expect.

```
# /var/cluster/caa/script/myFirstCAA_app.scr start
```

If that works, then verify that the stop entry point works as well.

```
# /var/cluster/caa/script/myFirstCAA_app.scr stop
```

This is a **very** simple example and testing your application resource action script may need to be more thorough. See section 23.5 for more information.

24.2.4 Validate, Register, and Start the Application Resource

Once the action script has been tested, validate the resource profile.

```
# caa_profile -validate myFirstCAA_app
```

If the profile validates, register the resource. For more information, see section 23.4.7.

```
# caa_register myFirstCAA_app
```

Once the resource is successfully registered, start the resource. For more information, see section 23.4.11.

```
# caa_start myFirstCAA_app
Attempting to start `myFirstCAA_app` on member `molari`
Start of `myFirstCAA_app` on member `molari` succeeded.
```

After starting the resource, relocate it for good measure.

```
# caa_relocate myFirstCAA_app
Attempting to stop `myFirstCAA_app` on member `molari`
Stop of `myFirstCAA_app` on member `molari` succeeded.
Attempting to start `myFirstCAA_app` on member `sheridan`
Start of `myFirstCAA_app` on member `sheridan` succeeded.
```

24.3 Dependent Resource

Creating a dependent resource is similar to the approach that we took in section 24.2 when creating a simple, highly available resource. The difference is that we must also create a resource (or resources) on which to depend.

Decide on the needs (or dependencies) of your application. If you have an application that connects to a database, for example, then you can define two application resources:

- `DBuser` – Create an `application` resource for the application that utilizes the database. Set the database application resource (`DB`) in either the `OPTIONAL_RESOURCE` or a `REQUIRED_RESOURCE` attribute list.
- `DB` – Create an `application` resource for your database.

Note, the resource names are made up and are not specific to any resource type.

Another example is an application resource that is used to backup a client system over the network. In this case the cluster acts as a backup server for other systems on the network. It stands to reason that the backup application should be located on a cluster member with a direct physical connection to the network as well as the backup media (tape and media robot). In this example, you can define four resources:

- `BackupNet` – Create an `application` resource for your network backup program. Set the network (`BackupNIC`), tape (`BackupTAPE`), and changer (`BackupROBOT`) resources in either the `OPTIONAL_RESOURCE` or a `REQUIRED_RESOURCE` attribute list.
- `BackupNIC` – Create a `network` resource.
- `BackupTAPE` – Create a `tape` resource.
- `BackupROBOT` – Create a `changer` resource.

Note, as with the previous example the resource names are made up and are not specific to any resource type.

For additional information on dependent resources, see sections 23.6.1 and 23.6.2.

24.4 CFS Server Relocation

An application is often only as useful as its ability to access application data successfully. If the application data were on a file system (and not on a raw device), it would certainly be more efficient to have the application resource and the CFS server located on the same server. Since there is currently no "CFS server" resource type that can be used to monitor the location of the CFS server for a file system and that your application resource can have as a dependency, here are a couple of possible solutions:

- Create an application resource that monitors and relocates a CFS server.
- Add CFS server resource and monitoring capability to your existing application resource.

IMPORTANT:

If you plan to relocate a file system in a multi-fileset domain, remember that the CFS server serves AdvFS file systems on a per-domain basis.

In other words, do not create a resource that relocates `know#ledge` to `member1` and another resource that relocates `know#where` to `member2`.

For more information, see Chapter 13.

24.4.1 CFS Server Application Resource

A CFS server application resource can also be implemented to create a simple, highly available application resource (see section 24.2) with the following considerations:

- Modify the `application.tdf` type definition file to add two user-defined attributes to file systems and mount points. Each of these attributes should be defined as a "`name_list`" type.
- Modify the "`start`" and "`check`" entry points in the action script to perform the CFS server relocation tasks.

24.4.1.1 Add USR_CFS and USR_MNT_PT User-defined Attributes

The `USR_CFS` attribute will be used to define the file system list, whereas the `USR_MNT_PT` attribute will be used for a list of mount points that should match up with the file system list (in fact the action script should check that this is the case).

```
   USR_CFS   =  cluster_root#root cluster_usr#usr cluster#var
USR_MNT_PT   =  / /usr /var
```

1. Save a copy of the original `application.tdf`[2] file.

```
# cd /var/cluster/caa/template
```

```
# cp application.tdf application.tdf.orig
```

[2] The `application.tdf` file is in the `/var/cluster/caa/template` directory beginning V5.1A/PK1.

2. Modify the `application.tdf` file.

   The following entries should be added to the file.

```
#!=========================
attribute: USR_CFS
type: name_list
switch: -o cfs
default:
required: no
```

```
#!=========================
attribute: USR_MNT_PT
type: name_list
switch: -o mp
default:
required: no
```

24.4.1.2 Creating a CFS Server Action Script

As mentioned in section 24.4.1, the "`start`" and "`check`" entry points to the action script should be modified to check the location of the CFS server for the list of file systems and relocate the CFS server if the member running the application resource is not the CFS server.

The following tasks will need to be added to the action script:

- Check to see if the file system is mounted.
  - If the file system is not mounted, either mount it or post a message and exit.
  - If the file system is mounted privately, exit because either the member mounted it so it **is** the CFS server, or the member did not mount it in which case it cannot be unmounted or relocated by the member.

The following piece of code (written in Korn shell) is one approach to checking the file system status.

```
ic=0
jc=0
for i in $_USR_CFS                            ← Loop through the list of file systems.
do

   (( ic += 1 ))
   for j in $_USR_MNT_PT                      ← Loop through the list of mount points.
   do

      (( jc += 1 ))
      if (( $ic != $jc ))                     ← Make sure the file system and mount point is the
      then                                      same place in the list.
        continue
      fi
      fs="$(mount | grep $i)" ; stat=$?       ← See if the file system is mounted.
```

```
    if (( $stat != 0 ))                              ← The file system is not mounted.
    then
      not_mounted $i $j                              ← Call the not_mounted function.
      jc=0
      break
    else
      if [[ $fs != *server_only* ]]                  ← Check to see if the file system is privately mounted.
      then
        cfs_relocate $i $j                           ← Call the cfs_relocate function.
        jc=0
        break
      else
        priv_mount $i $j                             ← Call the priv_mount function.
        jc=0
        break
      fi
    fi
  done
done
```

- Check the location of the CFS server.
- If the CFS server is not the member running the application resource, relocate the CFS server.

```
function cfs_relocate
{
  cfs="$(cfsmgr -F raw $2 \                          ← Get information from cfsmgr.
  | awk '$0 ~ ss { print $5 }' ss=$1 \               ← Search for the file system, get the CFS server, and
  | cut -d. -f1)"                                    ← return only the base CFS server hostname.

  member="$(hostname -s)"                            ← Get this member's base hostname.

  if [[ $cfs != $member ]]                           ← If this is not the CFS server…
  then

    cfsmgr -r -a server=$member -s $2                ← Relocate it.

    stat=$?
    if (( $stat != 0 )) ; then                       ← If the relocation was unsuccessful...
      return $stat                                   ← Return an error.
    fi
  fi
  return 0
}
```

There are some additional questions you may wish to consider (and even answer):

- What if the relocation fails? Is this acceptable or should you exit the script with a failure status?
- If there is a relocation failure, what was the error? Should you address and attempt to handle specific errors, or is any error fatal?
  - If the error is "`Not Served`", should you attempt to forcibly unmount the file system with the "`cfsmgr -u`" command and then attempt to mount the file system?

- If the relocation fails, should another attempt be made? If so, how many? When should you give up and return an error?

There is not just one answer to each of these questions. Use your best judgment and try a few options to see what works best for your configuration.

24.4.1.3 Creating a CFS Server Application Resource

In this section, we will create a CFS Server application resource that we'll name `cfs_common`. The `cfs_common` resource will be a "`favored`" resource and used to relocate the CFS server duties for `cluster_root`, `cluster_usr`, and `cluster_var` to `member1` (`molari`). Of course this resource (or a similar one) can be used as a dependency for another application resource.

We will use the `caa_profile` command with the following options:

- `-a` – Our customized CFS server script.
- `-o cfs` – Used to set the `USR_CFS` attribute variable.
- `-o mp` – Used to set the `USR_MNT_PT` attribute variable.
- `-o as` – Set `AUTO_START`.
- `-o ap` – Set `ACTIVE_PLACEMENT`.
- `-p` – Set the `PLACEMENT` to "`favored`".
- `-h` – Set the `HOSTING_MEMBER`.

```
# caa_profile -create cfs_common -t application -a cfs_relo.scr \
> -o cfs="cluster_root#root cluster_usr#usr cluster_var#var",\
> mp="/ /usr /var",as=1,ap=1 -p favored -h molari
```

Verify the resource profile with the `caa_profile` command with the "`-print`" option.

```
# caa_profile -print cfs_common
NAME=cfs_common
TYPE=application
ACTION_SCRIPT=cfs_relo.scr
ACTIVE_PLACEMENT=1
AUTO_START=1
CHECK_INTERVAL=60
DESCRIPTION=cfs_common
FAILOVER_DELAY=0
FAILURE_INTERVAL=0
FAILURE_THRESHOLD=0
HOSTING_MEMBERS=molari
OPTIONAL_RESOURCES=
PLACEMENT=favored
REQUIRED_RESOURCES=
RESTART_ATTEMPTS=1
SCRIPT_TIMEOUT=60
USR_CFS=cluster_root#root cluster_usr#usr cluster_var#var
USR_MNT_PT=/ /usr /var
```

24.4.2 Relocating a CFS Server from an Application Resource

Instead of having a separate resource for relocating file systems to a different CFS server, you can add logic to your application resource's action script to do the relocation(s).

You will need to modify your "`start`" and "`check`" entry points.

- Verify that the file system is mounted. If it is unmounted, should you mount it or fail to start the resource?
- Locate the CFS server for the file system.
  - If the member is the CFS server, no relocation is necessary.
  - If the CFS server is not the member, then relocate the CFS server.
- If the relocation was successful, start the application.
- If the relocation was unsuccessful, do you try again?
  - If so, you must determine how many times to attempt to relocate the domain.
  - You must also decide what action to take if you cannot relocate the domain.
    - Should the resource start anyway? Probably. Your users will still be more efficient using an application that is accessing its data across the cluster interconnect than not being able to use the application at all.

24.5 Private Storage Resource

With the advent of the CFS, all file systems are available to all cluster members. For normal cluster operations, this is probably what you want. However, what if you have data that you want to restrict to one member?

TruCluster Server supports the notion of privately mounted file systems (also know as partitioned file systems – see Chapter 13, section 13.4)[3]. A partitioned file system is mounted and accessible by one cluster member.

Why would you want a partitioned file system resource? If you have an application resource that uses data , which you do not want any other cluster member to be able to access, then a partitioned file system may be the solution. If you have application data that is on a UFS file system and you would like the file system to be mounted read-write[4] as well as have the file system highly available,

---

[3] Partitioned file systems were not supported in V5.0A.

[4] Read-write UFS support began in *TruCluster* Server version 5.1A but is restricted to a partitioned file system

then create a partitioned file system resource. Alternately you may have an application with which you would like to utilize a memory file system (MFS). In V5.1A, the MFS is supported as a partitioned file system.

What is a partitioned file system resource? It is an application resource that mounts and unmounts one or more file systems.

Implementing a partitioned file system resource is relatively straightforward.

- Create an application resource.

  In the creation of the application resource, one potential implementation detail to consider is placing the file systems and mount points in the resource profile as illustrated in section 24.4.1.1.

- In the "start" entry point, mount the file system.

```
# mount -o server_only kits#kits /kits
```

- In the "stop" entry point, unmount the file system.
- If it's possible that open files might be left on the file system after the application has been stopped, you may need to consider using the fuser(8) command to handle this situation should it occur.

24.6 Cluster Alias Resource

For a majority of applications, the default cluster alias should be sufficient. For those applications that need to be restricted to a subset of members or to change the load-balancing behavior, alternate cluster aliases can be defined. Generally speaking, though, managing cluster aliases should have nothing to do with CAA, except that resources may manage applications that use a cluster alias.

Why do we have this section then? There are certain situations where you may want finer control over the handling of the cluster alias than the cluster alias subsystem alone provides. For example, what if you want to restrict an alias to the member running an application resource, but the application does not start up a network daemon that can be set as an "in_single" service in the clua_services(4) file.

For example, you have an application (we'll call it "widget") that you would like your users to use. The widget is running on member1. The users telnet(1) to member1 and start using the widget. If member1 is unavailable, then the application is unavailable.

If you implement an application resource to manage the widget, you will want to tie a cluster alias to the resource such that if the resource is relocated, the alias follows the widget.

There are a couple of possible solutions to having an alias follow the widget:

- Use the cluamgr(8) command.
- Use the ifconfig(8) command.

24.6.1 Alias Resource Using `cluamgr`

Use the cluamgr(8) command to "join" the widget alias in the "start" entry point of the widget resource's action script. When the resource relocates to another cluster member, use the cluamgr command to "leave" the widget alias in the "stop" entry point of the widget resource's action script.

- Save a copy of the original application.tdf file.
- Add an attribute to the application.tdf file as follows:
  - If you want to use an alias name, create a "name_string" attribute.

```
#!==========================
attribute: USR_ALIAS_NAME
type: name_string
switch: -o an
default:
required: no
```

  - If you want to use an alias IP address, create an "internet_address" attribute.

```
#!==========================
attribute: USR_ALIAS_IP
type: internet_address
switch: -o aa
default:
required: no
```

  - If you need more than one alias, create a "name_list" attribute.

```
#!==========================
attribute: USR_ALIAS_NAMES
type: name_list
switch: -o al
default:
required: no
```

- In the "start" entry point:

```
# cluamgr -a alias=${_USR_ALIAS_NAME},join,rpri=1
```

```
# cluamgr -r start
```

- In the "stop" entry point:

```
# cluamgr -a alias=${_USR_ALIAS_NAME},leave,rpri=0
```

NOTE:

As of this writing, once a cluster alias is created, it survives until the cluster is shutdown regardless of whether any cluster members are currently members of the alias. In other words, even after the last cluster member uses the cluamgr command to "leave" the alias, the alias is still in existence. The last member to route for the alias will continue to respond to alias requests unless the rpri attribute is set to zero.

If there is a possibility, however slight, that the widget resource will be stopped, and you do not want your users connecting to the cluster when the resource is unavailable, you may want to consider the option in the following section.

For more information on the cluster alias subsystem, see Chapter 16.

24.6.2 Alias Resource Using ifconfig

Use the ifconfig(8) command with the "alias" option.

This option does not use the cluster alias subsystem, though it does allow you to add an alias to a network interface.

There are a couple of restrictions to using the ifconfig command with the "alias" option:

1. You must use an IP address and not an alias name when defining the alias.
2. You can only have one alias per interface.

In order to implement an alias using ifconfig:

- Save a copy of the original application.tdf file.
- Add the USR_ALIAS_IP attribute to the application.tdf file as shown in section 24.6.1.
- Create a "name_string" attribute (named USR_ALIAS_INTERFACE) and add it to the application.tdf file as follows:

```
#!==========================
attribute: USR_ALIAS_INTERFACE
type: name_string
switch: -o ai
default:
required: no
```

- In the "start" entry point:

```
# ifconfig ${_USR_ALIAS_INTERFACE} alias ${_USR_ALIAS_IP}
```

- In the "stop" entry point:

```
# ifconfig ${_USR_ALIAS_INTERFACE} -alias ${_USR_ALIAS_IP} abort
```

NOTE:

You can also tie a virtual MAC address using the `ifconfig` command as well.

- Add a "`name_string`" attribute (named `USR_ALIAS_VMAC`) to the `application.tdf` file as follows:

```
#!==========================
attribute: USR_ALIAS_VMAC
type: name_string
switch: -o av
default:
required: no
```

- In the "`start`" entry point:

```
# ifconfig ${_USR_ALIAS_INTERFACE} alias ${_USR_ALIAS_IP} \
> physaddr ${_USR_ALIAS_VMAC}
```

- In the "`stop`" entry point:

```
# ifconfig ${_USR_ALIAS_INTERFACE} -alias ${_USR_ALIAS_IP} \
> -physaddr ${_USR_ALIAS_VMAC} abort
```

24.7 Auto-Restart Restricted Resource

Many customers have taken to using CAA for more than just making an application highly available. Due to CAA's capability to periodically poll an application's state and take action if/when this occurs, why not use this functionality to automatically restart applications that may be multi-instance or even cluster-aware?

The implementation is straightforward with the key being in the "`check`" entry point. Unfortunately, we cannot detail how to implement a "`check`" entry point because determining an application's health is highly subjective and application-specific. We can, however, give you some guidelines.

- If you have a multi-instance or distributed application, create resources for each instance.
- Set the `PLACEMENT` to "`restricted`".
- Set the `HOSTING_MEMBERS` attribute to the member on which to restrict the resource.
  - If you are setting up multiple resources for a multi-instance or distributed application, set the `HOSTING_MEMBERS` attribute to one member per resource and do not duplicate.
- If you want the resource restarted on cluster boot, regardless of its state when the cluster was shutdown, set the `AUTO_START` attribute to "1".
- Set `ACTIVE_PLACEMENT` to "1".

24.8 Mutual Exclusive Resource

What if you have an application that has to run all the time but cannot run on the same member at the same time as another application?

In this section we will cover one possible solution for handling this type of scenario.

For the application that must run at all times, we will create an application resource named prodAPP. Our other application (that cannot run on the same member as prodAPP) will be called devAPP.

The prodAPP resource will be "favored" to member1 (molari), while the devAPP application will be "restricted" to member2 (sheridan). In this scenario, if both members are up, then both resources will be running on opposite members. The fun begins when member1 becomes unavailable.

If member1 is unavailable, prodAPP will relocate to member2, but prodAPP and devAPP cannot be running on the same member at the same time!

24.8.1 Creating the USR_MUTEX Attribute

In order for prodAPP and devAPP to know which resource is their "anti-resource", we will create a user-defined application resource attribute that will be used for this purpose. The attribute will be a "name_list" type named USR_MUTEX.

- Save a copy of the original application.tdf file.
- Add the following entry to the application.tdf file.

```
#!==========================
attribute: USR_MUTEX
type: name_list
switch: -o mx
default:
required: no
```

24.8.2 Creating the prodAPP Application Resource

The prodAPP application resource will be defined with the follow attributes:

- -B – Our prodAPP application.
- -h – The hosting member. In this case, molari.
- -p – The placement policy. In this case, "favored".
- -o as – Set AUTO_START.
- -o mx – The mutual-exclusive resource list. In this case, "devAPP".

Create the prodAPP application resource using the caa_profile command.

```
# caa_profile -create prodAPP -t application -B /code/caa/prodAPP \
> -o mx=devAPP,as=1 -h molari -p favored
```

In the "start" entry point of the action script for prodAPP we will need to add logic to check the status and location of devAPP. If devAPP is running on the same member, stop it. If devAPP is not running, and prodAPP is running on one of its favored members, start devAPP.

The following piece of code (written in Korn shell) is one approach to handle stopping and starting devAPP.

```
host=$(hostname -s)
memb=NO_MEMB

for i in $_USR_MUTEX                      ← Loop through the list of mutually exclusive resources.
do
  caa_stat -a $i -r                       ← Check to see if the resource is running.

  if (( $? == 0 )) ; then                 ← If the resource is running...

    memb=$(caa_stat -t $i \               ← Run the caa_stat(8) command.
           | tail -1 \                    ← Get the last line.
           | awk '{ print $5 }')          ← Return the member name where the resource is running.

    if [[ $memb = $host ]] ; then         ← If the member is the same as this member...
      caa_stop $i                         ← Stop the mutually exclusive resource.
    fi
  else
    start_mutex=0
    for j in $_CAA_HOSTING_MEMBERS        ← Loop the list of hosting members.
    do
      if [[ $host = $j ]] ; then          ← If we're running where we're supposed to...
        start_mutex=1                     ← Set a variable.
        break                             ← Stop the loop.
      fi
    done
    if (( $start_mutex )) ; then          ← If we're running where we're supposed to...
      for k in $_USR_MUTEX                ← Loop through the list mutually exclusive resources.
      do
        caa_start $k                      ← Start the mutually exclusive resource.
      done
    fi
  fi
done
```

24.8.3 Creating the devAPP Application Resource

The devAPP application resource will be defined by the follow attributes:

- -B – Our devAPP application.
- -h – The hosting member. In this case, sheridan.
- -p – The placement policy. In this case, "restricted".
- -o mx – The mutual-exclusive resource list. In this case, "prodAPP".

Create the devAPP application resource using the caa_profile command.

```
# caa_profile -create devAPP -t application -B /code/caa/devAPP \
> -o mx=prodAPP -h sheridan -p restricted
```

In the "start" entry point of the action script for devAPP, check the status and location of prodAPP. If prodAPP is running on a member where devAPP is restricted, then exit with an error so the CAA will not attempt to restart it.

The following piece of code (written in Korn shell) is one approach to insure that devAPP doesn't start if prodAPP is running on the same member.

```
host=$(hostname -s)
memb=NO_MEMB
for i in $_USR_MUTEX                      ← Loop through the list of mutually exclusive resources.
do
  caa_stat -a $i -r                       ← Check to see if the resource is running.
  if (( $? == 0 )) ; then                 ← If the resource is running...
    memb=$(caa_stat -t $i \               ← Run the caa_stat command.
           | tail -1 \                    ← Get the last line.
           | awk '{ print $5 }')          ← Return the member name where the resource is running.
    if [[ $memb = $host ]] ; then         ← If the member is the same as this member...
      exit 1                              ← Exit because a mutually exclusive resource is running.
    fi
  fi
done
```

24.8.4 Mutually Exclusive Resources in Action

We've created the devAPP and prodAPP application resources; modified the action scripts for each resource; and tested the action scripts for each resource (always test your action scripts before registering your resources!). So let's register and start the resources.

```
# caa_register devAPP prodAPP
```

```
# caa_start devAPP prodAPP

Attempting to start `devAPP` on member `sheridan`
Start of `devAPP` on member `sheridan` succeeded.
Attempting to start `prodAPP` on member `molari`
Start of `prodAPP` on member `molari` succeeded.
```

Verify that the resources have started using the caa_stat command.

```
# caa_stat -t devAPP prodAPP

Name            Type            Target     State      Host
------------------------------------------------------------
devAPP          application     ONLINE     ONLINE     sheridan
prodAPP         application     ONLINE     ONLINE     molari
```

Does the logic work in `prodAPP`'s action script "`start`" entry point? Let's see by relocating `prodAPP` to `sheridan`.

```
# caa_relocate prodAPP

Attempting to stop `prodAPP` on member `molari`
Stop of `prodAPP` on member `molari` succeeded.
Attempting to start `prodAPP` on member `sheridan`
Start of `prodAPP` on member `sheridan` succeeded.
```

If the logic worked, `devAPP` should be stopped.

```
# caa_stat -t devAPP prodAPP

Name            Type            Target     State      Host
------------------------------------------------------------
devAPP          application     OFFLINE    OFFLINE
prodAPP         application     ONLINE     ONLINE     sheridan
```

Attempt to start `devAPP`.

```
# caa_start devAPP

Attempting to start `devAPP` on member `sheridan`
Start of `devAPP` on member `sheridan` failed.
molari : Resource devAPP (application) cannot run on molari

Could not start resource devAPP.
```

The logic in `devAPP`'s action script "`start`" entry point appears to be working, but we've only tested the first branch of `prodAPP`'s action script "`start`" entry point when we relocated to `sheridan`.

Let's complete our test by relocating `prodAPP` to `molari`.

```
# caa_relocate prodAPP

Attempting to stop `prodAPP` on member `sheridan`
Stop of `prodAPP` on member `sheridan` succeeded.
Attempting to start `prodAPP` on member `molari`
Start of `prodAPP` on member `molari` succeeded.
```

If our logic worked, `devAPP` should have been restarted on `sheridan`.

```
# caa_stat -t devAPP prodAPP
Name            Type            Target    State     Host
------------------------------------------------------------
devAPP          application     ONLINE    ONLINE    sheridan
prodAPP         application     ONLINE    ONLINE    molari
```

24.9 CAA Example Using sysman

In this section we will create an application resource using "sysman caa".

```
# sysman caa
```

Figure 24-2 shows the main window you will see when starting "sysman caa".

Table 24-1 shows the main menu button and the caa_* command that will be executed.

The main CAA window displays the currently registered resources and their state. To create a new resource, select the Setup... button, which will bring a popup window as shown in Figure 24-3. To see the equivalent caa_* commands that can be used in lieu of the buttons on the setup menu, see Table 24-1.

24.9.1 Adding a Resource with sysman

Adding a resource using "sysman caa" is as simple as clicking on the Add... button from the setup screen (Figure 24-3) which will popup the "Add" window as shown in Figure 24-4.

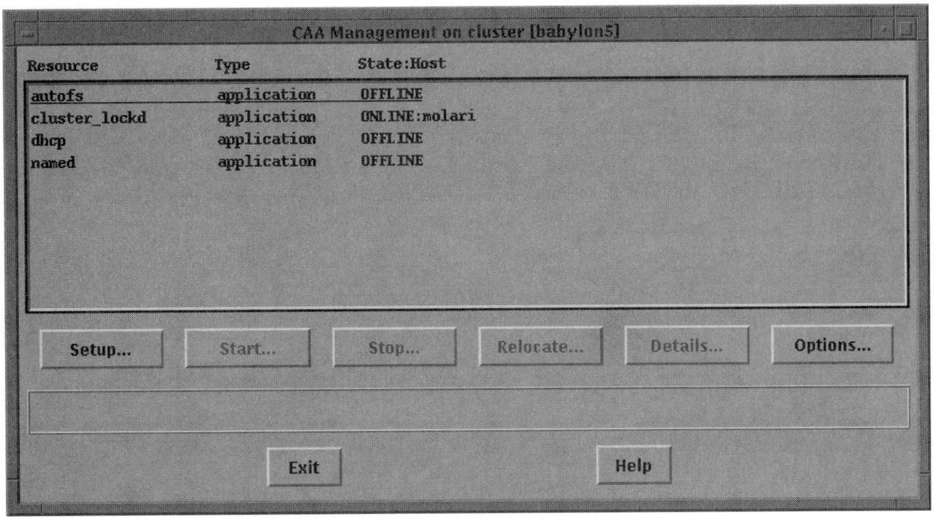

Figure 24-2: CAA Main Window

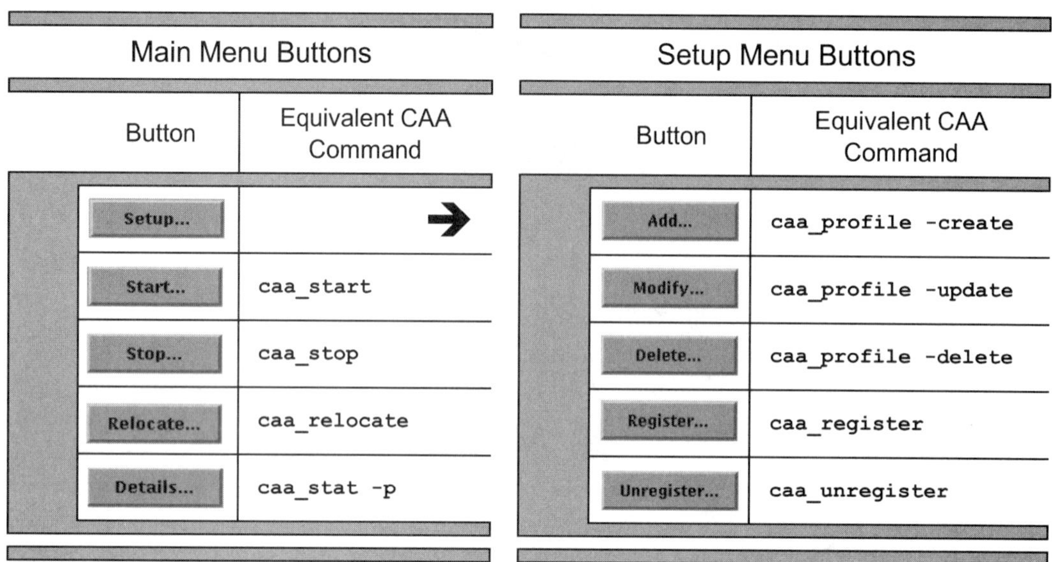

Main Menu Buttons

Button	Equivalent CAA Command
Setup...	➔
Start...	caa_start
Stop...	caa_stop
Relocate...	caa_relocate
Details...	caa_stat -p

Setup Menu Buttons

Button	Equivalent CAA Command
Add...	caa_profile -create
Modify...	caa_profile -update
Delete...	caa_profile -delete
Register...	caa_register
Unregister...	caa_unregister

Table 24-1: Main Menu and Setup Menu Buttons to caa_* Commands

Figure 24-3: CAA Setup Window

Figure 24-4: CAA Setup: Add Resource Popup and Resource Type Pulldown Menu

- Choose a resource name that is unique and relatively descriptive.

  In our example we have chosen to call our resource "memberUP" to indicate that a member is up if this resource is running somewhere in the cluster.

- Select the resource type using the pulldown menu.

  In this example we will create an application resource.

- Click on the Next > button to continue – this will pop up the window illustrated in Figure 24-5.

The next step is to input the required profile attribute that does not have a default value.

Resource		Required Resource Attribute without a default value
Application	–	ACTION_SCRIPT
Changer	–	DEVICE
Network	–	SUBNET
Tape	–	DEVICE

In our case, we will choose the application name to manage and the action script name. For a more complex application we would likely write our own action script. However, since we will be using a

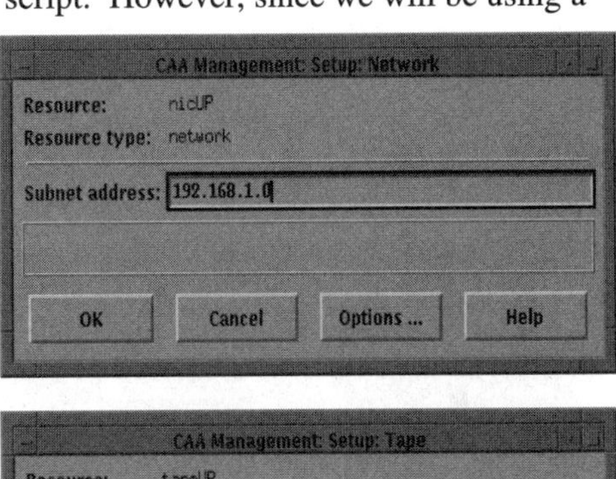

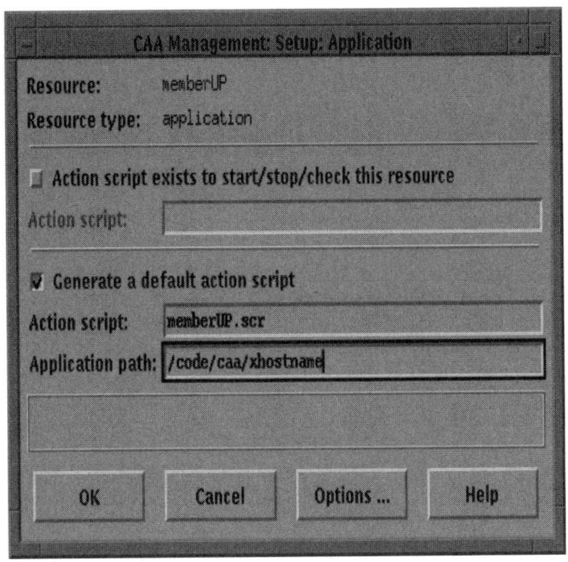

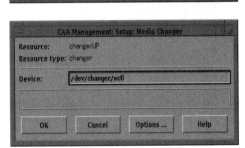

Figure 24-5: CAA Setup Resources

very simple Tcl/Tk application that we wrote (see section 24.2.1), we will choose to have a default action script generated, and we will simply indicate the path to our application. Choosing to generate a default action script causes "`sysman caa`" to copy the `template.scr` script from the `/var/cluster/caa/template` directory and inserts the application name and resource name in the appropriate spots within the script.

```
# grep -E "memberUP|xhostname" /var/cluster/caa/script/memberUP.scr
SERVICE_NAME="memberUP"
PROBE_PROCS="/code/caa/xhostname"
START_APPCMD="/code/caa/xhostname"
```

Note that the action script name is the name resource name with a "`.scr`" extension. Also note that the script will be located in the `/var/cluster/caa/script` directory by default. We recommend that all action scripts remain in this default directory.

At this point you can choose to take the default profile attributes by clicking the OK button. Or you can choose to customize the profile attributes by clicking the Options ... button.

24.9.1.1 Customize Profile Attributes

The Options popup window includes the default values for the remaining attributes. The Options popup window for each resource type is shown in Figure 24-6.

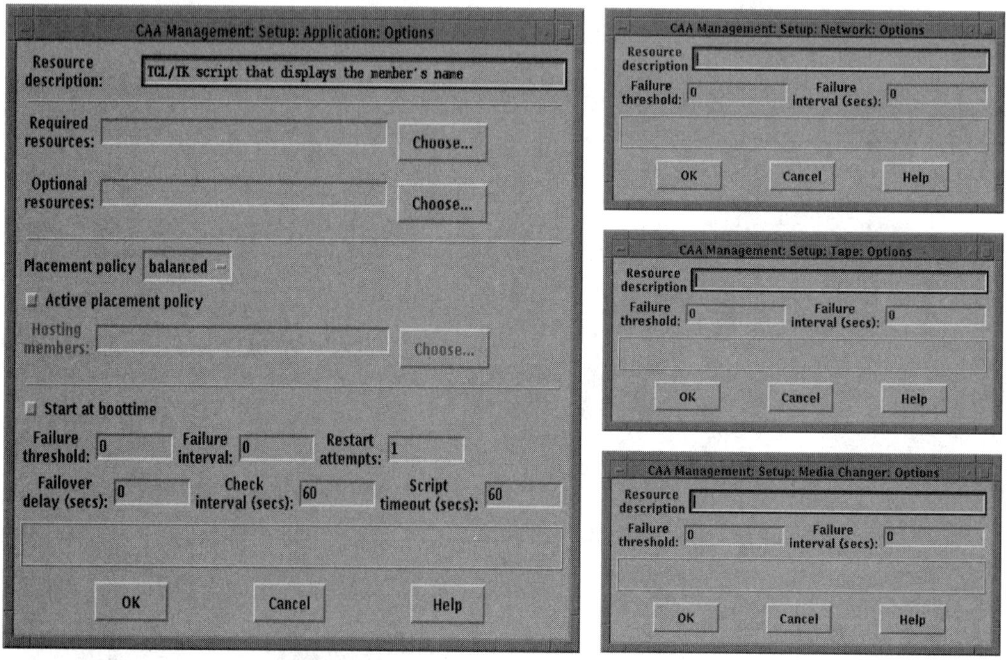

Figure 24-6: CAA Resource Options Pages

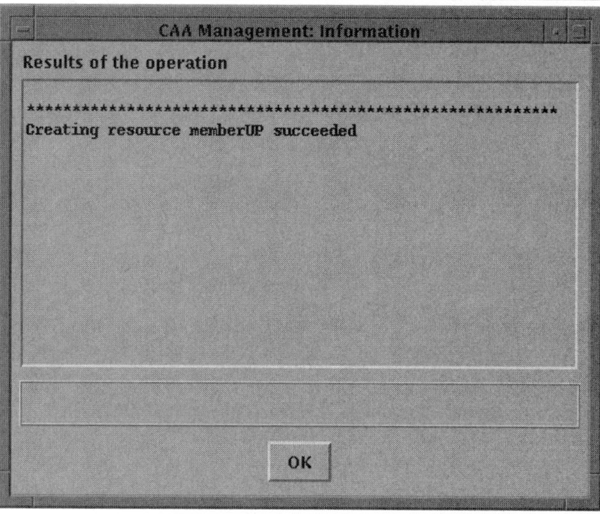

Figure 24-7: CAA Informational Popup

In our simple application resource we will take all of the default values except that we will add a resource description (the DESCRIPTION profile attribute). After adding the text for the resource description, click the OK button – this will return you to the Resource Setup popup window (Figure 24-5). Click the OK button again and the resource will be created (see Figure 24-7).

You will then be prompted to register the resource as shown in Figure 24-8.

There will be another informational popup letting you know that the registration was successful. It will look similar to the one shown in Figure 24-7 before the reminder to start the resource (the far right popup in Figure 24-8).

24.9.1.2 Modify the Action Script

Before we can start the "memberUP" resource, we need to make a couple of minor changes. The application that we chose to use — xhostname — is a typical X Window System application that is designed to run in the foreground; therefore we will need to modify the action script to launch xhostname in the background. Failure to do this would result in an action script timeout and would return an error to the resource manager, a condition that should be avoided. Furthermore,

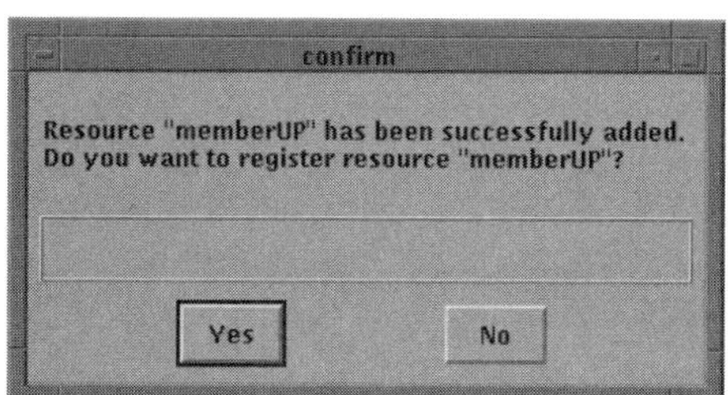

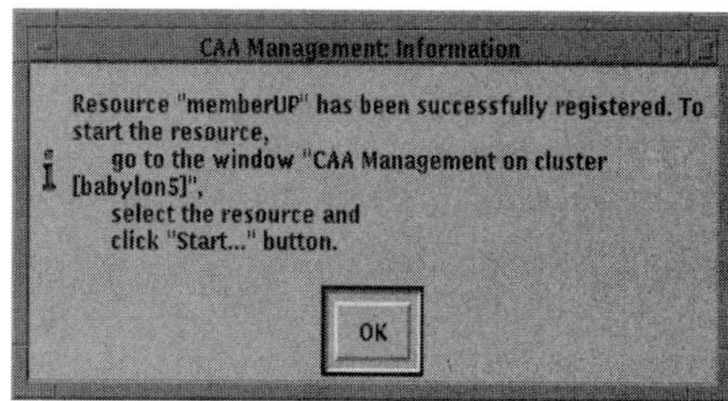

Figure 24-8: CAA Resource Registration Popup and Start Resource Informational Popup

since this is an X Window System application, it will require that we set the DISPLAY environment variable.

```
# diff memberUP.scr memberUP.scr.orig
315,316d314
< export DISPLAY="delenn:0.0"
<
322c320
<         out=$($START_APPCMD)&
---
>         out=`$START_APPCMD`
```

The diff(1) command above shows where we added the DISPLAY environment variable and where we modified the line where the application is started by inserting an ampersand (&). Note that we also replaced the grave accent (`) command substitution to the "$()" syntax for clarity.

24.9.1.3 Register, Start, Stop, and Relocate the Resource

Once the resource is created, select the resource and register the resource by pressing the Register... button as shown in Figure 24-3. Finally, you can start, stop, and relocate a resource by clicking on the appropriate button in the main CAA window as shown in Figure 24-2.

24.10 References

- The *TruCluster* Server Cluster Administration Guide.
- The *TruCluster* Server Cluster Highly Available Applications Guide.
- The *TruCluster* Server Technical Overview Guide.
- Reference pages (noted within the text).

25

Performing a Rolling Upgrade

One of the greatest maintenance benefits of *TruCluster* Server is the rolling upgrade. Performing a rolling upgrade allows for the update of the operating system and the cluster software without having to take down the cluster. This unique ability contributes to one of *TruCluster* Server's primary themes – high availability. In this chapter, we will discuss how to perform a rolling upgrade with little or no service downtime in the cluster.

So you're probably saying to yourself, "What the heck is meant by 'no service downtime in the cluster?' There's no way that this can be accomplished on a UNIX system." We're here to assure you that this is precisely what happens. During a rolling upgrade, one cluster member at a time is upgraded. As soon as the upgrade is complete, that cluster member is returned to operation and then another member of the cluster is upgraded. The impact on users accessing services on the cluster is minimal and in most cases, users are not even aware that a rolling upgrade is in progress.

If you think about it, the designers of the *TruCluster* Server software were ingenious for allowing the operation of a cluster in a mixed-version environment for the operating system and the cluster software components.

25.1 Tasks that Can be Performed in a Rolling Upgrade

There are three basic tasks that can be accomplished by performing a rolling upgrade:

1. Upgrade the base operating system and the cluster software from one version to the next.
2. Patch the current version of the operating system and cluster software.
3. Install a New Hardware Delivery kit (NHD).[1] For more information on the New Hardware Delivery kit, please see Compaq's *Tru64* UNIX New Hardware Delivery Release Notes and Installation Instructions.

---

[1] The cluster must be running at least *TruCluster* Server version 5.1A to use this feature.

TruCluster Server Upgrade Paths

If you are at...	and want to get to...	This is the recommended procedure
V5.1	V5.1A	Perform a Rolling Upgrade from V5.1 to V5.1A.
V5.0A	V5.1A	Perform a Rolling Upgrade from V5.0A to V5.1. Perform a Rolling Upgrade from V5.1 to V5.1A.
V5.0A	V5.1	Perform a Rolling Upgrade from V5.0A to V5.1.
V5.0	V5.0A - V5.1A	There is no direct upgrade path. Perform a Full Installation. Alternately, remove the V5.0 cluster software, perform an Update Installation of Tru64 UNIX and then install the TruCluster Server software.
V1.[56]*	V5.0A - V5.1A	There is no direct upgrade path. Perform a TruCluster Migration. See Chapter 26 for more information.

* - TruCluster Available Server Environment (ASE) or TruCluster Production Server (PS)

Table 25-1: TruCluster Server Upgrade Paths

While you can only perform one rolling upgrade at a time, you can accomplish multiple tasks as you perform the upgrade. What do we mean by this? Well, let's say that you want to upgrade from *TruCluster* Server version 5.1 to *TruCluster* Server version 5.1A and to install Patch Kit 1 for *Tru64* UNIX version 5.1A/*TruCluster* Server version 5.1A. This can easily be accomplished first by performing a rolling version upgrade followed by a rolling patch at the Install Stage[2] of the rolling upgrade.

25.2 Upgrade Paths for *TruCluster* Server version 5.X

As of this writing, the latest release of Compaq's *TruCluster* Server software is *TruCluster* Server version 5.1A. Table 25-1 provides upgrade paths for *TruCluster* Server version 5.X.

25.3 Stages of a Rolling Upgrade

A rolling upgrade of a cluster is accomplished through an ordered series of stages. These stages are represented in Table 25-2.

---

[2] See section 25.3, Stages of a Rolling Upgrade, for more information on the Install Stage.

Rolling Upgrade Stages

Stage	Description of Tasks to be Performed	Runlevel	Member	Time
Preparation	Backup the Cluster.	single-user or multi-user	Any	Time can vary greatly according size and number of file systems that are required to be backed up.
	Choose a Lead Member for the Rolling Upgrade.	multi-user		
	Update Firmware.	console	Lead	
	`# clu_upgrade -v check setup 1`	multi-user		
Setup	`# clu_upgrade setup 1`	multi-user	Lead	45 - 120 minutes
	Reboot **all** cluster members except the Lead member.		All but the Lead	
Preinstall	`# clu_upgrade preinstall`	multi-user	Lead	15 - 30 minutes
Install	`# clu_upgrade install`	multi-user	Lead	30 - 120 minutes
	Update Installation (`installupdate`) and/or	single-user		
	New Hardware Delivery (NHD) kit installation (`nhd_install`) and/or	single-user		
	Patch kit installation (`dupatch`)	single-user or multi-user		
Postinstall	`# clu_upgrade postinstall`	multi-user	Lead	< 1 minute
Roll	One member at a time, shutdown the system.	console	All but the Lead	15 - 30 minutes per cluster member
	Update the firmware.			
	Boot to single-user mode.			

	While in single-user mode:
	`# bcheckrc`
	`# update`
	`# swapon -a`
	`# clu_upgrade roll`
		single-user		

Switch	On **any** member, run "`clu_upgrade switch`"	multi-user	Any	< 1 minute
	Reboot **all** members one at a time.		All	Normal reboot time.
Clean	On **any** member, run "`clu_upgrade clean`"	multi-user	Any	30 - 90 minutes
Undo	Prior to the switch step, any or all steps can be undone. See section 25.6 for more information.	multi-user	varies according step being undone.	varies according step being undone.

Table 25-2: Rolling Upgrade Stages

The times specified in this table are approximate and depend on the speed of the system, the speed of the storage, and whether or not the command is being executed on the CFS server (for the cluster_root (or /), cluster_usr or (/usr), and cluster_var (or /var) file systems). Please also note that the time required for the Setup Stage can be quite lengthy (beyond 120 minutes) – depending on the number of nodes in your cluster. The reason for this is that copies of all system level files are made on disk.

25.4 What to Consider Before Starting a Rolling Upgrade

Disk space requirements are an important issue during any rolling upgrade of a cluster. As a general rule, there should be at least 50 percent free space in the root file system (`cluster_root#root`); 50 percent free space in the `/usr` file system (`cluster_usr#usr`); and 50 percent free space in the `/var` file system (`cluster_var#var`). If this is not the case, then either remove unwanted files from these file systems or use the `addvol(8)` command to temporarily add unused volumes to these file systems.

WARNING:

When adding additional unused volumes to these system-level file systems, please do not attempt to use unused disk partitions from the quorum disk(s). To do so will cause you a great deal of grief and possible downtime for the entire cluster.

A final word on disk space requirements: it is recommended that there be at least 50 MB free space on each cluster member's `boot_partition`. If this is not the case, then remove unwanted files from the member's root domain. If you are unable to free up any space in the member's root domain, please do not use the `addvol` command to add additional space. Instead, see the section in Chapter 22 on how to restore a cluster member's boot disk.

25.5 The Rolling Upgrade

Without further ado, let's show you how to perform a rolling upgrade, the stages of which are described in the following flow diagram (see Figure 25-1).

25.5.1 Preparation Stage

Preparing the cluster for the rolling upgrade includes several parts. Each of these parts must be completed before you can continue to the next stage of the rolling upgrade.

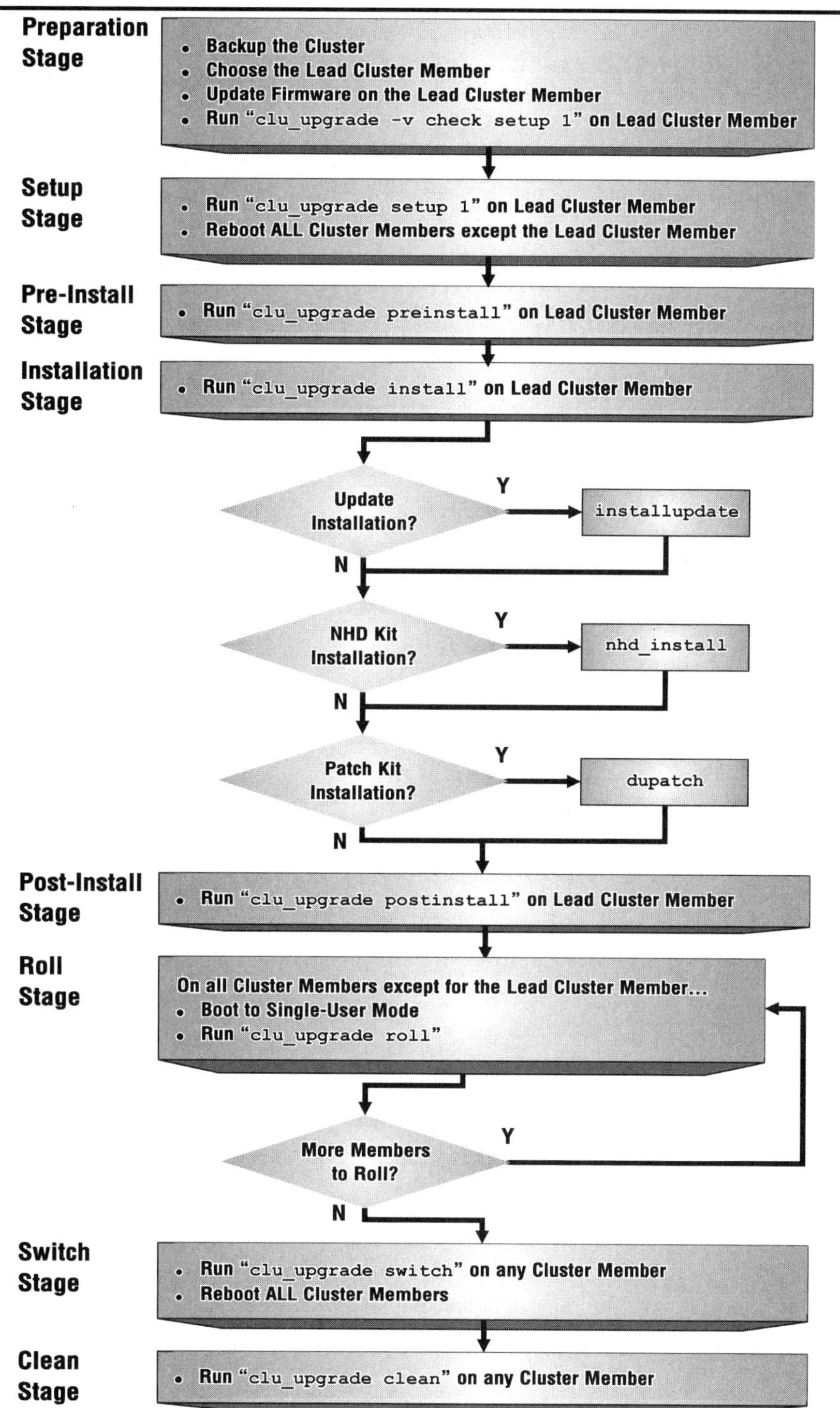

Figure 25-1: The Rolling Upgrade Flow

25.5.1.1 Determine which Cluster Member will be the Lead Member

The "lead member" is chosen as the first member of the cluster to be rolled. Normally, it is good practice to select the cluster member that is serving the root file system, the `/usr` file system, and the `/var` file system. The following provides an example of how to determine which cluster member is serving these file systems.

Let's find out which cluster member or system is serving `/`, `/usr`, and `/var`:

```
# cfsmgr / /usr /var

 Domain or filesystem name = /
 Server Name = molari
 Server Status : OK

 Domain or filesystem name = /usr
 Server Name = molari
 Server Status : OK

 Domain or filesystem name = /var
 Server Name = molari
 Server Status : OK
```

Or, you can use our cfs script.

```
# cfs | grep -E "cluster_root|cluster_usr|cluster_var"

molari            /                              cluster_root#root          AdvFS
molari            /usr                           cluster_usr#usr            AdvFS
molari            /var                           cluster_var#var            AdvFS
```

If one or more of these file systems (`/`, `/usr`, or `/var`) is being served by another cluster member, you can easily relocate this file system using the `cfsmgr` command.

```
# cfsmgr /var

 Domain or filesystem name = /var
 Server Name = sheridan
 Server Status : OK
```

```
# cfsmgr -h sheridan -r -a SERVER=molari /var
```

```
# cfsmgr /var

 Domain or filesystem name = /var
 Server Name = molari
 Server Status : OK
```

Now that we know which system is the server for these file systems, let's determine which `memberid` it is in the cluster.

```
# hostname
molari
```

```
# sysconfig -q generic memberid
generic:
memberid = 1
```

Or you can use the `hwmgr(8)` command:

```
# hwmgr -view cluster
Member ID        State    Member HostName
---------        -----    ---------------
    1            UP       molari (localhost)
    2            UP       Sheridan
```

In our example, the system known as `molari`, which is also cluster `memberid 1`, will be the lead member for the purposes of the rolling upgrade.

25.5.1.2 Back up the Cluster

In general, it is a good Systems Administration practice never to perform any type of major systems maintenance without first having a good and verifiable backup of your system.

NOTE:

We have noticed that while most Systems Administrators remember to back up /, /usr, and /var, the majority of folks forget about each cluster member's boot disk. Please, always remember to backup each cluster member's boot disk when you back up your cluster.

25.5.1.3 Update the Systems Firmware

New *TruCluster* Server software often takes advantage of the latest features that can only be found in the latest systems firmware updates from HP. It is essential to have the latest and greatest systems firmware in place before actually operating your cluster on the newly upgraded *TruCluster* Server software.

When does the systems firmware need to be upgraded? At any time before actually running the new TruCluster Servers software. In order to minimize downtime, in the case of the lead cluster member, the systems firmware for that node should be upgraded early during the Install Stage. In the case of the other cluster members, the systems firmware for each node should be upgraded before completion of the Roll Stage – see section 25.5.2.5 for a recommendation as to when to upgrade the systems firmware for the other cluster members. For more information on installing systems firmware, please see Chapter 5 on Installing *Tru64* UNIX.

WARNING:

Firmware upgrade of the KGPSA host bus adapter may alter Fibre Channel (FC) node name.

During the testing required to produce this chapter, we came across an issue and a warning from HP Support that has to do with upgrading firmware on the KGPSA.

Upgrading the firmware on the KGPSA may change the FC node name. "This upgrade cannot be taken lightly as the change in the FC node name changes connection status on the HSG80s on the *Tru64* UNIX platforms." If the storage system for the cluster "is using Selective Storage Presentation (setting entries into the Access_Enable table), then all these new connections will have to be renamed and the old connections deleted."[3]

The following is an example of these changes in the connections and how to correct them:

- `SHOW CONNECTION` before the KGPSA firmware upgrade:

```
BL5-HSG1> SHOW CONNECTION
Name         Operating system    Controller  Port    Address    Status    Offset
MOLARI1B01     TRU64_UNIX           THIS        2      000008     OL this      00
           HOST_ID=1000-0000-C921-92C9              ADAPTER_ID=1000-0000-C921-92C9

MOLARI1A01     TRU64_UNIX           THIS        2      000002     OL this      00
           HOST_ID=1000-0000-C921-93B0              ADAPTER_ID=1000-0000-C921-93B0
```

- `SHOW CONNECTION` after the firmware upgrade:

```
BL5-HSG1> SHOW CONNECTION
Name         Operating system    Controller  Port    Address    Status    Offset
!NEWCON02      WINNT               THIS        2      000008     OL this      00
           HOST_ID=2000-0000-C921-92C9    ADAPTER_ID=1000-0000-C921-92C9

!NEWCON03      WINNT               THIS        2      000002     OL this      00
           HOST_ID=2000-0000-C921-93B0    ADAPTER_ID=1000-0000-C921-93B0

MOLARI1B01     TRU64_UNIX          THIS        2      000008     offline      00
           HOST_ID=1000-0000-C921-92C9              ADAPTER_ID=1000-0000-C921-92C9

MOLARI1A01     TRU64_UNIX          THIS        2      000002     offline      00
           HOST_ID=1000-0000-C921-93B0              ADAPTER_ID=1000-0000-C921-93B0
```

3 Compaq Support Blitz TD 2807-C.

Notice that the two new connections, !NEWCON02 and !NEWCON03, are the same KGPSA adapters that appear in MOLARI1B01 and MOLARI1A01, but the firmware upgrade has changed the Fibre Channel Node Name or the HOST_ID on the connections. The system's old connections are now OFFLINE and the system cannot access any of the units that are presented with Selective Storage Presentation[4]. In a cluster and especially during a rolling upgrade, this would not be a very desirable situation but it can easily be resolved.

- SHOW CONNECTION after re-editing the connection entries:

```
BL5-HSG1> SHOW CONNECTION

Name        Operating system    Controller  Port    Address     Status    Offset

MOLARI1B01     TRU64_UNIX           THIS      2      000008      OL this   00
           HOST_ID=2000-0000-C921-92C9              ADAPTER_ID=1000-0000-C921-92C9

MOLARI1A01     TRU64_UNIX           THIS      2      000002      OL this   00
           HOST_ID=2000-0000-C921-93B0              ADAPTER_ID=1000-0000-C921-93B0
```

Notice that the old connections MOLARI1B01 and MOLARI1A01 were deleted. The new connection !NEWCON02 was renamed to MOLARI1B01, and !NEWCON03 was renamed to MOLARI1A01.

One final word about firmware before we proceed. If any of your systems in the cluster has an EISA bus, and most EV5 and EV56 Alpha based system had this, you must run the EISA Configuration Utility (ECU). The ECU is third-party software that was usually shipped on diskette with your system hardware. If you do not have a current ECU diskette, please contact your HP support representative for a replacement copy before starting the rolling upgrade.

25.5.1.4 Determine if the Cluster is Ready to be Upgraded

```
# clu_upgrade -v check setup 1
Retrieving cluster upgrade status
```

This verifies the following:

- There is no rolling upgrade in progress.
- All cluster members are running the same version of the operating system and cluster software.
- There are no cluster members running on tagged files[5].

---

4 For more information on Selective Storage Presentation, we will refer you to Compaq StorageWorks manual for the HSG80 Controller (ACS Manual).

5 For more information on tagged files, please see section 25.5.2.1.

- There is enough free disk space in which to perform a rolling upgrade of the cluster.

25.5.2 Setup Stage

During the Setup Stage, the following subtasks are performed:

- The rolling upgrade log is created and initialized. This file can be found in `/cluster/admin/clu_upgrade.log`.
- The "`clu_upgrade -v check setup`" command is reissued.
- A set of tagged files is created in preparation for the rolling upgrade. Tagged files are used so that the cluster can operate on two different versions of the operating system and cluster software at the same time. This is why there must be enough free disk space to perform a rolling upgrade.
- For all cluster members except the lead member, the `/etc/sysconfigtab` attribute `generic:rolls_ver_lookup` is set to 1. This allows the cluster members that have not yet been "rolled" to use the tagged files to operate.

Up to this point, the Setup Stage does the same tasks whether you plan to perform an Update Installation, an NHD Installation, or a Patch Kit Installation.

25.5.2.1 A Note about Tagged Files and How They Work

What's a tagged file and why should you care? As we stated in the previous subsection, tagged files are created in preparation for the rolling upgrade. Their primary purpose is to enable the cluster to operate on two different versions of the operating system and cluster software at once. Is it magic or just a clever trick? You be the judge!

First, a tagged file is usually created in the same directory as its original file. Each tagged file has an AdvFS property set on it. This is called a DEC_VERSION_TAG.

Next, if a cluster member's `/etc/sysconfigtab generic:rolls_ver_lookup` attribute is set to 1, then pathname resolution includes the determination on whether or not a specific file has an `.Old..` prepended to the file's name and whether the copy has a DEC_VERSION_TAG property set on it. If both of these conditions are met, then when an attempt is made to use the file, the request is redirected so that the .Old.. prepended file is used. See, it's magic!

Well, now that we have you thoroughly confused, let's try to simplify matters with an example. If you execute the command `/usr/sbin/dump` on a member that has not been rolled, then what actually gets executed is `/usr/sbin/.Old..dump`. Executing the same command on a member that has been rolled will execute the newly updated `/usr/sbin/dump` command.

You may find that this feature of allowing two different versions of the operating system and cluster software to co-exist will come in handy particularly when it comes to testing and verifying that your user applications work on the new version of the software.

25.5.2.2 Setup Stage for an Update Installation

The Setup Stage for an Update Installation also copies the cluster kit from the mounted CD (containing the *TruCluster* software installation CD) to `/var/adm/update/TruClusterKit`. This is done so that the cluster kit will be accessible during the Install Stage and the Roll Stage.

Please note that if your existing cluster is at *TruCluster* Server version 5.0A or at *TruCluster* Server version 5.1, you will see a slightly different version of output from the "`clu_upgrade setup 1`" command than if you were using *TruCluster* Server version 5.1A.

The following is the sample output of the "`clu_upgrade setup 1`" command, taken from a *TruCluster* Server version 5.1 system:

```
# clu_upgrade setup 1

This is the cluster upgrade program.
You have indicated that you want to perform the 'setup' stage of the upgrade.

Do you want to continue to upgrade the cluster? [yes]:yes
```

```
What type of upgrade will be performed?
1) Rolling upgrade using the installupdate command
2) Rolling patch using the dupatch command
3) Both a rolling upgrade and a rolling patch
4) Exit cluster software upgrade
Enter your choice:1
Enter the full pathname of the cluster kit mount point ['???']:/cdrom1/TruCluster
```

```
A cluster kit has been found in the following location: /cdrom1/TruCluster/kit/
This kit has the following version information:
'Tru64 UNIX TruCluster(TM) Server Software V5.1A (Rev 1312)'

Is this the correct cluster kit for the update being performed? [yes]:yes
```

```
Checking inventory and available disk space.
Copying cluster kit '/cdrom1/TruCluster/kit/' to '/var/adm/update/TruClusterKit/'.
```

The next sample output is what you would see at the Setup Stage if you were performing an Update Installation on *TruCluster* Server version 5.1A:

```
# clu_upgrade setup 1

This is the cluster upgrade program.
You have indicated that you want to perform the 'setup' stage of the upgrade.
Do you want to continue to upgrade the cluster? [yes]:yes
```

```
What type of rolling upgrade will be performed?
    Selection   Type of Upgrade
---------------------------------------------------------------------
         1      An upgrade using the installupdate command
         2      A patch using the dupatch command
         3      A new hardware delivery using the nhd_install command
         4      All of the above
         5      None of the above
         6      Help
         7      Display all options again
---------------------------------------------------------------------
Enter your Choices (for example, 1 2 2-3): 1
```

```
You selected the following rolling upgrade options: 1
Is that correct? (y/n) [y]: y
```

Please note that as *TruCluster* Server version 5.1A is the latest version, we have yet to test the Update Installation to a later version of *TruCluster* Server.

25.5.2.3 Setup Stage for a New Hardware Delivery (NHD)[6]

As of this writing, not much has been documented on what is required for performing a rolling upgrade of a cluster for a New Hardware Delivery. Based on available information, when a rolling upgrade for an NHD Installation is performed, at the Setup Stage, the NHD installation kit is copied from its source media to `/var/adm/update/NHDKit` for accessibility during the Install Stage. For more information on the New Hardware Delivery kit, please see Compaq's *Tru64* UNIX New Hardware Delivery Release Notes and Installation Instructions when this document becomes available.

25.5.2.4 Setup Stage for Installation of a Patch Kit

Unlike the Setup Stage for either an Update Installation or an NHD Installation, the Setup Stage for a Patch Kit does not do anything additional in terms of copying files for greater accessibility.

Again, if your existing cluster is at *TruCluster* Server version 5.0A or at *TruCluster* Server version 5.1, you will see a slightly different version of output from the "`clu_upgrade setup 1`" command than if you were using *TruCluster* Server version 5.1A.

The following sample output of "`clu_upgrade setup 1`" command comes from a *TruCluster* Server version 5.1 system:

[6] This is a feature of *TruCluster* Server version 5.1A or later.

```
# clu_upgrade setup 1

This is the cluster upgrade program.
You have indicated that you want to perform the 'setup' stage of the upgrade.

Do you want to continue to upgrade the cluster? [yes]:yes
```

```
What type of upgrade will be performed?
1) Rolling upgrade using the installupdate command
2) Rolling patch using the dupatch command
3) Both a rolling upgrade and a rolling patch
4) Exit cluster software upgrade
Enter your choice:2
```

The following is what you would see at the Setup Stage if you were performing a Patch Installation on *TruCluster* Server version 5.1A:

```
# clu_upgrade setup 1

This is the cluster upgrade program.
You have indicated that you want to perform the 'setup' stage of the upgrade.
Do you want to continue to upgrade the cluster? [yes]:yes

What type of rolling upgrade will be performed?
    Selection   Type of Upgrade
-----------------------------------------------------------------------
        1       An upgrade using the installupdate command
        2       A patch using the dupatch command
        3       A new hardware delivery using the nhd_install command
        4       All of the above
        5       None of the above
        6       Help
        7       Display all options again
-----------------------------------------------------------------------
Enter your Choices (for example, 1 2 2-3): 2
```

```
You selected the following rolling upgrade options: 2
Is that correct? (y/n) [y]:y
```

25.5.2.5 Verification of Setup Stage

The Setup Stage has been known to take a very long time – over two hours – on clusters greater than two cluster nodes or on older, more vintage AlphaServer architectures like AlphaServer 2100s. The reason for this is that system files are being copied into tag file sets. The greater the number of cluster nodes, the greater the number of system files that need to be copied, which takes longer to complete. Please have patience during this stage of the process.

The following is sample output from the Setup Stage from a two-member cluster. You should receive output similar to this on completion of this stage for your cluster:

```
Backing up member-specific data for member: 1
......
Creating tagged files.
............
The cluster upgrade 'setup' stage has completed successfully.
Reboot all cluster members except member: '1'
The 'setup' stage of the upgrade has completed successfully.
```

At this point, **all** cluster members **except** the lead member must be rebooted. As soon as the other cluster members come up after the reboot, they will be running on the tagged files.

25.5.2.6 One More Thing on the Setup Stage Before You Reboot...

If the firmware on each of these other cluster members has not been upgraded, we highly recommend that you take this opportunity to upgrade each system's firmware.

25.5.3 Preinstall Stage

The Preinstall Stage is executed on the lead member of the cluster only after the other cluster members have been rebooted at the end of the Setup Stage. The following subtasks are performed during this stage:

- Confirm that the cluster is ready to proceed with the upgrade by verifying that all members are running on the tagged files and that the lead member is not.
- An on-disk backup of the lead member's member-specific system files is made.
- The tagged files are verified and matched against their inventory files.

The following is sample output from the Preinstall Stage for an Update Installation:

```
# clu_upgrade preinstall

This is the cluster upgrade program.
You have indicated that you want to perform the 'preinstall' stage of the upgrade.
Do you want to continue to upgrade the cluster? [yes]:yes
Checking tagged files.
...................................................
The cluster upgrade 'preinstall' stage has completed successfully.
On the lead member, perform the following steps before running the installupdate
command:
# shutdown -h now
>>> boot -fl s
When the system reaches single-user mode run the following commands:
# init s
# bcheckrc
# update
# kloadsrv
# lmf reset

See the Tru64 UNIX Installation Guide for detailed information on using the
installupdate command.
The 'preinstall' stage of the upgrade has completed successfully.
```

This next sample output is from the Preinstall Stage for a Patch Kit installation:

```
# clu_upgrade preinstall

This is the cluster upgrade program.
You have indicated that you want to perform the 'preinstall' stage of the upgrade.
Do you want to continue to upgrade the cluster? [yes]:yes
Checking tagged files.
...................................................
The cluster upgrade 'preinstall' stage has completed successfully.
You can now run the dupatch command on the lead member.
```

25.5.4 Install Stage

Now that we have all the preliminaries out of the way, we are finally ready to get this show on the road. The Install Stage of the rolling upgrade is where we actually get to start upgrading the software. All stages previous to this have been in preparation of this stage.

All the tasks of the Install Stage are executed on the lead member. The commands for each of the tasks that can be executed are: `installupdate(8)` and/or `dupatch(8)` and/or `nhd_install(8)`[7]. See Table 25-3 for the combination of tasks that can be performed.

As of this writing, NHD installation kits have not been made available. Therefore, while the `nhd_install` command is mentioned here, no example of `nhd_install` output is provided.

TruCluster Server Rolling Upgrade Tasks

Tasks	Supported Version			Command(s)
	V5.0A	V5.1	V5.1A	
Update Installation	✓	✓	✓	`installupdate`
Patch Kit Installation	✓	✓	✓	`dupatch`
Update Installation and Patch Kit Installation	✓	✓	✓	1. `installupdate` 2. `dupatch`
New Hardware Delivery (NHD) Kit Installation	✗	✗	✓	`nhd_install`
New Hardware Delivery (NHD) Kit Installation and Patch Kit Installation	✗	✗	✓	1. `nhd_install` 2. `dupatch`
Update Installation, New Hardware Delivery (NHD) Kit Installation, and Patch Kit Installation*	✗	✗	✓	1. `installupdate` 2. `nhd_install` 3. `dupatch`

* - This is only supported if you have previously installed the NHD kit on a TruCluster Server version 5.1A cluster.

Table 25-3: Rolling Upgrade Tasks

For more information on this topic, we refer you to Compaq's *Tru64* UNIX New Hardware Delivery Release Notes and Installation Instructions when they become available.

25.5.4.1 Install Stage for an Update Install

Let's now follow the individual steps required to perform the Install Stage for an Update Installation:

1. Shutdown the lead member.

```
# shutdown -hs now
System going down IMMEDIATELY
...
```

2. Update the system firmware on the lead cluster member. Please review the Warning in section 25.5.1.3.

3. Boot to single user mode.

```
P00>>> boot -fl s
...
Loading vmunix ...
...
INIT: SINGLE-USER MODE
...
```

4. Manually run the `bcheckrc(8)` command to check and mount all file systems.

```
# bcheckrc
Checking device naming:
    Passed.
Checking local filesystems
Mounting / (root)
user_cfg_pt: reconfigured
root_mounted_rw: reconfigured
Mounting /cluster/members/member1/boot_partition (boot filesystem)
user_cfg_pt: reconfigured
root_mounted_rw: reconfigured
user_cfg_pt: reconfigured
dsfmgr: NOTE: updating kernel basenames for system at /
    scp kevm tty00 tty01 lp0 dmapi scp0 dsk0 dsk1 dsk2 dsk3 dsk4 dsk5 dsk6 dsk7
dsk8 dsk9 dsk10 floppy0 cdrom0 dsk13
Mounting local filesystems
exec: /sbin/mount_advfs -F 0x14000 cluster_root#root /
cluster_root#root on / type advfs (rw)
exec: /sbin/mount_advfs -F 0x4000 cluster_usr#usr /usr
cluster_usr#usr on /usr: Device busy
exec: /sbin/mount_advfs -F 0x4000 cluster_var#var /var
cluster_var#var on /var: Device busy
...
```

5. Execute the `kloadsrv(8)` command to start the kernel load server daemon, the `update(8)` command to flush data from memory and update the file system, and finally use the "`swapon`" command with the "`-a`" option to make all swap space available.

```
# kloadsrv
# update
# swapon -a
```

6. Make sure that all Software License Product Authorization Keys (PAKs) are active by resetting the License Management Facility (LMF).

```
# lmf reset
Combine OSF-USR ALS-NQ-2000NOV03-90 with OSF-USR UNIX-SERVER-IMPLICIT-USER
```

7. Now let's start the Update Installation by executing the `installupdate(8)` command. We recommend using the "`-nogui`" flag because it takes less time to complete and time is especially important when it involves anything that may impact users. For example, in one of our four-member ES40 clusters, an `installupdate` from V5.0A to V5.1 took 30 minutes longer with the GUI option than without.

```
# /sbin/installupdate -nogui /dev/disk/cdrom0c

Searching for distribution media...
Checking for installed supplemental hardware support...
Completed check for installed supplemental hardware support
*** START UPDATE INSTALLATION (Thu Nov 8 11:02:38 PST 2001) ***
    FLAGS: -nogui

Checking for retired hardware...done.
Initializing new version information (OSF)...done
Initializing new version information (TCR)...done
Update Installation has detected the following update installable
products on your system:

        Tru64 UNIX T5.1A-4 Operating System (Rev 1278)
        Tru64 UNIX TruCluster(TM) Server Software X5.1A-4 (Rev 619)

These products will be updated to the following versions:
        Tru64 UNIX V5.1A Operating System (Rev 1885)
        Tru64 UNIX TruCluster(TM) Server Software V5.1A (Rev 1312)

It is recommended that you update your system firmware and perform a
complete system backup before proceeding.  A log of this update
installation can be found at /var/adm/smlogs/update.log.

Do you want to continue the Update Installation?  (y/n) []:  y
```

As the system firmware has already been updated on the lead member, we can continue with the `installupdate`.

8. For our installation, while we want to select the kernel components, we do not have an interest in archiving obsolete files as we find that they are not very useful and take up valuable space. If you have accounting running, you may want to run a report on them first to see if anyone is using them and if not, then delete them.

```
Do you want to select optional kernel components?  (y/n) [n]: y
Do you want to archive obsolete files?  (y/n) [n]: n
```

9. The check for conflicting software has found four software subsets that are not compatible or will not be upgraded with this Update Installation. These software subsets are identified and will need to be reinstalled after the Rolling Upgrade has been completed.

```
*** Checking for conflicting software ***
-------------------------------------------------------------------------------
The following software may require reinstallation after the Update
Installation is completed:
        COMPAQ C++ Version 6.3 for COMPAQ UNIX Systems
        DEC C++ Class Libraries Version 4.0 for Tru64 UNIX
        DECevent
        Development Enhancement Tools for Tru64 UNIX
Do you want to continue the Update Installation?  (y/n) [y]: y
```

10. This section of the `installupdate` command will allow us to select which kernel options we would like for the new kernel that will eventually be built from the Update Installation. The selections that we have made support the environment in which our cluster is operating. Each Systems Administrator should determine the kernel options that best support his system's unique environment.

```
...
*** KERNEL OPTION SELECTION ***
    Selection   Kernel Option
--------------------------------------------------------------
        1       System V Devices
        2       NTP V3 Kernel Phase Lock Loop (NTP_TIME)
        3       Kernel Breakpoint Debugger (KDEBUG)
        4       Packetfilter driver (PACKETFILTER)
        5       IP-in-IP Tunneling (IPTUNNEL)
        6       IP Version 6 (IPV6)
        7       Point-to-Point Protocol (PPP)
        8       STREAMS pckt module (PCKT)
        9       Data Link Bridge (DLPI V2.0 Service Class 1)
        10      X/Open Transport Interface (XTISO, TIMOD, TIRDWR)
        11      Digital Versatile Disk File System (DVDFS)
        12      ISO 9660 Compact Disc File System (CDFS)
        13      Audit Subsystem
        14      All of the above
        15      None of the above
        16      Help
        17      Display all options again
--------------------------------------------------------------
Enter your choices, choose an overriding action or
press <Return> to confirm previous selections.

Choices (for example, 1 2 4-6): 1 2 3 4 8 11 12 13
```

```
You selected the following kernel options:
        System V Devices
        NTP V3 Kernel Phase Lock Loop (NTP_TIME)
        Kernel Breakpoint Debugger (KDEBUG)
        Packetfilter driver (PACKETFILTER)
        STREAMS pckt module (PCKT)
        Digital Versatile Disk File System (DVDFS)
        ISO 9660 Compact Disc File System (CDFS)
        Audit Subsystem
Is that correct? (y/n) [y]: y
```

11. A check is then made for file type conflicts. If obsolete files are detected, you are given the option to archive them, view them, or continue with the Update Installation. In our case, we were not really interested in archiving or viewing obsolete files. You may choose to do otherwise.

```
*** Checking for file type conflicts ***
        Working....
Obsolete files are files that were shipped with the previous version
of the operating system that the current version does not require.
Obsolete files are removed during the Update Installation.  To save
any of these files, archive them now.
        File Administration Menu
        ------------------------
        a) Archive Files
        v) View List of Files
        x) Return to Previous Menu
        Enter your choice: x
Continuing update install...
```

12. The Update Installation again checks to make sure that we have enough space in our file systems. As you can see, the designers of *Tru64* UNIX software are being very careful to ensure that there is indeed enough space to perform an Update Installation.

```
*** Checking file system space ***

Update Installation is now ready to begin software load. Please check the
/var/adm/smlogs/update.log file for errors after the installation is complete.

Do you want to continue the Update Installation? (y/n) [n]: y
```

13. The new version of the Operating System files is copied to a predetermined area for faster and easier access during the roll of the other cluster members. The upgraded *Tru64* UNIX Operating System is then loaded.

```
Copying the new version of the operating system files to
/var/adm/update/OSKit. This information will be used by the clu_upgrade
command to roll the remaining cluster members and should not be
modified in any way. This operation may take a while.
        Working....

*** Load Tru64 UNIX V5.1A Operating System (Rev 1885) Software Subsets ***

*** Starting protofile merges for Tru64 UNIX V5.1A Operating System (Rev 1885)

*** Finished protofile merges for Tru64 UNIX V5.1A Operating System (Rev 1885)
```

14. Finally, the newly upgraded *TruCluster* Server software subsets are installed and loaded.

```
*** Load Tru64 UNIX TruCluster(TM) Server Software V5.1A (Rev 1312) Software Subsets **
3 subsets will be installed.

Loading subset 1 of 3 ...

TruCluster Migration Components
   Copying from /var/adm/update/TruClusterKit (disk)
   Verifying
Loading subset 2 of 3 ...

TruCluster Reference Pages
   Copying from /var/adm/update/TruClusterKit (disk)
   Verifying

Loading subset 3 of 3 ...

TruCluster Base Components
   Copying from /var/adm/update/TruClusterKit (disk)
        Working....Thu Nov  8 13:09:18 PST 2001
   Verifying
3 of 3 subsets installed successfully.

*** Starting protofile merges for Tru64 UNIX TruCluster(TM) Server Software V5.1
A (Rev 1312) ***

*** Finished protofile merges for Tru64 UNIX TruCluster(TM) Server Software V5.1
A (Rev 1312) ***

*** Starting configuration merges for Update Install ***
...
Update Installation complete with loading of subsets.
Rebooting system with Compaq Computer Corporation Tru64 UNIX V5.1A
generic kernel for configuration phase...

Removing temporary update installation files...done.
...
```

15. The lead cluster member will reboot. When the system comes back up, the software subsets are configured on `member0` and then on `member1`. In this instance, `member1` is the designated lead cluster member.

NOTE:

You may notice that some of the configuration messages are stating that software subsets are being configured on `member0`. This is only the directory, `/cluster/members/member0`, on the cluster_root file system and not for cluster `memberid` 0.

16. After the configuration of all the software subsets, a new kernel will be built for the lead cluster member. The new kernel will be copied in place and the system is again rebooted.

```
...
rebooting.... (transferring to monitor)
...
The system is ready.
```

```
Compaq Tru64 UNIX V5.1A (Rev. 1885) (molari.gene.com) console
login: root
Password:

****************************************************************************
The cluster is currently in a rolled state and the software versions
that are available are different depending on which cluster member you
are on.  Additional information about the exact state of the system
can be obtained using the /usr/sbin/clu_upgrade command.
****************************************************************************
```

17. At this point in the Upgrade Installation, we are just about done with this stage. The next step will be to verify that the Install Stage is complete and successful. See section 25.5.5.1.

25.5.4.2 Install Stage for a Patch Kit Installation

We've seen the individual steps required to perform the Install Stage for an Update Installation. Now let's see what it takes to perform the Install Stage of a Patch Kit Installation:

1. Update the system firmware on the lead cluster member. Please review the Warning in section 25.5.1.3.
2. We are now ready to install the Patch Kit. Again, the following commands must be executed on the lead member.
   - If installing the Patch Kit from multi-user mode:

```
# cd /usr/patch_kit
# ./dupatch
```

← or where your Patch Kit is located

   - If installing the Patch Kit from single-user mode:

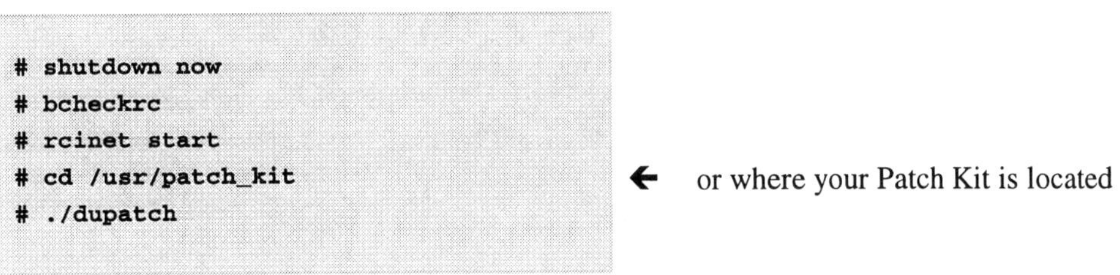

```
# shutdown now
# bcheckrc
# rcinet start
# cd /usr/patch_kit
# ./dupatch
```

← or where your Patch Kit is located

WARNING:

While you have a choice of installing Patch Kits in either multi-user or single-user mode, we agree with HP in recommending that the Patch Kit installations should be performed in single-user mode. Doing so will reduce the risk of another Systems Administrator causing unintentional issues.

As the contents of every Patch Kit vary from release to release, we won't bore you with the details here but instead refer you to the Patch Kit's Summary and Release Notes for expanded information. It should also be noted that Patch Kits have been known to take anywhere from thirty minutes to two hours to install. This depends on the number of patches in the Patch Kit and the type of server you are attempting to patch.

3. Once the `dupatch` command is complete, reboot the lead cluster member.

25.5.5 Postinstall Stage

The Postinstall Stage verifies that the Install Stage has completed and the Update Installation and/or the Patch Kit Installation and/or the NHD Kit Installation has completed successfully. This stage must be done on the "lead" member.

```
# clu_upgrade postinstall

This is the cluster upgrade program.
You have indicated that you want to perform the 'postinstall' stage of the upgrade.
Do you want to continue to upgrade the cluster? [yes]: yes
```

```
The 'postinstall' stage of the upgrade has completed successfully.
```

We would now recommend that you test the newly upgraded software before rolling the other cluster members to this new version.

25.5.5.1 Testing the Newly Upgraded *TruCluster* Server Software

First, let's test the Cluster File System by relocating a cluster file system between individual cluster members. In this example, we have just completed the `installupdate` on the server `molari`. The server `sheridan` has not been rolled to the new version of the *TruCluster* Server software yet.

```
# cfsmgr -v -a server /

 Domain or filesystem name = /
 Server Name = sheridan
 Server Status : OK
```

```
# cfsmgr -h sheridan -r -a SERVER=molari /

Recovering filesystem mounted at / to this node (member id 1)
Recovery to this node (member id 1) complete for filesystem mounted at /
```

```
# cfsmgr -v -a server /

 Domain or filesystem name = /
 Server Name = molari
 Server Status : OK
```

Let's test Cluster Application Availability management. In this example, we will be relocating the CAA service for `cluster_lockd` from `sheridan` to `molari`.

```
# caa_relocate cluster_lockd -c molari

Attempting to stop `cluster_lockd` on member `sheridan`
Stop of `cluster_lockd` on member `sheridan` succeeded.
Attempting to start `cluster_lockd` on member `molari`
cluster NFS Locking:
         cluster rpc.statd started
         cluster rpc.lockd started
Start of `cluster_lockd` on member `molari` succeeded.
```

```
# caa_stat cluster_lockd

NAME=cluster_lockd
TYPE=application
TARGET=ONLINE
STATE=ONLINE on molari
```

So what have we really tested here? Well, we have tested that the new *TruCluster* Server software that we have upgraded to work the same as the old software.

25.5.5.2 Testing Application Software on the Newly Upgraded *TruCluster* Server Software

The next step would be to test the application software on the newly upgraded *TruCluster* Server software. Let's face it, this is probably the most important part of this chapter – testing and verifying that everything is okay from the standpoint of the user application software. You do not have *TruCluster* Server installed because it's really cool… or maybe you do… but because of the advantages it provides to you and your user community. These advantages do not mean very much if your users' application software does not work properly.

We strongly recommend that you test your individual applications on the new *TruCluster* Server software before continuing any further. Please make sure that it runs the same on the new *TruCluster* Server software as it did on the old *TruCluster* Server software. Your next question is probably, "How can you compare if you are now running on the new software?" While the cluster is running the new *TruCluster* Server software on the lead cluster member, it is still operating on the old *TruCluster* Server software on all the other non-rolled cluster members.

25.5.6 Roll Stage

While the lead cluster member was upgraded during the Install Stage, upgrades to the remaining cluster members are performed during the Roll Stage. The Roll Stage is performed individually on each of the remaining cluster members – one at a time and in single-user mode.

The "`clu_upgrade roll`" command performs the following:

- Verifies that the member to be rolled is in single-user mode, is not the lead cluster member, and has not been rolled yet.
- Backs up all the member-specific files for the member to be rolled.
- Sets up `it(8)` scripts that will be executed on reboot. These `it` scripts actually perform the installation and update of the new software.

The resulting output of the "`clu_upgrade roll`" command very much mirrors what was done during the Install Stage. If a version update was performed, then the output from the "`clu_upgrade roll`" will look a great deal like the output from the `installupdate` command. The same will be true for the installation of a Patch Kit.

Now let's show you what really happens during the Roll Stage:

First we need to shut down this cluster member to upgrade the system firmware. Again, please review the Warning in section 25.5.1.3.

```
# shutdown -hs now
...
Halting processes ...
...
```

Next we need to boot the system into single-user mode. As soon as this is done, we use `bcheckrc` to check and mount all the file systems and the "`lmf reset`" command to reset all the License PAKs to make them active.

```
P0>>> boot -fl 0
INIT: SINGLE-USER MODE
#
```

```
# /sbin/bcheckrc
```

```
# lmf reset
Combine OSF-USR ALS-NQ-2000NOV03-99 with OSF-USR UNIX-SERVER-IMPLICIT-USER
```

Now let's start the roll or upgrade of this cluster member. Please note that one of the first tasks performed is backing up the member-specific files.

25.5.6.1 Rolling a Cluster Member after the `installupdate` Program

The output from rolling a cluster member after a version update installation will probably look very familiar. It should, as this is basically what occurred during the `installupdate` with a few differences at the end. For the sake of not being too redundant, we will note only the differences in this example.

```
# clu_upgrade roll

This is the cluster upgrade program.
You have indicated that you want to perform the 'roll' stage of the upgrade.
Do you want to continue to upgrade the cluster? [yes]:yes
```

```
Backing up member-specific data for member: 2
...
*** START UPDATE INSTALLATION (Thu Nov 8 13:39:22 PST 2001) ***
    Checking for installed supplemental hardware support...
Completed check for installed supplemental hardware support
Checking for retired hardware...done.
Initializing new version information (OSF)...done
Initializing new version information (TCR)...done
Initializing the list of member specific files for member2...done
Update Installation has detected the following update installable products on your
system:
        Tru64 UNIX T5.1A-4 Operating System (Rev 1278)
        Tru64 UNIX TruCluster(TM) Server Software X5.1A-4 (Rev 619)

These products will be updated to the following versions:
        Tru64 UNIX V5.1A Operating System (Rev 1885)
        Tru64 UNIX TruCluster(TM) Server Software V5.1A (Rev 1312)

It is recommended that you update your system firmware and perform a
complete system backup before proceeding.  A log of this update
installation can be found at /var/adm/smlogs/update.log.
Do you want to continue the Update Installation?  (y/n) []: y
```

```
Do you want to select optional kernel components?  (y/n) [n]: y
```

```
Do you want to archive obsolete files?  (y/n) [n]: n
```

```
FLAGS:

*** Checking for conflicting software ***
The following software may require reinstallation after the Update
Installation is completed:
        COMPAQ C++ Version 6.3 for COMPAQ UNIX Systems
        DEC C++ Class Libraries Version 4.0 for Tru64 UNIX
        DECevent
        Development Enhancement Tools for Tru64 UNIX
Do you want to continue the Update Installation?  (y/n) [y]: y
```

```
*** Determining installed Operating System software ***
*** Determining installed Tru64 UNIX TruCluster(TM) Server Software X5.1A-4 (Rev
619) software ***
        Working....

*** Determining kernel components ***
*** KERNEL OPTION SELECTION ***
```

```
    Selection   Kernel Option
--------------------------------------------------------------
        1       System V Devices
        2       NTP V3 Kernel Phase Lock Loop (NTP_TIME)
        3       Kernel Breakpoint Debugger (KDEBUG)
        4       Packetfilter driver (PACKETFILTER)
        5       IP-in-IP Tunneling (IPTUNNEL)
        6       IP Version 6 (IPV6)
        7       Point-to-Point Protocol (PPP)
        8       STREAMS pckt module (PCKT)
        9       Data Link Bridge (DLPI V2.0 Service Class 1)
        10      X/Open Transport Interface (XTISO, TIMOD, TIRDWR)
        11      Digital Versatile Disk File System (DVDFS)
        12      ISO 9660 Compact Disc File System (CDFS)
        13      Audit Subsystem
        14      All of the above
        15      None of the above
        16      Help
        17      Display all options again
--------------------------------------------------------------
Choices (for example, 1 2 4-6): 1 2 3 4 8 11 12 13
```

```
You selected the following kernel options:
        System V Devices
        NTP V3 Kernel Phase Lock Loop (NTP_TIME)
        Kernel Breakpoint Debugger (KDEBUG)
        Packetfilter driver (PACKETFILTER)
        STREAMS pckt module (PCKT)
        Digital Versatile Disk File System (DVDFS)
        ISO 9660 Compact Disc File System (CDFS)
        Audit Subsystem
Is that correct? (y/n) [y]: y
```

```
*** Checking for file type conflicts ***
*** Checking for obsolete files ***
*** Checking file system space ***

Update Installation is now ready to begin modifying the files necessary
to reboot the cluster member off of the new OS. Please check the
/var/adm/smlogs/update.log and /var/adm/smlogs/it.log files for errors
after the installation is complete.

Do you want to continue the Update Installation? (y/n) [n]: y
*** Starting configuration merges for Update Install ***
```

Up to this point, it would be rather hard to differentiate this output from the output from `installupdate`. This next section of output is unique for the Roll Stage.

```
The critical files needed for reboot have been moved into place. The
 system will now reboot with the generic kernel for Compaq Computer
 Corporation Tru64 UNIX V5.1A and complete the rolling upgrade for this
 member (member2).
```

```
The 'roll' stage has completed successfully.  This
member must be rebooted in order to run with the newly installed software.
Do you want to reboot this member at this time? []: yes
You indicated that you want to reboot this member at this time.
Is that correct? [yes]: yes
The 'roll' stage of the upgrade has completed successfully.
```

As soon as the cluster member finishes rebooting, it configures the individual software subset for `member2`.

After the configuration of all the software subsets is complete, a new kernel will be built for this cluster member. The new kernel will be copied in place, and the system is rebooted.

```
Saving /sys/conf/SHERIDAN as /sys/conf/SHERIDAN.bck
The system will now automatically build a kernel
       with the selected options and then reboot.  This can take
       up to 15 minutes, depending on the processor type.
*** PERFORMING KERNEL BUILD ***
...
System rebooting
```

This cluster member is now running on the new *TruCluster* Server software.

25.5.6.2 Rolling a Cluster Member after the `dupatch` Program

The output of a roll of a cluster member after a Patch Kit Installation is much simpler than a roll after an Update Installation.

```
# clu_upgrade roll

This is the cluster upgrade program.
You have indicated that you want to perform the 'roll' stage of the upgrade.
Do you want to continue to upgrade the cluster? [yes]: yes
```

```
Backing up member-specific data for member: 2
....
The 'roll' stage has completed successfully.  This member must be rebooted in order
to run with the newly installed software.
Do you want to reboot this member at this time? []: yes
```

```
You indicated that you want to reboot this member at this time.
Is that correct? [yes]: yes
```

After the cluster node is rebooted, the newly patched software subsets are installed and configured. Finally a new kernel is built and copied into place. The cluster member is again rebooted, but this time, when the system comes back up it will do so on the newly patched *TruCluster* Server software.

25.5.6.3 A Final Word on Rolling Cluster Members

The Roll Stage is not complete until each and every cluster member, except the lead cluster member, is rolled. If a cluster member goes down and cannot be rebooted before all cluster members are rolled, it is recommended that this cluster member be deleted from the cluster. You can always add this cluster member back after the Rolling Upgrade is complete and this system is repaired.

25.5.7 Switch Stage

The Switch Stage is where we actually turn on any new software features installed during the Install Stage. Until this point, after the Install Stage and prior to the completion of the Roll Stage, the cluster was actually operating on two different versions of the operation system and *TruCluster* Server software. One of the ways it does this is by making sure that active features between the different versions of the software are as compatible as possible. This is handled by effectively "turning off" or disabling any and all new features installed during the Roll Stage until the entire cluster is at the same version of the software.

In detail, let's see what happens when the "`clu_upgrade switch`" command is executed:

- First, it verifies that all cluster members have been rolled and that they are all operating off the same version of the operating system and the *TruCluster* Server software.
- The new version ID of the operating system and cluster software is then set in each cluster member's `/etc/sysconfigtab` file. This version ID corresponds to the running kernel.

This "`clu_upgrade switch`" command is executed in multi-user mode and on any cluster member. This command is only executed once and only on one node of the cluster.

```
# clu_upgrade switch

This is the cluster upgrade program.
You have indicated that you want to perform the 'switch' stage of the upgrade.
Do you want to continue to upgrade the cluster? [yes]: yes
```

```
Initiating version switch on cluster members
...
The cluster upgrade 'switch' stage has completed successfully.
All cluster members must be rebooted before running the 'clean' command.
```

After the "`clu_upgrade switch`" command completes, every member in the cluster must be rebooted one at a time. For the convenience of the System Administrator and the users, the reboot of each cluster member can be done over time.

CAUTION:

It should be noted that as soon as the Switch Stage is completed or the "switch thrown," you cannot issue any "`clu_upgrade undo`" commands.

25.5.8 Clean Stage

The Clean Stage is the final stage of the Rolling Upgrade. The "clu_upgrade clean" command performs the following:

- Verifies that the Switch Stage has been completed.
- Removes all the tagged (.Old..) files.
- Removes all the on-disk backups that were created by the clu_upgrade command.
- Removes the Kit installation directories: /var/adm/update/TruClusterKit, /var/adm/update/OSKit, and/or /var/adm/update/NHDKit.
- Creates a directory for the upgrade just completed in /cluster/admin/clu_upgrade/history/release_version. This directory contains the log files for each stage of the upgrade.

The following is an example of output from the "clu_upgrade clean" command:

```
# clu_upgrade clean

This is the cluster upgrade program.
You have indicated that you want to perform the 'clean' stage of the upgrade.
Do you want to continue to upgrade the cluster? [yes]:yes
```

```
.Deleting tagged files.
......................................................................
Removing back-up and kit files

The Update Administration Utility is typically run after an update
installation to manage the files that are saved during an update installation.
Do you want to run the Update Administration Utility at this time? [yes]:yes
```

```
The Update Installation Cleanup utility is used to clean up backup files created
by Update Installation. Update Installation can create two types of files: .PreUPD
and .PreMRG.  The .PreUPD files are copies of unprotected customized system files
as they existed prior to running Update Installation. The .PreMRG files are copies
of protected system files as they existed prior to running Update Installation.
```

At this point, the cluster is now operating on the newly upgraded software.

25.6 Checking the Status of the Rolling Upgrade

There will be times when you will want to check the status of the rolling upgrade or to verify where you are in the rolling upgrade process. The commands in Table 25-4 can be used to obtain the status of the Rolling Upgrade. These commands may be executed at any time provided that the Clean Stage has not been initiated.

Here is an example of the Rolling Upgrade status after the Roll Stage.

How to Check the Rolling Upgrade Status

Command	Function of the Command
`clu_upgrade -v` `clu_upgrade -v status`	Display the status of the Rolling Upgrade.
`clu_upgrade check [`*stage*`]`	Check to see if the specific *stage* can be performed. If the *stage* is not specified then a check will be made to determine if the very next stage can be performed.
`clu_upgrade started` *stage* `clu_upgrade completed` *stage*	Check to see if the specified *stage* has been started or has been completed.
`clu_upgrade check roll` *memberid*	Check to see if the specified cluster member (*memberid*) has been rolled to the new software.
`clu_upgrade tagged check [`*product code*`]`	A check is made to determine if a tagged file has been created for the specified product. If the *product code* is not provided, a check is made of all the tagged files versus all products installed on the cluster.

Table 25-4: How to Check the Rolling Upgrade Status

```
# clu_upgrade -v status

Retrieving cluster upgrade status.

Upgrade Status

Stage           Status                       Date
setup           started:                     Thu Nov  8 08:04:14 PST 2001
                lead member:                 1
                cluster kit source:          /cdrom1/TruCluster/kit/
                completed:                   Thu Nov  8 08:22:18 PST 2001

preinstall      started:                     Thu Nov  8 08:40:42 PST 2001
                completed:                   Thu Nov  8 08:41:12 PST 2001

install         started:                     Thu Nov  8 12:12:12 PST 2001
                completed:                   Thu Nov  8 13:15:33 PST 2001

postinstall     started:                     Thu Nov  8 13:34:25 PST 2001
                completed:                   Thu Nov  8 13:34:25 PST 2001

roll            started:                     Thu Nov  8 13:38:36 PST 2001
                members rolled:              1 2
                completed:                   Thu Nov  8 13:52:22 PST 2001
```

How to Undo		
Stage to Undo	**Command**	**Comments**
Setup	`clu_upgrade undo setup`	This must be executed on the lead member and no other cluster members may be running on tagged files. If there are cluster members running on tagged files then use the command **`clu_upgrade`** tagged disable ***`memberid`*** command to disable the tagged files on the specified cluster member.
Preinstall	`clu_upgrade undo preinstall`	This command must be run on the lead cluster member.
Install	`clu_upgrade undo install`	Halt the lead cluster member and then execute this command on any other cluster member. When this command is completed then boot the lead cluster member.
Postinstall	`clu_upgrade undo postinstall`	This command must be run on the lead cluster member.
Roll	`clu_upgrade undo roll` *`memberid`*	Halt the cluster member for which you wish to undo the Roll Stage then execute this command on any other cluster member. When this command is completed then boot the halted cluster member.

Table 25-5: How to Undo

25.7 Undoing a Stage in the Rolling Upgrade

Practically any stage, with the exception of the Switch Stage and the Clean Stage, can be undone. What do we mean? Well, we have the capability of undoing stages of the Rolling Upgrade. In the next table, we show which stages can be undone, how to undo the stage, and any comments related to this process. See Table 25-5.

25.8 Uninstalling a Patch Kit

Uninstalling a Patch Kit is very much like installing a Patch Kit – provided of course you opted to make the original Patch Kit installation reversible.

As outlined in this chapter, you would follow each stage of the Rolling Upgrade as if you were actually installing a Patch Kit. You would even execute the `dupatch` command but instead of following the instructions for the installation of the Patch Kit, you would follow the instructions for the un-installation of the Patch Kit. After the `dupatch` command is completed and the Patch Kit is completely uninstalled, follow the remaining stages for the Rolling Upgrade as you normally would.

25.9 Log Files for the Rolling Upgrade

Like many systems managers, we know that you are curious and will want to see "where the bodies are buried" for the Rolling Upgrade. Whether the Rolling Upgrade was successful or aborted, the directory that contains not only the logs, but also all the timelines when each stage is started or completed is in the `/cluster/admin/clu_upgrade/history` directory.

Let's take a quick look at the contents of this directory.

```
# pwd
/cluster/admin/clu_upgrade/history
```

```
# ls
Compaq.Tru64.UNIX.V5.0A.Rev.1094/  Compaq.Tru64.UNIX.V5.1.Rev.732-1/
Compaq.Tru64.UNIX.V5.1.Rev.732/
```

```
# cd Compaq.Tru64.UNIX.V5.1.Rev.732-1 && ls

clean.completed            roll.completed.member2
clean.started              roll.started
clu_upgrade.log            roll.started.member1
installupdate              roll.started.member2
installupdate.member       setup.completed
patch.completed            setup.started
patch.started              switch.completed
postinstall.completed      switch.completed.member1
postinstall.started        switch.completed.member2
preinstall.completed       switch.started
preinstall.started         tag_files.list
roll.completed             tag_files.miss
roll.completed.member1
```

The names of the files speak for themselves. We recommend that you take the opportunity to examine the contents of these files as you perform a Rolling Upgrade on a cluster.

25.10 Determining which Patches are Installed

Many systems administrators have asked us, "Given that the cluster has been patched, is there a quick way to determine exactly which Patch Kits are installed?" Actually, this is an easy and exceptionally quick process. The following shows two ways to determine which Patch Kits have been installed onto your cluster:

```
# dupatch -track -type kit

        * Previous session logs saved in session.log.[1-25]

- This dupatch session is logged in /var/adm/patch/log/session.log

Gathering details of relevant patches, this may take a bit of time
```

```
Patches installed on the system came from following patch kits:
----------------------------------------------------------------

- T64V51AS0001-20001114 OSF510
- T64V51AS0001-20001114 TCR510
- T64V51AS0002-20001204 OSF510
- T64V51AS0002-20001204 TCR510
- T64V51AS0003-20010521 OSF510
- T64V51AS0003-20010521 TCR510

                        NOTE

When a patch kit is listed, it does not necessarily mean
all patches on that kit are installed on your system.
```

Or

```
# grep KITNAME /var/adm/patch/log/event.log

KITNAME><T64V50AAS0001-20000718> TCR505, OSF505
KITNAME><T64V50AAS0001-20000718> OSF505, TCR505
KITNAME><T64V51AS0001-20001114> TCR510, OSF510
KITNAME><T64V51AS0001-20001114> OSF510, TCR510
KITNAME><T64V51AS0002-20001204> TCR510, OSF510
KITNAME><T64V51AS0002-20001204> OSF510, TCR510
KITNAME><T64V51AS0003-20010521> TCR510, OSF510
KITNAME><T64V51AS0003-20010521> OSF510, TCR510
```

Both examples show that Patch Kits 1, 2, and 3 are installed for *Tru64* UNIX version 5.1 and *TruCluster* Server version 5.1. For more information on the separate Patch Kits, we refer you to each Patch Kit's Patch Summary and Release Notes document.

25.11 The Non-Rolling Patch Upgrade

While the current patch strategy of performing a Rolling Upgrade is designed to provide the greatest amount of availability, many systems managers have indicated that this high availability option is not utilized for mission critical services. Although the cluster is up and available, as soon as the installation of a Patch Kit starts, the cluster is considered to be down and therefore unavailable. Understandably, systems managers want a solution to apply patches that is simpler, quicker to implement, and minimizes the number of reboots.

The cluster engineers at HP have come up with an inventive solution to this new requirement. Instead of performing a Rolling Upgrade for a Patch Kit, they will provide new functionality to allow for a Non-Rolling Patch Upgrade.

How would this work? The `dupatch` program will be modified to provide the option of patching the entire cluster as a single unit. `dupatch` will be run on one member of the cluster and once it completes the management of the patches, it will issue a command to the other cluster members to perform the patch propagation, the patch configuration, and the building of the individual kernels for each of the cluster members. This also means that while the Non-Rolling Patch Upgrade is in progress, there should be no users or user applications running on the cluster.

One note about the Non-Rolling Patch Upgrade process: because this uses the Event Management (EVM) subsystem[8] within *Tru64* UNIX, it is necessary that all cluster nodes be in multi-user mode with network services up and available.

This all sounds like a nice future feature right? As of this writing, preliminary testing has been quite impressive with the Non-Rolling Patch Upgrade. Using this new feature, the time to patch a three-node cluster on *Tru64* UNIX version 5.1 and *TruCluster* Server version 5.1 is approximately 36 minutes. An eight-node cluster took 1 hour 20 minutes.

When will this feature be available and on which versions of *TruCluster* Server? This new feature is scheduled to be introduced starting with Patch Kit 2 for *Tru64* UNIX version 5.1A/*TruCluster* Server 5.1A in late Spring 2002. It is not known if HP will provide this same functionality with later Patch Kits for V5.0A and V5.1.

25.12 References

- The *TruCluster* Server Cluster Installation Guide.
- The *TruCluster* Server Cluster Administration Guide.
- The *Tru64* UNIX and *TruCluster* Software Patch Summary and Release Notes.
- The *Tru64* UNIX and *TruCluster* Software Patch Kit Installation Instruction document.
- Compaq Support Blitz TD 2807-C.
- Reference pages (noted within the text).

[8] For more information on the Event Management (EVM) subsystem, please see Chapter 8 – the Event Manager.

26

Migrating to TruCluster Server

Migrating from *TruCluster* Production Server or *TruCluster* Available Server version 1.[56] to *TruCluster* Server version 5.X is a fairly significant task since you can't perform a "rolling" upgrade; in fact, you can't have a V1.[56] cluster connected to a V5.X cluster. There are tools, however, to help you migrate (we use the term "migrate" because it is a more accurate description of the process than "upgrade"). There are three basic migration options, and we'll discuss each one and illustrate the most popular. We will also raise some of the considerations and requirements necessary to move from the previous type of cluster to the new one.

We will cover the following:

26.1 Migration Assessment

Before beginning any sort of migration, you should assess your current situation to see what work needs to be done before a successful migration is performed.

26.1.1 Migration Issues

Consider this list of migration issues. You will have to address these before initiating your migration since many of them could turn out to be showstoppers if you don't plan ahead.

- There can be no sharing of the storage or cluster interconnect between a V1.[56] and V5.X clusters.
- Some additional hardware may be required.
  - Storage for new cluster-common file systems, member boot disks, and quorum disk.

- Cluster Interconnect (LAN or Memory Channel), which may not already be in place in many configurations (such as ASE-only configurations).
  - If you are currently using Memory Channel 1 and you will be adding newer systems to your cluster (such as the DS or ES series AlphaServers, which only support Memory Channel 2), you should be aware that Memory Channel 1 and Memory Channel 2 cannot exist (mixed) on the same rail. You should check the Supported Options web site to see what is supported.

    http://www.compaq.com/alphaserver/products/options.html
- Additional shared SCSI controllers to eliminate single points of failure.
- Additional network interface to reduce single points of failure.

- *Tru64* UNIX version 5.X is a major operating system upgrade, and you should read the Release Notes and Installation Guide to familiarize yourself with the various changes before diving in.
- Applications must be supported on *Tru64* UNIX version 5.X. It could be that the version of your production application supported on V5.X is very different from installation, configuration, and implementation. Know this before moving forward.
- There is a new AdvFS file system on-disk structure in V5.X. This change is only relevant for newly created file domains, and the previous format of the domain is compatible with V5.X. No update to the existing domain structure occurs during an OS upgrade.
  - The new on-disk structure allows tracking of more files in a domain and delivers better performance when creating and accessing files.
- The Logical Storage Manager (LSM) has on-disk changes that take effect during an `installupdate(8)`. These changes can be rolled back if you run `volsave(8)` before the upgrade (and save the files produced by `volsave`): `clu_migrate_save` runs `volsave`. Note: This ability to rollback the LSM on-disk structures is important if you upgrade; however, we recommend a fresh install of V5.X, not an `installupdate` to V5.X.
- *TruCluster* Server V5.X requires a new license (`TCS-UA`), which is member-specific; that is, it must be installed on each member.
- The UFS file system is not supported read-write cluster-wide (but is supported read-write while mounted exclusively on a single member as of V5.1A).[1]
- Multiple ASEs in a V1.[56] configuration are tricky and require special consideration but should rarely occur. See section 26.4.6 for more information on multiple ASEs.
- ASE-specific environment variables (such as `MEMBER_STATE`, `ASEROUTING`, `ASE_ID`, and `ASE_PARTIAL_MIRRORING`) do not exist in *TruCluster* Server.

[1] Using "`mount -o server_only`".

26.1.2 Migration Planning

Ask yourself these questions to get an idea of how you will migrate to the new version and what resources and hardware you'll need.

- How many systems are in the current cluster and will any of them be available for use in the migration? This is key if you choose migration option 3. The migration options are covered in section 26.3.
- What is the current version of the operating system and *TruCluster*? The migration tools require *TruCluster* V1.5 or V1.6.
- Are there additional PCI slots in the future members of a V5.X cluster? This is in case a cluster interconnect and/or additional storage card might need to be added.
- What is acceptable downtime for the migration? This maintenance window must be considered, especially if migration option 3, requiring some "hard" down time, is chosen.
- Are there scripts that reference *Tru64* UNIX version 4.X disk names (`/dev/rz23c`)? These will have to be modified (or symbolic links added) since *TruCluster* Server does not support the old device names. See `clu_migrate_save` output for the mappings.
- What applications are being used? These will have to be checked to see if they are compatible with *Tru64* UNIX version 5.X.
- What types of ASE services are being used? ASE services are like CAA resources in version 5.X. See Section 23.4 for more on CAA resources.
  - Disk services are not needed in *TruCluster* Server version 5.X because of the nature of shared storage.
    - You no longer have to associate an application resource with storage because the storage is accessible (with a few exceptions) from each member. You may, however, create CAA resources such that the application tries to locate the storage to the member that is running the application. See Chapter 24 for an example.
    - You need a CAA resource if you want to set the relocation policy and/or to set up start and stop scripts, which are combined into one script in *TruCluster* Server.
  - NFS services aren't required; instead NFS service is fully integrated into V5.X clusters. Clients can use the default cluster alias or another cluster alias for NFS mounting. See Section 20.4.2 for more about NFS Serving and Section 20.4.2.3 for the details about the `exports.aliases` file.
  - The old-style DRD services are also not needed, but you may need to create symbolic links to point to the new device names (`/dev/rdisk/dskN[a-h]`) for the application to run.
- What are the versions of SRM firmware, storage controller (HSx), and Host Bus Adapters (KxPxx)? These should all be updated to the latest version.
- Do you have single points of failure for the new cluster-common file systems or disks? You should use some combination of software and/or hardware mirroring for `cluster_root`, `cluster_usr`, and `cluster_var`. You can use LSM to mirror `cluster_usr` and

cluster_var. As of V5.1A, you can also mirror cluster_root and swap with LSM. The boot partition and CNX partition must be mirrored at the hardware level as of this writing. Since primary swap, the boot and CNX partitions are all on the same disk; it probably makes sense to mirror the whole disk at the hardware level. Note: if you follow our recommendations in Chapter 21, the member book disk can be restored in a matter of 10-15 minutes provided that the failing member didn't cause the cluster to lose quorum. So even if you don't mirror the member boot disk, you can recreate it rather quickly.

26.2 Migration Tools

There are four primary scripts that will help you migrate from V1.[56] to V5.X clusters. These scripts are part of the *TruCluster* Server kit found on the *Tru64* UNIX Associated Products CD (Volume 2) and are documented in the Cluster Installation manual. The specific subset name is TCRMIGRATE5xx. On your V1.[56] cluster, install this subset on each member. Here we show installing the kit from a V5.1A distribution.

```
# mount -r /dev/rz4c /mnt
# setld -l /mnt/TruCluster/kit TCRMIGRATE520
```

These scripts will be installed into the /usr/opt/TruCluster/tools/migrate directory.

- clu_migrate_check

  The clu_migrate_check script performs a check on the general hardware, firmware, and file systems. The clu_migrate_check script output will contain:

  - Hardware and firmware information.
  - List of unsupported hardware.
  - List of differences with V5 (for example, ASE-specific paths, separate start and stop scripts, etc.).
  - List of cluster IP addresses (ASE services).

  This is used in preparation for option 3 and possibly option 2.

- clu_migrate_save

  The clu_migrate_save script saves information about the system, the ASE, and how the shared storage is used by the ASE services and stores this data in /var/TruCluster_migration/<CLUSTER_NET>. This is used in either option 2 or option 3.

- clu_migrate_recover

  The clu_migrate_recover script restores the cluster configuration (LSM configuration, frees devices) in the event of a migration failure. This could be used in option 2 or option 3 but only on a failed migration attempt.

- `clu_migrate_configure`

  The `clu_migrate_configure` script configures the storage and file systems on the V5.X cluster using the data saved by `clu_migrate_save`. Of the four scripts, this is the only one that runs on the V5.X cluster. This is used in option 2 or option 3.

  Note: Use "`clu_migrate_configure -x`" to see what `clu_migrate_configure` would do without actually carrying out any of the instructions.

For more details about the `clu_migrate_*` scripts, refer to Chapter 8 of the *TruCluster* Server Cluster Installation Manual.

26.3 Migration Options

How then do you migrate a V1.[56] cluster to V5.X when you can't perform a rolling upgrade and you can't have the V5.X cluster connected to the V1.[56] cluster (in any way except possibly on a LAN)? You have three options from which to choose. These options are usually thought of as a trade-off between downtime and expense.

- Option 1:

  Create a separate cluster consisting of new systems and storage. Once this cluster is built and tested, migrate the functionality from the V1.[56] cluster to this new V5.X cluster. The problem is that few people have the luxury of obtaining this additional hardware.

- Option 2:

  Create a separate, perhaps limited cluster with new systems and at least enough storage to establish the cluster and test your applications. Once the new cluster is fully configured and tested, physically connect the old storage from the V1.[56] cluster to the new cluster. This option is slightly less expensive than option 1 but still requires additional hardware.

- Option 3:

  Upgrade the existing V1.[56] cluster using its hardware and storage. Remove and disconnect one member from the V1.[56] cluster, install and configure a standalone *Tru64* UNIX V5.X system, shut down the remaining systems in the V1.[56] cluster, connect the V1.[56]'s storage to the standalone V5.X system, configure the storage, create a single-member cluster, and then add the other systems to the new cluster. This option requires the least amount of additional hardware (perhaps some additional disks, HBAs, and LAN interconnect cards (if using LAN interconnects for the cluster interconnect)).

26.4 Migration Example

Let's run through our "option 3" example. We will mostly use existing hardware, configure and test the version 5.X cluster while a reduced version 4.X cluster continues our live production, then complete the migration with a minimum of downtime. If there is a problem with the applications or CAA resources, you will see how to return to the full version 4.X cluster.

26.4.1 Planning

Plan. We cannot emphasize enough the importance of planning your migration and your cluster layout. If you skip this step, you may be forced to rebuild the cluster in the not too distant future. Part of your planning process should include reading the *TruCluster* manuals. The *TruCluster* Server Cluster Technical Overview is a small manual, which you should read cover to cover because it will ground you in the *TruCluster* Server components and technology. Another crucial part of planning is determining which layered products you will need to upgrade. Don't gloss over this point because some of your layered products that run on V5.X could differ from your current version and therefore require learning an updated product.

26.4.2 Check Your Existing Hardware for Compatibility

After you've planned how the cluster will be laid out and migrated, you are ready to begin the process. Install the `TCRMIGRATE5XX` subset and run `clu_migrate_save` (to build the data that will automate part of the migration). Also run "`sys_check -escalate`" on each member (both as a precautionary measure – you want this data in case you have to recreate part of the V1.[56] infrastructure – and so you can see what hardware you have on the cluster). As a result of planning and reviewing the "`sys_check -escalate`" data, purchase any hardware necessary for the new cluster. This would also be a good time to consider converting any UFS file systems to AdvFS. If you convert the file system(s) now, you won't have to repeat the task should the migration fail to complete for some reason. Figure 26-1 shows our V1.[56] cluster starting point.

Note: By converting to AdvFS at this state, you will be taking the old AdvFS on-disk structure forward. You should, at a later time, convert to the new structure by creating a new file domain and restoring the data to that domain.

26.4.3 Divide and Conquer

Pick a member to remove from the V1.[56] cluster (this will be our V5.X cluster beachhead). Add any of the identified required hardware to that system. Also update the firmware and install *Tru64* UNIX V5.X on the removed system as seen in Figure 26-2. Notice that neither the storage nor the cluster interconnect is shared at this point. Remember, we recommend a fresh install of V5.X, not an `installupdate` to V5.X, because there are many major changes in the OS since V4.X (AdvFS, LSM, and clustering, just to name a few).

26.4.4 Create a *TruCluster* Server Cluster

Install *TruCluster* Server on your newly installed V5.X system. This is a good time to apply the latest patch kit. (Simply installing the *TruCluster* subsets does not create a cluster.) Also, you should partition your disks for the cluster-common file systems (`cluster_root`, `cluster_usr`, and `cluster_var`). Now run `clu_create` to create a single-member cluster. Your new "split" cluster should look something like Figure 26-3. Again, these are two completely separate one-member clusters.

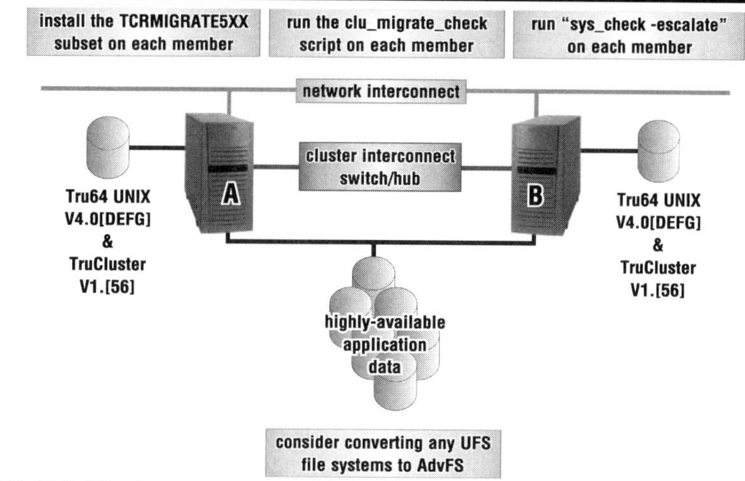

Figure 26-1: V1.[56] Cluster

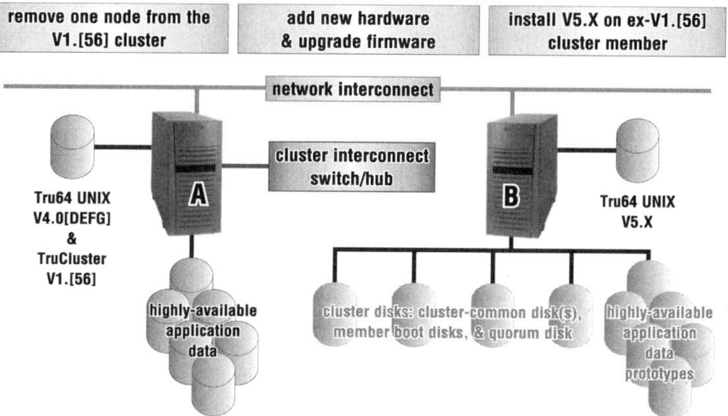

Figure 26-2: Preparing for the New Cluster – Install Tru64 UNIX

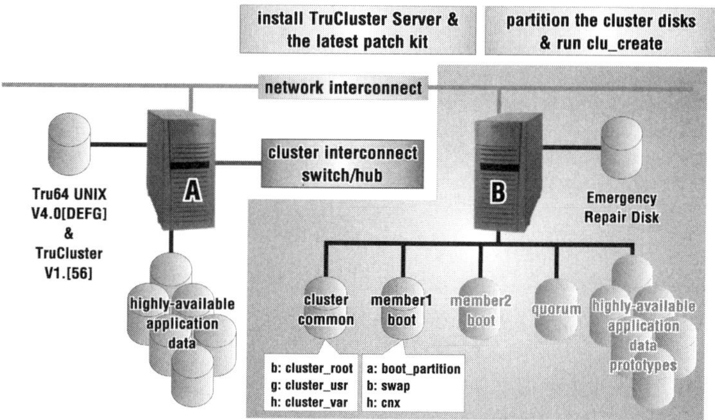

Figure 26-3: Create a One-Member TruCluster Server Cluster

26.4.5 Test CAA Resources

Install the applications and set up any test databases if necessary. Depending on the application, it may be best to install the application before running `clu_create` but reference the application's installation guide for further information. Create the CAA application resources for the ASE services that will be migrated to the V5.X cluster and test them. After testing, set them `OFFLINE` so that the production storage can be moved into the new cluster (in place of the prototype) as seen in Figure 26-5.

26.4.6 Gather the Configuration Data

On the V1.[56] cluster, make sure that none of the services have a placement policy to prevent services from running on the remaining node. (Otherwise we won't pick up that service, and the service won't be available during this phase of the migration.) Change the placement policy if necessary and run `clu_migrate_save`. Then set all of the ASE services `OFFLINE` (with an "`asemgr -x <service>`" command) in case you need to return to the V1.[56] cluster, and shut down the V1.[56] cluster (only one member in our example) as shown in Figure 26-4. Example `clu_migrate_save` output:

```
beginLog molari Thu May 16 15:24:22 EDT 2002
               TruCluster Migration Data Gather Tool
               _____________________________________

    ******************** Running preliminary checks ********************

    ********************** Backing up for Recovery **********************

Backing up console variables
    (to /var/TruCluster_migration/molari-mc0/ConsoleVars)

Backing up LSM configuration
    (to /var/TruCluster_migration/molari-mc0/Backup.d/LSM.d/)
voldg: Volume daemon is not accessible

Backing up disk labels
    (to /var/TruCluster_migration/molari-mc0/Backup.d/Disklabels.d/)
        Saving disk label for rz0
        Saving disk label for rz16
        Saving disk label for rz17
        Saving disk label for rz18
        Saving disk label for rz19
        Saving disk label for rz20
*** Warning: Cannot access /dev/rrz21c
scu: Unable to open device '/dev/rrz21c', ENXIO (6) - No such device or address

    *********** Labeling Disks for Device Name Mapping on V5.* ***********

Labeling disk label packids ...
Labeling device /dev/rrz0c with "@rz0"[2]
```

[2] The disklabel field "label" contains the name of the old device name: "label: @rz34."

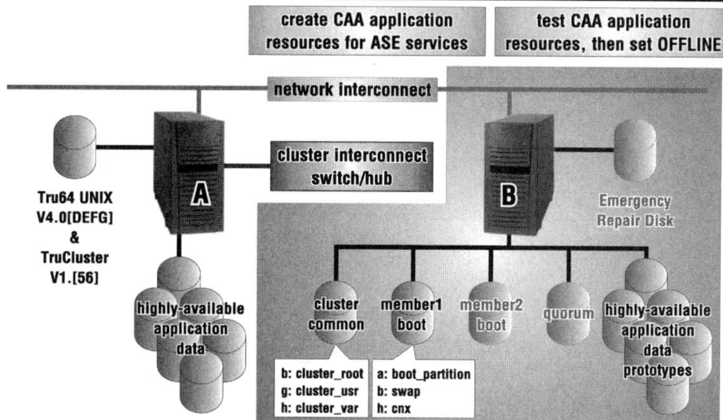

Figure 26-5: Create and Test Application Resources

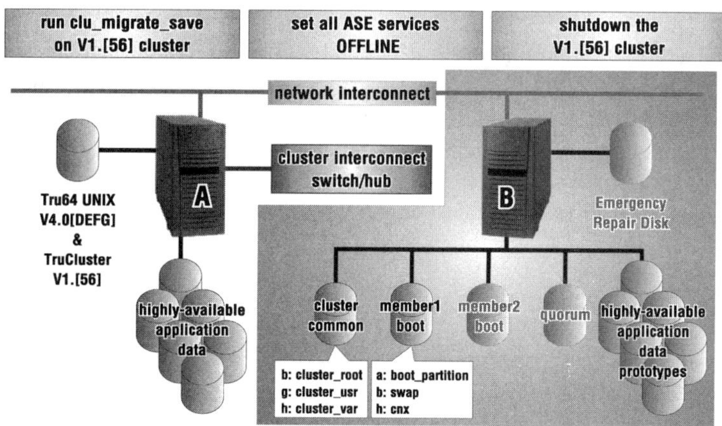

Figure 26-4: Save the Current Cluster's Configuration Information

```
Labeling device /dev/rrz16c with "@rz16"
Labeling device /dev/rrz17c with "@rz17"
Labeling device /dev/rrz18c with "@rz18"
Labeling device /dev/rrz19c with "@rz19"
Labeling device /dev/rrz20c with "@rz20"
*** Warning: Cannot access /dev/rrz21c
scu: Unable to open device '/dev/rrz21c', ENXIO (6) - No such device or address

    **************** Gathering Information for Migration ****************

Gathering ASE database information (might take a long time for large ASEs) ...

Saving ASE information ...
       LSM disk group information
       Distributed Raw Disk information
       AdvFS domain information
       Mount point information
       NFS export information
       Service information
       User-defined action scripts
```

```
    ******* Copy Migration Information to a Tru64 UNIX V5.* System *******

The directories containing the information gathered by this utility must be
copied to the system that will become the first member of the new cluster.  If
the /.rhosts file on that system allows access for root@molari,
this utility can copy these directories automatically.  Otherwise, manually
copy the directories after this utility exits.

Copy the directories? (y/n):
After this utility exits, copy the following directory and its contents to
the Tru64 UNIX system that will be the first member of the new cluster.

        /var/TruCluster_migration/molari-mc0/

Press Return to continue ...

    ***************** TruCluster Data Gather Completed *****************

Information regarding the gathered information can be found in the file:
  /var/TruCluster_migration/molari-mc0/README

A log of this session can be found in the file:
  /var/TruCluster_migration/molari-mc0/Log.d/clu_migrate_save.log
```

If you happen to have more than one ASE, it's possible that you could have the same device name (`/dev/rz10c`) referencing two different physical devices (once in ASE 1, and once in ASE 2). You could relocate all services to a single member in each ASE and run `clu_migrate_save` on each member holding all the services per ASE (which saves two sets of data). Once you have the V5.X cluster installed and all members added, run `clu_migrate_configure` twice (once for each set of saved data from the two ASEs), and then manually resolve any conflicts based on duplicate disk device names.

26.4.7 Apply the Configuration Data

As shown in Figure 26-6, move the data (storage) to the V5.X cluster and run `clu_migrate_configure` to configure the storage. Then test the application resources with the actual production data. By the way, "`clu_migrate_configure -x`" will show you what the script would do without actually doing it.

If testing is successful, continue with section 26.4.8; otherwise, return for now to the V1.[56] cluster by following the directions starting in section 26.4.11.

26.4.8 Connect the Other Member to the New Cluster

Add any required hardware to the other member; update its firmware; set the SRM environment variables (`bootdef_dev`, `boot_reset`, `auto_action`); and connect the "new" system back to the cluster interconnect and shared storage so that we can add it to the cluster as shown in Figure 26-7.

26.4.9 Add the Old Member to the New Cluster

As shown in Figure 26-8, run `clu_add_member` on the V5.X cluster to add the new member. Once `clu_add_member` is complete, you can boot the new V5.X cluster member, configure its network interface(s), and configure a quorum disk (at least we will configure a quorum disk since this is a two-member cluster).

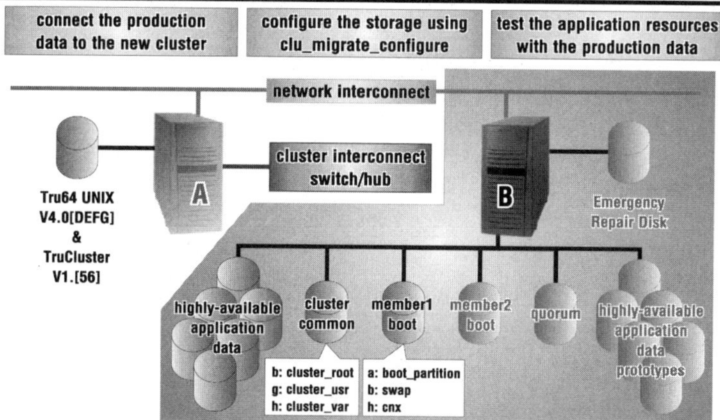

Figure 26-6: Apply the Configuration Data to the New Cluster

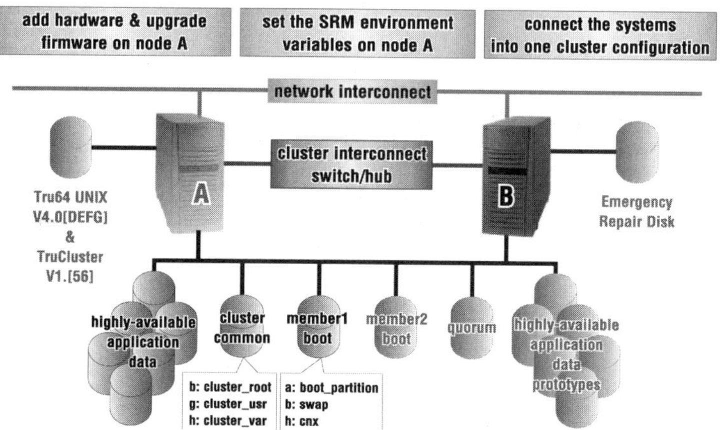

Figure 26-7: Connect the Second System to the New Cluster

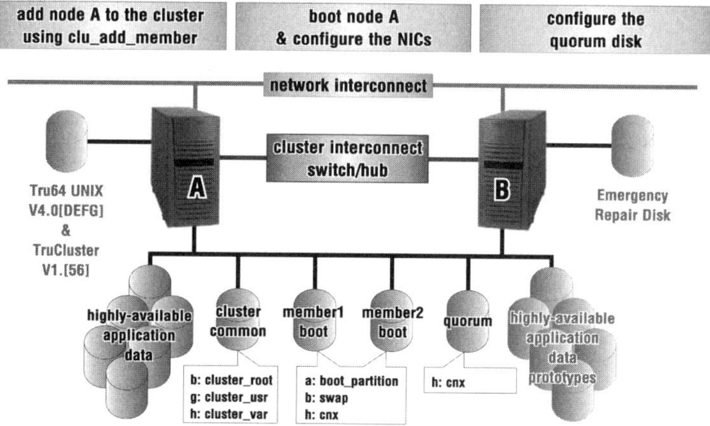

Figure 26-8: Add the Second System to the New Cluster

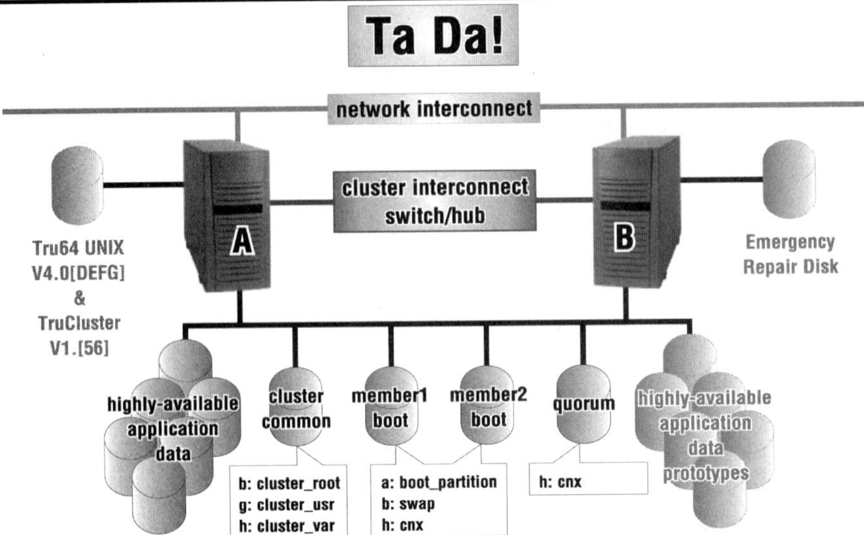

Figure 26-9: Welcome to TruCluster Server!

26.4.10 Admire New Cluster

If you've made it this far, congratulations! See Figure 26-9 for a picture of what the new migrated cluster looks like. Label the Emergency Repair disk as such and keep it for emergencies (i.e., in case you have to boot a non-clustered member to restore a root file system (see Chapter 22)).

26.4.11 Retreat to the V1.[56] Cluster

If the migration failed, reconnect the production data (storage) back to the V1.[56] cluster; boot the V1.[56] cluster (which consists of the one member); run `clu_migrate_recover` and set the ASE services ONLINE (`asemgr -s <service>`) as shown in Figure 26-10.

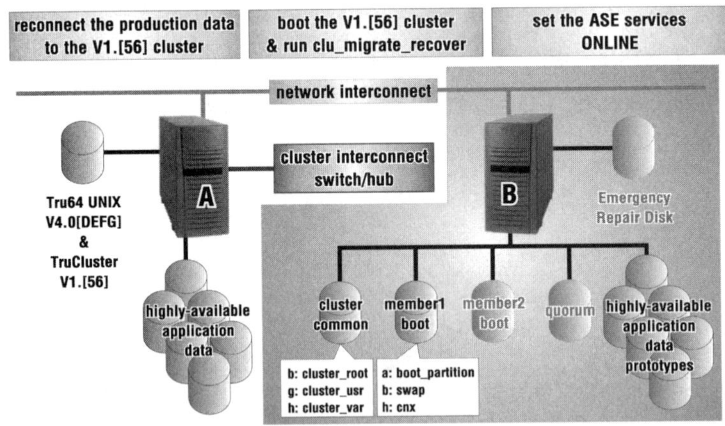

Figure 26-10: Failed Migration Recovery

If you wish to completely undo the migration, restore V4.0X/V1.[56] onto the removed node and add it back into the V1.[56] cluster.

26.4.12 Where's the Log?

A log of a successful option 3 upgrade can be found at:

http://www.tru64unix.compaq.com/docs/highavail/migration/migration_log.htm

26.5 Migration Benefits

1. More flexible configurations (can use LAN interconnect) – Chapter 3.
2. Single System Image (management) – Chapters 1 and 2.
3. Cluster File System – Chapters 2 and 13.
4. Performance benefits due to:
    a. CFS and "improved" DRD – Chapters 13 and 15.
    b. Ability to use newest AlphaServers.
    c. Ability to use newer, faster storage.
5. Improved manageability – GUI management interfaces – Chapters 5, 11, and 19.
6. Simplified installation/configuration – Chapters 10, 11 and 12.
7. General ease of system administration (LSM, software installation, etc.) – Chapters 14 and 19.
8. Cluster Alias (cluster or cluster subset appears as a single machine to clients) – Chapter 16.
9. CAA for high availability of single-instance applications and ASE-style start and stop scripts migrate easily – Chapters 23 and 24.
10. CAA allows resource dependencies, polling and auto-restart capabilities – Chapters 23 and 24.
11. CAA advantages over ASE (no need to manage storage in action scripts); more flexible dependency rules provide greater range of failover choices – Chapters 23 and 24.
12. Application compatibility (if an application runs on *Tru64* UNIX V5.X, it will run on *TruCluster* V5.X) – Chapter 3.
13. Great platform for large multi-node database applications – Chapter 3.
14. More scalable (easier to add members) – Chapter 11.
15. Support for Fiber Channel multi-path storage access – Chapter 4.
16. Larger storage configurations – Chapter 4.
17. Wide SCSI addressing – Chapter 4.
18. Improved AdvFS performance – Chapter 13.
19. Clusterized LSM (looks the same as LSM on a standalone system) – Chapter 14.
20. No requirement for symmetrical I/O configuration among cluster members – Chapter 3.
21. You'll be cool.

26.6 References

- The *TruCluster* Server Technical Overview Guide.
- The *TruCluster* Server Cluster Administration Guide.
- The *TruCluster* Server Cluster Installation Guide.
- The *TruCluster* Migration Workshop.
- The *TruCluster* Server Workshop.
- The *TruCluster* Server Cluster Highly Available Applications.
- Reference pages (noted within the text).

TruCluster Server Troubleshooting

Here, we take a look at problems we've seen and offer advice on what to do if you see them.

A.1 Troubleshooting

A.1.1 System/Cluster is Hung (or Appears Hung)

- Are there CNX messages indicating lost quorum? (Check /var/adm/messages.)

  If so, follow Chapter 17 suggestions for restoring quorum.

- Do the members respond to `ping(8)`?

  If not, the member(s) may be hung or suspended: force a crash (see section A.1.2).

- Try logging in as root at the console.

  If you can, check resources (memory, CPU, I/O, CFS) to see if something is swamped. Also check event logs and the console log.

A.1.2 System/Cluster is Hung II

If a single member is truly hung (doesn't respond to ping, you can't login at the console, no interactive processes are responding, etc.), you probably need to force a crash on the hung member (it could also be affecting the performance or responsiveness of the rest of the cluster). To do this:

1. Use the `dumpsys(8)` command on each responding member to copy a snapshot of memory to a dump file. By default, the `dumpsys` command writes the dump to `/var/adm/crash`, which is a CDSL to `/cluster/members/{memb}/adm/crash`.

```
# dumpsys
Saving /var/adm/crash/vmzcore.0
```

2. Use clu_quorum to make sure the cluster will not lose quorum when you halt the hung member. (Reference Chapter 17.)

3. Crash the hung member by manually halting the member and running "crash" at the console prompt.

```
>>> crash
```

4. Boot the previously hung member. During boot, savecore(8) runs and captures the dump in /var/adm/crash. If the system won't boot, try booting to single-user and collect the crash files manually:

```
# /sbin/bcheckrc
# /sbin/init.d/savecore
# /sbin/init.d/crashdc
```

This should create the crash files in the default location (/var/adm/crash).

You should send the crash files to HP Support for analysis.

A.1.3 System is Running Slowly

If your cluster member(s) is running slowly, you should run the usual tools to try and identify the subsystem and, if possible, the specific offending element much like on a standalone system.

- vmstat(1)

  You should have healthy idle time (usually non-zero), zero or near zero pageouts, and healthy free list size (greater than the vm_page_free_target – "sysconfig -q vm vm_page_free_target").

- netstat(1)

  Look for heavy activity and especially collisions (if Ethernet). Collisions greater than 10% of traffic are usually a bad sign, but this is not a hard and fast rule.

- collect(8)

  Use collect for just about all of your performance gathering needs, but the I/O stats are particularly helpful. Watch for any disks getting overwhelmed. What is considered overwhelmed? That's outside the scope of this book, but it's a factor of the HBA, storage subsystem, and individual disk(s) themselves. Historical data is also a good guide to see if disks (or anything else for that matter) are being exhausted more than usual.

```
# collect -s d
Initializing (10.0 seconds) ... done.

#### RECORD    1 (1032229234:0) (Mon Sep 16 22:20:34 2002) ####

# DISK Statistics
#DSK     NAME  B/T/L    R/S RKB/S  W/S WKB/S   AVS   AVW  ACTQ   WTQ  %BSY
   0   cdrom0  0/5/0      0     0    0     0  0.00  0.00  0.00  0.00  0.00
   1     dsk0  1/0/0      0     0    0     0 13.33  0.00  0.00  0.00  0.10
   2     dsk9  2/0/1      0     0    0     0  0.00  0.00  0.00  0.00  0.00
   3    dsk10  2/0/2      0     0    0     0  0.00  0.00  0.00  0.00  0.00
   4    dsk11  2/0/3      0     0    0     0  0.00  0.00  0.00  0.00  0.00
   5    dsk12  2/0/4      0     0    0     0  0.00  0.00  0.00  0.00  0.00
   6    dsk13  2/0/5      0     0    0     0  0.00  0.00  0.00  0.00  0.00
   7    dsk14  2/0/6      0     0    0     0  0.00  0.00  0.00  0.00  0.00
   8     dsk1  2/1/0      3   139    0     0 21.37  0.00  0.07  0.00  5.49
   9     dsk2  2/1/1     15  1943    0     1 22.83  0.00  0.36  0.00 21.47
  10     dsk3  2/1/2      0     0    0     0  0.00  0.00  0.00  0.00  0.00
  11     dsk4  2/1/3      0     0    0     0  0.00  0.00  0.00  0.00  0.00
  12     dsk5  2/1/4      0     0    0     0  0.00  0.00  0.00  0.00  0.00
  13     dsk6  2/1/5      2   170    0     0 30.42  0.00  0.08  0.00  6.69
  14     dsk7  2/1/6      0     0    0     0 17.50  0.00  0.01  0.00  0.70
  15     dsk8  2/1/7      0     0    0     0  0.00  0.00  0.00  0.00  0.00
  16    dsk18  2/2/0      0     0    0     0  0.00  0.00  0.00  0.00  0.00
  17    dsk19  2/2/1      0     0    0     0  0.00  0.00  0.00  0.00  0.00
  18    dsk20  2/2/2      0     0    0     0  0.00  0.00  0.00  0.00  0.00
```

In this case, dsk2 is getting some activity, but it isn't bad: 21.47% BSY (busy).

- `ps(1)`

  This command lists the current processes. If the performance problem is a single process, you'll get a good idea of that from this output. Using the "`pcpu`" keyword, you can see the current top CPU users.

```
# ps -eo pcpu,cputime,user,pid,comm | sort -r | head
%CPU        TIME USER        PID COMMAND
 5.2    16:40.18 monbot   1132662 monbot-2.3.7
 4.4    11:54:07 gry      1168434 xl8tl33tsp34Kd
 1.3     0:00.04 root     1138862 rshd
 0.6    02:46:58 root     1048576 kernel idle
 0.2    13:31.87 aey      1049022 more README
 0.0     9:17.01 root     1048808 evmd
 0.0     5:21.51 cjy      1052689 telnet justice
 0.0     3:04.06 root     1048692 update
 0.0     2:32.01 bly      1052606 ksh
```

We might have used "`ps aux | head`" here but the formatted output was difficult to read. You can use either command or roll your own.

- evmget(1)

  Using the EVM_SHOW_TEMPLATE, you can a define the information that is returned from the evmget, evmwatch(1), evmsort(1), and evmshow(1) commands.

```
# export EVM_SHOW_TEMPLATE=\
> "@timestamp (@event_id)\n[@priority] @name\n@@\n"
```

There are two cluster-related filter template files in the /usr/share/evm/filters directory as shown by the evf script that we wrote.

```
# ./evf -vd /usr/share/evm/filters clu caa

/usr/share/evm/filters

  clu.evf

    @clu:clu             ->  [name sys.unix.clu]
    @clu:cfs             ->  [name sys.unix.clu.cfs]
    @clu:cnx             ->  [name sys.unix.clu.cnx]
    @clu:drd             ->  [name sys.unix.clu.drd]
    @clu:member          ->  [name sys.unix.clu.member]
    @clu:shutdown        ->  [name sys.unix.clu.shutdown]
    @clu:wall            ->  [name sys.unix.clu.wall]
    @clu:caa             ->  [name sys.unix.clu.caa]
    @clu:clua            ->  [name sys.unix.clu.clua]


  caa.evf

    @caa:caa             ->  [name sys.unix.clu.caa]
    @caa:app             ->  [name sys.unix.clu.caa.app]
    @caa:cli             ->  [name sys.unix.clu.caa.cli]
    @caa:err             ->  [name sys.unix.clu.caa.err]
    @caa:res             ->  [name sys.unix.clu.caa.res]
```

By setting the EVM_SHOW_TEMPLATE and using the "@clu" filter, you can retrieve all cluster-related events that have occurred using the following evmget command.

```
# evmget -A -f @clu

29-Aug-2002 01:55:24 (13)
[200] sys.unix.clu.cnx.quorum.gain
CNX MGR: Node has (re)gained quorum (current votes 2, quorum votes 2)
...
```

When troubleshooting, it is often useful to cast a wide net and then draw it tight as appropriate (perhaps limiting the events to a specific time period); for example, to return all events that have occurred in the last two hours:

```
# evmget -A -f "[age < 2h]"

29-Aug-2002 03:36:14 (968)
[200] sys.unix.clu.drd.new_accessnode._hwid.105
DRD: Server molari selected for device 105
...
```

Once you find an event of interest, you can get more information by using the evmshow command with the "-d" option.

A.1.4 Parsing Events

Taking the event ID from the previous example, we can get more information as follows:

```
# evmget -f "[event_id = 968]" | evmshow -d

============================ EVM Log event ============================
EVM event name: sys.unix.clu.drd.new_accessnode._hwid.105

    This event is posted by a DRD client to indicate that it has
    selected a server as a new access node for the specified device.

======================================================================

Formatted Message:
    DRD: Server molari selected for device 105

Event Data Items:
    Event Name          : sys.unix.clu.drd.new_accessnode._hwid.105
    Cluster Event       : True
    Priority            : 200
    PID                 : 1061550
    PPID                : 1061518
    Event Id            : 968
    Member Id           : 2
    Timestamp           : 29-Aug-2002 03:36:14
    Host IP address     : 192.168.0.69
    Cluster IP address: 192.168.0.70
    Host Name           : sheridan.dec.com
    Cluster Name        : babylon5
    Format              : DRD: Server $server_name selected for device $_hwid
    Reference           : cat:evmexp_clu.cat

Variable Items:
    disk_type (STRING) = "SERVED"
    server_name (STRING) = "molari"
    _hwid (INT64) = 105
    reason_code (INT32) = 0

======================================================================
```

If the event you are focusing on happens to be a binlog event, the "evmshow -d" command will translate the event's binary information via DECevent (V5.0A, V5.1, and V5.1A) or Compaq Analyze (on V5.1B, if installed).

A.1.5 The "mc_diag -d" Command

In Chapter 4, we discussed using the mc_cable and mc_diag SRM console commands to verify that the Memory Channel hardware is functioning. In this section, we will discuss how to get additional diagnostic information (while at the console prompt) from the Memory Channel by using the mc_diag command with the "-d" option.

The "mc_diag -d" command displays eight fields of information:

- Link Control and Status Register (LCSR)
- Memory Channel Error Register (MCERR)
- Memory Channel Port Register (MCPORT)
- Cluster Interconnect Receive (from Memory Channel) Base Address Register (PRBAR)
- PCI Status and Control Register (CFG04)
- Configuration Longword (10H) Register (CFG10)
- Module Configuration Register (MODCFG) – Memory Channel 2 ONLY
- Port Online Status Register (POS) – Memory Channel 2 ONLY

You can obtain (or decode) information about the Memory Channel card's configuration from the output.

A.1.5.1 Standard Hub or Virtual Hub?

For example, you can determine if the card is configured in standard or virtual hub mode by looking at bit 2 of the LCSR field. If the card is in virtual hub mode, then looking at bit 31 of the MCPORT field will indicate VH0 or VH1 mode while bits 21:16 will indicate the node ID (or hub slot location in standard hub mode). See Figure A-1, Figure A-2, Figure A-3, and Figure A-4.

NOTE:

In a dual-redundant Memory Channel configuration, each card in the same system should be jumpered similarly. See section 4.4.1 for more information on configuring the Memory Channel.

```
>>> mc_diag -d

          LCSR     MCERR    MCPORT   PRBAR    CFG04    CFG10    MODCFG        POS
mca0 - 00084800 00000000 42420000 80000000 04000006 40000008 0000000b 00000001

          0000       01000010
```

Figure A-1: Memory Channel 2 Hub Configuration, Node ID 2 (Hub Slot 2)

```
>>> mc_diag -d

          LCSR     MCERR    MCPORT   PRBAR    CFG04    CFG10    MODCFG        POS
mca0 - 00084800 00000000 42420000 80000000 04000006 40000008 0000000b 00000001

          0000       01000010
```

Figure A-2: Memory Channel 2 Hub Configuration, Node ID 0 (Hub Slot 0)

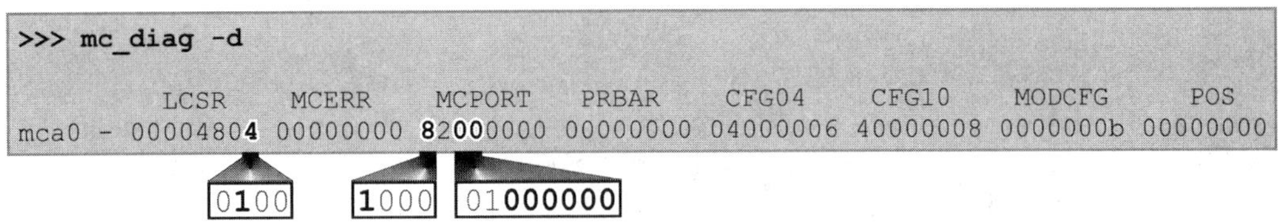

Figure A-3: Memory Channel 2 Virtual Hub Configuration, VH0

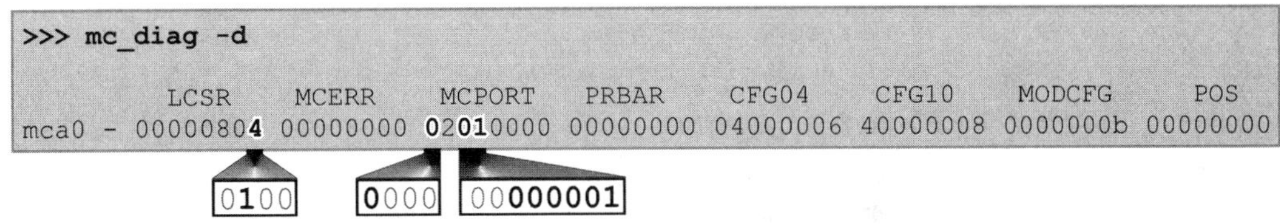

Figure A-4: Memory Channel 2 Virtual Hub Configuration, VH1

A.1.5.2 Memory Channel Address Space Window Size

In order for redundant Memory Channel rails to function with 512MB address space window size, each Memory Channel must be located in separate PCI buses. You can use the "show config" command to determine the location of the Memory Channel cards.

```
P00>>>show config
...
     Bus 00  Slot 08: DEC PCI MC
                                        mca0.0.0.8.0           Rev: 22, mca0
...
     Bus 01  Slot 03: DEC PCI MC
                                        mca1.1.0.3.0           Rev: 22, mca1
...
```

```
>>> mc_diag -d

          LCSR     MCERR    MCPORT   PRBAR    CFG04    CFG10    MODCFG   POS
mca0 - 00204800 00000000 42400000 80000000 04000006 40000008 0000000b 00000004
mca1 - 00204800 00000000 42400000 80000000 04000006 48000008 0000000b 00000004
                                                                  1011
```

Figure A-5: Memory Channel 2 Memory Window Size of 512MB

How can you determine the address space window size without looking at the card? Bit 2 of the `MODCFG` field indicates memory widow size. If bit 2 is not set, the address space window size is 512MB. See Figure A-5.

A.1.5.3 The `MCERR` Field

The `MCERR` field should always be zeroes. However, a non-zero `MCERR` field is not necessarily fatal. We have seen an instance where the Memory Channel on a DS10 system does not complete its power-up self-test before the SRM console is ready. If this happens, run the `init` command, which should clear the problem. If it does not clear the error, you can cycle power on the system. As a last resort to clear the error before logging a call with HP, power off the system and reseat the card.

For more information on the "`mc_diag -d`" bit fields, see Chapter 3 (Troubleshooting) of the Memory Channel Service Information Guide, which shipped with your Memory Channel hardware. The guide also contains additional tips for troubleshooting the Memory Channel hardware as well.

A.1.6 CNX Problems (quorum, CNX boot hangs, etc.)

If you experience quorum problems or the cluster seems to hang and CNX messages are displayed on the console, try setting the `sysconfig` debug values in `cnx:msg_level` (default 1) and `cnx:debug_msg_level` (default 0) each to 5 either at boot time (by modifying `/etc/sysconfigtab`) or in real time using "`sysconfig -r cnx <attribute>=5`". These settings cause more verbose CNX messages to be logged to the console, `/var/adm/messages` and `/var/adm/syslog.dated/current/kern.log`, and can help you or HP Support with additional clues about the CNX behavior in your cluster.

A.1.7 Unable to See Your Shared Storage from Your Cluster Members

This is usually a persistent reservation problem and should only happen in isolated situations. Refer back to sections 15.13 and 22.5 for details about I/O Barriers and when they might get in your way. You can check for persistent reservations from the perspective of the cluster with "`cleanPR show`":

```
# cleanPR show

      cleanPR Version: 1.5
...
 Checking device 5 1 100
                       Key Entry 0: 0x30001
                       Key Entry 1: 0x30002
                       Key Entry 1: 0x30002
                       Key Entry 3: 0x30001
                       Key Entry 6: 0x30001
                       Key Entry 6: 0x30002
                       Key Entry 6: 0x30001
                       Key Entry 6: 0x30002
...
Total of 5 devices found w/Persistent Reservations
Total of 0 devices cleared of Persistent Reservations
```

You can also check the devices on your storage controller (`HSG80> show <unit>`) to see if they are listed as "persistent reserved" under "State" in the output.

```
HSG80> show d100

    LUN                                       Uses             Used by
------------------------------------------------------------------------------

  D100                                        DISK30100
        LUN ID:       6000-1FE1-000B-1A40-0009-0361-3888-0062
        NOIDENTIFIER
        Switches:
          RUN                      NOWRITE_PROTECT          READ_CACHE
          READAHEAD_CACHE          WRITEBACK_CACHE
          MAX_READ_CACHED_TRANSFER_SIZE = 32
          MAX_WRITE_CACHED_TRANSFER_SIZE = 32
        Access:
                ALL
        State:
          ONLINE to this controller
          Persistent reserved
          NOPREFERRED_PATH
        Size:               17769177 blocks
        Geometry (C/H/S): ( 5258 / 20 / 169 )
```

If you find that indeed there are persistent reservations on your storage, you can boot the Emergency Repair Disk (which means shutting down the cluster) and use the "`cleanPR clean`" command to clear all the persistent reservations.

```
# cleanPR clean

                          cleanPR Version: 1.5

                                  WARNING

        This shell script will clear all Persistent Reservations
        from the HSX80 devices attached to this system.

                                  WARNING

Do you wish to proceed ? <y/n> [n]: y

        Removing Persistent Reservations from all HSX80 devices...

 Checking HSG80 at /dev/rdisk/dsk108a (SCSI #5 (SCSI ID #2) (SCSI LUN #100))
 Checking HSG80 at /dev/rdisk/dsk6a (SCSI #5 (SCSI ID #9) (SCSI LUN #15))

Total of 0 devices found w/Persistent Reservations
Total of 0 devices cleared of Persistent Reservations
```

If the "`cleanPR clean`" command doesn't resolve all the PRs, you can run the `scu` command manually to clear them.

```
# scu
scu> set nexus bus 2 target 0 lun 3
scu> preserve clear
```

WARNING:

Never clear persistent reservations from a cluster member! You will remove **needed** reservations. Always shut down the cluster and boot a standalone version of the OS, such as the Emergency Repair Disk, if you need to run the "`cleanPR clean`" command or if you need to use "`scu`" to clean them manually.

A.1.8 Upgrading the KGPSA Firmware Causes HOST_ID Changes

After upgrading the firmware on the KGPSA host bus adapter, the `HOST_ID` connection for the KGPSA may change. If this happens, any storage accessed through it that is isolated using selective storage presentation (SSP) at the HSG80 seems to "disappear." The reason it seems to disappear is that we use the `HOST_ID` to configure the connections at the HSG80 (when using SSP). If the

HOST_ID changes, the SSP settings no longer apply since the connection names are different. For example, consider one such connection:

Before the firmware update:

```
HSG80> SHOW CONNECTION

Connection
Name       Operating system    Controller  Port    Address    Status   Offset
UNIX01       TRU64  UNIX             THIS         2          000008      OL  this        00
           HOST_ID=1000-0000-C123-ABCD          ADAPTER_ID=1000-0000-C123-ABCD
```

After the firmware update:

```
HSG80> SHOW CONNECTION

Name       Operating system    Controller  Port    Address    Status   Offset
!NEWCON02    TRU64  UNIX             THIS         2          000008      OL  this        00
           HOST_ID=2000-0000-C123-ABCD     ADAPTER_ID=1000-0000-C123-ABCD
UNIX01       TRU64  UNIX             THIS         2          000008      Offline     00
           HOST_ID=1000-0000-C123-ABCD     ADAPTER_ID=1000-0000-C123-ABCD
```

Once discovered, you can quickly resolve this problem by deleting the old connection and renaming the new one at the storage controller (HSG80). See Chapter 4 for more information about storage configurations including selective storage presentation.

A.1.9 CAA daemon (caad) Doesn't Start When Booting

The explanation here is that there probably isn't a *TruCluster* Server license registered on that member. Each member must have the TCS-UA license. See the Cluster Administration manual (Chapter 11). The boot messages will probably look like this:

```
TruCluster Software is not licensed for use on this system.
This system will continue running but Cluster Application Availability
will not function.  Please install the TCS-UA license and reboot this member.Error:
CAA daemon not started.
CAA dependent system services will not start.
NFS mount daemon started
NFS export service started
Cannot communicate with the CAA daemon.

...

14-Sep-2002 18:01:37 [600] esmd: System Error: The CAA daemon has failed and cannot
be restarted
```

And you may also see messages in the /var/adm/messages file:

```
Sep 14 18:07:30 kyle vmunix: This cluster member is missing the TCS-UA license PAK.
```

A.1.10 CFS Boot Error When Mounting `cluster_root`

The first booting member gets CFS errors when trying to mount `cluster_root`. You may see an error message similar to:

```
WARNING: Magic number on ADVFS portion of CNX partition on quorum disk is not valid
```

This could be a problem with the quorum disk itself or a path to the quorum disk. See the Cluster Administration manual (Chapter 11).

A.1.11 CFS Boot Error When Mounting Boot Partition

When booting a member into an existing cluster, you may see an error:

```
cfs_mountroot: CFS server already exists for node boot partition
```

This usually is an indication that the `boot_parition` is currently mounted by another cluster member. Unmount the `boot_partition`.

A.1.12 Can't `umount` a File System that No Longer is Served by a Cluster Member

Use "`cfsmgr -e`" to see if the file system is being serviced. If it is "`Not Served`", you can use the "`cfsmgr -u`" command to forcibly unmount the domain. See Chapter 11 of the *TruCluster* Server Cluster Administration manual for details.

A.1.13 AutoFS File Systems Become Busy or Unresponsive

Forcibly unmount the AutoFS intercept points and `autofs` file systems served by the member. See Chapter 7 of the *TruCluster* Server Cluster Administration manual for details.

A.1.14 Anything Else "Unexpected" and Not Covered Specifically

Check the console, `kern.log,` and `daemon.log` in `/var/adm/syslog.dated`; `messages` in /var/adm; Compaq Analyze (`ca`); and `evmget` (and associated filters). Admittedly this is a wide net, but as you find problems or curious results in the above, you can narrow your approach. For example, if you find AdvFS I/O errors in the `messages` file, you might begin looking for storage errors with `ca` to diagnose a possible storage or controller problem.

A.2 References

- The *TruCluster* Server Technical Overview Guide.
- The *TruCluster* Server Cluster Administration Guide.
- The *TruCluster* Server Cluster Highly Available Applications.
- The Memory Channel Service Information guide (for MC1 – Order # EK–PCIRM–SV.B01)
- The Memory Channel Service Information guide (for MC2 – Order # EK–PCIMC–SV.A01)
- Reference pages (noted within the text).

B

Resources

This appendix provides references to additional resources – both print and electronic - for *Tru64* UNIX and *TruCluster* Server.

B.1 Programs and Scripts Used in This Book

All of the programs and scripts used in this book are available at the Digital Press and BRUDEN Corporation websites.

Digital Press – http://www.bh.com/companions/1555582591

BRUDEN Corporation – http://www.bruden.com

B.2 Educational Resources

BRUDEN Corporation is one of HP's approved training vendors for *Tru64* UNIX, OpenVMS, and *TruCluster* Server.

BRUDEN Corporation – http://www.bruden.com

B.3 Electronic Resources

There are many, many sources for additional information on UNIX on the Internet. The sources that we present were selected because we found them useful both in developing this book and in managing *TruCluster* Servers on a day-to-day basis. All websites and e-mail distribution addresses are accurate as of this writing; however, it should be noted that with the recent merger of HP and Compaq, we expect that many of these addresses will change.

B.3.1 Mailing Lists

B.3.1.1 Compaq Services' *Tru64* UNIX Patch Mailing List

HP's Compaq Services maintains a mailing list that automatically notifies subscribers of the latest patches on *Tru64* UNIX software products. To subscribe to this mailing list, please go to the following website: http://www.support.compaq.com/patches/mailing-list.shtml

B.3.1.2 Compaq Services' Security Mailing List

HP's Compaq Services also maintains a mailing list that automatically notifies subscribers of the latest security issues and patches on Compaq software products. To subscribe to this mailing list, please go to the following website: http://www.support.compaq.com/patches/mailing-list.shtml

B.3.1.3 *Tru64*-UNIX-Managers List

The *Tru64*-UNIX-Managers list (formerly Alpha-OSF-Managers list) is a quick turnaround troubleshooting aid for people who administer and manage Alpha AXP systems running HP *Tru64* UNIX (formerly Compaq *Tru64* UNIX (formerly Digital UNIX (formerly Digital OSF/1))). Its primary purpose is to provide the *Tru64* UNIX Manager with a quick source of information for system management problems that are time critical.

To subscribe to the list, send a message to `majordomo@ornl.gov` containing the command "`subscribe tru64-unix-managers`".

The *Tru64*-UNIX-Managers list is archived at: http://www.ornl.gov/its/archives/mailing-lists

B.3.2 USENET Newsgroups

There are several newsgroups that may be of particular interest to systems managers and administrators of *Tru64* UNIX and *TruCluster* Server. They are as follows:

- `comp.unix.tru64` – The primary *Tru64* UNIX newsgroup.
- `comp.unix.osf.osf1` – An archive of *Tru64* UNIX discussions.
- `comp.unix.osf.misc` – A miscellaneous *Tru64* UNIX discussion group.

B.3.3 WWW Resources (HP)

HP maintains several useful websites on *Tru64* UNIX products (including *TruCluster* Server) and on products that work with *Tru64* UNIX. As of this writing, the addresses to these websites are accurate; however, with the merger of Compaq and HP, we expect these website addresses to change.

B.3.3.1 The *Tru64* UNIX Homepage

HP's *Tru64* UNIX group maintains a very complete and up-to-date website dedicated to *Tru64* UNIX and *TruCluster* Server. Readers will find many links that are useful to the successful deployment and management of a *Tru64* UNIX or *TruCluster* Server system.

http://www.tru64unix.compaq.com

B.3.3.2 Online Documentation

HP's *Tru64* UNIX group maintains all of their *Tru64* UNIX and *TruCluster* Server documentation in an online and searchable format.

B.3.3.2.1 Tru64 UNIX Online Documentation

http://www.tru64unix.compaq.com/docs/pub_page/doc_list.html

B.3.3.2.2 TruCluster Server Documentation

http://www.tru64unix.compaq.com/docs/pub_page/cluster_list.html

B.3.3.3 Technical Updates

HP's *Tru64* UNIX group publishes the latest technical information on *Tru64* UNIX and *TruCluster* Server. Please monitor these websites for the latest information on these products.

B.3.3.3.1 Tru64 UNIX Software Product Technical Update Information

http://www.tru64unix.compaq.com/docs/pub_page/os_update.html

B.3.3.3.2 TruCluster Server Software Product Technical Update Information

http://www.tru64unix.compaq.com/docs/pub_page/tcr_update.html

B.3.3.4 Best Practices

Of all hardware and software vendors, we believe that HP's *Tru64* UNIX group is unique in having comprehensive and current Best Practices websites. Many systems managers and administrators have told us just how valuable these websites are to the successful deployment of systems.

B.3.3.4.1 Tru64 UNIX Best Practices Website

http://www.tru64unix.compaq.com/docs/best_practices/index.html

B.3.3.4.2 TruCluster Server Best Practices Website

http://www.tru64unix.compaq.com/docs/best_practices/clus_bps.html

B.3.3.5 Alpha Systems Firmware

The latest firmware for Alpha systems is available online from the following website:

http://gatekeeper.research.compaq.com/pub/DEC/Alpha/firmware

B.3.3.6 Patch Information

HP provides online access to patches for *Tru64* UNIX and *TruCluster* Server. The following websites provide easy access to patches and documentation on patches.

B.3.3.6.1 Tru64 UNIX and TruCluster Server Patch Documentation

http://www.tru64unix.compaq.com/docs/patch

B.3.3.6.2 Tru64 UNIX and TruCluster Server Patch Roadmap

http://www.tru64unix.compaq.com/docs/patch/roadmap.html

B.3.3.6.3 Tru64 UNIX/TruCluster Server Patches

http://www.support.compaq.com/patches

B.3.3.7 New Hardware Delivery Information

HP recently developed several websites on New Hardware Delivery in support of changes to the *Tru64* UNIX software products that provide functionality to new system hardware.

B.3.3.7.1 Tru64 UNIX New Hardware Delivery Documentation

http://www.tru64unix.compaq.com/docs/nhd

B.3.3.7.2 New Hardware Delivery Technical Update Information

http://www.tru64unix.compaq.com/docs/pub_page/nhd_update.html

B.3.3.8 Compaq Services Online Homepage

HP's Compaq Services homepage provides a variety of useful online services from call logging to problem diagnosis and more.

http://www.compaq.com/support

B.3.3.9 WEBES Homepage

The WEB-based Enterprise Services (WEBES) kit provides diagnostic tools (including Compaq Analyze) that can help analyze *Tru64* UNIX systems.

http://www.compaq.com/support/svctools/webes/index.html

B.3.3.10 StorageWorks Information

HP's StorageWorks group provides online information that is useful in setting up and managing the storage hardware necessary for the successful deployment of a *TruCluster* Server system. As the main HP StorageWorks website can be challenging to navigate, we have provided several links that should make it easier to access the necessary information.

B.3.3.10.1 StorageWorks HSZ RAID Controller Documentation

http://www.compaq.com/products/storageworks/array-and-scsi-controllers/HSxuserdocs.html

B.3.3.10.2 StorageWorks HSG RAID Array Controller Software (ACS) Documentation

http://www.compaq.com/products/storageworks/acs/documentation.html

B.3.3.10.3 StorageWorks Fibre Channel SAN Switch Documentation

http://www.compaq.com/products/storageworks/fcsanswitch816/documentation.html

B.3.3.10.4 StorageWorks Enterprise Virtual Array (EVA) Documentation

http://www.compaq.com/products/storageworks/enterprise/documentation.html

B.3.3.10.5 EVA Virtual Controller Software (VCS) Documentation

http://www.compaq.com/products/sanworks/vcs/index.html

B.3.3.11 Shareware and Freeware for *Tru64* UNIX

This website provides access to shareware and freeware for Tru64 UNIX.

http://www.tru64unix.compaq.com/demos/

B.3.4 WWW Resources (Non-HP)

B.3.4.1 The System Administration, Networking and Security (SANS) Institute

The SANS Institute's purpose is to allow computer security professionals, auditors, system administrators, and network administrators to share the lessons they are learning and find solutions to the challenges they face. The Institute's website contains valuable information useful to the management of any system on the Internet.

http://www.sans.org

B.3.4.2 UNIX Guru Universe

UNIX Guru Universe has long been one of the premier portals to information on UNIX. This website contains many useful links to information on UNIX.

http://www.ugu.org

B.3.4.3 Tru64.org

The Tru64.org website is the most comprehensive portal available for *Tru64* UNIX and *TruCluster* Server. It has lots of resources including mailing lists, articles, and FAQs all related to *Tru64* UNIX.

http://www.tru64.org

It should be noted that this website is not affiliated with HP.

B.3.4.4 *Tru64* UNIX User Group

The Encompass HP User Group is the former DECUS, US Chapter. Their website contains much useful information and many useful links related to *Tru64* UNIX:

http://www.encompassus.org

B.4 Supplemental Reading

As this book is focused on *TruCluster* Server, we have only lightly touched upon a number of topics in *Tru64* UNIX. To gain a more in depth understanding of these topics on *Tru64* UNIX, please consult the following books:

B.4.1 *Tru64* UNIX File System Administration (AdvFS, LSM, etc.)

Tru64UNIX File System Administration Handbook

Author(s): Hancock, Steven M.

Publisher: Digital Press, 2000.

ISBN: 1555582273

B.4.2 *Tru64* UNIX System Administration

Tru64 UNIX System Administrators Guide

Author(s): Cheek, Matthew; Fafrak, Scott; Hancock, Steven; Moore, Martin; and Yates, Greg

Publisher: Digital Press, 2002.

ISBN: 1555582559

B.4.3 *Tru64* UNIX Troubleshooting

Tru64 UNIX Troubleshooting: Diagnosing and Correcting System Problems

Author(s): Moore, Martin; Hancock, Steven M

Publisher: Digital Press, 2002.

ISBN: 1555582745

B.4.4 Oracle 9i on *Tru64* UNIX/*TruCluster* Server

Tru64 UNIX-Oracle9i Cluster Quick Reference

Author(s): Donar, Tim

Publisher: Digital Press, 2002.

ISBN: 1555582729

B.4.5 Miscellaneous Cluster Musings

In Search of Clusters

Author(s): Pfister, Gregory F

Publisher: Prentice Hall PTR, 1995.

ISBN: 0138997098

C

Index